THE EERDMANS CRITICAL COMMENTARY

David Noel Freedman, *General Editor*

Astrid B. Beck, *Associate Editor*

THE EERDMANS CRITICAL COMMENTARY offers the best of contemporary Old and New Testament scholarship, seeking to give modern readers clear insight into the biblical text, including its background, its interpretation, and its application.

Contributors to the ECC series are among the foremost authorities in biblical scholarship worldwide. Representing a broad range of confessional backgrounds, authors are charged to remain sensitive to the original meaning of the text and to bring alive its relevance for today. Each volume includes the author's own translation, critical notes, and commentary on literary, historical, cultural, and theological aspects of the text.

Accessible to serious general readers and scholars alike, these commentaries reflect the contributions of recent textual, philological, literary, historical, and archaeological inquiry, benefiting as well from newer methodological approaches. ECC volumes are "critical" in terms of their detailed, systematic explanation of the biblical text. Although exposition is based on the original and cognate languages, English translations provide complete access to the discussion and interpretation of these primary sources.

The Letter to

PHILEMON

A New Translation
with
Notes and Commentary

MARKUS BARTH

and

HELMUT BLANKE

WILLIAM B. EERDMANS PUBLISHING COMPANY
GRAND RAPIDS, MICHIGAN / CAMBRIDGE, U.K.

© 2000 Wm. B. Eerdmans Publishing Co.
255 Jefferson Ave. S.E., Grand Rapids, Michigan 49503 /
P.O. Box 163, Cambridge CB3 9PU U.K.

Printed in the United States of America

05 04 03 02 01 00   7 6 5 4 3 2 1

Library of Congress Cataloging-in-Publication Data

Barth, Markus.
The Letter to Philemon: a new translation with notes and commentary /
Markus Barth and Helmut Blanke.
p.   cm.   (The Eerdmans critical commentary)
ISBN 0-8028-3829-4 (alk. paper)
1. Bible. N.T. Philemon — Commentaries.
I. Bible. N.T. Epistles of Paul. English. Selections. 2000.
II. Title.   III. Series.

BS2765.3.B37   2000
227′.86077 — dc21
                                          00-028776

www.eerdmans.com

Contents

Contents

LITERARY, BIOGRAPHICAL, AND CONTEXTUAL ISSUES

NOTES AND COMMENTS ON PHILEMON

Contents

Abbreviations

AB	Anchor Bible
ABD	*Anchor Bible Dictionary*
ASV	American Standard Version
ATANT	Abhandlungen zur Theologie des Alten und Neuen Testaments
AThR	*Anglican Theological Review*
BAG	W. Bauer, *A Greek-English Lexicon of the New Testament and Other Early Christian Literature,* trans. and adapted by W. Arndt and F. W. Gingrich
BauerLex	W. Bauer, *Griechisch-Deutsches Wörterbuch zu den Schriften des Neuen Testaments und der übrigen urchristlichen Literatur,* reprint of the 5th ed. (Berlin: De Gruyter, 1971)
BBB	Bonner biblische Beiträge
BDF	F. Blass and A. Debrunner, *A Greek Grammar of the New Testament and Other Early Christian Literature,* translation and revision of the 9th-10th German ed. by R. W. Funk (Chicago: University of Chicago Press, 1961)
BDR	F. Blass and A. Debrunner, *Grammatik des neutestamentlichen Griechisch,* rev. F. Rehkopf, 14th ed. (Göttingen: Vandenhoeck & Ruprecht, 1976)
BT	*Bible Translator*
BTN	Bibliotheca theologica Norvegica
BWANT	Beiträge zur Wissenschaft von Alten und Neuen Testament
BZNW	Beihefte zur Zeitschrift für die neutestamentliche Wissenschaft

CBQ	*Catholic Biblical Quarterly*
CGTC	Cambridge Greek Testament Commentaries
CIG	*Corpus Inscriptionum Graecarum*
CIJ	*Corpus Inscriptionum Iudaicarum*
CR	Corpus Reformatorum
CSEL	Corpus Scriptorum Ecclesiasticorum Latinorum
EKK	Evangelisch-katholischer Kommentar zum Neuen Testament
ERE	*Encyclopedia of Religion and Ethics*
EVB	E. Käsemann, *Exegetische Versuche und Besinnungen,* vols. 1-2, 6th ed. (Göttingen: Vandenhoeck & Ruprecht, 1970)
EvTh	*Evangelische Theologie*
ExpT	*Expository Times*
FRLANT	Forschungen zur Religion und Literatur des Alten und Neuen Testaments
FS	Festschrift
GK	W. Gesenius, *Hebräische Grammatik,* völlig umgearbeitet von E. Kautzsch, reprografischer Nachdruck der 28. Auflage (Leipzig, 1909; Hildesheim: Olms, 1962)
HC	Hand-Commentar zum Neuen Testament
HNT	Handbuch zum Neuen Testament
HTR	*Harvard Theological Review*
ICC	International Critical Commentary
IDB	*Interpreter's Dictionary of the Bible*
Interp.	*Interpretation*
JAC	*Jahrbuch für Antike und Christentum*
JB	Jerusalem Bible
JBL	*Journal of Biblical Literature*
JQR	*Jewish Quarterly Review*
JR	*Journal of Religion*
KEH	Kurzgefaßtes exegetisches Handbuch
KEK	Kritisch-exegetischer Kommentar über das Neue Testament
KJV	King James Version
KNT	Kommentar zum Neuen Testament
LB'84	Die Bibel. Nach der Übersetzung Martin Luthers. Bibeltext in der revidierten Fassung von 1984 (Stuttgart: Deutsche Bibelgesellschaft, 1985)
LCL	Loeb Classical Library
LSLex	H. G. Liddell and R. Scott, *A Greek-English Lexicon,* reprinted from the 9th ed. of 1940 (Oxford: Clarendon, 1977)

LXX	Septuaginta, ed. A. Rahlfs (Stuttgart: Deutsche Bibelgesellschaft, 1935)
MeyerK	Kritisch-exegetischer Kommentar über das Neue Testament, begr. von H. A. W. Meyer (Göttingen: Vandenhoeck & Ruprecht)
MMLex	J. H. Moulton and G. Milligan, *The Vocabulary of the Greek Testament,* reprinted from the edition of 1930 (Grand Rapids: Eerdmans, 1980)
MPG	Patrologia Graeca, ed. J.-P. Migne (Paris: Migne)
MPL	Patrologia Latina, ed. J.-P. Migne (Paris: Migne)
MthSt	Münchener theologische Studien
NEB	New English Bible
NIC	New International Commentary on the New Testament
NJB	New Jerusalem Bible
NKJ	New King James Version
NovT	*Novum Testamentum*
NTD	Das Neue Testament Deutsch (Göttingen: Vandenhoeck & Ruprecht)
NTS	*New Testament Studies*
NTTEV	*Good News for Modern Man: The New Testament in Today's English Version* (New York: American Bible Society, 1960)
Pesh.	The Peshitta
PreisigkeLex	F. Preisigke and E. Kießling, *Wörterbuch der griechischen Papyrusurkunden mit Einschluß der griechischen Inschriften, Aufschriften, Ostraka, Mumienschilder usw. aus Ägypten,* vols. 1-3 (Berlin: Selbstverlag d. Erben, 1925)
RGG	*Die Religion in Geschichte und Gegenwart,* 3rd ed. (Tübingen)
RHR	*Revue de l'Histoire des Religions*
RNT	Regensburger Neues Testament
RSV	Revised Standard Version
RV	Revised Version (1881)
SBLMS	Society of Biblical Literature Monograph Series
SBS	Stuttgarter Bibelstudien
SBT	Studies in Biblical Theology
ScotJT	*Scottish Journal of Theology*
SegB	Segond Bible, rev. ed. (Geneva: Maison de la Bible, 1964)
StB	H. Strack and P. Billerbeck, *Kommentar zum Neuen Testament. Aus Talmud und Midrasch,* Bd. 3, 7 unv. Aufl., pp. 625-631 (Munich: Beck, 1979)
StUNT	Studien zur Umwelt des Neuen Testaments

Symm.	Symmachus's version of the OT in Greek (late 2nd cent. C.E.)
TDNT	*Theological Dictionary of the New Testament*
THAT	*Theologisches Handwörterbuch zum Alten Testament*
Theod.	Theodotion's version of the OT, in Greek (2nd cent. C.E.)
ThExH	*Theologische Existenz heute*
ThLZ	*Theologische Literaturzeitung*
ThWNT	*Theologisches Wörterbuch zum Neuen Testament*
TWAT	G. J. Botterweck and H. Ringgren, *Theologisches Wörterbuch zum Alten Testament*
TWB	*Theological Word Book of the Bible* (ed. Richardson)
UNT	Untersuchungen zum Neuen Testament
USQR	*Union Seminary Quarterly Review*
VetT	*Vetus Testamentum*
Vg.	Vulgate
WA	Martin Luther, *Werke. Kritische Gesamtausgabe* (Weimar, 1883ff.)
WMANT	Wissenschaftliche Monographien zum Alten und Neuen Testament
WuD.NF	*Wort und Dienst. Jahrbuch der theologischen Schule Bethel*
WUNT	Wissenschaftliche Untersuchungen zum Neuen Testament
ZAW	*Zeitschrift für die alttestamentliche Wissenschaft*
ZB	Züricher Bibel
ZNW	*Zeitschrift für die neutestamentliche Wissenschaft und die Kunde der älteren Kirche*
ZWTh	*Zeitschrift für wissenschaftliche Theologie*

Abbreviations of Classical and Medieval Works

Antiphon
 Or.   *Orationes*
Appian
 Bell. Pun.   Λιβυκή (*Punic Wars*)
 Rom. hist.   *Romanes historiae*
Aristotle
 NE   *Nicomachean Ethics*
 Pol.   *Politica*
 Rh.   *Rhetorica*
Ps.-Aristotle
 Oec.   *Oeconomica*
Athenaeus
 Deipnosoph.   *Deipnosophistae*
Augustine
 Ad Exod   *On Exodus*
 Civ. Dei   *De civitate Dei*
 Ep.   *Epistulae*
Barn.   *Barnabas*
Cicero
 Off.   *De officiis*
 Parad. St.   *Paradoxa Stoicorum*
 Prov. cons.   *De provinciis consularibus*
 Pro Val. Flacc. *Pro Valerio Flacco*

Clement of Alexandria
   Strom.   *Stromata*
Ps.-Clement
   Hom.   *Homilies*
Columella
   Rust.   *De re rustica*
Demosthenes
   Or. Phil.   *Philippic Orations*
Did.   *Didache*
Dio Cassius
   Hist. Rom.   *Historia Romana*
Dio Chrysostom
   Or.   *Orationes*
Diodorus of Athens
   Perieg.   *Periegeta*
Diodorus Siculus
   Bibl. hist.   *Bibliotheca historica*
Diogenes Laertius
   De clar. phil. vitis *De clarorum philosophorum vitis*
Diogn.   *Epistle to Diognetus*
Dionysius of Halicarnassus
   Ant. Rom.   *Antiquitates Romanae*
Duns Scotus
   Oxon.   *Opus Oxoniense*
Epictetus
   Diss.   *Dissertationes*
Eusebius
   Chron.   *Chronica*
Festus
   Gramm.   *Grammatica*
1 Clem.   *1 Clement*
Gregory of Nazianzus
   Carm.   *Carmina*
Heraclitus Ponticus
   Athen.   *Athenaia*
Hermas
   Man.   *Mandates*
   Sim.   *Similitudes*
   Vis.   *Visions*
Homer
   Il.   *Iliad*

Od.	*Odyssey*
Horace	
Sat.	*Satires*
Ignatius	
Eph.	*To the Ephesians*
Philad.	*To the Philadelphians*
Polyc.	*To Polycarp*
Rom.	*To the Romans*
Smyrn.	*To the Smyrnaeans*
Trall.	*To the Trallians*
Irenaeus	
Adv. haer.	*Adversus Haereses*
Isaeus	
Orat.	*Orationes*
Isocrates	
Paneg.	*Panegyricus*
Josephus	
Ant.	*Antiquitates*
BJ	*Bellum Judaicum*
Julius Caesar	
B Civ.	*Bellum Civile*
Justin Martyr	
Apol.	*Apologia*
Dial.	*Dialogue with Trypho*
Juvenal	
Sat.	*Satires*
Lactantius	
Div. inst.	*Divinae institutiones*
Livy	
Hist.	*Historia*
Macrobius	
Sat.	*Saturnalia*
Mart. Pol.	*Martyrdom of Polycarp*
Musonius	
Ep.	*Epistulae*
Origen	
C. Cels.	*Contra Celsum*
Ovid	
Am.	*Amores*
Ars am.	*Ars amatoria*

Pausanias
   Perieg.   *Periegesis*
Philemon Comicus
   frag.   *Athenaia, fragmenta*
Philo
   De decal.   *De decalogo*
   Deus immut.   *On the Unchangeableness of God*
   Jos.   *De Josepho*
   Leg. ad Gaium *Embassy to Gaius*
   Mos.   *Moses*
   Op. mund.   *De opificio mundi*
   Quod omn. prob. *Quod omnis probus liber sit*
   Spec. leg.   *De specialibus legibus*
   Virt.   *De virtutibus*
   Vita contempl. *De vita contemplativa*
Ps.-Philo
   Lib. ant. Bibl. *Liber antiquitatum Biblicarum*
Plato
   Cra.   *Cratylus*
   Ep.   *Epistolai*
   Grg.   *Gorgias*
   Leg.   *Leges*
   Menex.   *Menexenus*
   Phd.   *Phaedo*
   Phlb.   *Philebus*
   Plt.   *Politicus*
   Prt.   *Protagoras*
   Resp.   *Respublica*
Plautus
   Bacch.   *Bacchides*
   Mil.   *Miles gloriosus*
Pliny the Younger
   Ep.   *Epistulae*
Plutarch
   Coriol.   *Coriolanus*
   Crass.   *Crassus*
Polybius
   Hist.   *Historiae*
Polycarp
   Phil.   *Letter to the Philippians*
2 Clem.   *2 Clement*

Seneca
   Ben.   *De beneficiis*
   Constant.   *De constantia sapientis*
   Ep.   *Epistulae*
   Ep. mor.   *Epistulae morales*
Sextus Empiricus
   Math.   *Adversus mathematicos*
Sophocles
   frag.   *Hecuba, fragmenta*
Suetonius
   De gramm. et rhet. *De grammaticis et rhetoribus*
Tacitus
   Ann.   *Annales*
Tertullian
   Apol.   *Apologeticus*
   De bapt.   *De baptismo*
   De cor. mil.   *De corona militum*
Thomas Aquinas
   ST   *Summa theologiae*
Varro
   Rust.   *De re rustica*
Xenophon
   Hell.   *Hellenica*
   Mem. Soc.   *Memorabilia Socratis*
   Oec.   *Oeconomicus*
Ps.-Xenophon
   Athen.   *Athenaeus*

The Social Background:
Slavery at Paul's Time

Paul's Epistle to Philemon constitutes only a tiny part of the Bible, yet it deals with one of the most serious and scandalous forms of human existence: the life of a slave. The Philemon letter is so short that, written with a fine pen, it might fit on a postcard; its length does not exceed that of a little note or billet. But at stake is the issue of liberation from oppression and exploitation of human beings.

At first sight the presupposition and intention of the epistle can be summed up as follows: A pagan slave called Onesimus has run away from his master, Philemon. The owner was a respected member and benefactor of the Christian congregation in the small Asia Minor town of Colossae. The fugitive has found refuge with the apostle Paul, who, in pursuing his missionary work, has been imprisoned, probably in a large city. The conditions of Paul's captivity were so liberal as to permit him to benefit from services that Onesimus, after becoming a Christian, rendered to the propagation of the message of Christ. But while the apostle counts on his own forthcoming release from chains, he sends the slave Onesimus back to his master, together with the letter "to Philemon." In grateful recognition of the God-given love and faith that make Philemon a pillar and paragon of the congregation, Paul extends a warm personal plea for the reception of the returning fugitive as a brother. To underline his request the apostle formally pledges to pay in cash for whatever damages are incurred through Onesimus's escape. In addition, Paul expresses the hope that Onesimus might be voluntarily returned to the apostle in order to serve, substituting for Philemon himself, as a permanent helper in the gospel work. Paul hopes to be released in the near future and to visit Philemon. Then he will see with his own eyes whether and how his request has been fulfilled.

The fact that an explicit appeal for the formal release (manumission) of Onesimus is missing has puzzled readers of the Epistle to Philemon. For understanding the substance and message of this letter, at least a minimum of knowledge is indispensable regarding the conditions of slavery and of manumission at Paul's time, that is, between circa 10 C.E. and circa 63 C.E.

In the first half of the first century C.E., slavery was an essential and for all practical purposes unchallenged element of the Roman Empire's culture and economy. More than only Greek and Roman features of slavery are present in the society of peoples surrounding the Mediterranean Sea. Asia Minor had been colonized by Greeks from since about 1000 B.C.E., and after 189 B.C.E. stood under Roman control. It was the floodgate through which early and later Babylonian, Assyrian, and Persian features of slavery streamed into the central and western parts of the Greco-Roman world. Since in addition Egyptian, Phoenician, and — on a minor scale — Jewish customs may have contributed to the prevailing situation of slaves, it is misleading to speak of a uniform or of "the" ancient slave system. In actuality, the confluence and competition of manifold traditions and practices determined the life of slaves in the cities and regions where Paul had grown up, where he worked before and after his conversion, and to which he addressed his letters. At his time, the institution of slavery was exposed to changes on various levels. Agricultural and industrial developments began to make the keeping of slaves uneconomical. Political and social considerations spoke against the maintenance of slaves in huge numbers. Other interests contradicted mass manumissions. Humanitarian thinking and a continuous series of new laws moved at least toward a minimal protection of slaves.

The apostle Paul's sojourns in cities with large slave populations — among them Ephesus, Corinth, Syrian Caesarea, and Rome — gave this rabbinically trained Jew and born Roman citizen ample opportunity to be aware of both the stable and changing human and social and the legal and economical pressures and prospects under which slaves lived day by day.

The following sketch of main aspects of slavery at Paul's time is not based on newly discovered or hitherto unused ancient sources. No more than a summary is presented of the use and the evaluation made of ancient source material by scholars who are reckoned among the experts in this field.[1] One of them

---

1. See the bibliography for the Greek, Latin, and other sources, and for the secondary literature quoted in the following. My former assistants Charles Pleasant at Pittsburgh Theological Seminary (at present, teacher at the Community College of Allegheny County, Monroeville, Pa.), David MacLaghlan at Basel University (now professor of New Testament

observes, "There is no subject of ancient history more difficult to study and more beset with controversy and dispute."[2]

I. PROBLEMS OF AN ADEQUATE DESCRIPTION

a. Ideological presuppositions can influence the selection and interpretation of ancient texts. There is a passionately engaged humanitarianism that abhors and detests slavery in any conceivable form; there exists a specifically Jewish or Christian zeal for abolition of slavery in Europe, in North America, or elsewhere; conspicuous also is a Marxist concern in uncovering the brute material presuppositions of all cultures.[3] But emotional aversion alone does not guarantee that all available sources are duly weighted and every relevant facet of a slave's life in the ancient world is taken into consideration.

b. Different forms of slavery coexisted side by side or were mixed. Only in rare cases can generalizations be made. In almost every aspect the life of a house slave was distinct from that of the groups or masses working in the fields; in gold, silver, lead, or salt mines; in marble or lime quarries; or as rowers on galleys. Between the relatively privileged domestic slaves and those practically exposed to a slow and painful death stood what might be called a slave middle class, consisting of skilled craftsmen, secretaries, educators, nurses. In each case the character and status of the owner and his family influenced the treatment of the slave. Female slaves were used for other purposes than males. Existing laws — whether protective or oppressive — were not automatically heeded or

---

at the Atlantic School of Theology in Halifax, Nova Scotia), and Hans Rapp (at present, minister at the Evangelical Reformed Church in Frenkendorf, Switzerland) have collected, sifted, topically arranged, and evaluated the literature upon which the picture of slavery here presented is based. Without their careful and intensive work, I would not have dared to present a summary of the present state of research on ancient slavery. Still, mistakes and errors, eventual traces of prejudices or misjudgments go on my own account.

2. R. H. Barrow, *Slavery in the Roman Empire* (London: Methuen, 1928; reprint, New York, 1968), p. 98. In Appendix I, pp. 237-245, Barrow presents an annotated collection of Latin references from ancient historiographers, poets, and other writers, also from inscriptions. A similarly complete florilegium of Greek texts has not come to my attention.

3. Brief surveys on the nineteenth- and twentieth-century historiography on slavery are given in chap. 6 of J. Vogt, *Sklaverei und Humanität* (Wiesbaden: Steiner, 1965); N. Brockmeyer, *Antike Sklaverei*, Erträge der Forschung 116 (Darmstadt: WBG, 1979), pp. 16-73; Brockmeyer, *Ancient Slavery and the Ideal of Man* (Oxford: Blackwell, 1974), pp. 170-210; M. I. Finley, *Ancient Slavery and Modern Ideology* (London: Chatto & Windus, 1980), pp. 11-66. For the controversy between Marxist and non-Marxist evaluations, see esp. Brockmeyer, *Antike Sklaverei*; Z. Yavetz, *Slaves and Slavery in Ancient Rome* (New Brunswick, N.J.: Transaction, 1988), pp. 115-175.

enforced. The dividing line between slaves and free persons was not always sharply drawn or easily recognized. A slave could own one or more slaves; he could, within certain limits, possess private property. He could work side by side with his owner or with other free persons. Often a reasonably rich man's slave was better off than a poor citizen in possession of all civil rights. Also there were forms of a person's legal status in which elements of total dependence and of freedom were mixed.[4] In Egypt, which was, according to the Bible, the paradigm of a slave house, there existed completely dependent labor forms; but the servants were not treated as mere instruments or cattle. In turn, in Greece and in Italy formally freed ("manumitted") persons possessed, at least in the first generation, no more than a very limited freedom.[5]

c. Ancient slavery has, for better or worse, served its time and run its course. To describe its essence, its horrors, and maybe some alleviating circumstances, a modern historiographer cannot draw on his awareness of scandalous, oppressive conditions of his own time — though they may motivate him to study former systems of exploitation and to learn from them for his own stance in contemporary social issues. Indeed, conditions similar to ancient slavery still survive in some southern and eastern parts of today's world. Forced labor, exploitation, and brutal contempt of fellow human beings still exist everywhere, even in supposedly civilized countries. But the feudalism of medieval Europe, the treatment of black persons imported as cheap labor to Europe and the Americas, the proletariat created in the wake of industrialization, the recently abolished apartheid system of South Africa, and the grip in which nations of the Northern Hemisphere keep most of the Southern peoples — systems such as these are not simply the same as ancient slavery. For the latter was only in exceptional cases directly related to skin color, racism, nationalism, and work considered beneath the dignity of free persons. Among ancient slaves there were highly intelligent and well-trained people who did qualified work and had — especially at Paul's time — a fair chance of being eventually manumitted and/or of marrying into the owner's or another free person's family. Not only Marxist students of slavery but also, e.g., F. Nietzsche,[6] agree that in many aspects an ancient slave's treatment was better and his life conditions more secure than those of a nineteenth-century factory worker. A Greek or Roman master had a keen interest in keeping his slaves healthy and gaining their confidence. Only during a limited period did slave revolts lead to open slave wars. Since poor, free people only rarely showed solidarity with the rebelling slaves, it

---

4. Examples are the Helots in ancient Sparta, the metics in Athens, and the *coloni* (war veterans settled on state property) in the Roman provinces.

5. As Pliny the Younger's letters to Sabinianus (*Ep.* 9.21 and 24) show; see Annotation 4, pp. 86-87.

6. *Menschliches-Allzumenschliches* I. Ein Blick auf den Staat, p. 457.

would be misleading to treat slavery as the cause or a feature of a perennial class struggle between the rich and the poor.

d. Some historical problems regarding ancient slavery are solved in such contradictory fashion or so obscurely that it seems best to consider them unanswered and open. Were the great achievements of Greek culture and Roman order possible only on the basis of this one regrettable substructure? Was slavery an essential but ultimately catastrophic element of the economy that contributed to the decay and fall of the Roman Empire? Was debt enslavement on the way out in different parts of the ancient world? If so, was it because in the long run work done by hired helpers and employees proved to be cheaper than the maintenance of a slave in good and especially in bad times? Can it be upheld that philosophical philanthropic thought and progressive legal development, or that Jewish and/or Christian influence, played a decisive part in the final abolition of ancient slavery? While clarity and harmony among scholars dealing with such questions seem highly desirable, they certainly are not yet in view.

This observation cannot, however, prohibit an attempt to depict some of the main aspects of ancient slavery as they may implicitly or explicitly be reflected in Paul's Epistle to Philemon.

II. WAYS INTO SLAVERY

In antiquity four elements were constitutive of the Greek legal concept of freedom: the right to represent oneself in matters related to courts and property; the protection from forced seizure, without due process of law; the right to work and earn a living according to one's own choice; the liberty to go and live wherever one desired. Among these points, the first was decisive while the latter three might be impinged upon.[7] Roman definitions of freedom are even shorter: freedom is "the power to live as you wish," or consists of "doing whatever one pleases unless something is prohibited by force or law."[8] There were several ways to lose freedom, to be forced into slavery, or even to bow to its yoke voluntarily.

a. *War and piracy.* Just as in the great ancient Near Eastern empires of

7. This description of freedom is based on the Delphi inscriptions regarding the manumission of slaves, as elaborated upon by W. L. Westermann and summarized by S. S. Bartchy, *MALLON XPHΣAI: First-Century Slavery and the Interpretation of 1 Cor 7:21*, SBL Press, Diss. Series 11 (Missoula, Mont., 1973), pp. 42-43.

8. See, e.g., Cicero, *Parad. St.* 5.1.34, and Florentinus's and Justinian's Institutes 1.3.1; cf. A. Berger, *Encyclopedic Dictionary of Roman Law* (Philadelphia: Philosophical Society, 1953), p. 552.

Babylonia, Assyria, and Egypt, and in tiny Israel, so in Greece and Rome prisoners of war were made slaves — unless they were promptly redeemed. If compared with the barbaric custom of killing captive and wounded enemies, the profitable use made of former enemies by turning them into slaves at least saved the life of the defeated. Commercial gain was certainly the motivation of pirates and other man hunters. Free persons who were caught could either be used to extract ransom money from relatives or be sold on the market.

b. *Slave markets.* With daily rates of up to one thousand persons, the islands of Chios and Delos, the Greek cities of Athens and Corinth, in the Near East Tyre and Ephesus, in the West Rome and Syracuse were the most prosperous slave-trade centers. The majority of slaves sold on the market stemmed from the East.[9] Unless the number of slaves offered for sale exceeded demand, the price of an able-bodied adult equated in Greece, at Plato's time, and in Rome, in the days of Cicero, the yearly income of a free artisan. In the East[10] three annual wages of an employee were paid for a slave. In addition to the selling price, local and regional import, export, sales, and eventually manumission taxes had to be disbursed. In addition, the buyer was responsible for the payment of private debts the slave might have incurred under his former owner. The purchase of a slave was a capital investment that would bring a return only after one, three, or more years. Slaves were bought by states, cities, temples, real estate holders, industrialists, shop owners, and other private citizens. Just as in the Second Temple in Jerusalem, so probably also some early Christian congregations and bishops held slaves.[11]

c. *Self-sale.* Under the pressure of debts and other extreme needs, a free man could sell himself into slavery — if he so desired, together with his family. Solon's legislation in ancient Athens forbade this act of ultimate despair. Roman law made no provision for it. But in the Babylonian and Assyrian empires the majority of slaves consisted of debt slaves, not of prisoners of war. Much later, in the Roman provinces, self-sale could not be suppressed — though since

9. Following Livy, *Hist.* 35.49.8; 36.17.5, Jews, Syrian, Lydians, and Medes were "born for slavery"; cf. Cicero, *Prov. cons.* 10; *Pro Val. Flacc.* 65.

10. Including Israel, see Deut 15:18.

11. See below, n. 156, and F. Overbeck, "Über das Verhältnis der alten Kirche zur Sklaverei im Römischen Reich," in Overbeck, *Studien zur Geschichte der Alten Kirche* (Chemnitz: Schmeitzner, 1875), p. 211. In *1 Clem.* 55.2; Hermas, *Man.* 8.10; *Sim.* 1.8; *Apostolic Constitutions* 4.9, there are indications that church members were urged to redeem Christian slaves, or were commended for doing it. Equally, Jewish families or synagogues in the Diaspora ransomed, if possible, Jewish members from their pagan masters. Still, Ignatius, *Polyc.* 4.3, warns: let slaves "endure slavery to the glory of God that they may attain a better freedom from God. Let them not desire to be set free at the church's expense, that they be not found the slaves of lust." Similarly Tertullian, *De cor. mil.* 13: manumission may well lead to new enslavement in the world.

Emperor Augustus it was often more profitable for a slave owner to manumit slaves than to increase their number. There is evidence also of reasons for self-sale other than debt and poverty. The intention could be fraudulent when, e.g., a self-sale took place to prevent bankruptcy, to avoid falling into the hands of a heinous creditor, or to reclaim the lost freedom by legal tricks after the heat was off. Some early Christian documents speak of a noble reason for self-sale. Though the apostle Paul had warned church members "not to become slaves of men" (1 Cor 7:23), in about 100 c.e. a Roman bishop compares self-sale to the self-sacrifice of noble Gentiles when the money from it had been used for ransoming other Christians or to provide food for the needy.[12]

d. *Court sentences.* Insolvent debtors could be condemned by a court to slave labor or to become slaves. The same judgment could strike murderers, arsonists, tax evaders, draft dodgers; this way the number of state-slaves was increased or part of the damages suffered by the state or private persons was recovered. Some courts condemned vile criminals to a gladiators' school, to galley service, or to fighting wild animals. Greek city laws as well as special ordinances passed for Rome and Alexandria (Egypt) forbade that a local citizen became a slave in his own hometown; he had to be sold abroad. In Rome enslavement because of debts was made illegal no earlier than under the first emperors.[13] However, because private property rights and laws prevailed over social legislation, debt enslavement by court sentence continued throughout the empire.

e. *Exposure of children.* Unwanted children, especially girls, could be brought up or sold by their finders as slaves, prostitutes, or wives. Only if they could prove their free birth or were redeemed by their natural parents could they become free again.

f. *House birth.* When, by the middle of the first century b.c.e., the great Roman wars of expansion had come to an end and the influx of captives was drastically reduced, an increasing proportion of slaves were born and raised on the premises of slave owners. There were children begotten by the master and borne by female slaves; only a minority of them were eventually formally adopted, declared free, and made coheirs with the patron's legitimate offspring or relatives. Other house-born slaves stemmed from voluntary or enforced liaisons between male and female slaves. From a patron's viewpoint, slave breeding was much cheaper and also more desirable than slave buying. Unless a bought slave was a skilled artisan, a businessman, or a teacher of outstanding character,

---

12. *1 Clem.* 55.2. According to R. Knopf, *Lehre der zwölf Apostel, Zwei Klemensbriefe,* HNT, suppl. vol. (Tübingen: Mohr, 1920), p. 132, "concrete examples of the self-sacrifice here praised are not known from the old Roman congregation or from early Christianity." The *Apostolic Constitutions* (5.1.3), however, recommend this sacrifice.

13. Though Livy, *Hist.* 8.28, mentions a *lex poetali* of 311 b.c.e. that prohibits debt slavery.

for a long time or forever he would be trusted far less than a slave who had grown up under the master's eyes. At the time of Paul, the majority of slaves had never known freedom because they were house born. Slaves by birth seemed to contradict theories saying that slavery was a result of bad luck, brute power, or inhuman legislation. Rather, the existence of house-born slaves appeared to support the opinion that slavery had its foundation in nature, or — to use a medieval expression — in natural law.[14]

During the nineteenth century, scholarly estimates regarding the numerical proportion of slaves to the total population of the antique cities and states varied widely. More recent research comes to converging results. In ancient Babylonia and Assyria the number of slaves was insignificant. Slaves were found only in rich houses, and even there, between one and three formed the average while ten were exceptional.[15] In the great cities of Greece and Italy, as many as one-third of the inhabitants may have been slaves; in Corinth up to half.[16] In Italy the number of slaves was drastically increased after the Punic Wars in the West and the conquest of Eastern territories; between about 200 and 150 B.C.E. 250,000 prisoners of war became slaves. In the period of the slave wars (ca. 140-70 B.C.E.), as many as 300,000 slaves may have lived in the city of Rome. Still, by the time of Julius Caesar the markets for war prisoners were shriveling up. The maintenance of large numbers of slaves became a luxury only few citizens could afford — for showing off their wealth rather than economical gain. In the towns and rural districts of the Roman provinces, there lived far fewer slaves than in the great Roman and Greek political, trade, and industrial centers.

14. Aristotle, *Pol.* 1.1254a, 1255a, states, "From the hour of their birth, some (persons) are marked out for subjection, others for rule. . . . Some persons are by nature free, and others are slaves, and . . . for these latter slavery is both expedient and right." Cf. *Pol.* 1.1260b: "The slave exists by nature." The Greek language uses the same term *(physei)* to denote "by birth" and "by nature."

15. Following I. Mendelsohn, *Slavery in the Ancient Near East* (New York: Oxford University Press, 1949), pp. 116 and 121.

16. Athenaeus, *Deipnosoph.* 272b, mentions individuals who owned more than 1,000 slaves, and — though not without some signals of skepticism — for Athens in about 300 B.C.E., the figure of 21,000 citizens, 10,000 metics, and 400,000 slaves; for the small island of Aegina and its huge slave market, 470,000; and for the city of Corinth more than 460,000 slaves. Also Athenaeus quotes a writer who claims that "every Roman has an infinite number of slaves; in fact there are many who own 10,000, 20,000, or even more." Since H. Wallon, *Histoire de l'esclavage dans l'antiquité* (Paris: Hachette, 1847), p. 224, such numbers are considered exaggerated. Only on latifundia and in mines could one — very rich! — employer use so many slaves.

III. THE SLAVE'S DAILY LIFE AND LEGAL POSITION

In the western countries under Roman rule, large numbers of slaves were used in mines, on the huge rural estates (called latifundia), and on galleys. Sources for researching and describing the plight of these slaves are almost nonexistent.[17] The desperate situation of industrial and agricultural slaves is revealed by the fact that most of the great slave revolts originated in places where hundreds of thousands of slaves worked relatively near to one another, and in cities. For understanding Paul's Letter to Philemon, the broad issue of mass slavery cannot be neglected, but attention has to be focused primarily on the fate of house slaves living in relatively close contact with their owners.

Whether a slave's life was more or less tolerable, or was utterly miserable, was dependent on at least three factors: the treatment by the owners, the laws and customs regulating the master/slave relation, and the slave's own attitude and work. The relevance of each of these factors varied, depending on conditions of peace or war, on economic opportunities or pressures, on national affinities or tensions, on deep-rooted prejudices or developing philosophical and moral humanitarian ideas, on personal experiences, and on public opinion.

A. Good and Bad Masters and Slaves

There was a proverb saying, "As many enemies as (you have) slaves,"[18] and another, "Only the wise man is free, those wicked are enslaved."[19] References are

---

17. Plato's philosophical and political works, Aristotle's sociological and moral writings, as well as, e.g., Cicero's and Seneca's tracts and epistles deal with domestic slaves. Some details about the treatment of slaves who, as chain gangs or unfettered, worked on extended landed property are given by a relatively progressive ancient patron, Lucius Junius Moderatus Columella. In the first century c.e. he wrote — from the master's point of view — several books on agriculture *(De re rustica)*. In the course of his discussion of the most profitable use to be made of slaves (1.8.7-10), he advises, for instance, that an overseer should have "such qualities of feeling that he may exercise authority without laxness and without cruelty, and always humour some of the better hands, at the same time being forbearing even with those of lesser worth so that they may rather fear his sternness than detest his cruelty." From Columella's well-meant counsel conclusion can be drawn upon the widespread cruel treatment of slaves who in most cases never saw their owner and were not personally known to him.

18. See, e.g., Seneca, *Ep. mor.* 47.5; Macrobius, *Sat.* 1.11.13; Festus, *Gramm.* 349.23, as mentioned by S. Lauffer, "Die Sklaverei in der griechisch-römischen Welt," *Gymnasium* 68 (1961): 376.

19. Diogenes Laertius, *De clar. phil. vitis,* 7.121. In his *Paradoxa Stoicorum,* Cicero gives these words a Stoic interpretation: they concern the soul and the virtue of the rich and the slave, rather than their social status. Philo, *Quod omnis probus liber sit,* presents the same

---

made to "the natural brutality of slaves."[20] However, it would be presumptuous to derive from such dicta that everywhere and always all slave owners were of malicious intention and ruled with a merciless fist. Equally misleading would be the notion that all slaves were continuously thinking of flight, murder, or revolution and enjoyed, while bearing their yoke, nothing better than lying, cheating, and raping.

Seen through the master's eye, the slave was an expensive investment that had to bear dividends. At the same time, this piece of property was considered more than only a useful matter or a figure in a calculation. Aristotle called the slave a possession and an instrument but emphasized that this tool was "a living possession . . . which takes precedence over all other instruments," which are no more than "lifeless slaves." Among all possessions, slaves were esteemed as the most necessary and essential, though also the most troublesome.[21] If it was conceded that the slave has a soul, yet this soul was considered inferior to that of a woman or a child.

Slaves had *names* by which they were called — unless they were addressed

---

opinion. Following Plato, *Leg.* 6.776-778, some slaves, indeed, are more virtuous than a brother and a son; yet he considers it also true that the soul of a slave is utterly corrupt. For, as the wisest of the Greek poets, Homer (*Od.* 17.322-323), has observed, the far-thundering Zeus bereaves those enslaved of half of their reason. Slaves must always be suspected of plotting against their master; therefore they must be ruled with an iron hand, though not without justice.

20. Diodorus Siculus, *Ant. hist.* 34/35.2.13.33, quotes this phrase in order to disprove it by showing that slaves were brutalized to the point of despair; he stresses the wrong suffered at the hands of their masters. He advises the patrons to "treat their slaves gently. For heavy-handed arrogance leads states into civil strife and . . . paves the way for plots of slaves." Equally in 2.40, Diodorus attributes the start of violence between slaves and masters to cruel owners rather than to vengeful slaves. In 2.27, 36-37 the same author mentions masters who provided no food to their hardworking slaves but forced them to form foraging groups who would steal and plunder and kill in order to get something to eat.

21. Aristotle, *Pol.* 1.1253b; *NE* 1161b *(ktēma empsychon, empsychon organon)*; Ps.-Aristotle, *Oec.* 1.1344a. In *Pol.* 1254b, Aristotle observes that "the use made of slaves and tamed animals is not very different." The Latin historian Varro, *Rust.* 1.17.1, describes slaves as vocal, semivocal, and mute at the same time; for they speak like people, are semivocal like cattle, and serve as mute waggons. Correspondingly, following Aristotle, *NE* 8.1161b and *Pol.* 1.1254ab, the relationship between master and slave is like that between a craftsman and his tool, or the soul and the body, or the male and the female. It is "natural and expedient," so this philosopher teaches, that "the soul rules over the body, and that mind and reason exert authority." According to *Pol.* 1.1255b, "the abuse of this authority is injurious to both." At any rate, "the slave is part of his master, a living but separated part of his bodily frame." More texts from Plato and Aristotle will be cited in the subsection on philosophy, pp. 33-36. It was Aristotle rather than Plato who, by his political, sociological, and moral writings, decisively influenced not only ancient Greek and Roman but also medieval thought on slavery and corresponding practices.

10

by equivalents of the American "boy."[22] Unlike the sons of Romans who received numbers for names, such as Tertius or Quartus, slaves were not treated as numbers and not branded with figures. Some bore an outlandish name, e.g., Manes or Midas, indicating the country of their origin. Others were given names by their owners that expressed the master's expectation; examples are Onesimus = useful or profitable; Eunous = well-disposed, friendly; and Fortunatus = lucky man. Though within narrow limits, a slave was considered a person with a minimum of dignity.[23] These were slaves who on the day of their manumission accepted a new name — in most cases that of their master. They achieved two ends by this: they shed the slave name they may have hated, and they expressed their experienced or expected good relationship with the patron.

Unless slaves were exposed by absent landlords, mine owners, or factory owners to tough supervisors, or were kept by affluent citizens as status symbols, in most cases they worked together with their owners to fulfill the same tasks; many were dressed the same way, ate the same food, and lived in similar housing. However, useless or rebellious slaves were excluded from laboring at the side of free persons. Only very rich masters could afford wasting a slave's productive capability in mines or quarries. There the dangers inherent in the work to be done, and wanton treatment by slave drivers, would drastically threaten the health and shorten the life span of a slave.

In cities and on farmland, slaves were sometimes delegated to work temporarily for another master. With the permission of their owner and provided that they hand over most of their earnings to him, they could also hire out themselves. A reasonable master would organize the cooperation between himself and the slave after the rule that he would "require work and offer what is right"; in order to benefit as much as possible from a slave and make use of dormant capabilities, a master might train the unskilled or have him or her schooled by experts in a craft or in trade.[24] Because of their physical strength,

22. For details concerning Greek slave names, see M. Lambertz, *Die griechischen Sklavennamen* (Vienna: M. Lambertz, 1907), esp. 2.31; Bartchy, p. 61; and Lauffer, p. 379. See Annotation 1, pp. 83-84, for a summary regarding slave names and designations.

23. According to Lauffer, p. 385, "the favorite formulation that the slave is not a human being, but a matter, dates from the 19th century and corresponds to the ethos of the modern emancipation movement." Cf. n. 52.

24. Cicero, *Off.* 1.41; Seneca, *Ben.* 3.21.2. Following Ps.-Aristotle, *Oec.* 1.1344, the life of a slave consists of labor, punishment, and eating, and it is to be shaped in a way that his working capability does not suffer. He is to be treated neither all too crudely nor all too leniently. When he does the work of a free man, he is to be honored, deserves to be richly nourished, and should be humored by the permission to participate in festivities. Xenophon, *Oec.* 3.4; 5.16; 13.9, warns of brutality and recommends good treatment because it supports a good atmosphere at home. While a Roman slave owner had unlimited power over life and

education, intellect, or technical skill, slaves could sometimes do better work than their owners or other free people.[25] In most cases, whatever the work, the performance of free persons and slaves could lead to the same result and quality.[26] Slaves had an edge over free workers because only in exceptional cases were they drafted for military service.

If all the heavy, supposedly lower and certainly more depreciated basic and indispensable duties and chores had been fulfilled by slaves, the antique community would deserve the title "slave-holder society," and its economy the label "slave economy." Yet the instances were relatively rare in which a slave owner passed his or her life in luxury as an absentee landlord or landlady, or as an unproductive city capitalist busied only with counting his blessings. Rather, because in all occupations free people and slaves worked side by side, nineteenth- and twentieth-century class-struggle terminology is not appropriate.[27]

---

death, in Greece local laws imposed some restrictions. In Israel, Hebrew slaves stood under some legal protection, and wise men advised moderation. See Annotation 2, pp. 84-85, for a first look at slavery among Jews, and sec. VIII, pp. 53-83, for a description of the main lines of Old Testament and rabbinic teaching on slavery.

25. An early Roman writer of comedies made a master say to a slave, "am I your slave or are you mine?" (Plautus, *Bacch.* 163). Ps.-Xenophon, *Athen.* 1.10-12, in about 420 B.C.E., warned free men not to hit a slave at the work site because the person hit might be indistinguishable from a free worker, and argued "it is no longer profitable for my slave . . . to fear you. . . . For this reason we have set up equality between slaves and free men, between metics and citizens." Both the Roman comic writer and the Athenian patriot may well exaggerate, but they still contribute to the variety of relevant opinions.

26. In antique literature, attempts were made at listing the work to which slaves were assigned; see, e.g., Athenaeus, *Deipnosoph.* 6.267b-d. Among the slaves are agricultural workers, dockworkers, transport workers, treadmill workers, street cleaners, garbage removers; skilled laborers in dockyards, weapon factories, and other factories; builders (and wreckers) of houses, palaces, temples, streets, squares, shops, businesses, and private constructions, fortifications, canals, sewers, aqueducts; stonecutters and stone setters, masons, cabinetmakers, carpenters, metalworkers, potters, glassworkers, painters, seamstresses, beauticians, bathhouse attendants; delivery boys, scribes, postal couriers, accountants, buyers and salesmen, bankers, investors, authorized agents; in households: janitors, bodyguards, lamp carriers, gardeners, cleaners, stable boys, laundry workers, boudoir assistants, wet nurses, table servants, musicians and other entertainers, also private secretaries, educators of children, doctors; in city or state administration: record keepers, librarians, engineers, tax collectors, policemen — sometimes of higher rank than manumitted or freeborn persons.

When slaves were deemed fit for high positions in trade, administration, public service, or even at the emperor's court, they were usually manumitted. Actually they were used for checking free competitors for the same offices and were envied or treated as a threat to the privileges of those freeborn (W. L. Westermann, *The Slave System of Greek and Roman Antiquity,* 3rd ed. [Philadelphia: American Philosophical Society, 1964], p. 916).

27. Bartchy, pp. 86-87, refers to the review article by F. Villinghoff in *Gymnasium* 69 (1962): 269-286, in which the theses defended by Soviet-Russian scholars are discussed. Books

In addition, after about 50 B.C.E. the proportion of slaves to the total population was decreasing. As mentioned, this happened not only because of the diminished supply of slaves under the imperial Pax Romana and because of enlightened criticism of cruel slave treatment, but also because slave labor became more expensive than the work of free persons. Egypt instead of Sicily began to be the corncrib of Rome. Periods of poor harvests or a general recession were hard not only on slaves but equally on masters who had to feed them through this or that crisis.

An owner who expected his "animated instrument" to do good work and serve faithfully could not spare the expense of providing the slave with enough food, adequate clothing (e.g., of leather), an adequate roof over the head, and if need be doctoral care.[28] A decent funeral of slaves was prescribed by law, but not guaranteed. It was in the master's own interest to avoid conflicts, to control himself when meting out punishment, and to keep the slave in as good a mood as possible. Because of the expensive maintenance of a slave, it became more and more unlikely that within one to three years the market price of the slave would be recovered, and the value of the slave's work became clear profit. Though there were old families who treated slaves better than the newly rich,[29] there also were staunch conservatives who spurned what looked to them like an all-too-soft treatment.[30] There are examples of table community shared between master and slave; there were intermarriages. In Greece and Rome tombstones have been discovered on which masters praise the courage and fidelity of a slave who had, for instance, saved the master's life during a war or when fellow slaves planned revolt, arson, or murder.[31] Evidence does not exist that slaves

written or edited by H. H. Kippenberg, e.g., *Die Entstehung der antiken Klassengesellschaft* (Frankfurt: Suhrkamp TB, Wiss. 130, 1977), represent the Marxist viewpoint.

28. According to Xenophon, *Mem. Soc.* 2.4.2-4; 10.1-2, an affluent friend fallen ill might be neglected; but for a sick slave a doctor would be called.

29. As the Attican orator Isaeus, *Orat.* 8.41, observes; cf. Seneca, *Ep.* 47.14-15. The good olden times are recommended by Plutarch, *Coriol.* 24.5, when he writes, "In those days the Romans treated their slaves with great kindness"; slaves were punished only so much that they felt ashamed, and cruel actions of the masters were resented by the public. In analogy, e.g., Athenaeus, *Deipnosoph.* 6.263b; 267ef; 273a-e, notes a nostalgic reference to the time when everybody in a house or on a field did his own work, with his own hands, not having any slave. Even for the future, working without slaves is considered possible and desirable. Cf. Westermann, *Slave System,* p. 21.

30. E.g., Plutarch, *Cato* 5.1, 2, mentions the following principles of Marcus Cato, who lived from 214 to 149 B.C.E.: slaves must be treated like beasts of burden and used to the uttermost. May they sleep enough — then they will work all the harder. For having intercourse with his wife, a slave has each time to pay a price.

31. Plato, *Leg.* 6.776d: "We know of course that one ought to own slaves who are as docile and good as possible; for in the past many slaves proved themselves better in every form of excellence than brothers or sons, and have saved their masters and their goods and

used every national or economical emergency to start strikes or slow work, or to engage in sabotage or open rebellion. A slave well treated, trusted, and rewarded was — even when he was later manumitted — a living old-age insurance for the owner.

Slaves were permitted or could afford to go to the theater and to celebrate, together with free persons, on festival days. Especially the Saturnalia were an occasion on which a slave might be served at table by no lesser persons than his master and/or his mistress. It was considered wise behavior when time and again the master let freedom wink, that is, when he goaded and prodded his slave by speaking of eventual manumission.[32] Does this imply that "good service was the road to manumission"?[33] And does it mean that the life of a slave doing domestic work or of a slave artisan, shopkeeper, or secretary was tolerably good and protected? Certainly, when a master did not keep his word, hopes raised in a slave were frustrated.

And yet, many slaves were given more than good words. Even while they were still slaves, in Greece — just as earlier in the neo-Babylonian empire — there were masters who allowed skilled slaves to keep for themselves a fixed sum or a proportion of the proceeds of their work. When the owner possessed land or cattle, the slave could rise to a status resembling that of a tenant farmer and receive the right to use a part of the land and of the gains made for his own benefit. When he married into the owner's or another free family, a house or other things could become the slave's private property by testament. Slaves who acquired slaves of their own have already been mentioned. In Rome, although a master could not be forced to do so, out of his own will he was often ready to pay his slave or slaves more than only occasional tips or pocket money. Slaves received *peculium,* i.e., a fixed regular amount of which they could dispose with relative freedom.[34]

---

their whole houses." Cf. Dionysius of Halicarnassus, *Ant. Rom.* 12.6; Seneca, *Ben.* 3.18.4; 19.2-4, and passim; Philo, *De decal.* 167; Pausanias, *Perieg.* 1.29.7. The tragedian Euripides, *Helena* 728ff., lets an old slave say, "If then, I am born to be a slave, I should like to be reckoned among the noble slaves; having — if not the name — yet the heart and the mind of a free person. This is better than combining two evils in one person, an evil mind and submission to slavery." Documentation and discussion of "slave fidelity" *(Sklaventreue)* is given by Vogt, *Sklaverei und Humanität,* pp. 83-95. Whether a corresponding article or book on fidelity shown by masters toward sickly and aging slaves, even on *Herrentreue,* could ever be written, has not yet been demonstrated. Still, not all patrons were tyrants, rascals, and exploiters.

32. Xenophon, *Oec.* 5.16; Plato, *Plt.* 9.579a; Aristotle, *Pol.* 7.1330a; Ps.-Aristotle, *Oec.* 1344b; Cicero, *Pro Rabirio* 15; Philo, *Spec. leg.* 2.67; *Virt.* 123.

33. This formulation is A. M. Duff's in his book, *Freedmen in the Early Roman Empire* (Cambridge: Heffer, 1958), p. 14, and is taken up by Bartchy, pp. 82 and 104.

34. Delphi inscriptions of the early decades c.e. show that the Latin term *peculium* was transliterated in Greek. For a precise definition of *peculium* in Roman law, see Berger, s.v.

Some of the slave's money went into eating places and pubs, theaters and bawdy houses. Also the money could be used to move a slave's wife and children near himself. Slaves needed and spent cash to pay the membership fees of a collegium; others became adherents of a religious community, e.g., of one of the mystery cults; they paid for offerings to a (usually Eastern) deity. Some invested funds in their masters' business and thus became participants, shareholders, actually business partners. Others saved their *peculium* for preparing their separation from the master, that is, for defraying travel and living expenses during a planned flight. Again others saved money for paying the price — usually an amount exceeding the market value — for legal manumission by the owner or through the mediation of a temple.[35]

The features of slavery depicted so far do not suffice to declare that at Paul's time, in the Roman Empire, the average life of a house or city slave was fairly good, certainly tolerable.[36] Slaves would have had little or no reason to flee from their masters if their lot had generally been relatively easy during the first century c.e. The good work expected of a slave was not always stimulated by the master's good example or by honestly kept promises; therefore it was not always done out of the slave's free will. Masters used threats and had almost unlimited possibilities to punish a slave who actually or supposedly was guilty of idleness, neglect, mischief, and of displeasing his owner in any other way.

The most frequent form of punishment was beating. "You school a Phrygian by the whip," a proverb said.[37] Not only whips and goads were used

---

peculium, and W. W. Buckland, *The Roman Law of Slavery* (New York: Cambridge University Press, 1908; reprint, 1979), pp. 187-206.

35. When in ancient Babylonia and Assyria a slave died before he had spent his acquisitions and savings, his private belongings usually were seized by the master. Under Greek and Roman jurisdiction, however, only a part of the slave's property fell back to the slave's owner.

36. Lauffer, p. 377, states (trans. from the German original), "The slaves accepted their situation and had come to terms with it; . . . at its time slavery generally was a tolerable condition, a vital and over centuries well-functioning social institution . . . (which was) never as such put into question by the slaves themselves." Bartchy, p. 72, declares bluntly: "most slaves were treated well." As extreme alternatives to the ideology of a continuous class struggle (cf. n. 27), such opinions appear to be comprehensible. But they may well be as one-sided as the opposite generalization of permanent and total ill-treatment and misery of all slaves.

37. According to Xenophon, *Mem. Soc.* 2.1.15-17, Socrates answered the proposition, "by whips masters beat the laziness out" of their slaves, with his consent: "I make their lives a burden to them until I reduce them to submission." Plato, *Leg.* 6.777b-e, advises to punish a slave justly — and this not only by oral admonition; for the slave "is a troublesome animal and therefore he is not very manageable," being a "troublesome piece of goods." According to *Leg.* 7.793c-794a, "We ought neither add insult to punishment so as to anger them, nor yet leave them unpunished lest they become self-willed; and a like rule is to be observed with the free-born." Still much later, in about 300 c.e., the historiographer Diogenes Laertius, *De clar.*

to prod slaves, but also sticks — with the result that a chastised slave, though against his owner's intention and best interest, might be permanently maimed and crippled or even killed.[38] Unlike the custom of branding newly acquired slaves that prevailed in ancient Babylonia and was also carried out by the Romans in Sicily after the Punic Wars, in the Greek cities this cruel marking of slaves was probably not the rule. However, in the western parts of the Roman Empire a slave caught as a thief or fugitive could be branded FUR or FUG respectively.[39] Another way of marking a recaptured fugitive was to fix an iron collar bearing a warning inscription around his neck. Actual torture of slaves included exposure to heat or cold, and starving. Sometimes punishments were performed in public; a slave might be beaten and chased across the market by fellow slaves.[40]

For a slave who had killed his master, the death penalty was prescribed by law. It was usually carried out as slowly and cruelly as possible — e.g., by crucifixion.[41] Up to the time of Nero, in Rome the collective execution of all slaves on the premises where one slave had killed the master seems to have been undisputed. Under this emperor, in 61 c.e., a minority of the Senate in vain attempted to prevent a crucifixion of 400 slaves of the household of Pedanius Secundus, the prefect of Rome, who had been murdered by one of his slaves.[42] Since the owner of slaves was lord over their life and death — as much as he was free to dispose over the life and death of his own children — there was ample opportunity for extreme cruelty in the treatment of slaves, unless teachers of morals, an emperor, the Senate by laws, and public opinion imposed limits on tyrannical masters. Among the horror and atrocity stories circulating in the first century after Christ was that of a slave owner who fed his slaves to his lux-

---

phil. vitis 7.23, mentions a slave who while he was beaten said, "It is my nature to steal," and who received the answer, "and to be beaten, too."

38. Cf. Exod 21:20-21. In commenting on the Mosaic legislation concerning harsh punishment, Philo, *Spec. leg.* 3.141-143, discusses the legal and personal consequences to be borne by the master. When in the ancient Near Eastern empires fines were imposed on a person who had maimed another person's slaves, the fine was payable to the owner, not the victim; see S. Schulz, *Gott ist kein Sklavenhalter, Die Geschichte einer verspäteten Revolution* (Zürich and Hamburg: Flambert/Furche, 1972), for references.

39. The difficulty of selling such a slave on the market prevented money-conscious slave owners from taking this measure.

40. Torturous punishments are enumerated by, e.g., Galenus (ed. C. G. Kuhn, 5.17) and Seneca, *De ira* 3.3.6. Some slaves found guilty by a court or by their master were thrown before wild beasts or forced to become gladiators. According to Plutarch, *Coriol.* 24.5, cruel punishment performed in public was resented by eyewitnesses when they were in a holiday mood.

41. See Annotation 3, pp. 85-86, for details on crucifixion and other ways of executing slaves found guilty.

42. Tacitus, *Ann.* 14.42-45.

ury fish.[43] This story, including its surprising end, was spread around widely; it reveals that public opinion turned against extreme cruelty from masters.

The worst suffering under the institution of slavery was endured by *female slaves*. There exists little source and secondary material for writing a history of slavery that considers slave girls and women, but if this history could be written, it might uncover a repulsive uniformity in different cultures and periods — unlike the records of the lot of male slaves. A history of pain and tears and humiliation would be revealed — as is indeed the case in the biblical accounts of Abraham, Sarah, and Hagar (Gen 16; 21:1-21). In ancient Babylonia as well as in the culture presupposed by Homer, in the Greek and Roman cities, in town and country houses, a caught or bought or house-born slave girl became the maid of the lady of the house for all domestic purposes. As such, she was exposed to ever-changing wishes, including sadistic abuse.[44] At the same time, with or without the lady's consent, the female slave was an object of unlimited, at times perverse, sexual exploitation by the master, his male offspring, and his friends. Also she could be hired out to individuals or a brothel as a prostitute — just as were handsome young male slaves for sodomy.[45] It was assumed that lasciviousness and promiscuity were natural and welcome to all slaves, including those married.

A female slave was, however, not only supposed to give pleasure; she could also be expected to give birth to children who would increase the number

43. According to Seneca, *De ira* 3.40; Dio Cassius, *Hist. Rom.* 54.23.1-4, Vedius Pollio, once a slave, then a freedman, finally a very rich free Roman citizen, gave a dinner, and Emperor Augustus honored him with his presence. One of the slaves ruined a crystal vessel. In his ire, the host ordered — as he had often done before — the negligent slave to be thrown to the fish in his garden pool (the fish was a lamprey). The slave implored the emperor not to let him die this way. Augustus saved the slave's life by commanding that all crystal in the house be smashed and fed to the fish.

44. J. Leipoldt, *Die Frau in der antiken Welt und im Urchristentum*, 3rd ed. (Leipzig: Koehler and Amelang, 1965), p. 29, refers inter alios to Juvenal, *Sat.* 6.219 and 475ff.; Ovid, *Am.* 1.14.16ff.; *Ars am.* 3.239ff., for examples of cruel treatment.

45. Dio Chrysostom, *Or.* 15.5, observes that intercourse occurred not only in secret places. Musonius, *Ep.* 66.2, explicitly warns masters not to use enslaved girls and women for sexual satisfaction. For, so he argues, the male head of the house would certainly not wish his wife to turn to a male slave. Equally Seneca, *Constant.* 1.2, condemns sexual exploitation. Ps.-Demosthenes, *Ad Neaeram* 127, mentioned voices that were raised against the use of female slaves for prostitution. In his book, *Die Ehe im Neuen Testament,* ATANT 52 (1961), H. Baltensweiler refers to I. Bloch, *Die Prostitution,* vol. 1 (Berlin, 1912), pp. 364ff., for further examples. The Koran (XXIV 33) tells slave owners not to force into prostitution those slave girls who wanted to remain chaste. But it continues, "when someone yet uses force, then Allah is merciful and ready to forgive." Not only female slaves were sexually used. Though it is seldom mentioned in ancient literature, it was presupposed that male slaves could be submitted to homosexual exchange of favors; cf. Seneca, *Ep.* 47.7.

of the master's slaves. Slave women who had babies might become wet nurses to the patron's legitimate children; in this capacity they could ascend to a position of esteem and trust. Others proved their worth as assistants of the doctor who cared for the health of the master, his family, and his slaves. Chances were rare that a young or widowed master would marry a slave and thereby make her a free person. Hebrew and ancient Cretan law, as well as a Roman landlord's advice, contained elements that intended to protect a minimum of unfree women's dignity.[46] But this changed little or nothing: if male slaves had practically no legal rights, female slaves had even fewer. On the other hand, when in Rome a freeborn woman married a slave, her social rank was lowered. Unless she was very rich and influential, at best she had to be satisfied with the status of a freed woman *(liberta)*, which included obligations to the slave's master. In worse cases she became a maid *(ancilla);* either way, when her husband died before her, the master would inherit a substantial part of her dowry.

Despite the many hints so far given regarding the position of slaves before the law, details concerning changes of their legal status are still to be mentioned.

B. Changes in the Legal Position

"No part or lot in law has any slave"; "A slave person has no right"; "No obligation exists toward a slave"; "Over against slaves everything is permitted"; "A slave thou art, no right of speech hast thou."[47] These quotes seem to contain all that is known of the (absence of any) civil slave rights. And yet it is necessary to distinguish between temporal, regional, national, and local legislation. At the time of Paul, Roman legislation and court practice were harsher than Greek laws and customs had ever been. In Athens, for instance, a suit could be filed against a master whose behavior toward a slave appeared outrageous.[48] Since the first century C.E., Rome was in control of the Greek-speaking and other provinces, and cities such as Corinth and Ephesus could not avoid jurisdiction according to Roman standards. Still, there were also strong currents against total subordination to Rome. Neither universal nor provincial Roman law auto-

---

46. Exod 21:2-11; Deut 21:10-14; Law Code of the City of Gortyna (trans. A. C. Merriam, 2.14-15); Columella, *Rust.* 1.8.19.

47. Philo, *Quod omn. prob.* 48, cites the first and the last of these sentences from an unknown source that most likely is of Greek origin and may be dated back to the time of Solon and Lycurgus, whom Philo has mentioned just before. The second quote stems from the *Digesta* (of Paulus? Ulpian? Florentinus?) of the *Corpus iuris civilis;* the other two are culled from secondary legal literature on ancient slavery.

48. Athenaeus, *Deipnosoph.* 6.266ff.

matically prevailed over local traditions. Not only those parts of prescriptions and rulings that were or appeared to be unclear or self-contradictory, but the whole legal system of the occupying power, was ignored as much as possible, especially in Asia Minor, down to the third and fourth centuries c.e.[49] Therefore it must not be assumed that Paul's arguments in his Letter to Philemon are totally or primarily based on his acquaintance with Roman law and practice.

In addition, even Roman law, specifically regarding masters and slaves, was in the process of ever-new changes. State law, expressing a minimum of sociopolitical concern, was about to limit private law. Before the emperors' time private law had been the basis and the criterion of laws regarding slaves. Also, humanizing tendencies began to make themselves felt. Imperial legislation sometimes limped after changes that already had taken place. At other occasions, the laws and ordinances appear to have jumped ahead. At any rate, even where a statute explicitly prohibited cruel practices and encouraged a humane relationship between master and slave, the letter of the law could not guarantee voluntary implementation or enforce compliance. Progressive laws did as little compel a wicked slave master or mistress to stop tortures as reactionary laws prevented good slave owners from treating their slaves as fellow human beings. Certainly the first century c.e. was a time of transition in all issues related to slavery. In the following, starting from the status quo ante, the main steps taken in imperial legislation will be outlined.

Before the law and the courts a slave occupied a middle position between the owner's children and his cattle. The family head *(paterfamilias)* had the right *(potestas)* to decide over life and death *(ius vitae necisque)*, the work to be done, the place where the slaves had to live, and eventual sale on a slave market. While the lady of the house was also "under the hand" of the family head, she was in a slightly better position, but before the sons and daughters of the patron came of age, their dependence upon the father was as total as that of slaves.[50] Since a slave could not represent himself or herself in court, bought as well as house-born servants and maids were defenseless against charges raised against them. A slave's complaints against the owner, including legal matters regarding the slave's personal interests, were not admitted in court — unless a free person was willing to step in as representative. If the witness of a slave was heard in conflict cases between free persons, the slave's testimony was valid only when it was confirmed under torture. Even when money from relatives or from the slave's *peculium* was available for paying for the slave's release, the master could not be legally forced to grant freedom.

49. Bartchy, pp. 40-44 n. 104, gives examples.
50. In Dio Chrysostom, *Or.* 15.20, a drastic description is found of a father's full power over his minor sons. By law a father was entitled, e.g., to imprison, sell, or kill his child.

Thus the life of a slave was determined by the superior power and wealth of the owner. In ancient Rome, one of the worst possible results of law and order determined the daily life of the slave: legal traditions and customs cemented the relationship between the stronger and the weaker, the richer and the poorer. Slave laws made sure that the power holder was in the right, the underdog in the wrong. The people in possession of property were legally protected, and their common interests made them unite their forces, hold together, defend what they considered inherited rights.

Yet there were exceptions that prohibit the conclusion that, always and everywhere in the antique world, laws caused and revealed nothing but cruel suppression and exploitation of slaves. In 595 B.C.E. Solon prohibited the sale of a person for unpaid debts; also the self-sale of insolvent debtors was no longer permitted. Though the law prescribed the execution of a slave who had killed his master, after Plato's time the Athenians made the executions dependent on the verdict of a court. The killing of a slave for other grave offenses was legal, but the slave's master could renounce his right.[51] According to Roman law, a master who had killed a slave had to pay no more than a fine.

Still, a development took place. Before the Republic was succeeded by the rule of the Caesars, the slave had legally been not much more than a mere thing.[52] While the low esteem of slaves was never explicitly abandoned — except by philosophers and in the actual treatment of some slaves — laws passed in Rome under Augustus (31 B.C.E.–14 C.E.) and his followers revealed more and more the conviction that slaves were human beings and deserved to be treated as persons.[53]

In 18 B.C.E. the *Lex Julia de maritandis ordinibus* was still restrictive for women born as slaves: a senator must not marry a freedwoman. A potentially humanizing legislation begins with two laws that seem to contradict the slaves' best interest and yet could work out, especially with regard to manumission, in their favor. The *Lex Fufia Caninia* of 2 B.C.E. prescribes that freedom be granted solely to a limited number of slaves, that is, to a fixed proportion of the total number of slaves in the hand of one owner.[54] In 4 C.E. the *Lex Aelia Sentia* pro-

---

51. Columella, *Rust.* 1.7.2, warns masters not to exploit all that the law permits regarding a slave's treatment.

52. According to A. Ehrhardt, "Rechtsvergleichende Studien zum antiken Sklavenrecht," *Zeitschrift der Savigny-Stiftung für Rechtsgeschichte,* Roman. Abt., 68 (1951): 74ff., Lauffer, pp. 385-386, as observed in n. 23, questions the general application of this widespread opinion.

53. The following account is incomplete and contains gleanings from the works of A. Berger, W. W. Buckland, F. Lyall, M. I. Rostovzeff, and A. N. Sherwin-White, as listed in the bibliography.

54. One-half when there are 2-10 slaves; one-third out of 11-30; one-fourth out of 31-

vides that a slave owner must be at least twenty years old, a slave to be manumitted at least thirty;[55] that a female slave in order to be released for marriage with a free man must actually be married to him; and that no damage must result to a creditor by the emancipation of a slave — or else the manumission is null and void.

Again, in 19 C.E. the legislation appears to redound to both the advantage and disadvantage of slaves. The condemnation of a slave to fighting wild animals can no longer be pronounced by the private owner; the right to pass this judgment is laid into the hands of the prefect of Rome and the provincial procurators. On the other hand, a freed slave no longer receives the full Roman citizen's right but only a partial equivalent, the "Latin citizenship." This makes him a sort of resident alien, comparable to metics in Athens but superior to the status of Helots in Sparta. Still, in 20 C.E. the slave is promoted from a nonperson in court to at least some legal status before the magistrates and judges.

Under Claudius (41-54), in 47, a law was passed to protect incapacitated or rich slaves. The master can no longer simply throw them out and let them perish on the street or in a field; neither must he accelerate their death by any other means. If a slave can get to the Asclepius temple, he or she becomes free. From now on, a master who had killed a slave could be prosecuted and punished as a murderer.

At Nero's time (54-68), in 61, the prohibition to throw a slave to wild animals was repeated. While Domitian ruled (81-96), castration of slaves was disallowed. Especially during the reign of Hadrian (117-38), numerous progressive steps were taken. Punishable became the hijacking of persons for the purpose of selling them, the killing of a slave, the ill-treatment of slaves and their sale for indecent professions or as gladiators, and the separation of a slave from his parents, his wife, and his children. The right of slaves to acquire and possess property was asserted, together with the permission that they could freely dispose by testaments over 50 percent of their assets. Manumission — e.g., by municipal corporations in the provinces — was facilitated, and to the freed persons certain rights were granted.

100; one-fifth if there are more than 100. In theory, this law remained valid until the time of Constantine (306-37 C.E.). The fact that this emperor forbade the possession of Christian slaves by Jews and that, in addition, his successor, Constantius II (337-62), made it illegal for Jews even to own pagan slaves (see E. E. Urbach, "The Laws regarding Slavery, as a Source for Social History of the Period of the Second Temple, the Mishnah and Talmud," in *Papers of the Institute of Jewish Studies London*, ed. J. G. Weiss [Jerusalem: Magnes Press, 1964], p. 83), did not actually improve the fate of slaves. The only intention was to hurt the Jews.

55. According to an Egyptian version of this law ("Extracts from the Gnomon of the Ideologues," *Select Papyri*, LCL, 206.21), only a prefect was entitled to legalize the manumission of a slave under thirty years of age.

A law of Antoninus Pius's time (138-61) prescribed that a city prefect, if he found a slave's accusation of an excessively cruel owner well founded, could arrange the sale to another master. Beginning with the rule of this emperor, a fugitive's chance to find a safe asylum was increased. Finally, a rescript contained the threat of deportation or capital punishment to Jewish slave owners who circumcised their non-Jewish slaves.

Marcus Aurelius (161-80) declared the Roman law valid for the provinces. He also reconfirmed earlier ordinances that forbade the sale of slaves as gladiators, the use of slaves for shameful purposes, and the splitting up of families.

Septimius Severus (193-211) declared in about 208 that a master lost his honor when he cruelly manhandled a slave.

In the *Constitutio Antonina* (212) Emperor Caracalla (211-17) conveyed the full Roman citizen's right to all freeborn and freed men in the whole empire.

Since the years of Diocletian (284-305), the differences between the legal status of free and unfree persons were reduced — however, rather by the termination of privileges enjoyed by free citizens than by actual improvement of the slaves' lot.

Under Constantine (306-37) the severe punishment of a slave, including beating to death, was still tolerated and led to no legal consequences, but arbitrary killing of a slave was rated as murder and the branding and crucifixion of slaves were prohibited. The *Codex* of Theodosius (379-95) contains both elements that protect and features that alleviate slavery. Finally the *Codex of Emperor Justinian* (518; r. 527-67) established full equality between persons freed by manumission and persons born free. The emperor's code prescribed (in 7.4.14.2) that in ambiguous cases regarding a person's exact status, the "more humane judgment" should prevail.[56]

Indeed, these changes in law formed together no more than a trickle of oil upon an open wound, and the recurrence of some of the single drops reveals how ineffective some of them were, especially in the provinces. The first century B.C.E. *Lex Fabia de Plagiariis* (*Digesta* 48.15), which prohibited the harboring of fugitive slaves and imposed heavy fines on trespassers, was never rescinded. Other, more beneficial laws may never have been enforced in the provinces — with the effect that, e.g., Paul could either not know of them or not reckon with their enactment. And yet, especially those laws passed as a *Senatus consultum,* that is, as a decree of the rather conservative majority of the Roman senators, reveal an ongoing change that could — and eventually did — signal the demise of antique slavery.[57]

56. For details see Buckland, *Roman Law of Slavery.*

57. In many aspects, the successors of the ancient slave systems — the feudalism of the medieval Holy Roman Empire and, later, the import of slaves from overseas territories into Europe and the Americas — made things as bad as they ever had been, if not worse.

C. Feelings and Attitudes of Slaves

Very little source material is available regarding an antique slave's inner life and self-understanding. Under the influence of experienced slave fidelity and of Stoic thinking, the conviction emerged that a slave's virtues could well be far superior to those of the owner. But the consciousness of ancient slaves lies in a gray zone that defies scrutiny. Certainly in Greek and Roman comedies all kinds of slaves freely speak their mind. Still, many of the slaves appearing on the stage to make the people laugh have stereotyped characters, pronounce typologized opinions, and conduct themselves as the author and the spectators expect them to. Since the huge majority of slaves were illiterate, they could not leave to posterity written evidence of their thoughts and experiences. Those ancient writers who had been slaves themselves or stemmed from freed persons did not write autobiographies or use other occasions to wallow in frightening or humorous recollections.[58] What free or freed persons wrote in dramas, poems, epistles, and philosophical, moral, and legal tracts cannot be checked against slaves speaking for themselves with their own voices, gestures, tears — and smiles. In consequence, every picture drawn of ancient slavery is bound to be utterly defective and problematic.[59]

"No slave is really happy." "Eternal hatred . . . (is fostered) by a slave against his master."[60] "The slave prays that he be set free immediately." "I, desiring your affection, have conducted myself blamelessly, just as a slave wishes to be conciliatory in the interest of freedom."[61] "How can a person be happy while being a slave to anyone?" "Free people enjoy life and flourish, slaves labor to exhaustion and perish."[62] These statements are generalizations; they leave room for exceptions and contradictions. E.g., in a comedy a free man who works day by day as a hired hand complains, "How much better is it to have a decent mas-

---

58. Plato and Diogenes had been made prisoners and sold into slavery, yet were soon ransomed by friends. The Cynic philosopher Sion, the poet Terence, Horace's father, Epictetus, Dio Chrysostom, and several renowned artists, doctors, educators, and scholars had been slaves. Dio Chrysostom, *Or.* 15.2-12, has produced a fanciful dispute between a freeman and a slave that reveals that the slave by no means was ashamed of his social status.

59. Under the subtitle "The Slave's View of His Situation," Bartchy, pp. 82-87, tells the reader hardly more than that in the first century c.e. every slave hoped to be freed soon and had enough good reasons to expect manumission within a foreseeable space of time. Therefore, assumes Bartchy, it would be wrong to speak of a general "unrest among the slaves." But in Annotation 6, pp. 88-92, details of the slave revolts and wars will be mentioned. During the insurgencies, the slaves' own thoughts and capabilities became most distinctly tangible.

60. Philo, *Quod omn. prob.* 41; 1QS 9.21-23.

61. This way Bartchy, p. 85, interprets Epictetus, *Diss.* 4.1.33, and part of a Greek papyrus letter.

62. Plato, *Grg.* 491e; Heraclitus Ponticus, *Athen.* 12.512.

ter than to live lowly and badly as a free man."[63] Good masters could find partners in good, useful, and faithful slaves. More or less voluntarily, such slaves accept their fate and position.[64] Great achievements of ancient culture are at least as much due to slave labor as to the ingenuity of free people. It was slaves who made technical inventions that benefited not only the ruling or rich minority of the population but also the middle class — and the slaves themselves.[65]

The inner life of the slave, its potential development, and the threats to it became an object of special concern to Stoic moral philosophers. Yet before Stoic thought can be described, a look at the role played by religion in a slave's life is necessary.[66]

It is easy to understand why the classic Greco-Roman deities Zeus (Jupiter) and Hera (Juno) together with their Olympic, oceanic, and chthonic company and the half-gods, as worshiped on official occasions in the cities and the sanctuaries of the rulers and masters, exerted little or no attraction for the slaves. For the duration of some of the great festivals,[67] and at times of inner or external political turmoil, slaves were actually prohibited from seeking oracles or other comfort at the existing great temples. No one among the classic gods, the heroes, and the priests put the institution of slavery into question. However, as much as is known, this did not motivate slaves to declare themselves atheists or agnostics, or to condemn religion as such, e.g., as opium for people in their situation.

Slaves whose forefathers or who themselves stemmed from Asia Minor had favorites among less-known deities of their homelands. Others tried to in-

63. Philemon Comicus, *frag.* 277k.

64. Evidence of the term "their place," as it is used in English and American diction, seems not to exist in ancient literature. In Pauline writings — see Eph 6:5-6; cf. Col 3:22 — Christian slaves are exhorted not just to "please" their masters by "putting on a show" but to render their service "wholeheartedly . . . from the bottom of their hearts . . . with fervor." The suggestion made by Aristotle and other writers, that masters stimulate good work by speaking of eventual manumission (see above, n. 32), may not only have been heeded by wise or shrewd masters, but also may have motivated slaves to put their heart into their labor.

65. Seneca, *Ep.* 90.25-26, mentions windows that admit light through transparent tiles, vaulted baths with heating systems built into the masonry, the treatment of marble surfaces, and stenography.

66. Most important among treatments of this topic is F. Bömer, *Untersuchungen über die Religion der Sklaven in Griechenland und Rom,* vols. 1-4 (Mainz: Verlag der Akademie d. Wiss. u.d. Lit., 1958-63), esp. 1.29ff., 26f., 78ff., 105ff. While following Bömer, not too much weight is to be placed on the religious motivation of slaves; Vogt, "Sklavenkriege," in Vogt, *Sklaverei und Humanität,* pp. 20-60, esp. 37-48, has added indispensable corrections. For solid background information on religion in the Hellenistic and Roman time, see M. P. Nilsson, *Geschichte der griechischen Religion,* vol. 2, 2nd ed. (Munich: Beck, 1974), pp. 195-244, 345-384, 622-691.

67. See, e.g., Athenaeus, *Deipnosoph.* 6.262c.

terpret their masters' official gods in a sense favorable to their yearning for liberty. Again others sought refuge under the wings of deities known only in the region in which they were held captive. For slaves of eastern origin, the Syrian goddess Atargatis, also called Holy Aphrodite, the sun-god Helios or Mithras from Persia, or the god Men were guarantors of liberation. Slaves from other regions prayed to *Zeus Eleutherios (Jupiter Liberator),* Diana, Demeter, chthonic Sicilian deities, or house gods *(lares).* Similar special protection was attributed to the god Silvanus and the goddess Fortuna. Several slave revolts were started in the name of a deity. There were slave wars that had the character of not only national but also religious wars, in partial anticipation of the later crusades.

Gods and goddesses such as those mentioned were also worshiped by free people in the East and West, but slaves and other poor people most likely constituted the majority among the participants in these cults. There they had a welcome opportunity to meet and to feel equal to religious free persons. Foremost in mystery cults the earthly status of a worshiper made no difference. Slaves, deprived as they were of civil rights by civil law codes, had according to sacral law the capability to hold religious offices and to be respected as responsible functionaries.[68] Belonging to a religious community could therefore mean attaining some honorable position and increasing one's self-respect. Under the protection of his religious association, even a miserable, often beaten slave was far from the status of a thing or animal: he was accepted as a human being and could feel proud to be a servant of a deity. To be elected, accepted, and favored by a god could make a slave feel proud and help him survive the hardship endured from the hand of earthly masters. Papyri, inscriptions, and individual authors[69] reveal that members of a religious society were called "brothers." Religious attachment and engagement were especially attractive to slaves because in certain cults equality and brotherhood appeared to be realized for all persons.

Similar was the effect of joining one of the existing collegia in which slaves could meet on festival days or, if possible, on evenings of any day. A "college" consisted of a group of most diverse people who voluntarily and regularly met as a social club, a craft guild, and/or for providing to its members a decent funeral.

It was possible for a slave to participate in different cults and societies at the same time. The message and worship of God the Liberator from Egypt and

68. Schulz, p. 87, enumerates rights given in Roman sacral law to slaves and to sanctuaries they visited: in his relation to religion, a slave was a person, not a thing; a slave could bring offerings to gods, make valid oaths, and consecrate valuable oblations. The place where a slave was buried was protected.

69. Such as the astrologer Vettius Valens, 4.11.172.31, according to H. v. Soden, *TDNT,* 1.146.

of Jesus Christ the Redeemer seem to fit perfectly into the pattern of a slave's religious opportunities during the first century c.e. Slaves constituted the majority of the church members in Ephesus, Corinth, Rome, and perhaps everywhere. However, the intolerant attitude of, e.g., Paul, though not of some Corinthian church members, to other deities and cults did by no means support a merger or friendly coexistence of several religious attachments.[70]

The refuge a slave found in a religious community did not automatically make him a happy slave. Not even the mitigating conditions initiated for a slave under the early Roman emperors could prevent an ancient slave from anticipating the feeling and desire of American slaves: "I wanna be a slave no more . . . I wanna be free." Four ways of protest against the institution of slavery and the daily sufferings of a slave can be distinguished: (1) the frequently dearly paid-for escapist way, that is, flight from the master; (2) the violent alternative of murder, revolt, and open warfare; (3) the intellectual, spiritual, and moral way of philosophical consolation to which an increasing aversion of public opinion against slavery corresponds; (4) the formation of slave-free communities and the way of prayer — if by prayer is meant more than wishful thinking or turning away from faithful and courageous activity. Each of these methods in its own way can throw light on the content of the Letter to Philemon in some detail. In addition, the legal way into freedom, manumission, will also be discussed.

IV. FUGITIVE SLAVES[71]

The reasons for running away from the owners and seeking shelter elsewhere were probably always and everywhere the same: yearning for freedom or return to the family and home country, fear of the master's threats, experience of merciless treatment with or without cause, consciousness of some misdeed, hope at least for improved conditions under another employer.[72] But by far not all slaves who had been exposed to fear, beating, maiming, tortures chose to flee or

70. See, e.g., 1 Cor 8:4-6; 10:19-22.
71. The standard book on fugitive slaves and their fate is H. Bellen, *Studien zur Sklavenflucht im römischen Kaiserreich* (Wiesbaden: Steiner, 1971); reviewed by N. Brockmeyer in *Gnomon* 46 (1947): 182-187. According to Finley, pp. 111 (German trans. p. 212 n. 72), there exists source material for describing the flight of slaves in Rome and Italy, but not for slave flight in Greece and other Greek-speaking regions of the East — with the exception of Egypt. Cf. Buckland, p. 111, etc. For the ancient eastern empires see Mendelsohn, *Slavery*, pp. 58-64.
72. Philo, *Virt.* 124.

had a chance to escape. The great number of laws related to slave flight, the uncertain future of those runaways who had nowhere to go, and the prevailing practices of dealing with the recaptured were almost prohibitive. Except during great slave revolts, there appears to have been but scarce solidarity among slaves, and practically none at all with the poor among those free in the city and country proletariat. A very strong personal will, careful planning, and a state of extreme necessity were presuppositions of the attempt at a flight. The possibility of betrayal by a fellow slave had to be faced; the finding of food, clothing, and shelter was a daily problem; the risk of being found at a hiding place was to be borne; and harsh punishment after eventual recapture was certain. Because of the increasing chances to be legally manumitted, in the first century c.e. the number of escapees was probably lower than in preceding periods.[73]

Runaway slaves might occasionally find fellow sufferers, but on the whole they were shunned by people who feared for the consequence of associating with them and giving them food and/or cover. A fugitive was a lone wolf rather than part of an army. How could a person survive when, even more than before the flight, a civil law in his or her favor did not exist? The runaway was an outlaw who could be caught, starved, beaten, raped, and killed by anyone met anywhere, day or night.

One option for the runaway was joining a robber gang;[74] another was disappearing and merging among the throng of great harbor towns or other large centers such as Alexandria, Caesarea, Ephesus, Corinth, or Rome.[75] Fear would in most cases compel a slave to put the largest possible distance between the master and himself or herself. Again, not even beyond an ethnic or provincial border, or on another shore of the Mediterranean Sea, was safety assured. The name, accent, language, and behavior of the fugitive could prevent a kind reception by the local population and even contribute to detection. Whoever turned over such a person to the police, and finally to the irate owner, was richly rewarded. The risk of identification was great for the escapee — even

---

73. Evidence of the "armies of run-away slaves" of which E. Käsemann, *Essays on New Testament Questions Today* (Philadelphia: Fortress, 1960), p. 208, speaks, has not yet been produced, except for the period of the slave wars, between 140 and 70 b.c.e. But in Heb 6:18 all Christians are depicted as fugitives seeking to take hold of the hope that lies before them and that will not be frustrated.

74. An example to be dated a thousand years before the apostle Paul's time is offered by the community of "every one who was in distress . . . was in debt, and . . . was discontented" that gathered to David and whose captain he became when he was persecuted by King Saul (1 Sam 22:2). The rich farmer Nabal derided him as one of the "many servants who nowadays break away from their masters" (1 Sam 25:10). Obviously things related to slavery changed very little in the ancient world.

75. Epictetus, *Diss.* 1.29.59ff., speaks of a fugitive slave who, even while he is in a theater among the crowds watching a play, is in panic fear of being recognized.

27

when a seemingly permanent shelter and job were found. Because of the many unemployed free persons and freedmen who lived in poverty, the runaway's labor would be paid below a minimal rate; often the fugitive would be hungry, wet, and cold.

And yet, there also existed two ways to achieve at least the same if not a better life than had been endured before the flight: seeking asylum in the house of a free and, if possible, high-standing person; or entering the precincts of a temple that was permitted to offer refuge. These ways require special attention because the Letter to Philemon presupposes one or both of them.

Harboring fugitive slaves was prohibited by law in the East and West; whoever gave shelter, whether free man or free woman, freed slave or slave, trespassed existing strict laws and incurred, if denounced or otherwise discovered, heavy penalties.[76] A calculating fugitive who had met friends of his master in a personal way was well advised to appeal for temporary asylum at the door of an acquaintance of his patron. If possible, the slave would turn to a person of relatively high social standing. Roman law conceded that in this case the slave was not guilty of flight *(fuga)* in the full legal sense — if only the private asylum giver carefully examined the complaints of this slave and sent him back to his master, usually with a written request or recommendation how the prodigal should be received and treated.[77]

If both the fugitive and his protector wanted to stay together, the latter could offer compensation and, the owner's agreement provided, keep the slave for himself for lifelong service. Under given circumstances the asylum giver also was entitled to sell the slave on the market. For this reason, a slave's flight to the house of a free person did not mean certain freedom; rather it was an act of vol-

---

76. The Codex Hammurabi (dated in the eighth century B.C.E.) prescribes capital punishment for aiding and abetting flight. Sumerian and Hittite laws mention less severe punishments: either substitution of another slave or financial compensation to the owner. The Roman *Lex Fabia de Plagiariis,* mentioned on p. 22, corresponds in substance to the old Oriental legislation. See Mendelsohn, *Slavery,* pp. 58-59; Schulz, p. 29, for references.

77. The role of the asylum giver as an intercessor on behalf of a fugitive slave is beautifully exemplified not only by Paul's Epistle to Philemon but also by two letters, written about 110 C.E. from Rome, by Pliny the Younger. This high state official wrote letters in favor of a freedman who had run away from his patron. For the text of the two pertinent Pliny letters, see Annotation 4, pp. 86-87.

H. Grotius, J. B. Lightfoot, E. Lohmeyer, J. Knox, H. Greeven, E. Lohse, P. Stuhlmacher, and other commentators on Philemon have extensively referred to Pliny's epistles. R. Gayer, *Die Stellung der Sklaven in den paulinischen Gemeinden und bei Paulus* (Bern: Lang, 1976), pp. 258-266, offers a detailed comparison between Paul's and Pliny the Younger's arguments. Below, in the introduction to the literary issues raised by the Letter to Philemon, harmonies and differences between Paul's and Pliny's letters will be pointed out in order to throw light on the uniqueness of the biblical epistle. In the index of names at the end of this commentary, the page numbers will be listed where Pliny is mentioned.

untarily seeking a new and better master. Philo warmly recommends offering asylum, but he is aware that a "change of masters" rather than freedom is actually gained by fleeing slaves.[78]

When, however, the fugitive sought refuge at the home of a free person not befriended with his or her master, or of a friend who proved unable or unwilling to intercede, a bad situation ensued: neither the sacred duties and rights of hospitality at one's hearth nor the ancestor *lares* of the house protected the slave from forcible seizure by the owner, his delegates, or the city police; in addition, the host had to suffer grave legal and financial repercussions. Only Jewish law formed an exception to this general rule: according to Deut 23:15-16, an Israelite was forbidden by God to turn away or to extradite a runaway slave; the fugitive was entitled to choose a place and settle down near the residence of the asylum giver, and was not to be oppressed.[79]

Instead of seeking refuge in a private home, a fugitive could also apply for asylum in a temple.[80] Not all sanctuaries were asylum temples, and such temples were not everywhere within easy reach.[81] In the West, there appear to have been very few opportunities of this kind.[82] Eventually, statues of Roman em-

78. Philo, *Virt.* 124, while enumerating causes for a slave's flight, writes, "Do not disregard his plea. For it is a sacrilegious act to surrender a suppliant, and the slave is a suppliant who has fled to your hearth as to a temple, where he has a right to obtain sanctuary, and protected from treachery may preferably come to an honest and open agreement, or if that is not possible, be sold as a last resort. For though in changing masters there is no certainty which way the scale will turn, the uncertain evil is not so grave as the acknowledged." Regarding the last-quoted statement, Shakespeare obviously disagreed.

79. The prohibition of oppression indicates that the settled refugee did not become a free person but remained in a state of dependence upon his first host. Interpreters of the Deuteronomy text disagree on at least one point: Is it only the Israelite slave who is protected, or shall the Gentile ("Canaanite") fugitive benefit from the same privilege? Philo, *Virt.* 125, is very explicit in dealing with this issue: "This is his (God's) legislation about compatriots *and* foreigners, about friends and enemies, about slaves and free and (hu)mankind in general" (italics added). Jewish legislation will be discussed in more detail in sec. VIII, pp. 53-83.

80. When E. Lohmeyer, in his commentary on Philemon, *Die Briefe an de Philipper, an die Kolosser und an Philemon,* 13th ed., KEK 9/11 (Göttingen: Vandenhoeck & Ruprecht, 1964), p. 172, calls — perhaps hyperbolically — the "widespread asylum practice the religious correction added to the hardness of slavery in antiquity," he probably did not think of the role of temples as banking institutes that could profit from handling the fate of fugitives, as shown below.

81. The Gortyna Law Code (1.35-50) reveals that once upon a time any temple could be chosen. But in Athens this privilege was possessed only by the Thesaion, in Delphi by the temple of Apollo, in Ephesus by the Artemis temple, on the island of Chios by the Drimakos Sanctuary, in Caesarea by several yet not all temples, in Memphis — no earlier than under the Greek influence at the time of Ptolemaeus (323-285 B.C.E.) — by the Serapeum.

82. In, e.g., Diodorus Siculus, *Bibl. hist.* 36.3.3-4, a sanctuary at Palici is mentioned to which, in about 100 B.C.E., fugitives and rebellious slaves from Sicily resorted.

perors assumed a protective function. In all cases, the safety from persecutors that was found by reaching a temple or monument was only temporary. The priests offering asylum attempted either to reconcile master and slave or made provision for the slave's sale to another patron.[83]

When a female or male slave had escaped, the master was by no means condemned to swallow the loss and remain inactive.[84] Whether or not he took up the hunt himself, he could be sure of the support of other slave owners and people on his social level. When he asked for it, the city's or state's police apparatus, secret service, and — in case a slave had fled abroad — diplomatic service aided him to recover his property.[85] In addition, there were professional slave catchers (in Latin: *fugitivarii*) who — for a substantial fee, of course — would seek to trace and recapture the runaway. Fugitives would always feel hunted; wherever they were hidden, they would worry about being found out and recaptured. When after 150 c.e. the Roman slave legislation was declared binding for all provinces, Rome's elaborate system for capturing fugitives also found empire-wide imitation, with the effect that the probability increased drastically that a slave be caught in a police razzia. The potential number of traitors stemming from any stratum of the population grew when the fugitive's owner had published a warrant of apprehension and a reward for the seizure.[86]

When a slave returned of his own will because of the misery endured while on the run, or when he was forcibly returned by private persons eager for a reward, or by policemen, his fate depended entirely on the master. The slave might be whipped or beaten until he was a cripple; he might be branded on his head or arms; the skin under his feet might be burned off by glowing iron plates; a metallic collar with his name and address might be fixed around his throat; he might even be killed as a warning to fellow slaves. Still, killing a returned slave made the master's loss as great as it would have been without recapture. If the owner tried to sell the recovered fugitive, he had to guarantee to the buyer for a given period that the slave would not again run away.

83. See pp. 47-49.

84. Not every slave owner was probably willing to adopt the pessimistic attitude of Sir 33:31, "If you ill-treat him (the slave) and he runs away, which way will you go and seek him?" The search for a runaway may have been futile in many cases, yet in order to prevent other slaves from imitating a given example, intensive efforts had to be and were made for retrieving every fugitive, and there were promises of reward for giving useful hints or for catching the escaped person.

85. Plato, *Plt.* 9.578d-e, mentions this solidarity and calls it a reason why slaves were afraid to run away from their masters and eventually leave behind their own family members.

86. E.g., M. Dibelius, *An de Kolosser, Epheser, an Philemon*, 3rd ed., HNT 12 (Tübingen: Mohr, 1953), pp. 111-112, and its reedition by H. Greeven, pp. 34-36, reproduce the Paris Papyrus 10. For its text, see Annotation 5, pp. 87-89.

On the other hand, when an escaped slave had found refuge with a good and high-standing friend of the master's house and was voluntarily returned carrying an intercessory letter, there was the possibility of a benevolent, if not hearty, reception.[87] While the intercessor was free to combine emotional, moral, utilitarian, financial, selfish or altruistic, and other arguments to support his plea, and may have put the master under some pressure, the decision over the slave's fate was left to the owner exclusively.

Still, a slave could also turn to methods other than flight to do something for his liberation.

V. SLAVE REVOLTS AND WARS[88]

The Letter to Philemon in no way refers to a past, present, or planned violent action in which the slave Onesimus might have become engaged. However, precisely because for some slaves violence appeared to be an option as a way out of slavery, information about the cause, special features, course, achievements, and failures of slave revolts and wars contributes to understanding why the most radical method of rejecting slavery is not even touched upon in Paul's epistle.

Revolts took place foremost when and where slaves were amassed and employed in great numbers, as in mines and quarries, extended agricultural estates, or on slave markets. Slaves working as domestics, artisans, or in business and trade, especially the house-born among them, were less prone to use vio-

87. The legal technical term for such a letter was *pistis* or *logos asylias* (plea for safe conduct); see Lohmeyer's commentary on Philemon, p. 173 n. 3. Because such a script could contain no more than a warm request, it cannot be compared to a nineteenth-century American freedom letter, which was legal proof of valid manumission.

88. Among the ancient historiographers, the Sicilian Diodorus, *Bibl. hist.* 34.2.1-48; 3.1; fragment 36.1-11, constitutes one of the richest sources for the study of slave wars. Dependent upon Poseidonius of Apamea (in Asia Minor), writing under the influence of Middle Stoic moralism, and endowed with the gift to adorn his work with picturesque details, this man offers a vivid account of the Sicilian uprising. Ample information about Spartacus is provided by Appian, *Rom. hist., bella civilia*, 1.116-120, and by Plutarch, *Crass.* 8. While there is literature written by free men about the revolting slaves, none exists from the pen of the few educated leaders, not to speak of the crowds of the illiterate majority participating in the revolts. Still, it is known that they made propaganda for their cause, and that the news of their successes and failures spread rapidly over land and sea. Occasionally mimes were produced, and council meetings and court sessions were held. However, texts and reports written by revolting slaves have not yet been found. In the secondary literature, the chapter "Die Struktur der Sklavenkriege" in Vogt, *Sklaverei und Humanität*, pp. 20-60, is specifically concise and instructive.

lence, unless an unusual provocation had occurred. Even when a revolt shook the open country, city slaves preferred to side with the owners. Also, only in rare cases would other poor people join rebelling slaves; and if they did, their contribution was usually insignificant and their inclination to plunder discredited those they meant to support.

Uprisings of slaves took place in Greece, in several Greek- and Latin-speaking regions, and at the eastern coast of the Mediterranean Sea. Best known are the insurrections shaking Sicily, Asia Minor, and Italy between 140 and 70 B.C.E.[89] Among the most important and occasionally common features of the revolts and wars, nine are outstanding:

1. The treatment suffered from the hands of heartless owners and their employees was so bad and became so intolerable that the explosion of long-suppressed rage into violent actions was no surprise. It appeared to be fully justified — not only to slaves but also to sensitive people among those who, aware of the existing misery, described the slave wars as historians.

2. Only in exceptional cases did revolting slaves seek or find support among impoverished farmers and the poor in the towns and cities.

3. Eastern nationalistic and religious elements played so great a role in several of the great western risings that the slave wars formed part of the social, economical, cultural, and religious East-West tension of the time.

4. Leaders of the uprisings were charismatic personalities who sometimes claimed to be divinely appointed and impressed their followers by seemingly supernatural skills. Some of them liked to be called "kings," and liked to be treated as such. Not all leaders stemmed from the ranks of the slaves: a bastard and several dissatisfied or adventurous freemen were among them.[90] Nothing is known of a leading role of women.

5. When several revolts took place at the same time, the leaders refused to play the game of the legally established government and society; they did not compete with or fight against one another. Rather, one of the chiefs would subordinate himself to the other and be satisfied with the role of the king's general.

6. Only in one case was a program to form a new society and establish a heavenly city proclaimed. The revolts lacked a reflected ideological foundation and intended primarily to destroy, or rather to reverse, the existing social order. Slavery as such was not questioned or abandoned, but all

---

89. A survey of the classical slave wars is given in Annotation 6, pp. 88-92.

90. The stories told in Exod 1–2 of the birth, education, and first public appearance of Moses combine several of these traits.

powers were to be taken from the mighty and henceforth wielded only by former slaves.

7. Often the same stages of an uprising can be distinguished in different revolts. What begins with a plot and murder is continued in brigandage and guerrilla actions. Next, armies are formed and government troops are engaged in pitched battles. When trained, the slaves fight skillfully and bravely. They occupy and defend cities until by treason or on the battlefield they are defeated. They die as heroes, by suicide or on crosses.

8. During the years of the slave wars, government, citizenry, and populace were usually appalled and cringing with fear. The slaves fighting for improvement of their status and for freedom found no sympathizers outside their ranks, but were summarily dubbed "robbers" (which corresponds to the modern nomenclature: "terrorists") and treated as vile criminals.

9. The immediate result of the slave wars was a deterioration of the slaves' life and legal position. Yet, only a few decades after the last great threat to the established society, voices were emerging that asked for a different evaluation and treatment of all slaves.

In the course of these developments, Greek and Roman and Jewish intellectuals prepared the way for a nonviolent change of the lot of slaves. The increasing proportion of house slaves and changes taking place in the economy favored their noble reflections and intentions. For instance, the latifundia lost their monopoly of food production in the West; imports from the East, especially of wheat from Egypt, were cheaper. In addition, public opinion turned against the cruel treatment suffered by many slaves. Indeed, prevailing necessities as well as changing feelings permitted or encouraged the formulation of humane principles upon a philosophical and psychological basis.

VI. THE CONSOLATION OF PHILOSOPHY[91]

If there was any comfort for slaves at all, it had to be found in good treatment by their master, in the enjoyment of holidays or some free hours, in the hope eventually to be ransomed by a relative or to be manumitted by the owner. In addition, at least those slaves who found a way to attend performances of Aes-

---

91. This formula is borrowed from the abbreviated title of a work of Boethius (ca. 480-520 C.E.), a Roman statesman, philosopher, and prolific writer. Boethius was hardly the first to understand philosophy as a sort of cure of souls and as a guide to reasonable and moral conduct: Stoic teachers preceded him.

chylus's, Sophocles', and Euripides' tragedies, and of Aristophanes', Menander's, Plautus's, and Terence's comedies, could realize at least two things: how hard even the high and mighty were struck by ill fate, guilt, and misery; and how well a wise or shrewd, bold, if not impertinent slave could stand up to his master.

However, little if any consolation was forthcoming for that minority of slaves who could study Greek philosophy. More clearly and extensively than Plato, Aristotle[92] pronounces that by nature some people are slaves, that is, other persons' property (*Pol.* 1.1252a; 1254a). For those who are not free by nature, "slavery is both expedient and just" (1255a). "It is meet that Hellenes should rule Barbarians" (1252b); "for the superior in virtue ought to rule" (1255a).[93] Following Aristotle, both reason and factual experience disprove the thesis upheld "by some" (other alleged philosophers) that slavery is in violation of nature. In actuality, "it is expedient that one part of humanity should rule and the other be ruled."[94] "From the hour of their birth some are marked out for subjection, others for rule."[95] "The lower sort are by nature slaves, and it is better for them as for all inferiors that they should be under the rule of a master" (1254ab). This division of status, so the great philosopher of Athens avers, "originates in the constitution of the universe," that is, "in the predestined rule of the soul over the body." Only when nature is corrupted does the body appear to rule over the soul (1254a).

In summary, according to the sociopolitical ethics of Aristotle, slavery is a fact founded in nature and established by birth. Slavery reveals and epitomizes the moral superiority of the soul over the body and sanctions the dominion of the Greeks over the barbarians. Because it is natural it is rational — and vice versa. For the same reason it is also righteous, moral, and profitable. Though in the context mentioned (but see, e.g., *Rh.* 1.1273b) Aristotle does not explicitly speak of "natural law" or "a law of nature," he in fact explains slavery as an expression and application of the order of the universe.

Even before Aristotle (in the wake of Plato) had given literary expression to it, this view of the cosmos, of nature, and of reason was contested by other philosophers. Plato and Aristotle reject the references to nature made by the so-

92. In his *Pol.* 1.1252-1255. Compare with the following the statements of Aristotle mentioned above in n. 21.

93. Aristotle knows and regrets the fact that some noble Greeks have become slaves; Hellenes do not like to call fellow Hellenes slaves. He admits that this constitutes a foundation for differences of opinion.

94. Aristotle, *Pol.* 1.1254a.

95. As observed in n. 14, the Greek term *physei* may as well be translated "by nature" as "by birth." Centuries after the classical Greek philosophers, Latin writers such as Cicero, *Prov. cons.* 10; *Pro Val. Flacc.* 65; and Livy, *Hist.* 35.49.8; 36.17.15, still maintain that Jews, Syrians, Lydians, Medes (that is, Asians) are born for slavery.

called Sophists. According to the teaching of members of this group, nature and law strictly contradict another. By the good and beneficial order of nature all human beings are created equal. But the law made by human beings is a tyrant over humankind, for it seeks to enforce many things that are strictly opposed to nature, especially inequality. Following this conviction, all human beings are relatives, members of the same household, citizens endowed with the same basic rights. The differentiation between free and slave is man-made and imposed on humankind by superior power only. Therefore slavery is interference with nature. While the Sophists acknowledge that slavery is protected by law, they point out that all laws are products of human decisions, power relations, and anatural actions. Therefore slavery is unjust.

Relatively few names are known of those Sophists who fiercely denounced slavery. In the fifth century B.C.E., the famous Athenian orator Antiphon (*frag.* 44b, col. 2) questioned the prevailing opinion that by nature all human beings were destined to be either Greeks or barbarians. He argued that by nature all people were created equal and had all the same needs, as shown by the fact that they breathe through their mouth and their nose. With obvious displeasure Plato mentions the Sophist Hippias and refers to the similarly minded Trasymachos, who assumed that, from the beginning of history, laws and statutes had only limited validity because they were passed in favor of those in power and served no better end than to support those stronger than others. Aristotle mentions Alcidamas, according to whom the deity has set all human beings free and nature created no one to be a slave. In consequence, according to Alcidamas, all who had become prisoners of war and were now living as slaves ought to be released into freedom at once.[96] Xenophon, a historian and pragmatist rather than a speculative philosopher, observed that full democracy would be established by full participation of slaves in government.[97]

In summary, in antiquity the honor of the first to have protested slavery in principle and as a legal institution belongs to the often and much maligned Sophists. They declared the differentiation between slave and free an insult and infraction, directed against godhead and nature, and considered its fixation in positive law an injustice committed by the strong at the expense of the weak.[98]

---

96. Plato, *Prt.* 337c; *Plt.* 1.338a-340c; Aristotle, *Rh.* (scholiast) 13.1373b. Trasymachos's argument anticipates the criticism of the established order, as raised by Marxists and the Frankfurt School of Philosophy. In turn, the theological reasoning of Alcidamas reminds of the biblical statements according to which the liberation of Israel from Egypt is prototype and criterion of the treatment — and release! — of slaves in Israel.

97. Xenophon, *Hell.* 2.3.48.

98. Schulz, pp. 66-70, follows the example set by, e.g., W. Richter, "Seneca and the Slaves," 1965, pp. 206-208, when he proclaims the Sophists' "uncontested glory." The radical character of the Sophists' protest found late echoes in the stance of nineteenth-century

Still, the Sophists' call was not heard in the fifth and fourth centuries B.C.E. Dominant political and social, legal and economic traditions and institutions contradicted even the bravest of their voices and contributed to mute them.[99] Another, far less radical approach to condemning slavery was taken by later philosophers, even by the youngest branch of the Stoic school.[100] Under the aegis of the expanded Roman Empire and the ideology of a worldwide Pax Romana, individualism as well as cosmopolitanism were given a chance to develop. Still, the novel opportunities, concerns, and intentions reflected in Younger Stoicism need not obfuscate the Younger Stoics' dependence on the wisdom of great Greek tragedians, on radical opinions of Sophists — and also on the systematic constructions erected by Plato and Aristotle. Some quotes from classical Greek writers reveal the old quarries from which some building stones stem that were used by the Later Stoics.[101]

"The body is in slavery but the mind *(nous)* is free" (Sophocles, *frag.* 854n2). Euripides is much more prolific: "Nature does not bother one bit about laws"; "nature is the greatest"; "even when someone is of bad birth, the most important is virtue; the name makes no difference"; "the same birth by nature is noble and ignoble. Status pride is effected by time, through law. Reason and understanding are true nobility. They are given by God, not by riches"; and, as already quoted, "even when I am born to be a slave, I should like to be reckoned among the group of the noble slaves *(douloi gennaioi)*. Even when I don't have the name, yet I would have the heart and mind of a freeman. This is better than combining two evils in one self: a bad mind and the thralldom of slavery."[102] In *Hecuba* 864ff., the same poet argues that no mortal person is free since he or she is a slave to property, fate, the crowds, the laws and cannot act according to well-considered opinion *(gnomē)*. Unlike the Sophists, who held that the division between free and slave as established by fate and law was the main enemy of humankind, Euripides was exclusively concerned with the difference between good and bad persons. Since personal value, virtue, and morality of the individual were decisive for him, he did not consider slavery an ultimate threat

---

Christian abolitionists who declared "slavery is sin," and in the analogous pronouncement on apartheid made by the World Council of Churches in 1985 in Vancouver.

99. Sharp, though not unjustified, is W. Richter's remark, "as a matter of fact, Plato and Aristotle saved slavery"; see "Seneca und die Sklaven," *Gymnasium* 65 (1958): 207.

100. In textbooks and dictionaries it is customary to distinguish between Early, Middle, and Later, so-called Younger, Stoicism; see, e.g., Nilsson (see n. 66), pp. 257-268, 295-415, and Annotation 7, pp. 92-93.

101. For the following selection of quotes and for a summary observation, see esp. Richter, "Seneca und die Sklaven," pp. 207-210. The citations suffice to show that there is a humanism that precedes the writings of the Younger Stoics by centuries.

102. Euripides, *Ion* 854; *frag.* 520 N2; 526 N2; 810 N2; *frag. Alexandros; Helena* 728-733.

to humanity; freedom was real when there was peace of mind, and a slave could possess freedom no less than a free person. The unfree stood on the same level as those legally free — if only honesty and noblesse were found in the person's heart.

Perhaps from the comedian Menander stems a line that can be translated, "Serve voluntarily — and you will not be a slave!" Zeno's conviction was that "only the wise is free; bad people are slaves";[103] Philemon Comicus (*frag.* 22) makes one person on the stage say to another, "Even if he be a slave, Sir, he is no less a human being — if only he be (truly) human." Following Xenophon (*Mem. Soc.* 4.5.5), "the worst slavery . . . is the slavery endured by the incontinent," who, whether free or not, cannot control their passions and lusts.

Statements of Plato and Aristotle reveal that more could be learned from Athens's greatest philosophers than only an unconditional endorsement and whitewash of slavery. Socrates, the prototype and ideal philosopher for Plato and many later philosophers, let slaves as well as free persons benefit from his teaching and revealed by his life and death solidarity with persons in bondage. According to Plato (*Phd.* 62b-c; 61a), Socrates, though imprisoned by the state authorities, is in reality a captive of God and therefore God's property. He is a part of the deity's flock, in bondage to the divine owner. Therefore he must not flee — or commit suicide. As mentioned, Plato gives (in *Prt.* 337c) at least room to the Sophist who unfolds his view of natural equality as opposed to enforced legal slavery. In *Leg.* 776e-777a, Plato teaches that to treat slaves like brute beasts makes their souls fifty times worse; so he indirectly admits that slaves have souls. When in *Plt.* 9.577d-e he calls an enslaved soul a city under a tyrant, then in fact he admits that the soul of a free person might be enslaved to an evil lord. Following *Plt.* 308d-309a, true statesmanship subjugates to the yoke of slavery even those (free!) citizens who are "wallowing in ignorance and baseness." Interpreted in the best possible sense, this might imply that ultimately educated and virtuous slaves ought to go free!

Even more important are ideas that the Later Stoics may well owe to Aristotle. If really a master must rule over the slave just as the soul must marshal the body — as averred in *Pol.* 1.1254a — then it is presupposed that slaves, too, have a soul and can understand what the soul's dominion over the body should mean. Indeed, in *Pol.* 1259b-1260b, Aristotle teaches that slaves as well as women can have virtues — e.g., temperance, courage, justice. However, he is sure that a slave's virtue can never be equal to the master's, for it can only be measured with the gauge of the slave's subordinate status and work. Slaves need admonition even more than children. Following *Pol.* 1.1253a, all human beings are political animals — they are the best possible animal when they are brought

103. Diogenes Laertius, *De clar. phil. vitis* 7.121.

to perfection, the worst when separated from law and justice. Indeed, Aristotle concedes that even a slave may become perfect, that is, a perfect slave! In *Pol.* 1.1255b, the philosopher goes so far as to say that, since the slave is "a part of his master, a living but separated part of his bodily frame," it is natural for master and slave to be friends and to have a common interest. This relationship cannot be created by law and force because they produce the opposite, even enmity. More extensively the issue of friendship is discussed in *NE* 8.1161b: *qua* slave, a slave cannot be his master's friend, but *qua* human being. Thus at least by innuendo Aristotle expresses the hope that the same slaves he earlier called animated instruments or cattle may have the quality of humanity.

The conclusion must be drawn that Late Stoic teaching on freedom and slavery has its foundation in pre-Socratic, Platonic, and Aristotelian ideas. A spirit of humanity is recognizable. It reveals honest concern to find guidance and give counsel in good and evil days and situations, for the benefit of masters as well as slaves. Indeed, various accents were set by the Stoic teachers between about 50 B.C.E. and 200 C.E. in fundamental issues regarding slavery. Yet Younger Stoicists, such as Cicero, Seneca, Musonius, Epictetus, Dio Chrysostom, and finally Emperor Marcus Aurelius, basically maintain similar principles.

To wit: Slaves are human beings, not things, cattle, and mere objects and instruments. They have a soul, an inner life, and are capable of virtue. In a slave the battle between good and evil rages as much as in every free person. By nature, namely, as children of Zeus, they are as free as their masters. The differentiation between freemen and slaves is only nominal, and the distinction between Greeks and barbarians is invalid. If bad luck, brute force, or man-made laws erect barriers and produce inequality, the inner freedom given by virtuous conduct and the wisdom found in philosophy can make any person a king, if only base passions such as greed, arrogance, and fear of ill fortune, of death, of specific persons, and of the crowds are fought and overcome by strict self-discipline. Repudiated are the (Roman legal) definition of freedom as the capability to do whatever one likes and to move wherever one pleases, and the corresponding opinion that slavery is the worst of all evils. Freedom is not a sociopolitical status under the law; rather is it identified with the ever new decision for moral conduct. True freedom is inner freedom. A slave may be a better person than a master — as demonstrated by the imprisoned Socrates and the slave Diogenes.[104]

---

104. The best specific example of such teaching is offered by Seneca, *Ep.* 47 and *Ben.* 3.18.1-3. See Annotation 8, pp. 93-94; cf. Richter, "Seneca und die Sklaven." Epictetus has been the great herald of inner freedom, see esp. *Diss.* 1.4.18-21; 17.28; 2.5.5-6; 17.29; 3.22.38-39; 24.58-77; 4.1.1-37. According to him, whoever is willing to be free is free; cf. Horace, *Sat.* 2.7.83. In Philo's youthful work "Every Good Man Is Free" *(Quod omnis probus liber sit),* the distinction between external and internal, fake and true freedom is as clearly made as by

It may be impossible to decide whether the idealistic and dualistic separation of soul and body or the redefinition of freedom, whether sheer rationalism or a sincere human concern, was the prime mover among the many tenets and motivations combined in Late Stoicism. Though the term "brother" as used in, e.g., Sir 33:31; Philem 16, is not used by the Stoics to describe a virtually perfect master-slave relationship, the notion of brotherhood seems to tremble at least at the tip of Seneca's stylus.[105] But even if Seneca might have encouraged a wise master to call his slave "brother" and to treat him as such, the bare thought of a reciprocal address of the master by a slave would have been beyond his scope. Legal, political, social, and economic emancipation of the slaves was certainly not the goal at which the Stoic philosophers were aiming. Slave revolts and wars they do not even mention. Their intention was to reach and to liberate the human heart — whether it beat in a person embedded in wealth and power or in a miserably poor and oppressed man or woman. The cosmic and cosmopolitan, sincere and warm character of this philosophy did not prevent it from being spiritualistic and individualistic. If the advice given to masters and slaves was practicable, yet it did not go out for social change. Alteration or embellishment of the time-honored and seemingly unshakeable institution of slavery was not given primary importance or was left open — to an unknown future.

While it may be doubted whether this teaching and advice really conveyed substantial consolation to slaves, there is no question that it was comfortable for slave owners, including freed persons and emperors — if only they accepted, possessed, and exercised some humanity.

So many lines of the apostle Paul's utterance about slavery run parallel to Stoic teachings that it is safe to assume that the apostle did not only know of Stoic

---

Epictetus. If compared with Seneca, Philo, and Epictetus, the Bithynian Dio Chrysostom, *Or.* 14-15 — though he follows the same vein — sounds rather superficial. He makes rhetorical exercises rather than substantial contributions to the issue of freedom and slavery. He argues, for instance, that no human being can really be certain whether or not he or she be legally slave or free.

105. Seneca emphasizes equal birth, solidarity in temptations and aspirations, the capability of inner freedom, and the desirability of love. Why, then, does he not mention brotherhood, as did the French Revolution with its slogan "Liberté, égalité, fraternité"? Is there not an indissoluble co-inherence and mutual interdependence of freedom, equality, and brotherhood? Among the reasons for the omission, one may have weighed heavy: in Greco-Roman tradition, "friendship" appears to have ranked as high as, if not higher than, brotherhood. Even in the Bible brotherhood did not exclude tensions such as those between Cain and Abel, Esau and Jacob; the friendship between David and Jonathan was greater than any other intimate bond. When Jesus called John the Baptist, Lazarus, and his disciples his "friends" (John 3:29; 11:11; 15:13-15), his intention was certainly not to lower their status beneath that of brothers.

ideas and counsels but was also influenced by them.[106] It is much less certain, however, how much Stoicism contributed to the above-sketched changes in legislation and public opinion. As a necessary reaction against nineteenth-century idealism, since about 1930 a consensus[107] has been growing — even among Marxists and "bourgeois" scholars, especially historians — saying that among the active forces working against the institution of slavery as such, the impact of philosophical, psychological, and moral reflection was negligible or nonexistent.[108]

And yet, some early and several later effects of Stoic thought prohibit a denigration of that philosophical school. Columella's advice to slave owners, though far from being unselfish, is one example; Pliny the Younger's abovementioned letter to Sabinianus is another; Plutarch's critical evaluation of the older Cato's treatment of slaves is a third. Neither are to be ignored the public outcry against the ill-treatment of slaves, the almost defeated senatorial consent to the crucifixion of 400 slaves from the same household, finally Emperor Augustus's intervention on behalf of a hapless domestic. Throughout the Roman Empire, high and low people frequently watched performances of the tragedies of Sophocles and Euripides; of the comedies of Plautus, Sion, and Menander; and of other plays that demonstrated that servants were people, and some of them good or wise or funny persons. Stoic letters and diatribes could be read only by the relatively few educated among the slaves — with or without the consent of their owners. Still, the same dramas to which the Stoics partly owed their humanism conveyed their message to everybody, including the illiterate.

After it was earlier described[109] how some humanizing tendencies began

---

106. E.g., the Areopagus speech of Paul, as reproduced by Luke in Acts 17:22-31, contains (in v. 28) a quote from the Stoic Aratus; Paul's appeal to slaves, to work enthusiastically for their masters, and to masters, to let slaves receive what is just and equitable and to abstain from using threats (Col 3:22–4:1), reminds of Stoic counsels. In the third and fourth centuries C.E., a written correspondence between Paul and Seneca was fabricated in which the philosopher, though disturbed by Paul's poor style of writing, confesses his admiration of the apostle's deep thoughts. Here Seneca is depicted almost as a Christian. Slavery is not discussed in the correspondence, but the high ethical value of Paul's teaching is highly appreciated and is said to have impressed even Emperor Nero. See E. Hennecke and W. Schneemelcher, *New Testament Apocrypha*, vol. 2 (Philadelphia: Westminster, 1966), pp. 85-89. Cf. also J. N. Sevenster, *Paul and Seneca* (Leiden: E. J. Brill, 1961). After having been Nero's educator and counselor, Seneca was executed at the emperor's order.

107. Represented, e.g., by H. Greeven, "Die Sklavenfrage," in Greeven, *Das Hauptproblem der Sozialethik* (Gütersloh: Bertelsmann, 1935), pp. 34, 58-59; Westermann, *Slave System,* pp. 16ff., 166 (with some modification on pp. 104 and 216); Lauffer, p. 392; Richter, "Seneca und die Sklaven," pp. 201, 205-207, 213; Schulz, pp. 73-82.

108. The alternatives mentioned include political, legal, and above all, industrial and economical developments, together with the growing numbers of house-born and of manumitted slaves.

109. See sec. III.B, pp. 18-22.

to influence Roman legislation, at this place it is sufficient to mention only two examples of the reflection of Stoic thought in Roman law. In the *Digesta* 1.5.4.1, Florentinus states that "a slave is someone subjected to the dominion of another person according to the law of nations, but against nature," and Ulpian, in *Digesta* 1.1.1.4, bluntly writes into law that "by nature all people are equal." Later developments are no less impressive testimonies in favor of a delayed-action effect of Stoicism, among them the political and social changes taking place after the middle of the eighteenth century.[110]

VII. MANUMISSION — A LEGAL WAY OUT OF SLAVERY[111]

Among the many questions not yet unanimously answered by the interpreters of the Epistle to Philemon is the following: Did or did not Paul hope, expect, and urge Philemon to grant legal freedom to his runaway slave Onesimus?[112] If

110. In the Middle Ages, Thomas Aquinas, *ST* I qu. 96.4; II 2 qu. 57.3, harks back to both Aristotle (as quoted above) and Augustine, *Civ. Dei* 19.15, when he concedes no more than that slavery is part of secondary natural law; for, so he teaches, it did not exist in paradise but was the result of Adam's fall. Duns Scotus, *Oxon.* 4.d.36 qu. 1-2, was more explicit when he bluntly observed that slavery contradicted natural law. No earlier than in the abolitionist movement of the eighteenth and nineteenth centuries, at the side of biblical arguments also the Stoic heritage was given an interpretation that condemned institutional slavery as a whole and eventually led to its constitutional and legal prohibition and eradication — though not to the prevention of other forms of oppression and exploitation.

111. Special literature on slave emancipation includes G. R. Morrow, *Plato's Law on Slavery in Its Relation to Greek Laws* (Urbana, Ill.: University Press, 1939), pp. 95-110; Mendelsohn, *Slavery,* pp. 34-41, 46, 74-85; Duff, *Freedmen in the Early Roman Empire* (1928); H. Rädle, "Untersuchungen zum griechischen Freilassungswesen" (diss., Munich, 1969); N. Brockmeyer, *Antike Sklaverei,* pp. 122-125; Berger, articles on *libertinus* and related terms in *Encyclopedic Dictionary of Roman Law* XLIII, pt. 2, pp. 563-564, 575-577.

112. Th. Zahn, *Sklaverei und Christentum (in) der alten Welt* (Heidelberg, 1879), pp. 116-159; A. Jülicher, *Einleitung,* 3rd-4th eds. (Tübingen and Leipzig: Mohr, 1901), p. 98; Lohmeyer, pp. 191-192; P. N. Harrison, "Onesimus and Philemon," *AThR* 32 (1950): 276-280; F. F. Bruce, *The Epistles to the Colossians, to Philemon, and to the Ephesians,* NIC (Grand Rapids: Eerdmans, 1984), pp. 216-221; J. Knox, *Philemon among the Letters of Paul,* rev. ed. (New York: Abingdon, 1959; originally published, 1935), pp. 24-27, 36-37; S. C. Winter, "Paul's Letter to Philemon," *NTS* 33 (1987): 1, 4, 11-12; and others assume more or less tentatively that Paul wanted to achieve a legally valid manumission. Overbeck, p. 181, and Schulz, pp. 167-210, esp. pp. 180-183, are among the most radical exponents of the opposite opinion. In turn, there are scholars such as Greeven, "Die Sklavenfrage," p. 52, and Th. Preiss, *Life in Christ,* SBT 13 (London: SCM, 1954), pp. 32-42, who take a neutral stance. J. B. Lightfoot (pp. 408-409) and P. Stuhlmacher (*Der Brief an Philemon,* EKK 18 [Zürich and Braunschweig: Benziger Verlag; Neukirchen-Vluyn: Neukirchener Verlag, 1975], pp. 53-54) are among those

he did — why did he never explicitly formulate his wish? If he did not — how can his reticence be reconciled with statements made by him in other epistles about the freedom given and equality constituted by Jesus Christ?[113] Knowledge of the causes, the legal performance, and the effects of the emancipation of slaves can contribute to answering this question.

Being an academically trained rabbi, Paul was acquainted with old and contemporary Jewish laws and practices.[114] In addition, because he spent his early years in Tarsus, which, like the rest of Asia Minor, was under Roman dominion, and because of his later travels and activities in cities of Asia Minor and Greece and in Rome, he had ample opportunity to acquire more than a superficial knowledge of Near Eastern, Greek, and Roman ways of manumission.[115]

A. Motivations and Occasions

Only in rare cases would a slave not yearn and pray, work and if possible prepare means to become free.[116] Or else masters would not have summarily considered their slaves their enemies, and slaves would never have taken the risks of flight or revolt. Slaves enjoying a close relationship to the master could ask for conditions of an eventual release, and free members of their families or other friends could offer a sum for ransoming enslaved relatives. Still, there was no way to force a master who was unwilling to give freedom. Whatever would be

---

who feel unable to decide for either position. They agree that Paul's concern with the art of the matter, even the internal personal relationship between members of Christ's body, is so overriding that legal aspects are not taken under consideration (Dibelius and Greeven, p. 107). If this reasoning were correct, Paul's and the Stoics' attitudes would be practically identical. Decisive sociological arguments against a spiritualizing interpretation of the Letter to Philemon have been brought forward by N. R. Petersen, *Rediscovering Paul: Philemon and the Sociology of Paul's Narrative World* (Philadelphia: Fortress, 1985). Cf. also, e.g., R. Weth, "Diakonie am Wendepunkt," *EvTh* 36 (1936): 263-279, esp. 275-276 concerning Philemon.

113. E.g., 1 Cor 7:21-23; 12:13; Gal 3:28; 5:1, 13; Col 3:11.

114. See the next subsection.

115. In Greek the two words *apeleutheros* and *exeleutheros* are synonymous legal technical terms for denoting a freedman, equivalent to Latin *libertinus* or *libertus*. In 1 Cor 7:21, 23 Paul uses *apeleutheros* and mentions a price paid for manumission. In Philem 18-19 he promises to reimburse the legal owner for losses incurred by the flight, perhaps also by the earlier conduct of the slave. The expression for "freedom" that Paul uses in Gal 5:1 and 13 to describe the purpose of the redemption through Christ and of the Christians' calling, is also found repeatedly in the Delphi inscriptions pertaining to manumission.

116. See above, nn. 18, 32-33, 59, 61. Seneca, *Ep.* 80.4, writes of some slaves who "cheated their stomach" in order to save money for buying themselves out of slavery. Probably they sold food allotted to them, or did not buy that to which they were entitled.

offered by whomsoever — the patron had the right to retain his property. Again, when he had decided to let a slave go out free, the slave could not refuse.[117] In no case was the slave a legal person capable of negotiating or of appealing to a court in his or her own interest. However, there is evidence of slaves who — for reasons to be mentioned below — asked or begged masters to retain them for life, though they could not compel the patron to keep them.[118]

Several reasons could motivate a slave owner to give up a living part of his private property. (1) As already hinted at, the methods and costs of producing, handling, and trading goods could have been prohibitive. The market could develop in a direction that made it cheaper and less risky to employ free labor than to give, especially in bad years, shelter, food, clothing, medical care to slaves, not to speak of the problems of discipline and flight. For such reasons, manumission could be economically advantageous for the master. (2) Debt slaves had to serve no longer than for a given time span, usually up to the date when debts and expenses incurred for maintenance had been repaid. (3) Though it could be illegal, a slave owner occasionally released slaves by testament in order to spite unloved heirs or to thwart his creditors. (4) A slave who had done good work and proven faithful could be rewarded with his release. On the other hand, when a slave had fallen incurably ill or become old, the master could permit, or rather condemn, him to die as a free person. (5) The fertility of a female slave could be taken into account: she had increased the master's estate by giving birth to more slaves. By testament at the death of the master, a female slave could be classified as a wife or concubine. She could be declared, together with her children, legal heirs who were to be set free. (6) Even before his death, a master could give freedom to slaves who had become dear or indispensable members of the household or of the neighborhood, e.g., by marriage with a son or daughter or friend of the house. (7) To be admired by the community for magnanimity or for living up to humanitarian public opinion could also be a master's motive, as well as the desire to get rid of a lazy, useless, or slanderous member of the household. (8) When at the yearly Saturnalia celebration the roles of masters and slaves were reversed, masters might be reminded that according to the will of the gods slavery would not last forever. If they ever read or

117. Bartchy, passim, esp. pp. 98, 104-111, 118-119, 176, has convincingly shown that the statement made in 1 Cor 7:21 (lit. "if you can become free, rather use it") cannot mean "rather (remain a slave) and make the best use of this status." This verse and its context will be discussed more extensively below (pp. 191-200).

118. What is prescribed by Exod 21:6 und Deut 15:16 had analogues outside Israel — though without the ritual piercing of the slave's ear. Among non-Jewish authors, Suetonius, *De gramm. et rhet.* 21, demonstrates that sometimes slaves were treated so well that they preferred remaining in slavery to manumission. The case of slaves who after their emancipation yearned to be back under the hand of their masters will be discussed later.

heard of Stoic teaching, they might show an inclination to acknowledge the natural equality and eventual perfectibility of all human beings.

On the other hand, an entirely different cause could emerge for legal manumission. Under given conditions, emancipation in the interest and by decree of the community and its government superseded the protection of the master by the *ius civilis* (private law). When the existence of a city or state or king was threatened by war, and when the armed forces, constituted of free citizens, were too weak to meet and defeat the enemy, slaves were released in order to join the fighting troops and sailors.[119] In principle, following Greek tradition, neither slaves nor freedmen were either deemed worthy or forced to assist the defense of the freeborn people's fatherland. When other nations yet used slaves for this purpose, they proved thereby how barbarian and unwise they were. Those conscripted against their will might turn out to form a fifth column.[120] Still, before the battle of Salamis (490 B.C.E.), slaves were released so that they could fight as free men at the free citizens' side.[121] For their own freedom's sake and for a final struggle, the Athenians released 12,000 house-born slaves.[122] About 130 B.C.E., when Andronicus together with the slaves and the poor people supporting his revolt formed a threat to the rulers of Pergamum, the government of the city and its surroundings promised the metics they

119. According to a law of Solon, debtors who fought for Athens were unburdened of their debt and could not be held as slaves (Diodorus of Athens, *Perieg.* 1.79). In his description of King Philip's war against Athens, Dio Chrysostom, *Or.* 15.21, writes, "The Athenians, after the battle of Chaeronea, voted that slaves who would help them in the war would receive their freedom." Therefore, "if the war had continued and Philip had not reached peace with them too soon, many of the slaves of Athens, or rather, practically all of them, would have been free without having been emancipated one at a time by their respective masters." Jewish sages, as described by Urbach, pp. 79-83, discussed a special problem: some Hebrew slaves held by Jews joined Israel's troops in their battle against Gentiles, but contrived to be made prisoners by the enemies. They figured that the Jews would have to redeem them, and that being ransomed they would no longer be slaves. To meet this tricky attempt at being emancipated, one group of rabbis declared, under the protest of another, that redeemed captives would have to return into the ownership of their former masters.

120. Isocrates, *Paneg.* 123-124, blamed and condemned in one of his speeches those Greeks who by force conscripted slaves and had them fight against the army of their own fatherland.

121. For those who died in battle a — separate! — monument was built at state expense. Unfree men surviving a bloody encounter were at least once, in Sparta, amazingly rewarded (according to Athenaeus, *Deipnosoph.* 6.27) in a war against the Messenians. Though it had ended with a victory, the Spartans had suffered losses so heavy they feared the enemy might hear of this depletion of their manpower and attack anew, so they made some of the Helots who had fought at their side enter the bedrooms of the war widows in order to produce offspring. Later, the Helots who had found favor were made citizens.

122. According to Polybius, *Hist.* 38.15.3-4.

would be citizens, and told the freedmen and slaves that they would be raised to the status of resident aliens, if only they helped the local forces against the rebels.[123] But neither promises nor official manumission by the authorities was a guarantee for lasting freedom.[124]

Other methods of manumission were not limited to war conditions.

B. Normal Procedures

Three forms existed to carry out the legal emancipation of a slave.

The oldest was more or less informal: it took place in the frame of the master's home, according to private and family rights. Later, after mixed semiprivate and semipublic shapes had been tried out during a period of transition, state and corporation laws prescribed official performances. In addition, at all periods, there was a so-called sacral manumission, protected by the *ius sacrum* (religious law).

Though at the apostle Paul's time Roman laws passed under the emperors were supposed to determine all that was to be considered legal throughout the Roman Empire, many older Greek and Roman and Eastern traditions survived publicly or in hiding in Greece, the West, and Asia Minor.

In Greece, manumission occurred less frequently than in Italy, and the difference between a freed person and a slave was less conspicuous. Those freed could still be called "slave" *(doulos, doulē)*. There was no bestowal of citizenship; only the status of a "metic" (resident alien with limited rights) was achieved. The slaves manumitted before their owner's death had to accept and keep a contract *(paramonē)*. Its substance will be described later. Since the fifth century B.C.E., the act of manumission was no longer private and quasi-informal: laws prescribed that it be ascertained by testament, called out in the

123. Appian, *Rom. hist., Bella civilia,* 1.11, and Julius Caesar, *B Civ.* 1.34, record similar incidents during the Roman civil war. Vogt, "Sklavenkriege," pp. 43-45, gives more references. For details of the Sicilian and of other slave wars, see Annotation 6, pp. 88-92.

124. According Jer 34:8-22, in 588/587 B.C.E., slaves were liberated under pressure of Nebuchadnezzar's first attack on Jerusalem. But they were reinducted into bondage after the storm appeared to have passed over. Therefore Jeremiah announced God's judgment over the ruling classes of Jerusalem and Judea. Diodorus Siculus, *Bibl. hist.* 36.4.8, reports that in the course of a Sicilian revolt, both slave armies attacking a city and the urban defenders promised freedom to the urban slaves — if only they joined this or that side respectively. The slaves decided in favor of the defenders, were released, and contributed to their victory over the assailant; but as soon as the city's safety was restored, the emancipation was rescinded. In consequence, the cheated slaves left the city en masse and joined the revolt. In *Bibl. hist.* 36.3 the same author describes another event: the legal emancipation of some slaves motivated thousands of other slaves to revolt — with the result of a protracted slave war.

streets, in the theater, or before an altar. On the day of liberation, the slave — eventually also the manumitting master — would be wearing a felt skullcap, called *pilos*.[125] An inscription on stone or engraving in a vessel could confirm the validity of the manumission — a forerunner of the American freedom letters. Five percent of the released slave's monetary value had to be paid as city tax.

In Rome, according to the Twelve Table Law of the fifth century b.c.e., the patron originally retained some rights over the slave who had been set free. Centuries later a manumission could still be revoked, but a freedman could appeal to the prefect against a wanton revocation and the official had the power to protect the freedman if his claims appeared justified. An informal manumission was performed either by testament or by inviting the slave to share in table or festival community, or in the circle of friends, who served as witnesses.[126] The informal act was tax-free; it did not make the freedman a Roman citizen. As an intermediate form valid only during eighteen months within each five-year period, there existed until about 50 c.e. the *manumissio censu:* a slave who convincingly claimed to have been born a free citizen, who was supported by his master in his desire to become free, and who was accepted by the civil authorities for inscription in the voter's register became free and henceforth had the Roman citizen right. At Paul's time the safest way to grant and receive freedom was either by testament or by a letter written to the slave, who lived at another place than his owner. The letter had to contain a proper formula.[127] Or, in the *manumissio vindicta*, a high Roman state official had to give his consent to the master's wish and, in the presence of the master, touch the slave with a staff and declare him free.[128] As in Greece, a contract with a patron, requiring specific payments and works of the manumitted slave, had to be signed and a tax was to be paid. Unlike Greek custom, however, the freedman received Roman citizenship — though only to a limited extent, e.g., regarding suffrage. For major litigation, the patron remained the freed person's protector and representative but no longer possessed the power over his or her life and death. In some cases a manumitted slave ac-

---

125. In Rome this cap was called *pileus*. Its prototype was a helmet, as Homer, *Il.* 10.265, shows. A later analogy is the Jacobin cap worn during the French Revolution as a symbol of liberty and equality.

126. *Manumissio testamento, per mensam, in convivio, inter amicos* were the respective legal terms. Not yet found are antique records of general, empire-wide emancipation acts, such as passed under the presidency of Abraham Lincoln in December 1863.

127. Invalid was the wording "I wish ——— to be free" or the like; valid was a formulation such as "——— is free" or "I order that ——— be free."

128. Corresponding to, if not derived from, this ritual is the medieval granting of knighthood by the touch with a sword.

cepted the master's name in order to avoid his, say, Phrygian name reminding himself and others of his former slave status.

In Asia Minor, some features of manumission survived that were rooted in Babylonian, Assyrian, Persian, and Jewish legal traditions and customs. A slave could be released, sometimes together with his wife and children, when instead of a cash payment he offered to his owner another slave, a house, cattle, or land as a substitute. The place of transaction could be a city gate; the formula to be used by the master was "You are cleansed." In order to prevent a patron from reclaiming a manumitted person, the protection of a deity was invoked or the slave was declared a gift to a god or a goddess. Everywhere in the East and West, and at all times, temples had the right to play a major role.

C. Sacral Manumission

Delphi inscriptions, dated between about 200 B.C.E. and 250 C.E., proffer the most numerous and instructive examples of antique slave emancipation through the services of a temple.[129] One of these inscriptions reads, following the date: "The Pythian Apollo bought from Sosibius for freedom a female slave whose name is Nicaea, by birth a Roman, at a price of three silver minas and a half. Former seller according to the law was Eumnastos of Amphissa. He has received the price. The deed of sale was entrusted to Apollo for freedom."[130] This text shows that the act of sacred manumission was in fact a business transaction entrusted to a temple. Since the slave could not legally and commercially act on his or her own behalf, the flight to a temple that offered asylum was recommendable. Probably the attending priests would not be willing to expose themselves by making intercession for the runaway; also they had no right to serve as arbiters. Yet they could and would mediate by negotiating. A deal was worked

129. One of the earliest of three inscriptions describes the release of three Jewish handmaids, and another the manumission of "a Jew from the tribe of the Jews"; see Urbach, p. 13; A. Deissmann, *Licht vom Osten,* 2nd and 3rd eds. (Tübingen: Mohr, 1909), pp. 240-253; 4th ed. (1923), pp. 271-284; ET, *Light from the Ancient East* (New York: Doran, 1927; Grand Rapids: Baker, 1965), pp. 320-331; cf. Deissmann, *Paul* (New York: Harper Torchbooks, 1957), pp. 172-174, who was the first to draw successfully the New Testament scholars' attention to the numerous Delphi inscriptions and their potential relevance for understanding Pauline teaching on redemption.

130. This is the translation offered by C. K. Barrett, *The New Testament Background: Selected Documents* (London: SPCK, 1956), pp. 53-54. In the last-quoted sentence, the Greek text has *ōna;* unlike Barrett's version, "deed of sale," Deissmann translates it "purchase." Philologically, both versions are possible, but Deissmann's choice may well hide an important fact: the female slave had entrusted the required money to the temple — money she had taken from her *peculium* or that stemmed from other sources.

out by the priests and/or specialized businessmen, which was given the form of a contract between three partners: Apollo, the slave's legitimate owner, and the slave. The validation and publication of the arrangement were made by engravings on stone. In business and legal terminology, the whole act was an "intrustment sale." In its course the slave never became the property of Apollo.[131] The temple served as a bank[132] — which of course would ask for payment of a fee by the slave and/or the patron. This contribution to the mediator's expense substituted, incidentally, for a tax payment to the city treasury.

According to the inscriptions just mentioned, a person emancipated through the services of the Apollo temple would enjoy greater freedom than was immediately attainable after informal, formal, or state manumission. A sacrally freed male had access to courts, representing himself; not only he but also a manumitted female slave could possess private property without fear that in whole or in part it would be seized; they could freely choose which work they

131. In following A. Deissmann's lead, numerous scholars after him (sometimes with various accents as set, e.g., by F. Sokolowski, "The Real Meaning of Sacral Manumission," *HTR* 47 [1954]: 173-181; cf. Sokolowski, in the same volume, pp. 163-164, "Fees and Taxes in Greek Cults") stuck to the opinion that the slave seeking freedom first became Apollo's property, that is, a slave of Apollo, before he was actually manumitted and became free in the legal sense of this term. If this were true, the contracted transaction would deserve the name "legal fiction," as indeed Deissmann had suggested. In this case the apostle Paul, in turn, would have used, foremost in 1 Cor 7:22-23; Gal 3:13; 4:1-9; 5:1, 13; Col 2:14, a fiction as paradigm for describing the redemption by Christ! Corrections of Deissmann's view are found in Bömer, II, 1960, pp. 10ff., 135ff.; Rädle, pp. 56-88, 111-123; W. L. Westermann, "The Freedmen and the Slaves of God," *Proceedings of the American Philosophical Society* 92 (1948): 55-64. The counterarguments are conveniently summed up by Bartchy, pp. 121-125, and can even be augmented: the designation "slave of Apollo" is never found in the documents. If ever it had been used, it would have flatly contradicted the Greek and Roman conviction that religion served to make or keep a person free; cf. K. H. Rengstorf, *TDNT*, 2.261-269, and H. Schlier, *TDNT*, 2.487-496. Paul may not have known of the exact course of the Delphi procedure. A legal fiction was hardly a model for the intention and method of the same God whom Paul elsewhere calls righteous and whose great work is this: to make sinners rightous. In fact, a Delphi manumission was a kind of self-redemption by the slave even while it was mediated through clerical temple personnel. Paul, however, was far from proclaiming that freedom could be procured and secured out of humankind's own resources.

132. As indeed the treasure houses attached to ancient temples show. The Jerusalem temple was the depository of the half shekel (Matt 17:24); earlier one-third of a shekel (see Neh 10:32-33) temple tax had to be paid by every Jew in the world. The income from this tax, combined with the money flowing in during the great annual festivals, with prescribed and voluntary sacrifices that made money changing necessary, made this sanctuary probably one of the richest of the world; and its priests were well situated. The violent action taken by the itinerant preacher Jesus of Nazareth, according to Matt 11:15-18 and parallels, was as much resented as a threat to the religious establishment as it was to the economic system of that period.

48

would do, which occupation fit their wishes and gifts, and they were free to move wherever they liked. A *paramonē* contract would never have given him so much liberty.

Unless the cost of manumission was defrayed out of the slave's savings or a loan given to him, relatives, friends, or associations of benevolent people had to put up the money.[133] The enfranchised stood henceforth in a debtor relationship to those who had paid for his or her freedom — a bond that was moral as well as material and included services to be rendered to the magnanimous redeemer or redemptive group.

D. The Life of Those Freed

In Greek, a freedman was called *apeleutheros* (so in 1 Cor 7:22; Ignatius, *Rom.* 4.3) or *exeleutheros;* in Latin *libertus* or *libertinus*.[134] In cruel contradiction to many a slave's yearning and expectation, for an unknown proportion of those released from bondage enfranchisement meant transition not into better and easier but far worse conditions. "Once I am freed, he said, at once everything will be all right. I do not care for anybody, I speak freely and on an equal level with all people, I go where I want . . ." — with this soliloquy of a slave, Epictetus describes the hoped-for paradise. The philosopher continues, "Whereupon he is freed — but since he has nothing to eat, at once he seeks someone to flatter in order to get food; he hires out his body and suffers the worst. Even when somewhere he finds a crib he has fallen into slavery far worse than the former . . . ; he is unhappy, deplores himself and yearns back for the slave status." Finally Epictetus lets the freedman say, "What kind of evil did I suffer? Another person gave me shoes, clothing, food, nursed me, when I was sick — and I rendered him but some few services. Miserable man that I am now, since I have to serve

133. A *societas* founded by free persons and slaves for religious, cultural, professional, economical, or funeral purposes; an *Eranos* circle devoted to mutual assistance of its members; or a Jewish or Christian congregation were the sources from which help could be expected in emergencies. From these sources might come a loan or gift for the price of manumission. If permission was given by a law or an ordinance, such a group could carry out the manumission at its meeting place; see, e.g., Barrett, p. 53, for a synagogue inscription in the Crimea. Above, in n. 11, passages from *1 Clement,* Ignatius, *The Shepherd of Hermas,* the *Apostolic Constitutions,* and Tertullian that reveal reluctance of early congregations to redeem slaves were mentioned. No earlier than under the first Christian emperor, Constantine, was legal permission granted to the churches to perform a formal manumission, called *manumissio in ecclesia.*

134. *Libertus* designated his relation to the manumitting patron, *libertinus* his status among other persons, e.g., before the law and the courts. Corresponding female forms of these adjectives were used for freed women.

several people instead of one."[135] Even more blunt is another summary judgment: "Freedmen are still slaves."[136] The escaped man for whom Pliny the Younger wrote his warm letter of intercession was a freedman, not a slave![137] The motivation of his flight, however, and the circumstances of its enactment, the situation of the fugitive while out of his master's reach, and the uncertain treatment after voluntary or enforced return under the patron's power were practically the same as those of a slave. While in ancient Israel an emancipated slave *(hophshi)* became entirely free from his former master, documents found in Alalakh, Nuzi, Amarna, Ras Shamra, and Assyria demonstrate that the Near Eastern *hupshu* constituted a special class between the slaves and the free slave-owners.[138]

How large the proportion of this (lower) middle class was in relation to the total population is not known; in the eastern provinces of the Roman Empire it was probably much smaller than in the western, Greek and Italian, parts, for in the uncivilized East there were far fewer slaves and eventual manumissions.[139] At Paul's time, under the first Roman emperors, as mentioned earlier, a huge number of slaves were enfranchised; in Corinth, e.g., about one-third of all inhabitants were slaves, another third freed persons, the last third free people.

Not all members of the middle group lived and died in misery. Some may have succeeded in returning to the place of their origin.[140] Others managed to

---

135. *Diss.* 4.1.37. Epictetus had been a slave himself. Barrow, pp. 60-64, cites other, substantially parallel texts; see also Duff, pp. 50-142. After describing the miserable plight of a manumitted slave, Epictetus admits that some of those manumitted fared better. There were "emperor's freedmen" who had risen high. Yet the philosopher emphasizes how painful their way up to the position of knights or even senators was, and how much they might now be slaves of their passions, desires, fears, and similar emotions.

136. Quoted from Chrysippus by Athenaeus, *Deipnosoph.* 6.267b. Probably this sentence stated originally a socioeconomic fact; but it was eventually given a psychological and moralistic interpretation. E.g., Philo, *Quod omn. prob.* 156-157, writes: "We may well deride the folly of those who think, when they are released from the ownership of their master, they become free. Servants, indeed, they are no longer now that they have been dismissed, but slaves they are of the vilest kind, not to men, but to strong desires, to pot-herbs, to baked meats. . . . For as the proclamation (of their emancipation) cannot make them men of knowledge, so neither can it make them free, for that is a state of blessedness. It can only make them no longer servants."

137. See Annotation 4, pp. 86-87.

138. See R. de Vaux, *Ancient Israel, Its Life and Institutions*, vol. 1, 2nd ed. (New York: McGraw-Hill, 1965), pp. 80-96; French original (Paris: Du Cerf, 1961), pp. 137-138.

139. Therefore, even if the apostle Paul had explicitly or implicitly asked the owner of Onesimus to manumit his slave legally, and if Philemon had fulfilled the request, the situation of Onesimus might not have been really improved.

140. In the Po Plain, as mentioned in Annotation 6 (p. 91), Spartacus gave the Gallians

climb upward on the social ladder; among them were those who married into a noble family or were knighted and given high positions in the Roman imperial civil administration. No wonder this provoked the envy of freeborn aristocrats and of senators who spurned the very idea of "serving" an emperor. In the "good" families of Rome, especially the emperor's freedmen *(liberti)* were watched jealously and were by no means highly respected.[141] Within the Christian church, formal permission that freedmen — never slaves! — would become consecrated as priests and bishops was granted no earlier than under Pope Leo the Great.[142] Still, several freedmen became famous philosophers, poets, or artists.[143] In most cases, whether a freed person had a chance really to live on a level comparable to that of a freeborn citizen depended on the position of the manumitting patron.

In most normal cases the performance of manumission included the signing of a contract *(paramonē, pactum)* by which the male or female slave assumed the obligation to live and work on the master's property, and thus, practically speaking, became no more than a servant hired for a period of time or forever. More leeway was open to those obliged or permitted to live apart from their patron, in a workshop as artisans, in an office as clerks, or as traveling salesmen for the master's factory. They paid rent or delivered part of their gains. They were, in fact, still serving their patrons' order, and were serving them by day and by night.[144] If stipulated in the contract, it was possible for the former slave to gain total independence at a given time by paying a lump sum. Still, for the rest of their lives, those manumitted remained "freedmen" or "freedwomen of ———— ."[145] On the other hand, the patron had no longer the right over life

---

fighting in his army the chance to return home. But they preferred to turn south with Spartacus for more battles against their former owners and oppressors.

141. During the rule of some emperors, among them Claudius, Commodus, and Diocletian, freedmen actually ruled the empire — if contemporary (critical!) observations can be trusted. "Caesarism supported itself by emancipation," according to Lauffer, p. 395. Slaves manumitted by an emperor and called "Friends of the Emperor" are repeatedly mentioned by Epictetus in his *Diss.* 4; still, this moral philosopher considers them warning examples rather than paragons of virtue and of a fulfilled life. The case of Vedius Pollio, the nouveau riche ex-slave who entertained Emperor Augustus and in his majesty's presence intended to feed a slave to the fish, has been mentioned above.

142. According to Overbeck, pp. 205-207.

143. See above, n. 58, where several names were listed.

144. In Latin legal terminology, they owed the patron *obsequium, operae, officia, bona, reverentia, gratitutio* (obedience, occasional and regular services, material compensation, and gratitude). For details see W. Waldheim, *Operae Libertorum. Untersuchungen zur Dienstpflicht freigelassener Sklaven* (Stuttgart: Steiner, 1986).

145. Just as in 1 Cor 7:22 Paul calls a slave who is called by Jesus Christ, "a freedman of the Lord."

and death of the emancipated persons, and their children were considered born free.

This way a close bond would continue to exist that in most cases may have worked out in favor of the patron. For if, after the expiration of the *paramonē* in Greece and of the *pactum* in Italy, the former owner of the slave ever became impoverished, ill, or otherwise incapacitated, the ex-slave had to come to his or her assistance — or be labeled "ungrateful" and be treated by the public as well as by the law as a social outcast. By enfranchising slaves, a master could therefore create for himself an equivalent to social security and, in addition, have a faithful supporter in eventual troubles.[146] It was expected, however — though never enforced — that a patron would not let his ex-slaves suffer the extremes of deprivation.

The special status of the freed persons in relation to their masters had analogues in their standing within society as a whole.

In Rome, as already observed, only formally manumitted men received citizenship, not those freed in a private house-ceremony. Still, their civil rights were restricted. They had no access to the courts but needed protection and representation by their former owner; for the election of public office bearers, they had no franchise. In theory they could marry whomever they liked, but few were the persons of noble birth who would choose an ex-slave for a partner. They were entitled to write a testament, but part of their bequest still fell to their ex-owners. Freedmen were allowed or welcome to join the army or the navy, but never could attain to higher ranks. Only under the emperor's aegis could they become high magistrates in Rome or in the provinces. Sacerdotal offices were as much closed to them as was the dignity of senatorship. Since the year 19 c.e., the limited ("Latin") citizenship was clearly distinguished from full participation in "Roman" civil rights.

In Greece the life of a freed person was even more difficult. Indeed, those manumitted could own property, choose an occupation according to their liking and capability, and marry whomever they found willing. Still, before the law and in their status in society, instead of becoming citizens they counted no more than resident aliens, and the name *doulos, doulē* (slave) could not be shaken off. Yet bravery demonstrated in wartime or marriage with a respectable person could eventually help them attain full citizenship.

Details of a freed person's social-political status in Asia Minor are obscure. The mixed Greco-Roman and Near Eastern influence makes it probable that there, too, a freed slave enjoyed only very few of the free citizen's privileges.

---

146. Urbach, pp. 58-59, goes so far as to call Greek and Roman types of manumission "in many cases . . . but a legal fiction." He distinguishes them sharply from manumission by Jewish law, which "effected the slave's complete liberty and broke all bonds of servitude and obligation towards his former owner."

Slaves who did not find a place in administration or business, in manufacture or agricultural work, in another occupation, or in the arms of a rich or noble free person shared the lot of the unfortunate, homeless fugitive slaves. They became a part of the poorest among the city population; they were unemployed, perhaps unemployable, or were hired for occasional jobs together with other applicants for skilled or unskilled work; if they wanted to survive, many of them had to beg, to steal, or, as long as they were young enough, to sell themselves for male or female prostitution. So they joined the uncounted and anonymous mass of the proletariat — and disappeared in it. For them, the liberty gained turned out to be the freedom to die in utter misery of hunger and disease.

In summary, usually manumission meant access to a liberty fettered by so many strings and having its wings so drastically clipped that its effect was highly ambiguous, if not thoroughly undesirable, unpleasant, and miserable. This may have been one of the reasons why in the antique world slavery was neither seriously limited nor brought to an end by individual or mass manumissions. In fact, enfranchisement could at best turn out to be a slightly milder form of slavery, in the East and the West. The actual end of the ancient forms of institutional slavery was ushered in by economic and political, juridical and ideological changes.

VIII. OLD TESTAMENT AND LATER JEWISH TRADITIONS[147]

"In the whole of ancient society . . . slavery was taken for granted as a feature basic to political, economic, and social life. From this point of view, the Jewish people formed no exception." Even when "some sentiments of true humanity" were expressed "in classical Greek literature, in the writings of the Stoics and in

---

147. The source material used in the following stems from the Hebrew Bible, the OT Apocrypha, the Dead Sea Scrolls, Philo, Josephus, the Mishnah, and the Talmud. Among the Mishnaic and talmudic tracts, Gittin IV 4:1-6:2 (14b-45b); Jebamoth IV 12 (44a-48b), Kiddushin I 2-3 (14b-25a) are most important. References to Sifra Lev 25 are made as quoted by Urbach. In most cases, the Babylonian Talmud was consulted in the German version by L. Goldschmid, I-XII (Berlin: Jüdischer Verlag, 1930-36). The secondary literature is listed in the bibliography under the names of D. Daube, J. Jeremias, S. Krauss, I. Mendelsohn, G. F. Moore, S. Safrai, S. Schulz, H. L. Strack and P. Billerbeck, E. E. Urbach, R. de Vaux, W. L. Westermann, S. Zeitlin. The commentary of Strack-Billerbeck is mentioned more often than S. Krauss because of the easier accessibility and the larger number of literal quotes.

the Christian scriptures . . . neither in any of them nor in the Jewish sources is the slightest suggestion of any notion of the abolition of slavery." This sober summary statement was made by an eminent Jewish scholar and was directed against claims or apologies of modern Jewish abolitionists.[148] Neither ancient Hebrew legislation, historiography, and Wisdom Literature nor the scholarly interpretation of the Hebrew Bible in the Tannaitic and the Amoraic periods appears to contain substantial alternatives to the prevailing slave systems.[149] Not only were Jews enslaved to foreign masters, and not only did foreigners resident on Israel's soil possess Hebrew and Gentile slaves, but even members of the elect people — including priests — were slave owners. Since numerous biblical and postbiblical commandments presupposed slavery and did no more than regulate the treatment of slaves, there were but few pious Jews (such as Essenes) who ever thought of questioning and perhaps also abolishing slavery in their midst.

How could it happen that the possession of slaves was tolerated and endorsed, perhaps even sanctified in God's name and by his law, within in a nation whose history and faith, ethics and self-understanding were founded on liberation by its gracious Lord from Egypt, that paradigm of a "house of bondage"? Indeed, exploitation of the poor is radically denounced by Amos and other prophets, and the book of Deuteronomy contains several very humane laws, but slavery as such is never designated and condemned as a sin against God and the neighbor. Only centuries after the Reformation did Jewish and Christian abolitionists take up the struggle at that front (see Annotation 10, p. 96), and declarations such as "apartheid is sin" and similar protests against oppression and exploitation have been made only in the seventies and eighties of the twentieth century. What looks like, and might be called, a paradox in the

148. Urbach, pp. 4 and 93-94. Still, on p. 50 this author acknowledges the intention of the sages, if not to abrogate slavery as a whole, yet to reduce or abolish at least the enslavement of Jews by fellow Jews.

149. The conditions prevailing in the first two centuries C.E. can be deduced from Mishnaic *halacha* (the ethical and cultic doctrines), from Philo, from the parables of Jesus, and from Josephus. The Mishnah was compiled early in the third century C.E. by Rabbi Judah the Patriarch (ca. 135-220) and represents the so-called Tannaitic period. Another, new period began when *halachic* and *haggadic* (narrative) additions were made that called for an expansion of the Mishnah. After about four hundred years, the teaching and stories supplemented by sages in Palestine were collected and written down in the *Palestinian* (or *Jerusalem*) Talmud, those of the Babylonian-learned interpreters in the *Babylonian Talmud*. The so-called Amoraim had assumed the function of the Tannaites. Other, often later, complementations of the Mishnah, called *Tosefta*, are found in the *Baraitas* and the *Midrashin*, e.g., in the two Mekhiltas on Exodus and in the Sifra Leviticus. Even the latest documents of the second period may well contain elements of early Tannaitic conditions and teachings.

ancient and medieval Jews' attitude (and its analogue within the Christian churches) seems to be explicable as soon as a sharp distinction is made between state and private (or house) slavery.

Forced labor was imposed by, e.g., Ramses II (1290-1224 B.C.E.) upon the Hebrews living in Goshen, in the northeastern Nile Delta. Such a corvée was a temporary measure taken for the erection of state building projects, and it might be called state slavery. The same expression can be used for the status of Canaanite nations defeated by Israel during the conquest of the Promised Land, or later, e.g., by David (2 Sam 12:31). In 1 Kings 5:13-18 Solomon compelled "all of Israel" to bow their neck under this yoke. Jeroboam, first as spokesman for the house of Joseph, then in the name of all northern tribes, rebelled against the corvée laid upon Israelites. He and the people he represented resisted the practice that one member of a part of God's people did to another what a pharaoh had done to Israelite tribes in Egypt, and what the liberated tribes did not mind imposing upon defeated nations (see below, Annotation 9, pp. 94-96, for the pertinent texts).

But the existence of house slaves was accepted as a simple fact. Israel as a whole, as long as it was obedient and trusted its heavenly Lord, was a kind of slave of its God: it was redeemed and liberated in order to *serve* God, and for the construction of, e.g., God's house, the temple, it repeatedly, voluntarily, and even enthusiastically offered money and labor. Perhaps this was one reason the keeping of house slaves did not appear contradictory to Israel's own history experience, and why even a slave's work was accepted and appreciated as standing under God's protection. At any rate, the existing biblical laws regarding slavery, as also their learned interpretations, aim at regulating and within certain limits bettering the treatment of slaves, not at every dependent person's immediate and total emancipation.

The question whether Jewish slave legislation gave a minimum of protection solely to the Hebrew but not to foreign slaves has been answered in different, if not contradictory, ways. Leviticus 25:39-55 distinguishes between the obligations pertaining to Hebrew and alien servants. Only Israelite slaves must not be treated "harshly" by their masters, because both they and their owners are God's servants. But the Sabbath commandment reveals humane attitude most likely toward all slaves, whatever their origin and history. The Deuteronomic version of this commandment (5:12-15) asserts that the master of a house and all those dependent on him, including the cattle and the resident aliens, have to have their Sabbath rest because Israel was a slave in Egypt and was freed from bondage by God. In these verses, the rest to be granted manservants and maidservants is mentioned *twice*. In the Exodus version (20:8-11), God's own rest after the six-day creation work is given as a reason why men, women, children, and cattle shall rest on the Sabbath. Either way, the institution of domestic slavery is accepted. As shown in Annotation 14, no earlier than by Philo, about the time of Paul, was the Sabbath rest of slaves explained as a signal of their eventual emancipation.

A. The Loss of Freedom

Male and female non-Jews became slaves when, at the time of the judges and kings, Israel made people of Canaanite origin prisoners of war and/or when their fortified places were conquered.[150] While originally all Canaanites had to be killed, soon enough some members of the defeated people, especially women and children, were permitted to stay alive — and thereby to increase, together with other booty, the wealth and pleasure of the victorious conquerors of Canaan.[151] Also, whether they were Jews or Gentiles, slaves could be bought and sold; only the sale of a slave in his hometown or to a pagan buyer was prohibited,[152] what-

150. The Talmud's term for a non-Jewish slave is "Canaanite (slave)" — whatever had been the ethnic origin of a foreign slave now in the hands of a Jew. The curse pronounced by Noah over Ham in Gen 9:25-27, saying that Ham's son Canaan was to be "a slave to his brothers," stood behind this nomenclature. The Scripture passage was quoted to prove that foreign slaves to Jews had to be slaves forever and were to be treated severely. The treatment of a Jewish brother and neighbor, a so-called "Hebrew" or "Jewish slave" (Jer 34:9, 14, 17 and Neh 5:8), followed entirely different rules: release within a given period and no harsh measures. In the Talmud details of this distinction are discussed foremost on the basis of Lev 25:39-55, where indeed the two kinds of slaves and their life in Jewish houses are clearly described.

151. Judg 5:30; Deut 20:10-18; 21:10-14; Num 31:25-53; 1 Macc 8:10-11; cf. 1 Sam 30:2-3. At the time of David, Solomon, and the Hasmonean rulers, great numbers of foreign slaves were brought into Israel. Jewish captives in great numbers were sold abroad in slavery when Samaria and Jerusalem were conquered in the eighth and sixth centuries B.C.E., during the Greek and Roman invasions, during the Roman-Jewish war between 66 and 70 C.E., and under Emperor Hadrian. In the Old Testament, only one case is recorded in which Jews attempted to make slaves out of Jewish prisoners of war. According to 2 Chron 28:5-15, when Ahaz was king in Jerusalem, the Judean army was defeated by the forces of the Northern Kingdom, Israel; an immense number of the Judeans were killed in battle, but those taken captive were to be sold into slavery. Against this plan a prophet called Oded, supported by a few North Israelite army chiefs, intervened: God's curse would be upon those sinning this way. Finally a safe and honorable return of the captives to their homes was secured. According to, e.g., J. Pedersen, *Israel* (London and Oxford: University Press; Copenhagen: Povl Branner, vols. 1-2, 1926, vols. 2-6, 1940), 1.183-185, the figure 200,000 given for the caught kinsmen is certainly exaggerated. Kidnapping ("stealing") of free Israelites by fellow Israelites must have occurred — or else it would not have been threatened with capital punishment in Exod 21:16 and Deut 24:7. The commandment of the Decalogue "Thou shalt not steal" concerned not only movable goods but also persons, even kidnapping.

152. Slave trade is mentioned in, e.g., Exod 12:44; 21:2, 8; Lev 22:11; 25:42, 44-45;

ever price was offered.[153] Further, by court sentence a thief or an insolvent debtor could be condemned to slavery.[154] Finally, a hapless Jewish debtor could voluntarily give up his freedom — though only for a certain period, that is, until he had repaid by his labor what he owed or until the end of the sixth year of continuous service. Some Israelites had to sell their children or were deprived of them by force.[155] Children of a female slave or of a slave couple were the master's slaves;

Amos 2:6; 8:6; Eccles 2:7. The lamentation on Tyre in Ezek 27:13 refers to it. The worst biblical example of a Hebrew being delivered and sold abroad is the sale of Joseph by his brothers to traveling Ishmaelite traders for twenty silver shekels (Gen 37:20-28). Josephus (*Ant.* 16.1-5) reports that Herod the Great had sold housebreakers, in flagrant contradiction to the laws of the land regarding thieves, into slavery abroad. The Jewish historiographer adds the comment: "This penalty was not the act of a King, but of a tyrant and of one who held the public interest of his subjects in contempt."

According to S. Safrai, "The Jewish People in the First Century," in *Compendium Rerum Judicarum ad Novum Testamentum I 1-2*, ed. M. de Jonge, S. Safrai, et al. (Assen: van Gorcum, vol. 1, 1974, vol. 2, 1976), 2.625, in the Hellenistic period Jews "continued to keep slaves and even to engage in slave trade."

153. It was half as expensive to let a Hebrew slave work for you in a given period than to pay normal wages to a hired or employed worker, if the calculation of Deut 15:18 is correct. According to Gen 37:28, twenty silver shekels were paid for a slave; in Exod 21:32 the indemnification for a slave killed by a bull is thirty shekels — as much as Judas received for betraying Jesus. The Talmud makes the cash value dependent on the corporal fitness of the slave and suggests as an upper limit one mina and as a lower limit one-quarter of a mina, in analogy of the price of an ox. In StB IV 2, 716-722, talmudic statements are collected that reveal the conviction, "Slaves are like cattle." Still the Amoraic sages had various ways to answer the question whether only the body or both body and soul of the slave were the master's property; see StB IV 2, 709 and 716-722.

154. Gen 44:17; Exod 22:2-3; Isa 50:1. See Josephus's comments on the Jubilee Year in *Ant.* 3.282 (cf. the footnote to this passage in LCL, Josephus, *Ant.* 1-4, 454-455). According to this historian, the biblical text of Lev 25:39, which speaks of self-sale, actually means condemnation by a court for any serious trespass, not the voluntary self-sale of a debtor resulting from poverty. Philo, *Spec. leg.* 4.3, argues that a caught thief incapable of making restitution, as much as an insolvent debtor, "must be sold since it is only right that one who has allowed himself to become a slave by profit-making of an utterly lawless kind should be deprived of his liberty." Urbach, pp. 91-93, points out that, in the Amoraic period as late as the fourth century c.e., Jewish courts in Babylonia were given the right by the government to condemn Jewish lawbreakers to sale into slavery, including sale to pagan buyers. However, wherever the progressively humane legislation of the Greeks or Romans prevailed, debt slavery became discouraged or prohibited.

155. Self-sale or sale of children, whether to a Jew, a sojourner, or a stranger, was "regarded as an unmitigated disgrace unless one was compelled thereto by the pressure of poverty," according to Urbach, pp. 11-12. In the Bible, debt slavery is mentioned in, e.g., 2 Kings 4:1-7; Amos 2:6 (also 8:6?); Lev 25:39-43; Neh 5:5; Prov 11:29. On the other hand, exposure of unwanted children — who could be raised up and sold as slaves by Greek and Roman finders in their countries — appears to have been unknown among the Jews of the biblical

because they were house-born, they stood closer to their owner's family and were better trusted than persons bought on a market.[156] Among the buyers and keepers of slaves, and among those possessing house-born slave offspring, were the king (or: the state), temples, and individuals, including priests and rabbis.[157]

Geographical factors and socioeconomic conditions of the land of Israel made it impossible — save in a few exceptional cases — for a great number of slaves to be held by a single owner. There was no room for huge estates; coal and metals could not be dug up from underground or scraped from surfaces. Except for the time of David and Solomon, when slaves and/or forced labor were extensively used for construction work in the land and for faraway industrial enterprises, masses of slaves are never mentioned in the Bible except when a whole people or tribe was subjected to the corvée.[158] Still, even during the period of the exile, slavery existed among the Jews — if the reports are true saying that one out of six persons returning from Babylonia was a slave to a Jew.[159] In modern scholarship, for some time the idea was proposed and defended that at the period of the Second Temple, between Nehemiah and 70 C.E., in the wake of Nehemiah's spirited protest against Jews holding Jewish debt-slaves, consanguine people were no longer enslaved to Jews. This hypothesis has proven untenable.[160] In the New Testament period, "the ordinary Jew had at least one slave."[161] Slaves worked as domestics in the field or were entrusted with higher or lower administrative functions. Parading oneself, as done by Herod the Great, amidst an entourage of 500 slaves and freedmen was decried as un-Israelite behavior.[162]

The entry into slavery was marked by some rituals. In public the slave had to perform a humiliating duty such as carrying his master or opening his sandal strings. A bell could be fixed to the throat or garment of the slave. In some cases

---

time. Only the explicit prohibition of such an exposure by a Jewish synod of 140 C.E. indicates that there were Jews tempted to take that step.

156. Gen 17:12-13; Exod 23:12; Lev 22:11; Eccles 2:7. The possible increase of the number of slaves owned by Jews in the Hellenistic period, down to the time of the New Testament, was due to the birthrate among slaves rather than to other causes. This may well be the reason that the designation of a slave in the Greek book of Jesus Sirach is *oiketēs* (house servant) rather than *doulos* — though both terms were also used to denote free hired or employed persons (see above, n. 22).

157. See Annotation 9, pp. 94-96, for a description of the several groups and occupations of slaves in Jewish hands.

158. 2 Sam 12:31; 1 Kings 9:27; 2 Chron 8:18; 9:10.

159. Ezra 2:64-65; Neh 7:66-67.

160. See Annotation 10, pp. 96-97, for arguments marshaled on either side.

161. Safrai, 2.627; cf. Urbach, p. 32.

162. Josephus, esp. *Ant.* 16-17, mentions again and again with outspoken disgust Herod's departures from Jewish traditions.

the slave was branded. After the first century C.E., a ritual bath "in the name of slavery" was performed.[163]

B. The Legal Position and the Treatment of Slaves

TWO GROUPS OF SLAVES

In the Mishnah, the Talmud, and secondary literature, a sharp distinction is usually made between Hebrew and foreign ("Canaanite") slaves.[164] Within the Hebrew Bible, however, this difference and its consequences are explicitly discussed only once, in Lev 25:39-55. When a Jew has become a debt slave to a fellow Jew, the master must not rule over his "brother" with "harshness" (Lev 25:43, 46, 53), but shall treat him like a hired laborer (vv. 39-40) and release him when the Jubilee Year dawns or earlier if the slave pays with his own money for his liberation or is ransomed by his kinsmen (vv. 40-42, 47-49, 54); for Jewish slaves are all God's servants redeemed from Egypt (vv. 42, 55). Pagan slaves, however, who have been bought from aliens, and their families are permanent, bequeathable private property of Jewish owners — "forever" (vv. 45-47).[165] In Exod 21:1-4; Deut 15:12-15 an explicit reference to foreign slaves is not made, but it is made clear that (only) enslaved Jews — males in Exod 21, males and females in Deut 15 — are given the hope to be released after maximally six years of service. Just as in Lev 25:42, 55, so also in Deut 15:15 the liberation of Israel out of Egypt is the reason for the protection under which Jewish slaves stand.

In other biblical legal, historical, and sapiential texts, there is no explicit juxtaposition of Hebrew and Canaanite slaves, though sometimes it is obvious that either a Jewish or a non-Jewish slave is in focus.[166] Since the Sabbath commandment makes no distinction, *all* slaves are entitled and obliged by God to enjoy a weekly rest from labor, as much as free Jews.[167]

163. For details, see, e.g., Kidd 65a; 69ab; 148ab; Yeb 46a; more references in StB IV 2, 718, 722, 724.

164. E.g., Philo, *Spec. leg.* 2.122-123; Kidd I 2-3; StB IV 2, 698-716, 716-744; Urbach, pp. 9-31, 31-50.

165. Indirectly Philo, *Spec. leg.* 2.122, in an allusion to Lev 25, calls foreign slaves "slaves by nature." This corresponds to Platonic and Aristotelian teaching, saying that in principle Greeks could not be slaves or should not be made slaves because slavehood was proper for barbarians only.

166. In the Talmud, however, Lev 25 plays so great a role that the differentiation is never forgotten but played out with vigor.

167. Exod 20:8-11; Deut 5:12-15. Still, some sages of the Amoraic period attempted to restrict the validity of the commandment to slaves who had been circumcised. See Mekh Exod 21:8, as cited in StB IV 2, 725.

According to an ancient law, all slaves in Jewish possession had to be circumcised.[168] Therefore the sign of God's covenant was imposed — by force if necessary — upon newly acquired Gentile slaves. This price was to be paid for table community, Sabbath rest, and participation in Jewish festivals, not to speak of marriage into a Jewish family. Circumcision was not only physically painful, but to those affected it must have appeared as an act of barbaric cruelty or a product of a narrow nationalistic or bigoted mind.[169] Except for the Sabbath rest, the lot of foreign slaves in the hand of a Jew was not essentially better than the plight of a person owned by a Gentile.[170]

DEVELOPMENTS

Old Testament slave legislation between the time of the patriarchs and the destruction of the Second Temple, as well as its scholarly interpretation by the sages, in Jerusalem, Galilee, and Babylonia was certainly not identical or even compatible. Great changes took place — and not always for the better and more humane.[171]

168. Gen 17:12-13; cf. Exod 12:44-45; Lev 23:10-11; Deut 16:11, 14 (12:18). See Annotation 13, p. 99.

169. Urbach, pp. 40-45, and StB IV 2, 722, 725-727, have gathered (e.g., from Yeb 48b, Shabb 135b) evidence of talmudic discussions concerning the circumcision of foreign slaves. Opinions differed on the timing of the ritual. Was the newly bought slave to be circumcised at once, even against his will, or was he to be resold to a pagan if he proved "bothersome" to his Jewish owner who could not persuade him to accept circumcision within twelve months? Similarly divergent judgments existed and were permitted in respect to another problem: Could the owner of an uncircumcised slave eat the Passover? See G. F. Moore, *Judaism in the First Century of the Christian Era*, vol. 2 (Cambridge: Harvard University Press, 1901; 7th ed., 1954), pp. 18, 136; S. Zeitlin, "Slavery during the Second Commonwealth and the Tannaitic Period," *JQR* 53 (1962/63): 202-206; Safrai, 2.628-630. Below, the implications of circumcision will be further discussed.

170. When P. Billerbeck, in StB IV 2, 728, starts out to describe the Mishnaic and talmudic tradition pertaining to the treatment of Canaanite slaves, he does not neglect the humanizing traits present in the sages' teaching. And yet he calls the learned discussion of slavery "a dark sheet" in the history of the Old Synagogue. This judgment is not to be understood as merely one more malignant jab at Judaism from the Christian side. E.g., the great Hebrew University scholar E. E. Urbach concludes his discussion of "the laws regarding slavery" (p. 94) with the statement cited in the first paragraph of sec. VIII, p. 53. He denies flatly that the juridical treatment of slavery "is such as to add any very glorious chapter to the history of Jewish ethics . . . in the period of the second temple and that of the Mishna and Talmud." While in StB as much as in S. Zeitlin and the dictionaries consulted a seemingly balanced and harmonizing collection of rabbinical statements and stories is offered, Urbach carefully distinguishes between more and less humane attitudes in different periods.

171. See Annotation 11, pp. 97-98, for discussion of a progressive development of Jewish thought and practice in regard to slavery.

FUGITIVES

While slave revolutions and wars are not mentioned in the Jewish literature here discussed, the flight of slaves plays a considerable role. Unlike laws and customs prevailing among Gentile nations, in ancient Israel slaves who had escaped from their pagan masters were entrusted to the protection of a Jew or the Jewish community.[172] They were not to be sent back. The tractate Gittin IV 6:1-2 (45a) fully endorses the obligation to give protection to fugitive pagan slaves from abroad who seek shelter and security in the land of Israel — perhaps they intend to escape idolatry? Yet in the same passage a warning is uttered about abetting and aiding the flight of slaves.

Even in talmudic times, the situation of some slaves was so bad that murder of masters by desperate or irate slaves occurred. Such slaves faced the same punishment as any other murderer, but there is no indication of specifically torturous forms of execution. On the other hand, in the Talmud the Old Testament passage prescribing punishment of the master who killed his slave (Exod 21:20) is interpreted to mean that the master deserves capital punishment — just as if he had killed a free person (Exod 21:12, 14).

PRACTICE VERSUS LAW

At times laws were enacted, and later, interpretations were added that appeared to mark a progress toward more humanity. But in those cases contradictions still existed between legislation and legal comment on one side, and the actual treatment of slaves on the other. What was commanded or urgently recommended to Jews was often carried out as little as well-intended laws in Babylonian, Greek, and Roman history. A cynic would go so far as to say: laws and learned commentaries existed in order to be neglected. If slaves knew at all of the more humanitarian among the legal prescriptions, then beneficial laws must have looked to them like promises of a faraway, better future, rather than a bill of rights on whose ground they might have dragged a cruel master before a court. Arbitrary treatment of slaves, outbursts of impulsive cruelty, and pun-

---

172. 1 Sam 25:10; 1 Kings 2:39-40. No earlier than in Deuteronomic legislation (Deut 23:15-16) was extradition of fugitives prohibited and giving shelter and a livelihood prescribed. In *Encyclopedia Judaica*, 14.1657, this protection of fugitives is called a unique Israelite feature. Philo, *Virt.* 125, declares the law regarding fugitives valid for compatriots and foreigners. But, e.g., I. Mendelsohn, *IDB*, 4.389, and de Vaux, 1.135-136, assume that the statute was restricted to slaves coming from abroad — or else, it is argued, slavery would have been abolished at once. In turn, Mendelsohn affirms in his book *Slavery*, pp. 63-64, by reference to 1 Sam 30:15; 1 Kings 2:39, that in actuality foreign slaves were normally extradited.

ishment resulting in maiming or killing were certainly forbidden; but they were by no means prevented.

By making use of Old Testament narratives, laws, and counsels, of New Testament parables and of talmudic discussions, an outline can be drawn of the actual life of a slave in a Jewish house. The span and diversity of slave treatment become clear in the light of extremes on either side.

GOOD POSSIBILITIES[173]

Though the slave was property of the master as much as were land, buildings, and cattle, slaves — menservants and maidservants alike — had the right to be treated as human beings.[174] The master was expected to give his slave(s) the same quality of food, clothing, and shelter as he used for himself. Sometimes the slave's family could join him on the way into and out of slavery. Demeaning work could, at least of a Hebrew slave, not be extorted. The right to rest on the Sabbath day was assured by God's commandment. The participation in festivals was permitted. The slave could receive a *peculium,* just as Roman or Greek slaves did. Also the slave could possess — though not freely bequeath — private property, including land or a slave of his own. If no one among his kin paid for his release, and if he could save enough, the way to self-redemption stood open. After having received faithful service and good work, a wise master would abstain from threatening and abusing a slave. He would have an open ear for complaints, treat the slave as a child of God and brother, and even love him as he loved himself.[175] A proverb shows that on occasion a master might become totally dependent on his slave: "He who acquires for himself a slave, acquires a master."[176] Not only was a Hebrew slave to be treated like a hired hand, he also could rise to high positions and stand above free Jews and Gentiles.[177]

173. Humane ways of treating slaves were never completely extinct under prevailing harsh practices. Maimonides, *Guide of the Perplexed* 3.39, preserved earlier teachings and recommended them, even in the face of less humane prescriptions and examples of the Talmud that encouraged harsh treatment of non-Jewish slaves. Some of Maimonides' advice is included in the following.

174. The main rights, proclaimed in the name of God and written down in the law, are listed in Annotation 12, pp. 98-99.

175. Job 31:13-15; Sir 7:20-21; 33:29-31.

176. Kidd 20a, 22a; Arak 30b; cf. StB IV 2, 710.

177. "It is not fitting for a fool to live in luxury, much less for a slave to rule over princes"; "do you see a man skillful in his work? He will stand before kings"; "among three things that make the earth tremble (is) a slave when he becomes king" (Prov 19:10; 22:29; 30:22). "There is an evil which I have seen . . . I have seen slaves on horses and princes walking on foot like slaves" (Eccles 10:5, 7). Urbach, p. 33, gives examples of slaves risen high and

Heavy burdens and hated obligations could be imposed on female slaves. On the other hand, captured, bought, or house-born maids were also granted minimal, specific protection.[178] Hebrew as well as Canaanite girls and women served the lady and the children of the Jewish house; they could become the master's or his sons' concubines or wives or might be given in marriage to a fellow male slave, or even to a free Jew. Exodus 21:7-11 protects Hebrew maids and eventually grants them freedom, though not necessarily after the sixth year of their service. Deuteronomy 15:12-18 prescribes that Hebrew and foreign female slaves be emancipated in the seventh year, and Deut 21:10-15 gives the same right to complete freedom to a first loved and later spurned foreign woman — she cannot even be sold on the market.[179]

CIRCUMCISION AND BATH — FOR WORSE OR BETTER?

Most important among the eventually beneficial slave laws was the Old Testament commandment that foreign male slaves had to be circumcised (see nn. 167-168). Later legalized was a ritual bath "in the name of slavery"; a similar bath was prescribed for slave maids. While in most cases the bloody and painful circumcision rite probably could be performed by force only, it did enable a slave to participate in family meals and festivals, and it conferred on the slave the status of the lowest rank among the proselytes.[180] After circumcision and/or bath, slaves of both sexes held a kind of associate membership in the elect and redeemed people; foremost by marriage or testament, and after a second bath ("in the name of liberty"), they could become Jews and give birth to indisputably Jewish children, but even before their full incorporation in Israel they stood under a limited protection against wanton exploitation by their owners. While early in Israel's history a circumcised slave could be sold to a pagan buyer, the Tannaitic *halacha* forbade his sale to a Gentile living abroad. When the owner made such a sale, Jewish courts had the right to declare the slave free.[181] Normally, a circumcised slave remained a slave — until, at least in the-

---

quotes a talmudic statement, "The king's slave is as the king" — which reminds of the exalted power of the Roman emperors' slaves and freedmen.

178. Concise summaries are presented by, e.g., de Vaux, 1.134-135, in the French original of *Ancient Israel,* and Mendelsohn, *IDB,* 4.385-386.

179. In Kidd I 2 (16ab), the release of a Hebrew girl sold by her father into slavery is made mandatory when the maid shows the signs of puberty. Kidd I 2 and Ketub III mention measures in favor of seduced or raped female slaves.

180. See Annotation 13, p. 99, for details concerning the effect of circumcision.

181. Gittin 43b-45a; cf. Urbach, pp. 67-69.

ory, the blasts from the ram-horn announced the Jubilee Year and, with it, his freedom.

Therefore slave circumcision, at first sight a cruel way of assimilating the foreign-born to the culture and religion of the Jewish society, included an urgent invitation: slaves shall participate in the blessings experienced by Israel and the order given to this people.[182] The same people who had been enslaved in Egypt and were liberated by God's mighty arm in order to be free to serve the Lord alone — this nation was instructed to use the institution of slavery as an instrument of its mission among the nations, even as an open door for outsiders. Gentiles, too, were to become members of the redeemed people and to enjoy its privileges. "In effect these foreign slaves became a part of the Jewish people."[183]

Seen from this angle, the Jewish slave system contained three very specific traits: (1) It reminded every Jew that once, in the loins of his ancestors, he or she had been a slave — and, but for the grace of God, would still be. (2) It had a missionary quality, for it was a method to include Gentiles in the service of the liberating God and in the hope fostered by those belonging in his people — notwithstanding the hardship still to be endured in the service to a Jew. (3) It prevented faithful Jews from identifying Judaism with racism, for it contradicted an "ideology of pure blood," as it was developed among pagan and allegedly Christian nations in antiquity and down to the twentieth century. To a large extent, the Jewish congregations in the Diaspora — in Rome, e.g. — may well have been composed of Gentile-born, then enslaved, and later freed persons.[184]

BAD EXPERIENCES

"The reputation of slaves was no better among the Jews than in the rest of the world."[185] Disappointing experiences as well as sheer prejudice and pride resound in the suspicions and charges raised against slaves in general. A king quoted in GenR 61 (38a) answers the question, "Cannot a man do to his slave,

182. Cf. Isa 56:5-7 and Job 3:19.
183. Safrai, 2.630.
184. As S. Krauss, *Talmudische Archäologie* (Leipzig: Fock, 1911), 2.101, observes.
185. Quotes support this statement of Moore, 2.137: "Three love one another: proselytes, slaves, and ravens. . . . Five things Canaan commanded his children: love one another, love robbery, love licentiousness, hate your masters, and never speak the truth" (Pes 113b). "The more slave girls the more licentiousness; the more slaves the more robbery" (Aboth II 7). In StB IV 2, 729-733, rabbinical citations are gathered that reveal the utter contempt in which slaves were held: they are said to be lazy and sleepy, untrustworthy and impertinent, and to bring — with the exception of Joseph, Gen 39:5 — only losses to their masters. A dog has more honor than a slave. Slaves have to be treated like donkeys and are no better than cattle.

whatever he wills?" with a blunt "Yes." To call a fellow Israelite a "slave" was the greatest insult and foolishness imaginable: the person using the dirty name was put under the curse of Canaan.[186] This attitude of slave owners is not only a feature of the development of slavery in the period of the Amoraic scholars. What Exod 21:20-21, 26-27 says about the beating and the eventual maiming and killing of male and female slaves, and what Sir 33:24-28 recommends regarding the exploitation of the "donkey-like slaves" (see Annotation 2, p. 84), suffice to reveal how hard the daily life of most slaves must have been at all times. The Jewish people who knew slavery from their own past and who had been redeemed from it did keep slaves — as also did members of the early church. In general the treatment of all slaves was harsh — or else Lev 25:43, 46, 53 would not have forbidden precisely such "harshness," at least in the treatment of Hebrew slaves.

C. Manumission I: The Theological Foundation

In the biblical, intertestamentary, Mishnaic, and talmudic traditions, emancipation[187] of slaves has its solid basis in him who is called upon and proclaimed as the Lord God. In the preamble to the Ten Commandments God introduces himself as the one who wills, performs, and effects liberation. "I am the Lord your God, who has brought you out of the land of Egypt, out of the house of bondage" (Exod 20:2; Deut 5:6). Prophets and Psalms do not tire to remind Israel as a whole and its members individually that it is the Lord God who not only has freed Israel once upon a time but also remains true to himself by ever new acts of liberation. As freedom has been a gift of God, so it always will be.

Indeed, enslavement does still occur — and not only of individuals to individuals of Jewish or foreign origin. The inhabitants of the Northern and the Southern Kingdoms have to hear the threat and are not spared the announcement that they will be made captives and will be enslaved, and will finally have to experience the mass abduction into the Assyrian and Babylonian exiles. And yet slavery is in principle a matter of the past; it is not the final will and work of God. The prophets speak of the return of those dispersed, and within the slave law of Lev 25, in verses 42 and 55, God reminds the people of Israel that "they are my slaves whom I brought forth out of the land of Egypt; they shall not be sold as slaves. . . . I am the Lord your God." Equally in the Deuteronomic version of the Sabbath command-

---

186. A collection of pertinent references is found in, e.g., StB IV 2, 733, and IV 1, 310.

187. As before, after the example set by the translator of E. E. Urbach's often quoted essay "The Laws regarding Slavery" (p. 1), the nouns "manumission," "liberation," "emancipation," "redemption," "release" and the corresponding verbs are used as synonyms in the following — though subtle distinctions might be made.

ment (Deut 5:12-15), Israel's redemption from slavehood in Egypt is mentioned as the reason for granting rest to slaves. By the exodus from Egypt and at Mount Sinai, the covenant made by God with the patriarchs is confirmed and becomes more specific. As God is true to himself, so Israel is bound to be his chosen and redeemed people. Israel is constituted as the nation of those freed for good.[188]

To speak of God as the actual giver and guarantor of freedom means to relativize, if not to exclude, other potential sources and pillars of liberty. Freedom, whether given or taken away, is not in the hand of a wanton fate to which Olympic and other rulers as well as the most miserable human beings are helplessly exposed. Neither is freedom dependent exclusively on the benevolence of liberal masters. Finally, freedom — at least in the biblical sense of the synonyms used for it — is not achieved by self-redemption. Theology — that is, speaking of God, recognizing his will, and accepting his gift — is in both the Hebrew Bible and the later ancient Jewish writings indispensable to a sober and realistic discussion of justice and emancipation for slaves.

What the apostle Paul writes to Philemon about the slave Onesimus is not determined only by his freewheeling moods and intentions, nor does it reflect solely specific facts and the development of slave holding in his non-Jewish environment. Rather, even after the Damascus encounter, Paul remained a well-trained pharisaical Jew. Below, in the Notes and Comments on Philemon, the theological influence of his biblical and rabbinical training will have to be mentioned repeatedly.

At least four features distinguish the freedom granted and vouchsafed by God, according to Jewish literature, from conceptions of liberty as represented by secular ideologies and events.

1. LIBERATION IS CARRIED OUT IN THE FACE OF AND AGAINST THE OPPOSITION OF NOT ONLY OPPRESSORS, BUT ALSO OF THE OPPRESSED.

God's will is forced upon the pharaoh with a mighty hand and outstretched arm (Deut 5:15; etc.). Yet the Israelites, too, were extremely reluctant to accept

---

188. Only one prophet, Amos (9:7), goes so far as to declare that, just as Israel was brought up from Egypt, so also the Philistines from Caphtor and the Syrians from Kir were "brought up (into freedom)" by God, and only Hosea (8:13; 9:3, 6; 11:5 except in the Hebrew text) utters the threat that Israel, because in perfidy it broke the covenant made with it by God, will have to return to Egypt. As mentioned earlier, worship of *Jupiter Liberator* or of goddess Astargatis, who protected and liberated slaves, existed among slaves in Italy and Sicily. But accounts claiming to record a historic event and speaking of the unique act of liberation that is valid for the present and the future time have not been discovered.

Moses as God's authorized agent of redemption.[189] Murmuring, rebellion, and demonstrations in favor of returning to the fleshpots, cucumbers, melons . . . onions and garlic[190] occurred before and during the exodus. The people wandering toward the Promised Land that was "flowing with milk and honey" were more often than not unwilling recipients of God's bounties. As the pharaoh had to experience God's brute superior force, so Israel needed continuous persuasion and coddling through ever new warnings or punishments — and through acts of overwhelming patience and mercy. Without the pressure of God, which was hard in some instances and soft in others, the people of Israel would not have received and experienced the freedom, the sustenance, and the blessing that God had decided to grant. Indeed, the narrative, legal, prophetic, and hymnic parts of the Bible speak — as much and intensively as earlier and later philosophical, nationalistic, and socialistic freedom literature — of the oppressor's unwillingness to grant freedom to the subjugated part of the population. But they also have much to say of the recalcitrance of those groaning under oppression and exploitation. They, too, are capable, inclined, or even resolute to resist liberation — even their own redemption. Their obstinate resistance to Moses, his task, and his acts shows that they are slaves — poor, miserable people who love their fetters better than the freedom and the hard and long way leading to it. Not only do the hardened heart and enormous physical superiority of the tyrants resist liberation. There are also the foolishness, the fickleness, the lack of confidence and courage, even the sin, of those chosen to be free.

2. LIBERATION IS THE TRANSITION FROM A BAD TO A GOOD SUZERAIN.

Not only does God redeem "out of the land of Egypt, out of the house of bondage"; he also frees his people for a specific purpose: they shall be servants of the Lord God. The message of Moses to the pharaoh is, "Let my son go that he may serve me," "Let my people go that they may hold a feast for me ... to sacrifice to the Lord our God."[191] As already quoted, the social, legal, political basis of Is-

---

189. When in Rom 9:14-18 the apostle Paul refers to the book of Exodus, he emphasizes God's mercy toward Israel and God's power over Pharaoh in order to exemplify God's freedom of choice and action. According to Acts 7:20-36, the Hellenist Stephen challenged the Jewish crowd and provoked them to anger and violence. He had done no more and no less than accusing them of rejecting their liberation through God's elected servant Moses, and Moses himself.

190. Exod 16:3; Deut 11:4-6; etc.

191. Exod 4:23; 5:1, 3. Similarly in Exod 3:12, 18; 5:8; 7:16; 8:1 (Hebrew: 7:26), 20, 25-28; 9:1, 13, 24-26; 10:3; 12:31; Mal 3:17, service of God, holding a feast, and bringing sacri-

rael's slave legislation is, according to Lev 25:53 (cf. 25:42): "To me the people of Israel are servants; they are my servants whom I have brought forth out of Egypt." Therefore, liberation consists not only of separation from an evil foreign dominion. Rather its special intention, character, and power is to make the people free for entering the service of another lord, even of God. What good would be freedom from a miserable life if it did not become, at once, the freedom for a new and good life? The exodus accounts themselves and the later biblical references to the exodus do not discuss a dismissal into a social or moral void. They describe an acquisition that God makes in order to possess a special people for himself alone. Unlike Greek and Roman notions of the meaning of freedom and gaining liberty, in the Bible liberation is transfer of title and ownership from one master to another. Because of the difference between the former owner, the pharaoh, and the final owner, Yahweh, the new bondage into which Israel enters will be essentially different from the earlier one — although here and there service is rendered. "They are thy people and thy heritage whom thou didst bring out by thy great power and by thy outstretched arm" (Deut 9:29; etc.). The forced obedience once rendered to the pharaoh's brutal force, and the obedience to which the same pharaoh was compelled so that he finally let Israel go out free, were one thing; the service for which God had liberated Israel was another. After the shame suffered in Egypt, Israel was called to consider it an honor to belong to God and to serve him alone. *Deo servire summa libertas* (to serve God is the ultimate freedom) — this dictum expresses what God extended with redemption.

After being led out of Egypt, Israel is by no means free to do as it pleases. Voluntarily, though not without fear and trembling, this people enters and confirms its special relationship to God. Truth and loyalty, righteousness and love are the basic requirements of the covenant made by God.[192] A summary of the

---

fices are exchangeable terms for describing the purpose of the liberation. According to Exod 5:17; 7:8, 11, 24, Pharaoh was aware that the Israelites leaving the realm of his influence were bound to enter the power sphere of another lord. Cf. Jer 30:8-9, "I will break the yoke from off their neck, and I will burst their bonds, and strangers shall no more make servants of them. But they shall serve the Lord their God and David their king." In Col 1:13, a Christian hymn is quoted that praises God's work: "He has delivered us from the dominion of darkness and transferred us to the kingdom of the beloved Son."

192. Serving other gods, crouching before idols, behaving as the non-Jewish nations do — this would not only mean to misuse the freedom granted, but also to jeopardize and lose it, according, e.g., to Deut 4:19-20, 28; 6:12-15; 28:36-37; 31:20. In these verses, the verb "serve" is used to denote service rendered to idols. In analogy, following the apostle Paul, redemption by Christ has nothing to do with release into anarchy or license. Rather it is submission to the authority of Jesus Christ, which is even stronger than the power still wielded by sin, flesh, and death. In Paul's theology, too, liberation is transfer of sovereignty and allegiance. Just as in the books of Amos, Hosea, Isaiah, Deuteronomy, and also in many psalms,

proper use of the freedom given is found in Deut 10:12-21: what Israel owes to God is to fear and to love him and to keep his commandments. Only in this way does Israel answer and correspond to the love of God shown to his people — and not only to them but also to the sojourners who are as bare of rights as was Israel while it sojourned in Egypt. By serving the Lord, cleaving to him, swearing only in his name — thus Israel will praise God the redeemer. In Deut 33:3-5; 30:16-20, the Law given to Israel is described as a demonstration of God's love: he wants them to stay alive and remain free. Everywhere in the Bible the name "Servant of the Lord" is an honorary title.[193] A separation or sharp distinction between cultic and ethical service of God cannot be justified on biblical ground.

3. IN ORDER TO MAKE ISRAEL FREE AND SUSTAIN ITS FREEDOM, GOD SO HUMBLES HIMSELF THAT HE TAKES THE FORM OF A SLAVE.

Jewish teachers of the post-Mishnaic period have made an amazing collection of seemingly unrelated texts of the Hebrew Bible in order to demonstrate that what a slave usually does for his master, this God does for his people: (a) "The Lord your God bore you as a man bears his son," or "on eagle's wings"; (b) "I bathed you with water . . . I clothed you also with embroidered cloth and shod you with leather"; (c) "the Lord went before them . . by night in a pillar of fire to give them light"; (d) "He who keeps Israel, will neither slumber nor sleep"; (e) "the ark of the covenant of the Lord went before them . . . to seek a resting place for them"; (f) slaves used to bake bread for their masters, but he acted as their baker from heaven, for "Man ate from the bread of the angels."[194] The se-

---

so according to Paul's epistles faith and love and voluntary service are the way to keep the new covenant. To "be set free for freedom" does not permit one to "submit oneself again to the yoke of slavery" or use "freedom as an opportunity for the flesh" (Gal 5:1, 13; cf. 4:8-10; 1 Cor 8:9; 1 Pet 2:16). "You were bought with a price; do not become slaves of men" (1 Cor 7:23). In Rom 6:12-23, Paul extensively describes the service "to righteousness for sanctification" for which those justified and sanctified by grace are liberated.

193. Schulz, pp. 135-136, emphasizes that Abraham, David, and the prophets are often called this way, and he refers to Pss 19:11, 13; 27:9; 31:16; etc.; cf. 2:10; 100:2; etc., in order to demonstrate the employment of the Servant of the Lord title by every pious Jew; to Lev 25:42 for application to Israel as a whole; to Deut 34:5 for Moses; to Josh 24:29 and Judg 2:8 for Joshua. The same expression is used for Jesus of Nazareth, Paul, other individual Christians, and the whole congregation (Phil 2:7; Rom 1:1; Acts 4:29; etc.).

194. (a) Deut 1:31; Exod 19:4; (b) Ezek 16:9-10; (c) Exod 13:21; (d) Ps 121:4; (e) Num 10:33; (f) Ps 78:25. The pertinent texts from TanchB bishlah 10 (29b); ExodR 20 (82d); 25 (86C); NumbR 16 (182b) are quoted in StB IV 2, 718.

lection and composition of these uncohesive verses are certainly not carried out under the auspices of nineteenth- and twentieth-century literary-, form-, historical-critical, or of structuralistic and sociological exegetical, methods. Indeed, the sages' atomistic use of the Bible looks playful or rhetorical rather than scholarly. But since the Bible as read and interpreted at Paul's time has to be discussed at this place, the amazing result of rabbinical Bible study cannot be bypassed with silence or contempt. Jewish scholars thought it proper to point out God's humility, that is, the method of God by which he became and still is Israel's redeemer.[195] The same God, however, who labors so hard in order to liberate his groaning people, also does rest and, in addition, gives his rest to all those crouching under a heavy yoke.

4. THE SABBATH SIGNALS THE LIMIT AND END OF ALL SLAVERY.

Among the apodictic Ten Commandments, issued in the prescriptive and promising form, "You shall not . . ." and "you shall . . . ," the Sabbath commandment calls for sanctification of the Lord's day by complete rest (Exod 20:8-11; Deut 5:12-15). Not only all members of the chosen and redeemed people, but also their slaves and cattle and the resident alien shall abstain from work. In different Scripture passages, different reasons are produced for this statute. According to the manna story of Exod 16, especially verses 22-30, on six days God gives enough food to make the gathering of daily bread on the seventh superfluous. Exodus 20:11 uses God's own rest on the seventh day of creation as decisive argument. And Deut 5:15 avers that the redemption from Egypt shall be remembered on the Sabbath day. Probably from the Sabbath statute are derived and developed the casuistic commandments (introduced by "When . . .") regarding the release of Hebrew debt slaves after six years, or after seven times seven years, in the Jubilee Year.[196] In its weekly, its heptannual, and its fifty-year cyclical forms, the Sabbath ordinance reminds of the destiny that God has set for and within his chosen people, for slave owners and slaves alike. The Cre-

---

195. There are Old Testament texts that explicitly speak of the inseparable unity of God's majesty and humility. E.g., Isa 57:15, "I dwell in the high and holy place, and also with him who is of a contrite and humble spirit," and Isa 63:9, "in all their afflictions he was afflicted." The first half of the Christ hymn found in Phil 2:6-11 expresses admiration for the lowliness of the high Lord. Cf. Heb 2:10-15: through sufferings and death Christ was made perfect and became the leader to salvation. Among the Greek deities, the half-god Herakles also labors like a slave. However, in so doing he demonstrates heroically his superior power and skill, not his solidarity with poor and oppressed people.

196. Exod 21:2-4; Deut 15:12-15; Lev 25:40-41, 47-55.

ator's own rest, the bounty of him who provides food to the migrants in the wilderness, and the sociopolitical redemption from Egypt — these past events are neither to be forgotten nor ignored, for indeed they are the cause why the Sabbath is to be kept. The Sabbath is an intrusion into the labor and toil and drudgery of every week and every year; foremost to the slaves it announces a limit and end to the skinning and flailing, the sorrow and despair of every day. On the Sabbath, ox and ass and other cattle receive the right to rest. Certainly they will work all the better on the following weekdays, but to the slaves are donated, together with the physical rest and the chance to recover strength and usefulness, the right, hope, and guarantee of liberation and freedom in due time. While in Exod 21:2-4 the deliverance from Egypt is not explicitly connected with the seven-year cycle, the verses Deut 15:12-15 establish an essential bond between sabbatical rest and sociopolitical freedom.[197] At the time of Paul, Philo of Alexandria emphasized this connection.[198] Are the Sabbath rest and the hope for manumission a privilege granted to Hebrew slaves only?[199] Since the biblical command includes the cattle and the strangers living in the city gates, all slaves, including Canaanites — who were compared to cattle by Jesus Sirach and in the Talmud — were entitled to enjoy the rest prescribed for the holy day or any other festival. Indeed, the six- or the forty-nine-year limit set for retaining a slave pertains only to fellow Jews. But the Sabbath commandment includes foreign slaves. By working on a Sabbath, they would have desecrated the land and thereby hurt their masters badly.

The four just-mentioned features of the theological basis of manumission lead to the following conclusion: among the Jews emancipation from slavery is a gift of God, not a general human right found in nature or birth, in the depth of the soul or in the reason alone.

God's personal concern for the oppressed, his open ear for their cries, his action at a specific time, and his promise to remain true to himself — these are the presuppositions of emancipation. By his commandment God asserts his

197. According to 1 Macc 10:34-35, at the time of High Priest Jonathan, the Seleucid king Demetrius (162-150 B.C.E.) sent a letter to the Jews granting freedom to all Jews under his rule on "all the feasts, and Sabbaths and New Moons and appointed days, and the three days before a feast and after a feast." This letter may be a product of Jewish wishful thinking rather than of the royal chancellery in Syria's capital. At any rate, it is a testimony to the interdependence of Sabbath, holy days, and freedom. Josephus, *Ant.* 3.281-282, too, is a witness to the coherence of the weekly Sabbath, the heptannual Sabbath Year, and the Jubilee Year.

198. See Annotation 14, p. 100, for an amazing passage in one of this philosopher's writings.

199. The Damascus Covenant (CD 11.12) might but need not be understood as permitting a pagan servant, maid, or hired worker to be used for work on a Sabbath: no more is prohibited than to make them angry on that day. Still, the very strict Sabbath prescriptions in the context make this interpretation unlikely.

will to be remembered and celebrated as the redeemer. By faithful obedience the granted freedom is held fast. It is ultimately to be extended to all persons.[200] Freedom is not regarded as a natural human right; all the more it is a right given and protected by God.

D. Manumission II: The Casuistry of Performance

Though in Gittin 38a the Talmud calls the manumission of slaves the first of three ways in which a master loses his fortune, the Old Testament and earlier as well as later sages among its commentators discuss a great number of good reasons why a law-abiding Jew should and would give liberty to a slave.[201]

Manumission had to take place in conformity with certain rules. Since the Hellenistic period, a mixture can be observed of Jewish, Greek, Roman, and other procedures.[202] A document called *get,* equivalent to later freedom letters, had to be phrased in a legal and unambiguous way and handed out to the slave, though exceptions existed.[203] A public announcement of release was necessary.[204] In principle, the document and the proclamation of freedom were irrevocable.[205] A bath "in the name of freedom" had to be taken by the slave; it included the obligation to keep the Torah and eventually had the effect that henceforth in every regard the former slave was counted as a Jew.[206] Additional rituals of formal release in postbiblical times included the investment of the male slave with phylacteries; the task to read Torah verses in front of the Jewish congregation; the wearing of a special cap by the patron and the manumitted slave; or the marriage with a free Jewish woman. Mandatory steps were complemented by elective procedures. In the Hebrew Bible and later, the freed person was called *hophshi.* A statute contained in Deut 15:12-14, 18 obliges the manumitting patron to pay out to the released slave a substantial gift.[207]

---

200. As indeed some modern Jewish Passover liturgies affirm.

201. See Annotation 15, pp. 100-101.

202. As pointed out by Krauss, 2.98-100, and Urbach, pp. 60-61.

203. Rabbinical opinions differed when exceptional cases were discussed: see Gittin 38b.

204. Philo, *Spec. leg.* 4.4, calls this proclamation *kerygma.*

205. Jer. Gittin IV 4 (45d); jer. Jeb. VII 1 (8a); jer. Pea II 2 (29a).

206. Urbach, pp. 59-63, dates this bath no earlier than the second half of the second century c.e. If he is right, then the bath for freedom was not the forerunner of or the model for John the Baptist's and the early church's baptismal practice and formulae. There were cunning slaves who during their first bath ("in the name of slavery") attempted to proclaim, Now we are baptized for freedom! This trick was, whenever possible, frustrated by the application of force; see Yeb 45b-47b.

207. The farewell gift somehow resembled the gifts, loans, or spoils that the escaping

At least three elements distinguished Jewish manumission legislation from formal emancipation in other ancient slave systems. (1) God's law compelled the Jewish owner to manumit a slave as soon as the slave's relatives or the slave in person paid for his or her value or covered the not-yet-amortized debt. Neither a Greek nor a Roman patron could be forced to accept the payment and grant freedom. (2) Not only was it possible for the kinfolk of the enslaved to redeem their unfortunate relative, as indeed Lev 25:48-49 envisages by saying, "one of his brothers . . . or his uncle, or his cousin, or a near kinsman belonging to his family may redeem him," but rather, according to the Talmud, the members of the slave's wider family were duty-bound to do so, and if they didn't have the means, the whole Jewish community was obliged to pay for the release of the Jew who became enslaved to a stranger, whether nearby or in a faraway country.[208] (3) The Hebrew slave had the right to renounce emancipation and to seek a minimum of social security.[209] A ritual act, the piercing of an ear with an awl and the fixation of that ear to the doorpost of the slave owner's house, was prescribed for when a male slave wanted to remain a slave. Reasons for his wish may have included (always?) his love of the master, of the wife given him by the patron, and/or of his children who might not have been released together with him (cf. Exod 21:4-6).[210]

In the biblical, Mishnaic, and talmudic legal traditions, some passages speak only of the manumission of Jewish slaves — with special consideration also of Hebrew females; other passages speak of the release of Hebrews and Canaanites on an equal level; and very few speak of special cases when a foreign slave had to be given freedom. Hebrews who had sold themselves because of unpaid debts, or who were sentenced by a court to slavery because of debt or theft,

---

Israelites took out of Egypt, according to Exod 3:21-22; 11:2-3; 12:35-38. When the slave married a daughter, son, or friend of the master, the gift was equivalent to a dowry. Deut 15:7-11 reveals a distinctly social concern. The gift was to prevent the relapse of its recipient into that poverty that had led to the debtor's self-sale.

208. The sages interpreted the words "may be redeemed" and "may redeem" in Lev 25:48-49 (so in RSV; the translation in NEB is "shall have the right of redemption" and "may redeem") in the sense of "shall be redeemed" and "shall redeem." Indeed, a strict obligation to redeem is pronounced in Lev 25:25 — but this verse speaks of the Jewish slave's lost or sold real-estate property only, not of the slave's personal liberation. By insisting on the imperative meaning of vv. 48 and 49, the sages expressed — certainly in harmony with the whole Jubilee Year legislation of Lev 25 — a warm human concern: what was declared valid for property was all the more mandatory for the redemption of Hebrew brothers and sisters.

209. Greek and Roman slaves did not possess this right, but together with the pharaoh, though through other means, Israel was forced to accept God's liberation work. See Annotation 16, pp. 101-102, for details of repudiated manumission.

210. In Deut 15:16-17 the same statute is declared valid for female slaves, too; cf. Kidd I 2.

also Jewish children sold by their parents, were the first given the right to be free. Exodus 21:2-3 prescribes emancipation in the seventh year — for the male slave only, and for his wife if he has brought her with him under the yoke. As earlier mentioned, following Deut 15:12-14, male and female slaves are to be freed after six years of service; in turn, Lev 25:39-41 speaks only of the enslaved Hebrew brother — and he has to wait for the coming of the Jubilee Year as fixed by the calendar.[211] Following Exod 21:7-11, one of three conditions must be fulfilled before a Jewish female slave (sold by her father for paying a debt) can "go out" in freedom without payment: (1) the master's displeasure with her after he has used her sexually, (2) her marriage to one of his sons, (3) the reduction of food, clothing, and intercourse after the master has taken another wife. As mentioned in note 179, when a female slave child reached puberty, she had to be manumitted.[212] Deuteronomy 21:10-14 contains an unprecedented law that gives freedom to female Gentile captives: when the Jewish owner deems her beautiful (and humiliates her by sexual contact), he either must marry her (and thereby make her a free woman) or, if she displeases him, "let her go wherever she will." Slaves crippled by blows of their enraged masters had to be freed irrespective of their Hebrew or Canaanite origin, according to Exod 21:26-27.[213] Still, among the sages a passionate debate took place regarding whether it was ever permitted to manumit a Canaanite slave.[214] On the other hand, it was not contested that even for non-

211. Josephus, *Ant.* 3.282-285, speaks of the Jubilee Year only, not of the seventh year, and he mitigates its economic impact. Instead of mentioning persons who had sold themselves, Josephus discusses people condemned by a court to enslavement on the ground of transgression of any legal ordinance.

212. A slave girl is given less protection in Lev 19:20-21: if before her enslavement she had been engaged to be married (or, according to other versions of the Hebrew text, if she was another man's maid), the man who seduced or forced her to have intercourse with him was not required to be put to death with her for adultery but could get away with a guilt offering — after the elders had made the necessary inquiries. The girl might have faced a better future when she could remain in the house of her owner and eventually there could give birth to his child.

213. In the Talmud, various opinions on the meaning of this text are set side by side. It is, however, unlikely that the original wording intended to exclude Canaanite slaves, as is, e.g., suggested in *Encyclopedia Judaica*, 14.1658. In Israel, the life of every slave was under God's protection. The Hebrew slave is in mind when Jeb. 70b and other talmudic passages affirm that only the slave's body, not his soul or life, is the master's property. What the owner has acquired is no more than the capability of the slave to work; see Krauss, 2.89-90.

214. The group opposed to the emancipation of foreign slaves who had been bought on a market cited Lev 25:46 in support of their stance: "You may bequeath them to your sons after you to inherit as a possession for ever; you may make (perpetual) slaves of them," and therefore maintained that only Hebrew slaves were to go free in the seventh or fiftieth year or earlier if they were redeemed. These teachers understood the verb forms "you may bequeath them .. make perpetual slaves of them" as meaning "you must. . . ." The unlimited curse pro-

Jews a door was left open toward enjoying a share in the elect people's God-given freedom. This door was circumcision, as ordained by God for male foreign slaves and recognized in the manifold rabbinic arrangements for the steps to be taken by proselytes toward becoming full Jews.

Never was there a time when all biblical statutes were completely observed, not to mention enforced. Regarding practically every conceivable detail, already in Deut 15; 21; 23; and Lev 25, the slave laws contained in Exod 21 were either supplemented by additional casuistic statutes or adapted to the need of later periods. No wonder the Mishnaic as well as the Amoraic sages arrived at variant interpretations. Very often the ancient postbiblical literature offers and tolerates conflicting opinions.

It is uncertain whether the commanded release of Hebrew slaves was ever completely carried out for any extensive period of time.[215] Even thinner is the evidence for deciding whether that part of the Holiness Code that contained the Jubilee legislation (Lev 25:8-34) was ever implemented as a whole or in part. The Hebrew Bible alludes to the high hopes connected with that year only in Ezek 46:17; Isa 61:1ff.; cf. 58:6; Num 36:4. Of the books written in the intertestamental period and cherished by esoteric circles, solely the book of Jubilees (prologue; 1:14; 50:1-5; etc.), which was written during the Hasmonean period, between 153 and 105 B.C.E., and the Qumran Scroll 11QMelch refer to it. In the rabbinic literature, references to the Jubilee Year are equally scarce, according to G. F. Moore (*Judaism,* 1.340 n. 1; 2.146-147). Although the Targumin and Sifra Leviticus do not neglect or omit Lev 25, the prevailing opinion among Jewish scholars and other leaders appears to have been that after the Babylonian exile this great year of liberty was neither proclaimed by anyone empowered to do so, nor ever enacted.

---

nounced on Canaan in Gen 9:25-27 served as an additional proof text. See, e.g., Gittin 381b; Sofa 3ab; Berak 47b; cf. Krauss, 2.98; StB IV 2, 739; Urbach, pp. 53-56; Zeitlin, pp. 204-206.

215. E.g., Mendelsohn, in *IDB*, 4.388, doubts whether the prescribed manumission was enforced more effectively than its Babylonian counterpart: the legislated emancipation of debt slaves after three years of slave labor. Jer 34:8-16 reveals that the Deuteronomic version of the law was ignored before the fall of Jerusalem in 587/586 B.C.E., and Neh 5:5-13 shows that during the reconstruction period, in the second half of the fifth century B.C.E., the Old Testament laws regarding debt slavery were ignored — until Nehemiah called the Jewish slave owners to order. In a parable (Matt 18:34), Jesus of Nazareth presupposes that a defaulting large-scale debtor could be delivered to jail (that is, to bondage as a slave) "till he should pay all his debt." Within a six-year span, complete repayment of huge amounts owed was impossible. In 1 Macc 6:49, 53, however, it is recorded that briefly before 160 B.C.E., food was short in Israel because the land was given the sabbatical rest. Philo, *Spec. leg.* 2.122-123, speaks of the release of Hebrew slaves "in either the seventh year . . . or in the fiftieth." He recommends buying foreign slaves (who need not be treated with kid gloves and eventually released), lest domestic service be wanting!

As the introductory verses, 1-7, of Lev 25 show, the institution of that heptannual Sabbath Year was the source of the Jubilee and was to be crowned by it. In each fiftieth year, on the Day of Atonement — the book of Jubilees prescribes the forty-ninth year — trumpet blasts shall announce the beginning of the Sabbath of all Sabbath Years. Fields and vineyards are to be left uncultivated throughout the year; land mortgaged or sold shall return to the original owner(s); dispersed and enslaved family members are to be redeemed by the next of kin so that they can return home as free persons. As Isa 61:1ff. sums up the same legislation and expectation: this year means "good tidings to the afflicted (or, to the poor) . . . binding up the brokenhearted . . . proclaiming liberty to the captives . . . opening of the prison (or, of the eyes) to those who are bound . . . proclaiming the year of the Lord's favor and the day of vengeance of our God; to comfort all who mourn. . . ."

This Isaiah text was read by Jesus in the synagogue of Nazareth, according to Luke's Gospel (4:18-19), although without the reference to God's vengeance and to the comfort promised to all those mourning. However, in the first two beatitudes of the Sermon on the Mount (Matt 5:3-4; cf. Luke 6:20-21), together with those thoroughly poor (or, poor in spirit; cf. Ps 33:19 LXX), the mourners are specifically blessed and assured of ample recompense in the kingdom of God for what they lack at present. While in Lev 25 nothing is said about the person who will proclaim, with Jesus, that the great year has begun, now God's righteous and gracious order will prevail over disorder and inequality. Already in Isa 61 the herald of the year of grace is at least as important as the benefits the year brings. It is possible that the second Isaiah had in mind a royal servant of God such as Cyrus (Isa 45:1) or an obedient offspring of David's house (Isa 53:3) who would proclaim and thereby usher in the year of salvation and justice. Yet it is also possible that he thought of a new Moses or of Moses *redivivus,* or another eschatological prophet, or even himself. Again, since the Jubilee is mentioned in the priestly passages Lev 25; Ezek 46:17; Num 36:4; and 11QMelch, it cannot be excluded that the realization of the Jubilee Year was expected from a priest or priest-king of the end time, and that they were confident priestly control over its prescribed social and economical changes would be maintained. Certainly there must be reasons why inside and outside the Bible there are no clear-cut reports or hints saying that the Jubilee Year was ever observed.[216] Before and after the last book of the OT canon was written, those

216. Josephus, *Ant.* 3.280-286, declares "jubilee" *(yobel)* and "freedom" as synonymous terms and distinctly affirms the validity of the complete Jubilee legislation of Lev 25. To outstanding Jewish and Christian scholars, these three texts are not convincing. E.g., de Vaux, 1.269-70 (in the French original; see n. 138), calls the Jubilee Year "an ideal of social justice and social equality that has never been realized . . . a utopic law" that has "remained a dead letter." H. St. J. Thackeray, in a footnote to Josephus, *Ant.* 3.282 (LCL, p. 454), speaks of

interested in the extant social and economical order and its stability would certainly contribute to letting prescription and/or promises that must have looked to them revolutionary be neglected or forgotten — or, if hard pressed, would water them down by a spiritualizing interpretation.

And yet, according to Luke 4 and other NT passages, Jesus announced that the commandment and promise of the Jubilee Year would now be fulfilled. After reading the Isaiah text just cited, he proclaims, "Today this scripture has been fulfilled in your hearing" (Luke 4:21). Among other things, this statement presupposes that before Jesus' coming and before the beginning of his public activity, no one had been authorized by God to announce the dawn of this year and none of the poor and captives in the land had been given a chance to enjoy its benefits. Actually by reading and interpreting in his own way Isa 61:1-2, Jesus introduced himself to those present in the synagogue as the eschatological king, or prophet or priest, or all of them in personal union. Later chapters in Luke unfold the story of how Jesus indeed fulfilled the promise for the poor and the captives in an unprecedented way — when he addressed himself to the social and religious outcasts and ate with them at the same table, when he healed and fed them, when he pronounced forgiveness and expelled unclean spirits, then he revealed God's mercy and kindness "to the ungrateful and the selfish" (Luke 6:35-36) and took care of their material as much as their spiritual needs. No wonder the guardians of the religious, social, and economic status quo treated him as a blasphemer and handed him to the Romans for execution — so that he died in the midst of two condemned revolutionaries.[217]

---

abuses to which this law had led and which caused it to be "early in the first century AD . . . virtually abrogated by a *prosbol* of Hillel." According to J. Morgenstern, *IBD*, 2.1002; cf. *Encyclopedia Judaica*, 3.1213, this legislation was "entirely theoretical and unrealistic," and "never became effective in any manner."

217. Following Luke 4:28-29, immediately after Jesus' initial sermon, an attempt was made at killing him. The flight of his disciples, the rejection by the majority of the Sanhedrin, and the crucifixion by the Romans did not stop the proclamation and the signals given for the fulfillment of the Jubilee Year described in Lev 25 and Isa 61. After Jesus' resurrection his disciples took up his message and were enabled to give signs of their full power. By adding the book of Acts to his Gospel, Luke intended to show that the Jubilee Year announced did not end with the crucifixion but continued to be proclaimed by the church and to be confirmed by mighty deeds and severe sufferings. E.g., A. Trocmé, *Jesus and Nonviolent Revolution* (Scottdale, Pa.: Herald, 1973); J. H. Yoder, *The Politics of Jesus* (Grand Rapids: Eerdmans, 1972), equally before and after the so-called Social Gospel and liberation theologians, have pointed out that this announcement and the implementation of its contents are at all times as essential to the church's mission as at Jesus' and the first disciples' and apostles' time. The Jubilee Year lasts, if Luke's interpretation is accepted, to the last day of the present world and therefore is still unfinished. For a careful exegetical study of Luke's Jubilee theology, see R. B. Sloan, *The Favorable Year of the Lord* (Austin, Tex.: Schola, 1977). Cf. N. P. Lemche, "The Manumission of Slaves — the Fallow Year — the Sabbath Year — the Yobel Year," *VetT* 24 (1976): 38-59.

Not much information exists of the actual life of manumitted slaves among the Jews. The *hophshi* did not form a special group between the free and the slaves. Only the foreigners living in Israel with the status of resident aliens, as mentioned in Deut 23:16, formed such a group. A Hebrew freed person was not bound to his former master by an equivalent to the Greek *paramonē* or the Roman *pactum* that stipulated *officia* and *operae*. Though after having served faithfully and being treated decently a slave would owe and show gratitude to the ex-master, legally the freed person was completely free and independent of the former owner.

And yet the Talmud records rabbinical controversies that indicate restrictions. There were sages who insisted on an eventually lifelong service of those freed from slavery to the person or persons who — when the closest relatives were incapable of paying for the redemption — had acted as redeemer(s) and laid down the money required. Other controversies pertained to whether a former slave was qualified to reoccupy a communal office held before becoming a slave, or whether the freed person should inherit all the patron's property when it was bequeathed to him by testament, at the expense of prospective consanguine heirs. Some held that only a part of the possession could go outside the circle of the blood relatives. Finally, the spiteful statement, a manumitted "slave remains a slave," is typical of a very late stage of the development of the *halacha*.[218] There were foreign slaves who had a home to return to; they were entirely free to seek and find the way of life they chose or could afford. Still it is probable that the majority of manumitted Canaanite slaves were incorporated in Israel, as proselytes and/or by marriage. Especially at the court of Herod the Great, there were Gentile freedmen who rose to high positions. At the other extreme were freed persons who became destitute and, if they were Jews, dependent on the welfare organizations of the Jewish local communities in Israel or abroad.

E. The Essenes

The numerous ways and problems of acquiring, maintaining, treating, and manumitting slaves were avoided by a Jewish minority group, or by two closely related communities. The Essenes may or may not have to be distinguished from Therapeutae and/or the monastic movement to which the settlement of Qumran and the scrolls found in its vicinity bear immediate testimony.[219] No

---

218. See Urbach, pp. 14-15, 30-31, 35, 58.
219. They are described by Philo, *Quod omn. prob.* 75-80, esp. 79; *Vita contempl.* 70-72; *Hypothetica (apol. pro Jud.)* frag. 11.1-18 (mention of slaves in 4), and by Josephus, *Ant.* 18.5-

one in their congregations was a slaveholder; all forms of slavery and of dependent labor were shunned. They flourished probably between the Maccabean times and the Judeo-Roman war (66-70 c.e.), and they constituted — as much as is known today — the first and only religious and social, economical and juridical, even political and moral type of a slave-free society in the ancient world.[220] Members of the communities carried out all manual work, including the labors considered demeaning, with their own hands.[221] Among the strict rules of their carefully organized communities was the renunciation of all private property, of gluttony, and of loud talk. By their monastic order and common life, they intended to express and restore the heritage of the true and faithful Israel, the people of the covenant. The relatively small but brave and if need be bellicose group stood in radical opposition to the sacrifices and politics of the "wicked" Jerusalem priesthood. Though they were outsiders and did not engage in propaganda and proselytism among non-Jews, they were tolerated on Judean soil and respected even in a wider environment. John the Baptist and the apostle Paul (immediately after his conversion) may have been in touch with them.

---

22 (slaves in 21) and *BJ* 2.119-161 (without reference to slaves). Enthusiastic descriptions of their unique stance within the ancient world are found not only in socialistic literature but also in, e.g., Schulz, pp. 129-134, 185-189, and G. Kehnscherper, *Die Stellung der Bibel und der alten christlichen Kirche zur Sklaverei* (Halle, 1957), pp. 141-144. Bare of a dithyrambic mood is W. Schenk, "Der Brief des Paulus an Philemon in der neueren Forschung (1945-87)," in *Aufstieg und Niedergang der römischen Welt* II, *Der Prinzipat*, XXV 4, ed. W. Haase and H. Temporini (Berlin and New York: De Gruyter, 1987), 1339-1395, 1470-1471: in a footnote to the last pages of his report on recent Philemon studies, he calls the enthusiasm just mentioned, including its application to rigorous criticism of the apostle Paul, a "social-romanticist" attitude.

220. Still, the Covenant of Damascus, a document stemming from this group, presupposes in 11.12 and in 12.6, 10-11 that members of the community possessed Jewish and non-Jewish slaves. On the other hand, according to Gayer, pp. 96-102, the Zealots, too, were opposed to slavery — at least to debt slavery imposed upon Jews.

221. Philo and Josephus proffer various reasons why, of all things, slavery was not tolerated in the Essene or Therapeutae communities. Philo argues that they repudiated slavery because slave owners denied that equality which is established by "the statute of nature, who motherlike has born and reared all men alike, and created them genuine brothers, not in mere name, but in very reality, though this kinship has been put to confusion by the triumph of malignant covetousness, which has wrought estrangement instead of affinity and enmity instead of friendship" (*Quod omn. prob.* 79). Most likely Philo reproduces in these words his own distinctly Stoicizing thought rather than the Essenes' own reasoning. His awareness of the actual predicament of slaves is, however, revealed by his repeated request that slaves be given equal right to speak up in the household (*Quod omn. prob.* 48-59; *Spec. leg.* 3.138). Josephus's argument, in *Ant.* 18.21, is more concise: Essenes do not own slaves "since they believe that the latter practice contributes to injustice."

F. The Uniqueness of Jewish Legislation and Practice[222]

The foregoing description of the outstanding elements and tendencies in the Jewish traditions regarding slavery is now to be repeated, accentuated, and concluded by an elaboration of the differences from non-Jewish traditions. The specific Jewish contribution and contradiction to theory and practice of ancient slavery can be summed up under eight aspects.

1. Israel and each Jew are constantly reminded by Moses, the Prophets, and many Psalms that they have been slaves in Egypt. May other nations boast of having sprung from on high — Israel is satisfied with its lowly origin, as is David with his earlier shepherd service: this people is unashamed of its former slave life because it knows that he who revealed himself as the Lord hears the cries of the oppressed, redeems them, and promises, whenever national and personal misery abound, to come as Redeemer to the needy and/or penitent. To the Lord God Israel prays — unless it has forgotten him, distorts his worship, turns to idols, and seeks by political alliances to save itself. This Lord is remembered and celebrated in great festivals and in personal devotion. Therefore, for Israel freedom is a matter of grace and of faith. It depends on God's untiring faithfulness and is embraced by keeping his covenant. Liberation is the work of God, who has acted, does manifest himself, and will complete his work in history, even when he has to labor like a slave in order to fulfill his will. To remember the Lord God — this is the alternative to trust in a blind fate that condemns some people to be born for a life as slaves and secures for others the bliss of freedom. By no means may Israel worship a multiplicity of gods, among whom some protect the wellborn, powerful, and rich — while hardly any are protectors of the ignoble, the poor, and the oppressed.

2. For Israel, the opposite to enslavement under a tyrant means a better predicament than living in an empty space in which a nation, its leaders, and all its members would be delivered to the uncertainty, the potentials, and the whims of human desires and decisions. Liberation is in effect transition into the service of a good and gracious Lord who has redeemed his people. Israel, Moses, the prophets, and the wise men and women do not in principle fight slavery, submission, obedience, respect, fear; theirs is not the stance for a superior ideology, sociology, anthropology, or politics, and for them liberty is not an end in itself — as if it could and would solve all human problems. But as fear of

222. Cf. Annotation 12, pp. 98-99. An instructive survey, describing in seven points the distinct testimony and "the boldest steps" of Israel in the issues of slavery, has been made by Schulz, pp. 110-111. With some changes and additions, it has been used in the following, though unlike Schulz's procedure, not only Old Testament utterances are taken into consideration, but also intertestamentary evidence, together with Philo, Josephus, and developments reflected in Mishnah and Talmud.

God is proclaimed the beginning of all wisdom, so loyalty as God's covenant partners and keeping God's commandments are the purpose of liberation and the only way to remain free from the dominion of evil lords.

3. Just as by the exodus and the promise of future acts of liberation God interferes into the slave history of all nations and societies, so the Sabbath commandment interrupts the tramp of the masters' and the slaves' everyday life. Hebrew as well as foreign servants and maids are protected by the Sabbath. The observation of the one weekly holy day, as much as of its offspring, the Sabbath Year and the Jubilee Year, gives and expresses the hope for liberation and rest from all labor and toil.

4. The Jubilee Year legislation is replete with visionary elements concerning a just social order that protects foremost the weak, unfortunate, and poor among the people. If it is a vision and almost a utopia, yet it ought not be understood as the description of a socioeconomic revolution that actually took place twice every century after the codification of the Holiness Code. In the Bible, even apodictic laws such as the Ten Commandments are not bare of visionary, futuristic, promising dimensions. In the Hebrew original the imperfect tense is used, which includes a promise for the future, not the imperative. Each commandment is therefore also a promise. The covenant made by God with, e.g., Noah, Abraham, and David and the covenant renewed through the death of Jesus Christ are one-sided promissory obligations pronounced by God — but they also bind the human partners. A contract between persons of equal rank is something else.

5. Casuistic prescriptions and prohibitions guard the life, limb, and dignity of all slaves. Young female slaves are placed under specific protection, even when the master has had intercourse with them. Under specified conditions manumission must take place immediately and without payment. Families and children are less easily torn apart than in Greek and Roman practice. Fugitives from abroad could find an asylum in the land of Israel.

6. There is only one passage in the five canonical books of law in which a distinction is explicitly made between the treatment of Hebrew and Canaanite slaves: Lev 25:37-55. Other Old Testament texts treat unambiguously either Jewish or foreign slaves; again others leave it open whether one only or both groups are in mind. Frequently in the Talmud, and as it appears always in secondary literature regarding slavery in the Jewish society, are found elaborations on the differences. Indeed, masters are told to manumit Jewish debt-slaves — after a given number of years. Still, as little as God imposes freedom upon Israel by the force used against the pharaoh, as little can a Jewish master force a slave to choose freedom and leave the house. Despite all hardship to be endured for the rest of his life, there was also some protection from starving and utter destitution when a slave chose to renounce freedom. Jewish slaves could be re-

81

deemed at any time by their kinfolk or a Jewish congregation; but a foreign slave, especially when his work was useful and profitable for the owner, had hardly any hope for manumission. Exceptions, however, were also made in favor of non-Jewish slaves: a very faithful servant or maid, a foreign slave marrying into the master's family, and a slave maimed by the master's blows were given freedom or at least had the right to ask for it.

7. The biblical ordinance that foreign male slaves must be circumcised, and the postbiblical ritual of their and the foreign females' bath in the name of slavery, are not only measures to assimilate non-Jews into the Jewish household. Rather circumcision and bath threaten, undermine, and eventually destroy the distinction between Jew and (former) alien. Both acts initiated the incorporation into Israel that could be intensified by steps until the foreigner became, by a second bath, a proselyte of righteousness. Therefore, in the Jewish tradition neither nature nor birth, neither nationality nor religion, neither good fortune nor bad fate are considered sources or signs of a predestination that would make sure that a person was enslaved forever. Even Gentile slaves who in earlier years as captives of war — or since the exile, after being bought on a slave market — had become slaves in Jewish homes, could become Jews and serve God, the redeemer from slavery. Thus the cruel institution of slavery was used to proclaim the lordship of God over people of every conceivable origin, and the seemingly nationalistic and egoistical distinction between Hebrew and Canaanite slaves had to yield to the freedom found in the service of God.

8. The Jewish Essene and/or Therapeutae communities did not engage in mission to the nations. The fact that their members did not hold slaves could hardly impact the conduct of contemporary slave owners and the predicament of the slaves. And yet these communities were a pilot project that at various times and in a variety of forms would be admired, perhaps also imitated among non-Jewish secular and religious groups. No discussion of ancient slavery can ignore the testimony they bore in action, not just in words, to the equality, the brotherhood and sisterhood of all human beings. Together with all faithful Jews, the Essenes demonstrate that a firmly founded theology, thorough scripture study, and an intense yearning for help coming from God alone do not neglect, belittle, or destroy social ethics but generate and produce a new interhuman relationship in which power and riches do not have the last word.

This list of eight Jewish idiosyncrasies in slave experience, legislation, and treatment might be complemented by the enumeration of other traits that are common with Near Eastern culture, and of developments that reveal Greek and Roman influence. The idea of a highest God who is father, or of nature as the common mother of all human beings, existed among the Greeks even before it occurs in Jewish literature of the Hellenistic period. Good treatment of slaves, including their marriage into their owner's or another free family, as well as testamentary designation of them as heirs are found inside as much as outside Palestinian and Diaspora Judaism. Equally the estimation of slavery as a curse, the hatred between slave and master, the contempt shown for the weaker and dependent members of society, the meting out of cruel punishment, and other features are shared by the Jewish people with non-Jewish societies. There is nothing to boast of a superior morality and humanity in the development of the Jewish slave system. As earlier indicated, the same is true of the attitude of the early Christian church to slavery.[223]

In Israel as well as in the whole antique world, slavery was considered as indispensable as are machines for twentieth-century American industrialists and farmers. The apostle Paul and his utterances regarding slavery have to be understood against this background. Still, before consequences can be drawn for the interpretation of his Letter to Philemon, annotations will illustrate some important topics that have been barely touched on in the foregoing, and then a series of literary-historical questions pertinent to Philemon will be discussed in some detail.

ANNOTATIONS

1. Slave Names and Designations

Because, beginning in the last decades B.C.E., the number of manumitted slaves was growing, there was no longer a slave name that might not also have belonged to a free man or woman. Several Roman popes of the first two centuries had slave names, but this does not prove that all of them had been slaves or freedmen.

Very often a slave was not called by name. Not to be called by one's name was and is specifically humiliating. In a comedy concerning a bad slave who is given the name "hard-to-sell," the fourth century B.C.E. poet Epicrates makes a slave say, "What is more hateful than to be summoned with 'Slave, Slave . . .?'" according to Athenaeus, *Deipnosoph.* 6.262d. The Greek term used at this place

223. Overbeck, pp. 158-230, has shown that there is ample reason for the Christians to be ashamed of the ancient church's attitude to institutional slavery: it did not seriously question, criticize, or shake it. An exception appears to have been an obscure gnostic sect, the Carpocratians, mentioned by Clement of Alexandria, *Strom.* 3.2.6-10, esp. 6. Also Gregory of Nazianzus, *Carm.* 2.26, and John Chrysostom, *In Matthaeum* 63.4, have a few critical words against slavery as such.

is *pais*. Still, Athenaeus enumerates in the same context (263a-264f) a series of other addresses that were supposed to take away the sting of "slave." In Hebrew, *ebed* — as much as Ugaritic, Akkadian, east-Canaanite, and Aramaic cognates — means either a slave or a free (servant) or a political subject, a high adviser, a military subordinate, finally a worshiper of Yahweh or some deity. More than three hundred times the LXX translates *ebed* by *pais*, but *doulos, oiketēs,* and *therapōn* are also used. The Latin word is *servus*, a term that, just as its Semitic and Greek equivalents, also denotes a free, though in one or another way dependent, laborer.

Since the Hellenistic period the expression "Phrygian" designated a difficult, uncouth, or cowardly slave — as if to say, what else can you expect from a person coming from central Asia Minor? In his commentary on Philemon (1875, p. 378 n. 2), J. B. Lightfoot quotes Cicero's *De Flacco* 27 and other ancient writers' depreciative remarks that connect a slave's character and behavior with the region of his origin. Eunus, the leader of slave revolt in Sicily during the second half of the second century B.C.E., proudly called the revolutionaries "Syrians," according to Diodorus Siculus, *Bibl. hist.* 34.2.24. The term "slave," as used in Western languages, stems from the Middle Ages and reveals the contempt in which Europeans held eastern European Slavonic peoples. On the other hand, the Talmud occasionally states that "no slave has a legally recognised ancestry but is folk similar to the ass" (see Urbach, "The Laws regarding Slavery," p. 46 n. 119). Only to the name of a free person, not of a slave, belonged the mention that he or she was "the son" or "the daughter of ———." To the slave's name, if anything, the name of the master was added. In turn, the apostle Paul employs proudly for himself and other Christians the designation "slave of the Messiah Jesus"; so, e.g., Rom 1:1 and 1 Cor 7:22. Those who serve this Lord well are not deprived of their proper names; they gain rather than lose specific dignity, as the Pauline greeting lists show.

2. A First Look at Slavery in Israel

In the Old Testament, the Mishnah, and the Talmud, Hebrew slaves enjoy specific protection. They must not be treated harshly; a slave who is maimed by his master must be given freedom. However, when the cripple insists on staying in his master's house (because elsewhere his lot might be even worse), he can let his ear be pierced and fixed to the doorpost, and stay. A master who kills a slave is punished eventually by death (see Annotation 12). Still, counsel given to slave owners by a Jewish sage expresses not only the universal but also the prevailing Jewish attitude toward slaves. It is found only in the (Greek) LXX and the (Latin) Vulgate versions of the OT, not in the Scriptures canonized by the Jews and used as readings in their synagogues; the LXX and Vulgate were used primarily by Christians. In the RSV, Jesus Sirach (Ecclesiasticus) 33:24-28 (i.e., 33:25-29 or 30:33-38) has the following wording: "Fodder and stick and burdens for an ass, bread and discipline and work for a servant. Set your slave to work, and you will find rest; leave his hand idle, and he will seek liberty. Yoke and thong will bow the neck, and for a wicked servant there are racks and tortures. Put him to work, that he may not be idle, for idleness teaches much evil. Set him to work, as is fitting for him, and if he does not obey, make his fetters heavy." The next sentence (33:29) curbs the punishment of the lazy or malignant slave: "Do not act immoderately toward anybody, and do nothing without discretion." Again, the next two verses (33:30-31) remind the master to treat the slave as the master's other ego, that is, as a brother. There are textual variants to all these verses and quite a number of different interpretations.

G. F. Moore, *Judaism*, 2.137-138, does not believe that the author of this passage "was a particularly hard-headed master, or that the lot of slaves was greatly ameliorated in later times." Still, Job 31:13-17 suggests that slaves should be considered and treated as brothers, and Sir 7:20-21 (7:21-22) advises, "Do not abuse a servant who performs his work faithfully, or a hired laborer who devotes himself to you. Let your soul love an intelligent servant; do not withhold from him his freedom." These verses are preceded by an exhortation concerning the owner's wife and followed by wise counsels regarding cattle and children. Maimonides, in his *Guide of the Perplexed* 3.39, radically corrects the first-quoted part of Sir 33; he describes a reasonable treatment of slaves in line with the teaching of humane Stoic philosophers. Other writers attempt to dissolve the contradictions between Sir 33:24-28 on one side, and 33:29-30 and 7:20-21 on the other side, by suggesting that bad treatment is reserved for foreign slaves, good treatment for Israelite slaves. But the reasons they offer are not convincing, according to Urbach, p. 26. Another solution is proposed by P. W. Skehan and A. A. di Lella (in *The Wisdom of Ben Sira*, AB 39 [1987], pp. 402-406): a multitude of slaves is to be kept under sharp discipline; but if a (middle-class) Jew could afford to own no more than one single slave, then this servant had better be treated kindly.

At any rate, there is no single, unchangeable attitude of Jews toward slaves.

3. Crucifixion and Other Modes of Execution

After the end of the slave war headed by Spartacus, in 71 B.C.E., six thousand slaves were crucified at the Via Appia. This "evil," barbaric, slow, and humiliating form of execution was not only normal for the worst criminals and rebels, but was also often used for defeated military and political enemies. Before and during the time of the Roman dominion, it was used in the East and in the West. In Plautus, *Mil.* 2.4.372f., a slave defies threats because he knows that his own tomb, just as that of his father, his grandfather, and his forefathers, will be the cross. In Juvenal, *Sat.* 6.219-224, a slave owner cringes under the whimsicalness of his wife, who bluntly denies that a slave is a human being. Even if the slave is innocent, she insists on having the slave crucified: "hoc volo, sic jubeo, sit pro ratione voluntas" [this I will, such is my command; may my will prevail over reason!]. In several of Plautus's comedies, the expression "go to the cross" corresponds to the English "go to hell!" M. Hengel ("Mors turpissima crucis," in *Rechtfertigung,* FS E. Käsemann [Tübingen: Mohr, 1976], pp. 125-184; enlarged ET, *Crucifixion* [London: SCM, 1977]) has collected the ancient evidence in order to apply it to the Pauline preaching of Christ crucified. Plato, *Leg.* 9.865b-868c, demands that a slave be killed if he has murdered his master or another free person. This philosopher leaves the choice of manner of death to the victim's relatives. In turn, a master who had killed his slave needed at Plato's time no more than purification by a court and/or at a sanctuary. Later, however, a formal sentence was necessary to free a master of the charge of murder after he had killed a slave, or to permit the execution of a slave accused and found guilty of a gross crime.

4. Pliny's and Other Letters of Intercession

In the LCL edition of Pliny the Younger, two letters regarding a fugitive freedman (*Ep.* 9.21 and 24) are translated. The first reads as follows:

"To Sabinianus. The freedman of yours with whom you said you were angry has been (= come) to me, flung himself at my feet, and clung to me as if I were you. He begged my help with many tears, though he left a good deal unsaid; in short, he convinced me of his genuine penitence. I believe he has reformed, because he realizes he did wrong. You are angry, I know, and I know too that your anger was deserved, but mercy wins most praise when there was just cause for anger. You loved the man once, and I hope you will love him again, but it is sufficient for the moment if you allow yourself to be appeased. You can always be angry again if he deserves it, and will have more excuse if you were once placated. Make some concession to his youth, his tears, and your own kind heart, and do not torment him or yourself any longer — anger can only be torment to your gentle self. I am afraid you will think that I am using pressure, not persuasion, if I add my prayers to his — but this is what I shall do, and all the more freely and fully because I have given the man a severe scolding and warned him firmly that I will never make such a request again. This was because he deserved a fright, and it is not intended for your ears; for maybe I shall make another request and obtain it, as long as it is not unsuitable for me to ask and you to grant."

Pliny wrote a second letter (9.24) in which compliments and thanks are expressed to Sabinianus for yielding to the "authority, or if you prefer . . . the request" of the writer. At the same time Pliny gives "a word of advice for the future: be ready to forgive the faults of your household even if there is no one there to intercede for them." Reasons why the fugitive freedman was no better off after his manumission than a slave before his emancipation are discussed in VII.D (pp. 34-37).

Other ancient letters of recommendation were written by, e.g., a priest in about 346 C.E. in favor of "Paul the soldier" who had deserted. From the early fourth century stems an analogous letter of intercession written by Isidor of Pelusium (MPG, 78.277, #142). Just as in Pliny's epistles, in the last-mentioned scripts the recipients are asked to grant pardon to the repentant fugitives. All the more noteworthy, then, is that, in addressing Philemon, Paul explicitly neither mentions repentance nor begs for forgiveness. Among medieval letters of intercession are two in which Anselm of Canterbury pleads for a monk who has frivolously left his monastery and now hopes to return and be graciously received by his abbot. The result of Anselm's intervention is as unknown as that of Paul's (see ##140 and 141 in F. S. Schmidt, ed., *S. Anselmi Opera Omnia* III [Stuttgart: F. Fromme, 1968], pp. 285-288).

5. A Warrant of Arrest

The text Papyrus 10 is easily accessible in LCL *Select Papyri* II 234, pp. 137-138. The announcement was made by a private person. Obviously it is shaped after a previously established model. It is dated August 13, 156 (or 145?) B.C.E., and was first posted at public walls in Alexandria, Egypt, then also outside the city.

After the date, the original warrant reads, "A slave of Aristogenes, son of Chrysippus, of Alabanda, ambassador, has escaped in Alexandria, by name Hermon also called Nilus, by birth a Syrian from Bambyce, about 18 years old, of medium stature, beardless, with good legs, a dimple on the chin, a mole by the left side of the nose, a scar above the left corner of the mouth, tattooed on the right wrist with two barbaric letters. He has taken with him 3 octadrachms of coined gold, ten pearls, an iron ring on which an oil-flask and strigils are represented, and is wearing a cloak and a loincloth. Whoever brings back this slave shall receive 2 talents of copper; if he points him out in a temple, 1 talent; if in the house of a substantial and actionable man, 3 talents. Whoever wishes to give information shall do so to the agents of the strategus."

The figures mentioned were later changed: the reward was raised to three, two, and five talents respectively. The reduced compensation for catching the slave in a temple may have to do with the expected difficulties in prying him loose from the priest's hands. The high reward for finding the slave in a rich man's home may be connected to the fine the host had to pay for harboring the fugitive; a part of the substantial penalty would go to the slave's owner.

The papyrus ends with a description of another slave who also took valuables with him, and whose capture will be rewarded on the same terms.

6. Examples of Slave Insurrections

a. During the classical period of Athens and Sparta, masses of Attican slaves made use of wartime conditions to start revolts, as did the Helots of Sparta after a great earthquake. During the first half of the fourth century B.C.E., Plato, *Leg.* 6.777bc, mentions "the frequent revolts in Messenia," on the Peloponnese; cf. Thucydides, 7.27.5.

b. About 325 B.C.E., on the island of Chios, the slave Drimakos encouraged fellow slaves to form a robber gang in the mountains and led them in an attack on the rulers of the city and its defense forces. After his assault succeeded, he made a contract with the citizenry: he would regularly take no more from the city storehouses than a certain quantity; also he would receive and test slaves who flee from their masters and send back those lacking sufficient cause. Though eventually an award was set on his head, after his death the citizens built a sanctuary for this "kindly hero *(hērōs eumenēs),*" which also served as an asylum for fugitives. The slave and bandit has become a Robin Hood. David's flight from Saul (1 Sam 22:2) had similar consequences.

c. After the end of the Second Punic War in 201 B.C.E., armies of slaves were imported into Italy where the small farmers had been ruined during the two Roman wars with the Carthaginians. At first rich Roman knights left uncultivated much of the land they had bought at bargain prices. Soon enough they realized that they needed a huge labor force to look after soil and cattle on the newly formed latifundia. A series of revolts was the result: 198 B.C.E. in Latium (where surviving noble Carthaginians assisted Roman proprietors); 190 in Etruria; 185 in Apulia. Finally, while Rome was heavily engaged in external wars from Spain to Persia, the great revolts erupted:

d. Between 136 and 132 B.C.E., Eunus led the First Sicilian Revolt. He came from Apamea — a trade center not far east of Colossae, where Philemon and his slave Onesimus were living two hundred years later. A dreamer and diviner, a magician and healer, Eunus was one of the hungry, poorly clad, branded, partly fettered, and often crudely whipped mine or agricultural slaves.

He was provoked by the foolish, arrogant, and tyrannical lord and lady of the manor and answered by announcing that (his Asia Minor home goddess) Atargatis had revealed to him that he would be king. After murdering master and mistress, he was joined by slaves, robbers, religious and nationalistic enthusiasts, and they declared him their king. He assumed the name Antiochus, his wife became queen, and a court ceremonial was established for the "kingdom of Syrians" — though without Oriental divine titles for the monarch. He succeeded in conquering and holding the regional capital, and arranged public trials in the theater. While a great number of citizens were executed, enough were permitted to survive in order to be used in carefully organized industrial arms production. The number of his troops is said to have risen from 400 to 200,000 — but there is no way to verify these numbers. At the same time, also in Sicily, Cleon, a slave imported from the Taurus region, had made a similar journey from the slave pen to a robber band and to the leadership of a well-organized army of freedom fighters. His troops were capable of routing small and large units of Roman soldiers. The hope of some contemporaries did not materialize that Antiochus and Cleon, together with their armies, would eventually fight one another. Cleon subordinated himself to Eunus/Antiochus and served as his general. The joined forces of Eunus and Cleon were finally besieged and defeated when, supported by a traitor, the Romans conquered their capital, Enna. The survivors who were too slow to kill themselves or one another mutually were brought to death after protracted tortures. While Cleon died in battle, Eunus was left to die in prison — eaten by lice. Still, the news of this revolt spread like a prairie fire.

e. From 133 to 130 B.C.E., in the northwestern Asia Minor city of Pergamum, Andronicus — not a slave, but the bastard child of royal blood (his father: King Eumenes II, his mother: a flute player) — was the central figure in an unusual sequence of events. In a somewhat ambiguous testament, the childless king Attalus III, Eumenes II's successor, had promised freedom to Pergamum and other cities under his rule. At the same time, he had installed Andronicus as heir to the throne and executor of his last will. When his testament was contested by Roman provincial authorities and the well-to-do people of the city, Andronicus successfully appealed to the local slaves, to the half-free servants at the palace and in the temples, and to all the poor among the city's population. The disinherited prince associated himself — to use J. Vogt's formulation (*Sklaverei und Humanität,* p. 27) — with the disinherited proletariat. He became the poor man's and woman's king and promised riches to them — they would be citizens of the city that in the future would be called "Sun-City" (Heliopolis) and constitute a city of righteousness. A classless society would be formed, e.g., by granting sexual freedom to everybody rather than insisting on the implementation of marriage laws. This city would find imitation in the whole world. In summary, envisaged was a cosmopolitan solution to the problems of inequality, injustice, and poverty. Andronicus hired mercenaries to defend his creation, but regular armies put an end to all his aspirations.

Between 1532 and 1534 in Münster, Westphalia (Germany), a similar attempt was made to organize a messianic state. Inspired by Dutch and Frisian Anabaptists, the spiritualistic theologian *(Schwärmer)* B. Rothman (or Rottman) and a local cloth merchant, B. Knipperdolling, replaced private property by a communist economic order; monogamy by polygamy; official and private libraries by the toleration of but one book, the Bible; and the festival days of the church by frequently held love-meals at the marketplace, during which obstructing citizens were executed.

f. In 120 and 104 B.C.E., within the mining district of Laurium in Attica, several slave revolts took place (as described by S. Lauffer, *Die Bergwerkssklaven von Laureion*). During the same period, an insurrection occurred at Delos, the seat of a flourishing slave market. Meanwhile in Italy, in 105 B.C.E., Vettius, an adventurous son of a very rich Roman knight, released his slaves and made himself king over more than three hundred slaves who had left their masters to join him. To fight an *ad hoc* mobilized Roman army, he appointed a general who was promptly bribed to betray him to the Roman authorities. Defeated, Vettius and other survivors of the ensuing slaughter committed suicide.

g. During the same time, "turmoil and a very Iliad of woes possessed all of Sicily," as Diodorus Siculus, *Bibl. hist.* 34.6, phrased it. Especially between 104 and 100 B.C.E., in the east and the west of the island, revolts that had begun with the butchering of a master turned into raging wars. Sometimes impoverished free people, among them evicted farmers, joined the slaves. In the open country assassinations, robbery, and rape were the order of the day; only fortified cities, including the slaves living in them, resisted the "brigands' attack" on the silent majority. The Second Sicilian Revolt started when, for diplomatic reasons and under the pressure of Sicilian land and slave owners, by order of the Roman Senate 800 Bithynian slaves were given freedom. This limited emancipation act kindled high hopes in the myriads of other slaves from Asia Minor. In vain — for no additional manumissions ensued. The compressed masses of slaves exploded, inspired by two charismatic persons: Salvius and Athenion. A predecessor of them and his 2,000 followers had been quickly — by treason — overwhelmed in a mountain fortress. Salvius, a freedman, a flutist and skilled in divination, called up the Sicilian slaves to meet him en masse at the sanctuary of Palikan in eastern Sicily. He was promptly chosen their king in a formal assembly *(ekklesia)* and was henceforth called Tryphon (Luxurious Dandy). After some victories over inadequate government troops, he increased his army to over 30,000 well-trained combatants. His contemporary, Athenion from Cilici (Asia Minor), had as a slave in the west of Sicily risen to the position of manager of a huge estate. He was an expert in astrology and claimed to be elected and appointed by the gods to be king of the whole island. In his capital, Triakola, he surrounded himself with all the splendors of an elaborate court ceremonial. While only the most able-bodied revolutionaries were trained for war, Athenion took care that the majority worked on the land, looking after the cattle and the crops, and continued their former professional activities. Competition and dispute between King Tryphon and Athenion was avoided because Athenion subordinated himself to the former, as his general, though with the right of succession to the throne. Since Rome was weakened by the ongoing Civil War, it took years until enough loyal troops could be spared to suppress this great revolt.

h. The gravest menace to Rome and its social and political order was the insurrection and war of Spartacus between 73 and 71 b.c.e. The slave Spartacus from Thracia, sold on a Greek slave market to an Italian buyer, was put into the gladiator school at Capua; escaped with seventy-eight comrades; called upon Thracian, Gallian, and Teutonic slaves to revolt; and soon had an army of 100,000 people who were ready to fight for their freedom. Some poor farmers, shepherds, and field workers joined the movement. Weapons to replace their kitchen knives and pitchforks were taken from government transports and arsenals, and from defeated Roman units. Spartacus was an ingenious military leader, distinguished by human and heroic character traits. Combined with the woes of the simultaneously raging Civil War, he presented the worst threat to the Roman Republic since its foundation. Unlike Eunus, Andronicus, Vettius, Salvius, and Athenion, he had no aspiration for kingship and a royal court, but was the central figure within a triumvirate and had a war council at his side. Instead of promising a golden city and making laws and provisions for a new great society, he had only one single purpose: to lead the slaves back to their native places. Armies sent out to stop him were routed by his superior tactics. Captive Roman soldiers had to fight one another to death, just like gladiators. He succeeded in gaining control first over southern Italy, then over the Po Plain. When he wanted to dismiss the Gallians and let them cross the Alps and go home, he was urged to let them stay with him for an attack on Rome and final revenge on all oppressors. After turning south and realizing that he could not conquer Rome, and after being cheated by pirates who had agreed to transport his army by sea to Sicily, he retreated in the direction of Brundisium (today Brindisi) on the Salentine Peninsula, the "heel" of Italy. Time and again the motley crowd gathered around Spartacus thwarted the implementation of his plans and orders, thus causing his final downfall. A blockade, erected to cut him off from the main part of Italy, created famine and despair among his troops. He died on the battlefield while trying to break out. The last of his army were crucified.

Athenaeus, *Deipnosoph.* 6.272ff., speaks of "more than a million slaves . . . killed" during the great massacres. The figure may well be exaggerated, yet it reveals a tendency of public opinion in the centuries after the great revolts: revolutionary slaves were an enormous threat — but the ways chosen by them ended in catastrophes, not in the gain of freedom.

7. Three Phases of Stoicism

a. In the fourth and third centuries B.C.E., Zeno, Cleanthes, and Chrysippus are outstanding exponents of Early Stoicism. Chrysippus presents a radical philosophical/psychological reinterpretation of the terms "free" and "slave." Each word now denotes a disposition and quality of the mind rather than a social, political, or economic status. For all Early Stoics, the human mind is a reflection of the highest god Zeus, who is in person the world reason and the power urging and causing human beings to live virtuously. Only that person lives reasonably who is not enslaved to bodily needs and egoistical satisfaction but is spontaneously willing to serve the welfare of the community.

b. Spearheads of Middle Stoicism are Panaetius (185-111 B.C.E.) and Poseidonius (135-51 B.C.E.). The former rephrased and reshaped teachings of the older Stoicists in such a manner that to Romans they could appear to be an attractive combination of Greek education and Roman virtue. It is probably to his merit that the term *humanitas* was coined and became influential in the West. For Panaetius, ethics was not a matter of abstract thought, but all his philosophical endeavor aimed at assisting people to solve the problems of their daily life. Poseidonius combined expertise in natural science and mathematics with the results of historical and anthropological studies. He taught that the same *sympatheia* that bound or ought to bind nature and humankind together for a harmonious existence also connected or was to connect with one another all members of the cosmos, those far and those near, those high and those low. Conclusions regarding slavery were not yet explicitly drawn, yet a physical and metaphysical worldview was proposed that finally was able to affect the master/slave relationship.

c. The main representatives of "Later Stoicism," or "Younger Stoicism," are Cicero, Seneca, Musonius, and his disciples Epictetus and Dio (of Prusa) Chrysostom, finally Emperor Marcus Aurelius (d. 180 C.E.). There are reasons to include among the Late Stoics also the Jewish philosopher-theologian Philo of Alexandria, who, together with Seneca, was a contemporary of Paul. It is not impossible that the apostle knew of the writings of Seneca (and Philo?) and was influenced by them. The concept *humanitas* or equivalents come to full blossom in Cicero's and Seneca's works (e.g., Cicero, *Off.* 3.23; cf. 1.41; *Parad. St.* 5;

and Seneca, *Ep.* 47; *Ben.* 3); cf. note 104 (p. 38). Humanity is revealed by many means, but above all by a wise, educational, and quietly benevolent attitude foremost toward subordinate and weaker persons.

8. Seneca on Slavery

We here reproduce Seneca's thoughts in stylized logical order, rather than following their original development in *Ep.* 47 and *Ben.* 2.18:

Whereas
- A slave is not just a slave but first of all a human being, begotten the same way as free persons, living under the same sky, breathing the same air, dying as a free person dies (*Ep.* 47.1 and 10; *Ben.* 3.22.3);
- Fortune has equal rights over slave and free so much so that today's slave may be free tomorrow and vice versa (*Ep.* 47.1.9-11);
- There exists solidarity between all human beings inasmuch as all of them are slaves: some to greed, some to ambition, all of them to fear, an ex-consul to an old woman, a millionaire to a serving maid, a noble youth to an actress — and this because voluntarily they subjugate themselves to such slavery (*Ep.* 47.17);
- The soul of a slave may be that of a free person, and virtue is accessible to the freeborn and the slave alike; a slave can be just, brave, magnanimous, self-sacrificing, a benefit to others — and this out of his own free will (*Ben.* 3.18.1-4; 19.2-4);
- The slave status pertains only to the slave's body, which a master can buy or sell, not to the slave's inner part (the mind or soul), which is and remains ever free (*Ben.* 20.1);
- Slaves are enemies of the free only when ill-treated, but can be or are, as members of the same household, better friends than free persons vying for favors by blandishments (*Ep.* 47.5-8, 11, 16);

Therefore
1. A master should value and judge his slaves by their morality, not by the (base) servant work to which they are assigned (*Ep.* 47.13-14);
2. He should associate himself with his slaves on kindly and affable terms; to be specific: by inviting them to his table and by sharing food and drink with those worthy of this honor (*Ep.* 47.13-14);
3. He should seek friends among them, for there are slaves who resemble good material lying ready for the use of an artist (*Ep.* 47.16);
4. In brief, he ought to treat his inferiors as he would like to be treated by his

betters, making them respect and love rather than only fear him (*Ep.* 47.11, 17-18).

As this summary shows, Seneca — as much as his Stoic peers — follows the firmly established Aristotelian tradition of directing ethical advice to those members of the household who are considered superior. Only the master, the king, the husband, the father are deemed worthy and sufficiently important to be addressed. Obviously ethical discourse has here the form of a dialogue between free male persons, even the king, the husband, etc., on one side, and the philosopher on the other side. Short reactions of the author's free dialogue partner or partners may be included in the text — but no questions or responses of a slave.

And yet, Seneca also has counsel for slaves. H. Greeven ("Die Sklavenfrage," pp. 33-38) has collected the following quotes: "To serve philosophy — this is freedom" (*Ep.* 8.7); "freemen, freedmen and slaves are no more than names, arisen out of pride and injustice" (*Ep.* 31.11); "Whoever has learned to die, has unlearned to be a slave" (*Ep.* 24.10). Certainly statements such as these may apply to both masters and servants alike. Still, slaves are specifically addressed when Seneca writes, "Arise (from the lowest corner) and make yourself worthy of the deity" (*Ep.* 31.31) and "Be patient and submit yourself to the inevitable" (*De ira* 3.16).

9. State and Private, Secular and Sacral Slaves

a. State slaves were laboring during the reigns of David and Solomon, in the mines of Arabah, in the foundries of Ezion Geber, on ships, or in construction work, as mentioned in 2 Sam 12:31; 1 Kings 5:27-32 (vv. 13-18 in RSV and other versions); 9:15-21, 28; 2 Chron 8:18; 9:10. Some of them worked together with slaves of Hiram of Tyre. The forced labor to which the Gibeonites (Josh 9:19-27) and other Canaanites were subjected was similar to the yoke under which the tribes of Israel were pressed in Egypt. Forced laborers were not essentially better off than slaves; but although they were loaned out, they were not sold. As observed earlier, after God had liberated his elect people from Egypt, the tribes conquering Canaan after the conquest did enslave Canaanite nations, and the kings David and Solomon behaved in the way that was usual among other nations. At the beginning of section VIII, it was pointed out that neither in early nor in late Jewish biblical or legal and theological literature is a protest in principle raised against owning house slaves. The resentment, caused by the imposition of forced labor by Judeans upon free Israelites and exploding in Jeroboam's rebellion and in the secession of the ten northern tribes from the house of David (1 Kings 12), had nothing to do with a general repudiation or renunciation of slavery. At the time of the composition of the final edition of the canonical books of the Kings and of the Jews' return from the Babylonian exile, the descendants of Solomon's slaves were still slaves, according to 1 Kings 9:21; Ezra 2:55-58; Neh 7:57-60.

b. Since the exile — not yet in Ps 68:19 (18), where the equivalent *mattanot* occurs — temple slaves were called *netinim* ("those given" in LXX 1 Chron 9:2, "dedicated" or "consecrated") in the Old Testament; see B. A. Levine, "The Netinim," *JBL* 82 (1963): 207-212, and J. P. Weinberg, "Netinim and 'Söhne der Sklaven Salomos' im 6.-4. Jh. v.u.Z.," *ZAW* 87 (1975): 355-371; *TWAT*, 5.709-712. Originally, only Israelites were deemed fit for service at a temple, including the lowest labors. Under the pressure of unpaid debts or in order to fulfill a vow or urgent wish, Jewish parents sometimes "gave" a child into the hands of a priest. By his mother Samuel is "lent" rather than "given" to the Lord, for the length of his life (1 Sam 1:28). By Joshua, however, Gibeonites, too, were given functions fitting the *netinim* (Josh 9:27), and out of the war captives a king could make a donation to a temple for the same purpose. Thus the *netinim* became a group mixed of Jews and foreigners. Those 220 who had returned from Babylonia are listed by their families in Ezra 2 and Neh 7 — as though they all had been free Jews. After their arrival in Jerusalem, they were settled in a special building on the Ophel, near the temple, and stood under the direction of the priests, who in turn were subordinated to the Zadokite priests (Num 18:2; etc.). Since the time of David, the lowest possible rank in the hierarchy was reserved for the *netinim* — according to Ezra 8:20. But their name and their institutional function were most likely formed under Babylonian influence between the eighth and sixth centuries B.C.E. Ezekiel (44:5-8) reproaches his people for admitting "foreigners, uncircumcised in heart and flesh" to serve in the sanctuary. He exempts only the Zadokite priests from the charge leveled against the Levites because, together with Israel, the latter had gone astray from the Lord and served idols. Finally, according to Num 3:5-9, only Levites — and therefore no pagan foreigners — are true *netinim*, capable of ministering at the sanctuary under Aaron and his priestly sons. Henceforth, the temple slaves are "given," even by Moses' arrangement, to be attendants to the Aaronid priests. Numbers 8:14-19, cf. 18:6, reaffirms this by stating that exclusively Levites are "wholly given" to God, "taken" by God for himself, and "given as a gift to Aaron." Perhaps some of the remaining circumcised *netinim*, whether of Jewish or foreign origin, attained the rank of Levite. In the Mishnah, e.g., in Yeb II 4, the *netinim* still form a special, that is, the lowest, group in the population. Sons and daughters of the offspring of the Gibeonites must not be married to a Jewish woman or man; they rank with bastards and foundlings.

c. Bought and house-born slaves of priests are mentioned in Lev 22:10-

11. Unlike ordinary Jews, they were permitted to eat of the share a priest received of the sacrifices. When after a victorious battle the booty, including prisoners, was distributed, the priests were entitled to a portion of it. Josephus, *Ant.* 20.181 and 206, tells of slaves of some of the last high priests in Jerusalem who went out with bludgeons in order to enforce the delivery of those tithes that would legally have belonged to the poorer priests. In Pes. 57a, a corresponding act of plundering a temple storeroom is described.

d. Evidence of rabbis keeping one or several slaves is given by the frequent references of the Talmud to the good and evil days shared by Gamaliel II and his slave Tabi; see, e.g., Berak II 7 (16b) and BQ 74b. Urbach, "The Laws regarding Slavery," pp. 87-88, speaks of the wealthy rabbinic circles in fourth-century-B.C.E. Babylonia that paid state taxes for impoverished Jews and then treated these Jews "as their slaves to an excessive degree." No consensus existed among the sages whether slaves of rabbis could become rabbinical scholars (see Urbach, pp. 45-46).

10. Judaism and Abolitionism

The *Encyclopedia Judaica* (XVI 1657) speaks of "a strong Talmudic tradition" that, with the cessation of the Jubilee Year by the destruction of the First Temple (in 587/586 B.C.E.), the keeping of Hebrew slaves by Jews came to an end. StB IV 2, 698-699; Urbach, "The Laws regarding Slavery," pp. 3-7; S. Zeitlin, "Slavery," passim; S. Safrai, "Jewish People," 2.628-629; S. S. Bartchy, *Mallon Chresai*, pp. 31-32, mention the same hypothesis — in order to refute it. The thesis was based specifically on Gitt. 65a; Kidd. 69a; Arak 29a in the Babylonian Talmud. Supposedly postexilic Judaism was inclined to become an emancipation movement, at least of Hebrew slaves. Strong arguments, however, have been marshaled by the scholars mentioned against this opinion.

In the canonical and apocryphal Wisdom Literature slavery is presupposed, and it cannot be demonstrated that only non-Jewish slaves are meant when the treatment of slaves is described, especially in Prov 22:7; Job 31:13-15; Sir 7:21; 33:27-33; Jth 4:10; 7:27; 8:7, 22-23; 16:3. According to Jth 7, it is better, even for God's own people, to be captured and made slaves than to die; priority is given to survival, obviously in strict contradiction to slogans such as "better dead than red."

The Mishnah and Talmud extensively discuss the legal, moral, and economic issues of slavery. Anecdotes are passed around that illustrate the cordial relationship between Rabbi Gamaliel II and his slave Tabi.

High priests owned slaves (see Annotation 9); in several parables of Jesus, good and bad slaves play a major role. Philo, *Spec. leg.* 2.123, declares the keeping of domestic slaves "most indispensable" — it "should not be absolutely excluded. . . . For the course of life contains a vast number of circumstances which demand the ministrations of slaves."

11. Developments in Jewish Slave Laws and Customs

There are conspicuous differences between:

a. The earliest strata of the Abraham, Isaac, Jacob, Joseph sagas;
b. the Book of the Covenant (Exod 20:22–23:19), which reflects conditions arising after the conquest of the Promised Land and is in several instances much kinder to slaves than contemporary non-Jewish laws and customs;
c. the actual treatment of slaves in the monarchic period, according to narrative elements in the Samuel, Kings, and Chronicle books;
d. the concern shown for all those poor, and specifically for the slaves in Deut 15:2-3, 12-18; 20:10-18; 21:10-14;
e. the prophetic exposure and scolding of flagrant disobedience in God's people;
f. the voices of wisdom in Prov 22:7; Job 31:13-15; Sir 7:20-21; 33:24-31;
g. the actual status and treatment of slaves, as illustrated by parables of Jesus, especially Matt 18:23-34 and Luke 16:2-8.

There is not one law regarding slavery found in the Bible and later ancient Jewish writings, but there is a living process with high and low points, now pushing forward with humanizing intentions and then relapsing again into cruel customs. As shown in Annotation 2, the sage Jesus Sirach, for instance, combines in one and the same passage (33:24-31; cf. 7:20-21) shockingly cruel statements with the appeal for moderation, prudence, enlightened self-interest, and soul brotherhood. The noble words found in Job 31:13-15 in effect proclaim the fatherhood of God and the brotherhood of all human beings. And yet, what Jesus' parables reveal of social conditions prevailing in Palestine during the first century contradicts the idea that such sentiments were widespread or generally shared.

After the Greek occupation of Palestine, during the Hasmonean period, and after the Romans had conquered the land, fundamental changes did not occur. The same is true of the periods reflected in the Mishnah and Talmud, though some qualifications are necessary. It is one of the merits of Urbach to have shown in his article "The Laws regarding Slavery," that after 70 c.e. the Tannaitic sages' *halacha* stood nearer to the enlightened ideas of, e.g., the "younger" Stoic philosophers, than did the *gemara* of the Amoraim. For though in the Tannaitic period the discussion of slave laws moved in favor of the servants of Jewish extraction, only in the Amoraic centuries did the conditions of the foreign slaves' lives worsen. For this reason Urbach (p. 3; cf. p. 94) has warned of describing "the attitude of Judaism toward slavery in terms of a kind of movement toward complete abolitionism." Certainly the punishment of a master who has killed a slave, and the command that a slave maimed by his master must be manumitted (Exod 21:20-21, 26-27), can be considered, together with I. Mendelsohn ("Slavery in the OT," 4.388), sufficient reason to speak generally of "the humanitarianism of biblical legislation." Yet this can hardly justify S. Safrai's observation (made in "Jewish People," 2.629-630) of "a gradual withering away of the institution of slavery and its almost total disappearance" since the first century c.e. As a historiographer, Urbach is probably more careful than Safrai when he does not recognize such a progress but writes (p. 93), "the loss of Jewish political freedom, the general reduction to the level of slaves (after the destruction of the Second Temple) contributed to the tempering of the force of social idealism, and even contributed toward the reinterpretation of Jewish statute law and biblical rabbinical enactment in a spirit flatly contradictory to the sense implicit in the original promulgation," the occasional *obiter dicta* containing "sentiments of true humanity" notwithstanding.

At any rate, during earlier and later periods enormous cultural steps were taken from the days of Noah and Abraham to the subtle discussions of God's will in the Talmud, but slavery as such was never radically put in question. Only the Essenes formed an exception.

12. Human Rights Established by God

Wherever the covenant, the law, and the statutes given by God were observed, slaves in Jewish hands had the following assured rights — though a term equivalent to "general human rights" does not occur in the Bible or in the rabbinical literature:

a. Sabbath rest (Exod 20:8-11; Deut 5:12-15);
b. participation in the Passover celebration (Exod 12:4);
c. freedom of Hebrew slaves after six years' service, including the family if it had been brought into slavery together with the family head (Exod 21:1-4; Deut 15:12-18);
d. free choice to remain as a perpetual slave in the master's house (Exod 21:5-6; Deut 15:16-18);
e. emancipation of a female slave if her master has used her sexually and does not wish to keep her (Exod 21:7-11);

f. punishment — according to the Talmud: by death (but it is doubtful whether it was ever carried out; see StB IV 2, 737-739; Urbach, "The Laws regarding Slavery," p. 93) — for a master who has so badly hurt a slave that the slave has died on the same day (Exod 21:20-21);

g. freedom for a male or female slave when the master has caused the permanent loss of, e.g., an eye or a tooth (Exod 21:26-27);

h. a considerable parting gift from the flock, the threshing floor, and the winepress to a male or female slave released in the seventh year (Deut 15:12-15);

i. full protection to asylum-seeking fugitive foreign slaves (Deut 23:16-17);

j. manumission of all Hebrews, irrespective of the length of their work as slaves, every fiftieth year, in the so-called Jubilee Year, when also all pawned or sold fields return to their former owners, dispersed family members are allowed to go home, and the soil shall lie fallow.

Whether the last-mentioned among these statutes was ever obeyed is not certain. To repeat an observation made earlier, most likely the Jubilee Year was in actuality a program, a promise, or a hope — whose fulfillment had to wait; see Lev 26:8-24; Num 36:4; Ezek 46:17; Isa 61:1-2; Luke 4:18-19.

13. Circumcision and Covenant Membership

By his circumcision, a slave was "brought under the wings of the Shekina," that is, under the protection of God's glorious indwelling in the land, in the sanctuary, and among his chosen people — so Gen Rabba 47.29d formulates the benefit received by the cultic act. Certainly the legal rights and holy duties of a circumcised slave were limited, but no more than those of free Jewish women and children; see, e.g., S. Krauss, *Talmudische Archäologie*, 2.95. Only a full proselyte ("of righteousness") was entitled to have a share in all privileges and obligations of a Jew. Gittin 38b reveals that opinions differed regarding the question whether a slave dedicated to the sanctuary completely "belonged to the holy people," even when the dedication made him free. A drastic example of how free people could be induced or forced to circumcision is contained in Gen 34, the archaic account of the Shechemites' extorted subordination to the covenant ritual of Israel. Still, when Paul three times, in Gal 2:3, 14, and 6:12, strictly opposes circumcision imposed by force, he aims not at a general contemporary Jewish or Jewish-Christian practice, but rather at an aberration of former proselytes who had become Christians. A circumcision and complete subjection to the Jewish way of life, motivated by a panic fear of Jews after Esther's intervention (LXX Esther 8:17), and the imposition of circumcision upon the defeated Idumeans as a precondition of their staying in their country (Josephus, *Ant.* 13.257-258), were certainly not the normal way of Gentiles into God's covenant with Israel.

14. Philo on the Sabbath and Slave Liberation

Spec. leg. 2.66-69: "He (God) not only requires the free men to abstain from work on the Sabbath, but gives the same permission to men-servants and hand-maids, and sends them a message of security and almost freedom after every six days, to teach both .. an admirable lesson. The masters must be accustomed to work themselves . . . while on the other hand the servants are not to refuse to entertain still higher hopes, but should find in the relaxation allowed after six days an ember or spark of freedom, and should look forward to their complete liberation if they continue to serve well and loyally." Philo calls the "occasional submission of the free to do the menial offices of a slave, together with the immunity allowed to the slave . . . a step forward in human conduct towards the perfection of virtue, when both the seemingly distinguished and the meaner sort remember equality and repay to each other the debt incumbent on them. . . . For servants are free by nature, no man being naturally a slave." The combination of biblical and eschatological elements with traits of the Roman Saturnalia and of Stoic values and thoughts is typical of the syncretistic climate of Alexandria, Egypt, rather than of strictly rabbinical teaching. Yet it represents a current within Hellenistic Judaism.

15. Diverse Reasons for Manumission

Though in Mishnah Kidd. 102 and Talmud Kidd. 14b-22b only three compelling occasions for manumission of Hebrew males, and four grounds for releasing Hebrew females, are listed, the reasons discussed elsewhere in the Talmud are far more numerous. Many of them pertain to the emancipation of non-Jewish slaves. The authors of StB IV 2, pp. 679-709, 739-744, have compiled an almost complete collection:

a. completion of the years owed for amortizing a debt, at the latest with the sixth year;
b. the Jubilee Year — of which, if it was ever observed, some debt slaves might benefit very soon after their enslavement; others only in the last years of their lives; again others, never;
c. the refunding of the owner in cash, either by the slave himself or his kinsmen, for the debt amount not yet amortized by labor;

d. puberty signs in a girl sold into slavery by her debt-ridden father;
e. the maiming of a slave in consequence of beating suffered from the owner;
f. declaration of freedom by a freedom letter, or by testamentary installation of a faithful slave as heir;
g. marriage of a male or female slave to the owner's daughter or son, or to another free Jew;
h. release in critical wartimes (as in Jer 34:8-22; Josephus, *BJ* 4.508);
i. factual granting of rights that originally befitted only a free Israelite, such as permission given to a slave to marry a free Hebrew lady, to don the prayer shawl *(tefillin)*, to complete a deficient quorum at an assembly for worship;
j. the recognition of and payment for a religious vow made by the servant;
k. the attempt to sell a Jewish, eventually also a circumcised foreign, slave to a non-Jew or to a Jew living abroad;
l. the flight of a Jew from his master in the Diaspora, unless the slave was successfully reclaimed;
m. the master's dedication of a slave to a sanctuary;
n. the declaration that a slave had no longer a master (probably in extreme cases of the slave's uselessness or impertinence, or of impoverishment of the owner);
o. when a slave had belonged to two masters and only the first had manumitted him, a court could force the second to dispense with his half-property by accepting an IOU for the half-value of the slave, or else the half-free slave would not have been free to marry either a free or a slave woman and to fulfill the command of producing children.

16. Renounced Manumission

The Mosaic Law makes provision for slaves to refuse their emancipation and remain in their master's home. Exodus 21:5-6 and Deut 15:16 mention love of the master and the family as the only reason for a slave's remaining a slave. Some self-love may, however, not have been excluded in those cases when a slave was or had become bodily or mentally ailing, old, or otherwise seemingly useless. The right to have the ear pierced included the right to food, clothing, a roof over the head, and a minimum of care in critical situations. No wonder that for some slaves this minimal protection was preferable to the freedom of preslavehood days, the burden of an unpayable debt, or the unknown cost of future freedom. The master retaining a freedom-fearing slave did not get a bargain under all circumstances; rather he might lose through the deal and pay heavily for it. The stories of Israel's conduct during the years spent in the wilderness show what burden God and Moses had to bear because Israel was unwilling to accept freedom, even from the Egyptian yoke.

The rejection of emancipation had to be pronounced publicly — before God, as the RSV translates — that is, before the judges, as Urbach, "The Laws regarding Slavery," pp. 23-24, suggests. The symbolic piercing and fixing of the ear is allegorically interpreted in the Talmud: the ear was painfully treated, because it had not listened to vital pronouncements: either to the commandment prohibiting theft — in some cases, indeed, theft had led a person into slavery — or to the promise of freedom made to the members of God's people. The doorpost or door, in turn, was understood as the witness to the liberation out of the (prison-)house of Egypt, a witness that was now spurned when the (fool of a) slave preferred to stay inside. Talmudic utterances, gathered in StB IV 2, pp. 731 and 742, show that some manumitted slaves became dependent on communal charity.

At any rate, the sages did not look with favor on Hebrews who remained slaves voluntarily. Rejection of freedom was considered a shame not only for the slave but also for those of his wider family who might and should have intervened as redeemers or protectors. To renounce emancipation was as bad as repudiating the kingship of God, even of him who had broken the Egyptian yoke laid on Israel's neck in order to make the Jews his own servants (Lev 25:55). For this reason the refusal of liberation is made more and more difficult; see Kidd. 22b; Jerus. kidd. 59d; Tosephta BQ VII 3; cf. StB IV 2, pp. 700, 705-707; Urbach, pp. 10-12. The Targum Jonathan (on Lev 25) limits the duration of the permanent attachment of a slave to the owner: the male and female slave whose ear was pierced becomes free when the master dies or, at the latest, in the Jubilee Year.

Literary, Biographical, and Contextual Issues

Amazing agreement reigns among conservative and critical introductions to the NT and in commentaries and monographs on the Epistle to Philemon.[1] In the following, the abbreviation PHM will be used for this letter. PHM is accepted as authentically Pauline, whether or not a secretary has assisted the writer.[2] At least the words "If he has done you any wrong . . . charge it to my account. . . . I, Paul, shall pay you back" (vv. 18-19) had to be written by Paul's own hand. These sentences are formulated in exact legal-economical terminology and are an obligation of payment (an IOU) that is enforceable before any court.

There seems to be nothing really new that could be added to observations and evaluations made again and again. Here we will offer no more than a survey of special literary features, especially the attestation, canonization, and integrity, the vocabulary and style, the structure and logic of the text, and the historical-biographical problems related to the main persons mentioned. When, however, we compare the ways the master/slave relationship is discussed in this

---

1. The attacks launched by the old Tübingen School against authenticity are no longer supported by introductions ranging from Th. Zahn (Leipzig: Deichert, 1897) to A. Jülicher (Tübingen and Leipzig: Mohr, 3rd-4th eds., 1901), or from H. C. Thiessen (Grand Rapids: Eerdmans, 1952) and D. Guthrie (Downers Grove, Ill.: InterVarsity, 3rd ed., 1970) to H. Koester (Berlin and New York: De Gruyter, 1980).

2. Varieties of possible secretarial assistance are extensively discussed in, e.g., A. van Roon, *The Authenticity of Ephesians*, NovT Suppl. 34 (1974). For a summary see AB 34, pp. 40-41.

letter and in other Pauline contexts, more than a summary of harmonious opinions is necessary. In sections I-V the more formal literary questions, in section VI the biographical issues, and in section VII a comparison with similar or contradicting NT texts will be the main themes. Finally, section VIII will deal with issues related to the history of interpretation, including criticisms of the substance of PHM.

I. ATTESTATION AND CANONIZATION[3]

Papyri, majuscule, and minuscule codices, the Old Syriac and Old Latin versions, and citations found in Greek, Latin, and some Syrian church fathers contain parts or the whole of PHM. In consequence, manifold ancient MSS and texts are essential tools for finding or reconstructing a wording as approximate to the autograph as possible.

PHM is not contained in some of the best and most complete ancient MSS of the NT, and small is the number of fragmentary texts providing its wording or parts of it. In some cases the absence of this letter from a codex, a canonical list, or a version can demonstrate that, at the time and place of the document in question, PHM was not used for reading in public worship[4] and was therefore not "received" as part of the NT canon, neither eventually commented on by scholars. But not every absence of PHM demonstrates rejection of canonicity. The lines containing PHM may have been lost or destroyed incidentally, while contemporary canonical lists reveal its reception.[5] At any rate, a sufficient number of MSS have survived from antiquity to provide a fair certainty about the text.

Only one ancient papyrus, $\mathfrak{p}^{61}$, called Colt 5, contains some lines of PHM, verses 4-7. This papyrus probably stems from Egypt and was written no earlier than about 700 C.E. Still, the scribe appears to have copied a much older MS;

---

3. For the following, just as for the Translation, Notes, and Comments, Nestle-Aland's *Novum Testamentum Graece*, 26th ed. (1979), and *The Greek New Testament*, ed. K. Aland, M. Black, B. M. Metzger, and A. Wikgren, 3rd ed. (1966), have been used as main instruments.

4. As suggested by Col 4:16. The encyclical destination of apostolic writings is evident in Gal 1:2; James 1:1; 1 Pet 1:1-2.

5. When in the fourth century the collection of NT books received its present extension and limitation, the technical term for acknowledging — not creating — the canonical rank of a book was "we receive" (*dechometha* in Greek, *recipimus* in Latin). Canonization of apostolic books added the twenty-seven parts of the NT to the earlier canon of the early church, the Old Testament.

both the unknown, older MS and the codex to which p[61] may originally have belonged probably contained most or all of the Pauline epistles. A much older papyrus, Chester Beatty p[46], which is dated about 200 C.E. and may have reproduced the then-known complete Pauline corpus, includes Hebrews. However, the Pastoral Epistles and PHM are missing from the existing fragments. Between 150 and 250 C.E., Marcion, Tertullian, the Canon Muratori, and the so-called Marcionite Prologues are among the Greek and Latin witnesses confirming the canonical rank of PHM. Clement of Rome, Irenaeus, Cyprian, Hilary, Augustine, and especially Ambrose quote from the epistle. As much as is known today, Ambrosiaster, John Chrysostom, Jerome, and Pelagius wrote the first commentaries on it.

Among the oldest (second to fourth century) versions of the Greek text, the *Vetus Latina* reveals the early reception of PHM.[6] Among the fragments of the two Old Syriac versions, PHM is not represented. However, Ignatius, bishop of the Diocese of Syrian Antioch, in his letter to the Ephesians (1.3; 2.1; cf. 4.1), recommends a certain Bishop Onesimus highly — perhaps because he identified him with the slave mentioned in PHM and considered this letter Pauline. The National Syrian Church of Edessa (in the Euphrates region) did not treat PHM worthy of inclusion in its canon, nor did the fourth-century Syrian theologians Ephraem, Aphraates, and Apollinaris of Laodicea.[7]

Several important majuscule codices, dated between the fourth and ninth centuries, contain the complete Greek text or parts of it: ℵ (Sinaiticus); A (Alexandrinus); C (Ephraimi Rescriptus, only vv. 1-2); D (Claromontanus); F (Augiensis); G (Boernerianus; the codices D, F, and G offer both a Greek and a Latin text); H 014 (Euthalianus); I (Freer); and Psi (Mount Athos).

Among the minuscules that together with p[61] and the majuscules just enumerated constitute what in Nestle-Aland's twenty-sixth edition of the Greek NT is called Majority Text (M), the codices 33, 81, 104, 323, 365, 629, 945, 1739, and 1881 are most relevant.

In Egypt in 367, in Rome in 382, in Carthage and Hippo in 395 and 397, in the Syrian Church in about 500, PHM was endorsed as an integral part of the NT canon.

---

6. The different places occupied by PHM in ancient codices are listed in the Beuron edition of the *Vetus Latina,* ed. H. J. Frede, XXIV 2:1a, pp. 292-293; cf. the reprint of this list in K. Aland, *Neutestamentliche Entwürfe* (Munich: Chr. Kaiser, 1979), pp. 3-23.

7. For the history of canonization see, e.g., W. G. Kümmel, P. Feine, and J. Behm, *Introduction to the New Testament* (Nashville and New York: Abingdon, 1963), pp. 352-353; hereafter cited as Kümmel, *Introduction.* Kümmel takes up Th. Zahn's and J. Leipoldt's earlier elaborations. See also R. M. Grant, *A Historical Introduction to the New Testament* (London: Collins, 1963), p. 198. Frede, XXV 2:2, 1983, pp. 947-948, is convinced that in the Syrian Church PHM was excluded from canonical rank, rather than not yet accepted.

II. TEXTUAL INTEGRITY AND CRITICISM[8]

The textual transmission of PHM is as much and as little stable and reliable as that of most Pauline epistles. Compared with the thousands of variant readings to the Lukan and Johannine writings, the state of the PHM text looks fairly good. Dramatic, exciting, or disturbing alternatives to the Majority Text hardly exist. The variants offered by individual MSS — or some groups of them — do not really change the intention and substance of this one-page document.

A considerable number of variant readings will be discussed below, in the Notes to the verses where they occur. At this place a few examples will suffice.

Verse 5. The sequence "love and faith" differs from the order "faith and love" in the thanksgiving sections of Ephesians (1:15) and Colossians (1:4; cf. 1 Tim 1:14), but is adapted to them in a great number of Greek MSS and most Old Latin witnesses. In substance, "faith" put first corresponds to the phrase "faith working out in love," which Paul has used in Gal 5:6, and in the various triadic arrangements of faith, love, and hope in 1 Thess 1:3; 5:8; and 1 Cor 13:13; cf. Heb 10:22-24. In the better MSS, however, love precedes faith. While within the thanksgiving sections of Romans only faith is mentioned (in 1:8), in PHM the noun and the verb "love" occur much more often than faith and believing, in correspondence to the ethical rather than kerygmatic or polemic character of the epistle. Yet faith is by no means belittled. For immediately after verse 5, in the same context of thanksgiving, first in verse 6 Philemon's faith, then only (in vv. 7 and 9) his love, is mentioned. Either way it is not disputed that "love is the greatest" (1 Cor 13:13), the "bond of perfection" (Col 3:14).

Verse 6. The more trustworthy MSS have "to recognize every good (. . . *agathou*)," but a very small group, including Vg., adds the noun "work," so as to make the text say "to recognize every good work." Since even in his undisputed letters Paul does not mind speaking of "good work . . . good works . . . doing good," this addition does not necessarily contradict the justification by faith alone, which is proclaimed by the apostle foremost in Galatians, Romans, and Philippians. Still, the full sense of Philem 6 is narrowed when the reading "good work" is given preference. For "good" is not only the character or sum of what human beings are called and by God's Spirit enabled to do or can possess as a virtuous element of their character (*bonitas* is in some old Latin texts the translation of Greek *agathon* of Philem 14). Rather, according to Paul, "good" is above all what God gives (cf. James 1:17), that is, God's commandment, the

---

8. The Beuron edition of the *Vetus Latina* XXV 2:2, 1983, pp. 945-996, contains the best reconstruction of the Old Latin text and the most complete collection of Greek and Latin textual variants. For a list and discussion of most of the existing variants, see C. R. Gregory, *Textkritik des Neuen Testaments*, vols. 1-3 (Leipzig, 1900-1903), and the *Editio major* (to be) published by K. Aland.

gospel, salvation, faith, love, hope, the conscience, the will to obey, and other things, including earthly goods.[9]

Verse 7. In variant readings offered by the majority of the minuscule MSS, "much grace" is substituted for "great joy," and the past tense "has given me" (lit. "I had") is replaced by the present "we have." Sometimes instead of "for me" the text reads "for us." The most important codices do not support either of these readings, which indeed do not really change the meaning but emphasize that joy is a fruit of the Holy Spirit and therefore a gift of grace; cf. Gal 5:22; Rom 14:17. Whenever this joy is genuine, it is neither a passing mood or event nor a private possession, but is being shared by those in Paul's environment.

Verse 9. The English classical philologist Richard Bentley (1662-1742) has suggested that in the original script of PHM Paul called himself a *presbeutēs* (ambassador), not a *presbytēs* (old man). In effect, the reading "old man" adds a special emotional urgency to Paul's pleading and does not underline his apostolic and full power to give commands, as mentioned in verse 8. On the other hand, a self-pitying reference of Paul to his advanced age might create the impression that the apostle presents himself — only at this place, as never in other epistles — as a helplessly whimpering senior citizen or crippled veteran. All existing PHM have *presbytēs*. Among the widespread modern Bible versions, only JB translates "old man"; RSV mentions "old man" as a possibility, and NEB has simply "ambassador."

The conflicting interpretations need not stay in contrast forever, for the noun *presbytēs* can mean "ambassador" as well as "old man." Therefore Bentley's conjecture is ultimately superfluous. The context encourages the version "ambassador."

Verse 12. After the words "I am sending him back," many MSS add "but you — do receive him." Later, in verse 17, according to all early versions, Paul will indeed tell Philemon in the imperative form, "receive him." The middle form of *proslambanō* signifies a welcoming and warm reception, be it at home as a guest, at work as a colleague, or in all situations as a comradely companion and helper. The variant readings of verse 12 anticipate and duplicate the substance of verses 15-17: Paul expects that Onesimus will stay "forever . . . as a beloved brother . . . as a partner" at his master's side. However, the variant readings mentioned may well reflect a certain interest on the side of copyists and/or interpreters for the slave's permanent place under the hand of his earthly master — a concern that was not necessarily also Paul's own. When the better texts of verse 12 omit a reference to Onesimus's reception after his return, they leave

---

9. Rom 7:12-13, 18-22; 8:28-32; 10:15; 13:5; Gal 6:10; etc. So-called deutero-Pauline epistles concur with the wider use of "good"; see, e.g., 2 Thess 2:16-17; 1 Tim 1:5, 19; Titus 2:10; 1 Pet 3:10.

it open whether or not Paul, in writing verse 12, was preparing the way to expressing (in v. 13) his secret wish and hope that Onesimus return to him and definitely become a fellow servant of the gospel. In that case the restitution of Onesimus to Philemon might in reality be no more than a means toward another end, far from being the apostle's final intention.

Verse 25. The "Amen" appended to the final blessing is found in a good number of very important Greek MSS and in the Vg. Since a concluding "Amen" reoccurs for certain only in Gal 6:18 and in good, although not all, MSS of Phil 4:23, its use in Philem 25 is somewhat exceptional.[10]

III. VOCABULARY, LANGUAGE, AND STYLE[11]

A. Statistics

The Epistle to Philemon consists of about 330 words; slightly more than 140 different verbs, nouns, adjectives, conjunctions form the vocabulary. Among the New Testament writings, only the Epistle of Jude has a richer vocabulary in proportion to the totality of words used. Ten words in PHM never occur again in other Pauline letters, but are found in pre–New Testament sacral and profane Greek texts. Only *prosopheilō* ("to owe," v. 19) is not found in the LXX and is a *hapax legomenon* within the NT. In this letter the number of verbs and substantives is almost the same, while in the uncontested Pauline letters the number of

10. In Jewish worship "Amen" was the response of hearers to Scripture readings, to homilies given, and to prayers offered. Equally, saying "Amen" was early practiced in Christian congregations for answering the public reading of Paul's letters, a sermon, or a prayer. A longer formula is used in 1 Cor 14:25.

The suggestion that PHM had been written in a shorter form by Paul himself, and that the letter in its present shape includes later interpolations, was made by H. J. Holtzmann, "Der Brief an Philemon, kritisch untersucht," *ZWTh* 16 (1873): 428-441, but has for good reasons remained insulated.

11. The statistical data presented in the following are culled from R. Morgenthaler, *Statistik des neutestamentlichen Wortschatzes* (Zürich and Frankfurt: Gotthelf Verlag, 1958), esp. pp. 38ff., 44ff., 164, 173-178. For a detailed study of the vocabulary and its relationship to that of other Pauline letters, see W. Schenk, "Der Brief des Paulus an Philemon in der neueren Forschung (1945-87)," in *Aufstieg und Niedergang der römischen Welt* II, *Der Prinzipat* XXV 4, ed. W. Haase und H. Temporini (Berlin and New York: De Gruyter, 1987), pp. 1339-1395.

Among the monographical studies on style and character of PHM, P. L. Couchout, "Le style rhythmé dans l'épître de Saint Paul à Philémon," *RHR* 96 (1927): 129-146, has found much attention. In his commentary on PHM, E. Lohmeyer but slightly varies from Couchout's proposals for the distinction of poetic lines and verses.

verbs prevails over that of nouns; in Ephesians, Colossians, and First Timothy, substantives surpass verbs in ratios between 3:2 and 8:7. Also noteworthy is the proportion between the total number of verbs and substantives on one side and of all other sorts of words on the other. In no other Pauline letter is the proportional frequency of other words as high as in PHM. In all his letters, Paul speaks emphatically of his personal relationship to those addressed, but in PHM the occurrence of the emphatic pronouns "I" and "thou" is specifically dense.[12]

At the beginning of the use and exploitation of such word statistics, and even more so after computers were used for the same purpose, subtle or wild consequences were drawn for adjudicating the genuineness or spuriousness of letters preserved under the name of Paul. However, among all Pauline epistles, PHM demonstrates that differences between occurrence and ratios of specific words do not suffice for that purpose. As already stated, PHM is generally considered genuine. Specific situations and themes were and are sufficient cause for one and the same author to vary language and diction. In linguistic regard, PHM stands about halfway between the uncontested Pauline letters and Ephesians/Colossians.[13]

B. Types and Families of Words and Styles

1. *Liturgical, religious, or strictly theological* is the vocabulary of the benedictions at the opening and the end of the letter. Not only there but also in the epistle's central sections, references are made to God our Father, the Lord Jesus Christ, and the gospel; to grace, peace, thanksgiving, brotherhood, love, faith, knowledge; and to the special service to be rendered by Christians.[14] Also the repeated use of the "divine passive" (in vv. 15 and 22) and probably the mention of "rest" (vv. 7, 15, 20; cf. Heb 3:11–4:11) are elements typical of religious diction.

12. In the twenty-five verses of PHM, *egō* is used 4 times (once in vv. 13 and 20, twice in v. 19). Elsewhere in Paul, the average occurrence of *egō* as an emphatic reference of Paul to himself (not counting the genitives, datives, and accusatives of this pronoun) is roughly one per chapter: 5 times in the 10 chapters (combined) of Colossians and Ephesians; 8 in the 6 of Galatians; 19 in the 16 of First Corinthians; 11 in the 13 of Second Corinthians; 4 in the 4 of Philippians; 18 in the 16 of Romans. The use of "we" and "you" and of the corresponding forms and possessive personal pronouns might be added to this statistic and would confirm the exceptional character of the diction of PHM.

13. Cf. AB 34B *(Colossians)*, introduction, p. 57. T. A. Robinson, "Grayston and Herdan's 'C' Quantity Formula and the Authorship of the Pastoral Epistles," *NTS* 30 (1984): 282-288, excludes PHM, because of its brevity, from the statistics offered of the vocabulary of the other Pauline epistles. Yet the protest raised by Robinson against using *hapax legomena* as proof or disproof of authenticity can be applied to PHM, too.

14. Vv. 2-9, 13-14, 16, 20, 22, 25.

2. *Intimate, cordial, family-warm* elements abound in most verses of PHM. God the Father; Paul as an earthly (though figurative) father of Onesimus and Philemon; brothers; a sister and child born in prison; the common life of people under one roof and among other members of the congregation; love and faith and sharing in the same good and its fruit; the pain of separation; the surprise of a homecoming prodigal or fugitive; a respected person's forthcoming visit — of this kind are the family motifs spread over the epistle. Paul declares that Onesimus is his very heart; the slave is worthy to be received the way the apostle would be received; he is Paul's representative for Philemon and in his house. To pave the way to that reception, Paul forgoes the use of his apostolic title and the application of his ministerial full power. His counseling is nondirective, consisting of mere innuendoes.

Imperative verb forms are found only in verses 17, 20, 22, and when in verse 20, despite all signs of calculated reticence, the noun "obedience" is used, it is in the context of the expression of Paul's full confidence in Philemon's voluntary compliance and overflowing generosity. Essential to the whole epistle is the dominance of a language of the heart. Here an affectionate appeal is made to constructive emotion.

3. In no other Pauline letter are *legal and commercial* vocabulary and formulations found as densely as in PHM. Nearest to this letter stands Colossians with its references to a deposit made at a safe place and an IOU deleted in favor of the saints.[15] In Colossians this diction provided surprising imagery for expressing the message and effect of the gospel, but in PHM it has more than only metaphorical significance.[16] It gives the letter the character of a social action, directly related to a burning contemporary issue.

The inclusion of the literal sense of law and business terms and sentences is a consequence of the issues addressed in this letter. At stake are the right to private property, the infraction of this seemingly unshakeable order, the damage caused by a slave's flight, and the question of how a runaway is to be treated when returning. Paul did intervene, as it were, as a self-appointed *amicus curiae,* and he formulated his intercessory plea as if he were Onesimus's advocate or a priest at Delphi specializing in mediating between runaways and their masters. To do this he had to speak in the plain terms of contemporary bargaining. Obviously he was not only expert in God's holy law and in the question of its

15. Col 1:5; 2:14; cf. AB 34B, Introduction A, n. 2.
16. Pliny's similar letter on behalf of an escaped and sent-back runaway freedman was quoted above, in Annotation 4 to the "Social Background" (p. 86). So far, the most intensive and fruitful presentation of the interrelationship between the social problems of Paul's environment and his message (of another, eternal and symbolic divine universe!) has been made by N. R. Petersen, *Rediscovering Paul: Philemon and the Sociology of Paul's Narrative World* (Philadelphia: Fortress, 1985).

application to daily life, but he was also fully aware of current legal and commercial conditions and requirements.

Both Hebrew and non-Jewish legal customs and traditions are endorsed when in PHM the family terms "father," "mother," "sister," "child" describe interpersonal relationships that include legal obligations. Of course mutual love and faithfulness cannot be substituted by anything else. In Deuteronomy and many a prophet love, righteousness, truth, and voluntary goodness *(ahabah; emeth/emunah; ṣedeq/ṣedaqah; ḥesed)* are almost synonyms for the designation of the loyalty owed to the (legal!) covenant established by God between himself and his chosen people, and for the mutual relationship of its members. Not in vain do old and new, Jewish and secular marriage contracts go into details of the partners' economical obligations. Unless love is the basis, core, and purpose of righteousness and unless justice is the essential external form and mark of love, both love and law are perverted. Therefore, especially in PHM, Paul skillfully intertwines family with legal terms and arguments. They are neither opposites nor mutually exclusive.

Paul's spiritual fatherhood, established by the conversion of Onesimus under the apostle's care (Philem 1; cf. 1 Cor 1:14-15; Gal 4:19; 2 Cor 6:13), makes him intercede for the slave (Philem 8-17) and offer payment. For damages caused by a minor child the father must pay; when an adult child has misbehaved, the father out of sheer love for the child may cover the loss incurred by others. In turn, Paul could not even jokingly allude to a total and lifelong indebtedness of Philemon to himself, neither could he hope for a personal profit from this intimate relationship, unless Philemon had been, just as later Onesimus, converted by Paul and was therefore considered a spiritual son. The mutual indebtedness expressed in verses 18-20 is one aspect of the love that welds parent and child together.

Further legal and/or commercial connotations may be found in other verses.[17] The formula *eis Christon* (v. 6: "into, for, or toward Christ") looks equivalent to its use in the baptismal liturgy (see, e.g., Rom 6:3). On the basis of 1 Cor 1:12-15, its longer form (baptizing) "in the name of Christ" is understood by some interpreters to mean "on the account of Christ," as if by baptism a person became the property of Christ. Less contestable are the implications of "appealing on behalf of . . ." (Philem 9-10); "sending back" (v. 12, especially if this verb should have the same significance as in Luke 23:7, 11, 15, and Acts 25:21 where it certainly means "referring to a higher court for decision"); "for you" (which in Philem 13 expresses a legal substitution); *gnōmē* (v. 14, if rendered in English by "verdict" rather than by "opinion" or "consent"); "separat-

---

17. As observed and emphasized by recent articles of Sara C. Winter and of P. Lampe. For the titles and summaries, see Annotation 3, pp. 227-228.

ing" (v. 15; the same verb means "divorcing" in 1 Cor 7:10, 11, 15; Matt 19:6; Mark 10:9); "have back eternally" (v. 15, meaning possession without temporal limit and without the possibility of later recall); "have a guest room ready" (v. 22; this request is as crisp as a modern order by telex for the reservation of a hotel room).

As N. R. Peterson (*Rediscovering Paul,* p. 78) observes, such "themes, however literal or metaphysical, raise the fundamental issue of the economy, the integrity, of the brotherhood," even "of the social economy of the brotherhood." Paul is a sober and competent realist. Even while he is witness to his Lord, he is a devoted churchman, a pragmatic herald of love and faith. The combination of several styles of diction contributes to the persuasiveness and charm of PHM.[18]

C. A Private or/and Official Letter?

The question "private or official?" has created intensive debate. Arguments have been brought forward in favor of the first and the second theory, but also with the intention to reject the alternative altogether.

1. A STRICTLY PERSONAL COMMUNICATION

PHM is called a private letter mainly because of the following facts: in the address, three proper names precede the mention of the house church; later, the second-person singular pronoun *sy* (thou) and its genitive, dative, and accusative forms *sou, soi, se* are frequently used; the vocative form "brother" and the corresponding singular form of the verbs occur in verses 2c, 4-8, 10-23. It is first of all the ethical decision of the one individual, Philemon, for which the apostle asks. Not in vain have the collectors of the Pauline corpus and the NT

18. J. Knox, *Philemon among the Letters of Paul,* rev. ed. (New York: Abingdon, 1959; originally published, 1935), p. 9, cf. 13, calls PHM "one of the most charming letters ever written . . . carefully and skillfully"; although it has (p. 26) "quasi business character," it "suggests with some hesitation and indirection" what Philemon is expected to do. J. Müller-Bardorff, "Philemonbrief," in *RGG,* 5.331-332, speaks of "an exceedingly amiable letter, not without humor and brotherliness towards the slave." B. M. Metzger, *The New Testament: Its Background, Growth, and Content* (New York and Nashville: Abingdon, 1965), p. 234, considers PHM a "model of the art of letter writing, revealing . . . simple dignity, refined courtesy, and warm sympathy. It also illustrates the way in which existing human relationships may be made means of expressing Christian love."

An ample collection of high appraisals is offered at the beginning of an unpublished commentary on PHM by the Romanian scholar H. Binder.

codices, and the compositors of canonical lists, placed only one name at the top of the text. In addition, in the address Paul calls himself "prisoner" rather than "apostle" or "servant" of Christ; the latter titles are used in official letters to churches (cf. the first verses of the Pastoral Letters), except in Second Thessalonians. In Philem 8 and 14, Paul renounces his right to make use of his apostolic authority. When writing PHM, Paul did not intend to pronounce a final opinion or judgment on slavery in general.[19]

2. AN OFFICIAL CHURCH LETTER

Not only Philemon, Apphia, and Archippus, but also the congregation meeting in Philemon's (according to the postscript: also in Apphia's) house is addressed in verses 1-2 and thereby encouraged and entitled to participate in the slave owner's decision. While Paul hides his full power to extend commands, he yet mentions Timothy as coauthor (v. 1)[20] and undergirds his appeal by calling himself Christ's, the Messiah Jesus', prisoner and ambassador (vv. 1 and 9) and by expecting "obedience," even beyond the call of duty (v. 21). As already observed, this letter is a model of nondirective eye-to-eye pastoral counseling: here brothers convene with other members of the same family. While the apostle explicitly uses the words "I" and "thou," "we" and "thee," "mine" and "thine," he does not fail to refer also (in vv. 3, 6, 22, 25) to "us," "you," "our," and "your." Because previously the Christians in Colossae have learned by experience what a dear, cooperative, beneficial brother Philemon is, they have the right and duty to be eyewitnesses of the effects of Paul's letter. Actually, they are more than just Philemon's environment, and much more than mere observers or watchdogs. By being addressed together with the one brother in their midst, they are made responsible participants in all that Paul writes and Philemon will do. The slave's owner has to make up his mind in such manner that his decision and the congregation's decision are harmonious and that the way he chooses to go is the congregation's, and vice versa. Therefore reasons exist for saying Philemon is a church letter. Already about 400, those disputing the canonical value of this let-

---

19. Kümmel, *Introduction*, p. 246, formulates carefully that PHM "stands closest to a private letter." But A. Deissmann, *Paul*, Torchbook 15 (New York: Harper, 1931), pp. 215-216; Müller-Bardorff, 5.331; G. Bornkamm, *Paulus* (Stuttgart, Berlin, Cologne, and Mainz: Kohlhammer, 1969), p. 100; and E. Schweizer, *Der Brief an die Kolosser*, EKK (Einsiedeln: Benziger; Neukirchen: Neukirchener Verlag, 1976), pp. 27-28, unambiguously affirm the private character.

20. As at the beginning of First and Second Thessalonians, Second Corinthians, Philippians, and Colossians.

ter with the argument that it was only a private letter dealing with a private affair were contradicted by Chrysostom and Jerome (see sec. VIII, pp. 203-205).

By its inclusion in the NT canon, it was recognized that all congregations and all members of the church are factually addressed and had better recognize the letter's inspiration, authenticity, and authority.[21]

3. A COMBINATION OF PRIVATE AND OFFICIAL

The contrast between the arguments so far mentioned can be dissolved as soon as the alternative "private or official?" question is rejected. According to E. Lohmeyer, there is an epistolary and liturgical tradition that has all the traits of the "fixed scheme of a congregational letter" and yet also has a private character. J. Knox calls PHM an "altogether extraordinary letter" that not even remotely resembles in its form "papyrus letters and other ancient letters, because many people are involved in a private letter in order to control compliance."[22]

However, could perhaps the form of a private letter to an individual be an artistic literary device comparable to the fictitious letters of, e.g., Plato, Abelard, and C. S. Lewis? The etymological meanings of the names Philemon, Apphia, Archippus, Onesimus evoke as beautiful and meaningful implications and associations as the names borne by the persons in John Bunyan's *Pilgrim's Progress*.[23] Still, the form of PHM is far from artful fiction. Only in a real letter, concerning a special historic problem, can elements such as the following appear in combination: mention of a coauthor and of a special house church; greetings from persons also listed in the letter to the Colossians; reference to very specific events and situations; mere hints, innuendoes, implications instead of clearly formulated wishes or commands.

For these and other reasons, PHM resists an interpretation that calls it ei-

---

21. E. Lohse, *Colossians and Philemon* (Philadelphia: Fortress, 1971), p. 187 (hereafter cited as *Philemon*), observes that PHM "is not a mere private letter. . . . Rather it is a binding message from the Apostle. Although Paul foregoes mentioning his official titles. . . ." Cf. W. H. Ollrog, *Paulus und seine Mitarbeiter. Untersuchungen zur Theorie und Praxis der paulinischen Mission*, WMANT 50 (Neukirchen-Vluyn: Neukirchener Verlag, 1979), p. 104, and S. Winter, "Paul's Letter to Philemon," *NTS* 33 (1987): 1-2.

22. E. Lohmeyer, *Die Briefe an die Philipper, an die Kolosser und an Philemon*, 13th ed., KEK 9/11 (Göttingen: Vandenhoeck & Ruprecht, 1964), pp. 174-177; Knox, pp. 51-52. Cf. n. 24.

23. The four names may be etymologically translated "Bosom Friend," "Darling," "Horse-master," "Useful." In Philem 10, 11, 20, Paul does indeed play around the root meaning of "Onesimus" by speaking of his usefulness and of the profit the apostle himself has enjoyed and hopes to enjoy.

ther only private or only official. When one member of the church is given apostolic guidance, the whole congregation is included in the admonition.[24]

D. Rhetorical Devices

At least four oratory ingredients spice the language and style of PHM. None of them is unique within the Pauline epistles, but in PHM they are combined with special skill.

1. DRAMA

Paul's approach to Philemon is as dramatic as would be the rhetorical procedure of a contemporary orator who, appointed to act as defense or prosecution attorney for somebody or some cause, took his stance before a judge, a council, or a town assembly. Paul pleads in favor of Onesimus in a most dramatic way, just as he speaks up in, e.g., Galatians, Romans, First and Second Corinthians for the true gospel, for stable faith, and for decent conduct. The earlier-mentioned liturgical, emotional, juridical, and economical elements of his diction express the manifold dimensions and contribute to the power of the ongoing drama. While Colossae was too small and insignificant to have a theater, some of its inhabitants will have had the opportunity to watch a play that one way or another reflected the life, feelings, experiences, and aspirations of every human being. Now a special drama, domestic and yet also of public interest, is unfolded before the eyes of the Christians in Colossae. Each of the main actors in the Paul-Philemon-Onesimus drama urges those present to identify themselves with this or that tragic or comic character and scene. Below, in section VI (pp. 128-150), the cast and development of the drama will be described in some detail.

24. Cf. Immanuel Kant's categorical imperative. Its original meaning, according to which personal, private ethical decisions have to be such as might become the basis of universal legislation, is here reversed. A convincing theological and ethical reason for the intertwinement of private and official elements has been proffered, e.g., by Th. Preiss, *Life in Christ*, SBT 13 (London: SCM, 1954), pp. 33-34, 66: "In the body of Christ personal affairs are not private." Similarly G. Friedrich, "Der Brief an Philemon," in *Die kleineren Briefe des Apostels Paulus*, ed. H. W. Beyer et al., 10th ed., NTD 8 (Göttingen: Vandenhoeck & Ruprecht, 1965), p. 183, writes, "In the Christian congregation personal legal things have no longer purely private character when a matter is at stake which concerns two members of the same congregation." Cf. U. Wickert, "Der Philemonbrief — Privatbrief oder apostolisches Schreiben?" *ZNW* 52 (1961): 230-238; C. F. D. Moule, *The Epistles of Paul the Apostle to the Colossians and to Philemon*, CGTC (Cambridge: University Press, 1968), pp. 18-19 n. 6.

2. CONTRASTS

PHM bristles with contradictory elements and yet aims at their combination. Individuals, especially Philemon, are addressed, but also the house church (v. 2). Love and faith are mentioned and discussed separately, and yet they are held together as if by nature they formed a hendiadys (vv. 5-7). We repeat: what Philemon as an exemplary church member has amply proven in the presence and for the benefit of many men, women, and children, this he shall neither hide nor withhold when Onesimus is restored to him (vv. 5-7, 9-20). Paul makes a humble request to which Philemon is expected to react with obedience, but this compliance has to be voluntary and spontaneous (vv. 8-9, 14, 21). Useless Onesimus has proven useful and is trusted to prove even more so (vv. 11, 13, 15). The slave is not just a protégé of Paul, but rather the apostle's own heart or alter ego (vv. 12 and 17). Temporal separation will turn out to lead to eternal belonging in the master's home (vv. 12, 15); now the slave will be a brother (v. 16). Poor Paul in prison pledges to make cash payments (vv. 18-19). Whether or not master Philemon has a right to compensation for damage suffered, this slave owner is a debt slave of Paul (vv. 19-20) and ought to work in the apostle's service — unless he prefers to let Onesimus work for Paul (v. 13). The debtor Paul claims the rights of a creditor![25]

The contrast motifs are developed so far as to become paradoxes, and the paradoxes in turn may be understood at best as playful and humorous, at worst as subtle extortions. Paul is not alone with his request for a brotherly reception and treatment of Onesimus: Timothy and the group sending greetings add to the weight of Paul's request. Philemon is not only Paul's "dear brother" (variant reading of v. 1) but also, since he was converted by Paul, his lifelong indebted child (v. 19b). The master ought to receive and love the slave as a brother — because both Onesimus (v. 10) and Philemon, as sons of Paul, *are* already brothers! Is, perhaps, Paul too far away and all too restricted in his movements, and incapable of enforcing obedience? The public reading of his letter in Philemon's house and the forthcoming visit of Paul (vv. 2 and 22) certainly will make Philemon comply.

One group of potentially dramatic motifs, however, is intentionally and conspicuously absent from PHM: the application of Paul's apostolic authority; a comparison of Paul with the lawgiver Moses; the citation of one or several words of Christ; the claim that Christ speaks through his messenger; other possible references to inspiration; finally a threat of curse or excommunication.[26]

---

25. Especially Lohmeyer, p. 182, emphasizes such contrast.
26. Paul compares his service to that of Moses in 2 Cor 3; words of Christ he quotes and inspiration he claims in, e.g., 1 Cor 7:10-11 (cf. Acts 20:35); 1 Cor 2:6-16; 7:40; 2 Cor

3. HEBREW ELEMENTS

The language, diction, and style of PHM are Greek but include Jewish features.[27] Here a Semitic way of thought and speech is cast into Hellenistic rhetoric, both being used, according to E. Lohmeyer, with perfect mastership. Hebrew poetic lines, stanzas, and chiasms contain "parallel members"; the substance of one statement is repeated, clarified, crowned by a contrast, or enhanced by a second sentence coined in other words. So in Philem 4-5:

> v. 4: Always I give thanks to God
> when in my prayer I ask him to remember you.
> v. 5: For I am hearing of your love and your faithfulness which you
> show to the Lord Jesus and all saints.

In the latter verse love may be specifically related to all the saints, faithfulness to the Lord Jesus. And, as already pointed out, the sequence of first love, then faithfulness, is reversed in verses 6-7. Several subdivisions and the letter as a whole use the *inclusio* (ring-composition) pattern and deploy analogies: The word "grace" dominates the initial and the final benedictions (vv. 3 and 25). The house of Philemon is the meeting place of a congregation and shall soon have Paul as a guest (vv. 2 and 22). "Love" occurs in verses 1, 5, 7, 9, before the reception of Onesimus as a dear (lit. "beloved") brother is explicitly asked for in verse 16. What Philemon is and does for Paul and the congregation, he shall also be and do for the returning slave. In substance, though without employment of the word, "gift" is a motif to which allusion is made in various ways. Grace and peace, love and faithfulness are gifts of God. As it were giftwise, Paul sends Onesimus back, pledges to pay for damages, and will be a guest in Philemon's house (vv. 12, 18, 19, 22). Voluntarily Paul renounces his power to give orders; voluntarily he sends the slave back — and spontaneous shall be the response and conduct of the earthly master (vv. 8, 9, 12, 14, 16, 18). The congregation's prayer for Paul's coming corresponds to the apostle's prayer for the host of the congregation (vv. 4-7 and 22). The idea of community is resumed in the appeal to partnership (*koinōnia* and *koinōnos* in vv. 6 and 17). "The good" Philemon does recalls "every good (gift)" mentioned earlier (vv. 6 and 14). Three times the letter speaks of the heart, and twice of the rest being given to it (vv. 7, 12, 20).

13:3. On the other hand, in Gal 1:8-9 and 1 Cor 16:22 he threatens with a curse, and in 1 Cor 5:4-5 he speaks of a temporal excommunication carried out in cooperation of himself with the Corinthian congregation and the power of the Lord Jesus.

27. Couchout, pp. 129-146, and Lohmeyer, pp. 176 and 181-183, have elaborated on this theme at about the same time.

Bible versions that render the PHM text in indented and parallel lines, with spaces between strophes, do not (yet?) appear to exist. But E. Lohmeyer in his commentary, and P. L. Couchout in his article on literary style, have chosen this way of presenting the text in print. Couchout reconstructs eight stanzas consisting of eight lines each. Every word of the letter, from the first to the last, is treated as an essential part of the structure.

Lohmeyer (p. 176) observes that in Philem 4-7, just as in other Pauline thanksgiving sections, "language and rhythm lift themselves above human discourse and are oriented toward the festival form of a psalm." In the central part of PHM (vv. 8-20), Lohmeyer distinguishes twenty-four poetic lines, grouped in three strophes of equal length.

Bold attempts of this kind display the skill of translators and expositors. But the artistic subtlety and beauty of Paul's style do not suffice to prove that all Pauline writings have the form of a hymn or poem. The apostle is done enough honor when his style is called *Kunstprosa* (prose art).

Features such as repetitions, analogies, and resumptions of the same words or motifs can occur in every carefully written Hellenistic letter, be it private or official. In many regards, the style of Pliny the Younger's letters to Sabinianus resembles the diction of PHM. But the praise of God and of love expressed in Paul's letters by all the stylistic means mentioned — this praise is unique. In Holy Writ as well as in all good literature, language and form are inseparable from the substance. The Hebrew elements in the style of PHM correspond to the Jewish presuppositions of some of the arguments proffered in this letter. Because the OT and later Jewish roots of PHM have been neglected in all too many commentaries and monographs, they will be discussed later more extensively.

And yet, PHM also contains features that might be ascribed to an entirely different source:

4. HUMOR

In contrast to the doctrinal style of Romans; to the irony and sarcasm found in Galatians; to the apologetic, wailing, and aggressive passages of Second Corinthians; and to other idiosyncrasies of other letters, in PHM the use of contrasts is a sign and means of underlying good humor. Humor is, according to Wilhelm Busch, "where one laughs, in spite of it," even in the face of grave situations.

The mighty apostle of the omnipotent Lord Christ is a prisoner in Roman hands (vv. 1, 9-10) and chooses the role of a beggar before Philemon (vv. 8-9). The child Onesimus was created by a father in chains (v. 10), who was, according to some versions of verse 9, an old man! A pun is made on the name Onesimus ("Useful") in verse 11. God's purpose in permitting separation was to establish eternal union (v. 15). Paul and Philemon are business partners, and Onesimus can substitute for Paul by being the third man in this association (v. 17). Philemon is much deeper in debt to Paul than the apostle eventually is to the slave owner (vv. 18, 19). Paul hopes confidentially that he will benefit from Philemon — not only materially but by finding rest for his troubled heart (v. 20). Overflowing obedience is the sum of complete voluntariness (v. 21). A man whose chances for quick release from prison were less than certain invites himself to a private home for the near future (v. 22). All or at least a part of these elements can be considered, or are, humorous.

It is not certain whether Paul intended this impression, and whether Philemon was capable and willing to appreciate jokes pertaining to his relationship to Onesimus and to Paul. But together with other earliest hearers and readers of PHM, modern readers are by no means prevented from responding with a smile or a chuckle. The dreadfully serious issue of the slave Onesimus's future is treated cordially and almost lightly — a fact that reminds of the role of slaves in Greek and Latin comedies. Obviously bitterness is neither the only nor the best way of reacting to grave issues. Indeed, Philemon has a hard choice to make, but the decision-making process is sweetened as much as possible — by humor.

IV. STRUCTURE AND LOGIC

No dispute exists regarding the subdivisions of PHM. The logic is clear and convincing: on the ground of given and accepted presuppositions, conclusions are drawn that are consistent with the premises. When and wherever the will and the courage exist to make use of human reason, to apply its findings to attitudes, decisions, and actions, the arguments of PHM make good sense.

In formal regard, four parts can easily be discerned:

a. Address and Opening Greeting (vv. 1-3)
b. Thanksgiving and Intercession (vv. 4-7)
c. Request for a Voluntary Decision (vv. 8-20)
d. Personal and Liturgical Conclusion (vv. 21-25)

In the main part or core of the letter (vv. 8-20), subsections have been distinguished. E. Lohmeyer suggests that three things are described in succession: the present situation (vv. 8-12), the past (vv. 13-16), and the future of Onesimus

(vv. 17-20). P. Stuhlmacher observes in verses 8-20 "a stepwise rhetorical movement of thought": verses 8-12 contain Paul's plea without use of apostolic authority; verses 13-16 constitute concrete wishes for Onesimus's future at Paul's side and for the brotherly reception of the returning refugee, acknowledging Philemon's freedom and right to make his own decision; and verses 17-20 offer palpable requests for the treatment of the slave — as if Onesimus were Paul in person. Recognizing a careful rhetorical order, J. Gnilka calls verses 4-7 proem, verses 8-16 argument, and verses 17-19 epilogue.[28]

The logical interrelation between the personal and liturgical frame (vv. 1-3 and 21-25) and the central sections (vv. 4-7 and 8-20) reveals extreme care and tact in Paul's approach to Philemon. The apostle begins by showing his gratitude and joy. He has received gratifying information on Philemon's role in the congregation; Paul's extended contact with Onesimus has been most fruitful and enjoyable. The positive information and experience make him expect the best of all persons mentioned (vv. 4-16). Then only does Paul proceed to mention or hint at potentially negative possibilities.[29] According to verses 1-7, a firm reality underlies Paul's hope and intervention regarding the future relation between master Philemon and slave Onesimus. It is based on three pillars: (1) the prevenient and everlasting grace and peace of God, as revealed, upheld, and guaranteed by Jesus Christ; (2) the effect of God's creative grace and peace: the existence of a historical social body on earth, the church, which assembles to celebrate the good done by God and expects its members to do what is good; (3) Philemon's personal contribution to the life of the congregation and to the pleasure of Paul. We repeat: the apostle feels entitled to expect that Philemon will be as full of love toward Onesimus as he already is in his relation to Paul and all the other Christians.

Not in vain do main themes and motifs occurring in the description of the basis of Paul's thought recur in the rest of the epistle: nothing is superfluous, redundant, or baroque. This is Paul's logic and argument:

> Since God in his grace has taken the congregation into his hand,
> in order to sustain it as one body with many members,
> Philemon can and will not refuse to prove his love and faithfulness to the
> one church member whose name is Onesimus.

---

28. Cf. Lohmeyer, pp. 181-83; P. Stuhlmacher, *Der Brief an Philemon*, EKK 18 (Zürich and Braunschweig: Benziger Verlag; Neukirchen-Vluyn: Neukirchener Verlag, 1975; 3rd ed., 1989), p. 36; and J. Gnilka, *Der Philemonbrief* (Freiburg: Herder, 1982); L. White, "The Structural Analysis of Philemon," *SBL Seminar Papers* (1971), 1:1-47, was not available to me.

29. As Petersen, pp. 73 and 293, observes — with the effect that the priority of good news, of the gospel over the law, is clearly established.

It is characteristic of the ethics unfolded in PHM that it can neither be understood nor implemented without recourse to the good news on which it relies and is to confirm. Far from presenting a law before or without a gospel, or from forcing a person under the yoke of Bible texts or the man Paul, the letter exemplifies what evangelical ethics can and must be: practical and specific but nondirective; appealing to human dignity and freewill decisions yet far from displaying or planting a moral superiority complex; constructive, though not of a system of virtues and rules, but of freedom and joy. In the Sermon on the Mount, the Epistle of James, and First Peter, ethics is much more than an eventual appendix to gospel proclamation and faith. Ethical conduct is depicted as the way to bear, in action and in suffering, an existential and social witness to Christ. The ethic of these documents as well as of PHM and other Pauline letters can therefore be called kerygmatic or evangelical ethics.[30]

Just as Jesus' proclamation is logical and yet contains paradoxes, so also PHM's logical structure does not exclude tensions, contradictions, even paradoxes such as those mentioned earlier. The question whether among the Pauline statements about slaves there exists a conflict between PHM and other New Testament letters will be discussed later, in section VII.

V. DATE AND PLACE

As stated, prevailing scholarly opinion today accepts PHM as a genuine letter of Paul.[31] However, no agreement exists concerning time and location of the writing of the billet. The answers given to at least three open questions predetermine the guesses or results concerning the origin of PHM: (1) Are all four Captivity Letters (Philippians, Ephesians, Colossians, and Philemon), perhaps also Second Timothy, not to speak of First Timothy and Titus, stemming from the same city and period? (2) Are Colossians, Ephesians, and Second Timothy authentic, and if so, how relevant are their biographical information or hints? (3) Are the places and dates of Paul's itinerary recorded in the book of Acts, in their totality or at least partly, reliable? Since these issues are solved in widely divergent ways, opinions about PHM's date and place are also divided.

J. Knox (pp. 27-28) observes, and the contradictions between post-Knoxian

---

30. J. Zmiejewski, "Beobachtungen zur Struktur des Philemonbriefes," *Bibel und Leben* (Düsseldorf) 15 (1974): 276-296, sums up the substance of Philem 8-20 by pointing out three facts: (1) PHM is an official, not a private, letter; (2) Christ is proclaimed in the form of admonition rather than of preaching; (3) not only one specific slave is a brother, but all Christians are brothers.

31. Nineteenth-century exceptions will be mentioned below, in n. 53.

chronologies of Paul confirm the fact, that the available materials are not sufficient for giving final answers. Knox, this distinguished expert in PHM studies, admits that the understanding of this letter will hardly increase substantially by knowledge of Paul's actual situation at the time of its writing. Because this letter has not fallen from heaven and would be misunderstood if comprehended as a timeless script, various theories about its origin have yet to be recorded. In question are: a captivity of Paul in Ephesus between 53 and 57, in Caesarea at the Sea between 59 and 61, or in Rome between 61 and 63. If Paul died one or two years earlier or later than 63, the dates for Caesarea and Rome have to be changed accordingly. Among the arguments for either place are the following.[32]

a. *Rome between 61 and 63.* The capital of the Roman Empire is favored by many expositors.[33] Literary evidence for Rome exists in some ancient — though not in all the oldest — Greek manuscripts.[34] Several forms of a postscript to PHM contain the words "written from Rome." While such appendices are not a part of the original text, they do not necessarily transmit false information. If Colossians is genuinely Pauline and was dispatched from Rome, then also PHM can hardly have been written at another place and time. For almost exactly the same coworkers are near Paul and send greetings to the Colossians and to Philemon. Rome was a favored place of refuge for runaway slaves. In the crowded city they hoped to be safe from private and official hunters. Here they could hope to find work and/or a protector. And here existed the rare chance to eventually move up the social ladder as high as the status of the powerful "emperor slaves." If not succeeding in one of these ways, they might survive by begging or joining a revolutionary or criminal group, or disappear unnoticed in the crowds of the slums.[35]

In Rome, Paul was kept in a relatively loose form of captivity, as Luke states in Acts 28:16, 30. Fellow workers, among them Luke, were free to visit him or were held in the same cell or compound.[36]

---

32. The substance of AB 34 (*Ephesians,* vol. 1), pp. 50-52, and AB 34B *(Colossians),* pp. 126-134, is here resumed and augmented.

33. In commentaries and monographs on PHM, and in introductions to the NT, Rome is proposed by as diverse interpreters as, e.g., Thomas Aquinas, Martin Luther (WA, 25.76), H. Grotius, J. B. Lightfoot, L. Cerfaux, J. Schmid, A. Robert and A. Feuillet, F. F. Bruce, B. Metzger, C. F. D. Moule, Th. Preiss.

34. L, P, perhaps also 048, certainly the MSS belonging in the Koine group; Aland's Majority Group is largely identical with the formerly called *Koine* family.

35. A certain Epaenetus, whom Paul mentions in his letter to Rome (16:5) as a member of the Roman congregation and calls the first convert to Christ in Asia Minor, may have been a slave who went to Rome in order to find a refuge and/or friends. If, however, Rom 16 originally should not have been the conclusive part of Romans, but of, e.g., Ephesians, this argument is invalid.

36. In 2 Tim 4:17 Paul writes out of a stage of his captivity when "Luke alone is with

Obviously, social contact and conversation with free persons and fellow captives were possible. By receiving and giving information and counsel, by dictating or suggesting letters, in common Bible study and prayer Paul was enabled to care for nearby and faraway congregations and individuals, and so to continue his pastoral work.

A first argument against the Roman theory is not very solid: the self-invitation of Paul to Philemon's house for a visit in the near future (Philem 22) is assumed to conflict with the apostle's clearly stated intention to travel westward from Rome to Spain, and therefore not to return to eastern regions (Rom 15:24, 28). Still, just as at earlier occasions (cf. Rom 1:9-13; 2 Cor 1:15-17), Paul may once again have been forced to change his travel plans. He had declared the faith of the Christians in Rome a signal to "the whole world" (Rom 1:8). Even without reaching Spain, he could write of the worldwide spread, fruit bearing, and growth of the gospel (Col 1:6). The concluding verse of Acts avers that after his release from prison, though under slight restriction, Paul preached the gospel in Rome "openly and unhindered." Certainly even during his stay in prison there were still periods in which he counted on the chance to be acquitted by the emperor's court. Only the latest among the Captivity Letters reckons with his near condemnation and death.[37] The Pastoral Epistles include hints that Paul will travel east of Rome. Especially the close connection between PHM and Colossians, if the latter is considered as authentic as the former, supports the Roman origin of PHM.

Still, other reasons proffered against Rome might be stronger: (1) If not only Hierapolis and Laodicea, as indeed the Sibylline Oracles (12:280; cf. 3:345; 5:318) affirm, but also Colossae (so Eusebius, *Chron.* 2.154) were destroyed by

---

me"; 2 Tim 1:17 makes it probable that Rome was the place. The so-called "we" reports in Acts (16:10-17; 20:5-15; 21:1-18; 27:1–28:16) suggest that Luke was traveling with Paul during all his missionary journeys except the first. Among the other companions of the apostle, the Thessalonian Aristarchus had been with Paul on his way to Rome (Acts 27:2; cf. 19:29; 20:4); the same man was a fellow prisoner of the apostle at the time when Colossians (4:10) was written, but was among the free visitors of Paul according to Philem 24. The Colossian Epaphras, by whom the congregation at Colossae had been founded and by whom the imprisoned Paul was informed about the life and love of the Christians in Colossae (Col 1:7-8), is not called a fellow prisoner in Col 4:12, but shares the prison with Paul according to Philem 23. See the detailed study of Paul's relationship to his companions in W. H. Ollrog's work cited in n. 21. Regarding the possibility that Paul was in a Roman prison not only once but twice, see below, n. 48.

37. The hints regarding impending death, which are given in Phil 1:12-23, esp. 20-22; 3:12-14, 20-21; 2 Tim 4:6-8, do not completely suffocate the sparks of hope glimmering in, e.g., Phil 1:25; 2:24; 4:4. Equally, when Second Timothy was written (esp. 4:16-18), there was still a slight chance that Paul would survive his trial. Travel plans formulated elsewhere in the Pastoral Epistles confirm this; see n. 48.

an earthquake in 61/62 C.E. and made completely uninhabitable, then letters sent to those places in, e.g., 63 might have gone to nowhere or to ruined houses. (2) The geographical distance between Rome and Colossae is enormous. Therefore a flight from central Asia Minor to the capital of the empire would have been most difficult, risky, and expensive for Onesimus.[38] Earlier, the same distance and cost factors would have been weighing also on Epaphras, who from Colossae had gone out to meet, inform, and help Paul, and on Tychicus and Onesimus when they brought Paul's letter to the Colossians and to Philemon.[39] (3) It is difficult to imagine that Paul, while kept in prison in Rome, could expect in the foreseeable future to be a guest in Philemon's house in Asia Minor (Philem 22). (4) If one presupposes that the Captivity Letters were all written from the same location, the prison site in the praetorium and in "Caesar's house," which is mentioned in Phil 1:13; 4:22, may, but need not, be pointing to Rome. Such buildings existed also in the provinces.[40] (5) The Epistle to Philemon, studied without side-glances toward Colossians and Philippians, contains no hint in favor of a Roman provenance.

All arguments *against* Rome are eventually buttressed by concrete proposals of other cities.

b. *Caesarea at the Sea, circa 60.* The book of Acts (23:23–26:23) describes extensively Paul's two-year captivity in a Roman provincial center: Caesarea was the capital of Palestine and the seat of the procurator. Paul's imprisonment in that city was temporarily as lenient (24:23) as his later captivity in Rome. Therefore some, if not all, Pauline letters from prison might have been of Caesarean origin.[41] This place was close enough to the central parts of Asia Minor to be visited by the Colossian Epaphras and by the fugitive Onesimus; it possessed an asylum temple. There friends were permitted to attend to Paul's needs (24:23), and it appears natural that from there Paul could expect to go to Colossae for a visit (Philem 22). Although Acts 24–26 do not speak of far-reaching mission work organized or performed by Paul from the Caesarea base, yet even there he used unique opportunities to proclaim Christ, the resurrection and hope, before the procurator, Felix, Festus, and King Agrippa.[42]

---

38. Even if Philem 18 is understood to mean that Onesimus stole the necessary funds from his master.

39. Col 1:7-8; 4:7-9, 12; Philem 12, 23.

40. For instance, in Jerusalem and Caesarea, according to Matt 27:27; John 18:28, 33; 19:9; Acts 23:35.

41. M. Goguel, M. Dibelius and H. Greeven, E. Lohse, Bo Reicke, and others favor this choice, while E. Haupt, E. Lohmeyer, W. G. Kümmel, W. Bieder are wavering between Rome and Caesarea.

42. Acts 25:10-12, 25; 26:32; 28:19.

Again, it is impossible to be certain. In none of the Pauline letters is Caesarea ever mentioned. Whether 2 Tim 4:16 was written from Rome or from Caesarea, Paul's assertion is surprising that during his first legal defense nobody came to his assistance. At least when Col 4:14, Philem 24, and 2 Tim 4:17 were written, Paul was with Luke — the same man who, according to the "we" sections of Acts (see n. 36), together with the apostle and Aristarchus, went on board in Caesarea for the journey to Rome (Acts 27:2). However, those five biblical chapters (Acts 22–26) that describe Paul's stay in Caesarea are not phrased in the form of a "we" report. Luke and Aristarchus may have joined him only at the last moment before the apostle's embarkation to Rome. Aristarchus had been, together with others, Paul's companion in Ephesus, Macedonia, Greece, and Troas (Acts 19:29; 20:4-5). Indeed, Luke and Aristarchus send greetings to Colossae and Philemon. But no evidence exists that they could have done so only from Caesarea. Finally, Paul's hope to be free soon enough for a visit in Philemon's house looks highly adventurous, if not crazy, if it was fostered in Caesarea. Those among the Jerusalem and Diaspora Jews who hated Paul passionately would certainly have seized and killed him as soon as he left the gates of the prison in that city.[43]

c. *Ephesus.* The lack of conclusive evidence either for Rome or Caesarea has made necessary the search for a third option. A respectable group of scholars favors Ephesus.[44] The Marcionite Prologues state that Colossians was written from Ephesus.[45] This city, the capital of the province of Asia Minor, recommends itself because of its relative proximity (ca. 100 miles as the crow flies) to Colossae. Epaphras's journey to Paul, the delivery of Colossians to Colossae by Tychicus, Onesimus's flight to Ephesus and return to Colossae, and Paul's planned visit at Philemon's house would therefore be manageable without major obstacles and risks.[46] In Ephesus Paul stayed for at least two and a half years. In this city he established a school that became a mission center for Asia Minor.[47] There industrious, devoted, and trusted fellow workers such as Timothy and Aristarchus would form a close circle around Paul. Except in Philippians, whenever Paul mentions his chains in the Captivity Letters he appears to retain

43. Cf. Acts 20:3; 23:12-15, 21, 27, 30; 24:1-9; 25:2-3, 7, 11, 15, 24; 26:21.

44. A. Deissmann, G. S. Duncan, W. Michaelis (as mentioned in AB 34, p. 51 n. 211) have been stipulating an Ephesian captivity of Paul and the corresponding origin of the Captivity Letters in Ephesus. J. Knox, E. Lohse, W. Marxsen, A. Suhl, S. Schulz, R. Gayer, J. Gnilka, P. Stuhlmacher, and H. Binder have followed their example more or less tentatively.

45. As quoted by Moule, p. 22.

46. Col 1:7-8; 4:7, 8, 12; Philem 12, 22. It is noteworthy that Tacitus, *Ann.* 3.60-61, speaks of an Ephesian delegation to Emperor Titus that hoped to clean Ephesus of the charge of harboring, in e.g. the famous Artemis temple, masses of escaped slaves.

47. See AB 34B, introduction, nn. 17, 61, 101, 132.

hope; an appeal of his case to the Caesar in Rome was not yet necessary during a captivity in Ephesus.

On the other hand, when Paul sent Tychicus *to* Ephesus (Eph 6:21-22; 2 Tim 4:12), he could not have sent him out *from* Ephesus. In 1 Cor 15:32 and 2 Cor 1:8-11 the apostle mentions tribulations and threats to his life but does not speak of imprisonment. This is confirmed by Acts 18:19–20:1, where much is told of Paul's activities in Ephesus but nothing of an incarceration. This argument from silence lacks definite persuasiveness but may yet, if combined with positive statements, have some weight. We repeat: in 2 Tim 4:11 and 16 the apostle states that "Luke alone is with me," and that no one sided with him — but all deserted him "at my first defense." Whether Luke was always in Ephesus when Paul was there is uncertain. But it is certain that in that town Paul had a reliable circle of supporters. All of this may not defeat but can weaken the Ephesus theory.

In summary, convincing proof cannot be delivered either for Rome, for Caesarea, or for Ephesus.[48] Rome may still be preferred to the other possibilities because, just as Ephesians and Colossians are twins, so also Colossians and PHM bear signs of stemming from the same author, the same place and situation, at about the same time.

The question whether PHM was written before or after Colossians will be discussed in section VI below.

---

48. Yet another alternative to placing and dating PHM might be taken into consideration. What if it ever could be demonstrated that all of the three Pastoral Epistles (First and Second Timothy, and Titus) were authentically Pauline in their present wording, and if great emphasis were laid upon the biographical utterances contained in them? In that case Paul was set free after his (first) captivity in Rome as it is described in Acts 28. Then he made at least four additional journeys: (1) After or before going to Spain or instead of carrying out the Spanish plan (Rom 15:24, 28), he traveled to Ephesus and Macedonia (1 Tim 1:3). (2) He evangelized Crete and founded the congregations on that island that Titus was later to strengthen (Titus 1:5). (3) He made final visits in Corinth, Troas, and Miletus "before winter" (2 Tim 4:13, 20). (4) He planned to spend a winter in Nicopolis, east of the Adriatic Sea (Titus 3:12). On the first and third of these journeys he might, on short notice, have intended to visit Philemon in Colossae. In this case Caesarea, Ephesus, as well as many other cities might be the place where PHM was written, if not Colossians and Ephesians, too, between about 63 and 65. Then it was a second captivity in Rome that ended with Paul's execution between ca. 65 and 67.

There is one additional theory, also based on the assumed authenticity of the Pastoral Epistles. J. A. T. Robinson, *Redating the New Testament* (London: SCM, 1976), pp 70-84, proposes that these letters were written between autumn 55 and fall 59, that is: First Timothy after First Corinthians; Titus between Romans and Philippians; Second Timothy after Philemon, Ephesians, and Colossians. On pp. 70, 76, 83-84 Robinson seeks to explain why the stylistic differences of the Pastoral Epistles fail to demonstrate that an author other than Paul was at work.

At this place, still another geographical problem requires attention: Was PHM really sent to Colossae, or, unlike Colossians, was it destined for another city? Several reasons speak in favor of the slave owner's residence in Colossae: Tychicus and Onesimus bring Colossians, of course, to Colossae (Col 4:7-8). Onesimus, Epaphras, and Archippus lived in that town, or at least had very close connections with the local church (Col 4:12, 17; Philem 2). The *Haustafel* contained in the Epistle to the Colossians (3:18–4:1), especially the master/slave section 3:22-25, provides a perfect foreplay, summary, or postlude of what Paul has to say about Onesimus and to Philemon. Therefore, for a long time it was considered self-evident and indisputable that PHM went to a house situated in Colossae.

However, tentatively in the middle of the nineteenth century, and most vigorously since 1927, it has been proposed that Archippus rather than Philemon was the owner of Onesimus, and that Philemon lived in Laodicea, a major center with which the tiny and insignificant Colossae never could compare. Bold and interlocking reasons are proffered by J. Knox in his book *Philemon among the Letters of Paul*, 1935 (cited in the following from the revised edition of 1960), in favor of these two theories. In Col. 4:17 Archippus is described as a deacon in the church at Colossae, and the congregation is urged to tell him to "fulfill the service" that he had "received in the (name of the) Lord." This "service" is supposed ultimately to mean that the deacon's former slave, dear brother Onesimus, be voluntarily transferred to Paul, so that he can henceforth work with the apostle in the "service in the bond of the gospel" (Philem 13 and 21). In the verse immediately preceding Paul's indirect but urgent appeal to Archippus, in Col 4:16, the apostle speaks of a letter "from Laodicea" that is also to be read in Colossae, in exchange with the reading of Colossians in the Christians' assembly at Laodicea. Since Paul does not speak of a letter "*to* the Laodiceans," he must have in mind, so it is argued, a letter delivered first to a member of the Laodicean church, even Philemon, in order that this man then hand it to the real addressee, Archippus. In this case the Laodicea letter mentioned in Col 4:16 is not lost — as is commonly assumed — but is present in the church's NT canon under the title "To Philemon." Actually, however, Philemon was expected to do more than forward the letter "*from* Laodicea" to Colossae, whereupon Christians at Colossae would add pressure on Archippus to do what Paul expected of him, and to do even more than the epistle actually spelled out (Col 4:16-17; Philem 21).[49]

On the other hand, Col 4:7-9 rather favors the tradition that PHM, together with Colossians, went directly to Colossae, through the hands of Tychicus, proba-

---

49. For a more complete sketch of J. Knox's contribution to PHM research, see Annotation 1, pp. 225-226.

bly briefly before the earthquake struck the town in 61/62. It would be completely unusual to mention in Philem 1-2 the real addressee only at the third place, after Philemon and Apphia. There is no solid evidence to demonstrate that Archippus was the main person addressed by Paul. In the body of PHM, the frequent use of second-person singular verb forms and of the words "thou" and "thine" contradicts the assumption that anybody other than the first named recipient of the letter, a hospitable house owner in Colossae, even Philemon, was addressed. Just as Timothy is mentioned only in Philem 1 and never again in this letter, so Archippus seems to be forgotten after verse 2.

Later-to-be-discussed parallels exist between the *Haustafel* of Colossians (3:18–4:1), especially between its uniquely intensive and extensive section treating the master/slave relation in 3:22–4:1, and PHM as a case study. It is hardly fortuitous that the verb *adikeō* (doing wrong) is used by Paul in the treatment of the same subject only in Col 3:25 and Philem 18.[50] Certainly similar issues were burning also in other cities and congregations, but written evidence for Laodicea does not exist in the Pauline letters. Finally, Archippus is never called *agapētos* (beloved, dear) by Paul, while an appeal to "dear Philemon" to extend the love shown "to all saints," also to the returned slave, makes good sense (vv. 1, 4-7, 16).

Two additional reasons speaking against the Laodicean hypothesis may seem of little value but can be appended: Marcion knows two Pauline letters to Colossae: one of them is PHM. And the fifth-century Theodoret of Cyrrhus, living no more than a few days' traveling time from Colossae, informed the readers of his commentary on Philemon that in Colossae Philemon's house is "preserved to the present," a statement that, in view of the earthquake of 61/62 and later catastrophes of the same kind, is less than completely reliable.

After the discussion of such seemingly trivial literary-historical problems, now the way is free for much more important and dramatic issues.

VI. DRAMATIS PERSONAE

PHM makes the reader participate in a drama that runs its course from one act and scene to another and terminates open-ended, yet with the prospect of a happy end.[51]Who are the persons and which are the tensions, conflicts, retard-

---

50. As stated by H. Blanke in AB 34B, in the notes on Col 3:25, both masters and servants are warned of "doing wrong." The context forbids excluding the masters from this warning. Col 4:1 exhorts the slave owners to give and to do what is "right and proper."

51. Petersen, pp. 24-29, 45, 57, and passim, has with great energy elaborated on the

ing elements, and solutions provoking fear and love, and also smiles and pleasure, in the hearts of those watching the play?

Pliny the Younger's letters of intercession (quoted in Annotation 4 to the
"Social Background," pp. 86-87) present a drama that is mainly taking place in
the soul of the fugitive. The steps in the development and progress of the escaped freedman's psyche — from evil done to guilt feelings and regret; from
confession before a self-chosen father confessor to absolution by the deeply
moved listener; from the start of a new life to the display of astonishing virtue
— are movingly depicted. Pliny's heart has been so deeply moved by them that
he has become an intercessor for the fugitive and urges and expects the letter's
recipient, Sabinianus, to also move away from his no-longer-justified anger and
reveal what a magnanimous person he really is.

By no means does Paul's letter exclude or hide psychodramas in all persons concerned, as the repeated mention of the "heart" (*splangchna,* vv. 7, 12,
20) and the use of the earlier-observed "language of the heart" show. But PHM
does not contain the material for drawing exact psychographs. When compared
with Pliny's letters, in Paul's epistle the rich vocabulary, available for describing
the way and means and results of progressing from vice to virtue, is conspicuously absent. Paul respects and protects, as it were, the privacy and intimacy of
psychic events. His letter focuses on an interpersonal drama, even on action,
and changes taking place between God and humanity, and between different
human beings on earth. Indeed, there are strangely moved hearts; but they do
not obfuscate the priority of the social I-Thou relation, between God and
earthly persons. Thus the scenery is wider than the human soul, and the dramatic conflict and its solution are not limited to the victory of the soul, or of
virtue, over the base body and its intemperate passions.

Since the drama takes place between several persons rather than mainly
in the psyche of one admirable individual — is then God or Christ reduced to
the rank of other human actors? Indeed, in PHM frequent references are made
to God and Christ, as in other letters also to the Holy Spirit. But unlike Greek
plays, in PHM the deity's superior power is not just a tacitly recognized background element, nor is it reduced to the saving intervention of a *deus ex ma-
china.* When Paul mentions the Lord, he speaks and reminds of the creator of
all things, who at all times and everywhere wields incomparable power, who

---

"story" reflected in PHM, esp. on the drama and its divine and human actors. (Cf. also
D. Soesillo, "The Story Line in Translating Philemon," *BT* 34 [1983]: 424-426.) This way he
draws attention to anthropological and sociological dimensions of Paul's theology. Petersen
succeeds in offering a new key to understanding the life, message, and work of the apostle
Paul. Still, he may go to an extreme, if not too far, when untiringly (on pp. 127, 131-132, 151,
181-182, 164-165, 260, 265, 294-295) he speaks of several "masks" the apostle puts on — in
order later to drop them again.

fills all things, who is all in all.[52] For this reason, in the drama of the slave owner and his fugitive slave, God and the Lord are not additional persons in the interaction of equal agents and forces in psychic developments and in interhuman affairs. The incomparable central place and function of *theology* and *Christology* will be described below, in section VII, when their place in the *Haustafeln*, in the unity formulae, and in PHM is treated thematically.

The main parts of the social drama on earth are played by three persons: Paul, the author of the letter; Philemon, the slave owner; and Onesimus, the slave who has run away and is now being sent back to his master. Auxiliary roles fall to eight less conspicuous persons: the coauthor (or scribe?) Timothy; the relatives or close friends of Philemon, Apphia and Archippus; and five fellow workers of Paul whose names are also known from Colossians and who by sending their greetings in fact support the requests formulated in the letter. Around the chief and supporting actors, on stage are also a minor and a larger chorus group in order to fulfill essential functions: the congregation meeting in Philemon's house, and "all the saints" who enjoy Philemon's love, faith, and liberality. These groups pray for Paul, and to the first the apostle conveys God's blessing (vv. 2-3, 5-7, 22, 25). Just as the angels in the book of Revelation, and not entirely different from the role played by cheerleaders on American football fields, so the members of the house church and the saints in all the world accompany, watch, support, lament, or enjoy the ongoing action. All those assembled in Philemon's house do not yet lift up their voices during the drama described in PHM; but they will certainly do so later, after the public reading of the letter, and perhaps not only once.

Only the protagonists shall now be introduced. Soon enough it will become apparent that no more than fragments are known of their history, character, intention, work, and effect. Still, what is known of them is enough to arouse sympathy with them, even a laughing or weeping participation in the vital decisions they made earlier or will make in the future.

A. Paul, His Situation and Intention

1. *Known* with a fair amount of certainty are the following things: PHM was dictated or written by Paul himself. Denials of authenticity and unity of the epistle have survived for only a few decades.[53] Even if Timothy served as a

---

52. As, e.g., 1 Cor 15:23-26; Col 1:12-20; Eph 1:17-23; 4:4-6 confess extensively, and 1 Cor 8:6 and Rom 11:36 in crisp omnipotence formulae.

53. Knox, p. 28 n. 21, mentions F. C. Baur, *Paul the Apostle* (London, 1875), pp. 80-84; W. C. van Manen, "The Epistle to Philemon," *Encyclopedia Biblica* (New York, 1902), cols.

scribe (except for vv. 18-19), the text is Paul's own. This verdict is not even shaken by those declaring that Ephesians definitely and Colossians most likely are spurious. So the author of PHM was a historically well documented person: Paul, the man who stemmed from the Jewish Diaspora in southern Asia Minor, was a Roman citizen and an ardent rabbinical scholar. He was a lawyer-theologian of pharisaical orientation before he was forced into Christ's service and became the Lord's most important apostle to the Gentiles.

On his missionary journeys Paul had never visited Colossae and Laodicea. The travelogues contained in Acts are confirmed (or influenced?) by Col 1:7-8 and 2:1: the Christians of these Lycus Valley cities (a varied reading of Col 2:1 adds Hierapolis) had never met Paul face-to-face. Evidence exists, however, of a close acquaintance between Paul and at least five earlier or later residents of Colossae: Epaphras, who had founded the congregation, who had told Paul how much its members loved one another, and who continuously was praying for the Christians in Colossae, Laodicea, and Hierapolis (Col 1:7-8; 4:12-13); Philemon, who receives a very personal letter; Apphia, who is simply called "sister" but may have been cohostess of the house church; Archippus, who according to Col 4:17 is far from perfectly fulfilling his ministry in and to the church in Colossae; and Onesimus, who, when he left Colossae, was not yet a member of the local congregation and yet could not fail to give Paul a picture of its life, on the basis of his own impressions and experiences. Probably both Epaphras and Philemon drew Paul's attention specifically to one social problem: the master/slave relationship.

When Paul received the information and reacted to it, he was in prison.[54] At the time of writing PHM, he was convinced of being released soon (Philem 22). According to both letters, as also to Romans and Second Corinthians, Philippians and Second Timothy, the apostle considered his captivity an essential and by far not regrettable part of the spiritual warfare to which he was called. To some of his coworkers he gives the title "fellow soldiers."[55] Captivity

---

3693-3697; Holtzmann, pp. 428ff. Kümmel, *Introduction*, p. 246, adds the name of C. Weizsäcker, *The Apostolic Age*, vol. 2 (1893), p. 283.

54. Philem 1, 9, 10, 13-23; Col 4:18; cf. Col 1:24, 29; 2:1. The term *desmios* (captive) is used in Philem 1 and 9, and in Eph 3:1; 4:1; 2 Tim 1:8; *desmoi* (fetters, bonds) occurs in Phil 1:7, 13-14, 17; Col 4:18; 2 Tim 2:9. In Acts 16:23-24, 27, 37, 40; 22:4; 26:10, the word *phylakē* (prison) is used, which, however, in Paul's own writings occurs only in 2 Cor 6:5 and 11:23. The context always contains a qualification: although earthly authorities retain him, the apostle is Christ the Lord's prisoner. In Eph 6:20 he calls himself humorously an ambassador "in chains" *(en halysei)* for the gospel's sake.

55. In Col 1:29 and 2:1 (cf. 1 Tim 6:12; 2 Tim 4:7) Paul calls his life an *agōn* (struggle) and his daily activity a continous *agōnizomai* (struggling). Epaphroditus, Archippus, and the congregation participate in it as comrades-in-arms (Col 4:12; Phil 1:30; 2:25; 2 Cor 10:4-6; cf. Eph 6:10-20).

is an occasion to live up to the spiritual warfare for which a Christian is drafted and for which he is equipped.

Especially in PHM, Paul's present imprisonment stands in direct relationship to the main topic of the epistle. A prisoner of war — unless he was killed on the spot, could escape, or was released for cash — was sold and became a slave. Therefore a certain equality exists between the apostle and the slave Onesimus, except that Onesimus has sought to escape human bondage while Paul (unlike, e.g., Plato) had never been a slave of any human being. Just like Socrates and every good Stoic, and even more like Jesus himself, he did not attempt to shake off the chains. The apostle accepted and was bearing great sufferings not for his own but for Christ's and the gospel's sake.[56] The repeated references to his captivity in PHM therefore demonstrate Paul's empathy and sympathy with Onesimus. Because of the existential solidarity between a prisoner and a slave, Paul urges Philemon to treat Onesimus as Paul's own heart, his self, or alter ego (Philem 10, 16-17; cf. 22). Briefly stated, Paul's intervention and intercession on behalf of Onesimus comes not only from the bottom of his heart but is confirmed by the apostle's very existence and current predicament.[57]

Obviously Paul proceeds in another way than, e.g., Andronicus and Spartacus, the militant spokesmen and leaders of slaves who at their own time had fought for emancipation.[58] Also his stance is different from that of much later great preachers, social reformers, and/or revolutionaries who demanded human rights and justice not only for slaves but also for all who were poor.[59] Yet the difference between the arguments and methods need not contradict or exclude his full solidarity with the slave Onesimus's past, present, and future. He knew that Christ had become poor, and he accepted and followed voluntarily the charge to "remember the poor," especially those of Jerusalem (2 Cor 8:9; Gal 2:10; etc.).

---

56. The most extensive enumeration is found in 2 Cor 11:26-33.

57. In PHM Paul omits, however, not only the self-title "apostle" but also the title "servant" that in, e.g., Rom 1:1; Gal 1:10; 2 Cor 4:5 (and in a variant reading of 10:7) he employs, displaying both humility and pride. He does not ask Philemon to remember (a) that Jesus Christ himself had become a "servant," (b) that Philemon himself must behave as a slave of Christ, and (c) that, by receiving Onesimus as a brother, the master would receive Christ himself (cf. Matt 25:31-46). Such omissions may be fortuitous, but they also may be a sign that Paul does not consider servitude as a value of its own right that by all means has to be preferred to free movement and decision, and to voluntary action and spontaneous love.

58. For Andronicus and Spartacus see above, "Social Background," Annotation 6e and 6h, pp. 89, 90.

59. Paul is distinctly not the first in the row of, e.g., Bernard of Clairvaux and Joachim of Fiore, Savonarola and Thomas Müntzer, Karl Marx and Friedrich Engels, Leonhard Ragaz and Walter Rauschenbusch, Che Guevara and Helder Camara.

While PHM gives ample testimony to Paul's spiritual fatherhood and brotherhood regarding his "child" and "brother" Onesimus, the apostle also reveals an equally intimate concern for the slave's master. It is not just a matter of form that he calls Philemon "dear" and "brother." He thanks God and is heartily pleased by Philemon's relation to God and the church members. The apostle pronounces God's blessing on him and all those meeting in his house, however rich or poor they may be. He is confident that Philemon will fulfill voluntarily whatever is expected of him, will do even more than only receive Onesimus as a dear brother, and will bid welcome to the visiting apostle. Paul and Philemon have the same interests; they are business partners, debtors, and creditors at the same time. The proven and future usefulness of the slave will be a benefit for Philemon as well as for Paul.[60] Paul's solidarity with the master is as cordial and total as that with the slave.

This way Paul proves to be neither an unmoved mover nor an incompetent meddler in the life of those to whom and about whom he writes. The love he shows is far from cool neutrality. He has the best for each one of them in mind, and he admits freely that he himself does and will also gladly benefit from Onesimus's and Philemon's compliance with his wishes and hopes.

2. *Unknown* is, however, an even greater number of things, because clear-cut information cannot be derived from Paul's letters as a primary, and from Acts as a secondary, source. Frequently in the history of interpretation, the knowledge gaps regarding the specific circumstances presupposed and discussed in PHM have been filled with more or less wild guesses and theories. It would be useful to know but is not known, (a) whether a slave was kept, for anyone and for any reason, in Paul's paternal home at Tarsus; (b) whether Paul himself had ever owned a slave, with the opportunity to prove himself a wise or foolish master; (c) whether the apostle had ever experienced *long* periods of loneliness, cold, hunger, etc. Certainly he had repeatedly endured manifold and extreme sufferings, to the limits of what seems humanly possible, and often he had to reckon with violent death,[61] yet being a Roman citizen by birth, he still could enjoy a minimal legal protection that was not available to a slave. (d) Unknown also is how soon, how much, and how consciously he was influenced by current humanistic trends in moral philosophy and slave legislation.

Other open questions have already been touched on. Neither Caesarea nor Ephesus nor Rome is the indisputable cradle of PHM. The exact conditions of Paul's imprisonment can hardly be reconstructed. He may have been chained

---

60. See Philem 1, 7, 20; vv. 2, 4, 7; vv. 3-7, 25; vv. 9, 14, 21, 22; vv. 17, 18, 19; vv. 11, 20 respectively. In effect, almost every verse expresses the most intimate imaginable I-Thou relationship.

61. See, e.g., 2 Cor 4:7-12; 6:4-10; 11:23-29.

behind bars to a cold stone wall, or he may have been permitted to move relatively unhindered, while living in a private home (cf. Acts 24:23; 28:16, 30). It is not certain whether PHM was written earlier or later than Colossians. The fellow prisoner Aristarchus (Col 4:10) is not yet or no more in captivity when he is counted among the free fellow workers of Paul in Philem 24. Epaphras is still free according to Col 4:12, but captive together with Paul according to Philem 23. Colossians expresses no hope for a quick release of Paul, but Philem 22 presupposes his acquittal in the near future. The generalizing admonition to slaves and masters contained in Colossians may have been evoked by Epaphras's report on the congregation (Col 1:7-8) or, before or after Paul's conversations with this "dear fellow worker," by the different stories Onesimus had to tell from his own perspective. Unambiguous is the information provided by Col 4:7-9, saying that Onesimus accompanied Tychicus when the latter brought Colossians to those addressed. It is most likely that PHM was mailed through the hands of the same persons — as one of the spurious postscripts to Philem 25 states — but whether Onesimus himself carried and handed out the letter concerning himself cannot be ascertained.

More important are issues related to the substance of PHM. No doubt Paul wrote this letter because he loved and trusted the master as well as the slave (Philem 9-17, 21; Col 4:9). But consider also the following possibilities: (a) It cannot be definitely stated whether for better or worse there were also hidden persuaders at work to make Paul kindly intervene for Onesimus, while yet the slave was sent back home — where not only good but also evil might befall him. Had perhaps Onesimus himself timidly or boldly urged Paul to take this step "for love's sake" (v. 9)? Or had another Christian such as Epaphras or the whole congregation in Paul's environment wished and urged that the slave be sent back? Most likely they would have made the condition that Paul write a covering letter whose content and effect would be totally unlike King David's command to Joab regarding the soldier Uriah (cf. 2 Sam 11:14-26). Paul's decision to act and write as he did may as well have been strictly his own, made in lonely majesty, as it might have been the result of consultations and the rejection of other possibilities. (b) In PHM there is — unlike other Pauline texts[62] — no reference to Christ's immediate return and to the end of the present aeon. It is

---

62. First and Second Thessalonians; 1 Cor 7:19-31, esp. 29-31; Rom 13:11. In Eph 6:8-9; Col 3:24-25 Paul reminds both slaves and slave owners of the impartiality of the impending Last Judgment. Among newer interpreters, S. Schulz, *Gott ist kein Sklavenhalter, Die Geschichte einer verspäteten Revolution* (Zürich and Hamburg: Flambert/Furche, 1972), pp. 138ff.; A. Suhl, *Der Brief an Philemon* (Zürich: TVZ, 1981), p. 216; H. Conzelmann and A. Lindemann, *Arbeitsbuch zum Neuen Testament* (Tübingen: Mohr, 1975), pp. 223-224, cf. 418, e.g., refer to such texts to explain why Paul does not attack slavery as such nor propagate a revolutionary change of the existing order.

unknown whether the eschatological orientation of Paul's ethics made him consider social change superfluous for the time being. (c) Might it have been one of the apostle's and/or congregation(s)' concerns to attain, or maintain, cultural and moral respectability within their environment — a civic reliability that might have been put at stake or lost when the existing social order was questioned or attacked?[63] This argument is widespread, for the *Haustafeln*, the "fear" of the political authorities required by Rom 13:1-7, and Paul's contribution to the return of Onesimus to his place seem to support it. The acculturation theory is a complement or consequence of a strictly eschatological interpretation of Paul's ethics. (d) In addition, it might be guessed or proposed that Paul either trembled at the prospect that sooner or later a hunter of fugitive slaves would apprehend Onesimus, with evil consequences also for the apostle himself and the congregation.

Interpretations of PHM that, consciously or not, build on a selection or combination of alternatives such as those just mentioned are bound to be more fanciful than reliable. What is not known cannot be treated as if it were certain.

Puzzling and controversial is the answer to a final question: What did the pleading and exhorting apostle really want Philemon to do in response to the letter? Four diverging answers have been given, based on individual verses that were given supreme rank above other statements.

a. After his return to Colossae, Onesimus is to remain his earthly master's slave. Paul is willing to recognize God's providence that permitted Onesimus to escape only in order to make him return as a slave "forever" (v. 15). However, while the slave system gave the slave's owner enormous power over his property, Philemon is urged to renounce his power and right — as much as Paul does by not using his apostolic authority. Voluntarily Philemon shall receive and treat Onesimus as a dear brother and partner, instead of punishing and oppressing him (vv. 16-17). Before God and humankind the slave is now to possess and enjoy the same dignity and right as his master. If this was Paul's intention, then he aimed at a reform of slavery, not at abolition. A warm interpersonal family relationship was then to replace the rights claimed by rich and powerful owners.

b. Or Paul had eventual emancipation of Onesimus in mind — a normal legal manumission that would be, however, for a given period limited by a contract between the releasing patron and the released person. The *pactum* to be made would include future economical cooperation between the two, and also moral obligations that need not be fixed in writing (cf. v. 21).

c. Paul might have secretly hoped for immediate manumission free of any

---

63. Appeals to what is "decent" and "fitting" *(prepon, anēkon, kathēkon)* among Jews, Greeks, and Christians are made in 1 Cor 10:32; Eph 5:3-4; Col 3:18; 4:1; Phil 4:8; Philem 8.

legal bonds, except the display and growth of mutual love. The unconditional gift of freedom to a slave might contain the opportunity of cordial brotherly relations between the two free persons on an equal level (v. 16). But the same liberation might also expose the *libertus* to grave temptations and hardships. Certainly Paul's forthcoming visit to Philemon's house (v. 22) will permit the apostle to check whether and how far the slave's present owner has complied with the apostle's wish. There are interpreters of 1 Cor 7:21 who assume that Paul presupposes the right of a slave to refuse manumission of both the restricted and the total forms.[64]

d. J. Knox is outstanding among the promoters of a last possibility: Paul wanted Onesimus to be sent back to himself. The loan or transfer of a slave by his owner to another person was legally possible. Paul was convinced that Onesimus could be more useful when he shared in the apostolic service of the gospel than he could be to Philemon. Then it is the intended transfer of Onesimus to Paul that the apostle does not spell out in writing, yet expects Philemon to arrange voluntarily (v. 21). If Philemon complies, Paul himself will have a profit — not only of Onesimus, who will cooperate with him, but actually of Philemon himself, whose magnanimity meets with Paul's own: Philemon permits Onesimus to leave, and Paul permits Philemon to let the slave be a substitute for the owner's person (vv. 11, 13, 20, 21). In the latter case he would either send Onesimus to Rome or, rather, permit him to follow Paul on his journeys after the apostle has visited Philemon. Then Paul's intention was not so much to free Onesimus *from* this or that bondage, as to set the slave free *for* full-time cooperation in mission work.

The last-mentioned hypothesis has the strongest support from a combination of several individual verses. But since its main base, the wish uttered in verse 13 to have Onesimus work with Paul in the future, is phrased most tentatively, the other options cannot simply be excluded. Paul's counseling is so nondirective that ample room is left for Philemon to answer the letter by actions of his own choice. When Paul speaks of "obedience" in verse 21, he may mean obedience to God, to himself, or to Philemon's conscience. Since Paul never does exactly state his wish, the intention of the letter — except the request for voluntary obedience shown in a brotherly relation between Philemon and Onesimus — has its place among the unknown elements. PHM is open-

64. Above, in sec. VII (pp. 41-53) and in Annotation 16 of "Social Background" (pp. 101-102) the different modes, terms, and consequences of manumission have been discussed. Literature in favor of Onesimus's quick release or opposed to it was listed there in n. 112. E.g., Kümmel, *Introduction,* p. 246, and Stuhlmacher, p. 43 n. 108, find nothing in PHM that would suggest emancipation. But Moule, p. 275, is sure that manumission, though not mentioned, was implicitly intended. For a study of 1 Cor 7:21 (possible refusal of manumission?), see sec. VII.C, pp. 191-200.

ended, as are in their own ways several parables of Jesus. The first and later listeners and readers have to make up their own mind how the dramatic story shall end, and to take corresponding action.

B. Philemon, a Good Man and a Slave Owner

1. *Known features.* When Paul wrote to Philemon, the latter was a successful middle-class citizen, owner of a house large enough to host a house church and to have, in addition, at least one guest room available for a visitor. Also he owned, whether for work in his business or household, or as a status symbol, at least one slave.[65] Since he could not have made Paul's acquaintance in Colossae, he must have had reasons and means to travel, be it alone or, for convenience and safety's sake, accompanied by a slave. Philemon had been a Gentile by birth but never a proselyte — or else Paul would probably have alluded in his letter to the Law, the Prophets, and/or the Writings of the Old Testament, and to Jewish customs.[66] Under Paul's influence Philemon became a Christian, "owing" henceforth "himself" to the apostle (Philem 19) as much as a spiritual or physical child was in obligation to his father. Since Onesimus was not yet a Christian when he escaped from Philemon, the patron at the time of his own conversion either had not yet acquired the slave or had not insisted on the slave's baptism together with the "whole house."[67] Once converted by Paul, Philemon has proved to be so faithful to God and useful to the apostle that Paul calls him not only "dear brother" but also "fellow worker" (v. 1).

In verses 4-7 the apostle expresses his "great joy and encouragement" because Philemon's love and faith include not just the apostle but also "all the saints," especially all members of the church of Colossae. Paul is pleased and

---

65. Enthusiasm for class-struggle terminology might count the slave owner Philemon among the "bourgeoisie" whose interests usually coincide with those of the "capitalists." But if Philemon had been very rich, owner of great enterprises such as mines, large arable lands, mass-production factories, or transport galleys, he would rather have lived in Hierapolis, Laodicea, or farther west or east in an industry and trade center such as Ephesus or Apamea, than in the insignificant town of Colossae. Also he would hardly have had the opportunity for the close brotherly relation to Onesimus for which Paul is pleading.

66. When Paul knows that Jews and proselytes are present and influential in a congregation he addresses, as when writing to the Romans, he includes into doctrinal and ethical contexts references to the OT. Often he fights traditional interpretations of the Bible and proposes his own. For the appeal contained in PHM, the prohibition of treating a slave "harshly" and praise of a brotherly conviviality could easily have been buttressed with references to Lev 25:43, 46, 53; Job 31:13-15; Sir 7:22-24; 33:29-31.

67. As apparently it was usual in the congregations, according to 1 Cor 1:16; 16:15; Acts 11:14; 16:15, 31-33; 18:8.

encouraged because by and in Philemon's love their "hearts are given rest."[68] The hospitality offered to the (whole?) congregation in Philemon's house is probably but one of the many a "good work" to which variant readings of verse 6 bear testimony. Epaphras had apparently conveyed to Paul only good news about Philemon, and if Onesimus had added other information, Paul did not mention it, or simply did not care for it. For Paul and the congregation, Philemon was a good man, personally respected and in good standing.

The many salubrious facts are, however, matched by yawning gaps in the available knowledge of Philemon's person.

2. *Unknown matters.* Neither the origin and education nor the professional occupation and age of Philemon are known. Vulgate, and in its wake Thomas Aquinas, understood Philem 9 to mean that the slave owner was of about the same age as the apostle; when he counted about sixty years, he was considered and considered himself "an old man" *(cum sis talis, ut Paulus senex)*. But usually, if in this verse *presbytēs* is to be translated "old man," the interpreters (correctly) assume that Paul speaks only of his own advanced age. Nobody can prove whether Philemon was ever married, and if so, to whom. Numerous ancient and modern expositors assume that Apphia was his wife and that, perhaps, Archippus was their son. Still, neither Apphia nor Archippus need have been so closely related to Philemon. The (spurious) postscript of PHM avers that Philemon and Apphia were co-owners of the slave Onesimus — but not even common ownership by a man and a woman always was based on marriage. According to the *Apostolic Constitutions* (7.46), but without confirmation by an earlier source, Philemon was bishop of Colossae. Calvin (CR, *Calvini Opp.* 52.411) is convinced that he was "from the order of pastors"; a "private person" would not be called "cooperator."

No evidence exists about when, where, and how often Philemon had met Paul, and how long they had known each other. The slave owner may have seen and heard Paul in one of the cities visited by Paul on the first, second, or third missionary journey recorded by Luke in Acts. E.g., Philemon may have been a resident of Ephesus, Troas, or Miletus before he settled in Colossae, or he may have traveled occasionally to a west-coast city from Colossae.

Also obscure is the relationship between Philemon and Onesimus. If Onesimus was a house-born slave, the possibility cannot be excluded that Philemon was his physical father.[69]

---

68. The religious and eschatological significance of "rest" in Heb 3–4 is competently discussed by O. Hofius, *Anapausis*, WUNT 11 (Tübingen: Mohr, 1970). In PHM, "rest" may include the same sense.

69. The surprising emphasis with which Paul states, according to a poorly attested-to variant reading of Philem 10, "I *(egō)* have begotten him," and the exclusive, spiritual parent-

It is not known how he treated the slave.[70] Good treatment, including hints or promises related to eventual future manumission, was not only in the slave's but also the master's best interest. Also PHM leaves open whether Onesimus was made to labor with due respect for his inherited or acquired skills.[71] It is not certain whether any, or how much, care was taken for his health and relative happiness; whether the customary *peculium* (pocket money) was paid or withheld; and whether promises related to emancipation were broken. There is no foolproof evidence that before or by Onesimus's flight Philemon really had suffered damage for which compensation could be made in cash.[72] Therefore it is far from self-evident that Onesimus alone was responsible for the break between himself and his owner.[73] Indeed, there is no reason to belittle or doubt Paul's outgoing praise of Philemon's value for all the saints. Paul probably is not polishing up a dirty apple when he describes the function and excellent standing of this slave owner in the Christian community (Philem 1-2, 6-7). And yet there always have been and are Christians resplendent in their relation to superiors and equals within their communities, while under their own roof and in dealing with family and house matters they were and are far from impeccable. Not all Christian slave owners have followed Aristotle's advice to let freedom wink and to treat ever faithful servants as potential friends. Probably very few ever heeded Seneca's counsel to let good slaves eat at the family table. There

---

hood of Paul indicated by all readings of this verse may suggest this possibility but do not suffice to demonstrate that Onesimus was a bastard.

70. He might have tolerated so much of the slave's conduct that Apphia — if she was his wife and/or co-owner of Onesimus — grew as jealous of him as was Sarah when, according to Gen 16, she forced her husband to send his natural child Ishmael into the desert. Or a female member of Philemon's family might have failed in her erotic approaches to Onesimus, forcing the slave out of the house — as, according to Gen 39:6-20, was experienced by Joseph in Potiphar's residence. Yet Philem 11 seems to demonstrate that Onesimus ran away after having been a "useless," or simply a bad, servant. Despite the economical loss incurred, in this case Philemon might have been pleased at the happy riddance of a man too young to be legally manumitted. In addition, the master might have gladly renounced setting the official or private machinery in motion for retrieving and punishing the fugitive.

71. Onesimus's uselessness (v. 11) may have been caused by the slave's character and conduct; but as well it might be traced back to the master who compelled the slave to do work for which he was not fit, or to spend his days doing things below his capabilities. Apparently before Onesimus came to stay with Paul, the slave's potential usefulness was neither discovered nor trained nor enjoyed.

72. Paul leaves it open whether the master really has a claim upon reimbursement and full satisfaction. He introduces his promissory comment by a condition: "*If* he (Onesimus) has done any wrong *(ei de ti ēdikēsen se)* or owes you anything. . . ." In n. 82 it will be shown by which means Onesimus might have wronged Philemon.

73. In Annotation 2, pp. 226-227, possible prejudices and their causes will be mentioned.

may not have been too many who did what, in harmony with Stoic teaching, biblical and apocryphal texts such as Job 31:13-15; Sir 7:20-21; 33:30-31 described and recommended as a wise person's behavior: treating slaves as brothers and even loving them. Because in Philem 16 Paul asks the master to receive Onesimus from now on as a "dear brother," the conclusion can hardly be avoided that earlier he had not treated him this way. The eventual wrong committed by Onesimus may have been minimal; much greater may have been the injustice inflicted on the slave by the master. To repeat an earlier observation: in Col 4:1 Paul calls on Christian masters to let their slaves have what is "right and proper" — obviously this was not done automatically.[74] First Peter 2:19-20 speaks of slaves "suffering unjustly" from the hands of hard masters, without an indication that only non-Christian slave owners could be guilty of wantonness and cruelty.

Actually, far too little is known of the everyday relationship between Philemon and Onesimus before the breakup to permit a verdict. Between kindness abounding and disgracing meanness there are many stages, and both occur in crude and paradoxical mixtures. Paul is not fighting windmills when in the *Haustafeln* he exhorts masters to abstain from threats and to remember that in God's judgment they are not to expect preferential treatment (Eph 6:8-9; Col 3:25–4:1). First Timothy 6:17-19 shows that precisely the "rich" among the Christians were in need of admonishment not to be haughty, but "to do good, be rich in good deeds, liberal and generous." Not only the slaves but also their masters are in need, every day anew, to put on the "new person," even Jesus Christ himself in whom and by whom all of them are "one."[75] Although Philemon received a personal letter, he could not dodge or avoid hearing Paul's voice also in Colossians when the latter epistle was read (more than only once!) in front of the whole congregation, including its exhortations directed at masters.

Unknown is, finally, the reaction of this slave owner to Paul's intervention. Certainly it is hard to imagine that the love and faith given to Philemon out of God's grace (Philem 4-7), Paul's appeal for voluntary obedience (vv. 8-9, 14, 21), the public reading of Colossians and PHM, and finally the apostle's an-

---

74. For the combination of "right and proper" *(to dikaion* and *isotēs),* see the Greek and Latin quotes collected by, e.g., J. B. Lightfoot, *Saint Paul's Epistles to the Colossians and to Philemon* (1875), p. 296, note on Col 4:1, and Lohse, *Colossians,* p. 162 n. 74. The meaning of *isotēs* will be discussed below in Annotation 7, pp. 231-232. It is noteworthy that Paul expects Christians to follow not only what the Bible, Jewish or synagogal or church traditions, or he himself has been and is spelling out. Rather he tells them in Phil 4:8, "Whatever is true, whatever is honorable, whatever is just, whatever is pure, whatever is lovely, whatever is gracious, if there is any excellence, if there is anything worthy of praise, think of these things."

75. Gal 3:28; Eph 4:17-24; Col 3:5-11. Cf. 2 Cor 5:17.

nounced visit would fail to make Philemon comply. However, while Pliny the Younger's twenty-fourth letter reveals that the appeal made in the twenty-first was successful, the New Testament conveys no information on Philemon's reaction and Onesimus's final status.[76]

C. Onesimus, a Fugitive Returning to His Master

1. *Known things.* Since his birth if he was house-born, since he was acquired by Philemon if not, he was a certain man bearing the name "Useful" or "Profitable." This name was given to the slave in order to express what his owner expected of him. While the omission of Philemon's and Paul's coworkers' patronyms may reveal intimate friendship, Onesimus shares with the other ancient slaves the shame that he is not called "son of ———." If ever he had a prehistory to his enslavement, all reminders of it were intentionally deleted and consigned to oblivion.[77] It is most probable that when Onesimus fled from his master's home, met with Paul extensively, and was sent back under the protection of Paul's letter, he was still a young man. In view of uncountable risks, it took courage and skill to prepare and carry out the flight from his master. A wife and children are never mentioned; most likely there were none. The flight without them would have been a mean and selfish act, and with them, practically impossible. Paul does not explicitly ask for Onesimus's manumission: one of the reasons may well be the *Lex Aelia Sentia* passed by Emperor Augustus in 4 c.e., which prohibited emancipation of slaves under thirty years of age. If the runaway Onesimus is the same man as that Onesimus who about forty years later was bishop in Ephesus, then his age at the time PHM was written would have been about twenty years, and he would have had the respectable age of about sixty when he became head of the congregation at the large harbor city.

That Onesimus had run away from his master is unanimously presupposed by practically all readers and scholarly expositors of PHM. Recent attempts to deny that Onesimus had broken law and order are not (yet?) persuasive.[78] Explicit is the information contained in Philem 10: the slave became a Christian under the direct influence of the captive Paul. Equally plain is the af-

---

76. Literary sources and open possibilities for Onesimus's location and occupation *after* his eventual manumission will be mentioned later, in n. 88.

77. A reverse judgment on the lack of information about a person's origin is passed in the Epistle to the Hebrews (7:1-3). The legendary king-priest Melchizedek of Salem was "fatherless, motherless, without genealogy," and the lack of a patronymic made him resemble Jesus Christ and qualified him to be a "priest forever." In the Gospels, however, Jesus is called the Son of David, of Joseph, of the carpenter — or of God.

78. See Annotation 3, pp. 227-228.

firmation of Col 4:7-9: the converted fugitive became a "faithful and dear brother" to Paul and other persons. He was sent to Colossae (Philem 12) and went, together with Tychicus (Col 4:7-9), voluntarily in order to deliver what Paul had written, and to convey information on the apostle's situation.

Opposite the limited number of ascertained facts stands a wide array of matters withdrawn from firm knowledge.

2. *Elements unknown.*[79] As to his birth, Onesimus may have been a Phrygian by origin, a member of that people whose name was proverbial among Greeks and Romans — all slaves from Phrygia were supposed to be lazy, impertinent, bad persons. If Onesimus was born free, then he had become enslaved under miserable conditions — as a foundling, as a captive of war, through the slave market, by a court sentence due to a crime or unpaid debts, or by means of self-sale. It is, however, equally possible that he was born on Philemon's precincts, either as a son of enslaved parents or, as already mentioned, as the result of an intimate dalliance of the master with a domestic slave girl or woman. In the last-mentioned case Onesimus would have had better chances, although no legal right, for decent treatment and eventual manumission.

Unless the name Onesimus was imposed on him when he was born in Philemon's house, he may have had another, perhaps barbaric and hardly pronounceable name before he was enslaved. It is not known whether "Useful, Profitable" liked the titular name by which he introduced himself to Paul any better than a black American slave liked to be called "boy."

Also in regard to Onesimus's *education, skills,* and *actual work* done in Philemon's house, trade, shop, stable, or fields, no more than guesses are possible. It is not certain but probable that Onesimus knew more than only one language and was able to converse with people of different social levels. He also may have learned to read and to write, that is, to do more than a janitor's, a handyman's, or a luggage-carrier's work. Because Paul hopes and wishes to have him help in the gospel's service (Philem 13), it is reasonable to assume that Onesimus was capable of fulfilling "usefully" the duties of a secretary, a travel manager, and a companion. Perhaps Onesimus had proved to Paul that, in addition to possessing skills, he also was willing and strong enough to endure stress, disappointment, want, and pain.

---

79. J. Knox himself, in his bold attempt to understand PHM in a new light, speaks of "any number of questions to which the letter gives no answers" and of "the meagre facts we have" (p. 15; cf. 26). Fifty years after Knox, J.-F. Collange (*L'épitre de Saint Paul à Philemon* [Geneva: Labor et Fide, 1987], p. 16) provides a sharp warning. "Les choses ne sont pas aussi nettes . . aussi simple" as to provide glib answers for a problem that may have been created by asking the wrong questions. A. Suhl (*Der Brief an Philemon*, e.g., p. 39) confesses to be bewildered by the information, arguments, and advice presented in Paul's letter. Cf. J. F. Spiegel, *Ich will Freiheit. Der Weg des Sklaven Onesimos* (Wuppertal: Oncken, 1992).

It is commonly assumed that Onesimus's *character* and *qualities* had changed from bad to good and from base to elevated. The reason, means, and dates of that transformation or new creation are supposedly well known, as are the process and/or hour of his conversion to Christ under Paul's fatherly guidance. The drama has been given the shape of a melodrama. Having Paul for a spiritual father and having been (re)born in the dismal circumstances of a prison (Philem 10), this slave has been depicted as a model of a "new man." Indeed, total transformation and new creation are taught and promised by Paul and in First Peter to Gentiles converted and baptized in the name of Christ. Also they are reminded to put off the old and put on the new person. No longer are they to be ruled by the devil and by death, by foolishness and obstinacy, by debauchery, filth, and all kinds of immoral thoughts and actions. For already now they are resurrected from sin and death in order to lead a new life.[80] As other Pauline letters, so also PHM gives testimony to a total reversal and renewal of the inner and outer, personal and social life of a person who has been grasped by Christ.[81]

Obvious in PHM are the earlier-listed contrasts between former uselessness and newly gained usefulness (Philem 11), of temporary separation from the master and return to him forever (v. 15, cf. 12), of a mere slave and a beloved brother (v. 16), of the injustice and wrong (possibly) done in the past and the liberal compensation for damages that is now offered (vv. 18-19).

And yet, as little as Paul had cared for what the honorable leaders of the Jerusalem church "once had been" (Gal 2:6), so little does he care for revealing either the past of Onesimus or the causes and events that made the slave run away. For the apostle it is enough that Philemon's slave is now a "faithful and beloved brother" (Col 4:9; cf. Philem 16), who is returning to his place with a blank check in hand. All-too-curious students of PHM shatter at Paul's reticence to inform about Onesimus's earlier character and life, his conversion, and his present and future usefulness. Philemon, the apostle, and other persons near them will have known more facts than are actually spelled out. Must later readers and listeners of this epistle fill in the gaps by fanciful, if not fantastic, guess work? Good intentions notwithstanding, no more than novelistic fiction

---

80. Eph 2:1-10; 4:13-31, esp. 17-19; Col 2:11-14; 3:1-11. In corresponding texts, such as Gal 6:15; Rom 6:1-23; 2 Cor 5:17; Eph 2:14-18; Titus 3:1-7; John 3:1-8, new creation and rebirth through the Holy Spirit are gifts of God to Jews as well as to Gentiles. The significance of the term "inner person" *(esō anthrōpos)*, used in Rom 7:22; 2 Cor 4:16, cannot be discussed at this place.

81. There are NT texts such as John 3:3-8; Titus 3:5 that speak of the Holy Spirit as the means of new birth. According to the OT, the judges, kings, and prophets of Israel were equipped by the Spirit of the Lord to fulfill their ministries. E.g., Saul was promised after his anointing that the Spirit of the Lord would turn him "into another man" (1 Sam 10:6).

is produced when Onesimus is portrayed first as a hard-boiled rogue and perfect scoundrel, then as an edifying example of personal conversion and moral rearmament.[82] Before finding Paul and becoming his spiritual child, at his own risk Onesimus by his flight had broken contemporary political and social law and disturbed the economic order. Still, no reason exists to assume that he considered his escape from Philemon a crime against heaven or before his owner. Neither does PHM contain any indication that in Paul's opinion Onesimus's flight was a sin against God or a neighbor. Unlike Pliny the Younger, the apostle does not write of a moving confession of misdeed, of heartbreaking repentance, of serious vows made by the fugitive that ought to be met by pardon and forgiveness from the patron. Attempts made by Christian expositors to demonstrate that individual recognition of sin, rebirth, and virtuous behavior alone can dissolve the injustice of slavery, oppression, and exploitation are not supported by the text and substance of PHM.

Black-and-white paintings of the old and the new Onesimus certainly disregard that, according to Paul's preaching and teaching in 2 Cor 4:16; Col 3:5-13; Eph 4:13-31, the investiture with the cloth of a "new person" is not over and finished when sin is followed by awareness of guilt, repentance by forgiveness, confession by baptism. "Newness of life" is a way on which to "walk" (Rom 6:4); in order to "bear fruit" the saints have to grow as much as the gospel is fruitful and grows in them (Col 1:6, 10). The Christ garment donned in baptism makes necessary a struggle forward in daily ethical decisions and under much suffering, and the investiture will be perfect no earlier than the day when the earthly tent of present human existence will be clothed over by the eternal abode prepared by God.[83] In all his epistles Paul implicitly or explicitly exhorts his beloved spiritual brothers, sisters, and children to live up to their (high) calling. While it can be considered certain that Onesimus still had to grow, it is unknown how far he was on the lifelong way from hearing to believing the gos-

---

82. Usually onlookers of pictures of heaven and hell, or of the Two Ways, find the conduct and fate of the wicked and lost much more interesting than the illustrations of the blessed state of the virtuous. So also Onesimus's former wickedness has drawn more attention than his later virtue and bliss. Without any evidence, the slave has been depicted as a typical "Phrygian," a man who in the past had been lazy, dumb, slanderous, wicked, a thief who embezzled funds, hurt his master's business, or cheated others — so much so that Philemon became liable for damages. E.g., Lightfoot, pp. 377-378 and 409, offers an almost ridiculous catalogue of Onesimus's faults. He is convinced that in the conditional clause in v. 18 ("If he has done wrong . . .") "the case is stated hypothetically but the words doubtlessly describe the actual offense of Onesimus."

83. For details of this threefold teaching on the "old" and the "new man," see Comment V.A-C on Eph 4:22-24 in AB 34A, pp. 536-544, and the bibliography, p. 824. In PHM (v. 6) the formula *eis Christon* (toward Christ) signals the eschatological, as yet unattained dimension of obedience to all that is "good."

pel, from spiritual babyhood to maturity — a path leading through uncounted ups and downs, not sparing the traveler disappointing relapses and perhaps perplexing jumps forward.

Additional open problems exist in regard to the turning points in Onesimus's life.

Why did the slave leave his master?[84] If Onesimus was a perfectly clever rascal, his flight might not have been the result of a spontaneous decision but of extensive preparation. Still, as earlier stated, the responsibility for the slave's flight might also have been Philemon's. In that case Onesimus may have acted out of sudden and sheer despair. Finally, mutual disappointment, hatred and contempt between master and slave may have been so intense that, just as among estranged married couples, coexistence under one roof was no longer humanly bearable.

How did Onesimus fare during his flight? Nobody knows the troubles he had seen before he met Paul. It is unknown whether the slave escaped alone or as member of a group; whether he kept to himself or temporarily joined a (robber?) gang; whether he finally met Paul in Ephesus, Caesarea, Rome, or another city. Even if at times he may have disappeared in the crowds of city slums, it is possible that for weeks or months or years he had experienced loneliness, hunger, cold, panic, and/or despair — rather than solidarity and help from fellow fugitives, other social outcasts, or some Christians he had met by chance. Utter want may have driven Onesimus to regret his flight and inspired in him the idea that he might or should return to his master. It is possible that when Paul first saw him, Onesimus was in rags, sick with disfiguring diseases, and/or near starvation. No doubt, such possibilities make good material for psychological or historical novels that evoke, just as ancient tragedies, fear and love. Not even academic students of PHM can abstain from mixing vestigial elements of compassion with Onesimus, under drab and dry literary and historical comments. Yet, unlike Pliny the Younger in his plea to Sabinianus, Paul does not intend to stir up emotions. Also he does not depict Onesimus as a legendary and tragic Robin Hood or Billy Budd. Historical fiction may reveal and communicate more than only grains of truth related to a given period and its protagonists; its details may reveal more than a mere statistical historiography could ever do. Still, it cannot take the place of historical interpretation of a given text.

How did Onesimus find the apostle?[85] The fugitive may have met Paul by

---

84. The questionable answers given by S. C. Winter and P. Lampe are discussed in Annotation 3, pp. 227-228. D. Dormeyer, "Flucht, Bekehrung und Rückkehr des Sklaven Onesimus. Interaktionale Auslegung des Philemonbriefes," *Der Evangelische Erzieher* 35 (1983): 214-229, discusses psychological and pedagogical aspects of Onesimus's case.

85. Some answers to this question are composed by J. Reid, "The Message of the Epistles: Philemon," *ExpT* 45 (1933/34): 164-168.

sheer coincidence — and was, under some suspicion, temporarily incarcerated in the same cell Paul had been thrown into before or after Onesimus joined him. But it is as well possible that the slave had met Paul when the apostle was still free, and that he heard him speaking in some town of Asia Minor where also Philemon was meeting the apostle. Or, through Epaphras or another Christian, or by mere hearsay, he may have had some knowledge of Paul and his message. Perhaps drops or sparks of the apostle's message of freedom and unity in Christ, as expressed in, e.g., Gal 3:28; 5:1, 13; Col 3:11, had come to his attention. But it is most uncertain whether he ever had heard, before he met Paul, of the servanthood of Jesus Christ (cf. Phil 2:6-11) and of the apostle's urgent counsel that slaves serve their masters voluntarily, wholeheartedly, in all things (cf. Col 3:22-23; Eph 6:5-7). For several reasons, on one leg of his flight Onesimus may have inquired about Paul and asked where he might find him. This inquiry might have been made on the slave's own initiative or by following the advice of chance acquaintances.

Perhaps he expected from the apostle support in his yearning for liberty, equality, and dignity — not only comforting words but also some action. Yet it cannot be excluded that originally he hoped for no more than a material gift of charity. Because he was not yet a Christian before he met Paul, he also may have considered the cell or the rented room in which Paul lived an asylum temple comparable to the Apollo temple at Delphi. Also he might have assumed that the *lares* and *penates* (house deities) of Paul's place would protect him from ill fate, or that Paul's person was as good as, or better than, an emperor statue to which he might cling for protection from prosecutors.

The idea that Onesimus should return to his master may have been the fugitive's own, unless it was suggested to him by comrades-in-misery before Paul took it up. The same is true of the decision to return to Colossae with a recommendation letter in hand, written by a friend of his owner.

But it is also possible that, without any specific expectation, Onesimus looked for Paul just because he had heard that Paul was a lawyer or a man experienced in sufferings and troubles of all kinds, or simply a trustworthy and compassionate fellow. In the process of tracing Paul's current whereabouts, Onesimus may — incidentally or intentionally — have been helped by local Christians. Yet it is questionable whether they would have helped a non-Christian fugitive and considered Paul's place an easily accessible station on an underground railroad. If only it were known which among these many alternatives made Paul write the way he did: each one of them throws a different light on the substance of his letter and entails more than only various shades of interpretation.

What happened during the meetings between Paul and Onesimus? What Onesimus told Paul about the reason(s) and course of his flight, and whether

Epaphras, the founder of the congregation at Colossae, confirmed details concerning the house of Philemon, is not known. Perhaps Onesimus made excuses and accusations, showed anger or also contrition, sweated or trembled or wept while he spoke. Perhaps he was pleading guilty, but also expressed his wishes and hopes. But we don't know how often he saw Paul, and Paul's letter fails to deliver details of the exchanges between himself and the slave, even of variant scenes during their encounters, whether they were highlights or crises. Paul certainly spoke to Onesimus about Jesus Christ, and the slave obviously had reason to believe and trust Paul. Still, no evidence exists regarding the progress of the mysterious operation of the Holy Spirit of which the NT elsewhere speaks when it tells that preaching is followed by faith, and that confession and conversion are confirmed by baptism and joining a congregation, especially at its eucharistic meal. Psychological and pedagogical curiosity is left unsatisfied. No imitable patterns are provided for how to proceed in person-to-person mission work and counseling in order to benefit people in need of love and help.

Possible changes in Onesimus's character and conduct have already been mentioned. The designation of Onesimus as a "faithful, beloved (or: dear)" brother and useful person in Col 4:9 and Philem 11 makes it certain that Paul and Onesimus were frequently and extensively together and that Onesimus had moved far toward deserving such praises. It is not known, however, by which sort of work for Paul or for others the fugitive became worthy of the apostle's recommendation. He may have proved useful by physical work such as cleaning and washing, shopping and cooking; by skilled assistance as a scribe and as a communicator with outside persons; or by combining these and other activities. The young man Onesimus may have brought along, gained, or increased in the capability to fill such functions while he was near Paul. When, in the presence of the apostle and/or in the company of fellow workers of Paul, the past, present, and future of Onesimus were discussed, nobody can know how hesitant, taciturn, inventive, or active Onesimus was. He might himself have been the first to suggest that returning to his master would be the best course to take. Perhaps Paul himself was spiritually enriched and comforted by what the slave thought, said, and did.[86] Unknown is whether there was always a consensus;

---

86. A comparison between two groups of verses — cf. Philem 10-12, 15, 16 with Philem 11, 13, 18; Col 4:9 — leads to this conclusion. In the *Haustafeln* of Ephesians and Colossians, slaves are treated as thinking, feeling, and active subjects who make their own decisions and bear no less than the master's responsibility for a good mutual relationship. In the exhortations to slaves found in 1 Tim 6:1-2; Titus 2:9-10; 1 Pet 2:18-25, only the slaves are addressed; so again they are treated as responsible persons; they are expected to be active, however low and weak their position, not just to tolerate their fate. Especially according to Titus 2:10, they can prevent the doctrine (namely, the gospel of Jesus Christ) from becoming a curse word and being put to shame, and shall "adorn the doctrine of our Savior God in ev-

perhaps only after protracted deliberation did all parties agree on the slave's return to Colossae. The expression "I sent him back" (*anepempsa*, in Philem 12) certainly does not indicate that Onesimus was sent back in chains or handcuffed to Tychicus. Rather he will have started homeward voluntarily, whether or not he carried Paul's letter to Philemon in his own hand or pocket. Though Paul made him return, the slave probably felt treated as a free agent. He would have misunderstood the apostle's intention, method, and teaching if he had assumed that he was handled like a piece of mail gone astray that can or must be returned to the sender.[87]

How were Onesimus and the letter received and what became of the slave? Although literary evidence is missing, there are several reasons for assuming that Onesimus did not again take to his heels or die during his return trip to Colossae, and that after returning he lived.

Certainly Calixt I, bishop of Rome between 212 and 222, who was contested by the antipope Hippolytus because of his suspect Christology and all-too-lax penitential practice, had made his way from slave pen, through activities as a money changer, to the highest ecclesiastical position. The Apostolic Canons, as quoted by H. B. Swete in his edition of Theodore of Mopsuestia's *Commentaries on the Pauline Epistles* (p. 264 n. 10), prescribe that a slave be elected as bishop only with the consent of his master — or else *anatropē* (capsizing, upturning) will occur. "Our Onesimus" is mentioned as an example of such a consent by the master that led to the manumission of slaves found worthy of election, and of their being "sent out from their homes" for their new duties. But it is not certain whether the biblical Onesimus is meant. A letter of

---

ery regard." Thus in their own way they will be missionaries defending and recommending the faith they and the congregation confess. Following 1 Pet 2:15-16, together with all Christians they shall "by doing right put to silence the ignorance of foolish persons" and "live as servants of God." These commands include the Christians' relation to human institutions such as the state.

87. Inasmuch as Paul's written advice is directed to the master exclusively, it corresponds to Plato's, Aristotle's, the Stoics' approach to slave problems. Almost without exception they give advice to the king, the husband, the father, the slave owner: they should behave wisely, virtuously, justly, benevolently toward those ruled by them. But just as cattle are the property of and completely dependent on their owner, so women, children, and slaves are, in relation to those who own them, no more than the body is to the soul. The body with its passions has to be kept under the soul's control (see esp. Aristotle, *Pol.* 1.1252a-1260b, and other texts quoted above, in "Social Background," sec. VI, pp. 33-41). While Aristotle admits that "it seems absurd to say that they (those in dependent positions) have no virtue," he also states that "it is manifest that the masters ought to be the source of such excellence" (*Pol.* 1.1259a, 1260a). On the other hand, Paul's as well as Pliny the Younger's appeal in favor of a fugitive recognize changes having taken place in those who have escaped from their owners. These changes are to be followed by the hoped-for insight and the open arms with which the escapees are to be received.

Gregory of Nazianzus (MPG, 37.149ff.) admonishes a lady to manumit a slave who against his will had been elected and consecrated bishop. Finally, a tomb erected by a freed slave to his master Marcus Sebastius Philemon that has been found by archaeologists, may have been paid for by the biblical Onesimus (J. Massingberde-Ford, *Revelation*, p. 420).

The literary, historical, and archaeological evidence is so scanty that a legal court never would, and biblical interpreters hardly should, consider the case closed. It is unlikely that Onesimus was manumitted immediately after Paul's letter arrived: he was probably still too young to be legally emancipated. As stated, for this reason Paul could not even ask for his freedom. If Onesimus was ever sent back to Paul on a lend-and-lease or gratis-forever basis, he yet may never have reached the apostle and worked in his company for months or years.[88] At any rate, even in the probable case that Philemon fulfilled Paul's secret wish, it is uncertain whether Paul could in the expected way ever "profit" from the slave owner's magnanimity and generosity (Philem 20-21). According to Jerome's and Theodoret's commentaries on PHM, Onesimus died as a martyr in Rome. Erasmus is reticent in mentioning this information.

The result of this introduction of the protagonists in the Philemon/ Onesimus/Paul drama looks meager. The abundance of things unknown dwarfs the fairly certain information. The more care that is invested in exegetical procedure, the more Socrates, Nicholas of Cusa, and other seekers for truth are confirmed when they admit that "we know that we don't know" and are satisfied with a *docta ignorantia* (scholarly ignorance). Lacking vital background information, a literary, historical, and theological exegesis of PHM is bound to be tentative, free from the claim to bring or have matters under control.

When Paul passionately, subtly, and humorously advised Philemon how to receive and treat his slave, he certainly did not intend to solve the problems of the institution of slavery in general. Neither a dictate to all employers, nor church or state legislation pertaining to slavery, nor a timeless philosophy of the master/slave relationship can be derived from the case study PHM offers.

---

88. If PHM was written from Caesarea, Onesimus might have sought Paul in this city — but he might have arrived too late, when Paul had already been transferred to Rome. Presupposing that PHM stems from Rome, Onesimus might again have arrived too late because Paul had (between his assumed two captivities) already left the town for a journey either to Spain or back to eastern regions as suggested by the Pastoral Epistles. The fact that the letters to Timothy and Titus never mention Onesimus may indicate, though they do not conclusively demonstrate, that Philemon's slave never met Paul again. Finally, if all sections of the Pastoral Epistles should be spurious, and if Paul was never released from his (first) captivity but was executed not too long after dispatching PHM, Onesimus could never have seen Paul again.

And yet, other texts of the NT provide more information on Paul's stance. There are contexts that must not be bypassed if ever the unique character of PHM is to be appreciated.

VII. PARALLELS AND DIVERGENCIES IN PAULINE LITERATURE

Similar or the same issues pertaining to the master/slave relationship as are treated in their own way in PHM are also taken up in *Haustafeln* such as that found in a rather complete form in, e.g., Col 3:18–4:1 and in more fragmentary shape in 1 Tim 6:1-2. The theme recurs in formulae of confession that praise the unity of all humankind in Christ (see, e.g., Gal 3:28), and in an excursus made by Paul on the divine calling of slaves (1 Cor 7:17-24). In addition, pertinent to the topic of PHM are also a host of additional texts that speak of the following:

a. Jesus Christ, the servant of God;
b. Paul and other Christians, also non-Christian state officials who are servants of Jesus Christ or of God;
c. "new persons" created in Christ out of formerly separated hostile individuals and groups;
d. the mutual coherence, dependence, and responsibility of weak and strong members of Christ's body, the church;
e. love as the key and basis, center and sum total of the commandments and the spiritual gifts;
f. humility fitting all Christians whatever their status in church and society;
g. the brotherhood and sisterhood of God's children, created and protected by the firstborn, Jesus Christ.[89]

Whenever in the NT one of these or similar topics are treated or alluded to, either complete harmony with the substance of Paul's shortest letter, PHM, can be observed, or slightly different accentuations, or tensions and perhaps

---

89. Passages typical of the topics mentioned are: Christology: Gal 2:17; Phil 2:5-11; Rom 15:8; Christian and non-Christian servants *(douloi* or *diakonoi)* of God: Rom 1:1; 13:4; Gal 1:10; Phil 1:1; Col 1:7, 23, 25; 4:7, cf. 17; new creation: 2 Cor 5:17; Eph 2:15; members of Christ's body: 1 Cor 12; Rom 12:4-5; Eph 1–5; love of the neighbor: 1 Cor 13; Gal 5:6; Col 3:14; Eph 5:1-2; 1 Pet 4:8; James 2:8-10; 1 John 4:21; humility: Rom 12:10; Eph 4:1-3; Phil 2:3-4; children of God under the Firstborn: Rom 8:15, 29; 14:15; Gal 4:5-6; Eph 1:5; Col 1:18; 1 Cor 8:11.

even contradictions to other Pauline statements, resist the reconstruction of a seamless Pauline ethics. At this place, space permits an intensive comparison of PHM with no more than the *Haustafeln*, the unity formulae, and the description of the implication of God's call.

A. *Haustafeln*[90]

In the framework of the *Haustafeln* (HT in the following) in Eph 5–6 and Col 3–4, slaves and masters are admonished separately but in immediate succession. Regularly the same social setting is presupposed: the servants and their lords live close together in the frame of a house. In the ancient languages "house" often means more than merely the space covered by a roof. The term can include all persons and things under the direct care and control of one owner. The HT do not discuss the situation and obligation of capitalists owning thousands of slaves (e.g., absentee landlords) or the treatment and conduct of galley, mine, or latifundia slaves.

In *Did.* 4.10 and *Barn.* 12.7 the instruction appears to be limited to conditions under which both masters and slaves were Christians. As previously mentioned, a slave owner converted to faith in Jesus Christ could have all members of his household baptized with him. But the special mention made of such family baptisms may demonstrate that not always and everywhere would the whole "house" be included — just as it also proved impossible for some Jewish households under all circumstances to circumcise all non-Jewish slaves. The slave Onesimus became a Christian only *after* he had proven "useless" to his master and fled to Paul (Philem 10-11). Just as the Pauline marriage counseling concerns not only baptized couples but also mixed marriages (1 Cor 7:12-16), so the advice given to slaves and masters includes situations when only the slave or the master was a church member. In urban settings such as Corinth, the congregation included "not many wise after human standards, not many mighty, not many well-born" but a majority of socially weak, low and despised people, even of "have-nots" (1 Cor 1:26-29; 11:22, 30). Among them, slaves and other poor people who did not possess a house or the means to live in luxury would

---

90. Cf. the Glosses on Eph 6:1-9 in AB 34A, pp. 754-758; the literature mentioned on pp. 824-825 of the same work; and H. Blanke's Comment *"Haustafel"* on Col 3:18–4:1 in AB 34B, pp. 462-475. The term *Haustafel* is used here and in the following for convenience' sake — although archaeological evidence for stone, wood, metal, or papyrus tablets listing the duties of the several members of an ancient household has never been found.

In Annotation 4, pp. 228-230, the question will be briefly discussed whether *Haustafeln* in principle express a moralism and adaptation to secular bourgeois standards that contradict the radicalism of "eschatological" NT ethics.

certainly constitute the majority. It can be assumed that the composition of the Colossian and Ephesian churches was similar to that of Corinth.

The HT oblige Christian servants to obey their lords, irrespective of whether the latter are Christians. Equally, the HT are binding for Christian masters who own one or several Christian or non-Christian slaves. Among the "crooked" slave owners mentioned in 1 Pet 2:18, there may have been both believing and nonbelieving lords; they are to be served with the same respect and loyalty. First Timothy 6:2 indicates that probably only in exceptional cases were Christian slaves in the service of Christian masters. Even then, the slaves may be tempted but are not entitled to despise their owners: they are obliged to "serve all the more."

While in the HT masters are told to treat equally, with equity and justice, all their slaves,[91] PHM discusses a very special attitude toward one believing slave.

In Ephesians and Colossians, the direct appeal to slaves precedes in order and exceeds in length the address to the masters. In both letters the slave exhortation concludes with a reference to the impartial judgment of God — to which all persons are and will be exposed (Col 3:24-25; Eph 6:8-9). Actually this reminder holds together the admonitions directed to the slaves first and then to the masters. When all HT verses speaking of the Last Judgment are understood to pertain to both servants and lords, the imbalance between the two addresses no longer exists, for then the masters are as extensively and intensively admonished as the slaves.

The HT of Ephesians contains at its beginning (5:21) a unique element. The headline of the words concerning the three social partnerships, husband/ wives, parents/children, masters/slaves, consists of an urgent call for *mutual* service: "Because you fear Christ, subordinate yourselves to one another."

The slave/master admonitions of 1 Tim 6:1-2; Titus 2:9-10; 1 Pet 2:18-20 differ from those of Eph 6:5-9 and Col 3:22–4:1 inasmuch as only slaves are addressed. On the other hand, PHM is directed exclusively to a slave owner and his closest friends (and relatives?). Still, among the members of the house church there will also have been slaves who, upon hearing Paul's letters read before them, would rejoice in Paul's intervention for Onesimus and would join the free people present in exerting some moral pressure upon Philemon.

What, then, is the message of the HT, and how does it compare with the contents of PHM?

---

91. Equal treatment of all slaves corresponds to OT legislation regarding Sabbath rest, circumcision, compensation for crippled slaves, ill-used maids, and provisions for released persons. Still, the NT antiquates the sharp distinction made in Lev 25 and in the Talmud between Hebrew and Canaanite slaves.

1. CONCERNING SLAVES

In the HT, Christian slaves are told to *obey* their masters with fear and trembling and to serve and honor them from the depth of their hearts.[92] The letter addressed to Philemon looks like either a precedent to the general directives given in the HT or their practical application: Paul "sends back" a fugitive slave to his place under the hand of his master!

In Col 3:22 and Titus 2:9 the range of the expected obedience appears to be unlimited, pertaining to "all things," just as in Eph 5:24 married women are told to subordinate themselves to their husbands "in everything," or as in Eph 6:1 and Rom 13:1-7 the obedience of children to their parents and the subordination of all Christians to the political authorities appear to be unconditional and bare of any restrictions. Does this voluntary submission include the slave's, the wife's, the child's, the political subject's duty to yield to, e.g., enticement or compulsion to participate in idolatry, in criminal methods and wicked acts? Are the slaves forbidden self-defense when they are exposed to sexual assaults by the master and to seduction by the mistress or their offspring? Indeed, the OT stories of Joseph and Daniel give examples of such situations; but they also show how a wise person meets them. These stories as well as all the epistolary admonitions, including the HT, belong in the Wisdom Literature that teaches that fear of God, not of human beings, is the beginning of all wisdom. "Watch carefully how you conduct yourselves — not as fools, but as wise persons" (Eph 5:15). High above the "fear and trembling" before the master stands the fear and trembling in face of God's grace (Eph 6:5; Phil 2:12; cf. Heb 13:6). The HT, as much as 1 Cor 7:17-24, encourage wives, children, slaves, all Christians to live decently and true to their calling by God. No excuse is given to them to plead helpless, innocent, and free of responsibility. Though their social position is weak or low, they are not delivered to the whims and wantonness of those stronger than they are.[93]

How intimidating fear based on evil experiences and nasty threats, how difficult obedience, and how strong the temptation to commit acts of sabotage or open rebellion may have been for a slave — this is frankly admitted in 1 Tim 6:1-2: here the term "yoke" (of slavery) is used. Obviously some slaves despised and disobeyed their Christian masters. As mentioned before, 1 Pet 2:18-19 speaks of owners who were less than kind, gentle, sensible. Without cause they

92. Eph 6:5-18; Col 3:22-25; 1 Tim 6:1-2; Titus 2:9, 10; 1 Pet 2:18-25; cf. *Did.* 4.11.

93. Total and unrestricted submission to earthly authorities is not expected of the Christians of the apostolic period, as, e.g., the texts mentioned in Annotation 5, p. 230, show. Cf. also n. 99.

inflicted sufferings upon their slaves, and were — probably not only in the eyes of their slaves — "crooked" *(sklēroi)* personalities.

And yet the HT call for obedience and service. Even when Paul asks Philemon to receive the returned fugitive as a beloved brother and useful partner, the apostle does not exclude that Onesimus remains a slave. By all means a slave is to "do good" (Eph 6:8; 1 Pet 2:20) and to prove "useful" (cf. Philem 10). "All the more" is his or her place to fulfill a social function, if and when he or she and the master or mistress are Christians (1 Tim 6:2). However, would not Onesimus eventually be manumitted if Philemon fulfilled Paul's secret wish and sent the slave back to the apostle? Even then Onesimus would experience no more than a substitution of a new master for the old: he would have to "serve" as an aide to the work done by the apostle (Philem 13).

In Col 3:23 Paul tells slaves to "*work.*" The surrounding verses reveal that he means hard, good, faithful work. Once, in 1 Cor 9:6, Paul ironically mentions his own and Barnabas's right not to work, but in fact he renounces that right and lives as a hard worker, laboring under heavier loads than the other apostles, confident that his labor will not be in vain (1 Cor 15:10, 58). The slaves are not the only ones he drives to work. Especially in the letters to the Thessalonians, all Christians are commanded to work hard to fulfill the will of God by doing what is good for all people, and what will please the Lord.[94] Just as wives are exhorted in 1 Pet 3:1-2 by their conduct rather than by words to "win" their husbands for faith in Christ, so also slaves can and shall by their attitude and work demonstrate that their faith is authentic. More than only a testimony within the domestic walls is in mind. A public apologetic and missionary function of the slaves' subordination and honest work is explicitly mentioned in 1 Tim 6:2 and Titus 2:10. Their good conduct has the purpose "that the doctrine (of Christ, i.e., of the gospel) not be defamed" and that "in every thing they may adorn the doctrine of God our Savior." Thus slaves are called to prevent blasphemy and to add luster to the message and ethics proclaimed in Christ's name. They share fully in the calling of all Christians, "to

---

94. 1 Thess 2:9; 4:11; 2 Thess 3:10; Rom 2:10; 12:2; 15:7; Gal 6:9-10; Phil 2:16; Eph 4:28. Petersen, pp. 103-124, emphasizes the value attributed by Paul to his own and his fellow workers' hard labor. Not even Pauline texts, such as Rom 4:4-6, that seem to depreciate works in favor of sheer grace contradict Paul's positive attitude to work and good works. Exclusively "works of law" (esp. circumcision, Sabbath keeping, heeding the dietary legislation) he declares useless for justification by God. "Works of law" are something else than honest human activity in the service of God in following the holy, righteous, good, and spiritual law God has given (Rom 7:12, 14, 22; cf. 3:31). By the (un-Jewish!) term "works of law" Paul understands a legalistic kind of obedience that presumes that a selection of some few commandments and acts of service can substitute for fulfilling the whole law — by love; see esp. Rom 3:27-28; 4:9-12; 13:8-10; Gal 2:16; 3:10-12; 5:14. This sort of slavish obedience is the opposite of the freedom of God's children (Gal 3:23–4:7).

work out their salvation with fear and trembling; for God is at work in you, both to will and to work for his good pleasure," and to "be blameless and innocent, children of God without blemish in the midst of a crooked and perverse generation." Thus they "shine as lights in the world" (Phil 2:12-15).

Philemon's love and faithfulness, manifested in his service to God and for the benefit of the Colossian church (Philem 4-7), are by no means shown to a monopoly of socially and legally free persons. Whether Onesimus's future is to stay with his earthly master or to return to Paul for mission work on a large scale — he will be "useful" and he will be loved, both as a person and a church member (Philem 10, 13, 16).

The idea of *giving orders* to a dependent person — not any orders but only *such* that are "proper" — occurs in Philem 8, and the mention of obedience in verse 21 fits it well. But in this letter commandments and their implementation have a most particular place: Paul renounces his right to give orders and expects an entirely voluntary decision from Philemon (vv. 8-9 and 14), even while he trusts Philemon's "obedience" (v. 21). Unlike the HT, here "obedience" is clearly expected of the master rather than the slave. Just as according to the HT the slaves' obedience has to be spontaneous and voluntary,[95] so also the master's has to come of his free will. Later, in the detailed discussion of verse 21, the paradox of a *voluntary obedience* will be more intensively considered. According to Paul, both masters and slaves have to decide freely and from day to day anew. As stated earlier, it is not known whether Paul softly or harshly compelled Onesimus to return to Colossae, or whether Onesimus himself had first suggested this act of extreme humiliation. At any rate, Onesimus will have started hopefully. Philemon, however, is pressed, if not extorted, by a long array of arguments to carry out Paul's appeal.

Among the passages addressed to slaves of human masters, 1 Pet 2:18-23 is the only one to speak explicitly of the slaves' *suffering* and *conscience*.[96] A distinction is made between well-deserved punishment for poor or negligent work and sufferings inflicted willfully or mischievously on good and faithful workers. Unjust suffering is to be endured in the "awareness of God" (RSV: "mindful of God"). The conscience makes the slave realize that it is "grace"[97] (of God) to be

---

95. They are to be faithful and to serve and work "not seeking to please human persons by putting on a show," but "wholeheartedly . . . from the bottom of their heart . . . with fervor" (Eph 6:5-7; Col 3:23), and "for conscience' sake" (1 Pet 2:19).

96. For some introductory remarks about the use of the term "conscience" in the NT, see Annotation 6, p. 230.

97. Or "pleasing (God)." The Greek word *charis* occurs twice in 1 Pet 2:19-20 and eight times in the rest of the epistle. In current versions of First Peter, for these two verses a variety of translations of *charis* are chosen that differ from the usual NT sense of this noun. KJV has "thankworthy," with "thank" offered as an alternative; RSV reads "approved" in v. 19 and "ap-

chosen to walk in Christ's footsteps, in following him who suffered for the slaves just as for all human beings — without having sinned (1 Pet 2:21-25). Therefore in his daily life and in manifold sufferings of which the master knows little or nothing, a slave can be a better model of a follower of Christ and witness to the Lord than his master. In writing to Philemon, Paul does not mention external and internal afflictions suffered by Onesimus — though the slave may have told Paul many a sad story. However, it is certain that if Onesimus should return to Paul and serve under him, he will have to bear his share in the apostle's professional sufferings, as they are mentioned, e.g., in Col 1:24. No slave, least of all a servant of Christ, can avoid tribulation.

In the hortatory address to slaves, both connections and contrasts are made between the slaves' *service to Christ the Lord (or to God) and their obligation to their earthly masters.*[98] The dialectic relationship is pointed out with various emphases in the different HT, but regularly a christological or theological argument is essential of the parenesis (exhortation).

Are the earthly lords declared to be transparent — so much so that the HT simply affirm that above, behind, or within the earthly masters stands the Lord Jesus Christ, so much so that work for them is service rendered to Christ? Indeed, according to Eph 5:21-22, the mutual subordination of Christians to one another is first exemplified by the subordination of wives to their husbands: it is a voluntary readiness for service "as to the Lord." Yet Paul is far from adorning a prevailing patriarchalism with a halo. For neither husbands nor parents nor slave owners are in any way placed on a level nearer to God and Christ

---

proval" in v. 20; JB uses "merited," and NEB "a fine thing," in both cases. Vg. sticks to *gratia,* and both the old and the revised Luther versions, together with ZB, follow the Latin tradition and translate "grace." Because in Pauline theology (Rom 3:24, 28; 4:4; Gal 2:16; etc.), just as in First Peter, grace stands opposite to merit and meritorious works, those versions are not convincing that give *charis* in 1 Pet 2:19-20 a meaning different from its significance in all other occurrences in First Peter (see 1:2, 10, 13; 3:7; 4:10; 5:5, 10, 12). The author of First Peter could easily have chosen another clear term for indicating merit, pleasure, or acceptability.

98. In the Greek of Eph 6:5 and Col 3:22, the term here translated "earthly" is *kata sarka,* lit. "according to the flesh." While it is obvious that for Paul the earthly lords' status is infinitely lower than that of the Lord in heaven, the formula "according to the flesh" does not necessarily have the bad connotation it possesses when in the OT, in Paul, and in the Fourth Gospel it is the opposite of "in" or "according to the (Holy) Spirit." For Paul tells the slaves to use their relation to earthly masters for working for and serving "the Lord and not human persons" (Col 3:23; Eph 6:7). They shall not only "seek to please" their masters on earth, but shall do the will of God as "servants of Jesus Christ" (Col 3:22-23; Eph 6:6) — a will that, according to the Lord's Prayer, is to be fulfilled on earth as much as it is in heaven. Whether Col 3:24b is to be understood as an indicative or imperative ("you are serving" or "do serve") is not certain. Either way this verse, together with Eph 6:6 ("do God's will as servants of Christ"), seems to come close to the affirmation: by and in serving your earthly masters, you slaves serve the Lord, not the flesh.

than women, children, or slaves. Also the mighty are not denoted as Christ's or God's primary or exclusive representatives on earth. Not even one of them is called God's image — the way Adam and Christ are honored with this title — nor are they called his messengers, the way Paul describes himself. No earlier than in *Did.* 4.11 and *Barn.* 19.7 a (Christian) earthly master is explicitly called a "type" (*typos,* image, or representative) of God. Obedience to the master has its source and standard in Christ's servanthood: in his subordination to God the Father (Phil 2:6-8; 1 Cor 15:28). Christ's innocent suffering is the way on which wives and slaves as much as all Christians can safely walk.[99]

The same standard and criterion prevails in PHM: the master/slave relationship is neither a closed circle nor an absolutely necessary and self-contained, not to speak of deified and timeless, system. Rather, again and again references are made to the one God and Lord on whom all earthly slaves and lords depend.[100] They are not permitted to live according to their own laws and to do their own thing, however it pleases them. Paul presupposes in Philem 3-8, 25 that when Philemon and Onesimus became Christians, were baptized and became members of a congregation, they acknowledged and confessed the divine Lordship over all lords and powers (Col 1:15-20; 1 Cor 8:5-6; Phil 2:10-11). Later, the specific christological traits of the HT and of PHM will be scrutinized more extensively.

99. In the HT the earthly bearers of authority and the heavenly Lord are far from treated as joint managers — as if husbands, parents, masters had the same claim and right as has Jesus Christ over the physical and spiritual life of women, slaves, children. Neither an automatic nor a miraculous conflation of heavenly and earthly authority is suggested. Also the HT do not speak of a sacramental presence of the Lord in, with, and under the several lords; neither do they promote a veneration as is sometimes shown for transubstantiated, transfunctionalized, or transsignified eucharistic elements. Even if it has to be admitted that the breviloquy "subordinate yourself . . . obey as to the Lord" (Col 3:23; Eph 5:22; 6:7) seems to permit a sacramentalistic interpretation, yet the more elaborate formulae "as is proper in the Lord" and "this is pleasing the Lord" (Col 3:18 and 20), and above all the descriptions of Christ's unique and inimitable rulership, love, and sacrifice (esp. in Phil 2:6-11; Eph 5:25-27; 1 Pet 2:21-25), prohibit a tacit deification or idolization of earthly lords. Neither husbands nor parents nor slave owners decide over the right attitude to be taken by wives, children, and slaves. The will and work of God, as incarnated solely in the Lord Jesus, stands above those wielding earthly power. Under no circumstances does Christ stand closer to the strong than to the weak.

100. God and Christ are the source of blessing, love, and faith, according to the framework of PHM (vv. 1-7 and 25). Within the body of the letter (vv. 8-20, explicitly in vv. 8, 9, 16, 20), Christ the Lord is mentioned: (lit.) "*in Christ* I am free to give you orders . . . as a prisoner (in the service) of Christ . . . a brother in the flesh and *in the Lord* . . . to make use of you *in the Lord.*" An implicit reference to God is made in v. 15: the passive, "he has been separated (from you) for an hour," is a so-called *passivum divinum:* it refers to God, who has intended the temporary separation of the slave from the master. Cf. v. 22; it is God alone who can make possible Paul's visit in Philemon's house.

The *eschatology* contained in the HT is as weighty as their Christology. In Ephesians and Colossians the Last Judgment and the punishment and reward it brings are essential motives for the slaves' and the masters' conduct. What the Lord in heaven will impose upon or grant the slaves is not dependent on the earthly masters' unfair or fair, minimal, occasional, or continual retribution for the work done by slaves. God's judgment will come upon slaves and masters equally and impartially. Slaves are not to expect preferential treatment on the ground of their utter dependence, poverty, and suffering. According to the HT, neither by nature nor because of their conversion are all those kept in bondage good and just persons — as little as all slave owners are naturally and incorrigibly bad and unjust. All slaves and all masters will be judged according to what they have done.[101] Far from being irrelevant or damaging for ethical thought and action, in the whole NT eschatology is the source, criterion, and scope of the proper conduct of Christians.[102] Briefly stated, "the same good which a person performs — whether slave or free — this he (and she) will receive from the Lord" (Eph 6:8). In the HT, there is neither an explicit denial nor an affirmation of the threat and promise (formulated in the Gospels and in 1 Thess 5:2; Rom 13:11-12; cf. Phil 4:4-6) saying that the Day of the Lord will come like a thief at night and only little time is left until the judgment will come. The brevity of the interim is most emphatically pointed out in Paul's marriage counseling (1 Cor 7:29-31; cf. 1 Pet 3:7; Eph 5:25-27), but is equally important for understanding the admonitions given to slaves and masters.[103]

---

101. Col 3:24–4:1; Eph 6:8-9. Paul describes *God's* judgment (Rom 14:10) according to the good and bad works, for instance in 1 Cor 3:12-15; Rom 2:5-11; Gal 6:7-10. Does then Paul endorse, without any qualms and essential changes, some prophetic, Deuteronomistic, pharisaical, and rabbinical notions of the Last Judgment? In 2 Cor 5:10 it is the judgment throne *of Christ* before which "each one will receive good or evil, according to what he (or she) has done in the body." According to Paul, the judgment of the "Lord" described in the NT takes place in God's as well as in Christ's court. The supposedly most Jewish book of the NT, Revelation, has its center in the chapters, 4–5, in which God gives all power over life and death into the hands of the "slaughtered Lamb" and yet speaks of the deeds of the saints that follow them (Rev 14:13). Equally in Paul's theology the christocentric justification by grace and faithfulness alone, without works of the (misinterpreted and misused) Law, is complemented by the judgment according to works. See AB 34 on Eph 2:10, esp. Comment VI, pp. 242-251, for an attempt to show that there is no real contradiction, in spite of apparent tensions.

102. As especially Amos Wilder has shown in several essays and books, in contradiction to an opinion of Reinhold Niebuhr. See, e.g., A. Wilder, "Kerygma, Eschatology and Social Ethics," in *The Background of the New Testament and Its Eschatology*, ed. W. D. Davies and D. Daube, FS C. H. Dodd (Cambridge: University Press, 1956), pp. 509-536.

103. In practically identical wording, *Did.* 4.11 and *Barn.* 19.7 remind the masters that slaves set their hope upon the same God.

The second coming of Christ, the parousia, is never explicitly mentioned in the HT and in PHM. In PHM there are no references to the Last Judgment and to eventual rewards or punishments. On the other hand, in Eph 4:13, i.e., sometime before the Ephesian HT begins in 5:21, the final glorious appearance of Christ is mentioned. Colossians 1:5, 23, 27 mention hope, and 3:4 spells out its substance: "When the Messiah appears, our life, then you, too, will appear with him in glory." Therefore Philemon and the other Christians in Colossae could not be ignorant of the eschatological scope of Paul's theology and counseling, including his plea for Onesimus. Still, the main theme of PHM is love, not eschatological hope — just as the central theme of Romans is faith. The traces of hope yet present in PHM pertain neither to judgment, afterlife, or eternity, but to the warm reception of Onesimus as a brother, and of Paul as a guest in Philemon's house (Philem 16-17, 22).

2. CONCERNING SLAVE OWNERS

In some of the HT, no special words are directed toward masters.[104] What in Colossians and Ephesians is said to masters hardly amounts to general principles blown into the air. Rather Paul gives directives made necessary by emotions, conflicts, and tensions within the patrons' heart, and in their dealings with the slaves in such cases as in Colossae by Onesimus's flight; in Corinth and Ephesus by women's emancipation attempts (see 1 Cor 11:2-16; 14:34-36; Eph 5:21-34; 1 Tim 2:11-12); in Rome by the temptation (of enthusiasts?) to withhold respect and taxes from state officials (cf. Rom 13:1-7; Matt 22:17-21; Titus 3:1; 1 Pet 2:13-17). In Col 4:1 the advice to the masters consists of very few words: aware of the common heavenly Lord of slaves and slave owners, the latter are "to grant their slaves all that is just and proper" *(to dikaion kai tēn isotēta)*. According to Eph 6:9, the patrons are to do the same good to their servants as the slaves do in their masters' service, that is, be industrious, honest, reliable; it is the same impartial Lord in heaven who is the protector and judge of all of them. While not all slave owners were oppressors of the poor, or were rich, living in luxury and belonging to the highest social strata, yet the warnings and recommendation extended to the rich in 1 Tim 6:17-19 — not to speak of their

---

104. The absence of directives for masters in First Timothy, Titus, and First Peter does not demonstrate a general tendency to consider slaves in greater need of firm advice than masters. For in *Did.* 4.10-11, after lords are first admonished extensively, then only follows a shorter appeal to slaves. The masters are warned against giving commands grounded on bitterness toward Christian male *and female* slaves and are reminded of the impartiality of God's calling and of the work of God's Spirit in both those who own slaves and those who are owned. *Barn.* 19.7 returns to the Colossian and Ephesian sequence: first slaves, then masters.

blunt condemnation in Luke 6:24-26; James 1:10-11; 2:5-6; 5:1-6 — may be added as a corollary to the HT directives addressed to the masters: "Charge them not to be haughty, nor to set their hope upon uncertain riches but on God who richly furnishes us with everything to enjoy. They are to do good, to be rich in good deeds, liberal and generous, thus laying up for themselves a good foundation for the future that they may take hold of the life which is life indeed." Although poor people such as the slaves will certainly benefit from a master's good works, in this text an appeal to the spiritual self-interest of rich Christians is made. The liberality and generosity of the rich are means to attain to the same superior gain that also lies in store for other Christians whose works please God.

In their moral appeals to masters, Plato, Aristotle, and Stoic philosophers are much more eloquent and specific than the HT. The potential of the immortal soul in both slaves and masters is acknowledged and emphasized in various ways. The existing social order, even the institution of slavery, is accepted, sometimes defended, sometimes adorned as an opportunity to display humanity, but rarely questioned. Equality by nature, love, friendship, solidarity in the quest for virtue — such ideas and ideals contribute to the comfort that philosophy had to offer (see "Social Background," sec. VI, pp. 33-41). It looks as if the admonition to the masters, as found in the HT, had nothing or very little to add to the philosophers' humanizing counsels. This opinion is, however, valid only when the frequent mention of Christ or the Lord, and the reminders of the Last Judgment in the HT, are counted as irrelevant.

Earlier it was stated that the note sent by Paul to the slave owner does not only concern the private relationship between Paul and Philemon, or between Philemon and his slave Onesimus. Rather the past, present, and future of the slave for whom the apostle intercedes are embedded in the existence and history of Paul himself, of Philemon, of the local congregation, of Paul's fellow workers in the worldwide mission, and above all, of the gospel itself. Paul is convinced that the love attested in the gospel and poured out by the Holy Spirit is capable of arching over differences based on social status and social structures. Only in PHM the words directed to a master are centered in the master's proven love and the call for even more love — to be demonstrated by voluntary and cordial brotherhood with the returned slave.

In order to praise and provoke this love, Paul approaches Philemon in a manner different from his general admonition of masters in the HT. At least five differences can be mentioned:

a. Paul renounces a right that he has as an imprisoned ambassador of Christ. He does not use his full power to give an order and then to compel Philemon to fulfill his secret wish to have the "useful" Onesimus work with the apostle, or his outspoken appeal to receive and treat the slave as a brother (vv.

8-11, 13, 14, 16). This renouncement is one of the logical bases of the request extended to Philemon to do likewise by forgoing his right to punish the returned slave.

b. In 1 Cor 7:21, but never in the HT, the idea occurs that a Christian slave's future full-time occupation and life may take place outside the present master's dominion. More specifically according to Philem 13, the deepest wish of the apostle is to have Onesimus at his side. On the other hand, in 1 Cor 7:20-24 Paul anticipates what the HT, too, aver: As an earthly master's slave, a person can be fully obedient to his or her divine calling. Under all circumstances a slave is enabled by God to enjoy the freedom to which Christ has liberated all Christians (cf. Gal 5:1, 13). But to Philemon Paul suggests his preference: Paul would wish (v. 13) that, of all things, the brotherly reception of the returned fugitive issue in Onesimus's full-time (professional) service to the gospel.

c. Unlike other contexts in which all Christians are called children of God, the HT do not mention the possibility or necessity that slave masters, by treating slaves decently, recognize their equal status and abandon all recourse to structural social privileges. Philemon, however, is reminded of being a child of Paul as much as Onesimus is the apostle's child (vv. 11 and 19b), and that the indebtedness to the spiritual progenitor includes, if need be, lifelong service. Paul does not suggest that Philemon leave his home and congregation to join Paul in his mission work. Yet when he shows ready to accept Onesimus's service as a substitute for the slave owner's duty to serve Paul (v. 13), the apostle reminds Philemon of the firm claim he has on the service of this man.

d. In the HT Paul's role regarding master/slave issues appears to be restricted to that of a teacher of more or less timeless ethics, though his advice may also have been applicable to very specific occasions. He teaches that human lords be served according to "God's will" and "in the fear of the Lord," as is "proper in the Lord" and "pleases the Lord" (Eph 5:21; 6:6; Col 3:18, 20, 22). In addressing Philemon, Paul assumes and fulfills a much fuller and deeper function, revealing an overarching personal involvement in both the master's and the slave's factual and concrete existence. In PHM he speaks explicitly of the exemplary life of Philemon within the frame of the congregation, of his own apostolic suffering in captivity, of a fatherhood that makes children and brothers of master *and* slave, and of the apostolic wish, need, if not also right to be served in his mission work by both or either of them.[105]

---

105. According to Petersen, esp. p. 260, the apostle's existential involvement in a burning social issue of his time is the key to understanding all Pauline letters. This thesis is a necessary antidote against a narrow literary and comparative-religion interpretation of the apostle. In none of his letters does Paul miss an opportunity to apply a given topic to himself and to show what it meant for his own life.

e. In the HT Paul appears to support and confirm the masters' traditional rights and to let the slaves unilaterally bear the burden of the status quo. To those among Paul's interpreters who consider the HT genuine, Paul's stance may look utterly conservative. His intention seems to be to sanctify and glorify the keeping of house slaves with religion — if only the masters do what the most humane among contemporary counsels advise them to do. PHM, in turn, appears to have little if anything different to offer: the apostle sends the escaped slave back to his owner. However, the harmony between HT and PHM is not complete, for PHM offers glimpses at a possible social change. When the addressed man complies with Paul's request, things will never be completely the same again. This holds true whether Onesimus remains under the hands of his master in Colossae or is permitted to change places and work, by going to rejoin Paul and assist him, e.g., as a secretary. Also an eventual manumission of the slave cannot be excluded from the apostle's imagination or hope, as 1 Cor 7:21 indicates.

The different accents set in Pauline writings and the corresponding various interpretations of Paul — as an archconservative here and as a mildly progressive social thinker and instigator there — have to be tested in the light of the main reasons proffered for the stance taken. In all Pauline letters, within the passages pertinent to slavery, references to Christ do occur. It has now to be shown why they should not be treated as baroque ornaments but as essential parts of the social ethics proposed by the apostle.

3. EQUALITY AND HUMANITY THROUGH CHRIST

In his instructions for slaves and masters Paul presupposes the difference of their positions. But he asks for mutual respect and for good work(s) to be done on both sides of the social demarcation line;[106] indirectly, yet in fact, he affirms the full and equal humanity of lord and servant. In Colossians and Ephesians, both are separately addressed and both are told to remember before whose impartial court of justice they will have to give account of their deeds, and from whom they will receive their just reward. Before God, and therefore also for Paul and all Christians, they are on an equal legal footing. Greek and Latin moral philosophers could not refer to that court, neither to the omnipotence of

---

106. A maximal interpretation of the intended reciprocity is required by Eph 5:21: "Subordinate yourselves to one another." In loving his wife the husband precedes, or responds to, her voluntary subordination to him. See AB 34A, Comment V.C, pp. 708-715. More restrictive expositions would limit the meaning of the formula "the same good" in Eph 6:8 to "doing good," in relying on God's assistance at present as much as on his eternal award in the future.

that righteous judge, the God of Israel and the Father of Jesus Christ. When, only once in the NT, the abstract term *isotēs* is used, it signifies fairness rather than *égalité* in the political and social sense of the French Revolution and many a democratic constitution.[107] Still, the absence from the NT of a single abstract noun or cognate adjective denoting equality does not prevent the HT from giving testimony to the common humanity of masters and slaves.

The potential and actual humanism of the HT has another basis than the humanitarian traits found in enlightened Greek and Latin moral teaching.[108] At the place of natural law stands God, whose philanthropic promise and will are revealed in Israel's Scriptures and whose rule over the life of all persons, including the structures and institutions shaping their existence, is established through Jesus Christ. Reference to everybody's equal birth and death is absent in the HT, yet present are crisp formulae or lengthy excursions that sing or speak of Christ, his love, his service. The dualistic split between spirit and matter, the corresponding tension between soul and body, the capability of the immortal soul to battle and defeat physical passion and lusts were no longer fundamental. Rather in the HT or in their contexts, the rule of the risen Christ and his Spirit, as manifested in spiritual gifts such as faith and love, is the source of wisdom and ethical conduct. No longer does the criterion of moral behavior consist of the sum of timeless, semidivine virtues, or of the teaching and model character of persons such as Heracles or Socrates. Now it is proclaimed and believed that the Last Judgment lies in the hands of the one Lord Jesus Christ who is in person the standard and protector of humanity, even the "Man" par excellence (see Eph 4:13). In rewarding the good and punishing the evil done by slaves and masters alike, this judgment may in some regard resemble the *lex talionis*: the story of Dives and Lazarus (Luke 16:19-31) in its own way illustrates the judgment verses of the HT. However, it makes a difference whether a blindfolded goddess Justitia or Jesus Christ, through his own compassion and omnipotence, is the impartial judge.[109] New Testament ethics is based on the

107. See Annotation 7, pp. 231-232, for further remarks on equality.

108. Among the philosophical reasons for considering and treating slaves as human beings rather than as cattle or useful but disposable and potentially dangerous instruments and things, the following have been outstanding: the distinction between the law of nature and man-made laws; Zeus, the father of all human beings and created things; the womb of a mother out of which all persons are born; the conflict raging within all humankind between virtue on one side and base needs, lusts, and passions on the other side; the profit expected from a well-treated and faithful servant; and the great equalizer, Death, who makes no distinction between free and slave.

109. The cosmic character and validity of God's power and will are broadly unfolded in the praise of Christ that is formulated in Eph 1:10, 19-21 and Col 1:15-20. The incarnation, death, and resurrection of Jesus Christ stand in the foreground of Eph 2:11-18; Col 1:19-22; 2:9-11, 20; 3:1-3; 1 Pet 2:21-25; cf. Phil 1:6-11. For the indispensable operation and

proclamation of Christ. Christology and eschatology are inseparable and fulfill the same essential function. Christ, who has come, does rule now, and will come again, is the basis and source of all ethical counseling. For only he holds the divided parts of humanity firmly together. Him the counselor is trusting, and because of him he also is confident that the persons in lower and higher places whom he addresses will follow his advice. Unless exhortations issued out of faith, all admonitions would be legalistic and moralistic, certainly not evangelical.[110]

Within the HT and similar NT discussions of the main social relationships, short references to Christ can be distinguished from extensive christological utterances. In, e.g., Eph 5:22-33, marriage counseling includes, in poetic as well as in prosaic diction (vv. 23, 25-27, 29, 32), a moving proclamation of Christ's love and care. According to Phil 2:1-11, Christ's self-humiliation to the status of a servant and his exaltation to universal Lordship (vv. 6-11) are ground and model of the mutual unity and humility of the church members. In 2 Cor 8–9 the combination of a seemingly inexhaustible number of motivations for charitable giving in favor of the Jerusalem church has its heart and finds its peak in the proclamation of Christ who became poor in order to make many rich (8:9). When in 1 Pet 2:18-25 slaves are urged to subordinate themselves to good and to bad masters, the hymnic praise of Christ's innocent suffering for sinners undergirds and crowns the admonition. Ethical teaching need not only remind us of Christ; it also is an occasion and instrument to proclaim him.

Neither the length or intensity of the explicit Christ proclamations, nor the sparse and crisp references to the Lord, suffice to demonstrate the late, postapostolic, spurious origin and character of the texts mentioned. The hymnic christological passages may be pre-Pauline, but they are obviously fully endorsed by the apostle. The brief, as it were formulaic, references to Christ that prevail in, e.g., the HT of Col 3:18–4:1 correspond to the equally crisp mentions of Christ in Philem 8-22. Since PHM is unquestionably Pauline, the Colossian HT do not prove the opposite for Colossians. All the more, it looks surprising and seems to discourage the assumption of authenticity of the Pastoral Epistles, that in 1 Tim 6:1-2 and Titus 2:9 God and the teaching of the Savior are essential to the admonition while Christ seems not to be explicitly mentioned. In no

---

the many fruits of the Spirit, see Eph 1:13-14, 17; 2:18; 3:5, 7-12, 16; 4:3-4, 23, 30; 5:9, 18; 6:17-18; cf. Gal 5:16-25; Rom 8:1-27. While in Col 1:8 reference to the Spirit is made only by an adjective, at the end of *Did.* 4.11 and in *Barn.* 19.7 the Spirit is emphatically mentioned. Whenever a reference to the Spirit is made, God's and/or Christ's universal and eschatological power is meant.

110. Conflicting opinions regarding the substance of these observations will be sketched in Annotation 8, pp. 232-233.

case, however, least of all in the Pastoral Epistles, do the HT make sense without the context in which extended christological hymns and confessions precede or follow the ethical instructions.[111] The fact that, in one way or another, Christology and ethics always are joined together shows that a strict separation of the two has no basis in biblical texts. Since Colossians and PHM were written and dispatched at the same time, addressed to Christians living at the same place, the brief christological hints of Philem 8-22 most likely presuppose Philemon's and his house church's awareness of the elaborate Christology displayed in Col 1 and 2.

All references to Christ in ethical contexts intend to reveal that the tension and hostility between male and female, patriarchal and infantile, slave-owning and enslaved persons can only be overcome by the interference of a third party. According to Paul, apart from the superior power and right of God manifested in Jesus Christ, there is no ethics of unity and peace.[112] The purpose and effect of the divine intervention is this: neither of the divided human groups can claim victory over the other. All glory is due to God alone. The "one mediator between God and humankind, the person of Jesus Christ (incarnate and crucified)" of whom 1 Tim 2:5-6 speaks, is not only mediator between heaven and earth but also the only peacemaker between the sexes, the generations, the free and the slaves. No HT without explicit or implicit mention of HIM!

And yet PHM also contains elements that sharply distinguish it from the teaching of the HT.

4. THE SINGULAR WITNESS OF PHM: CHRISTOLOGY BY SOCIAL INVOLVEMENT

A superficial look at PHM might lead to the conclusion that this epistle is far less Christ-centered than the ethical instructions given in other undisputed Pauline and in so-called deutero-Pauline epistles. Absent here, for instance, is praise of Christ the redeemer and liberator, as found in 1 Cor 7:20-24; of Christ the model of an innocent person's suffering, as in 1 Pet 2:18-25; of Christ the loving and caring Lord, as in Eph 5:21-27, 28-32. Present is, on the other hand, an apostolic voice that reveals, as was earlier observed, a deep personal involvement in the history and welfare of both a slave and his master. In the HT a gen-

---

111. See Col 1:12-23; 2:9-15; Eph 1:4-14, 17-23; 2:11-22; 3:14-21; 1 Pet 1:18-21; 2:4-10, 21-25; 3:18-19; 1 Tim 2:4-6; 3:16; Titus 3:4-7; etc.

112. Later, the paradigmatic character of reconciliation and peace between Jews and Gentiles will be discussed on the basis of Eph 2:11-23; 3:5; Gal 3:28; etc.

eral address is directed as it were from far away, if not from high above, to all Christian servants and lords alike. But PHM is written out of an immediate and warm human concern in two individuals whose names suggest the nature of their owners. With both Onesimus and Philemon Paul identifies himself fully, although in very specific ways.

Onesimus "is my own heart" (Philem 12); "receive him as you would me" (v. 17); "if he has done any wrong or owes you something, charge it to my account. . ." (vv. 17-18).[113]

Paul and Philemon are business "partners" (v. 17);[114] what is "useful" for the master is also "profitable for me" (the apostle) (v. 11); he who is a beloved brother especially for Paul, is all the more so for Philemon (v. 16).

All three, Paul, Philemon, and Onesimus, but also others, are called brothers in verses 1-2, 7, 16, 20 — because God is their common divine Father. Still, Paul also is the spiritual father of Onesimus (v. 10) and Philemon "owes himself" to Paul as a spiritual child does to his progenitor. Similarly in Rom 4 and Gal 3, Abraham, the father of Israel "according to the flesh," is the spiritual father of believing Jews *and* Gentiles. As the latter are children of God *and* of Abraham and therefore mutual brothers, so also Philemon and Onesimus are brothers not only because of God, but also because they are spiritual children of the same human person, with whom they can stay, or who can visit them.

The close family relationship includes usefulness of the brothers to one another. Onesimus, the former no-good, is now "useful" to Paul and Philemon (v. 11), who as business partners have a common interest (v. 17); Paul is not ashamed to "take advantage" of Philemon's indebtedness to him (vv. 19-20).

The profit Paul expects from the family relationship to himself and between slave and master has an internal and an external dimension. Internal and yet total is the "rest" given by Philemon to the "hearts of the saints" in Colossae and elsewhere (v. 7). Paul hopes to be granted by Philemon the same rest for the benefit of his own "heart" when the latter brotherly receives the returned fugitive (v. 20).[115] External, though close to Paul's heart, is the effect of Philemon's response on the daily work of Paul. At stake is whether the apostle loses a dear

---

113. Luther writes in his "Vorrede" to WA *Deutsche Bibel*, 7.292-293: "Paul acts exactly as if he were himself Onesimus who had done wrong" (trans. according to E. Th. Bachmann, ed., *Luther's Works*, vol. 25 [Philadelphia: Fortress, 1960], p. 390, and as quoted by Lohse, *Philemon*, p. 188).

114. Pliny the Younger, *Ep.* 9.21, tells the freedman's patron that the fugitive had approached the intercessor as if Pliny were one and the same person as the patron: "He clung to me as if I were you."

115. Pliny, *Ep.* 9.21, does not explicitly mention a benefit for himself but writes of emotions in the psyche of both the patron and his escaped freedman: "You loved the man once and I hope you will love him again. . . . Do not torment him or yourself any longer."

companion or gains his permanent cooperation. Paul feels entitled to draft and enroll Philemon, but magnanimously makes a great concession: he is ready to accept the slave Onesimus's service as a substitute for the master's conscription (v. 13).

It looks as if these and other traits of interhuman trust might adumbrate or make superfluous an explicit testimony to Christ, and as if the call for co-humanity expressed in mutual love could move an explicit confession of faith in Christ into the background. Has then the proclamation of Christ been replaced by the display of human concern and the quest for immediate good works?

An affirmative answer is impossible, for only at first sight is PHM void of theological and/or christological depth. In this letter the theologically founded Christology has a specific form and character that distinguish it from the contents of the HT as well as from other occasional parallels in Pauline letters. Here the apostle speaks of himself and acts in a way capable of reminding Philemon again and again of no one and nothing else than Jesus Christ himself. When Paul announces his willingness to renounce his apostolic authority and yet extends his plea "as an ambassador and prisoner of the Messiah Jesus" (vv. 8-9), he resembles Christ, who hid his divine glory but who, just in being God's suffering servant, became worthy of the most glorious name (Phil 2:6-11). In 2 Cor 13:3 Paul asserts that "Christ is speaking in me," and in 2 Cor 5:18-20 he elucidates the contents and means of such speech: after praising God's own complete, perfect, and valid work of "reconciling the world in Christ," he is "beseeching on behalf of Christ [JB; cf. NEB: in the name of Christ] to be reconciled to God."

As a fully authorized representative will always bear the marks and colors of the sender's own character and power, so the apostle of Christ follows and resembles the Lord for whom he speaks. Christ's delegate is the more trustworthy, the clearer, stronger, and more numerous his identification marks are. Captivity (Philem 1, 10, 13), "being an ambassador in chains" (Eph 6:20), and joyful bearing of sufferings (Col 1:24; Eph 3:13; etc.) are features of Jesus Christ's own life, of which Philemon will necessarily think when Paul mentions his present situation.

Other elements in PHM point in the same direction. Paul's plea for the runaway Onesimus (vv. 9-11, 16-17) is in its own way a reflection and actualization of Christ's high-priestly intercession — as described foremost in the Epistle to the Hebrews, but also mentioned by Paul in, e.g., Rom 3:25; 8:34.[116]

---

116. To quote again Luther, from his "Vorrede" to WA *Deutsche Bibel*, 7.292-293: "What Christ has done for us with God the Father, that St. Paul does also for Onesimus with Philemon. For Christ emptied himself of his rights (Philip 2:7) and overcame the Father with love and humility, so that the Father had to put away his wrath and pride, and receive us into

Paul expects voluntary obedience and service — as the Son had offered to the Father and expected from his followers.[117] Paul is aware that reconciliation has a price: he is willing to pay for Onesimus, just as Jesus Christ paid (an infinitely higher price) for reconciling enemies to God and to one another.[118] The love shown and taught by Christ is in Paul's teaching the core and sum of the law (Rom 13:8-10; Gal 5:13-14; Col 3:14), and true love Paul reveals and expects in writing to Philemon. Christ alone has the right to claim and use as his property those redeemed by him; his "calling" obliges the freeborn and the slave alike to be his servants (1 Cor 7:17-24). Paul raises, though only in the form of a wish or suggestion, the same claim when he describes Onesimus as his son and Philemon as his lifelong and total debtor (Philem 10, 19). The fugitive as well as Philemon, or the first in place of the latter, should serve the spread of the gospel and thus prove "useful" (Philem 11, 13, 20).[119] Christ's parousia and God's judgment will decide the validity and value of Paul's conduct and labor (Phil 2:16; etc.). For Christ's second advent Christians long and pray (1 Cor 16:22; Phil 4:4-5; etc.). In PHM there is no explicit reference to the eschaton. Instead, Paul announces his forthcoming visit to Philemon's house (Philem 22). So Paul himself will see what fruit his appeal to the slave owner has brought.

Far from substituting himself for Christ, inadvertently or intentionally Paul makes his actions and instructions resemble those of Philemon's, Onesimus's, his own, and all other Christians' recognized common Lord. Elsewhere the apostle calls himself a model to be imitated by all Christians. In addressing Philemon, he gives many an example of how an imitator can speak and act.[120] By reference to his own situation and work, by his intercessory appeal to Philemon, by his willingness to pay, by his promise to appear in person — in brief, by his existence — Paul proclaims and verifies his faith in Christ. Narrations about Christ, hymns to his praise, creedal formulae, explications and ap-

---

favor for the sake of Christ, who so earnestly advocates our cause and so heartily takes our part. For we all are his Onesimuses if we believe."

117. Compare Philem 8-9, 13-14, 19-20 with Phil 2:6-8; Rom 5:19; 1 Cor 9:16-18; Eph 6:5-7; Matt 6:10; 26:39, 42, 45-46; Heb 5:7-8; 10:5-10; John 1:35-51; 6:66-69.

118. Gal 1:4; 3:13-14; 4:5; 1 Cor 7:23; Eph 2:14-18; 1 Pet 1:18-21; etc.

119. There is hardly a difference of meaning between the intention of the wordplay on the name Onesimus (useful) in Philem 10-11, the verb *chraomai* (to use) in 1 Cor 7:21, and the word *onaimēn* (to take advantage) in Philem 20.

120. In Phil 3:17; 2 Thess 3:9; 1 Tim 1:15-16 (cf. 4:12; 1 Pet 5:3), Paul designates himself as type *(typos* or *hypotypōsis)* of all who are to be saved, and in 1 Cor 4:16; 11:1; 1 Thess 1:6; 2 Thess 3:7, he requests that his example be followed. But just as he never calls a slave owner a "type" or "image of Christ," so he also abstains from using such a designation for himself. The titles "servant," "apostle," "ambassador" are good and honorable enough (Rom 1:1; Gal 1:10; 2 Cor 4:5; 5:20; etc.). He does not aim at Socrates' status in Platonic and Stoic teaching, not to speak of hero worship or idol worship in his own honor.

plications of Christ's coming, death, and resurrection are abundant in other parts of the New Testament. They issue in urgent calls for followership and discipleship, for repentance and conversion, for faith and love. They are the basis of the great churches' "orthodox" teaching. They possess a quasi-objective character because they proclaim who Christ is; what he did, suffered, and will do; and what power and right he has to invade and renew the created world, and to change and save human life. Such witness to Christ is by no means belittled or forgotten in PHM; it is presupposed that the recipients of this letter share in it.

The Christology of PHM is, however, more indirect, subjective, and suggestive. In view of a very specific social-conflict situation and the several agents who are its exponents, the epistle unfolds the effect of Christ's intervention in human affairs. Here, to use a bold formulation of Martin Luther, one person becomes Christ to his neighbor.[121] Christ is not only revealed *to* and *through* the apostle Paul, but also *"in"* him (cf. Gal 1:16). In Paul Christ lives, and the apostle lives "in Christ's faithfulness" (Gal 2:20). Other epistles elaborate on the correspondence between Paul's and Christ's weakness and strength (e.g., 2 Cor 12:9; 13:4). Those elect are destined to become "conformed to the image of God's Son" (Rom 8:29) and to be "transformed from glory to glory . . . through the Lord Spirit" (2 Cor 3:18). In their body they carry around the death of Jesus in order that in the mortal flesh also the life of Jesus may become manifest (2 Cor 4:10-11). Just as God's own faithfulness to Israel is reflected in Paul's unselfish and unshakeable loyalty to the Jewish people (Rom 9–11), so God's and Christ's own love is poured out and at work in the apostle and in the congregation (Gal 2:20; Rom 5:5; etc.).

The resemblance and parallel functions of Christ and of his elect servant(s) are neither a privilege of the apostle(s) alone nor placed into the foreground of PHM alone, as the texts just cited show. But only in writing to Philemon does Paul presume to be so transparent for the Lord above, in, and around him that he omits explicit christological proclamations and excursions.

What is said in the HT about the immediate impact of Christ on social divisions and tensions may look hard for women, children, and slaves. It seems to be all too general to take care of very specific and singular conditions. In PHM the same right and power of Christ are expressed in a much more persuasive

---

121. In the German text of *The Freedom of a Christian* (1520), Luther speaks of "becoming to my neighbor as much a Christ as Christ has become for me." What is here translated "a Christ" may as well be rendered by "a Christian." The Latin text, however, is unambiguous: "becoming each one to the other a kind of Christ (Lat. *Christus quidam*), so that we be a correspondence (Lat. *mutuum*) of Christ and Christ be the same in all, that is, true Christians" (WA, 7.35, lines 34-35; p. 66, lines 27-28).

form. For here Paul's warm concern for the slave Onesimus and his master Philemon is obvious.

The apostle's stance in social matters and the christological basis and heart of his position are even more explicitly manifested in another group of passages:

B. Oneness and Unity Confessions

Christology and sociology are an indivisible whole — according to three unity-in-Christ formulae found in Pauline letters. In the following, the abbreviation UF will be used for the singular and the plural of these formulae.

Gal 3:(27-)28	1 Cor 12:(12-)13	Col 3:(10-)11
(27 You all who have been baptized in [the name of] Christ have put on Christ.)	(12 For just as the body is one and has many members and all the members of the body, though many, are one body, so also the Messiah.)	
	13a For by one Spirit we are all baptized in one body,	(10 Put on the new man who is made new for knowledge according to the image of his creator.)
28a There is neither Jew nor Greek,	13b Jews or Greeks	11 Here there cannot be [a division between] Greek and Jew, circumcised or uncircumcised, barbarians, Scythians,
there is neither slave nor free, there is neither male nor female;	or slaves or free,	slave, free,
28b For you are all one in the Messiah.	13c and we were all made to drink of one Spirit.	11b but Christ is all in all.

Because these three passages appear to contradict flatly the substance of PHM, they require discussion at this place. The cited UF state boldly that the differences between free and slave are immaterial "in Christ," that is, where Christ's reign is manifested, confessed, and accepted, even in his body, the church. The formulae presuppose the existence of anthropological social differences and distinctions and their formerly divisive consequences. But they flatly deny their relevance in the present and future, after Christ has come. On the other hand, in harmony with the counsel given in the HT that slaves obey their masters, according to PHM Paul sends the slave Onesimus back to his master — as if the refugee were no more than a lost piece of property that a law-abiding (Greek or Roman) citizen of course would restore to its owner. Philemon is enabled to regain control over his slave, and Onesimus is again submitted to his earthly lord's will and decisions. Indeed, if and when the master heeds Paul's request for a brotherly reception and treatment of the slave, the mutual relation between both will no longer be the same as before Onesimus's escape. And yet the apostle appears neither to question nor to urge abolition of existing property rights, least of all the institution of slavery.

Has then Paul changed his mind? Or does he contradict himself, because — his fervent proclamation of Christ's rule and realm notwithstanding — in PHM, as an ethical counselor, he yields to the pressure of prevailing social conditions and situations. Is he then just a calculating opportunist whose theory and practice fall widely apart? These questions call urgently for an answer.

Before the common elements of Gal 3:28a; 1 Cor 12:13b; and Col 3:11 can be discussed, each one of their overtures, that is, the contents of Gal 3:27; 1 Cor 12:12-13a; and Col 3:10, requires attention. In the above synoptic presentation, for clarity's sake these proems have been bracketed.

1. THE PRELUDES

In Gal 3:27 Paul speaks of the baptism that in Galatia as well as everywhere else was the external form of confessing sin and hope for forgiveness, and thus of joining the church. The words (lit.) "baptized in Christ" distinguish this baptism from other water rituals.[122] The formula is used in Rom 6:3 and Gal 3:27 as an abbreviation of "baptizing in the name of Christ."[123] Above, in our translation of

---

122. E.g., from the purification acts prescribed for daily life and festival worship by the priestly Jewish writings and the Qumran community (e.g., Matt 15:2; Acts 6:2; 1QS 3.6-12), from the ritual performed by John the Baptist and his disciples (Acts 19:1-6), or from the lustration and rebirth rituals belonging in mystery cults. While John 4:2 affirms that Jesus' disciples did baptize years before his crucifixion, according to Matt 28:19 and Mark 16:16 the church's baptism was instituted no earlier than by the risen Christ. Certainly Acts 2:38 and the mention of baptism upon, in, or into the name of Jesus Christ in manifold stories of the whole book of Acts and in some epistles show that from the beginning this baptism was the door of entry into the Christian community. Just as by and in Jesus' Last Supper the Lord's Supper has been instituted, so probably also Jesus' baptism by John the Baptist is the original institution of that baptism that was later confirmed by words of the resurrected Lord.

123. When in 1 Cor 1:13-15 Paul mentions the absurd idea of a baptism "in the name

Gal 3:27, the words "the name of" were added before "Christ" in order to avoid three widespread interpretations saying that "baptizing into Christ" means: either immersion into Christ — as if the Lord were a fluid or a sphere; implantation into Christ — as if he were a tree or an incomplete statue; or drowning into the death or embedding into the tomb of Christ — as if Jesus had been executed and buried in water! In baptismal contexts, especially in Acts, the words "in the name of..." mean more than only authorization by Christ, and something else than the transfer of property from one side of a ledger to the other, or from one to another proprietor. Problematic is also the notion of a mystic sweet communion, as generated by the experience of a mysterious cultic miracle. The "calling out in the name of the Lord" *(qara' beshem adonai)* of which Gen 4:26; 12:8; 13:4; 21:33; etc. (cf. Acts 2:21; James 2:7) speak, is more likely one of the hermeneutic keys to the formula. It means proclamation, adoration, confession. In the baptism performed by church ministers, it is not only the baptizing clergyman or clergywoman who calls out and calls upon the name of the Lord; those being baptized participate actively in proclamation and prayer.[124]

The expression "putting on Christ" hardly alludes to the clothing of those baptized in a white garment. No evidence exists to demonstrate that, since the earliest days of the church or within the time span of Paul's missionary activities, the basically simple baptismal rite had been liturgically enriched by the manifold symbolic elements and actions that were later added. To put on the weapons of light is, according to Rom 13:12, 14, equivalent to putting on the Lord Jesus Christ (cf. Eph 4:24; 6:11, 13-17). The metaphor "putting on" includes various senses: Jews may think of the investiture of the high priest, a pagan citizen of the *toga virilis* donned to mark the transition from adolescence to mature manhood, and a soldier of the preparation for battle. Always the person solemnly clothed enters, assumes, and begins to fulfill a specific service. According to all Gospels, Jesus himself began his public ministry on earth with his baptism in or near the Jordan River. Paul discusses baptism in ethical context exclusively, not in order to define it as a means or guarantee of justification and salvation. Only within strictly eschatological contexts does the formula "put-

---

of Paul," he reveals his and the congregation's acquaintance with the formula "in the name of..." that prevails in Acts and recurs also in Matt 28:19.

124. Because in the Hellenistic Greek of the NT times the middle as well as the passive form of a verb can mean "to let oneself be..." (see BDF, 307 and 314), neither in Rom 6:3-4 nor in Gal 3:27a can the versions "they let themselves..." or "you have let yourselves be baptized" be totally excluded. An active participation of those baptized is certainly presupposed in Gal 3:27b: "you have put on Christ." A well-attested reading of 1 Cor 10:2 uses the *middle* form of *baptizō* for describing Israel's baptism by the Red Sea and the clouds! In all readings of Acts 22:16, the middle occurs: (lit.) "let yourself be baptized and washed from your sins, calling upon his (Christ's) name."

ting on . . ." describe an immediate, total change of the person who is being clothed; then the apostle speaks of the transformation of the mortal into a spiritual body (1 Cor 15:53-54; 2 Cor 5:1-10). Elsewhere he attributes the change to the operation of the Holy Spirit — e.g., in the passage next to be commented upon.

In *1 Cor 12:13a* Paul proclaims the effect of baptism with the Spirit. In 12:13c he uses the word "to drink" (which might as well be translated "to water"; see 1 Cor 3:6-8) in order to signify the abundant gift and manifestation of the Spirit that the Corinthians have experienced and of which they boast. "Soaking with Spirit" would be a version combining both meanings. According to 1 Cor 12:13, it is the Spirit alone who has made the Corinthians drunk. Only the Spirit is the means by which they are joined to Christ and made members in one body, even in Christ's (1 Cor 12:3, 12-13, 27).[125] In Eph 2:18 the combined function of Christ and the Spirit in giving access to God is crisply stated: "Through him (Christ) and in one single Spirit, the two (Jews and Gentiles) have access to the Father." According to 2 Cor 3:17-18, "The Lord *is* the Spirit!"

Colossians 3:10 contains the words (lit.) "made new for knowledge according to the image of his creator." These words offer a variety of possible translations and interpretations that cannot be discussed here.[126] The verse resembles Gal 3:27-28: here and there the UF is introduced by a reference to him or to that which is to be "put on" or has already become the garment always to be worn. While in Gal 3:28 Christ is the garment put on once, even in baptism, in Col 3:10 the saints are called to a continuous renewal. They are told in imperative form to don the new man and to strip off the old man and his pattern of behavior. In the interpretation of Eph 4:22-24 and Col 3:8-10, it was discussed who the old man and the new man might be,[127] and what it might mean that the putting-off and putting-on terminology is used in baptismal and in ethical, as well as in eschatological, contexts. Most likely in Pauline theology the old and the new persons (the *palaios* and the *neos* or *kainos anthrōpos*) who have been or are to be "put on" and "off" are Christ and Adam respectively.[128] Therefore generalizing translations such as "old" and "new nature" or "self" conceal rather than reveal the apostle's intention.

125. In Annotation 9, pp. 233-235, the interrelation between water baptism and Spirit baptism will be discussed.
126. See AB 34B, pp. 412ff., for a detailed discussion.
127. In AB 34A, pp 505-511, 536-545 (cf. the bibliography on p. 824), and AB 34B, pp. 406-414, arguments were offered that suggest the identity of the old man with Adam, of the new with Christ.
128. See Rom 5:12-21; 1 Cor 15:21-22, 45-49, and compare Gal 3:27 and Rom 13:14 with Eph 4:24 and Col 3:10.

2. MINOR DIFFERENCES BETWEEN THE FORMULAE

Each one of the unity confessions in Gal 3:28; 1 Cor 12:13; and Col 3:11 contains distinctive features. Only in Col 3:11 does the chiasmic enumeration of "Greek and Jew, circumcised and uncircumcised" (lit. ". . . circumcision and uncircumcision") repeat the contrast between God's elect people Israel and the nations. This duplication emphasizes the prior and exemplary rank of the overcoming and abolition of the mutual Jew/Gentile segregation and the potential dominion of one group over the other.[129] Oneness and unity in Christ — in Eph 2:11-17 and Col 1:20 they are called peace and reconciliation — replace now the former hostility against God and between human groups. Barbarians and Scythians are listed only in the Colossian catalogue, male and female only in Galatians.[130] While Christ, the Messiah,[131] according to all three texts, is the unifier and unity in person, only in 1 Cor 13:12 and 13c (cf. 12:3-4) is the Holy Spirit also praised as the agent, the means, and the demonstration of oneness. Following Gal 3:28, there *"is"* now neither Jew nor Greek, etc.; according to Col 3:11, however, there *"cannot be"* (any longer)[132] the former estrangement and enmity between heavenly and earthly powers and between the hostile camps on earth (cf. Col 1:20-21). For in Israel's Messiah the persons on either side of the social division lines "are all one" (Gal 3:28b) and "Christ is all in all" (Col 3:11b).

.

129. As often in Paul, so in these verses the mention of a "Greek" does not only include Greek nationals or Greek-speaking persons all around the Mediterranean Sea. Rather the term *Hellēn* is used as a synonym of those outside or without the holy law of God (Rom 1:16; 2:12; 3:21; 1 Cor 9:20-21), even of the nations (Heb. *goyim;* Gk. *ethnē*). In Col 3:11 the poetic parallel to *Hellēn* is *akrobystia* (uncircumcision), which confirms that more than only Greek nationals are subsumed under the term *Hellēn*.

130. Among the barbarians, the Scythians were considered the worst, even as superbarbarians. The couple male/female has been introduced by variant readings also into Col 3:11.

131. When in the Greek text the article is set before *christos*, or when in other passages *christos* precedes *Iesous*, the Messiah title of Jesus, i.e., his function and honor, is meant rather than only a part of his proper name. He stems from Israel, fulfills promises given to this people, and can be understood only on the basis of his relationship to God's elect nation. (See sec. VII.B.3.b, pp. 178-179, for examples of OT precedents and promises of Jesus Christ.) Before he came, the nations had been "apart from the Messiah, . . . strangers to the covenants based upon promise, . . . bare of hope and without God," according to Eph 2:12.

132. Other versions of the Greek *ouk eni* are, e.g., "there is no room for . . ." (JB), "there is no question of . . ." (NEB), "there is no . . ." (Phillips), or "there is no longer" (E. Lohse).

3. COMMON ELEMENTS IN THE CONFESSIONS

At least four problems are posed by the similarity and harmony of the three UF: To where can their origin and seat in the early church be traced? Which biblical roots and parallels may be relevant for their interpretation? How much are they unique to the Bible? Is it necessary to speak of a contradiction to the ethical admonition given in the HT and in PHM?

a. Origins and Functions

An uncontestable explanation of the root or *Sitz im Leben* of the UF has not yet been proposed.[133]

(1) The three catalogical enumerations of human groups that culminate in the words "all one in the Messiah," "all . . . of one Spirit," "Christ is all in all" may be cultic; they may, e.g., stem from a baptismal liturgy. In this case the UF belongs in the celebration of a sacrament. Perhaps the preaching and/or baptizing minister pronounced it; or it was a response of the person or persons baptized; or it was part of a hymn sung by the congregation.[134] Certainly the mention of baptism in Gal 3:27 and 1 Cor 12:12 favors the sacramental understanding.[135] But it is not

---

133. H. Lietzmann, *An die Korinther, I und II*, 3rd ed., HNT 9 (Tübingen: Mohr, 1931), p. 63, speaks of "a formula which he (Paul) apparently used quite often." Wisely he leaves it open whether the formula is pre-Pauline or Pauline, and which among its three shapes may be the oldest, the intermediate, and the latest.

134. The direct address to "you" in Gal 3:27-28 suggests the minister; Col 3:11 might contain a confessional response of those baptized; the pronoun "we" in 1 Cor 12:13a and c is typical of hymnic confessions made by the congregation.

135. Lietzmann, p. 63; R. Bultmann, *Theology of the New Testament*, vol. 1 (New York: Scribners, 1951), p. 311; and H. Conzelmann, *Der erste Briefe des Paulus an die Korinther,* KEK 5 (1969), pp. 249-250, together with a host of earlier or later interpreters are convinced that in 1 Cor 12:13 the words "into one body" describe the purpose and effect of baptism. But Conzelmann contradicts Lietzmann's opinion that the UF "is a disturbing interruption of the straight flow of argument and introduces (in vs 13b) a completely independent mystical sequence of thoughts." On the other hand, both Lietzmann and Conzelmann deem it possible that the soaking with the Spirit of which v. 13 speaks, if it be not an additional image for baptizing, refers to the Lord's Supper (cf. 10:4).

According to ever repeated intimations of Petersen (e.g., pp. 156-158, 210-213, 218, 239, 243, 254-257, 267), baptism is the one indispensable means and mark of separation from the structures of the present world, of entering the "antistructure" of the church and God's kingdom, of receiving the Spirit, and of adoption by God into the childhood and brotherhood of the Christians — in brief, of becoming a new creation. Dominated by sociological concerns, Petersen may well overestimate the function of the sacrament and attribute too little weight to the free operation of the Spirit, to which Luke in Acts and Paul in his letters bear testimony much more frequently than to baptism with water.

fail-safe: although the church's baptism "in (the name of) Christ," whenever it is mentioned in the NT, always is the water ritual that is performed on each believer, it is certainly not simply identical with, and simultaneous to, the ever free and new outpouring and manifestation of the Spirit. In First Corinthians, Paul presupposes that the Spirit's abundant presence is continuously experienced, not just once. In addition, Col 3:11 and its near context do not mention either water baptism or Spirit baptism. On the other hand, the First Epistle of Peter may well reflect a baptismal liturgy and confession, but it does *not* contain a UF.

Indeed, several alternatives exist to the hypothesis that the sacrament of baptism is the instrument by which union with Christ is effected.

(2) The UF have been understood as outbursts of early Christian enthusiasm.[136] A connection with the performance of baptism (or the Lord's Supper) might but need not necessarily exist if this theory could be proven true. During any formal or informal worship service, individual prophets may have spoken up in the sense of the formula,[137] or any church member may have been inspired to confess the Lordship of Jesus (cf. 1 Cor 12:3) by praising him as the One who has brought together and reconciled most diverse people. In voicing their enthusiasm, these persons in fact would have anticipated the perfect, peaceful state of humanity that was promised for the future world, after Christ's return (parousia) at the end of the present evil aeon, and after the resurrection of the dead.[138] From this doctrine, which in modern times is called "realized eschatology," a devastating ethical libertinism, and lawlessness, could easily issue. The NT mentions Hymenaeus and Alexander, who taught that "the resurrection has already occurred." First Corinthians and other letters mention members who drew the conclusion that "all things are permitted to me"; "let's continue in sin that grace may abound"; or "we have no sin."[139] In 1 Cor 6:12; 10:23

---

136. Esp. K. Stendahl, *The Bible and the Role of Women* (Philadelphia: Fortress, 1966), represents this view and does not hide his own enthusiastic agreement with the revolutionary confession of equality in Christ. He regrets the concessions made elsewhere to exigencies to which the apostle and the congregations yielded under the pressure of their social environment.

137. See 1 Cor 14:1-5, 24, 29, 31-32, 37, 39; Eph 2:20; 3:5; 4:11 for New Testament prophets; women were amongst them, as 1 Cor 11:4-5 shows. According to 1 Cor 14:26, when the congregation convenes, "each one has a hymn, a lesson, a revelation, a tongue, or an interpretation." The UF might stem from such a hymn, lesson, revelation, tongue, or interpretation.

138. As described in, e.g., 1 Thess 4:13-17; 1 Cor 15:12-57; 2 Cor 5:1-10; Eph 4:13; Rev 19–22. Cf. Matt 22:30: "In the resurrection they neither marry nor are given in marriage, but are like angels in heaven." According to Conzelmann (p. 250), the UF express "an eschatological . . . by no means empirical . . . invalidation of human differences."

139. In 2 Tim 2:17-18; 1 Cor 6:12; 10:23; Rom 6:2; and 1 John 1:8, the quoted sentences or the use made of them never expresses the doctrine and ethics of an apostle. Rather,

and everywhere in 1 Cor 14, Paul imposes conditions and strictures on the validity of the freedom slogan "all is permitted" and on the usefulness of all-too-free-flowing inspired speech. According to Gal 5:1 and 13, he had to combat the misuse of freedom among Christians. But neither the necessary warning nor the sharp polemics against legalistic or libertinistic "works of the flesh" prevented Paul from urging, of all people, the Corinthians and Galatians to live up to the UF.

(3) Further, "mysticism" can form a key to understanding the UF.[140] The unity with Christ might be basic for unity among persons of different social standing, for reasons lying beyond the efficacy of a church sacrament and beyond the anticipation of the eschaton by enthusiastic persons. In mysticism, rational induction or deduction, the personnel and the tools of organized religion, and the pounding on texts and doctrines are replaced by personal emotion and feeling, individual experience of the transcendent yet all-embracing and omnipresent divine reality. Mysticism knows a certainty greater than what established priests and sanctified sacramental elements can convey, even an intimacy and identification with the deity that in some extreme cases has been formulated "I am Thou, and Thou art me." A mystical interpretation of the UF by no means excludes theories referring to sacramental enthusiasm. There is, as especially A. Schweitzer (see n. 140) has suggested, a sacramental mysticism that transcends the straits of anti-institutional individualism. In turn, even the sacraments, especially the Lord's Supper, can not only be the occasion of enthusiastic outbursts, but also the *Sitz im Leben* of christocentric mystical hymns. Still, the opinion that Paul has to be understood as a mystic is

---

in their context enthusiastic libertinism is refuted and condemned with all available verbal means. Cf. also 2 Pet 2 and the Epistle of Jude. G. Eichholz, *Die Theologie des Paulus im Umriss* (Neukirchen: Neukirchener Verlag, 1972), pp. 278-283, suggests that the whole of 1 Cor 7, that is, Paul's statements on men and women and on slavery, be "read and understood as a rebuttal of enthusiastic ethical attitudes." However, J. Gnilka, *Der Kolosserbrief* (Freiburg: Herder, 1980), p. 189, observes in regard to Colossians that the role of enthusiasm is relatively reduced.

140. Deissmann's book *Paul;* A. Schweitzer's *The Mysticism of Paul the Apostle* (New York: Holt, 1931); and, among the commentators of First Corinthians, Lietzmann are outstanding representatives of this view. Lietzmann, p. 62, explains 1 Cor 12:12-13 by speaking of a "mystical truth," of the "mystic" reference to Christ himself rather than to a uniform social body, and of the ensuing "mystical notion" of the church, the body of Christ. Representing a dominant Roman Catholic tradition, L. Cerfaux, *La théologie de l'Église suivant Saint Paul* (Paris: Du Cerf, 1965), pp. 207-209, elaborates on "the mystic notion of a life whose source is Christ," and "the mystic identification . . . which is identity and parable at the same time . . . with the body of Christ." A discussion of mysticism and a selection of pertinent literature are contained in AB 34, pp. 384-394 and 419-420. Among the opponents of explaining Paul as a mystic is, e.g., Bultmann, pp. 311, 328, etc.

not undisputed, and the mere fact that several theories can be bundled does not suffice to validate any one of them or their combination.

(4) The UF may have a slightly different shape in Galatians, First Corinthians, and Colossians, because in each case the phrasing was an original Pauline creation. It could have been invented and formulated spontaneously, ever anew for and in each letter, in order to meet a need of the recipients and/or to clarify the context — by pointing out that Jesus Christ alone is the ground and means, standard and purpose of all elements of doctrine, church order, and individual conduct. In this case, in substance the formulae correspond to the various ways Luke described the earliest Christian community in Jerusalem: They were "one heart and one soul" and were assembled (lit.) "toward the one" *(epi to auto)*. Their mutual sharing and communion were the essential expression of their common faith in Christ, even of their faithfulness to him.[141] Within Paul's epistles, equivalent effects and demonstrations of reconciliation and peace are mentioned, especially when he urges the saints to be reconciled, to be of one mind, and to praise God together with one voice.[142]

b. Biblical Roots and Parallels

The meaning of the UF is best explained on the background of OT précis: Israel's confessions of the one God who has chosen and created one people to be his special property. In addition, parallels to the proclamation, One God — One People!, are found all over the NT.

(1) *In the OT,* in Jewish liturgies, in legal and prophetic books, and in visionary and scholarly literature, the praise of God who is one and the expression of gratitude for belonging in his one people are inseparable. Israel and each one of its members are, as it were, in the heart and in the hands of God. Israel's Holy Scriptures affirm that it has pleased God to create and call, send and guide, claim and judge specific persons. In those chosen by God every human being, especially the Jews, are to recognize prototypes and representatives of themselves.[143]

Adam and Eve demonstrate that humanity is created in God's image and destined to live as such. The election of the Gentile Abram makes him the fa-

---

141. Acts 2:42-47; 4:32; cf. 1:15; 2:1; *1 Clem.* 34.7.

142. Reconciliation: e.g., Rom 5:10-11; 11:15; 2 Cor 5:18-20; 13:11. Peace: Eph 2:14-17; 4:3; Col 1:20; Phil 4:7. One mind: Rom 12:16; 15:5-6; 1 Cor 1:10; 2 Cor 13:11; Phil 2:2; 4:2; cf. 1 Pet 3:8; one voice: Rom 15:6.

143. The question whether or not an understanding of God or Christ as a "corporate personality" is adequate to explain the interrelation between the One who is in heaven and his one people on earth will be briefly discussed in Annotation 10, pp. 235-236.

ther of both Israel and many nations. God causes Moses to lead Israel out of Egypt and to transmit and represent the law and statutes given from Mount Sinai, in the wilderness, and on the fields of Moab. Contempt of Moses and of the Law means to lose the freedom granted by God. When a man such as Achan by his theft sins against God, the whole people has to suffer (Josh 7). Because God is faithful to his chosen servant David, this lowborn king represents all the maligned and suffering members of God's people. "In David," so a great number of the Psalms aver, they can first pour out their lamentation and then yet conclude with the praise of God. Whenever after David's time a king sins, Israel is reduced and punished. But a good king given to them, such as Hezekiah and Josiah, ushers in release and victory for many. Prophets anticipate in their suffering and intercession the punishment that will befall many. The rendering of the NT term *Ho Christos* by "the Messiah" (see n. 131) reminds of these royal and prophetic precedents. The mysterious figure called "Son of Man" in Dan 7:13 is, in the same chapter (v. 27), interpreted by an angel to mean "the people of the Most High." On the Day of Atonement, the high priest bears before God all the sins and all the guilt of the whole people.

Thus, in a rich variety of modes, many are included in one person; the many are represented by the one chosen servant. The history of God with his one people and with the many nations is always focused on specific personalities who are given their high rank by the Lord alone.

(2) *According to the NT,* the comprehension of many in one culminates in Jesus Christ. He is sent by God, speaks in God's name to the Jews, and sends them out to the nations. He intercedes before God for friend and foe; he serves God in his life and death, and he is judged and justified by God alone. A rich variety of concepts, images, stories, and doctrines unfold his dominion over the many and their representation and salvation by him.

Outstanding in Paul's writings is the figure of one body and many members.[144] Together with other NT authors, this apostle also speaks of a temple being built of many parts; but Paul alone emphasizes its foundation upon Jesus Christ and its growth toward the one capstone, Christ. In the Fourth Gospel, First Peter, Hebrews, and Revelation the imagery of the one good shepherd and his one flock is outlined at length or briefly alluded to. The metaphors of the vine and the olive tree and of their branches are used by John and Paul respec-

---

144. In 1 Cor 12:7-30, esp. in vv. 12-13 and 27, the apostle speaks in a physical as well as figurative way of the multiplicity of members in one body: "As in one body we have many members . . . so we, though many, are one body in Christ"; cf. Rom 12:4-5. In Ephesians and Colossians, the one body/many members relationship is complemented by an elaboration on the exclusive dominion of Christ, the head, over the body with its many members. This does not contradict the witness of undisputed Pauline letters, for already in 1 Cor 11:3 Christ is called "head."

tively. Literal and metaphorical at the same time are the numerous Gospel passages speaking of Jesus' call to follow him, and the verses in Acts and Hebrews in which Jesus Christ is called the Leader and/or Perfecter of salvation and faith.[145] Obviously, there are many ways of proclaiming the unity of many persons established by and in him, the one Son and Messenger of God.

Harder to understand but no less pertinent are texts speaking of the preexistent Son. They affirm that his election by God and the love of the Father for him include all those (to be) redeemed. Also he is depicted as the firstborn brother whose prime right as an heir makes certain that the junior children will also receive their share. By the eternal Logos's incarnation the whole of humanity is assumed into community with God. The loneliness, the temptation, the weakness, the fear and suffering of the Son of God embrace every form of human frailty and failure.[146] Also his table communion with publicans, sinners, Pharisees, and disciples (who are about to betray him and deny him) has to be mentioned at this place.

Basic is always the theme, "one God — one redeemed people," "one Lord or head — one body or church," "one shepherd — one flock."[147] The same pattern is displayed in narrative and doctrinal, liturgical and figurative descriptions; physiological and botanical, architectural and economical, legal and moral, parental and matrimonial, priestly and sacrificial analogies and images compete with one another. Some elements are common; others correct one another mutually and prevent one-sided misinterpretations.[148] All of them show that the word "one" can signify much more than only the quantity of the number one. Oneness in the Bible is understood as the source and experience of a quality, that is, of a singular origin that creates plurality, of a continuity that fosters both progress and reform, of a power that effects slow or sudden change, of a will that calls for obedience, and of a faithfulness to which only faith and love are fitting responses.

---

145. Temple: 1 Cor 3:11, 16-17; Eph 2:20-22; 1 Pet 2:2-4. Shepherd: John 10:1-16, 27; 1 Pet 2:25; Heb 13:20; Rev 5:6-14; 7:9-17; etc. (if *arnion,* "lamb," includes the meaning "bellwether," as some commentaries suggest). Tree: John 15:1-6; Rom 11:16-24. Leader (and perfecter): Acts 3:15; 5:31 (Heb 12:2 RSV).

146. Preexistence: Rom 8:28-29; Eph 1:4-6. Firstborn: Rom 8:29; Col 1:15, 18; cf. Heb 1:6; 2:12-13; Rev 1:5. Incarnation: John 1:1-18; Heb 2:14-18. Temptation, weakness, and fear: Matt 4:1-11, 26, 36-44; 27:46; Heb 2:15; 4:14–5:8; cf. 2 Cor 13:4.

147. Exod 20:2; Deut 6:4; 1 Cor 8:5-6; Eph 4:4-6; John 10:16; etc.

148. Manifold titles of Jesus are collected in, e.g., Mark 14:61-62 and John 1:35-51. Even more are discussed in books on the "Christology of the NT." A rich collection of the descriptions of the church has been offered by, e.g., P. S. Minear in his book *Images of the Church in the New Testament* (Philadelphia: Westminster, 1960), again with the result of mutual complementation and correction. Neither "Lord" nor "people of God" can exhaust all aspects of the interrelation between the One and the many.

The formula "all are one in Christ" and the enumeration of those who constitute "all" are at the same time a proclamation of Christ's uniqueness and of the place and obligation of humankind. He is not only an individual: the Gospel stories and the apostolic proclamation reveal that "in" his heart, his words, his deeds, his death, his resurrection, his dominion, and his Spirit "many" or even "all" human beings are gathered together and included (cf. the texts mentioned or quoted in n. 153). In Rom 5:12-19 the words "the many" and "all" are used as synonyms.

In turn, the many or all are not just the sum of totally equal individuals. In the UF, the HT, and elsewhere, Paul distinguishes various groups: Jews and Gentiles, males and females, married and single people, parents and children, masters and slaves, etc. Each group can be offered a specific consolation and admonition. The proclamatory, evangelical praise of the all-embracing Christ always issues in an urgent, sometimes imperative appeal to those for whom Christ came, died, and was raised. They are to live, to act, to suffer, and to hope in conformity with his Lordship and under the impulse of his Spirit, rather than as slaves to the exigencies of bodily needs and social pressures of the environment (see, e.g., Rom 8:12-15).

Paul never tires of the phrase "in Christ."[149] In his diction it means the eternal inclusion of those elected in God's Son, the ministry fulfilled by Jesus on earth, and the church created by his death and resurrection, through the outpouring of the Holy Spirit and the preaching of the gospel. In Christ — here lies the basis of Paul's ethical instructions.[150]

The most authentic, concise, and precise interpretation of the formula "in Christ" is contained in the UF. Here Paul's Christology, anthropology, and sociology as well as his ecclesiology and ethics are three times bound up in one single and simple sentence. At least three elements are melted into an indivisible whole: Jesus Christ as he is in eternity and in time, the church living in the period between Pentecost and Christ's parousia, and the urgent call for the

---

149. See AB 34, pp. 69-71, for a discussion of the local, historical, mythical, mystical, existential, sacramental, ecclesiastical, or eschatological meanings that have been discovered in these two words. Often, though not always, the words "with Christ" are found in eschatological contexts. In Rom 6:3-8, 11, references to the death, crucifixion, resurrection, and life "with Christ" are summed up by the mention of deadness to sin, and of life for God "*in* the Messiah Jesus." The expression "in Adam" is an inverted reflection of the term "in Christ" (1 Cor 15:27). In Rom 5:12-21 Adam is called a "type of Christ," because by Adam the life of many or all human beings was similarly affected and determined as it is now "much more" by Christ. Positive parallels to the "in Christ" formula are the Pauline references to Abraham's children who, like the patriarch, live from God's promise and by faith alone: believing Jews and Gentiles are of yore and forever blessed "with" the believing Abraham (Rom 4:1-24; Gal 3:6-9, 14, 16-18, 29).

150. Often, esp. in ethical contexts, the synonym "in the Lord" is being used.

demonstration of brotherhood and sisterhood among all human beings, especially among Christians. Christ is hailed as the King who in his own way rules over all. Thanks is given to God, for "from the power of darkness he has redeemed us and has transplanted us into the realm of his beloved Son" — so Col 1:13 formulates the great change that has taken place. Where Christ, the universal Lord (Phil 2:10-11; etc.), rules, there he is the vertical and horizontal bond of unity. By the faith and love of the Christians this blessed tie is acknowledged and publicly exhibited. It is not an imperishable human capability or possession, neither does it establish a claim upon God or the right to impose dictates upon nonbelievers or believers. Rather the bond of unity is a continuously renewed gift of God. The testimony to Oneness given in Gal 3:28; 1 Cor 12:13; and Col 3:11 agrees with that of the High Priestly Prayer contained in the Gospel of John. The unity given by God is stronger than human relapses into enmity toward God and hostile segregation among humankind.[151]

c. Outstanding Features

Unique features of the UF complement and crown the elements shared with other biblical passages.

(1) The formulae confront hearers and readers with an extremely bold and absolutist, concentrated and universal description of Christ and the church. How can a sober member of the human society dare to affirm that "there is neither Jew nor Greek . . . slave nor free . . . male nor female; for you are all one" or "here cannot be Greek or Jew . . . slave, free, but Christ is all and in all" (Gal 3:28; Col 3:11)? What could sound more unrealistic or outrageous, scandalous or utopian for every pragmatist among the recipients and later readers of Paul's letters? Sheer enthusiasm suffices as little as the attribution of supernatural effects to the sacraments to give a solid foundation to the confession of unity in Christ. Whatever be the functions of inspiration and sacra-

---

151. For Paul it is certain that nothing in the creation can separate those for whom Christ died from the love of Christ and of God (Rom 8:13-39). Because love and faith are gifts of God, he starts most of his epistles, after the address and benediction, with the expression of his gratitude to God. The most beautiful demonstration of the promise and the need of perpetual renewal of God's gift is contained in the prayer of Jesus. According to John 17:21-23 (RSV), Jesus himself asks "that they all may be one; even as thou, Father, art in me, and I in thee, that they also may be in us, so that the world may believe that thou hast sent me . . . and hast loved them as thou hast loved me." While in John 17 the unity of the Father and Son is the basis and source, model and criterion of the oneness of the Christians, in 1 Cor 12:4-7 and Eph 4:4-6 the trinitarian unity of God, the Lord, and the Spirit underlies the same assertion.

ments in the life of the church, behind and above them exists a specific cause for making people enthusiastic and urging them to celebrate baptism and the Lord's Supper. Actually, the biblical UF can be pronounced only by such people who are convinced that by Christ, by the outpouring of the Spirit and in view of the Son of Man's parousia, an enormous change in world government and in interpersonal relations has taken place. Basic to this conviction is the present, future, and eternal Kingship of God, who "in Christ" invades, faces, and overcomes the present world with its chaotic estrangement, divisions, and hostility.

However, another story appears to be told by, for instance, Stephen's sermon and martyrdom, the summary reference to the dark world's uncomprehension and/or rejection in John 1:5, the accounts of Jesus' passion and crucifixion, the suffering experienced by the apostles and the congregations founded under their influence, the religious and social splits ravaging many a congregation: Neither Israel as a whole, nor Jesus' first and later disciples, nor the majority of the Gentiles agree in confessing that Jesus Christ is their Lord, Savior, and Reconciler. They did and do not live up to their repentance, faith, and love for which the gospel is calling. Such observations seem to contradict and yet cannot simply prove untrue or annul the Gospels' and the Epistles' message of events that have taken place quasi-objectively — of events that evoke a subjective response from persons too long divided by religious, social, national, or cultural differences. "Many" still remain true to the call extended to them, even when they are ignored, contradicted, and fought with all available means.

A palpable demonstration of the effective impact of God's Kingship upon the present world is the church, the deficiencies of its public testimony notwithstanding. In prayer and at the Lord's Table Jews and Gentiles, men and women, free and oppressed people meet and eat together as equals whenever the church is true to its founder and his Spirit.[152]

While the unity described in the formulae is essentially related to the church, it is not restricted to it. Jews and Gentiles, males and females, free persons and slaves exist not only inside the church. Even while no more than a small minority of the population living around the Mediterranean Sea had so heard the message of Christ that they believed, accepted, and heeded it, the substance of the message of Christ always concerned the cosmic dominion of Jesus

---

152. Petersen's *Rediscovering Paul* is the most impressive recent sociological attempt to show that "the symbolic universe," even the reality of God and the power of his fatherhood and Kingship, of which Paul speaks, is no less real, present, actual, and valid than the present earthly structures. By its "antistructures" to the orders of the present world, that is, by brotherhood and love, the church reveals that even in the midst of the sinful and divided contemporary world, the new life and order given by God are real and can and shall be experienced.

Christ and the reconciliation of all things (see, e.g., Col 1:15-20), not only of the Christians.[153] Because the UF possess a universalistic dimension, they are relevant for each and every human being, a reminder of, and an appeal to, the reality of which they speak. Only when Jews and Greeks, people of Jewish and of Gentile origin, of the male and female genders, free persons as well as slaves are declared to be included "in" Christ's reach and realm, then the unrestricted full power of Christ is proclaimed.[154]

It is probably intentional rather a sign of superficial social analysis that in the UF the structures of human existence and society are always described in binary terms. Indeed, the either/or categorization presupposes fundamental bi-polarity and bypasses the reality and phenomena of additional — e.g., hybrid — groups; there were slaves who also were owners of slaves, not to speak of her-maphrodites, homosexuals, and lesbians. However, every personal and social difference, competition, hatred, and enmity ultimately emerge out of the con-flict of two opposites. As soon as two obvious antagonists find the way to one another in peace, additional adversaries cannot stand aloof. The universal need for peace and unity can be met solely when again and again the two most prominent and representative exponents of hostility are reconciled. As the UF catalogues of pairs vary in some details, they are meant to be representative or exemplary rather than complete or exhaustive. They form as comprehensive *and* wide-ranging an intimation of human diversity and conflict as do modern summary distinctions between white and colored, rich and poor, oppressor and oppressed.

(2) In the lists enumerating the human pairs, "Jew and Greek" always oc-

153. The wall of separation and hostility torn down by Jesus Christ was, according to Eph 2:14-16, the wall between all Jews and all Gentiles and between all creatures and God. Correspondingly, the peace made by Christ means reconciliation of *all* humankind with God and of all divided human groups with one another. While they were still sinners and enemies, Christ has died for all people (Rom 5:6-10). Because he has died "for" them, all have died with him or in him in order also to be raised with him (2 Cor 5:14-15; Rom 6:3-11). Paul boasts of the cross of Christ alone because through it "the world is crucified for me, but also I for the world" (Gal 6:14). The term "body of Christ" only seemingly denotes a closed society; as shown in AB 34, pp. 198-199, this formula has a missionary dimension. The church is not an end in itself but a lighthouse for the benefit of the world (Eph 3:10; 5:8; etc.). As an am-bassador of Christ and in his name, the apostle urges acceptance of the reconciliation — on the basis of God who "in Christ has been reconciling the world." Three times in the one verse, Col 1:28, Paul emphasizes his responsibility for "every person." Earlier it was mentioned that the HT admonition includes situations in which one social partner was not a member of the church.

154. Specifically hurtful to a conceited human self-consciousness is a hint given in the Col 3:11 catalogue. It suggests that just as all human beings are either Jews or Gentiles, free or slave, so they also belong in the company of either barbarians or superbarbarians (cf. n. 130), as if there were no other choice than being either a boor or a bum!

cupies the first place.[155] Especially in Eph 2:11-22 the contrast between Israel and the nations, and the elimination of their mutual exclusion and enmity, are treated as paradigmatic for all interhuman diversities and their replacement by peace. The HT in the same letter (5:21–6:9) shows how in daily life the peace made by Jesus Christ is to be honored by husbands and wives, parents and children, slave owners and slaves. The church is a community of persons among whom each has not only a distinct origin, history, and present status but also a specific character and orientation. No more than anybody else are church members uniform drops, grains, or sand corns. For each one of them has special dignity and right, coupled with special obligations.

Unity in diversity is essential of the congregation. This multifaced social unit thrives on the interaction of the diverse spiritual gifts given to each member respectively (1 Cor 12–14; Rom 12:3-8; Eph 4:7-16). Actually the church does not live without the variety of people who move into and within it, and go out as missionaries. If the church is compared to a house or temple, its most important features are the manifold workers cooperating in it, and its open windows and doors. Certainly it is not dependent on walls — the walls are to be broken through by gates open day and night, as the vision of the heavenly Jerusalem indicates (Rev 21).

The definite access, insertion, and incorporation of Gentiles into the one household and people of God constitute the main difference between the old and the renewed covenant. Only with limited rights and duties had women,

---

155. The emphasis with which Paul in Rom 1:16; cf. 3:29; Acts 13:46, etc., pronounces that "the gospel is the power of God for salvation for the Jew first, and for the Greek" does not contradict but emphasizes the unification of both in Christ. For far from any competition, Paul's own special appointment to be apostle to the Gentiles complements Peter's "apostolate to those circumcised" (Gal 2:7-9; cf. Acts 15). In contradicting historical dogmas created by the Tübingen School, J. Munck, *Paul and the Salvation of Mankind* (Richmond: John Knox, 1959), has shown that in questions of mission there existed no essential difference between Paul and the Jerusalem church. Both supported the mission to Jews *and* to Gentiles wholeheartedly, though they assumed a different sequence. The mother congregation upheld the priority of the proclamation to Israel. Paul, however, after the rejection of the gospel by many Jews, was convinced that the conversion of Gentiles to Christ would precede the salvation of all Israel and thus make the Jews jealous. He expected that only after the nations' procession to Zion would the Jews also recognize their Redeemer (Rom 11:25-27). Passages describing differences, tensions, and conflicts, such as James 2:8-11; Gal 2:1-21; 3:22; Rom 2:12-13; 3:21-31; 11:28-32; Eph 2:1-9; Acts 10; 11; 15; 1 Tim 1:12-16, ultimately affirm the equal standing of Jews and Gentiles before God. Because in Gal 2:15 *hamartōloi* (sinners) is the predicative noun of the whole sentence and urgently suggests the translation "we are sinners of Jewish origin, not of Gentile provenience," all these texts agree in stating that there is no difference between the Jews' and the Gentiles' captivity in sin and death — although only the Jews were sinning against the Law given to them, while the Gentiles are sinners without having the Law. All are justified and saved by grace alone.

children, and slaves formerly belonged to the community chosen and created by God. But Jesus Christ opened the door to equal freedom and dignity even for those who within Israel were not free adult males. High- and low-standing outsiders belong to his people. Christians who might be tempted to form a closed shop or who might tend to treat the church as an end in itself resemble the persons resisted by Paul; they limited the access to God by stringent conditions and looked askance at Paul's mission work among the Gentiles. The church of which the apostle speaks cannot be secured by walls: after Jesus Christ has abolished the one great wall between God and the divided groups of humankind, no one is entitled or obliged to keep upright or to reerect any other fence (Eph 2:14; Gal 2:18).

If Jews and Gentiles, then those near and those far, then insiders and outsiders are joined together and reconciled by and "in Christ" (Eph 2:13, 17, 19). The presence of as yet inadequately trained believers (called *idiōtai*) and of obvious "unbelievers" in the assembly for worship is presupposed in 1 Cor 14, especially in verses 21-25. Excommunicated is only such a church member who seeks to introduce pagan ways of life (1 Cor 5; Eph 5:5). "Unworthy" are those Christians who, instead of "receiving one another," try to enjoy and celebrate even in the church the differences between the rich and the "have-nots" (1 Cor 11:17-21, 27-33).

(3) In each of their three different versions, the UF affirm that something new has been made of the members of the formerly divided and hostile groups: "in Christ" they are now "one." While only Gal 3:28 contains the explicit statement "you are all one in the Messiah," the parallels in First Corinthians and Colossians are equivalents of the same assertion.[156] Obviously this oneness is something new, for explicitly Eph 2:15-16 speaks of "one new person," that is, "a single new person," who "is created in Christ . . . out of the two . . . through the cross in one single body."[157] In 2 Cor 5:17 Paul affirms, "if anyone is in Christ, this person is a new creation (or: creature)." Similarly, in Gal 6:14-15 he proclaims that the effect of Christ's crucifixion is "a new creation," displacing

---

156. 1 Cor 12:12-13: because of the baptism of "all by one Spirit . . . in one body" as well as by drinking "of one Spirit" that was offered to all, "the many . . . are one body." Col 3:10-11: "Put on the new man. . . . Christ is all and in all."

157. The translation of *kainos anthrōpos* by the words "new man," which has been taken up from a broad tradition in my commentary on Ephesians (AB 34-34A), needs correction. In contrast to the Greek text, the version mentioned suggests that the new creature is male, not female. Appropriate is only another literal and inclusive version of Eph 2:15: "a single new person." The new person is the bride of Christ, even the church as she is described in Eph 5:22-32. In Paul's marriage counseling, the oneness of the many with and in Christ is the basis and prototype of the union of a husband with his wife, that is, of their "becoming one flesh" in the sense of Gen 2:24.

the validity and value of the former antagonism between those circumcised and those uncircumcised.

The newness and oneness in Christ affect every individual person. There will be conversion, rebirth, confession and growth of faith and love, specific deeds, sufferings and sometimes even small or great achievements. But the new unity is not to be identified with an individual psychic or collective, sacramental, enthusiastic, or eschatological transformation or transport out of this world into angel-like status and nature![158] Christians are not called to be disembodied spirits. Being sent *into* the present world, they are never instructed to flee and escape *from* it. They do not live in heaven though they are already citizens of it, and they are not residents of a cloud-cuckoo-land. Rather, before the parousia of Christ and the transformation of their bodies by resurrection, they are, as much as every human being, "flesh and blood" or "flesh and bone."[159] According to Col 1:15-20, not only is the reconciliation of all creatures due to Christ, but also their very creation and subsistence. Although Paul has experienced a rapture "in the body or outside the body" into the third heaven and

158. Neither an asexual or hermaphroditic, nor an ageless or atemporal, nor an economically irresponsible form of human existence is envisaged by Paul. Such existence might include exemption from all social, economical, cultural conditions, bonds, and obligations. It would suggest a uniformity that would deny and destroy what according to the biblical creation accounts is essentially human. A rather suspect variant reading of Gal 3:28 has *hen . . .* instead of *heis en Christō* (one thing, instead of one person, in Christ). It is unlikely that in this verse Paul intended to speak of a sexless, timeless, work-free nature and status of the newly created humankind. Rather he intended to speak of oneness and unity in diversity. Every part of Pauline ethics, esp. the HT, reveals not only Paul's realistic awareness and assessment of the various temptations and pitfalls, possibilities and opportunities related to sexuality, generation gaps, and social status. As will be shown in the interpretation of 1 Cor 7:17-24 (pp. 191-200), the fact is taken most seriously that those who are Christians now, have been met by God's call and can live according to that call in widely diverged personal situations. However, God's calling does not simply bless the existing condition — for instance, urge continued business as usual and getting married as considered normal. Neither does God's call bluntly announce "everything is permitted." In Pauline theology the presupposition of the heavenly calling is the subordination of all principalities and powers (that is, of the structures and institutions of created life) under the feet of Christ. Not in vain are HT found in only those Pauline epistles in which first the dominion of Christ over all powers, structures, and things has been proclaimed. Without the substance of Eph 1:19-23; 4:10; Col 1:15-20; 2:14-15, the HT found in later parts of these epistles would have no solid basis.

159. Gal 1:16; 1 Cor 15:50; Eph 5:29-30; cf. Heb 2:14; 5:7. Often but not always in Paul's theology the connotations of "flesh" are bad. This is the case when, e.g., in Rom 8:1-13 and 7:16-25 and John 3:6, just as in OT precedents such as Isa 31:3, flesh and spirit are set in opposition. Then "flesh" means weakness because of evil desire and subjection to sin. Very often, however, both in OT and Pauline theology flesh signifies the personal and social life in a body, even the physical bodily existence. Life on earth is a gift of God, willed and created and guided by God, and as such, together with all creatures of God, "very good" (Gen 1:31).

paradise (2 Cor 12:2-4; cf. Rev 4:1), he is aware that together with all Christians he lives "*in* the flesh."

But living within the limits set by bodily existence, that is, being exposed to sexual, historical, economical, etc., conditions, inclinations, and lapses, Christians are neither bound nor permitted to conduct their lives "*according* to the flesh" (Gal 2:20; Rom 8:12; 2 Cor 10:3). At the same time they are accepted as thoroughly human beings *and* strictly prohibited to follow inclinations and practices that among Gentiles are considered natural and normal. In consequence, it is possible to speak of their "paradoxical" existence.[160]

This way of life is never a private path and enterprise. Christians are always in community with fellow believers and always live within a world that seldom reacts with applause,[161] but most frequently with amazement, rejection, or open hostility. A social rather than an individualistic interpretation is necessary whenever the oneness in Christ is to be properly understood. The "one new person" created by Christ (Eph 2:15) always consists of at least two different individuals, one a Jew, the other a Gentile; one free, the other a slave; one male, the other female. Uniforms would serve neither external nor internal peace. The description of the church as one body having many members, as

160. Pauline passages describing the paradox are 1 Cor 4:10-13; 7:11-21; 2 Cor 6:4-11; cf. 12:9-10; 13:4, 9. Among these texts, 1 Cor 7:29-31 sounds definitely absurd when it requires the impossible: "Let those who have wives live as though they had none, and those who mourn as though they were not mourning, and those who rejoice as though they were not rejoicing, and those who buy as though they had no goods, and those who deal with the world as though they had no dealing with it." Before and after these puzzling statements the text affirms, "The anointed time has grown very short" and "The form of this world is passing away."

The seemingly absurd character of the paradoxes has often been explained by reference to the earliest Christians' hope for the immediate second coming of Christ and the end of the present world, even by their so-called *Naherwartung*. Only for a very limited number of days, weeks, or months, not for hundreds or thousands of years of church history, a good part of NT ethics would then be relevant. In that case "interim ethics" may be a fitting concept for describing the ethics of Paul, and also of the Sermon on the Mount. But the delay of the parousia does not invalidate the fact that all parts of the NT, including the book of Revelation and the Pastoral Epistles, expect of Christians extraordinary and amazing conduct even after the death of the last of the first disciples. It may be added that a new phase in the study of the historical Jesus and of Paul has been initiated by, for instance, M. J. Borg, "A Renaissance in Jesus Studies," *Theology Today* 45 (1988): 280-292; Borg, *Jesus — a New Vision* (San Francisco: Harper, 1988), and Petersen in his previously mentioned book, *Rediscovering Paul*. Instead of *Naherwartung*, the key of interpretation would then have to be found in the "revolutionary wisdom" teaching of Jesus (and of Paul), that is, in all they say about the impact of the Kingship of God (which sociologists may prefer to call the "symbolic universe") on the structures of the world as experienced now by all human beings.

161. In, e.g., 1 Cor 10:32; 2 Cor 6:8; Phil 4:8, Paul presupposes that Christians could find favor in their environment; cf. Luke 2:52; Acts 2:47.

given in 1 Cor 12 and elsewhere, reveals that the oneness and unity created in Christ protect diversity, and that diversity is an essential contribution to oneness and unity.[162] So also the UF remind church members that other persons are not just alter egos, their own self repeated or duplicated in equivalent copies. Diversity is constitutive of the new society created by Christ. This community proves by its very existence that difference and diversity need not mean unbridgeable gaps, insoluble tensions, mutual contempt, hatred and warfare, but can be and are overcome by reconciliation and peace. Now diverse persons are complementing one another without losing their identity.

As unique as Christ is among other personalities in human history, so unique is the church among other social groups.[163] Actually Christianity is and has to remain a strange element.[164] It is not forced to fit into or conform with the ideas and practices found in other bodies. As the church is depicted by Paul, its internal social order and its stance within the prevailing social structures of the environment are not based on the victory of a stronger over a weaker person or group, of a majority over a minority, or of a reverse superiority.

Despite weakness, self-contradiction, internal splits, and manifold denials, treasons, and defeats, the church is according to the UF a historical reality. Here many are assembled by, in, and around the one, Christ.

Is such teaching in harmony with Paul's intention and action regarding Onesimus and Philemon?

d. Contradictions to Philemon?

It appears that two things are mutually exclusive: the unity or equality in Christ as proclaimed in Gal 3:28, etc., and the subordination of one human group to another in submission to the one common Lord of which the HT and PHM

162. In order to discuss problems of ecumenism at the close of the twentieth century, O. Cullmann has gone so far as to give a book the title *Einheit durch Vielfalt* (Tübingen: Mohr, 1986); ET, *Unity through Diversity* (Philadelphia: Fortress, 1988).

163. Perhaps because in 1 Cor 10:32 Paul distinguished three human groups, Jews and Greeks and the church of God, the *Epistle to Diognetus* 1 speaks of a "new race" and Clement of Alexandria, *Strom.* 6.5.41, of the "third race." Cf. the term "Christendom" (*Christianismos*) used by Ignatius of Antioch in his letters to the Magnesians (10.1 and 3), Romans (3.3), and Philadelphians (6.1). Ignatius was the first to equate Christianity with an "ism," even the *Christianismos*. Equivalent might be later attempts to define the corporate and communal character of the unit created by Christ as a "new religion" or "new nation."

164. The Pauline texts quoted in n. 160 for exemplifying the paradoxical nature of the life in Christ also reveal the miraculous, unique, and seemingly offensive character of the church's existence. A moving description of the strangership and isolation of the Christian community in the present world is found in *Diogn.* 5.

speak. On one side stands the enthusiastic conviction that God's Kingship has come and has been established, on the other the "sobriety" of which the Pastoral Epistles (1 Tim 2:2; 3:4, 8, 11; Titus 2:2, 7) explicitly speak. To formulate the same tension in secular terms: here a fine principle or utopia — there a pragmatic accommodation to the social structures prevailing in the present world; or, here a revolutionary impetus — there an unshaken conservatism.[165] Could it be that Paul wavers back and forth between an illusionary idealism and bone-dry realism, without any chance ever to reconcile them? It might well be that in his letters he expresses the same tension as every Christian who with the Lord's Prayer jubilantly confesses that the kingdom, the power, and the glory are already God's alone, and yet humbly expects and asks, "Thy kingdom come." Have the accents set by Paul changed at different times, under varying conditions? Among the many revelations he received and heeded (Gal 1:16; 2:2; 1 Cor 2:10-12; 2 Cor 12:1-4), those given later may have clarified or corrected those given earlier. Faced with the misuse of freedom by antinomian and/or enthusiastic church members,[166] he may have had good reason to pull back loose reins. Serving his Lord from the depth of his heart and to the best of his capability, he may have been forced several times to change his mind.

Yet it is not necessary to conclude that for such reasons Paul's teaching on Christ, the church, and ethics is so ambiguous, so frustratingly dialectical, or so uncomprehensible that it cannot possibly be useful for later generations. Rather, just because Paul's message and ethics are not timeless but bear marks

---

165. Lightfoot, pp. 389-392, expresses his conviction that, after the laying down of the "universal principles" by Paul, slavery was "doomed." Indeed, before and after Lightfoot abolitionists were hardly bothered by the injunctions of the HT and the return of Onesimus to Philemon. E.g., G. Kehnscherper, *Die Stellung der Bibel und der alten christlichen Kirche zur Sklaverei* (Halle, 1957); Schulz, *Gott ist kein Sklavenhalter;* and K. Stendahl in the booklet mentioned in n. 136 dislike the contradictions found in Paul or denounce the brakes the apostle himself and/or church leaders after him had put on an immediate and radical social change. But Eichholz, p. 283, quotes A. Schlatter (see n. 139) for supporting the thesis that Paul, while rejecting revolutionary violent changes, does not exclude social change as a consequence of the gospel. Similarly Stuhlmacher, e.g., pp. 42-48, 69, does not consider PHM an antienthusiastic document, yet speaks of the danger that the church may unwillingly identify itself with a "social emancipation movement." Still, referring to 1 Cor 7:21, Stuhlmucher asserts that Paul favors emancipation, "even at the risk of enthusiastic misinterpretation." A radical criticism of Stendahl's arguments and conclusion is found in J. H. Yoder, *The Politics of Jesus* (Grand Rapids: Eerdmans, 1972), pp. 176-177 n. 22. As an alternative, on pp. 163-192 Yoder combines the message of the UF and of the HT under the chapter heading "Revolutionary Subordination," which takes up K. Barth's earliest, though later corrected, interpretations of Rom 13:1-7 (in *Der Römerbrief,* 1st ed. [Bern: Bäschlin, 1919], pp. 375-391; 2nd rev. ed. [Munich: Kaiser, 1921], pp. 465-475).

166. To which First Corinthians; Rom 6:1-2; Gal 5:1, 13; cf. 1 Pet 2:16; Jude; and 2 Pet 2 bear testimony.

of his and the addressed congregations' varying conditions, they can be relevant to specific needs of generations of later times, under changed circumstances. Whenever readers of Paul feel inclined either to applaud an enthusiastic interpretation of the UF or the alleged law-and-order ideology of the HT and PHM, they are in danger of forming an image of Paul that conforms to their own predilections. Actually, there are signs that UF, HT, and PHM do not totally contradict or exclude one another.

Christ is mentioned only briefly in the HT and in PHM, yet he is the same Christ who is praised in the UF as the place, the agent, the power of unification and common life. Here and there, the existence of the church is presupposed as the basis and frame of ethical decisions. The voluntary obedience expected in the HT and PHM does not contradict the freedom and equality in Christ affirmed by the UF. Above all, the same love of the neighbor *and* the enemy, which is the bond of perfection and the fulfillment of all commandments,[167] is implicitly proclaimed also in the HT and explicitly mentioned again and again in PHM. While these hints are not sufficient to dispel or simply negate tensions within Pauline ethics, another text of the apostle not only forces the issue but also contributes to its solution by a way other than a cheap compromise.

C. The Discourse on God's Calling

In the RSV, the wording of 1 Cor 7:17-24 is the following:

17 Only, let every one lead the life which the Lord has assigned to him, and in which God has called him. This is my rule in all the churches.
18 Was any one at the time of his call already circumcised? Let him not seek to remove the marks of circumcision. Was any one at the time of his call uncircumcised? Let him not seek circumcision.
19 For neither circumcision counts for anything nor uncircumcision, but keeping the commandments of God.
20 Every one should remain in the state in which he was called.
21 Were you a slave when called? Never mind. But if you can gain your freedom, avail yourself of the opportunity (footnote alternative: make use of your present condition instead).
22 For he who was called in the Lord as a slave is a freedman of the Lord. Likewise he who was free when called is a slave of Christ.

---

167. Col 3:14; Rom 12:9-21; 13:8-10; Gal 5:14; 1 Cor 13. In the three letters where they occur, the UF precede the praise of love, and Paul's discourse on freedom in Rom 8 precedes his statement on love. According to Paul, unity and freedom in Christ are never without love.

23 You were bought with a price; do not become slaves of men.

24 So, brethren, in whatever state each was called, there let him remain with God.

The RSV translation of verses 18-19 and 22-23 is true to the Greek text, but for verses 17, 20-21, and 24, words are chosen and meanings suggested that are disputable, if not misleading. Not all of the grave problems inherent in these eight verses can be discussed at this place.[168] If at all Paul's stance on slavery is to be explained not only on the basis of the HT, the unity confessions, and PHM, then an elaboration on two central problems is necessary: (1) the exact meaning of the command, (lit.) "Everybody remain in the calling by (variant reading: in) which he was called" (1 Cor 7:20; cf. vv. 17-18, 21-22, 24), and (2) the interpretation of the sentence, (lit.) "You were called as a slave — don't care; but if you can become free — use it all the more" (v. 21).[169] Only on the basis of

168. A complete interpretation of 1 Cor 7:17-24 would have to treat questions such as these: (a) Do these verses, within the whole of 1 Cor 7, form an excursus added for good measure, or are they the summit, center, and ultimate criterion of all other issues discussed in this chapter? (b) Does the costly redemption of Jews and Gentiles by the blood of Jesus Christ presuppose or suggest a "doctrine of atonement" either on the lines of a legal commercial satisfaction of God (as described by Anselm of Canterbury) or of a demonstration of overwhelming love (as depicted by Abelard)? (c) Why is the paradox of the Christians' simultaneous freedom by Christ and slave-service to Christ basic to a Christian's life, as indeed Luther proclaimed it to be at the beginning of his tract *The Freedom of a Christian* (1520)? Two other problems have been discussed above in sec. VII.B (pp. 170-191) and in "Social Background," sec. VII.C (pp. 47-49): (a) the combination of the pairs Jew/Gentile, free/slave, male/female, and the priority of the reconciliation of the people of God with the nations; (b) the problematic derivation of Paul's doctrine of redemption from the ("fictitious") sacral manumission practiced at Delphi.

169. The solution of these problems is facilitated neither by the crisp tone of the two quoted sentences nor by their closest context, vv. 17-24. According to 1 Cor 1:26-29; 11:17-22; 12:13, the contrast between persons of ignoble and of noble birth; rich house-owners and poor harbor, house, or shop workers; ever-hungry proletarians and overeating gluttons; free persons and slaves had created tensions and even splits among the members of the Corinthian congregation, affecting both their daily life and their assemblies for worship. Paul had received information from Chloe (1 Cor 1:11) and perhaps through Stephanas, Fortunatus, and Achaicus, the carriers of a letter of the Corinthians to Paul (16:17). At least four topics were proposed to Paul in writing for an answer: sexual contacts between men and women (7:1); edibility of sacrificial meat stemming from idol temples (8:1); spiritual gifts or persons (12:1); collection for Jerusalem (16:1). But among this information and these questions the slave/master issue does not rank prominently. What the apostle writes about free persons and slaves in 7:17-24 appears to be incidental rather than central; it is an illustration and example rather than the treatment of an acute problem in its own right. The same is true of the Jew/Gentile issue: it finds a fuller treatment for the benefit of the Corinthians (after brief allusions to it in 1 Cor 10:18-22, 32, and perhaps in the discussions of idol meat and of the col-

a careful study of the meaning and function of the key terms "call" and "calling," "being able to become free," and "using" (without an explicit object) is an answer to the following questions possible.

Does Paul consider and treat slavery as an institution, status, or occupation ordained and sanctified by God? Does Paul's eschatological orientation motivate him to counsel or to command slaves to remain slaves forever, irrespective of chances to become manumitted, or does he urge social change and emancipation, though not by violent means? In one case he is ultimately a supporter of the ruling powers, in the other he not only tolerates but implicitly works for and encourages social change.

Together with the HT and Rom 13:1-7, PHM seems to foster a conservative understanding of Paul. But the UF, combined with at least one exposition of 1 Cor 7:21 saying that every chance to become free must be used, appear to contradict this opinion. The history of Pauline interpretation shows that even when 1 Cor 7:21 was understood to support emancipation by manumission, yet Paul was most frequently depicted as a protector of the sociopolitical status quo.

1. THE IMPASSE OF TRADITIONAL INTERPRETATION

In Bible versions and exegetical literature, two main schools of thought can be distinguished.

a. The scholarly majority assumes complete harmony between PHM and 1 Cor 7:21; it makes Paul look like a man who lacks genuine concern about the social status of Onesimus and other slaves. First Corinthians 7:21 is translated, "If you can gain your freedom, make use of your present condition" (RSV, fn.) or, "even if you have a chance of freedom, you should prefer to make full use of your condition as a slave" (JB), or "choose rather to make good use of your servitude" (NEB, fn.), or similarly.[170]

---

lection for the saints in Jerusalem) only in 2 Cor 3 and 11. At any rate, Paul's excursus regarding God's calling (1 Cor 7:17-24) does include in vv. 21-23 an explicit discussion of the interrelation between free and unfree persons.

170. In the ancient church, e.g., Ignatius, Ambrosiaster, Chrysostom, Severian, Pelagius, Cyril of Alexandria, Theodoret, Vg., and Peshitta. In the classical Roman Catholic tradition: Peter Lombard, Thomas Aquinas, W. Estius; also modern Bible scholars. Among Protestant interpreters: ZB; C. K. Barrett; H. Bellen; J. A. Bengel; G. Bornkamm; W. Bousset; H. Conzelmann; W. M. L. de Wette; G. Eichholz; R. Gayer; E. J. Goodspeed; H. Greeven; A. von Harnack; E. Käsemann; G. Klein; W. G. Kümmel; J. Leipold; H. Lietzmann; E. Lohse; W. F. Orr and J. A. Walther (AB 32, pp. 215-216); F. Overbeck; Petersen, p. 198 n. 172; H. Schlier; W. Schrage; S. Schulz; A. Schweitzer; A. Steinmann ("Zur Geschichte der Auslegung von I.Kor. 7-21," *Theolog. Revue* 16 [1917]: 340-348); K. Stendahl; H. Weidinger; B. Weiss; J. Weiss; H. D. Wendland; U. Wilckens.

b. After the words *mallon chrēsai* (lit. "use rather"), a minority of expositors interpolate an allusion to "freedom" rather than to the state of enslavement. They offer a paraphrastic translation of the whole sentence such as "if a
chance of liberty should come, take it" (NEB) or "if you can gain your freedom,
avail yourself of the opportunity" (RSV).[171]

The arguments available in favor of the first and second schools include
the following.

For the hypothesis that a slave has to remain a slave:

a. In 1 Cor 7:8, 11, 20, 24, 40, that is, in the context of 1 Cor 7:21, the verb
"remain" *(menō)* repeatedly plays a decisive role and always means staying in
the present state or condition. No change is recommended to the man circumcised and the uncircumcised, and to the single and to the married person!

b. In 1 Cor 7:20 the noun *klēsis* (lit. "calling, call") not only sums up the
result of *kaleō* ("to call," in vv. 17, 18, 20, 21, 22, 24) but also specifies the sense
of this verb in 1 Cor 7. In verse 20 *klēsis* therefore can or must mean "station in
life, position, vocation."

c. Jesus Christ became and was a slave *(doulos)* voluntarily, according to
Phil 2:7, and Paul is convinced that to accept suffering with and for Christ is essential for the imitation of Christ crucified. Therefore being a slave and suffering as a slave can be gladly accepted by those slaves who are Christians.

d. Paul announces that only a very brief time is left for living under the
present conditions; for the time is nigh when at Christ's parousia heaven and
earth will be totally renewed by God himself (1 Cor 7:29-31; 1 Thess 4; Phil
4:5). This makes changes in social relations superfluous. Whatever is wrong and
bad now, cannot be reformed or improved. Freedom and justice cannot be established by human beings, least of all by political zealots. God alone on his
own day will transform the world.

e. Early Christianity had to strive for acceptance and respectability in
contemporary society. Therefore it had to invalidate suspicions or accusations
of being a subversive political, cultural, or economic liberation movement.

f. Israel's exodus history notwithstanding, in old Israel and even at Paul's
time the possibility existed among Jews that a slave voluntarily rejected the
manumission offered (Exod 21:5-6; Deut 15:16-17).

g. PHM and the HT confirm the advice given in 1 Cor 7:21. Peter
Lombard and Thomas Aquinas argue that a slave who continues to serve his
master not only prevents slander of God's name and of the gospel teaching (cf.

---

171. Ancient church and Reformation time: Ephraem, Erasmus, Luther, Calvin, Beza,
KJV. Among nineteenth- and twentieth-century scholars: C. H. Dodd, F. Godet, J. C. K.
v. Hofmann, J. B. Lightfoot, J. Moffatt, C. F. D. Moule, K. H. Rengstorf, A. Schlatter,
E. Schweizer, P. Stuhlmacher, P. Trumann ("Die Chance der Freiheit," *Biblia* 56 [1975]: 344-
368), Th. Zahn.

1 Tim 6:1; Titus 2:10) but also becomes heir of a better freedom granted by God. Already Ignatius (*Polyc.* 4.3), the *Gospel of Philip* 114, and Cyril of Alexandria had emphasized that by being and remaining a slave a servant avoided being victimized and enslaved by unbridled lusts.

These arguments lead to the conclusion that the internal freedom available to a slave who chooses to remain a slave attains to a goal higher than external social freedom. In this regard, then, the apostle's attitude resembles the comfort offered by the Stoics: he recommends in 1 Cor 7:21 that slaves renounce possible emancipation, because being a slave is a unique opportunity to display the virtues of a Christian.[172]

Yet there are counterarguments supporting the thesis of the second school, which understands Paul as a man who encourages slaves to seek freedom and seize every opportunity to gain it. These arguments can show that PHM ought not be quoted in favor of the conservative interpretation of 1 Cor 7:21, but rather as a document promoting social change.

a. The evidence adduced from Greek literature outside the NT for *klēsis* (calling) in the sense of occupation, professional status, or condition within society does not survive closer examination. Ample evidence exists in undisputed and disputed Pauline writings, also in the rest of the NT and in the apostolic fathers, that God's calling (*klēsis* and *kaleō*) pertains to something other than an earthly occupation and status. Certainly it reaches persons who are burdened or pleased with their places and functions in society. One makes his living, e.g., as a fisherman, the other as tentmaker (and as a delegate of the Sanhedrin, in addition); here is a publican and there a noble scribe or scholar. But the election and investiture into such an occupation or social group is never described as a divine call.[173]

b. When in the HT Paul tells the slaves to serve their masters humbly and faithfully, and when the fugitive Onesimus is sent back to his master, eventual emancipation from earthly bondage is by no means excluded. On the contrary, in 1 Cor 7:21 the words "if you can become free, use it all the more" plainly reveal an often overlooked element of Paul's concern and counsel for slaves. At first sight the slightest trace of interest in their liberation seems to be absent from, or at least completely hidden under, the apostle's utterances concerning slaves: according to the HT, nothing else counts than voluntary submission to the masters, and according to PHM Paul has taken the responsibility for Onesimus's return to Philemon. But the question of occasions for emancipation in 1 Cor 7:21 throws a new light on the HT and on PHM. It is most likely

---

172. Under the title "Verzicht auf Freilassung als asketische Leistung," in *JAC* 6 (1962), pp. 177-180, H. Bellen discusses the possibility that a slave's renunciation of manumission was a step proper for ascetics.

173. See Annotation 11, pp. 236-238, for a discussion of this translation, its origin, its implications, and the lack of philological evidence to support it.

that the apostle, when he wrote or dictated the HT in the letters to the Colossians and Ephesians, thought of the fact that a slave's good and faithful work would pave the way into liberty; and it is certain — because of the contents of Philem 13 — that Paul hoped secretly in the depth of his heart that Philemon would be set free by his earthly master for service at the apostle's side.

c. There is another, much weightier and deeper reason for stating that Paul reckons with emancipation at a given moment. Jesus Christ is proclaimed by Paul as the foundation and model of faith and life. This Lord is not only obedient, hard-suffering, and finally crucified the way a rebel or revolting slave would be; he is also raised from the depth of his servant-slave existence to the highest honor and glory. All over the world, to all persons on earth he can reach, Paul speaks of Jesus Christ in order that Jews and Greeks can participate as free children — not as "slaves to men" (1 Cor 7:23b) — in this Lord's life and glory, even while they still have to bear their share in his labor, suffering, and dying.[174]

The imagery of an ascertained inheritance and of a sure harvest is used for illustrating the relationship between the miserable present and the promised glorious future. They are related to one another as the transitory is to the final, as the means is to an end.[175] Being a slave and being a master — both states are elements of the world that passes away. Far from sanctifying slavery as the apostle is alleged to do in the HT and in PHM, Paul reminds the Corinthians in 1 Cor 7:21 that this institution has holes and openings for attaining equality and freedom. The apostle would flatly contradict all he said in the UF if he failed to exhort slaves to seize every opportunity of being manumitted.

d. The liberation by Christ of which Paul speaks[176] is not restricted to the gift of internal freedom. Indeed, freedom and peace of the soul (as also proclaimed by Stoic philosophers and as exemplified by Socrates' renunciation of an illegal escape from prison) were not unknown to Paul — or else he could not have spoken with joy of his sufferings (Col 1:24; Eph 3:13; etc.). But the UF of Gal 3:28, etc., not only express an emotional, perhaps mystical feeling, but are also basic to the congregations' life and order, e.g., at the Lord's Table. When Paul writes to Philemon of his planned visit (v. 22), he expects in the near future to be bodily freed from prison. As long as the apostle completely identifies himself with Onesimus (vv. 11 and 17), how can he foster a hope of freedom for himself unless he has the same confidence for the slave?

e. Indeed, a Jewish slave could repudiate manumission and choose to remain attached to his master's home as his ear was fixed to the doorpost. However, in Greek and Roman legal and historical, moral and poetical literature a

---

174. 1 Cor 4:6-13; 2 Cor 4:7-14; Rom 4:25; 6:5; 8:14-19; Phil 2:5-11; etc.
175. Gal 3:23–4:7; Rom 7–8; etc.
176. In 1 Cor 7:22; Gal 2:4; 3:13; 5:1, 13; Rom 6:18; cf. 8:21.

renouncement of manumission is never mentioned as a viable option. The translation of 1 Cor 7:21 in the sense of "rather make use of being a slave" suggests that Paul wanted all slaves who had a chance of freedom to take the desperate step of the Jewish slaves mentioned. It is probable that the contempt in which later rabbis held the ear-pierced Jewish slaves was not entirely strange to Paul. If so, then he could hardly counsel Christian slaves to choose that way.

The arguments supporting the first school are no less weighty than those favoring the second. The names of excellent scholars deciding for the one or the other option are most impressive (see nn. 170 and 171). Most likely it is impossible to tip the balance or break through the logjam. On either side Paul is interpreted in a way that seeks to protect him from the accusation thrown against him from the other quarter. If then in each case the apostle is pushed into the defendant's bench, the principle *in dubio pro reo* cannot be applied.

Or is there a compromise solution, saying that Paul intentionally may have chosen ambiguous language because he combined conflicting opinions within himself and had no other way than uttering them in mutually contradictory statements? Even such a compromise achieves no more than replacing the search for the true meaning of a text with a desperate shrug of the shoulders. In addition, it is also possible that the impasse faced by the expositors of 1 Cor 7:21 is caused by the exegetes' fixation upon a misleading alternative. Such alternatives exclude the victory of one school over the other and also defy a compromise and reconciliation between both. Perhaps the choice offered between Paul an archconservative and Paul a liberation theologian presupposes and imposes upon the text modern categorizations that cannot serve as suitable keys to understanding the apostle's mind, work, and words.

2. ANOTHER EXPOSITION

S. S. Bartchy's earlier-mentioned book, *Mallon Chresai,* is a great leap forward, after the discussion of this one verse had become stale in spite of lights thrown on it from opposite sides. As earlier observed, among the studies written by biblical exegetes on slavery in antiquity and especially at Paul's time, Bartchy's work offers the most instructive and circumspect orientation, together with a careful evaluation of the primary and secondary literature listed in the bibliography below.

Bartchy translates 1 Cor 7:21 in a novel way and provides arguments that so far have not been used, and thereby renders superfluous the strife between the two schools mentioned.[177] According to him, this verse "could be para-

177. Bartchy's exposition shares one element with both traditional interpretations,

phrased: 'But if indeed you are able to be manumitted . . .' or, 'if indeed your owner should manumit you, by all means [now as a freedman] live according to God's call.'"[178] On the ground of Bartchy's careful study of slavery at Paul's time, the main, double-pronged argument that supports his thesis can be summed up as follows:

a. According to Greek and Roman legislation and custom, a slave could not force his or her master to grant freedom. Therefore the words "if you can gain your freedom" cannot presuppose the following possibilities: that a slave could require and would be granted liberty, if only (1) sufficient payment was offered to the owner, out of the slave's own savings or from relatives; (2) after a slave's escape from the master's home a temporary cover and/or protector was found (in the worst case a robber gang, in better cases a friend of the master ready to intercede, or an asylum temple specializing in mediation between slaves and masters); (3) a slave had found so distant and safe a place that the master had no chance at all to retrieve the fugitive. For whatever was offered, whatever happened upon the initiative of a slave — it was still exclusively the master's privilege to decide over the future of his property. An example of the one-sided power of the socially superior person to release or to retain a man of lesser status is found in Acts 26:32: "This man could have been set free *(apolelysthai edynato)* if he had not appealed to Caesar."

b. The words (lit.) "rather make use" cannot be based on the assumption that, after a master had decided to release a slave, the person to be manumitted was free to accept or to reject the emancipation at will. Rather, in that case the slave had no other choice than to accept freedom and leave his patron's house, the risk of a much more miserable future notwithstanding. In a context not directly related to manumission but applicable to it, Seneca (*Ben.* 3.19.1) states, "servus non habet negandi potestatem" [a slave has no legal power to say no]. For several reasons,[179] manumissions were so frequent at Paul's time that Emperor Augustus passed laws that limited their number.

---

and another with only the second. (a) He asks for an object to the verb "using" *(chraomai)*, although in 2 Cor 13:10 the apostle Paul — just as before and after him Plato, Xenophon, LXX, Josephus, Epictetus, and papyri — employs the verb in an absolute sense, that is, without spelling out *what* is to be "used." For references see Stuhlmacher, p. 45 n. 112. (b) When Bartchy supplies *klēsis* (calling) as the intended object, he understands the noun to mean, in agreement with unquestioned lexical evidence and general NT usage, God's calling that is summed up in Christ, by authorized spokesmen of Christ, and depends on continuous confirmation by the Holy Spirit. As shown in Annotation 11, pp. 236-238, Paul does not mean by it an earthly occupation that has been allotted to a person by the Creator God or by the voice of worldly conditions, long before Christ's and the Spirit's coming.

178. Bartchy, pp. 158-159; cf. 120, 154, 183. For the reasons mentioned in the following, see esp. pp. 87-91, 98, 104, 111, 118, 172-183.

179. Such as, faithful service over many years, marriage of a slave into the owner's or a

From the grammar, syntax, and logic of 1 Cor 7:21; from the structure of the context; and from parallel statements of Paul in other letters, Bartchy derives additional arguments in support of his stance.[180] All of them lead him to the conclusion (p. 159 and elsewhere) that, according to Paul, neither circumcision nor uncircumcision, neither enslavement to an earthly master nor sociopolitical freedom bring a person nearer to God. Much more, all Christians, under all circumstances and conditions of their life in the society and culture of their environment, have to heed the call of God. Their one duty is to "keep the commandments," to let "faith work out in love," and to live as a "new creation in Christ."[181] Therefore near the end of his book (on p. 133) Bartchy offers the following version of 1 Cor 7:17, 20-21, and 24: "In any case, let each live his life in accord with the fact that the Lord has distributed [faith] to him and that God has called him. That is what I teach in all our congregations. . . . Each person should continue in that calling into which he was called. Were you a slave when you were called? Don't worry about it. But if, indeed, you become manumitted, by all means [as a freedman] live according to [God's calling]. . . . Each one should continue to live in accord with his calling [in Christ] — in the sight of God."

Opposite the expected unconditional trust in God's holy call and to answering that call in faith and by love would be to despair in view of continued earthly bondage and wanton misuse of freedom eventually gained.[182] As was earlier observed, in 1 Cor 7:20-24 primarily slaves are addressed, while the HT of Ephesians and Colossians contain corresponding appeals to the masters. The Epistle to Philemon imposes upon the master alone the responsibility to let faith and love determine the master/slave relationship. In all cases, as summaries of Paul's preaching, and counseling such as the UF, reveal, the congregation of Christ knows the way to exemplify, by the special interrelationship of its members, a new order of life. This order neither continues nor glorifies the sociopolitical present order; also it is not the effect of a revolutionary program carried out by desperate and yet courageous persons. Rather from day to day the new order, called by N. R. Petersen an "antistructure," has to be sought and found anew. In 1 Cor 7:17-24, freedom at any price and by any means as well as

---

friend's home, troubles with lazy or recalcitrant slaves, economic conditions in periods of crisis. See sec. VII of "Social Background," pp. 42-45.

180. Because they are accessories rather than basic elements of his thesis, they are not enumerated at this place.

181. 1 Cor 7:19; Gal 5:6; 6:15; 2 Cor 5:17.

182. By bearing his chains gladly for Christ's and the church's sake, Paul himself is an example of enduring captivity to the glory of God (see, e.g., Col 1:24; Eph 3:13; 6:20; Phil 1:12-14; 4:4; 2 Tim 4:6-8). Warnings of the misuse of liberty are found, e.g., in Rom 3:8; 6:1-2, 15; Gal 5:1, 13; 1 Pet 2:16; cf. Ignatius, *Polyc.* 4.3.

permanent slavery are equally rejected. Instead, the apostle speaks of a service to Christ that makes service to earthly masters bearable, and of a freedom that enables persons "all the more" to respond to God's call and to shoulder responsibilities in the human society. More important than freedom from an old yoke is the freedom *for* service to the one Lord, Christ, even in the time left before the parousia and the Last Judgment.

VIII. HISTORY AND ISSUES OF INTERPRETATION

Throughout the course of the church's history there have existed various interpretations and applications of PHM. The lack of an overarching harmony is caused by obscure and ambiguous elements in the text. The author's intention appears to be unequivocal: because Philemon and Onesimus are members of the church, Paul entreats the slave owner to receive and treat the returning slave as a dear brother. However, the apostle does not specify the manner and extension of social change implied in this request. Is he primarily expecting — in harmony with Stoic teaching of his time — an inner change, issuing, e.g., in a humane attitude of the master and in humble and faithful working habits of the slave? Or does Paul implicitly ask for manumission, and immediate and final termination of the master/slave relation? Although other issues have to be faced too, in the search for a proper understanding of PHM almost two thousand years of interpreting and applying the letter have been confronted with this grave alternative.

A. Samples of the Variety

The first person expected to understand the letter was Philemon. For him, correct interpretation would mean immediate compliance. If to Philemon several passages sounded obscure, or if he hesitated to act according to sufficiently clear statements, then the persons addressed together with him would be ready to help. Apphia, Archippus, and the other Christians meeting in the same house, if need be also the carriers of the epistle, Tychicus and/or Onesimus (Col 4:7-9), would gladly assist the solution of exegetical problems. In addition they would exert heavier or slighter pressure to lead the way from hearing and reading Paul's words toward acts of obedience.

At least four ways existed for Philemon to react properly. (1) He could keep Onesimus at his place as a house slave. By considering and treating him henceforth as a brotherly friend, he would go beyond the more general counsels given to masters in the *Haustafeln*. (2) He could fulfill the suggestion timidly made by Paul in Philem 13: he could loan or donate Onesimus to the apostle, as an assistant in Paul's mission work. (3) He could manumit Onesimus. Then Onesimus would acquire the status of a freedman and would for several years still be economically and morally bound to his patron, while also enjoying some legal protection. (4) He could grant instantaneous, unconditioned freedom to the slave. Thereby he might either expose Onesimus to the vicissitudes suffered by many ex-slaves or open the door to Onesimus's slow or rapid social ascent, e.g., to the rank of a bishop of Ephesus, of an employee in city administration, if not of a respectable emperor slave.[183]

It is most likely that Philemon responded as positively and completely to Paul's letter as his understanding and good will permitted, and that the fellow Christians in his environment appreciated the effect of the letter. Or else neither Philemon, nor the local congregation, nor any other church would have protected PHM from getting lost or being forgotten. But even if it were known which one of the four ways, or which other way, Philemon had chosen to enact his understanding of the letter — no evidence exists that Paul was ever informed of Philemon's decision and accepted it as fulfillment of the letter's intention.

In the *Haustafeln* of Col 3:22–4:1 and Eph 6:5-9, there existed under Paul's name clear indication of how PHM was to be interpreted. If these household codes are genuinely Pauline, they form a key to Paul's intention. If, however, as is the case for a majority of historical-critical exegetes, they are ascribed (together with 1 Tim 6:1-2; Titus 2:9-10; 1 Pet 2:18-20) to a Pauline school, they still offer insight into a very early interpretation of PHM. Since even in undisputed letters Paul himself takes what today is called a conservative stance,[184] there is no reason for assuming that the *Haustafeln* essentially contradict the apostle's own proclamation and ethical directives.

Further clues to an early interpretation of PHM are offered by Ignatius, the bishop of Syrian Antioch. In the first six chapters of his *Letter to the Ephesians,* there are so many parallels to the style of PHM that literary dependence

---

183. Recent extremes of opinion are represented by, e.g., A. Suhl, "Der Philemonbrief als Beispiel paulinischer Paränese," *Kairos,* n.s., 15 (1973): 267-279, and Fr. J. Hinkelammert, *The Ideological Weapons of Death: A Theological Critique of Capitalism,* trans. Philip Berryman (Maryknoll, N.Y.: Orbis, 1986), pp. 144-150. The first affirms that "emancipation is not considered" (p. 276); the second, that Philemon would certainly excommunicate himself and become a slave of sin if he did not manumit Onesimus on the spot (pp. 147-148). See n. 112 to "Social Background" (p. 41) for the names of other commentators who discuss this issue, and of scholars who refuse to choose between these alternatives.

184. In Rom 13:1-7 regarding voluntary subordination to political authorities; in 1 Cor 7:17-24 concerning circumcision, marriage, and slavery.

cannot be excluded. In *Eph.* 1.3; 2.1; and 6.2, Ignatius recommends a man called Onesimus who is now bishop of Ephesus and a model of a Christian. It is not certain whether the Onesimus mentioned in PHM and Bishop Onesimus were the same person and eventually collected and edited Paul's letters. Still, the possible identity of the two Onesimuses has been passionately upheld by several scholars, and it has inspired moving stories told to or written for young Christians in order to demonstrate the stages and results of a teenager's conversion and emancipation.[185]

On the other hand, Ignatius of Antioch did not support liberation of slaves in principle. In his letter to Polycarp (4.3), he warns of slaves who desire to be redeemed at the church's expense. Did they, perhaps, point to the precedent of Philem 18-19, where Paul had offered to reimburse master Philemon for losses incurred? Or did they refer to the redemption of family members who had become enslaved, as prescribed in Lev 25:47-49? At any rate, Ignatius shared the Stoics' misgiving against emancipation: freed slaves might become "slaves of lust."

The next step of PHM interpretation consists of the inclusion of this letter in lists of books that together with Israel's Holy Scriptures were read in divine worship, and which eventually were interpreted carefully by Christian scholars. Reasons such as the following contributed to its spread and esteem: Paul was considered its author; in this epistle he treated, if only in a specific case, the worldwide problems posed by slavery; here he showed a warm and friendly face in order to plead for a man in dire need of intercession; and with this letter in hand, church members could rebut enemies of the Christians who suspected or accused them of fostering social unrest. According to J. Knox (*Philemon*, pp. 80-82), the canonization of PHM was due to its close connection with Colossians, especially since it was believed to be the letter "from Laodicea" mentioned in Col 4:16. Among the first to accept PHM as unquestionably Pauline, and therefore as part of the New Testament canon, was Marcion; in this regard (the heretic) Marcion was followed by his declared en-

---

185. E. J. Goodspeed, *The Meaning of Ephesians* (Chicago: University Press, 1933), pp. 79-165; Goodspeed, *Introduction to the New Testament* (Chicago: University Press, 1957), pp. 222-239; Goodspeed, *The Key to Ephesians* (Chicago: University Press, 1956), pp. xiv, xvi; and J. Knox, *Philemon among the Letters of Paul*, 2nd ed. (London: Collins, 1960), pp. 85-92, are the modern fathers of this theory. J. F. Spiegel's earlier-mentioned novel of Onesimus's way into freedom (see n. 79) finds it "easy to imagine" that behind the bishop praised by Ignatius "the former slave Onesimus is hidden" (p. 171). "Saint Onesimus" is the name of a kindergarten in Athens. However, Stuhlmacher (p. 18) follows Lohse (*Colossians and Philemon*, p. 186) when he doubts whether the two men called Onesimus are one and the same person. He believes that the stylistic elements common to Ignatius's *Ephesians* and PHM stem from general Christian parlance, rather than reveal literary dependence of Ignatius.

emy, Tertullian (*Adversus Marcionem* 5.21), and by the Canon Muratori, at the end of the second century.

Yet there was also opposition. Only few church fathers reveal, between about 380 and 420, arguments used against the incorporation of PHM into the canon.[186] They mention: Christ did not always speak through the apostle Paul; convincing marks of inspiration are missing from PHM; there is no substantial discussion of Christ and of the church; the specific relationship of a long ago, deceased master and his slave is bare of perennial significance; the whole matter is too trivial to have been taken up by Paul himself; or, if yet he was the author of PHM, the letter is all too brief and insignificant to be edifying. Neither Chrysostom nor Jerome nor Theodore of Mopsuestia mention the names of the individuals or groups who rejected PHM for such reasons.

In the commentaries of these Fathers, PHM is used as an instrument for fighting certain monastic and enthusiastic movements. In second-century Rome there existed a Gnostic sect, the Carpocratians, who rejected slavery in principle. In the fourth century Eustathius of Sebaste was followed by a group of monks in Asia Minor. The Eustathians opposed not only the keeping of slaves but also marriage, private property, and fasting.[187] A Donatist branch, the raving and raging gangs of the Circumcellions, made the established church tremble in North Africa: the call for the release of all slaves was considered a threat to law and order. However, the existing literary sources hardly suffice for the conclusion that all opposition to PHM had its roots in a more or less chaotic enthusiasm, and that the endorsement of this letter was motivated solely by an antienthusiastic attitude.[188]

---

186. In the East, John Chrysostom (d. 407), *In epistolam ad Philemonem commentarius* (MPG, 42.701-720), and Theodore of Mopsuestia (d. 428), *In epistolam B. Pauli ad Philemonem* (H. B. Swete, ed., *Theodori episcopi Mopsuesteni in epistolas B. Pauli commentarii II* [Cambridge: University Press, 1882], pp. 258-285, esp. 262). In the West, Jerome (d. 420), *Commentarius in epistolam Pauli ad Philemonem liber unus* (MPL, 26.635-656, esp. *Praefatio* VII). Lightfoot, p. 383, offers extensive quotes from the Greek text of Chrysostom, the Latin of Jerome, and the ambiguous Latin versions of Theodore.

In the following, frequent use was made of the chapter "Auslegungs- und Wirkungsgeschichte," in Stuhlmacher, pp. 58-66. Stuhlmacher, in turn, repeatedly refers to the first part of E. Eisentraut, *Des heiligen Apostels Paulus Brief an Philemon* (Würzburg, 1928) — a book that has not become accessible to me.

187. Chrysostom (*In epistolam ad Philemonem commentarius*, p. 704) reacts against persons who claim that "Christendom has brought into life the overthrowing of all things," and who assume that "violence is the solution." Theodore complains (p. 262) that a great many of his contemporaries "upset all things of the present life" because "they no longer distinguish between slave and master, rich and poor, those subjected to rulers and those ruling over others."

188. In his commentary on PHM (pp. 58-59; cf. 65-69), Stuhlmacher suggests that it was the church fathers' antimonastic and antienthusiastic attitude that made them support the canonicity of PHM and motivated them to write commentaries on this epistle.

Chrysostom describes the usefulness of PHM the following way: Paul gives an example to all Christians of how to intervene on behalf even of a refugee, a highwayman, and a thief. Onesimus is an example of how even a very bad man can become a decent person. Here it can be learned that it is not fitting to lure a slave away from an owner. A slave is to remain in his status; also he may eventually convert the master, as suggested by 1 Cor 7:16 and 1 Tim 6:1.

Theodore of Mopsuestia (d. 428) appeals especially to Rom 13:1-7 in order to demonstrate that the status differences of the present time correspond to God's will; therefore slaves have to obey their masters. The humility of the great apostle's plea for a miserable slave is a model for all Christians. Forgiveness, as it is to be granted to Onesimus, is a greater gift than social freedom. Since the slave is now a brother of Philemon, he may even be willing to accept suffering.

Such expositions of PHM do not simply endorse contemporary law and order. They recommend that slaves be treated very humanely — just as Stoic teachings had done.[189] Chrysostom is the first among the most famous Fathers to utter misgivings about the institution of slavery as such. In commenting on NT books other than PHM, he affirms that slavery is the result of sin and greed. Together with the status of women in marriage, of children under their parents, and of subjects in relation to their governments, it is a system of oppression that is due to the sin of Eve, Ham, and Nimrod. Gratitude for God's grace should lead to a new attitude toward children and the poor, and to the manumission of slaves. After a revolt that shook Syrian Antioch, Chrysostom called upon the Christian masters to grant their slaves freedom. If they were unwilling to do so, then two or three masters should be content to be served by one commonly owned slave. When Chrysostom preached in this vein, he did not think of revision of city or state legislation but of the decision and action of believing individuals. For him, fairness shown to slaves was a matter of personal and private ethics.[190]

---

189. F. Overbeck, "Über das Verhältnis der alten Kirche zur Sklaverei im Römischen Reich," in Overbeck, *Studien zur Geschichte der alten Kirche* (Chemnitz: Schmeitzner, 1899), pp. 158-230, passes a harsh judgment when he affirms that, instead of protesting against slavery, since the fourth century the Christian teachers fostered a "sort of Stoicism" that had become "insipid and weak" (p. 225), and that the church caused fewer social changes between the years 300 and 600 than the emperors between the beginning of our era and the year 300 (p. 177). For the following description of Chrysostom's stance, see Overbeck, pp. 196-198, 217-218.

190. See the treatises *De statuis* and the *Homilies* on Matthew, Romans, and Ephesians. E.g., in *Homily* XL on 1 Cor 10, he asserts that slavery is a penalty of sin, but that even this punishment was annulled by Christ. Therefore, so Chysostom teaches, it is not necessary to keep slaves — or one, or at the most two slaves must suffice. Slaves held by Christians ought to be taught some skills so that they can provide for their livelihood, and then they should be set free.

In his comments on PHM, Jerome praises voluntary goodness as is expected of Philemon. He distinguishes between two laws: the eternal law of the Spirit (and of brotherhood and freedom) and the temporal law of earthly bondage. The first does not abrogate the second. Ambrosiaster (late fourth century, in Rome),[191] in turn, points out Paul's humility, the moral consequences of Onesimus's conversion, and the blessings of brotherhood between master and slave.

In later interpretations,[192] similar comments are repeated — until Thomas Aquinas, in his *Summa theologiae* rather than in the *Super epistolas S. Pauli lectura,* teaches that according to secondary natural law (that is, in consequence of Adam's sin), some people are slaves.[193] In his commentary on PHM, Thomas observes that Paul's appeal to Philemon fully corresponds to Sir 33:31: "If you have a servant, treat him as a brother." Also he states that in sending back the escaped slave, the apostle does not contradict Deut 23:15-16 — the text that prohibits the extradition of a runaway slave to his master. For, so Thomas argues, the cordial intercession of Paul for the slave and the absence of a threat to Onesimus's life created a situation that was not discussed in Deut 23. Other contributions of Thomas will be mentioned below, in our verse-by-verse interpretation.

Erasmus's commentary on PHM fills only a few pages.[194] He makes faithful use of Jerome's, Ambrose's (i.e., Ambrosiaster's), Theophylact's, and Theo-

---

191. *Commentarius in epistolas Paulinas,* MPL, 17.503-507, and CSEL, LXXXI 3.

192. E.g., of Theodoret of Cyprus in the fifth century, of Primasius in the sixth century (whose commentary on the Pauline epistle is an orthodox reedition of Pelagius's exegetical work), and of Theophylact in the second half of the eleventh century. Since Oecumenius (sixth century), the shape of biblical interpretation was increasingly a collection of quotations (a florilegium) derived from earlier Fathers. The medieval *Catenae of the Greek Fathers* has been edited by J. A. Cramer in Oxford, 1944, and contains in vol. 7 the excerpts from PHM commentaries. As a literary genre, the *Catenae* is comparable to the selections from the *Pandecta* (a collection of valid laws) produced by lawyers on order of Emperor Justinian (519-65). Another parallel is formed by the *Sententiae* (anthologies of dogmatic statements) widely used in the Middle Ages. The commentaries on biblical books intended not only to elucidate obscure elements by drawing from the insights of the past. They also adduce references to contemporary opinions in order to emphasize the current relevance of the text. The legalistic form of these commentaries does not necessarily contradict the religious character of most biblical books. E.g., the apostle Paul, in consequence of his rabbinical training, often proposed theological arguments in juridical diction. Especially the theme of PHM called for the combination of religious and legal elements.

193. *Opera Omnia,* vol. 21 (Paris: Vivès, 1876), pp. 553-560. The influence of Aristotle and of Stoic philosophers on Thomas's understanding of slavery was mentioned above, in n. 110 to "Social Background," p. 41.

194. See *In Novum Testamentum annotationes* (Basel: Froben, 1535), pp. 702-704.

doret's expositions, and admires above all the apostle Paul's humility and sensibility. To the humanist, the apostle proves himself a true humanist.

In the prologues *(Vorreden)* to the German New Testament (1522 and 1546), Martin Luther, in no more than fourteen lines of text, added new dimensions to the earlier interpretations of PHM. He understood this letter, this "masterful lovely example of Christian love," as a combination of pastoral, juridical, and christological concerns. As already quoted,[195] Luther observed that Paul identified himself with the guilty Onesimus and that all Christians are Jesus Christ's Onesimuses. According to Luther, a Christian renounces his rights, just as Paul had done when he abstained from giving commands to Philemon, and as Philemon is to do by not punishing the slave. Paul's intercession for Onesimus corresponds to Christ's intervention for all of us: by such love and humility God's wrath can be overcome.

In Luther's lecture on PHM (1527),[196] the same elements reappear. Philemon 8 shows that Philemon is "taken up" or "framed *(gefasst)* in Christ," and that Christ stands between Paul and the slave owner. In addition, the Peasants' Revolt of 1525 and the controversies with Thomas Müntzer[197] have left marks on this lecture of Luther: now the Reformer emphasizes the great sin Onesimus had committed in misusing the "Christian liberty" — by being a thief, by running away, and by refusing to do his duty. The words "whom I have sent back" (Philem 12) are declared to be the sum of the whole epistle, for by these words Paul "does not abrogate slavery." Rather by this phrase the status of a slave is "reconciled." With this interpretation PHM was made a trump card in the battle against the *Schwärmer* (spiritualists) of the Reformation period. However, unlike later Lutherans, the Reformer himself interpreted 1 Cor 7:21 as meaning "if you can become free, seize the opportunity for freedom."

John Calvin[198] is more dependent on the early church and medieval exposition of PHM than is Luther. The sociopolitical stance taken in the PHM commentaries of the two Reformers is practically the same. Yet Calvin is even more explicit than Luther. In commenting on Philem 20, he states, "faith in the gospel does not upset the political order, neither are the full power and the lordship of the master over the slaves invalidated. . . . The master's role over the

---

195 From WA, *Deutsche Bibel,* 7.292-293, above in nn. 113 and 116.

196. *Vorlesung über die Briefe an Titus and Philemon,* WA, 25.64-78.

197. Müntzer placed personal experience of Christ higher than a doctrinary definition of justification by faith. His main concerns were the liberation of the oppressed from the tyranny of their rulers and exploiters, and the formation of a Christian democracy. Ideas, goals, and methods that centuries later were called communist were anticipated by him. He died as one of the leaders of the Peasants' War in 1525, after heavy tortures.

198. *Commentarius in epistolam ad Philemonem* (1551), CR 80, *Calvini opera,* 52.437-450.

slave which is permitted by the law, is not taken away." Philemon "is told no more than to receive the slave humanely, after granting him forgiveness." However, this qualified endorsement of slavery is spiced by a special element that will play a major role later, in pietistic commentaries: Onesimus is depicted as a man who before his conversion was an outstanding rogue, even "a vile slave and a thief, and a tramp in addition." By his flight Onesimus demonstrated that "he was customarily and habitually resolutely fixed upon depravity." Solely by the grace of God did this scoundrel become a "memorable model of repentance" — though usually "the inner life of a slave is so corrupt that barely one out of twenty ever comes to a good end." Still, the power of God and assistance from the human side can have the effect that even such a person is reborn and made new (on vv. 10 and 16).

This interpretation is strongly reflected in the attitude of several evangelical groups during the post-Reformation centuries: personal conversion counts more than the concern for radical social change; the legality and validity of the present social structure can and will be overcome no earlier and by no other means than the establishment of God's kingdom, after the end of the present age. Calvin himself did not always prove so reticent. In the 1559 edition of his *Institutio* (4.20.30-32), he wrote of the right of subordinate political authorities, who were exposed to the injustice and whims of a tyrant, to resist the person who perverted God's good order — if need be, by force.[199]

Huldrych Zwingli exerted great influence on the government, the politics, and the society of Zürich. But his interpretation of the New Testament does not include commentaries on the Pastoral Epistles and PHM.

The great humanist, historian, lawyer, and Dutch patriot Hugo Grotius (1583-1645) wrote in his later years commentaries on the books of the Old and the New Testaments. He introduced a new element into scholarly Bible interpretation: he explained the several parts of the Bible in the light of their historical background and their place in the social life of the Jews, the Christians, and the nations. In his exposition of PHM,[200] he was probably the first to refer to Pliny the Younger's intercession for a runaway. Being an expert in Roman law, Grotius showed that Paul's intervention on Onesimus's behalf was a completely legal step and left untouched the master's right over the slave. For "the doctrine of the gospel does not remove status differences," as little between masters and slaves as between rulers and those ruled (on Philem 15). By his books on the law of nations, states, and communities, Grotius had earlier in his life estab-

199. John Knox of Scotland, Oliver Cromwell, and the fathers of the American Revolution have shown that Calvin's influence was capable of leading to great social and political changes.

200. In the frame of his *Annotationes in Novum Testamentum* II (1646, pp. 779-786, re-edited Paris, 1759), pp. 831-837.

lished his European fame as a great sage. He became the father of post-Reformation natural law theories by arguing, e.g., that because God is the creator of nature and reason, and because he is the ultimate source and protector of law, the will of God and natural law neither contradict nor exclude one another mutually. It is of the essence of humanity, if the latter is understood as "sociability," to possess a sense of what is right and to live according to it. While natural law acknowledges the fact of self-love, it requires the taming of self-love by love of the neighbor. Superior power of one segment of society does not suffice to legitimize existing social relations. For Grotius, PHM confirmed the synthesis in which ethical, religious, and rational foundations of law are inseparable and complementary.[201]

Two Roman Catholic commentaries, published only a few years after Grotius's death, follow the medieval pattern. In their expositions of PHM, Cornelius a Lapide and William Estius appear not to have taken notice of the Reformers' and Grotius's exegetical contributions. Still, whether consciously or not, they pay respect not only to the tradition in which they stand but also to the battle cry *sola Scriptura*.[202] For they compare and examine the opinions of the church fathers very carefully in the light of the literal meaning of each verse of PHM. Very skillfully they discuss those variant readings of the Greek text that have become accessible through printed editions of the Greek New Testament, and they dare to question claims for a monopoly of the current edition of the Vulgate. Cornelius a Lapide and Estius refer to Ignatius of Antioch as a source from which to derive that at a ripe age Onesimus became bishop of Ephesus. Cornelius a Lapide (on p. 816) reveals pastoral concern when he treats PHM as a model of showing how to deal with the poor and with servants. Estius describes Paul's solidarity with Onesimus in a unique way: the apostle has the slave as much "in himself" as Mary had in herself the child Jesus; the runaway is Paul's alter ego.

201. Stuhlmacher, p. 61, avers that, on the whole, Grotius's exegetical work lacks edifying value and dogmatical dimensions. But since for Grotius there was no legal question or social relation that was not also ethical and religious, Stuhlmacher's judgment may miss Grotius's intention and achievements. An excellent brief presentation of H. Grotius's life and work is made by E. Wolf, *Grosse Rechtsdenker*, 4th ed. (Tübingen: Mohr, 1963), pp. 253-310. For the religious character of Grotius's reflection on law, see esp. pp. 262, 279-281, 289-290. Grotius was deeply influenced by Aristotle and the Stoics, but he also was a Protestant indebted to Calvin's utterances on law. He defended those dogmas on which Roman Catholic, Reformed, and Lutheran Christians agreed, but he was persecuted by Dutch Reformed and rejected by Lutheran orthodox theologians, because he sided with the Arminians (Remonstrants).

202. Cornelius a Lapide, *Commentaria in omnes Divi Pauli epistolas*, rev. ed. (Antwerp, 1656), pp. 816-30; W. Estius, *In omnes Divi Pauli apostoli epistolas* (Paris: Quesnel, 1652), pp. 880-886.

Why, then, did the apostle not explicitly ask for manumission? In his explanation of Philem 16, Estius gives four answers: (1) Onesimus must not harvest freedom as reward for his flight and theft. (2) Since slaves are a useful part of property, Paul will not extend an "all too cumbersome petition" to Philemon. (3) First Corinthians 7:21 consoles the slave: You were called while being a slave? Don't bother! (4) The law of love does not require from Philemon the release of Onesimus, for it is applicable only according to given circumstances; not for everyone is it useful to be free. Therefore not even love compels slave owners to bereave themselves of the slaves who are indispensable for maintaining the masters' families.

It is obvious that by this kind of reasoning, Estius sanctioned the social and economic status quo: there were affluent Christians who owned slaves, and slave trade was a lucrative business. On the other hand, the same author appears to have been aware that Paul, by sending back Onesimus to his owner, may have contradicted his own proclamation of the freedom and equality of all God's children.

According to J. A. Bengel,[203] the words "more than a slave . . . in the flesh" (Philem 16) reveal that Paul expected Onesimus to be granted the status of a freedman. In all editions of Bengel's *Gnomon,* a "most private matter" is treated in PHM, while yet this letter "offers a specimen of highest wisdom (by showing) how Christians are to treat civil matters on the ground of higher principles."

The development of the historical-critical methods of exegesis and the increasing accessibility of ancient nonbiblical texts issued, in the nineteenth and early twentieth centuries, foremost on German soil, in an abundance of scholarly commentaries.[204]

After F. C. Baur with small success had attempted to disprove the Pauline origin of PHM, mainly philological and historical detail problems such as the Roman or Caesarean origin, the date, the purpose, and the result of the letter were intensively discussed. The question whether this kind, warm, and beautiful billet really pressed for Onesimus's emancipation, or whether the slave remained a slave in Philemon's house, was answered in various ways or left open. Prevailing was the conviction that Christendom does not know differences of status and rank, and that Christian brotherhood is independent of a person's social and economical position, while yet an ethical halo sanctifies the prevailing social order and may eventually pave the way toward some reforms.

203. Not yet in the first edition of his *Gnomon Novi Testamenti* (Tübingen: Schramm, 1742), pp. 889-890, but in later editions.

204. On pp. 62-64, Stuhlmacher's book on PHM contains a crisp description of the contribution made to PHM exegesis by J. F. von Flatt, W. M. L. de Wette, F. Bleek, H. A. W. Meyer, K. von Hofmann, E. Haupt, P. Ewald, and A. Schlatter.

Under the influence of the secular and/or religious emancipation movements of the middle of the nineteenth century, J. B. Lightfoot wrote his commentary on PHM, in 1875, and published revised editions in the same year and in 1879. He admits[205] that, at Paul's time, "to prohibit slavery was to tear society into shreds"; "the Gospel never directly attacks slavery as an institution"; the NT "is not concerned with any political or social institutions"; in PHM, while "the word 'emancipation' seems to be trembling at [Paul's] lips," "yet he does not once utter it"; this idea "has been marred by revolutionary violence."

Lightfoot concludes that church fathers such as Chrysostom and Theodore of Mopsuestia display "occasionally timidity and excess of caution" and therefore are "at fault." For Lightfoot, PHM is the main proof that the NT "lays down universal principles which shall undermine the evil (of slavery). . . . A principle is boldly enunciated which must in the end prove fatal to slavery. . . . Henceforth it was only a question of time. Here was the idea which . . . must disintegrate this venerable institution. . . . The Christian idea was not a dead letter . . . it is towards this goal that Christianity as a social principle has been always tending and still tends" — though "there have been shameful exceptions now and then." "It is a broad and patent fact that throughout the early and middle ages the influence of the church was exerted strongly on the side of humanity in this matter," as "the rapid strides towards emancipation during the present generation" show in Britain, Russia, and the United States, although the interior of Africa still lags behind.[206]

Lightfoot is confident that a peaceful evolutionary process is already spearheaded by Christendom and will lead to necessary social changes. Personal conversion is the key and the door to that change; nonviolence is the only method to promote it. What Luther and Calvin had sown on the ground of patristic and medieval traditions was watered by Lightfoot and taken up by a majority of twentieth-century evangelical groups. Renewal of the individual by personal rebirth became the alternative to developing Marxist ideas, programs, and means for a radical change of the prevailing social, political, and economic order.

However, since the end of the nineteenth century, the interpretation of the NT, under the influence of Johannes Weiss's and Albert Schweitzer's studies of the role of eschatology, took a new turn. The kingdom of God preached by Jesus was, according to the synoptic Gospels, originally understood as an otherworldly reality that was to break in from the beyond with the glorious re-

---

205. Already in the first edition (pp. 389-395), from which are culled the following quotes. All other references to Lightfoot in this volume are based on the 1st ed.

206. Against the idealism, optimism, and triumphalism of a stance such as Lightfoot's, not only historians and populists influenced by K. Marx and F. Engels, but also, e.g., Overbeck, "Über das Verhältnis," have raised rigorous protests.

appearance of Jesus Christ. His "parousia" was expected for the near future, within the life span of some of the first disciples. It was held that according to his undisputed letters, Paul shared in this hope.[207] The brief interval between Christ's resurrection and his return made the prevailing social conditions irrelevant to the substance of the gospel and gave the apostle's moral teaching the character of "interim ethics." Because immediate and worldwide political and social and economic change by human hands was far from his mind and missionary intentions, he wrote passages such as Rom 13:1-7 that required subordination to the powers that be; he sent the fugitive Onesimus back to his master; and he abstained from telling Philemon to manumit his slave on the spot.[208] Inner freedom, cordial love among Christians, and the willingness to accept the sufferings of the present time were the order of the day and formed alternatives to legalistic, enthusiastic, or zealotic ways of shaping a Christian's life.

The relevance of eschatology in the preaching and teaching of Paul cannot be questioned. It is surprising that it was not discovered earlier. While scholarly twentieth-century commentaries and discussions of Pauline ethics never ignore the influence of eschatological elements, divergent conclusions are drawn from them: (1) Large parts of Paul's admonitions are considered disproved by the nonappearance of Christ, and therefore as so time-bound that they are no longer to be respected as binding for the modern church. (2) The apostle's eschatological orientation is affirmed — though it is no longer identified with the hope for the parousia during the earliest disciples' lifetimes.[209] But it is understood as a compelling reason for Christians to wait and to suffer, and to tolerate unjust suffering — until God himself changes all things, on the Lord's Day. Abstention from engagement in radical sociopolitical action becomes then the rule for Christians. (3) The essence and function of the church is so approximated to the eschatological Kingship of God, that all Christians are called, already at the present time, to participate in all honest attempts at forming a new social order. The last-mentioned alternative will be discussed later in some detail, under the heading "The Challenge of Liberation Theology" (pp. 214-221).

An original, stimulating, and widely accepted contribution to PHM studies has been made by John Knox in his book *Philemon among the Letters of Paul* (1935;

---

207. As a comparison of, e.g., 1 Thess 4:15; 1 Cor 7:29-31; Rom 13:11; Phil 4:5 with Matt 10:23; 16:28 par. shows.

208. E.g., Conzelmann and Lindemann, pp. 224-225, cf. 418-419, summarize the consequences of this view for the interpretation of PHM.

209. W. Schrage, *The Ethics of the New Testament* (Philadelphia: Fortress, 1988), pp. 13-40, 181-186, 234-235, etc., demonstrates that the eschatological character of NT ethics does not depend only upon the *Naherwartung*.

enlarged ed., 1960). The literary and historical questions upon which Knox has concentrated, and the solutions proposed by him, are described below in Annotation 1 (pp. 225-226). They scarcely touch on theological and ethical issues.

Leonhard Ragaz, a Swiss exponent of what in the United States is called the Social Gospel movement, has not written a commentary on PHM. Still, within a general discussion of Paul's ethics,[210] he discusses the apostle's request for subordination and makes some explicit statements about the substance of PHM. He considers Rom 13:1-7 and 1 Cor 14:33b-36, which prescribe subordination to the Roman state and the silence of women during divine worship, non-Pauline interpolations, dating from a later period. Paul himself is called "apostle of liberty . . . a revolutionary, not a reactionary," rather a "carrier of a world revolution *sans par* except Jesus." Paul stands for "the great world revolution of the Kingdom of God" and for "the holy anarchism of the whole Bible" — although his genuine concern for the weak is somewhat mitigated by fear and lags behind the freedom of Jesus. It is wrong to condemn him as a conservative or reactionary, notwithstanding the "stark patriarchalistic character of the *Haustafeln*." Only because Paul relies on the revolution to be made by God himself does he resist preliminary reforms for which the time was not yet ripe. At his period revolts had no chance of success. In his Letter to Philemon "Paul does not require abolishment of slavery but accepts the limitation of inner emancipation which is so gloriously described." Since in PHM the apostle addressed "not free people but solely a congregation," he had, unlike Moses and the prophets when they spoke to Israel, nothing to say about political rights and active participation in effecting social changes. To God's own great future revolution corresponds, in Ragaz's understanding of Paul, inner freedom manifested in mutual love and in the sharing of all goods.

Ernst Käsemann affirms that despite contemporary slave revolts and "armies of run-away slaves," Paul accepted the slave system of antiquity as a matter of fact, which on occasion, that is, in PHM, he even endorsed.

Helmut Thielicke speaks of a secret invalidation *(Unterwanderung)* of slavery by Christianity. He is convinced that PHM contributed to the solution of this problem: this letter shows how the antinomy between the legal (Roman) and the moral (Christian) order is dissolved when step-by-step the superiority of the moral over the legal system antiquates unjust current conditions.[211]

210. See L. Ragaz, *Die Bibel — eine Deutung,* vol. 6 (Zürich: Diana-Verlag, n.d.), pp. 86-95, esp. 92-93; the work was written between 1941 and 1943, and has been reprinted, Fribourg and Lucerne: Edition Exodus, vol. 4, 1990.

211. Käsemann in an essay on Rom 13, originally published in 1961; ET, in E. Käsemann, *Essays on New Testament Questions Today* (Philadelphia: Fortress, 1960), esp. pp. 208-209. Thielicke, *Theologische Ethik* II (Tübingen: Mohr, 1955), pp. 550ff.

Peter Stuhlmacher[212] confirms the exegetical tradition that understands PHM as a call to "the congregation and the Church" to live and behave in conformity with the social patterns of the environment. At the same time, he concedes that an opposite interpretation of the letter is also relatively correct — an exposition that emphasizes the "socio-critical implications of the Gospel" and reckons with the eventual release of Onesimus. Just as Adolf Schlatter,[213] so Stuhlmacher proffers a more or less conservative attitude. The main danger is seen as lurking in an enthusiasm that might "devour the gospel in a social emancipation movement." Stuhlmacher questions "whether or not the direct transposition of Christian liberty into social impulses lies in the present ecclesiastic interest." But he admits that — if congregations today truly abided by Pauline principles — Paul's and the early Christians' ideas of full brotherhood and equality would lead to new ways of interpretation and of social life.

Alfred Suhl[214] differs from earlier PHM commentators in at least one regard. While sooner or later most of them break out in praise of Paul because he wrote such a personal, warm, charming, and/or humorous letter, Suhl observes that Paul's request for a voluntary, brotherly, and loving attitude of the master to the slave "borders on extortion with candy and stick." "This letter is (properly) understood then only when for a good while the reader has taken offence at the manner in which Paul is proceeding here." These observations suggest a question to be asked concerning many earlier expositions of PHM: Might not the applause given to the apostle's procedure be a cover-up for gratification at the sanction Paul appears to grant to the existing social order?

An important exponent of a dramatic new turn in the study of PHM (and of all of Paul's letters) is a monograph of Norman R. Petersen.[215] According to Petersen, the puzzles of PHM can be solved by the application of combined linguistic, structuralistic, and sociological methods. This is his position: In this letter the secular story of an imprisoned messenger of Christ and the equally worldly story of a conflict between a master and a slave are taken up and bound into the story of an entirely different world. Petersen uses the term "symbolic universe" for the realm in which God alone is Father, Christ alone is Lord, love is the only all-pervasive power, and all human beings are united in a brotherhood that is both material and spiritual. As an ambassador of the symbolic universe, Paul has to represent in person and to announce the onslaught of the di-

212. *Der Brief an Philemon*, pp. 42-48, 65-69.

213. In his *Erläuterungen zum Neuen Testament* II (Stuttgart: Calwer, 1909), pp. 861-866.

214. Suhl, *Der Brief an Philemon*, esp. p. 39; Suhl, "Der Philemonbrief als Beispiel paulinischer Paränese," esp. pp. 272-275.

215. His book *Rediscovering Paul* was frequently mentioned in the preceding section; see the index of names at the end of this volume.

vine order upon and into the sphere of the earthly institutional structures. At issue is the impact of the eternal upon the passing away, of the eschaton upon the temporal. It is essential of the church to be an antistructure, an alternative to the existing secular institutions. The church is the place where already at the present time a beginning is made of the replacement of divisions, enmities, and all forms of oppression by a new order of communal life. To this function of the church, that is, to the new human society, PHM is so pointed and vital a testimony that this epistle can be considered the key to the whole of Paul's theology.

So far no earlier study has attributed greater relevance to PHM than Petersen's.[216] Even if on occasion his formulations are weird and his arguments less than impeccable, yet the intention and direction of his research are relevant. Social ethics and its palpable manifestation in the constitution and formation of new social relationships are far from being an appendix or an eventual implication of the proclamation of God's kingship and righteousness. Rather they are the very essence of the proclamation of the gospel and of faith.

This insight has developed into a worldwide movement that will be described in the following.

B. The Challenge of Liberation Theology

"Theology of liberation" is the name most frequently used for a movement in which Christian congregations and their pastoral leaders are engaged in order to live and act according to the social, political, and economic substance of the gospel of Jesus Christ. In diverse forms this movement exists in almost all parts of the globe.[217] While it has roots and precedents in the proclamation and ac-

---

216. On p. 175 n. 21 Petersen himself states, "Commentators have not previously entertained the sociological implications that we have been exploring."

217. Outstanding among the various types and widely known authors of this theology are, since about 1960, in the United States the "black theology" and James H. Cone; in Latin America the base communities' "theology of liberation" and Gustavo Gutiérrez; in Korea the "Minjung theology" and Byung Mu Ahn; in South Africa the groups fighting apartheid, whose creed is formulated in the *Kairos Document* produced inter alios by Frank Chicane; in Italy the Roman Catholic and Waldensian "Grass Roots Movement" and Giovanni Battista Fransoni. Their impact on traditional and established theological ways is manifest, and literature relative to the main concerns and methods of liberation theology is abounding. The World Council of Churches' Anti-Racism Program and the Ecumenical Seoul Conference of 1990 on Justice, Peace and Preservation of the Creation endorse main features of it, while declarations of the Vatican Congregation for the Doctrine of Faith have condemned it passionately in 1984 and 1986. Least known are perhaps the signs of an emerging Jewish and Palestinian liberation theology: Nain Stifan Ateck, *Justice and Only Justice*, rev. ed. (Grand Rapids: Eerdmans, 1989), and Mark H. Ellis, *Towards a Jewish Theology of Liberation* (Grand

tion of earlier radical spiritual church members and groups,[218] it is yet a bold challenge to both the traditional academic theological work and the pastoral guidance so far offered by the higher and lower clergy. Now all church members are urged to rediscover the core of the gospel, to expose their faith and their attitudes to a thorough renewal, and to live as a community that no longer condones the misuse of power structures and the factual oppression, exploitation, and hunger among the majority of the earth's population.

In the following, attention will be focused on only one of the movements just mentioned: the Latin American theology of liberation[219] — though it is far from forming a uniform or complete whole.[220]

1. THREE ESSENTIAL FEATURES

a. Theology of, for, and by the People

Since the second century, scholarly theological work among Christians was, as far as is known, in most cases carried out by men. They sought to treat and solve problems of truth, order, and conduct in the light of Jesus Christ's com-

---

Rapids: Eerdmans, 1989). There are, further, Christian scholars leading or participating in the worldwide women's liberation movement in order to make vital contributions to a theology of freedom, justice, and equality.

218. See Annotation 12, pp. 238-240.

219. Main features of the survey presented in the following stem from Gustavo Gutiérrez, *A Theology of Liberation, History, Politics, and Salvation*, trans. and ed. Sr. C. Inda and J. Eagleson, rev. ed. with a new introduction (Maryknoll, N.Y.: Orbis, 1988; Spanish original: Lima, Peru, 1971); Leonardo Boff, *Church, Charisma, and Power: Liberation Theology and the Institutional Church*, trans. John W. Diercksmeier (New York: Crossroad, 1985; Portuguese original: Petropolis, Brazil, 1981); E. J. Beker and J. M. Hasselaar, *Wegen en Kruispunten in de Dogmatiek* IV (Kampen: Kok, 1987), pp. 79-101; P. Eicher, ed., *Neue Summe Theologie* (Freiburg: Herder, 1989), 2.237-271; cf. 3.473-503, esp. 483, 489, 497-498; the declarations of the Episcopal Conference meeting in Medellín, Colombia, in 1968, and in Puebla, Mexico, in 1979; and numerous essays about the Bible study done in base communities, published in journals such as *Reflexion, Paginas, Servir, Pastoral Popular, Solidaridad, Sal Terra, Revista de Teologia y Ciencias Humanas*, by, e.g., G. Gutiérrez, P. Richar, E. Dussel. Among Latin American Protestant protagonists of liberation theology, J. Míguez Bonino is best known. It is noteworthy that at least some evangelical and fundamentalist, free church or sectarian groups in their own way also develop a liberation theology of the kingdom of God.

220. Vital differences exist between several arguments and tendencies of this theology. Among others, the variations concern the question of a general revelation and presence of God in all liberation movements on the earth; the fact and the temptations of Marxist influence; the definition of the multifaceted concept "the people"; the special function of the church; the subordination owed to a recalcitrant institutional church; and/or the need or permission to engage in violent action.

ing, death, and resurrection. Unlike, for example, Paul, Matthew, and the author of Hebrews, they made their reflections and drew their conclusions more according to the standards of contemporary philosophical and ethical schools than in the footsteps of Israel's prophets, priests, and wise men. Similarly, throughout the Middle Ages and to the present day, university- and seminary-trained people have worked out this theology in libraries, in their studies, lecture halls, and/or monasteries. A certain distance from the maddening crowds, the noise and unrest of streets and marketplaces, of crammed and otherwise unhealthy housing has appeared to be a precondition of that work.

Liberation theologians do not in principle deny the potential value of academic school theology. But they insist that other carriers and methods of theological study may be even more necessary and relevant. Since the end of the Second Vatican Council (1962-65), in many of the Latin American base communities — their number is estimated at about 150,000 — poor, hungry, and oppressed persons meet for Bible study. They ask for the substance and the implementation of faith in God. In Hebrew terminology, the materially indigent and spiritually humiliated are the 'ani and 'anaw. In liberation theology they are sources and agents for working out the essence of the gospel; no longer are they and their poverty at best occasional subject matters of theology. Since, according to the Bible, God himself has opted for the poor, they are, even in their poverty, God's own people. Therefore in their voices God himself speaks and is heard. The old slogan *vox populi — vox dei* (the people's voice is God's voice) is given a new foundation.

Inasmuch as scholars and pastoral agents, among them bishops and parochial priests, nuns, and monks, listen to the voice of these people, declare their solidarity with them by deeds, and participate in the struggle for justice, they have a legitimate function among the poor and are relevant theologians.

In other words, theology is no longer a theory hovering above, about, or beyond the really existent earthly conditions of life. Rather, theological work is now understood as a practice aimed at changing the world. Truth is no longer treated as a timeless abstract but has ethics for a criterion. If truth fails to mean justice and freedom, it is equal to a mere phantom.

b. Jesus Christ's Victory on the Cross over the Powers of the World

Christology is the heart of liberation theology. Jesus Christ is the redeemer of the world, a gift of God's sheer grace that excludes the notion of human self-liberation. The historical Jesus came to the poor, healed the sick, and fed the hungry. He was rejected by the religious and political power holders of his time, and when he died on the cross he revealed full solidarity with all those dying under oppression. His resurrection is the triumph of life over the powers of injustice and death that dominate the world today as much as in Jesus' day. The poor and needy of Latin America experience the sinful and deadly energy of those powers in the economic dependence of their countries on the industrialized nations and the heavy hands of the local agricultural, industrial, trade, and banking power holders. Those rich care little or not at all for the food, clothing, shelter, and health of the huge majority of the people. When the poor would look up to the leaders of the church and expect help from them, they find themselves confronted by the alliance between altar, throne, and money — and therefore they turn to Christ and the Bible.

Liberation theologians know well enough that personal sin can and shall be overcome by the cross and the resurrection, by repentance and forgiveness — so much so that sinners will be reconciled with God. But they insist that structural sin and starvation can never be reconciled. The causes and the consequences of the present "system's" sin must be revealed by careful social analysis and must be resisted and abolished. Even if a new and just social order cannot be realized at once, there is yet and all the more God's promise that Christ will ultimately be victorious, and this pledge gives courage and patience to endure, to suffer, and to do everything possible for a change of present-time conditions. After all, the eternal *logos* of God has become incarnate and has taken the form of flesh and bone, of activity, of suffering and rising in the midst of the powers of sin and death. God's word and will are to be continuously incarnated in the realms of matter and of labor, of the crying needs and of the striving for justice.

c. The Power of the Spirit

Liberation theology can be briefly defined as a theology of the Holy Spirit ("pneumatology") or of the kingdom of God. These descriptions do not belittle but expound the christological core. For God's universal rulership is established by the resurrection of the crucified Christ, and by the gift and operation of the Spirit that made Jesus the Messiah of the Jews and the Gentiles. The same Spirit was poured out through the exalted Lord; it continuously reveals and explains him, and it manifests his living presence. According to 2 Cor 3:17 and other texts,[221] the Lord Christ, the Spirit, and freedom constitute an indissoluble whole. For the Kingship of God manifests itself and is experienced in the ongoing destruction of the yokes of ignorance and oppression, want and death. It is the Spirit that inspires the proclamation of the King of all kings and gathers

---

221. Esp. Luke 4:18-21; 11:20 (Matt 12:28); John 8:32, 36; Rom 8:2, 21; Gal 5:1, 13; James 1:25; 2:12.

persons of all kinds to celebrate him. The Spirit makes those downtrodden and voiceless conscious of their high calling and therefore of their true selves. As in the past it made brave apostles out of desperate disciples, so even now it effects consciousness and rebirth of those who cannot help themselves. By the power of the Spirit they are made to realize their God-given potential to assume responsibility. The Holy Spirit inspires and sustains human creativity, exerted in the service of a new humanity and a transformed society in which freedom and justice are held together by love. By the Spirit, human beings become God's co-operators. This Spirit causes and helps people to pray for the coming of God's kingdom, but also teaches them publicly to act according to the substance of their petitions. It manifests itself and becomes palpable in the charisms given to the members of Christ's body.

And yet the presence and power of the Spirit are not restricted to baptized persons only. Rather the worldwide yearning and striving for truth, justice, love, and freedom are evidence of the Spirit's operation, too. And not only the poor and the destitute, but also the rich and mighty are in need of that Spirit. They, too, live under the promise that God's Spirit will be poured out over all flesh. When the term "kingdom of God" is used, what is meant is the spiritual rule of God that is extended over the total life of individuals as well as over the yet existing social, political, and economic structures.

No longer can theology therefore be misused for a justification of the status quo in church and world. Neither can "kingdom of God" mean no more than a program to be realized by human good will and action alone. This term describes more than a better beyond that never touches the present world; it is not a utopia. Much more this kingdom is, by the power of the Spirit, a revolutionary force that moves the whole world toward justice and peace — to become a new creation. Because justification by grace engages humanity to cooperate with God, it can no longer be separated from sanctification.

Obviously, among the forces attacked by this christological and pneumatological theology are not only worldly powers but also, if need be, the institutional church and its traditional teachings and attitudes. Reproach is sometimes directed at both Roman Catholicism and Protestantism: while the first confides too much in the mediation and implementation of God's gracious gifts by the proper organs of the church, the second is suspect of internalizing and spiritualizing salvation. However, since the Eucharist and on occasion also Mariology stand in the center of Latin American liberation theology, this theology is far from being antichurch in principle. Rather it works for a reformation of the church so that its mission into all the world may be properly accomplished.

2. THE RELATION TO PAUL

At first sight, liberation theologians cannot have much use for Paul. This apostle's idea of Christendom appears to be individualistic, and his seemingly conservative stance in ethical matters looks irreconcilable with his pronouncements on freedom and equality in Christ.[222]

And yet a majority of liberation theologians esteem Paul highly — for reasons such as the following: (a) This apostle stated explicitly that God's Son became poor and took upon himself the form of a servant in order to make the poor rich and to let those under the yoke of the Law and of earthly powers become free children of God. (b) This learned messenger of Christ taught clearly that a literal understanding of the Holy Scriptures is no good unless it is inspired by the same Spirit that has previously blown into the prophets and wise men and women of Israel. (c) This teacher, church founder, and counselor has shown that and how Israel's experience of the exodus can be applied to the temptations of Christian communities: always God protects his migrating people in the face of a hostile world. (d) What Paul confessed in the unity formulae, this he put into practice when he protested the misuse of the Lord's Supper in Corinth, where the rich had segregated themselves in a scandalous way from the have-nots. This apostle placed mutual love, service, and sharing in the center of his ethics.[223]

However, the same Paul is also under suspicion of being an archconservative type of man who reproduces Jewish traditions and mixes them with non-Jewish, popular-philosophical elements in order to uphold (if not to justify) the social structures of his time. For even when the apostle speaks of love, the factual domination of stronger or higher persons over those considered weaker appears to be accepted as an order established and protected by God.[224]

---

222. A primitive view of Paul is exemplified by an early black theologian, Albert B. Cleage, *The Black Messiah* (New York: Sheed & Ward, 1968), p. 4. He compares Paul with Jesus: "Paul preached individual salvation and life after death. We as black Christians suffering oppression in a white man's land do not need the individualistic and otherworldly doctrines of Paul and the white man." However, "Jesus was a revolutionary black leader, a Zealot, seeking to lead a Black Nation to freedom."

Just as church members passionately engaged in the struggle for sociopolitical changes sometimes have troubles with Rom 13:1-7 and its parallels in the so-called deutero-Pauline epistles, so also do many feministic theologians consider several Pauline utterances on women and marriage an obstacle to women's liberation.

223. (a) 2 Cor 8:9; Phil 2:6-11; Gal 3:23–4:11; (b) 1 Cor 2:9-16; 2 Cor 3:13-18; (c) Rom 4:23-24; 1 Cor 10:1-13; (d) 1 Cor 11:17-22, 27-34; Rom 13:8-10; Gal 5:13-14; Col 3:14.

224. In his description of Pauline ethics, G. Theissen, *Studien zur Soziologie des Urchristentums* (Tübingen: Mohr, 1979; ET in paperback, Edinburgh: Clark, 1990), pp. 267-271, 286-287, uses the term *"Liebespatriarchalismus."*

No wonder there are liberation theologians who take a critical attitude toward Pauline statements on the relationship between church and state, and between husbands and wives, parents and children. Therefore even the instructions concerning the servants' subordination to their lords are no longer treated as an unshakeable foundation of the church's social ethics and stance in today's world.[225] Whoever has a heart beating at the side of the poor and oppressed appears for this reason to be compelled to see in the return of Onesimus to his master (Philem 12) an act by which ancient state, family, and economic orders are sanctioned and the dignity of an asylum-seeking fugitive is scandalously betrayed.

All the more remarkable is the first elaborate commentary on PHM that was written under the influence of and for the Latin American base communities. José Comblin, *Epistola aos Colossenses è épistola a Filemon*, elaborates carefully on the Pauline unity formula of Col 3:11, which combines individual with social renewal (pp. 67-68). Still, he suggests on pages 72-74 that the *Haustafel* of Col 3:18–4:1, with its call to the subordination of wives, children, and slaves, may not be as authoritative as the core of Paul's message. For, so he argues, the whole of Colossians may lack apostolic authenticity; and the *Haustafel* may contain nothing more than a gist of Jewish ethics, taken up for the benefit of the Gentile Christians of Paul's time. The words "in the Lord" signal, according to Comblin, solely or primarily the limit of subordination due to the stronger social partners.

On pages 85-107 he explains PHM as an authentic, wonderful, and inspiring letter of Paul, written from Ephesus. He calls it a condensed expression of the gospel of Paul that proclaims the realm of freedom created by the power of the Spirit. His view of PHM obviously corresponds foremost to that of N. R. Petersen, which was summarized above (pp. 213-214). According to Comblin,

---

225. A blunt rejection of the apostolic counseling pertinent to these fields is represented among German scholars, far from the frame and shield of an elaborated liberation theology, by Kehnscherper, *Die Stellung der Bibel und der alten Kirche zur Sklaverei*, and Schulz, *Gott ist kein Sklavenhalter*. As earlier stated, Overbeck, in his study "Über das Verhältnis," not only intended to disprove the claim of some contemporary church historians that Christianity effected the abolition of slavery; he also accused the apostle Paul (on pp. 179-181) of being indifferent to the continuation of this institution.

More recently, Peter Eicher, a European protagonist of the Latin American theology of liberation, in his essay "Die Anerkennung der Anderen und die Option für die Amen," in *Auf der Seite der Unterdrückten. Die Theologie der Befreiung im Kontext Europas*, ed. P. Eicher and N. Mette (Düsseldorf: Patmos, 1989), pp. 10-53, esp. p. 52 n. 82, attempts to relativize Pauline statements by writing, "In focusing his attention upon building congregations, Paul hardly has an eye for the social misery of society. . . . No contribution is made by drawing conclusions from a historical analogy between the situation of the early Christian minority and the power of modern Christendom."

Jesus Christ, the Spirit, and freedom are not only indivisible but are in effect identified. The love *(agapē)* to which PHM appeals again and again is not only a subjective reality and denotes much more than the bourgeois concept and attitude of *amor*. It is a revolutionary practice and means full solidarity. No longer does it tolerate domination, however subtle its shape; no longer is it satisfied with a modification and attenuation of the misery and injustice of the present conditions. Rather it transforms the world by creating and shaping a new society whose members live together as free partners.[226]

Comblin points out emphatically that freedom and equality, as envisaged by Paul for Onesimus in PHM, are essentially and therefore indissolubly connected with the expected voluntary response of Philemon. Unless the liberation process is carried out by free will, there will be no social freedom. Therefore Paul abstains from putting any pressure on the slave owner and consciously avoids asking in so many words for the slave's manumission. For, so Comblin argues, slave laws as imposed on ancient Israel according to the OT could at best alleviate a slave's predicament. Also the laws passed after secular revolutions have — as experience shows — not really changed society but have issued in new oppression. Only by *agapē* in the sense of the gospel is the material reality of life being effectively changed. Wherever spontaneous love, this gift of the Spirit, rules the day, the social orders will be really renewed.

In view of such an interpretation of PHM, those polemics miss the mark that summarily accuse and condemn liberation theology as a victim of Marxist influence — whether these attacks stem from the Vatican, a South American dictator, or another source.[227]

---

226. The exegetical results of the like-minded F. J. Hinkelammert have been mentioned in n. 183.

227. Still, some minor criticisms may be appropriate. (a) Comblin (on p. 89; cf. 72) sees in Israel's history and in the Old Testament solely a legalistic attempt to mitigate the plight of slaves. He bypasses the relevance of the exodus accounts and the references of Prophets and Psalms to the liberation of captives, of exiled Israel, and of individual members of this people. (b) Comblin is convinced that Philem 11-12 in effect mean the destruction of slavery, but he has no comment on the words in v. 12, "I send him (Onesimus) back" — as though these verses did not show that there is no basic contradiction between PHM and the *Haustafeln*. (c) On p. 105 Comblin concedes that for social change laws are necessary, and on p. 75 he admits that it was impossible for early Christianity to impose emancipation upon the ancient society. The church had to rely on the power of God's Spirit and of love. But on the same page he states that the liberation would eventually be effected by economic and cultural dynamics. By making these concessions, the author reveals his sobriety — but he also contradicts what he elsewhere says about the Spirit's operation and the church's mission.

C. A Survey of Charges and Their Rebuttals

In this final subsection to the introduction of PHM, a digest is to be presented — not of the earlier-mentioned philological and biographical issues connected with the form and substance of Paul's shortest letter, but of actual and potential indictments directed against it and of defenses erected in its favor. The summary will be phrased provocatively in order to engage the reader in dialogue with the apostle himself and with the impact of PHM on the shape, the value standards, and the actual stance of church and society.

1. INDICTMENTS

a. Concerning the Form of Paul's Request

The letter to Philemon is too short and the case of Onesimus too trivial or ephemeral for a serious discussion of the grave problem at hand: the wicked and pernicious institution of slavery.

In his diction, Paul combines and intermingles family, liturgical, juridical, and commercial terminology. This is not only artistically done, but it is also a clever device. By speaking of God and by praising Philemon's good standing, the apostle appears to prod and cajole the slave owner into compliance. Sober business talk or a sensible program for shaping a new society would be more direct. The multitude of arguments and motivations proffered to Philemon amount to a subtle way of extortion.

The absence of a direct command, e.g., to manumit Onesimus on the spot and the insistence on the recipient's free and personal decision barely hide the fact that PHM is an example of most directive counseling. Not in vain does the epistle culminate in the mention of abundant obedience that will be ascertained when the apostle visits Philemon (Philem 21-22).

If this be the way Christians motivate one another, at least a raising of eyebrows is appropriate, and perhaps other ways of curing souls and offering advice look preferable.

b. Concerning the Substance of PHM

Instead of denouncing and fighting slavery in principle, Paul acknowledges the slave owner Philemon's rights over his servant, together with the duties of the slave Onesimus. While facing the conflict situation that had provoked the slave's flight, the apostle appears to have no more in mind than appeasement.

By sending Onesimus back, he proved himself a law-abiding Roman citizen. Was he then simply afraid of legal consequences of harboring a fugitive, even of possible disadvantages for his own person as well as for the continuation of his mission work? If so — then his love did not (in contradiction to 1 John 4:18) expel his fear.

Be it admitted that Paul identifies himself so much with Onesimus that he calls the slave his own heart, and that he intercedes with all means for the escapee who is now being returned to his owner. The slave is taken seriously and is respected as a person. And yet, the wording of PHM is such that the slave always is the object of decisions and actions taken or to be taken by two men, Paul and Philemon — who each in his own way possesses and wields power. Certainly the apostle nobly renounces making use of his authority, and the slave owner is urged to use the household head's full power in a humane way. But Onesimus's own voice remains mute, his opinions and wishes and decisions are never mentioned. Though in person he is a fruit of gospel proclamation, his own contribution to preaching the gospel is but a secret wish and hope of the apostle (Philem 13).

In Philem 11 and 13 Paul speaks of the former uselessness and the present and future usefulness of the slave. In verses 2, 5-7 he mentions the contribution of the slave owner to the life of the congregation, and in verses 7 and 20 he describes his own profit from Philemon's past and future conduct. The criteria used for interhuman relations appear to be flatly utilitarian. Such standards may be proper for evaluating a tool or a cow. Yet a person's dignity calls for an affection that is not only determined by services rendered to other persons.

The apostle seems to overestimate the power of personal conversion and the effect that a community of believing brothers and sisters has on the existing power structures. Paul fails to show how an unjust system can ever be changed by a minority group that renounces the use of violence and in Christ's name accepts suffering with gladness.

Above all, Paul appears to be reproachable because by sending back Onesimus, he contradicts his own glorious statements on the freedom of a Christian and the equality of all persons before God. It looks strange that the same apostle who proclaimed Jesus as Pantocrator (universal ruler) over the soul and body of all human beings and over all angelic, demonic, or human institutions, traditions, and authorities now contributes to restoring the fugitive slave to the owner. The use made of Paul's proclamation, in the course of almost two thousand years of church history, certainly feeds the suspicion that no more than a consolation of the soul is effected by Christ's coming, as provided by the hope for a future total peace and happiness, on some faraway heavenly meadow.

Accusations of this kind are motivated by the concern that something radical must be said and done for the liberation of all poor and oppressed people. On the other hand, such indictments also reveal how little attention is given to the whole of PHM's form and substance and how superficial and malevolent certain conclusions can be. For this reason the pleas and judgments contra PHM have not been left uncontradicted.

2. DEFENSES

In order to explain and excuse Paul and PHM, among others the following arguments have been used:

Paul was a child of his time, and he was aware only of the urban social and moral problems of slavery, not of the condition of industrial, rural, and naval slaves. He may have known of the failures of Spartacus and his like, of the consolation offered to slaves and masters by Stoic teachers, and of developments in public opinion and in Roman legislation, which had humanistic traits. But he did not intend to reform structures and institutions of the whole world in which he lived, worked, and suffered. As the household codes show, his attention was focused on the nucleus of every society, the narrower and/or larger family.

The apostle's concern was the founding and building of congregations through the proclamation of the unadulterated gospel of Jesus Christ. This task prevented him both from making a scholarly analysis of the worldwide forms of oppression and misery and from elaborating on a program of better political, economic, and social order.

The Christian congregations consisted of so small and unimportant a minority and were so constantly exposed to suspicion, slander, and persecution that the apostle proved wise and realistic when he discouraged zealotic attitudes. He relied on the virtual benefits of the Pax Romana and on the fact that Judaism enjoyed protection as a *religio licita*. Therefore he hoped that by a quiet and peaceful life the local Christian congregations could gain respectability even within a hostile environment and thereby increase the chance of spreading the gospel further abroad.

The conviction that God alone could overcome, by creating a new world, all presently existing forms of injustice and misery, and the expectation that Jesus Christ's parousia would take place very soon, exerted a laming influence on human initiatives on the public level. Therefore it appeared superfluous, if not frivolous, to attack problems and scandals that could and would be solved by God alone.

Admiration and gratitude are due Paul because the humility manifested in PHM is sincere, the trust in the power of love is disarming, and the omnipresent charm is heartwarming. Neither scholars surrounded by books and bound by strict academic discipline who enjoy relative freedom and security nor political activists who are ready to mount barricades and are daily facing new challenges, chances, and pitfalls are entitled to criticize this letter. For the voice raised by a persecuted and imprisoned person is so wise and clear that it always prevails over petulant mumbling and stentorian verdicts.

Obviously the weight and persuasiveness of the several indictments as well as of the defenses are unequal. Still, some of the apologies contribute more to put Paul's authority for today into question, and to impede and prevent necessary social changes, than do the suspicions or the zeal of those who attack or ignore PHM outright.

So much for the situation of Paul in a court of twentieth-century moral judges.

After the Annotations that now follow, a detailed and extensive word-by-word and verse-by-verse exegesis of PHM will complete this commentary. There is no newly discovered literary or archaeological evidence upon which this exposition of the epistle's text could be built. Instead, the urgent social and ethical quest of our time has to be taken seriously during each phase of interpretation — even the need and yearning for a radical opposition to hunger, oppression, and homelessness, and for the realization of freedom, justice, equality, and peace for all. While consisting of only very few lines, Paul's Epistle to Philemon makes a vital contribution to thought and action — not as a dictate or patent solution, but as a voice worth hearing. To be reexamined is not only the light thrown on each puzzling element of PHM by uncounted Pauline utterances, but also the function of this letter as a possible approach to a better understanding of all main themes of Paul's theology.

ANNOTATIONS TO THE INTRODUCTION

1. Theses of John Knox

J. Knox was not the first promoter of the idea that PHM was sent to Laodicea rather than to Colossae. In the first edition of his *Philemon among the Letters of Paul,* 1935, pp. 38-47, he mentions as forerunners K. G. Wieseler, *Chronologie des apostolischen Zeitalters* (Göttingen, 1848), pp. 431ff., 450ff.; E. J. Goodspeed, *New Solutions of New Testament Problems;* and Goodspeed, *The Meaning of Ephesians,* pp. 6ff. Cf. J. Knox, "Philemon and the Authenticity of Colossians," pp. 144-160.

At least five daring hypotheses are woven into one plaid. Formulated in free style and sequence, their substance is the following: (a) Archippus was a deacon in Colossae, while Philemon lived in Laodicea. (b) Archippus, not Philemon, was the owner of Onesimus and was factually addressed in the letter called "To Philemon." Laodicea, however, was the last postal transit station before PHM reached Colossae. (c) The letter "from Laodicea" mentioned in Col 4:16 is not lost, neither is it, as assumed by Marcion, identical with Ephesians, but is the letter "To Philemon." The crude Latin makeup, known under the name "To the Laodiceans" (for its text see E. Hennecke and W. Schneemelcher, *New Testament Apocrypha*, vol. 2 [Philadelphia: Westminster, 1966], pp. 128-132), cannot possibly be considered authentically Pauline. (d) The purpose of Paul's genuine letter is to make Archippus release the slave so that Onesimus might in the future work at the apostle's side. (e) Onesimus was finally manumitted and became bishop of Ephesus (as already J. B. Lightfoot and T. K. Abbott had tentatively suggested). This bishop fulfilled a prominent role in collecting Paul's epistles and preparing them for canonization.

Knox's bundled missiles have created considerable excitement. Although major and minor elements were soon criticized or modified, scholars from diverse camps have expressed their admiration and respect for Knox's novel approach. Among them are E. Lohmeyer, P. N. Harrison, H. Greeven, C. F. D. Moule, W. Schmauch, F. F. Bruce, and P. Stuhlmacher. Critical modern introductions to the NT never fail at least to mention Knox's theories.

2. Prejudices against Onesimus?

Ancient and later, including modern, commentaries on PHM, also monographs on Pauline ethics, appear to have a tacit understanding: it is the slave who had been guilty, not the master. So, e.g., W. Schrage recently in his *Ethics of the New Testament*, p. 234, speaks of the "pardon" and "forgiveness" Philemon shall grant to Onesimus. The terms "penitence" and "pardon" occur in the letter of Pliny the Younger addressed to Sabinianus (see "Social Background," Annotation 4, p. 86), not in Paul's epistle. Pliny offers a remote parallel to PHM rather than a never-failing key. No more than a hint in the opposite direction is given by N. R. Petersen, *Rediscovering Paul*, p. 286 n. 118, when he writes, "Onesimus may have fled because he found Philemon to be a bad master."

The common prejudice against the slave is not supported by solid evidence drawn from PHM; rather it may be the result of a bias on the side of interpreters. A full commentary on PHM stemming from the sociologically oriented Frankfurt School and/or inspired by Marxist thought has not yet come to my attention. If it ever should be written, it would probably point out that PHM was almost exclusively expounded by men who were scholarly monks,

priests, or pastors, established church leaders or academic lights, living in relatively safe positions, with better or worse domestics at hand. With very few exceptions, professional theologians are among the last to shed class prejudices.

The prevailing consensus was bound to evoke passionate contradiction as
it was voiced, for instance — although without special reference to PHM — in a
South African antiapartheid manifesto, the *Kairos Document*. Here it is the
starved, exploited, oppressed people whose cause, as it were, by definition is
righteous, while all political, economical, and ecclesiastical wielders of institutional power are depicted as instruments of the devil.

3. Onesimus — Not a Fugitive?

Sara C. Winter, "Methodological Observations on a New Interpretation of
Paul's Letter to Philemon," *USQR* 39 (1984): 203-212; Winter, "Paul's Letter to
Philemon," *NTS* 33 (1987): 1-15, is deeply indebted to J. Knox but intends to go
further. A feeble hint given by Knox (on p. 15) that had been carefully introduced by the word "perhaps" and immediately rejected by other interpreters, is
developed into a full-blown scholarly hypothesis. Ms. Winter is convinced that
Onesimus had not run away from his master (Archippus, not Philemon!) but
had been delegated to bring a message or gift to Paul and to be his assistant for a
given time. Paul then sent the slave back several years before he wrote
Colossians (4:17), the letter in which he intimates that Archippus had not fulfilled the service expected of him. The "service" would have consisted of sending back the slave to Paul for assistance in his mission work. The Letter to
Philemon, now taken for a letter to Archippus, had been written earlier in order
to make the owner agree to the manumission and permanent return of the
slave to Paul. For Winter, the references to the former uselessness of the slave
(v. 11), to the sending back (v. 12), to the separation from the owner (v. 15),
and to the possible wrongdoing of Onesimus (v. 18) do not suffice to substanti-
ate the traditional flight hypothesis. Rather, lexicographical evidence suggests,
so she maintains, a better version of some key terms in PHM than has become
customary: *Parakalō peri* in verse 10 does not mean "I beseech *on behalf of . . .*"
but "I ask *for* (Onesimus)." The verb *anapempō* in verse 12 does certainly not
exclude the physical return of the slave to his legal owner but signifies, just as in
Luke 23:7, 11, 15; Acts 25:21, "I relegate him to a higher court for decision,"
even to the judgment of Archippus. *Gnōmē* in verse 14 therefore has the meaning "decision" (of the high court to which Onesimus is sent).

However, Winter's assumption that PHM was written several years before
Colossians is contradicted by the almost identical greeting lists in PHM and in
Colossians. No explanation is given why Onesimus is called "useless" before,

227

under Paul's influence, he became the opposite. Neither Archippus nor the Colossian congregation would have charged and trusted a man who was not yet a member of the congregation to bring gifts and news to Paul and eventually to become a useful supporter of the apostle's work. Most of the counterarguments against Knox's theories apply to Winter's daring proposal, too.

F. F. Bruce, in his commentary on Philemon (1984), deems it possible that Paul's intercession was made necessary by Onesimus's overstaying a leave of absence granted to him, rather than by the actual flight of the slave from his master.

P. Lampe, "Keine 'Sklavenflucht' des Onesimus," pp. 135-137, quotes Roman lawyers from the first three centuries c.e. in order to demonstrate that Onesimus's voluntary separation from his master Philemon was *not* a flight punishable by law, but the legitimate intention and attempt to find and engage a friend of his master who would intervene on his behalf. B. M. Rapske, "The Prisoner Paul," pp. 187-203, fully endorses this view; Onesimus was "fleeing to Paul as an *amicus domini*" (p. 201).

Lampe seems to overlook the fact that only the *acceptance* of a letter of intercession exempted the slave from official or private prosecution, and from subsequent punishment — if he was caught after his escape. Neither the search for a person who might intervene nor an oral or written plea in the slave's interest *automatically* assured impunity and liberty.

4. *Haustafeln* I — The Opposite of Pauline Ethics?

Rules for domestic slaves are found in Col 3:22-25; Eph 6:5-9; 1 Tim 6:1-2; Titus 2:9-10; cf. 1 Pet 2:18-25. A synopsis of these five NT texts is presented, for instance, by E. G. Selwyn, *First Epistle of St. Peter,* p. 430. Among the apostolic fathers, *Did.* 4.9-11; *Barn.* 19.5-7; *1 Clem.* 21.69; Polycarp, *Phil.* 4.2–6.3 might be compared. Without consequences for the interpretation, masters and slaves are not always denoted by the same terms in these texts. Slaves are usually called *douloi;* in 1 Pet 2:18 the noun *oiketai* reveals distinctly that *house* slaves are in mind. Slave owners are mostly called *kyrioi,* yet in 1 Tim 6:1-2; Titus 2:9; 1 Pet 2:18, and in the postscript to Philem 25, *despotai* is used as equivalent. *Kyrios* occurs frequently as a title or address of Jesus Christ or God — but also *despotēs* is used in this sense. The bad connotation "despot" is a sign of later developments.

A great number of critical scholars still assume that, together with the letters to Timothy and Titus and the First Letter of Peter, the Pauline scripts containing HT are products of a "Pauline School" rather than genuinely apostolic. Since the time of F. C. Baur, recently especially by Rudolf Bultmann and Ernst

Käsemann, the so-called deutero-Pauline epistles are being collectively considered exponents of "early Catholicism" — that is, of an abyss into which are relegated, for good measure, Matthew and Luke, too, not to speak of the majority of the apostolic fathers. Indeed, extensive comparison as made above between PHM and the HT, which supposedly ought to coincide with a comparison between a genuine and several spurious letters of Paul, would be superfluous if its results were already known and indisputable. Then it would suffice to state that Paul's eschatological ethics is irreconcilable with narrow house-bound moralism and cultural accommodation; warm personal involvement with cool hierarchical church regimentation; voluntary compliance to the demands of love with a suffocating legalism that suppresses freedom and inventive spontaneity; etc. Yet since it is all too easy to work with such generalizations, a harder and if possible less prejudiced way of inquiry has been chosen, for at least four reasons:

a. In the HT as well as in PHM God and Christ are repeatedly mentioned, in each case very briefly only but still with the implicit claim that the master/slave relation can and should be an existential witness to God and Christ rather than blind submission to current Greek, Latin, Hellenistic-Jewish, or legally established church standards and rules.

b. When Paul sends Onesimus back to his master (Philem 12), he acts in full accordance with the substance of HT admonitions to slaves: to subordinate themselves to their masters.

c. By "receiving" all the NT letters bearing Paul's name into their canon, the Christian churches have accepted the supposed deutero-Pauline letters as being equally authoritative for their preaching, doctrine, and practice as PHM. The history of interpretation and application (in German: *Wirkungsgeschichte*) reveals no essential difference between the impact of PHM and of the HT.

d. In AB 34 (*Ephesians* I, Introduction VI, pp. 36-61) and AB 34B (*Colossians,* introduction, pp. 114-125), reasons have been proposed for why at least Ephesians and Colossians may still or again be treated as authentically Pauline.

In summary, when the HT are despised and/or condemned as spurious, then also, in the wake of, e.g., F. Overbeck, "Sklaverei"; G. Kehnscherper, *Sklaverei;* and S. Schulz, *Gott ist kein Sklavenhalter,* PHM is likely to fall victim to the expositors' ire. For PHM does not contain an alternative to the HT. The accusation of lacking consistency with other Pauline ethical personal texts, that is, of missing ethical radicalism and courage, can be thrown against PHM as well as against the HT.

All the more it is necessary to observe not only parallels but also details that might help to qualify prejudices and generalizing judgments. E.g., N. R. Petersen, *Rediscovering Paul,* p. 289, believes that only in the (pseudo-)Pauline HT "there is no a priori reason (presupposed) for there being a conflict between the responsibilities" (of being a master in the world and a brother in the church) — while PHM, even in the face of conflict, calls for a one-sided decision.

5. Unconditional Surrender?

According to Rom 13:1-7, the Roman state is "a servant of God," because it is "instituted by God" — or rather is "subordinated to God" the way all creatures, principalities, and powers are. Whether they are good or evil, through Christ's victory and dominion over them they are already now subject to God or are in the future to be put under Christ's feet (Rom 8:20-21, 38-39; 1 Cor 8:5-6; 15:25-28; Phil 2:10-11; Col 1:15-20; Eph 1:19-22). The debt owed by Christians is, according to Rom 13:8, love of the neighbor. State officials at the tax office, in toll-booths, on the street are such neighbors; love is shown by paying "tax and toll, reverence and respect to those to whom they are due" (Rom 13:7 NEB). The exact wording of the dicta "Give to Caesar what is Caesar's, but to God what is God's" and "We must obey God rather than human persons" (Matt 22:21; Acts 5:29) may, at the time when the HT were written down, not yet have been known to all Christians. But the validity of the first of the Ten Commandments, which forbids for all realms of life service of any God other than the Redeemer and Lord, is reflected in early confessions and creeds (such as 1 Cor 8:5-6; Eph 4:4-6). This commandment dominates the ethics of the first Christians to the extent that they accept willingly persecution and suffering. Therefore subordination "in all things," as requested in the HT, does not mean subservience to totalitarian claims and practices. In Titus 2:9-10 the word "all" occurs no less than three times. Subordination "in all things" is to be an expression of "all good faithfulness" (toward the master *and* to God); to serve faithfully means to adorn the gospel "in all aspects" (i.e., "among all people"). All things fine and beautiful are in mind, rather than whatever tyrannic and/or mad master, husband, father, Caesar, or state official may demand. Not *all* HT mention "all things."

6. Conscience

NT usage and meaning of the term *syneidēsis* (conscience) differ from non-Christian Greek use for at least two reasons:

   a. Conscience is not a natural, innate anthropological capability or disposition but is created, inspired, and measured by God, who has revealed himself in his Son and through his Spirit.

b. A Christian's conscience does not only warn of evil a person might be inclined or resolved to commit; it also does more than merely punish — the way the Erinyes did — bad actions that have actually been carried out. Rather it exerts a positive function: it applies what is known of God's will to individual decision and conduct. It gives direction, courage, endurance, wisdom.

Ephesians 6:8 and Col 3:24-25 contain reminders of that which the slaves "know" *(eidotes)*. Ephesians 6:9 and Col 4:1 refer to the same awareness present in the earthly lords. The appeal to knowledge, either possessed or to be revived concerning the Lord's impartial and inescapable judgment, is considered a motive and power strong enough to enable servants and lords to act wisely and to fulfill their responsibilities. Just as the mentioned texts from Ephesians and Colossians, so also Rom 13:5 and 1 Pet 2:19 discuss subordination. The latter two passages mention the conscience instead of referring to knowledge, but they most likely mean the same. If interpreted according to its etymological origin and sense, Greek *syneidēsis,* as well as Latin *conscientia* and its cognates in Western languages, mean "co-knowledge" or "shared awareness." The "conscience of God," as 1 Pet 2:19 calls it, if literally translated, means awareness of God and his will related to a specific situation. It may be defined as the subjective reflection and voice of the revelation and direction coming from God. According to above all Lukan, Pauline, and Johannine passages that do not contain the word "conscience," it is the Holy Spirit that conveys this information, awareness, and application to the requirements of the moment. To have an awake and active conscience means, to use the formulation of Phil 2:5, to "have the same mind in oneself as (is) also in Christ Jesus."

7. Equality

"Equality" is the proper translation of *isotēs* in 2 Cor 8:12. But in Col 4:1 its sense is equivalent to the adage *suum cuique,* with its Greek precedents and its prominent position in Latin legal and moral tradition. It signifies fairness, equity, giving each one according to his or her need and performance. The verses Rom 13:3-4 take up the best contemporary legal-political philosophy of the state when they affirm that the ruling powers are rewarding the good and punishing the evil; see W. C. van Unnik, "Lob und Strafe durch die Obrigkeit," pp. 334-343. This description of the purpose of the state corresponds to modern expectations of a constitutional state (in German: *Rechtsstaat*). Since in the HT the term *isotēs* occurs solely in a verse addressed to masters, it does not lack a patriarchal, benevolent connotation.

Then, outside the HT, together with other church members also, slaves are called brothers, and when in, e.g., Philem 16 Paul requests a brotherly treatment of Onesimus by Philemon, not even the proclaimed brotherhood means indiscriminate egalitarianism. For not only in the whole Bible but also in other narrative, legal, and religious traditions, the position and rights of a firstborn brother excel those of the junior(s). And when Paul calls his fellow Christians, foremost his fellow workers, "brothers," he by no means forgoes his fatherly rights and duties vis-à-vis his "children." The work to be done by his coopera-tors stands on the ground of his work as foundation layer (see, e.g., 1 Thess 2:11-12; 1 Cor 3:5-10; 4:14-15; Phil 2:22).

8. *Haustafeln* II — Dubious Christianization?

In their discussions of the HT, M. Dibelius, *An die Kolosser, Epheser, an Philemon,* pp. 48-50, his pupil H. Weidinger, *Die Haustafeln,* and a great num-ber of later interpreters promote a common hypothesis. They consider the HT admonition as an originally non-Jewish and non-Christian, Greek and Roman, foremost Stoic way of moral teaching that was eventually, with more or less skill, imitated and adorned with a minimum of biblical elements, first by Helle-nistic Jews, then also by Christians. The stepwise adoption of the HT pattern of moral instruction by Christians is visible in the progressive "Christianization." Now the HT met the need and wish of postapostolic Christianity to accommo-date itself to the cultural standards and moral values of the environment — but stood in radical contrast to the earliest eschatological message and ethics of Je-sus and his apostles.

Other scholars have used a similar (form- and tradition-critical) method as Dibelius and have come out with different results. For instance, E. G. Selwyn, *The First Epistle of St. Peter,* 2nd ed. (1947), esp. pp. 17-33, 419-439, refers back to A. Seeberg, P. Carrington, and other authors who have elaborated on the use of early (oral and eventually written) Christian catechism. Selwyn establishes a connection between the ethical parts of First Peter, the Pauline epistles, and other parts of the New Testament and the *halachic* (hortatory) words of Christ as they are transmitted in Q (the assumed common source of Matthew and Luke) and by Mark (pp. 23-24). Selwyn recognizes that passages such as the HT contain "the original substratum, a fusion of Jewish and Gentile thought which may well have originated in Hellenistic Judaism" (p. 436). But on the same page he affirms that "occupying the middle part of the scene, are outstanding ele-ments of common teaching which are indisputably Christian." The concession that in Col 3:18-21 the words "in the Lord" may easily be a Christian gloss not-withstanding, Selwyn's thesis gives the explicit references in the HT to Christ much greater weight than they have in Dibelius and his followers. In favor of Selwyn's view speaks the fact that Jesus' teaching, as reported in Matt 19 and

Mark 10, distinguishes and holds together the three social relationships constituted by marriage, parenthood, and the contrast between rich and poor. The sequence of the treatment of the three topics is the same as in the HT of Ephesians and Colossians, and only slightly at variance with the order of the OT
commandments regarding parents, adultery, and theft. The Evangelists affirm
that during his ministry on earth Jesus himself was challenged by specific encounters and questions to give specific ethical directives, and that he had specific words to say to husbands and wives, to parents and children, and about the
calling of rich people and the discipleship in poverty. Therefore the directives
given in the HT may well stand high above a cheap adaptation to contemporary
institutions, moral principles, and practiced customs. They need not contradict
Jesus' and the apostles' eschatological message. Even apocalyptical predictions
include the call for patience and wisdom; see, e.g., the book of Daniel; Rev
13:10; James 5:7-11.

9. Union through Baptism?

When Jesus was baptized by John, the witness given by the baptizee contained a
correction of the Baptist's expectation and testimony, according to Matt 3:14-
15. In the scholarly interpretation of NT baptismal texts, a clear and sharp distinction between water baptism and Spirit baptism is seldom made. Texts such
as John 3:5 and Titus 3:5 are adduced in order to demonstrate that, in contradiction to John's baptism, in the church's baptism ("in the name of Christ")
water *and* Spirit are simultaneously means and gifts, related to one another as is
a sign to the thing signified. But John 3:5 and Titus 3:5 probably speak exclusively of the Holy Spirit's operation. Among the exegetical reasons for this thesis are the following.

a. The word *pneuma* (Spirit) occurs in John 3:5-8 five times, the word
"water" only once, at the beginning. The line of thought leads away from fluids
essential for natural generation and birth and toward the Spirit given and coming from above.

b. Passages such as Ezek 36:25-27 and Ps 51:7, 10-12 stand in the background of John 3:5-8 and are the key to understanding this text. They speak of a
very specific water that is given by God alone and that, unlike the water used in
human cultic ceremonies, really cleanses from impurity, gives a new heart, and
effects obedience to God's commandments.

c. Johannine parallels confirm the identity of the water given by Jesus
with the Holy Spirit: In John 4:13-14 Jesus promises to supply water that prevents future thirst and becomes a source bubbling into eternal life. According to
John 7:38-39, what Jesus says about faith in him, who is the origin of streams of

living water, refers to the Spirit the believers will receive no earlier than after Jesus' death.

d. The term *paliggenesia* (rebirth) that occurs in Titus 3:5 is usually considered a synonym of the personal "birth from above" described in John 3:3-13. Does it really mean the immediate result of the baptism performed by a minister or a priest? Indeed, according to Plutarch, in the myths and mysteries of Dionysos and of Osiris, in the *Corpus Hermeticum*, and in a fragment of Terentius Varro, *paliggenesia* signifies individual regeneration and is probably associated with a cultic event, just as it also is used in magic texts. Tertullian, *De bapt.* 5, appears to interpret Titus 3:5 and baptism in the light of mystery cults. However, an attestation of pagan mysteries effecting rebirth occurs only later than the date of the last NT book, and another, earlier cosmic sense of *paliggenesia*, mediated through Jewish usage, has influenced the meaning of the term in the NT much more strongly than a second-century and later sense of the same word ever might have done. In Stoic, perhaps also in Pythagorean, sources, and frequently in Philo, *paliggenesia* signifies the renewal of the world, a new creation of the whole cosmos. Among Jews this cosmic renewal does certainly not exclude individual persons; it can mean restoration of life and to life. Already the LXX version of Job 14:14 contains the phrase *heōs an palin genōmai* ("until I am reborn"; see BAG, p. 611, and TWB, 1.686-689, for more references from biblical and nonbiblical literature). However, in Jewish writings as well as in Matt 19:28 and probably also in Titus 3:5, "rebirth" denotes foremost a universal and probably also an eschatological, even an apocalyptical, event related to God's final judgment over heaven and earth. If Titus 3:5 meant no more than a cultic-sacramental individual renewal, the scope of the saving work of God would be unduly narrowed down. A cosmic-eschatological interpretation in the sense of washing by Christ's blood and of the Pentecostal shaking of the whole world's foundation might much better express the meaning of this text.

e. Especially the baptism stories of Acts 8:9-24 and 10:44-48 reveal that in the early church the human act of baptism with water had two distinctive meanings: (1) Frequently it is a prayer in action offered by penitent sinners for pardon — even for that constructive, creative, and edifying forgiveness that is essence and effect of the coming, the gift, and the work of the Spirit. Indeed, John the Baptist had announced that the coming Judge would bring the fire that cleanses the heart and the Spirit that totally renews it. Jesus had promised to give this Spirit, and the disciples and apostles took up the same conviction and became eyewitnesses of its fulfillment (Mark 1:8; Acts 1:5; 2:33, 38; 19:1-7). In 1 Pet 3:21, baptism with water is defined as an *eperōtēma*, that is, an application or stipulation made "to God . . . for a good conscience," and it is explicitly denied that baptism with water is or effects the immediate removal of the filth of sinful flesh. The verses Acts 8:12-17 exemplify a considerable lapse of time between the (water) baptism in the name of the Lord Jesus and the fulfillment of the urgent prayer of Peter and John for the gift of the Spirit.

(2) In other stories narrated in Acts, baptism is the confirmation of the manifest presence of the Spirit. This presence is revealed when the members of the congregation speak in tongues. Not even Gentiles by birth are excluded from this gift (Acts 10:44-48; 11:15-17; cf. Matt 28:19; Gal 3:1-5). The church's baptism with water is the act by which Christians recognize that *God* adds members to the church. According to Paul, the baptism of Jews and Gentiles has the function of a burial. It confirms that those baptized have already — on the cross! — died with Christ, and just for this reason have a sure hope of resurrection with him (Rom 6:3-11; Col 2:11-12; cf. 1 Cor 15:3-4). In Acts 8:9-13, 18-24 the notion is discussed that the Spirit, this gift that only God can give, can be manipulated and communicated by the use of certain "means." This idea is attributed to the magician Simon and rigorously condemned. Not even the laying on of hands is a quasi-magic instrument. According to Acts 8:15, 17, the imposition of hands is an act of intercessory prayer — just as baptism itself is a prayer, following 1 Pet 3:21.

10. Corporate Personality?

The psychological and sociological concept "corporate personality" seems to be a patent key for explaining the oneness and unity confessions. After J. Pedersen, *Israel*, had prepared the way for its use by his studies on the soul in Israelite thought and life, H. W. Robinson, "The Hebrew Concept of Corporate Personality," *BZNW* 66 (1936): 49-62, and A. Johnson, *The One and the Many*, have elaborated on it. Inter alios, T. W. Manson, *The Servant Messiah*, has made extensive use of this term for the interpretation of several NT texts.

The idea of an inclusive, collective, representative individual person in whom a larger or smaller group is comprehended is widespread in the history and culture of Semitic and other (not only ancient Near Eastern) peoples. It has a vital function in the self-consciousness, the value system, and the social order of many a group and its individual members. A Prime Man, a Patriarch, a King, also an actor, musician, or sports hero, may fulfill this function.

Israel of old as well as the church in the first and later centuries lived in the midst and were a part of contemporary culture even when they were considered and treated as strangers. But the notion of corporate personality does not suffice for explaining the Pauline UF. Just as the God of Abraham, David, and the prophets had a unique function in the history and literature of Israel, so in Paul's theology Jesus Christ incarnate, crucified, and risen transcends in his relation to "many" and to "all" the boundaries of an exclusively psychosociological interpretation. Cf. AB 34 (on Ephesians), pp. 195-196.

11. A Divine Call into Slavery?

The comprehensive Greek-English lexicon of the New Testament by Walter Bauer, translated by W. F. Arndt and F. W. Gingrich (cited as BAG), s.v. *klēsis,* p. 437, states that in 1 Cor 7:20 *klēsis* is to be translated "station in life, position, vocation."

This translation is supported foremost by Lutheran theologians of the nineteenth and twentieth centuries. Though in his German Bible versions of 1522 and 1546 Luther interpreted *klēsis* in 1 Cor 7:24 in the sense of heavenly, divine calling (not of social status and occupation), first in a sermon on John 21:19-24 (WA, 10, 1:1, 306-311) and later more often he saw God's own call fulfilled in the *befehl, stand, ampt* (command, status, office) of the factual social condition and position of the believers, in correspondence to his doctrine of the general priesthood of all believers. His intention was to show that every person in every occupation, not only monks and nuns, were entitled to consider their daily tasks and work an assignment and gift of God. In sections XVI, XXVI, and XXVII of the Augsburg Confession of 1530, this idea has received dogmatical status. K. Holl, "Die Geschichte des Wortes Beruf," pp. 189-219, has dug up roots of Luther's stance in medieval mysticism, in Jean Gerson, Gabriel Biel, and Desiderius Erasmus. Holl considered it "genuinely Lutheran" in ethical matters to understand "as harmonious the internal calling, which is heard in the gospel, and the voice heard from the [secular, professional, occupational] things themselves and their necessities" (p. 219). Max Weber, in his essay "Die protestantische Ethik und der Geist des Kapitalismus," in Weber, *Gesammelte Aufsätze zur Religionssoziologie* (Tübingen: Mohr, 1928), has made additional contributions to the deployment of a Protestant *Berufsethik.*

How solid is the philological basis of an interpretation of *kaleō* and *klēsis* in 1 Cor 7:17-24 that equates *Berufung* and *Beruf,* that is, heavenly calling and earthly vocation?

In contrast to the translation of *klēsis* prescribed by BAG for 1 Cor 7:20, the great *Greek-English Lexicon* compiled by H. G. Liddell and R. Scott (cited as LSLex), just as other Greek-English dictionaries, lists among other nonreligious meanings of this term, "calling into court, summons, invitation to a feast, name, appellation." According to LSLex, an equivalent to "professional occupation" is not suggested by any text outside or inside the NT; for the translation of 1 Cor 7:20, "*calling* in a religious sense" is considered proper. S. S. Bartchy, *Mallon Chresai,* pp. 10-25, extensively discusses modern opinions regarding the meaning of *klēsis* in this verse. He arrives at the same result as LSLex. However, probably in order to defend the tradition that can be traced back to Luther, if not to earlier theologians, Holl (p. 190) is willing to credit the apostle Paul with a "keen re-coinage" of the term *klēsis*, even in the sense of status or professional situation in life. Equally H. Lietzmann, *An die Korinther*, p. 32, concedes that parallels to 1 Cor 7:20, i.e., to the use of *klēsis* in the sense of status or profession, do not exist. And yet Lietzmann translates this verse, "everybody shall remain in the state, in which he was called." According to Weber (p. 63), there is no Greek word corresponding to the German *Beruf* (with its affinity to religious *Berufung*), while A. Bonhoeffer, *Epiktet und das Neue Testament*, p. 39, suggests that Greek *prosōpon* may have included the meaning "position in life." The plural *klēseis* (lit. "calls") occurs in Dionysius of Halicarnassus, *Ant. Rom.* 4.18, but never in the NT. Does this text support the idea that Paul, although he uses the singular exclusively, described the calling of a slave as one among other occupations planned and established by God? When in the passage mentioned Dionysius uses the plural *klēseis*, he means by it the Latin term *classes*, which indeed denotes societal ranks, corresponding to English "(social) classes." These ranks are not called classes because of a divine call extended to each individual member of each existing group. It is most unlikely that Paul intended to sanctify and glorify a class system by the notion of an eternal divine plan carried out through the distribution or imposition of diverse calls upon Christians and non-Christians.

What, then, is really God's "call" or "calling" according to the NT and related early literature? It is an "upward call" (Phil 3:14 RSV) or a "call to the life above" (NEB). It is "holy" (1 Tim 1:9), "great and august" (Hermas, *Man.* 4.3.6). It is denoted as a "heavenly call" in Heb 3:1, as a "promise" in *Barn.* 16.9, and as a "hope" in Eph 1:18; 4:4. Also the word "calling" is used as a parallel or synonym of the sum of the gifts of grace (Rom 11:29), of election (2 Pet 1:10), and of salvation by grace alone (2 Tim 1:9). One and the same calling is extended to each and all members of the congregation (1 Cor 1:26; Eph 4:4; *1 Clem.* 46.6). Paul prays to God and admonishes all Christians to walk worthy of it (2 Thess 1:11; Eph 4:1). They are to confirm it by their conduct (2 Pet 1:10).

Passages such as those just mentioned are cited by K. L. Schmidt in the article *kaleō*, etc., in TWB, 3.491-493; K. Barth, *Church Dogmatics* III/4, pp. 600-607; and S. S. Bartchy, *Mallon Chresai*, pp. 133-137. These authors conclude that "it is always God who calls in Christ," with emphasis on the words "in Christ." Thus they oppose the idea that in 1 Cor 7:17-24 Paul speaks of a call and appointment by God the Father and/or Creator, or even by creation, creaturely orders, or prevailing circumstances, that would precede, underlie, and imperatively determine a Christian's life and conduct. According to the NT, the "calling with a call" (1 Cor 7:20, cf. 24; Eph 4:4; 2 Tim 1:9) is not split up into calls, as if one was identified with a natural or historical human status and the other with the revelation and mission given through Christ and his Spirit. Also there is not one call for slaves, women, children, and another for masters, men, and parents. Rather all people — everybody, including the slaves — are urged to walk in Christ's footsteps (1 Pet 2:21). All church members are "called saints" (1 Cor 1:2; Rom 1:6-7; 8:28; Jude 1). Only when Paul calls himself *klētos apostolos* (called by God to be apostle, Rom 1:1; 1 Cor 1:1) does he refer to a special appointment and function within the church and the world — but not to his secular occupation, e.g., as a tentmaker. The diverse "spiritual gifts" *(charismata)* create, use, correct, augment, or crown for a common good purpose talents and physical or spiritual endowments given to single persons or groups. While these gifts are necessary for the common life and the worldwide mission of the many members of the one body of Christ, they are never given the name "calls."

Karl Barth (pp. 605-606) rejects the first and prefers the second school of interpreting 1 Cor 7:17-24, and paves the way for Bartchy's solution when he writes, "A Christian is not called to be circumcised or uncircumcised, free or slave; he is called precisely in the state in which he is. He must always be true, not to the state, but to his calling within it, as this man with this historical background and history. . . . The [earthly] vocation of a man can never be understood . . . as a kind of prison in which he is shut off from other possibilities . . . as a stronghold by whose thick walls man is protected from the varied and far too extensive demands of his divine calling."

12. Precursors of the Theology of Liberation

Liberation theology has its roots in the biblical accounts, reminders, and applications of Israel's redemption and exodus from Egypt. Among the additional pillars are early and late laws and statutes, e.g., concerning the Jubilee Year, which provided protection to those indigent; Amos's, Hosea's, Isaiah's, and other prophets' protests against oppression, and their promises in favor of the poor; the charges and expectations that Israel's kings should and would by a righteous government shield the widows and orphans (Ps 72:4, 12-14, etc.); those psalms that contain desperate and/or confident prayers and songs of destitute persons and groups, e.g., Hannah's (and the virgin Mary's) praise of God who dethrones the high and mighty in order to exalt and feed the lowly people (1 Sam 2:4-10; Luke 1:52-53); Jesus' programmatic Nazareth sermon that culminates in the proclamation of the Jubilee Year (Luke 4:18-19); the blessing of the poor and oppressed and the corresponding condemnation of the rich and mighty, as found in Jesus' own preaching and in the Epistle of James (Luke 6:20-26; James 1:9; 2:5-7; 5:1-5); the advice and promise given to the rich young ruler and to the disciples of Jesus (Mark 10:17-27, 42-45, etc.); and the description of the first Jerusalem congregation's solidarity with the poor (Acts 2:42-46; 4:32-37; cf. Gal 2:10; Rom 15:26).

In the course of church history, Oriental monks were the first who individually (as Anachorets) or in groups (called cenobites) chose poverty for God's and Christ's sake. By living as ascetics, they protested against the lifestyle increasingly preferred by affluent Christians, bishops, congregations, and churches — a way of life determined by the possession and protection of earthly goods and security. In the West, the earlier-mentioned Circumcellions intended to force the whole church to renounce riches. Augustine advised clerics to live as poor people — though he permitted them a share in property held by the congregations. Benedict of Nursia required individual poverty of the members of the order he founded. But the Benedictine monasteries as well as other medieval monastic communities relied on communal property rights. Albigensians, Cathari, Waldensians, and Joachim of Fiore condemned the riches of the church of their time, which included the employment of slaves. These groups were declared heretics. But when Francis of Assisi decided without compromises to follow in Christ's footsteps, and when he taught his followers to accept material poverty as inseparable from spiritual humility and mystical solidarity with the poor Christ, he found papal approval for the rule of his order. However, eventually even the Franciscan settlements became owners of extensive possessions. John Wycliffe took up the fight against the rich church, on the basis of intensive Bible studies and inspired by the humility of Christ. Unlike Francis's, his teaching was opposed by the official church.

The Reformation of the sixteenth century reaffirmed for all Christians the blessing of, and the request for, poverty "in Spirit" (cf. Matt 5:3). But the monastic or zealotic ideal of individual material poverty was now converted into the obligation of all Christians to do works of charity, and of the whole church to build and sustain poorhouses and eventually to assume responsibility for the maintenance of orphanages, hospitals, and schools. As previously mentioned, Thomas Müntzer and other radicals employed violence in favor of their own conceptions of freedom and justice. The radical wing of the Reformation was resisted and at least temporarily defeated by the alliance of the church with the contemporary princes, the aristocracy, and/or the up-and-coming upper-middle-class bourgeoisie.

In the post-Reformation centuries, the scholars' church retreat into a doctrinal and hardly ethical orthodoxy was challenged by Pietists who founded and sustained hospitals, schools, and other institutions in order to let the light of faith and love shine upon poor people. The Age of Enlightenment produced and supported humanistic and rationalistic ideas that soon enough led to great social and political effects: to the French and the American Revolutions. These ideas also influenced the nineteenth-century abolitionist and Social Gospel movements that reminded the churches emphatically of their special obligation and responsibility for the poor, exploited, and oppressed.

The suffering of the black slaves and their right to liberation; the exploitation of industrial and rural workers, including their wives and children, and their struggle for fair wages and participation in decision making; the crying of the hungry all over the world — these past and present facts determine the thought and work and suffering of the modern liberation theologians. Even when their analysis of the present social, economical, and political situation contains or resembles Marxist features, their theological work is an evangelical challenge to the whole church.

Notes and Comments
on Philemon

I. THE ADDRESS (VV. 1-3)

VERSE 1

From Paul, a prisoner of the Messiah Jesus and from my brother Timothy to our dear fellow worker Philemon.

The usual sequence of Oriental edicts, official letters from superiors to inferiors, and private correspondence of the Hellenistic period is followed in almost all New Testament epistles: first the sender's name, then the addressee's name, finally a good wish.*

The authenticity of the Letter to Philemon and all its parts cannot be seriously questioned. The words "I, Paul, with my own hand have written (this)" (v. 19) most likely pertain to the whole letter, not only the declaration of indebtedness. As in Gal 6:11 (but unlike 2 Thess 3:17; Rom 16:22; Col 4:18), Paul does not indicate that a secretary's service was employed for writing down, on dictation, the main parts of the epistle. Solely a postscript in a hardly reliable ancient manuscript affirms that Onesimus functioned as scribe. In section V of "Literary, Biographical, and Contextual Issues" (pp. 121-128) it was shown that stronger reasons suggest dating PHM in Rome between the years 61 and 63 than in Caesarea between 59 and 61 or in Ephesus in the mid-fifties.

A prisoner. This description of Paul's current predicament is repeated in various ways in verses 10, 11, 13, and 23. It assigns to PHM a place in the company of the other three "Captivity Letters": Philippians, Ephesians, and Colossians. Inasmuch as Second Timothy may be authentic to a large extent, it belongs in the same group. In the good MSS containing the opening of PHM, Paul calls himself "prisoner" rather than "apostle" or/and "servant." Four answers can be given to the question of what Paul may have intended and effected by referring so early in PHM to his captivity.

1. He reveals his humility and anticipates what he makes explicit in verses 8-9 and 14: he cannot and will not give orders to Philemon; he relies on volun-

---

*In the following Notes, commentaries, monographs, and other works interpreting PHM are cited or summarized under the respective authors' names only. When no page number is given, a comment on the currently exposited verse is being quoted or a summary made. Works other than commentaries, etc., are referred to by a short form of their title. The full titles of the commentaries and other publications, and publication data, are found in the bibliographies.

tary compliance and may count on a certain amount of compassion. Still, Paul exerts a special sort of pressure. "How could Philemon reject an appeal penned within prison walls and by a barnacled hand?" (J. B. Lightfoot).

2. Suffering for Christ's sake is for Paul himself a reason to rejoice (Col 1:24; etc.). When he is driven to play a fool's role, then he declares his weakness and his exposure to danger to be reasons for pride and boasting (2 Cor 11:1, 16, 21, 23-30; 12:9-10). According to, e.g., E. Lohmeyer's commentary on Phil 2:11–4:9 (pp. 111-177) and on Philem 1, Paul's authority as a martyr was even greater than his full power as an apostle.

3. The situation and legal position of a prisoner are close to those of a slave. Prisoners of war were sold on the market and became slaves. Even when a person kept in prison was not always literally fettered in a wooden stock, to the wall, or to guardian soldiers (cf. Acts 12:6-7; 16:24-26), and when domestic slaves did not work tied together as a chain gang, captives as well as servants were "in bondage." *Dēmōs,* derived from *dama(z)ō* (to tame, to bind, to subject), was the old Greek word used by Homer and Euripides for a slave, and the terms *desmios* (prisoner) and *desmoi* (chains, captivity) that Paul uses in Philem 1, 9, 10, 13 are derivates from the verb *deō* (to bind, to tie, to fetter). Since in other letters (e.g., in Rom 1:1; Gal 1:10) Paul calls himself a "slave," it is possible that by naming himself a "prisoner" in verse 1, he was paving the way for later expressions of his full solidarity with the slave Onesimus. Onesimus is called Paul's own heart, and the reception of the slave is declared to be equivalent to receiving the apostle himself (v. 12). In brief, his state as a captive places Paul at the side of the slave rather than of the master. The apostle utters his plea from the depth.

4. In addition, Paul's patience in captivity may have been an example for Onesimus on how to survive under adverse circumstances.

Common to these four explanations is the assumption that the meaning of "prisoner" and of "captivity" in verses 1, 9, 10, 13 is literal. Indeed, Paul was a physical victim of Emperor Nero's attitude to the Christians and of the worldwide Roman law-enforcement agencies: he was Caesar's prisoner. E. R. Goodenough, who in his essay "Paul and Onesimus" disputed this, has not found successors. Philemon 9 is usually understood as giving a hint of the relatively recent date of the apostle's imprisonment: "now also a prisoner." As a fellow prisoner, Epaphras, who was not yet (or no more) kept captive when Col 1:7-8; 4:12 were written, is with him (v. 23). All Captivity Letters, foremost the references to the praetorian guard (or to a praetor's residence or a government building) and to "Caesar's house" in Phil 1:13 and 4:22, confirm the detention of Paul by human hands and in a local prison. In 2 Cor 6:5 and 11:23 Paul explicitly speaks of "prisons"; the term "my fetters" occurs in, e.g., Phil 1:7, 13, 14, 17, and in a variant reading of Philem 10. It is certainly physical bonds that Paul in Eph 6:20 humorously equates with an ambassador's ornamental chains. In the wake of Paul, Polycarp (*Phil.* 1.1) called such bonds "most becoming the saints"; they are "diadems of those truly chosen by God and our Lord."

In view of the horrible conditions prevailing in ancient, medieval, and later prisons, it is possible to consider captivity and martyrdom inseparable. Indeed, in Acts 20:23 imprisonment *(desma)* and tribulation *(thlipsis)* are practically equated, and in 2 Cor 11:23 "labors . . . imprisonments . . . beatings . . . dangers of death" are enumerated in succession — almost as synonyms. Paul is convinced he has suffered more than any other servant of Christ.

And yet it is not necessary to imagine the imprisoned Paul exclusively in a dark and wet cellar, plagued by hunger, thirst, and cold, surrounded and almost eaten up by rats and vermin, scourged day by day during heavy interrogations, broken down by humiliations, sorrows, and hopelessness. For he could claim the preferential treatment due a Roman citizen (cf. Acts 22:24-29). Before he was legally condemned, he had to be kept in a state of sufficient physical and mental health to be visited by officials and eventually to appear in court. Acts 23–28 contain vivid scenes of Paul's life as a prisoner in Caesarea and Rome: Friends could visit him, supplying him with food and clothing, bringing news and taking messages. By giving oral counsel and instruction, and by dictating or writing letters, he was able to continue his missionary work. When he was temporarily released, he did this, according to Acts 28:31, "openly and unhindered."

Philemon 22 shows that when the apostle wrote to the slave owner, he expected to be released in the foreseeable future. At that time, if the hints given in Acts 28:16, 23, 30 can be trusted, Paul lived by himself "in a rented room."

For these reasons the self-designation "prisoner" in Philem 1 is hardly a self-pitying call for compassion; neither is it conscious self-aggrandizement. Rather it reminds Philemon that he is not addressed by a free man, but by a person under human bondage. When in other letters Paul calls himself apostle and servant, his dependence on Jesus Christ is in mind: he is no longer the Sanhedrin's delegate *(shaluᵃh)*, and, unlike Plato, he never was a human person's slave. But whenever in PHM he refers to his captivity, he means more than only his physical and temporal incarceration by the Romans. He is also and primarily captive of another authority, and in a different sense:

A prisoner of the Messiah Jesus. Despite the absence of the Greek article before *Christou,* the position of this word *before* "Jesus" indicates that *Christou* has the function of a title. In Philem 3, however, *Christou* is posed after "Jesus" and is therefore treated as part of the proper name of the Lord.

In verse 1, as much as in verse 9; Eph 3:1; cf. 2 Tim 1:8, Paul rejects the idea that at present he might be no more than Caesar's prisoner. He is in bondage to the "King of the Jews" who in the OT is sometimes called the Anointed

One (Messiah). Since Claudius's time, emperor slaves and emperor freedmen played an increasing role in the administration of the empire. Paul emphasizes that he is ultimately bound only to and by Christ. In analogy, he calls himself a "prisoner in the Lord" in Eph 4:1 and speaks of the "captivity of the gospel" in Philem 13. Equivalent is probably the formula "bound in the Spirit" in Acts 20:22. Certainly physical imprisonment by the Romans is not excluded by this terminology. Still, to E. Lohmeyer the genitives in the formulae "prisoner of the Messiah, . . . of the Lord . . . of the Gospel" are to be understood as subjective genitives: Jesus Christ and the gospel are the powers that hold Paul captive. In that case the walls of the prison are not made of stone, neither the fetters of iron: "prisoner" is used as a metaphor.

This does not mean that by an act of subtle sublimation and spiritualization Paul attempts to forget or take easily his physical predicament in order to lift himself and the recipients of PHM out of the reality of the present world and into a higher level of truth. According to Plato's *Kriton* and *Apology,* Socrates' detention in prison was a symbol of the soul's imprisonment in the body. The spirit of the noble, wise, and good man was capable of making the walls transparent and of transcending them. The Stoics elaborated on this freedom of the mind and of the virtues that could blossom within prison walls — and even in a slave. In PHM, however, the literal meaning of prisoner and the historical condition of Paul on earth are not dissolved in the fire kindled by the tinder of the spirit. The apostle retained (as much as did Philo, that master of allegorical Bible interpretation) the literal and historical sense of language at the side of the metaphorical use of words. According to Philem 16, Paul expects that (lit.) "in the flesh and in the Lord" Onesimus will be received lovingly. Equally the apostle's captivity has a double nature, one being this-worldly, the other rooted in the kingdom not of this world.

How are the two bondages related to one another? Which of them in its own way is real and determines Paul's existence, work, and thought? They are not of equal weight. As earlier mentioned, Norman R. Petersen *(Rediscovering Paul)* has made a vital contribution to understanding Paul. Although not explicitly, yet in effect he has shown how different are the apostle's stance and teaching from at least two widespread thought patterns regarding human existence in the conflict of diverse obligations. There are the classic Greek tragedies revealing how men and women are crushed and perish between the claims for allegiance raised by diverse deities. And there is the two-realms doctrine that, since Martin Luther, has exerted great influence on the ethical attitude and acts of many Christians. Petersen has paid special attention to the phrase "prisoner of Christ Jesus" and to why in Philem 1 Paul does not call himself a prisoner of the state. "Worldly realities," such as being either a free man or a prisoner, are, according to this author, "transformed for him (Paul) by virtue of what he is in

Christ." The formula "in Christ" denotes, in the diction chosen by Petersen, the "symbolic universe," that is, all that is known to Paul and proclaimed by him of the grace and the rule of God the Father and Christ the Lord, including the brotherhood of the church founded on love and faith. This "symbolic universe gives a new and different meaning to his (Paul's) worldly experience . . . the reality of the world as seen from within the world is replaced by the reality seen from the Church. For Paul there is only one reality" (p. 188). Slave, prisoner of Christ, ambassador, and apostle are "functional equivalents" (p. 128). "By using the language of worldly positions ('ambassador,' 'prisoner'), the apostle also absorbs them into his churchly position ('of Christ Jesus'), and thereby overcomes the reversal of the status suggested by his imprisonment." Paul expects the same "ameliorated reversal" from Philemon. This man is to be reversed "from being Onesimus's master in the world to being his brother in the Church" (p. 77).

Petersen uses verbs such as "transform," "replace," "absorb," "overcome" for pointing out that God's rule does not annihilate present worldly conditions of existence but takes care of them in a most gracious way. God establishes an incomparable new reality — not only in the far future but already now and here on earth. Paul uses a less complicated terminology: In, e.g., Phil 1:12-14 he speaks of the interrelation between the claims and the control of Caesar on one side, and of Christ on the other. He affirms that what has happened to him (the apostle) "has all the more served the advance of the Gospel." Therefore his imprisonment "in (or: for) Christ became revealed" and encouraged others "without fear to speak the word of God." Paul distinguishes between the hidden and the revealed character of his imprisonment, and he holds the two together. What at first sight is evil and depressing, is in reality good and encouraging. Only by revelation do the real cause, sense, and purpose of the apostle's corporal captivity become known — to himself as much as to people among and for whom he works and writes. Whenever he calls himself a prisoner of Christ, he says as much as: I do not mind, and don't you mind, my present physical bondage in Roman hands; for even in this state I'm in the good hands of Jesus Christ.

And from my brother Timothy (lit. ". . . from the brother . . ."). The term "brother" signifies not only a descendant from the same father and/or mother, or another close relative, sometimes including a husband or a sister. In their correspondence, rulers sometimes address one another this way. Members of the same nation or religious communities (e.g., of Israel, the Essenes, mystery cults, funeral societies) considered themselves and were expected to treat one another as brothers.

In the NT the fatherhood of God together with Christ, the firstborn brother, constitutes the congregation as a brotherhood united by love (*adelphotēs*, 1 Pet 2:17; 5:9; *philadelphia*, e.g., 1 Thess 4:9; Rom 12:10). As the mention of "sister Apphia" in Philem 2 and other sisters in other letters shows, this brotherhood always includes sisters. Scandals, lawsuits, hypocrisy, social tensions, personal strivings, and "false brothers" were a threat to the close community (see 1 Cor 5:11; 6:8; 8:12; 11:17-22; Gal 2:4; 2 Cor 11:26; etc.), but they confirm rather than obliterate the fact that the church was as real and palpable a community as any other social body. Whenever the congregations were true to their character and mission, they formed an alternative to social structures based on the exertion of power (cf. Matt 20:25-28; 2 Cor 12:10). Petersen uses sociological language when he describes the church as an "antistructure" in the midst of institutions relying on power. Philemon 8-9 reveals that Paul renounces the use of apostolic authority that he might claim — and does exert according to other letters. While in Philem 7 and 20 he collars the slave owner by calling him kindly and pointedly "brother," at this place the specific function of brother Timothy calls for elucidation.

Excursus: Timothy

The NT contains three sources and types of information regarding Paul's coworker Timothy. Critical interpreters attribute highest value to Paul's undisputed epistles, limited reliability to the Acts of the Apostles, and weaker historical trustworthiness to the Pastoral Epistles.

1. Alone or in company of other assistants of Paul, Timothy repeatedly is mentioned as a cosender of a Pauline script (see First and Second Thessalonians, Second Corinthians, Philippians, Colossians — and PHM). Details of his association with the apostle and the journeys he made as Paul's successful delegate to Thessalonica and Philippi are offered in 1 Thess 3:2-6 and Phil 2:19-24. Between being sent to these Macedonian cities, this "dear and faithful child of the Lord," who "has proclaimed Jesus Christ" and "does the work of the Lord the same way as I do," was dispatched also to Corinth. He was given the delicate assignment of redressing scandalous disorder in the local congregation (1 Cor 4:17; 16:10-11; 2 Cor 1:19). This mission turned out to be a failure: Titus had to replace Timothy, and only this second envoy of the apostle was crowned with success (2 Cor 7:6, 13-14; 8:6, 16, 23). Whether the anonymous "brother" sent with Titus (2 Cor 8:18, 22; 12:18) was again Timothy is not clear. At any rate, whenever Paul mentions Timothy, he speaks of him with special love and respect. This associate is, at the same time, Paul's child and brother and great helper. According to Phil 2:22, he served the apostle in the mission work as a son serves his father.

2. In the Acts of the Apostles (16:1-3), Luke reports that Timothy was born in Lystra (in Asia Minor, about two hundred miles east of Colossae). In the same city he had become "a disciple" — perhaps even before Paul's second arrival. His Jewish mother — in deference to his Greek father? — had omitted to have him circumcised but, in order to permit his access to synagogues and Jewish homes in Paul's company, the apostle himself marked him with this "sign" (Rom 4:11): it showed that he belonged in Israel. Timothy was frequently a companion of Paul, made travels to various cities as the apos-

tle's delegate, and finally waited for him in Troas in order to follow him southward on the way toward Jerusalem (Acts 17:14-15; 18:5; 19:22; 20:4). Acts does not reveal that a specifically close bond existed between the apostle and Timothy. The last information given speaks only of Timothy's departure with Paul from Troas: nothing is reported on his stay near Paul in Jerusalem, in Caesarea, on the ship transferring the apostle to Rome, or in the empire's capital.

If arguments from silence were admitted as evidence at all, these lacunae in Acts would contradict the hypothesis that the three Captivity Letters bearing Paul's and Timothy's names stem from either Caesarea or Rome. Ephesus would then be the most likely origin. The Epistle to the Hebrews (13:23) speaks of "the brother Timothy" who was recently released (from prison) and will eventually, in the near future, visit the recipients of the letter. This Timothy might well be the same man as the associate of Paul mentioned in Paul's letters and in Acts. But Hebrews reveals nothing of the location of the prison.

3. Presupposed that anything genuine is contained in the letters addressed to Timothy, they were written toward the end of Paul's life. According to these epistles, Timothy is (as "bishop") responsible for the congregation in Ephesus (1 Tim 1:3; 2 Tim 1:15, 18; 4:12) and needs advice and encouragement. After Paul has already in 1 Cor 16:10-11 and Phil 2:23 hinted at the youth of Timothy, 1 Tim 4:12; 2 Tim 2:22 make explicit that even at a late stage of Paul's life this trusted cooperator was still a young man. The names of his grandmother and mother are mentioned, and it is affirmed that both ladies were sincere believers even before Timothy became a Christian (2 Tim 1:5); according to the better MSS of 2 Tim 3:14-15, the grandchild and child was taught by them and knew the Holy Scriptures (the so-called Old Testament) ever since his babyhood.

It is not known whether Timothy ever had become acquainted with Philemon and Onesimus — be it in Colossae, Ephesus, or elsewhere. But his youth placed him at the side of the slave. Was he really a coauthor, or is his relation to Philemon as loose as that of the persons enumerated in Philem 23-24 who joined Paul in sending greetings? Indeed, in Rom 16:21-23 Timothy is the first among those who are greeting the Romans; among them is "Tertius who wrote the epistle." While it cannot be excluded that Timothy fulfilled secretarial duties, it is very unlikely that in the case of PHM he made smaller or larger contributions either in substance or as technical aid (cf. v. 19). E. Schweizer (*Der Brief an die Kolosser,* pp. 25-27) assumes that a document from Timothy's pen is in our hands: the Epistle to the Colossians. (The introduction to the commentary on Colossians in AB 34B will not support this hypothesis. An ancient letter has still to be found in which a pupil of a great master attempts to honor his teacher in an inauthentic letter bearing first the name of his teacher, then the imitator's name.)

Timothy is still remembered when Paul calls the main addressee *"our* dear fellow worker" and Archippus "*our* fellow soldier." But beginning with verse 4 (except in the better MSS of v. 6 and in a spurious variant of v. 7), the first-person singular of the personal and the possessive pronouns ("I . . . of me . . . me . . . my") convey the impression that Timothy was not really coauthor of PHM. Equally, after he was named as cosender, he appears to have been forgotten completely in, e.g., Phil 1:3; Col 1:23-25, 29; 4:7-13. In addition, in 1 Thess 3:2-6 and Phil 2:19-24 Paul speaks of the cosender Timothy as though the latter were not sitting at his side. PHM contains no stylistic idiosyncrasies that would betray another writer than Paul himself. Since Timothy was well acquainted with both the Scriptures and Paul's preaching, teaching, and writing, he would hardly have failed to imitate Paul by using scriptural arguments and citations; but Colossians and PHM stand out among the apostle's letters by the absence of OT quotations and allusions to specific Scripture texts.

However, the possibility remains open that Paul had discussed in some detail with Timothy the substance of what he was to write to Philemon. If so, then PHM stems out of brotherly agreement, is directed to brothers (vv. 2, 7, 20), and calls for brotherhood.

To our dear fellow worker Philemon. Among the monographs on Paul's cooperators, see especially W. H. Ollrog, *Paulus und seine Mitarbeiter,* and E. E. Ellis, "Paul and His Co-Workers." A glimpse of the few things known of Philemon and some of the many circumstances not known was offered in subsection VI.B of "Literary Issues" (pp. 137-141); in section V (pp. 127-128) it was stated that Philemon most likely lived in Colossae rather than in Laodicea (as J. Knox had suggested when he equated PHM with the letter "from Laodicea" mentioned in Col 4:16).

Paul first calls Philemon *agapētos.* Because the literal translation "loved" sounds ugly in English and "beloved" reminds of recently deceased relatives, the adjective "dear" could not be avoided, although it is often used in a superficial and trite sense. "Lovable" or "amiable" (E. Lohmeyer: *liebwert* and *liebenswert*) would be even less fitting, for Paul describes his factual, close, cordial attachment and solidarity — not just the potential of Philemon to be loved. He might as well have used the term "brother," as indeed he pointedly does in verses 7 and 20. In other letters (e.g., in Rom 1:13; 7:1, 4; 12:19; 1 Cor 10:14; Phil 2:12 (variant reading); 1 Cor 15:58; Col 4:7, 9; cf. James 1:16, 19; 2:5) the appellations "dear (ones)," "brothers," "dear brothers" are synonyms and mutually exchangeable. Onesimus is to be received by Philemon as a "dear brother" (Philem 16).

The unique combination of "dear" with "fellow worker" in Philem 1 poses a problem not only for the translator but also for the expositor. It looks strange that in the Greek text the conjunction "and" (*kai*) holds the attributes together but also separates them. Does *kai* here have the so-called "epexegetical" sense, or does it remind of an additional element in the close relation between Paul and Philemon? In the first case Paul would love Philemon only inasmuch as he does a specific work in support of the apostle. Philemon is then loved primarily or solely because of his usefulness as a worker. Indeed, "useful" is and will be the returning Onesimus (vv. 11 and 13), and to draw profit from Philemon is what Paul hopes (v. 20). But there are certainly also other reasons and ways to love a person! In the second case, a slight distinction is made between Paul's personal and his ministerial relation to Philemon. Since the apostle expects that Onesimus "in the flesh and in the Lord" will be received as "a dear brother" (v. 16), the apostle may attempt to distinguish between his own cordial feelings and his indebtedness to the work done for the gospel and the church.

Neither the wording in Philem 1 nor the fact that Paul the person and Paul the servant of Christ are as inseparable as concentric circles (see foremost Galatians, Second Corinthians, and Philemon) permits a decision. The apostle is so emotionally engaged in his work that he does not permit himself any feelings outside the service in which he stands. In other letters, in the lists of those greeted or sending greetings, the praising and tributes confirm the co-inherence of the personal and the ministerial realms.

Equivalent words such as "dear one," "fellow worker," "brother," "fellow soldier," "fellow servant" are often combined to form groups of two or three. In Phil 2:25 no less than five laudatory attributes are concatenated to praise Epaphroditus. In most cases when individual names are mentioned, outstanding persons are so described whose work consists of founding churches or strengthening existing congregations. As earlier cited, a fellow worker "does the work of the Lord just as I do" (1 Cor 16:10). Women are among these coworkers of Paul. Several of them are mentioned in the greeting list of Rom 16, one in Philem 2. Such workers stand in a special relation to God and to the apostle, to one another and to the congregations.

1. As laborers on God's plantation and building site, they are not only servants but "fellow workers of God" himself (1 Cor 3:9; cf. 1 Thess 3:2 and its variant readings). Just as Paul himself hopes not to labor in vain, so God's co-operators will be rewarded according to the kind of work they have done (Gal 2:2; 4:11; Phil 2:16; 2 Tim 4:8; 1 Cor 3:12-15; cf. 2 Cor 5:10). In Philem 6 and 14 Paul daringly anticipates God's judgment: he states that Philemon has done good work. Elsewhere he observes that the work of a faithful fellow worker is being done "in Christ . . . in the Gospel of Christ . . . for the kingdom of God" (Rom 16:3, 9; 1 Thess 3:2; Col 4:11).

This high estimation of work and labor does not contradict the utterances of Paul on justification by faith rather than by works — as exemplified by Abraham, who "does not work but believes in him who justifies the ungodly"

(Rom 3:28; 4:3-5; Gal 2:16; 3:6-24). Paul declares useless for justification solely "works of Law" (i.e., selected acts of obeying the Law, such as circumcision, Sabbath keeping, and dietary observations), but he never rejects, either for himself or for others, the fulfillment of the whole Law by love in a life led actively, devotedly, responsibly, and fruitfully (see, e.g., Rom 12:1-2; 13:8-10). Once Paul compares the work done by himself with the accomplishment of other servants of God, including the achievements of those who were apostles before him. Then he states self-consciously, "I have worked harder than any of them" (1 Cor 15:10).

2. Instead of mentioning *God's* fellow workers, Paul can also speak of *my* fellow workers (e.g., in Rom 16:3, 9, 21; Phil 4:3; and Philem 24). They are indispensable as delegates of the apostle. Not only Timothy and Titus do their best in, e.g., Corinth, but the "fellow servant" Epaphras appears to have founded the congregation at Colossae; he tells Paul of the Colossians' love and "wrestles consistently in his prayers for their perfection" (Col 1:7-8; 4:12). The colleagues do more than only inform the apostle of good and/or bad events in local churches. Also their contribution is not exhausted by the support they give to his teaching, preaching, counseling, admonishing, and praying. Provided with means and delegated by the Philippian congregation, a man such as Epaphroditus is also "a servant of the need" of Paul: he cares for the apostle's food, clothing, and health. Such persons are sometimes called apostles of the congregations (2 Cor 8:23; cf. Rom 16:7; Phil 2:25; Col 1:7-8).

As fellow workers of Paul, they are all dependent on Paul and cannot claim to be his equals. Yet among themselves, the cooperators stand on the same level. When the opinions of two of them diverge, a third is discharged to rush to their aid and reconcile them (Phil 4:2-3). Although a scribe's or secretary's service is different from that of an occasional emissary or a locally established "bishop," "deacon," or "elder" (cf. Phil 1:1 with the Pastoral Epistles and Acts 20:17-36), there is no hierarchy. Only their relation to Paul is very special. While *he* calls them *his* cooperators, no evidence exists that they would ever reciprocate by addressing and treating him as *their* fellow worker. (In analogy, a modern factory manager or office head who is wont to address his labor force and office staff collectively or individually as "dear cooperators" will hardly encourage them to call *him* "our fellow worker.") In 1 Cor 4:17 and in the address of the letters to Timothy and Titus, Paul calls his trusted helpers his "children" rather than his "brothers." According to 1 Cor 3:6, 10, the apostle has planted and laid the foundation before coworkers have watered the plantation and built upon the ground laid.

The functional difference between the apostle and his dear fellow worker Philemon is confirmed by Philem 8, 19, 21: Paul retains the authority to give orders, Philemon as a spiritual child of God owes himself to the apostle, and "obedience" is firmly expected. In one regard, however, Philemon's position may well be distinct from that of other fellow workers: he is trusted to comply with Paul's wishes completely out of his own free will (vv. 9, 14, 21).

3. A coworker's service rendered to God and Paul is always to the benefit of a community and its members. They are called "fellow workers for the joy" of others; Titus "is my partner and toward you a fellow worker" (2 Cor 1:24; 8:23). The instruction and guidance Paul gives his students, friends, helpers, and delegates does not aim at founding an academic school for scholarship's sake. Certainly he does not attempt to deliver the one gospel of Christ that has been preached (Gal 1:6-9) into the hands of "early Catholic" orthodox teachers or inflated hierarchs. Solely the foundation, the protection, and the encouragement of congregations are the purpose of their training in, e.g., Ephesus (cf. Acts 19:9).

When fellow workers own a house and have the necessary resources, they can do a work for the (apostle and) congregation that Paul himself cannot perform: they can receive and host brothers and sisters at their place and care for strangers who come in and go out, e.g., as evangelists. In Corinth a certain Gaius was hosting Paul "and the whole church" (Rom 16:23). Another Gaius, a church elder, is praised in a much later letter (3 John 1, 5-8) as a loyal man who demonstrates his love and does good work. Not only does he receive wandering missionaries in his house, but he also provides for their material needs when they leave. In turn, in Philem 4-7 Paul thanks God for good deeds of love and faithfulness from which all the saints have profited.

It is not known whether Philemon had distinguished himself as a fellow worker already when he had first met Paul and become a believer, be it at Ephesus or elsewhere. Philemon 19 ("you owe yourself to me") presupposes their earlier personal encounter. But it is possible, too, that only in Colossae had he undertaken his praiseworthy activity, for in Philem 5-6 Paul states that he had solely *heard* of Philemon's love, faithfulness, and good work. E. Lohmeyer suspects that Paul knew but little of Philemon and that the choice of general terms such as "love," "faith," "all the good" reveals "a substantial distance" between the writer and the recipient of PHM. Still, the great number of very personal and warm elements in this letter contradict this judgment.

Actually, by calling Philemon "our dear fellow worker" Paul lays on the man a hand that is warm and heavy at the same time. Its warmth will be felt when it turns out that love is the main theme of the epistle; its pressure when Paul appeals to Philemon: May he, by receiving Onesimus as a brother, continue and crown the praiseworthy work carried out so far!

VERSE 2

To our sister Apphia, to our fellow soldier Archippus, and to the congregation in thy house.

To our sister Apphia (lit. "To Apphia, the sister"). Apphia is a Phrygian name frequently found on ancient inscriptions. On a tombstone discovered in the ruins of Colossae is written "Hermas to his wife Apphia, the daughter of Trypho" (*CIG*, III 1168n 4380k 3; see also Dibelius and Greeven, p. 111). In one or another form of spelling, *appha* is "a term of endearment used by brothers and sisters, also by lovers" (LSLex, 1953, p. 232). It means as much as darling, sweetheart, or sweetie. Since the name Philemon reminds of *philēma* (kiss), the first two persons addressed in PHM appear predestined to form as intimate and ideal a couple as Philemon and Baucis: Philemon the liberal host, Apphia the gracious hostess of the house church, and both — as a late postscript to PHM indicates — the common owners of the slave Onesimus.

The majority of ancient MSS, though not the most reliable among them, have "to our dear Apphia" rather than "to our sister. . . ." Theodore of Mopsuestia, in following the reading (lit.) "dear loved one," distinguishes between the true love in the apostle's mind and the "shameful passion" of sexual love of which the majority of Paul's contemporaries would think whenever *agapē* (love) or a cognate term was used. If Paul had written to *Apphia tē agapētē* ("to the loved Apphia") rather than "to our sister Apphia," it would have sounded like "to my sweetie darling" — with unwanted mental associations. When another early Christian writer turns to a whole congregation rather than to an individual woman, he honors her with the address "elect lady" and "elect sister" (2 John 1, 13).

The term "sister" in Philem 2 expresses the same love and respect and recognizes the same function as the appellation "brother" in verses 1, 13, 16, and 20. "Paul gives men and women the same honor" (Theodore of Mopsuestia, 2.265, 269). In the "brotherhood" of the church, every adult female member was a sister. This community was one of the rare places where "love for brothers and sisters" (so *philadelphia* ought to be translated in 1 Thess 4:9; Rom 12:10; Heb 13:1; 1 Pet 1:22; and 2 Pet 1:7) overcomes the iniquity perpetrated by and in male-dominated societies.

Because of his utterances on a wife's subordination to her husband, and in view of the injunction that the married women "keep silence in the churches" (Eph 5:21-33; etc.; 1 Cor 14:34-35; cf. 1 Tim 2:11-12), Paul is suspected or found guilty of being an exponent of patriarchalism. However, when in 1 Cor 7:1-16, 25-40 he discusses intimate and social matrimonial matters, he describes the equal rights of husbands and wives, and of all who may consider marriage. And he calls for *mutual* subordination in Eph 5:21. According to 1 Cor 11:5, there are women who pray and prophesy publicly in divine worship. "There is neither male nor female: for you all are one in the Messiah" (Gal 3:28).

This pertains specifically to fellow workers in the service of God, of Christ, of the apostle, and of the congregations. The majority of terms Paul uses for describing the indispensable contributions made by men, he employs also for female cooperators. The work of women was not limited to caring for bodily needs. According to J. Brutchel, *Die Maria-Marta-Erzählung* (cf. D. A. Csányi, *Optima Pars*, pp. 5-78), it was not because of her caring for a meal but because of her total absorption, sorrow, and trouble for that work alone that Martha was once harshly treated by Jesus (Luke 10:38-42). Numerous distinguished female fellow servants receive special greetings, foremost in Rom 16:1, 3-6, 12-13, 15. Some are saluted because they do manifold heavy and painful work *(kopiaō)* in the Lord's service: "Sister" Phoebe, being a "deacan" [*sic*] of the Church of Kenchreae (the seaport of Corinth), is expected to travel to Rome (or Ephesus?); she is worthy of an honorable reception and every necessary material support; she has become a *prostatis* (outstanding as leader, protector, or administrator, if one of the senses of the corresponding verb stands behind this title). In several ways she has cared for and assisted many persons, including Paul (Rom. 16:1-2). Prisca (alias Priscilla) is sometimes mentioned before her husband, Aquila. Prisca and Aquila had not only assembled house churches in Rome, later in Corinth, and finally in Ephesus, but also had worked and traveled with Paul, risked their neck, given minute explications of the message of Christ to, e.g., the learned Alexandrian Apollos. They deserve thanks from Paul and all Gentile Christian churches (Rom 16:3-5; 1 Cor 16:19; 2 Tim 4:19; Acts 18:2, 18, 26).

Indeed, Apphia's contribution to the spiritual and physical life of the Christians in Colossae was probably no less important than Philemon's. She is certainly expected to have a say when the returning slave enters the door and when a decision about his future is made. Archippus, the next person mentioned in the address of PHM, perhaps has also been a leader of the congregation. He will have added his opinion. Since according to Col 4:17 his "service" was not flawless, Apphia's name may have been placed ahead of his.

There is a whole bouquet of well-meant guesses regarding the special bonds between Philemon, Apphia, and Archippus. Since the days of John Chrysostom, Theodore of Mopsuestia, and other church fathers, Apphia has been declared Philemon's wife. In addition, sometimes Archippus was considered their son. But Pelagius left it open whether Apphia was Philemon's physical sister or his wife. In old Egyptian dynasties, marriage between brother and sister was necessary or permitted in order to keep the divine royal bloodline clean. In biblical stories of the patriarchs, a married woman is repeatedly (Gen 12:13-19; 20:2-7; 26:7-11) called her husband's sister. When in Hellenistic Greek letters (see, e.g., LCL, *Select Papyri* I, ##97, 105, 155, 158; but see the footnote to #137) a husband calls his wife "sister," an old Oriental tradition is continued. But in commenting on Philem 2, J. Knox suggests that Apphia might have been Archippus's wife or mother. Supported by the Catholic tradition, A. Robert and A. Feuillet (*Introduction à la Bible*, p. 513), and H. Binder among Protestant expositors of PHM, affirm that Philemon was married to Apphia "without doubt." On the other hand, for instance, W. G. Kümmel (Kümmel, Feine, and Behm, *Introduction*, p. 246) sees no adequate reason to make Apphia the wife of Philemon and the mother of Archippus; he prefers to assume that the lady lived in the same house as those two. Not even one of the various hypotheses can be solidly proven. The fact that Aquila and Prisca were a couple when they were hosts to a house church in various cities does not suffice to bind Philemon and Apphia equally closely together.

The conflicting opinions just mentioned will be relevant for understanding the whole of PHM. At least one common concern unites those expositors who bank on close family ties between those first addressed in the letter. These bonds need not necessarily be an obstacle to living as members of the "household of God" and "in the Lord." Wife, children, and slaves formed so close a community in the ancient house that they were baptized together with the husband, father, and master when the latter became a disciple of Christ (according to 1 Cor 1:16; Acts 16:25, 31-33; etc.). The desired reception of Onesimus as "a dear" brother has two dimensions, as Philem 16 points out: he is "brother in the flesh" because, after returning, he is again a member of the natural family; and "brother in the Lord" because henceforth he is to be loved and respected as a member of the congregation. This prevents a strict and clean separation of family obligations on one side and of responsibility for the life of the congregation on the other.

One fact speaks distinctly against the consanguinity of the first three recipients of PHM. If Philemon and Apphia had been a couple, and even more if Archippus had been their son, it is hard to explain why Onesimus was not baptized before his flight. Philemon 10 reveals that he became a Christian no earlier than after meeting Paul in his prison. Further, when (in 1 Cor 16:19 and Rom 16:5; also in Col 4:15, variant reading) Paul mentions the house church meeting at the home of the couple Aquila and Prisca, he speaks of the assembly in "their," not in "his," home. In Philem 2, however, he writes to Philemon about "the congregation in thy house," and in verse 22 he begs the man rather than the lady to prepare a room. Not even a hard-boiled patriarch would be so rude toward the lady of the house.

Paul's acquaintance with Apphia cannot be dated. Since he had never been in Colossae, he may have met her face-to-face on one of his journeys somewhere in Asia Minor, or he knew her through favorable information received from Epaphras, the founder, teacher, and close friend of the Colossian church (Col 1:4, 7-8; 2:1; 4:12).

W. Estius and other expositors mention Greek and Latin martyrologies that tell of Philemon's and Apphia's death by stoning at Emperor Nero's time.

To our fellow soldier Archippus. Only in Col. 4:17 is Archippus mentioned again: "Tell Archippus: Look that you fulfill the ministry which you have taken over in the Lord." Two things are evident, and the third may be implied: (1) This man had assumed a ministry in the church. (2) He did not yet fulfill it completely. (3) He may have been absent from Colossae when Colossians was written or publicly read ("Tell him . . .").

In Philem 2 no more is said of him than that he is Paul's, Timothy's, Philemon's, and Apphia's "fellow soldier." Since he is directly addressed together with the other recipients of PHM, and since an honorable title is bestowed on him, Paul now presupposes that·Archippus lives in Colossae and is not yet or no longer in need of admonishment. The ambiguities inherent in Col 4:17, and their apparent contradiction to the complimentary address in PHM, have been tackled in various ways:

When, in harmony with Theodore of Mopsuestia and later traditions, although unlike Chrysostom, to this day (e.g., by H. Binder) Archippus is treated as Philemon and Apphia's son, then he is usually considered a relatively young member of the church of Colossae. Perhaps the ministry *(diakonia)* entrusted to him was that of a deacon *(diakonos,* in a spurious postscript to PHM); if so, then he did not have the responsibility of a presbyter or bishop (cf. Phil 1:1; 1 Tim 3:8, 12). Still, because *diakonia* and *diakonos* can as well mean any high or low function in God's, Christ's, the gospel's, Paul's, or a congregation's service, Archippus may also have exerted "some higher function than the diaconate properly so called": e.g., that of a "priest" (Lightfoot, pp. 43 and 310) or even a bishop. According to Luther (WA, 25.71), he was a citizen and bishop of Colossae, and in the latter capacity ranked higher than the rich Philemon, who had no more than material things to contribute to the congregation. The Syrian *Apostolic Constitutions* (7.46, end of fourth century) lists Archippus as bishop of Laodicea. E. Lohmeyer limits himself to calling him a church leader. P. Stuhlmacher declares him to be the successor of Epaphras. Finally Sara Winter ("Paul's Letter to Philemon," p. 2) follows J. Knox when she suggests that Archippus gave "particularly financial aid" to the congregation, serving as a sort of manager. Although indeed, in Acts 12:25, the formula "fulfill the ministry" is used for the collection and delivery of money, there is no evidence for such a specification and limitation of Archippus's ministry; neither LSLex nor BAG, s.v., supports Winter's interpretation.

Among all expositors of PHM, John Knox has done most in order to lift Archippus out of the pool of hardly known cooperators of Paul and into a relatively bright light (see "Literary, Biographical, and Contextual Issues," sec. V, p. 127, and Annotation 1, 225-226). On pages 49-61 he argues inter alia as follows: Because in Philem 2 the reference to "thy house" follows shortly after the name Archippus and is very distant from the mention of Philemon in verse 1, Archippus is the owner of the hospitable house, not Philemon. Therefore all the other second-person singular pronouns in this letter (lit. "thou," "thee," "thy," etc.) are addressed to Archippus. This man, rather than Philemon, was also the master of Onesimus. Knox considers one ancient papyrus letter sufficient proof for concluding that the first-named among several addressees need not be the person mainly addressed. According to Knox, Philemon lived in Laodicea, not in Colossae. His function was therefore first restricted to forwarding PHM "from Laodicea" (Col 4:16) to Colossae and then serving as the ultimate executor and custodian of the letter by watching over the implementation of Paul's wish regarding Onesimus. What the apostle really requested and hoped for was that Onesimus be returned to him as a helper in the service of the gospel, so Knox argues on the ground of Philem 13. At any rate, the high praise formulated in Philem 4-7 and the subtle pressure exerted in the following verses fall upon Archippus. This man is the "brother" (vv. 7 and 20) who is implored and prodded in verses 8-22 and greeted in 23-24 by persons in Paul's environment. But Archippus had not yielded immediately; he had been negligent in "fulfilling his ministry," that is, in sending Onesimus back to Paul. Therefore the Colossians were urged to have a serious word with him.

Toward the end of section V of "Literary, Biographical, and Contextual Issues," we offered reasons that speak against these theories. J. B. Lightfoot had located the same Archippus at Laodicea. He suggested that this "priest" had given a bad example of lukewarmness to his rich flock that well deserved the scolding pronounced in Rev 3:15-17.

Lightfoot, no less than Knox, is building on uncertain ground. Only one thing is sure: In Philem 2 Paul calls Archippus "our fellow soldier." Military imagery is repeatedly found in other Pauline letters.

Only one other person is explicitly designated as Paul's fellow soldier. Epaphroditus is called brother, coworker, fellow soldier, (church)-apostle, and minister of Paul in succession, without clear differentiation between value and rank of the several functions.

The term "fellow soldier" belongs in that group of Pauline utterances in which the whole of the apostle's and every Christian's, especially the outstanding "fellow workers'," daily life is described as a spiritual warfare and a hard struggle (*agōn;* Eph 6:10-20; 1 Thess 2:2; 2 Cor 10:3-4; Rom 15:30; Col 1:29; 2:1; 4:12; etc.; see AB 34A, pp. 758-806, for a discussion of the military metaphors).

When the imagery is borrowed from an athlete's struggle, such as in racing, wrestling, or boxing (Gal 2:2; 5:7; 1 Cor 9:24-27; Phil 1:27; 4:2-3; cf. Heb 12:1), no equipment is mentioned. Yet when special armor is included in the figurative speech, then the arms as well as the energy and wisdom to use them are treated as gifts of God (Eph 6:10-17; Col 1:29; etc.).

Which opponents are faced by the fighters? In the legend of Jacob's fight at the Jabbok River (Gen 32:24-32), the patriarch wrestles with God in order to receive his blessing. Untiring, intensive prayer is drastically described as a fight with the Lord. So also in Eph 6:18-20; Rom 15:30; and Col 4:12 prayer is the form and substance of the Christian's warfare — as if to say that God himself is to be attacked and overcome. In other contexts, other enemies can be distinguished. While Satan himself can be squashed under the feet of the saints solely by "the God of peace" himself (Rom 16:20), the members of the church have to wage a defensive war against the onrush of principalities and powers, be they political, cultural, or psychic (Eph 6:11-14: "stand . . . withstand . . . !"; Rom 8:35-39: "who can separate you from the love of the Messiah . . . ?"). Heresies emerging within the church have to be resisted, as especially Col 2 shows. Even from within each Christian vile attacks have to be continuously faced. In the struggle for victory, according to 1 Cor 9:24-27, Paul has to beat his own body roughly to exert strict self-discipline. As Rom 7:14-21 shows, a servant of God is in his person a battlefield between the impulses coming from his own body and the holy will and law of God. James 4:1 speaks explicitly of warding off the lusts stirring in the bodily members, and 1 Pet 2:11 warns of the attacks on the soul carried out by fleshly desires.

In consequence, a soldier in God's service has to suffer continuously. He is not a hero by nature but knows fear and trembling. Such a soldier is tempted, and sometimes stumbles, falls, and is failing. The soldier is dependent on advice and encouragement. The help Paul offers is not given from the position of a Napoleonic general on yonder hill, neither by the modern battle leader giving orders from a bombproof shelter. Equally, the support the congregation of Colossae is to give Archippus, according to Col 4:17, is expected to come from persons who within themselves are tempted by dangerous doctrines and ethics.

It is not known when and where Paul saw Archippus bravely fighting at his side. Was it when the apostle "fought with wild beasts in Ephesus" (1 Cor 15:32) in the mid-fifties? Or had Paul only "heard" through Epaphras (Col 1:7-8) of the man's engagement? The term "fellow soldier" certainly points to participation in a struggle that ends no earlier than with death (cf. Phil 3:12-14; only in 2 Tim 4:7 does the apostle look back on the good fight fought and the race finished by himself).

And to the congregation in thy house. In verse 4, Greek *sou* will have to be translated "thee"; so also here the translation of *sou* by "thy" must be chosen, its archaizing sound notwithstanding. For "your house," just as "remember you," would suggest that the house in question was the common property of Philemon, Apphia, and perhaps Archippus, too, and that Paul's thanksgiving included all three persons equally. But the Greek is unequivocal; the pronoun is used in the singular form.

It was already mentioned that, according to John Knox, Archippus rather than Philemon is the house owner and highly praised church member to whom Paul really addresses PHM. As already stated, one of the reasons adduced by Knox was that the name of Archippus, not of Philemon, stands nearest the reference to "thy house." Again, it would be most unusual in ancient epistolography if the substance of a letter were addressed to a person named in the third place.

Solely in PHM does a congregation that meets in the house of a church member have a place in the letter opening. Other Pauline epistles are either church *or* private letters, never both — although in their own way both types have an official character (see "Literary, Biographical, and Contextual Issues," sec. III.C, pp. 112-115). Whenever outside PHM Paul refers to what today is called a "house church," he does it, except in 1 Cor 1:16, toward the end of his letters. These groups send or receive special greetings. Similarly in Hellenistic papyri letters (see, e.g., LCL, *Select Papyri* I ##133-134, 138, 166-167), family members of the person addressed are saluted — but there is no mention of them at the start of the same letters.

What is known of early Christian assemblies in private domiciles?

Excursus: House Churches

Many passages in Acts (1:13; 2:46; 5:42; 10:2ff.; 12:12; 16:15, 31-34; 18:7-8; 20:8, 20; cf. Luke 19:9; 1 Tim 3:13) confirm the Pauline references to house churches (in 1 Cor 1:16; 16:19; Rom 16:5, 14-15, 23; Col 4:15; PHM). They had been formed since the first days after Easter and Pentecost. The baptism of many a "whole house" (i.e., of all members of a smaller or larger family, including children and slaves) contributed to the spread of this form of congregational meetings. The *Haustafeln*, too, show how relevant the house community was for the life and ethics of early Christianity.

A good bibliography and summary of the biblical, archaeological, sociological, and religious dimensions of the early house churches is found in P. Stuhlmacher, *Philemon* (1955), pp. 70-75. Before him, e.g., F. V. Filson had drawn special attention to them ("Early House Churches," pp. 105-112). On German soil in recent years, especially H. J. Klauck, *Hausgemeinde und Hauskirche im frühen Christentum*; J. Gnilka, *Philemonbrief* (1982), pp. 17-33; and M. Gielen, "Zur Interpretation der paulinischen Formel *Hē kat' oikon ekklēsia*," pp. 109-125, have further elaborated on this topic.

While for diverse reasons not all would-be followers of Christ gave up their family ties and earthly possessions for their Lord's, the kingdom's, and the gospel's sake (Luke 9:57-62 par.; 18:18-30 par.; Acts 4:36–5:10), other female and male disciples remained house owners. They used their earthly possession for the benefit not only of the local congregation but also of the apostle Paul and other migrating messengers of Christ. Not in vain is hospitality recommended in, e.g., Rom 16:23; 2 Tim 1:16; 4:19; 3 John 5-8.

Following the evidence of Acts, the formation of house churches began in Jerusalem even while Christians could still meet and publicly speak in the precincts of the temple. But because they were excluded more and more from the temple and the synagogues, the early Christians were forced to follow the example given by Diaspora Jews who, if they could not build a synagogue and meet in it, assembled in private homes for worship. Houses were also used for the performance of mystery cults, and for the meetings of funeral societies and collegia. In the Roman Empire the Jewish religion was for a long time treated as a *religio licita,* just as service rendered by non-Jews within their own four walls to the *penates* and *lares* (household deities) was officially tolerated. The meeting of Christians in houses therefore secured for them a certain legitimacy.

In the literature of the second and third centuries, references to the existence of house churches are scarce (see below). Archaeological evidence is proffered by one or two church rooms in a home at Dura Europos (in the Euphrates Valley). While the house in question may have been built in the first century after Christ, the decorations (frescoes) on the walls of the room(s) used as a meeting (and cult) place can be dated 232-33 c.e., about the same time as the earliest frescoes in Roman catacombs. The house was discovered in 1931/32 and ranks among the prime exhibits of the Art Gallery of Yale University, New Haven. It is not known whether the room(s) contained an altar, an elevated seat for the bishop, or other elements considered essential for preaching, teaching, prayer, singing, and sacraments. Since as early as the middle of the second century when Justin Martyr (*Dial.* 41; 116-117) denotes and explains the Eucharist as a sacrifice brought to God rather than as a meal, it may well be that already at his time an altar was erected in the rooms used for communal worship. The "House of Philemon" shown to visitors in Colossae according to the fifth-century commentary on PHM by Theodore of Mopsuestia, cannot have been the original building mentioned in Philem 2, for the whole town was destroyed by an earthquake in 61/62. After it had been rebuilt promptly, it was finally leveled by a new earthquake in 692. Among the Asia Minor churches addressed in Rev 2–3, the congregation of nearby Laodicea figures prominently, while Colossae is not mentioned.

In view of the average size of first-century houses owned by persons of some means, no more than forty persons may have assembled in one room. The thesis of M. Gielen (pp. 109-125) that Pauline references to house churches imply the existence of but one house church in each city is disputable: one letter was sent to the Christians in Colossae and another to Philemon. In addition, in Col 4:15 "brothers in Laodicea and Nympha and the congregation in her (or his? or their?) house" are separately greeted. That the Corinthian Gaius is called host to the whole congregation (Rom 16:23) might mean that all Christians living in the large city of Corinth are welcome to enter his house, but it need not exclude the existence of other hospitable homes. When an "upper room" was used (Acts 1:13; 20:8), it was called "large" when it offered room to an assembly of about a dozen persons, according to Mark 14:15. In the School of Tyrannus at Ephesus, where Paul for two years instructed missionary cooperators (Acts 19:9-10), the apostle probably rented a relatively small room, hardly the *Auditorium maximum.*

In the post–New Testament literature of the first three centuries, house churches are mentioned only in the *Martyrion of Justin* 3.3 and in the *Pseudo-Clementine Recognitions* 71.2. Since in the absence of specific church buildings no other rooms existed for the worship of the persecuted minority, there was no need to mention house churches. But when with Emperor Constantine the persecution found an end and imperial donations made the erection of (basilica-rotund or cross-formed) church buildings possible, private homes no longer remained the prime location of the Christians' solemn assembly. Now architecture, sculpture, and painting in honor of Jesus Christ began to develop fully, and rituals could be developed in ever richer forms.

Hence, structures made of stone and wood, built with solid walls, were separating the church from the world — irrespective of the work of Christ, who, according to Eph 2:14-18, had broken down all that formed a wall between Jews and Gentiles. An internal division preceded, accompanied, and followed the external distinction and separation of the cult center from secular domiciles: The clergy was distinguished and given a place apart from the laity. Conducting a service became the privilege of specifically trained and ordained persons. Analogous had been the transition in ancient Israel from the slaughtering of the Passover lamb in every house to the Deuteronomic regulation (Deut 12) according to which only priests at the temple were authorized to perform sacrifices. And yet Jews making the pilgrimage to Jerusalem still celebrated the Passover meal in private houses. As long as Christians met in secular houses, they followed this order in their own way: one priest and sacrifice — on Calvary! Many assembled for worship in homes in Jerusalem and all over the world!

Among Roman Catholic interpreters of PHM, W. Estius (p. 881) has tried to counteract a potential or actual tendency of Reformation-time theologians who saw in the early Christian house churches a precedent for a congregation-centered form of common worship and church order. Estius contradicts Erasmus explicitly when he states, "[House] Church is not the name of whatever sort of assembly, but of the well organized meeting of the faithful in which, in accordance with the purpose of the Christian religion, some rule, others are being ruled, although they are members of one single house and family." Today, within both the Roman Catholic and the Protestant churches, strong movements attempt to recognize and restore the basic function fulfilled by the early house churches — even when this creates tensions with the dominant hierarchy.

In Philem 2 Paul makes the house church in Philemon's home a co-addressee of his letter. Obviously he esteemed highly all that the assembled Colossians owed to the hospitality and liberality of their host. In honor of Philemon he describes this extensively in verses 4-7. At the same time, however, the apostle has also the main substance and purpose of the present letter in mind: he makes the assembled community co-responsible for the implementation of his concern — the brotherly reception and treatment of Onesimus (vv. 8-21). All those worshiping together, men and women, the rich and the poor, those more and those less educated, including slaves and children, are charged and enabled to exert some pressure on the slave owner, if ever he would prove reluctant to fulfill Paul's expectations. F. F. Bruce (pp. 200, 206) is convinced that the inclusion of the house church among those addressed is equivalent to greetings extended to groups of Christians at the end of other Pauline letters. The unique place at which mention is made of the house church in PHM reveals Paul's confidence in this form of solemn assembly. All those present are expected to hear the reading of his letter, to ponder its substance, and to assist one another in making decisions and taking action. This is more than only a kind greeting.

While the decision to be made by Philemon and his future permanent attitude toward Onesimus are very personal matters, they are yet not so totally his private affair that they are nobody else's business. If modern terminology be proper to the interpretation of an ancient document at all, then Paul aims not only at the democratic and humane result of personal and communal decision, but also at a democratic and humane decision-making process. Even if (as, e.g., E. Lohmeyer, p. 175, and N. R. Petersen, *Rediscovering Paul*, pp. 297-298, presuppose) Philemon should have been not only lord of the manor but also leader of the Colossian congregation, he cannot and must not decide in lonely majesty.

Therefore, at the time of Paul, the appeal to the house church made in Philem 2 was an almost revolutionary innovation. It makes the personal letter to Philemon an official letter, regarding a public, political, and economical issue. PHM announces an invasion of privacy and reveals that every distinction and separation of personal from social matters contradicts Paul's thought and intention. In other words: Paul's ethics is social ethics.

Not only an individual and a community, but also the church and the world, are paradigmatically juxtaposed in the phrase "congregation in thy house." The "house" (*oikos* or *oikia*) is the building and/or the family living in it, including the slaves. The originally distinct significance of the two Greek terms was fading away even before the time of the NT. "House" represents the basic earthly human structure of life in space and time. The "congregation" (*ekklēsia*) is the assembly of citizens of heaven who have become aware of God's Fatherhood and Christ's Lordship and who by word and deed and suffering bear public testimony to their conviction. Often the present "world" (even when its motivations are religious, as especially the Fourth Gospel shows) reacts to the existence of the church with blindness, contempt, slander, hatred, persecution, or with the attempt to infiltrate, reduce, and seduce the strange lady by subtle or crude means. Since Emperor Constantine (306-37) the church, in turn, has used unspiritual methods to make its will and power felt.

A very special mutual relationship between church and world is signaled by a house church. The meeting of Christians in a domestic frame fulfills a missionary function. It can include criticism and renouncement of traditional ways of life; it can initiate by its example slow or fast reforms in its environment; finally it can effect sanctification of daily life. The use of material things as well as the decision for spiritual priorities can be changed by it. Interpersonal relations will never be the same again as soon as love replaces deified major and minor virtues. Sanctification of a "house" means no less than a vigorous attack on the dualistic distinction between sacred and profane. The inscription of the words "Holy to the Lord" on the bells of the horses and the use of household pots as "bowls before the altar" of which Zechariah (14:20-21) has spoken prophetically, is anticipated by the existence of a house church.

An ethical doctrine stipulating that a Christian's allegiance can or must be divided between the house and the congregation is therefore discouraged. It seeks to ignore the factual invasion, occupation, and transformation of the house by a kingship that is not of the present world. Because Philemon is host to a house church, he cannot treat the relation to his slave as a purely secular matter, as if it had nothing to do with the faith and love shared by all Christians.

VERSE 3

Grace and peace to you from God our Father and the Lord Jesus Christ.

This same formula of initial blessing is found in many Pauline epistles and in 1 Pet 1:2; 2 Pet 1:2; Rev 1:4. Paul might — after using in Philem 2 the term "thy house" — have pronounced a blessing upon "thee," even upon Philemon alone. But he sticks to the traditional wording "you" (in the plural form). The blessing formula has been extensively discussed in, e.g., AB 34. At this place the discussion of selected constituents can suffice. It has to be shown that and how for the whole of PHM, this blessing lays the ground and fulfills a vital function. Certainly it transcends the role of a liturgical ornament.

The apostolic blessing replaces the wish for good health that is often found in contemporary Greek private letters. Obviously it is not part of the trite triplet (of, e.g., ##88 and 99 of the LCL collection of *Select Papyri*) that follows the pattern: How are you? — I hope all is well — I am fine.

Frequently in modern language versions, the verb "may" is added to the original text and placed at the beginning of a biblical blessing. But this interpolation is misleading. In spite of the suggestion made by, e.g., BAG, s.v. *charis*, the optative *eiē* (may there be) does not belong in the formula. More than a vague hope or wish loaded with religious embroidery is meant. Together with the benediction at the end of the epistles, the blessing places the totality of the epistle in the frame of the congregation's worship and lays, if not imposes, God's blessing upon those assembled.

Soon enough among the earliest Christians, not only readings from the Hebrew Bible or from vernacular versions of it but also the public reading of apostolic scripts became an essential part of the liturgy (Col 4:16; cf. Rev 1:9-11; chaps. 2–3; 22:18-19). The voices of NT prophets and apostles were listened to with the same respect as those of Moses, the prophets, the priests, David, and the Wisdom teachers. As did the benedictions pronounced by the patriarchs, so also the NT blessings combine prayer with proclamation. They affirm that those gifts that God alone can offer are given here and now and in the future.

By the pronouncement of God's blessing, Philemon and all persons in his house are urged to become aware of the intrusion made from outside into their lives — an invasion made not by an enemy, but by God and Christ. In the Bible the terms "visiting, visitation" *(paqad, pequdah, episkeptomai)* denote the coming of God from on high, be it for punishment or for salvation (e.g., 1 Sam 2:21; Luke 1:78). When God manifests himself this way, he always is active and brings his own gifts. The blessing puts the recipients of PHM under God's and Christ's full protection. Having such a Father as God is, they are special children. With such a Lord over them as Christ, they are servants in a unique sense. Just because of their total dependence, they have a particular dignity, strength, and task. They are entitled and equipped to form a community and to live together as a society whose character and conduct are unlike the forces and structures of the Hellenistic world in which they live.

Indeed, contemporary Greek letters that deal with great and small personal matters occasionally mention prayer and thanksgiving directed to a god or several deities (see, e.g., LCL, *Select Papyri* I ##97, 111-112, 115-116). But the invocation of superior powers sounds like a formality and appears to have little or nothing to do with the sender's main concern. Paul introduces him from whom all blessings flow most distinctly. When he speaks of the Father and the Lord, he uses sociological terms that make sense to everybody. But when he says God the Father together with the Lord Jesus Christ is the source of blessing, he declares that God is another father than Zeus (Jupiter means Zeus-father) or a biological progenitor and head of a household, and that Jesus Christ is a Lord unlike the emperor or any earthly slave owner. He speaks of the Father of Jesus Christ (Rom 1), of all families (Eph 3:14), and of the Lord of all lords (cf. Rev 19:16), even the "Lord" to whom "all knees shall bow in honor of God the Father" (Phil 2:10-11).

Paul does not intend to proclaim two gods. Only later, supposedly in honor of Jesus Christ, a few important theologians (Justin Martyr, *Dial.* 56; *Apol.* 1.13; Irenaeus, *Adv. haer.* 2.28; Origen, *C. Cels.* 5.39) came near such a proclamation. The apostle refers to that God who has fully revealed himself and has established his Kingship on earth through his Anointed One.

At present only Christians call the Father of Jesus Christ "our Father" and Jesus Christ "our Lord" (1 Cor 8:5-6; etc.). But Paul's thought and mission work have an eschatological dimension: he builds as much on the future victory of God's Kingship as upon its manifestation in the history of Israel, in the death and resurrection of Christ, and in the present operation of the Holy Spirit.

According to Paul, the bond that holds the Christians together as brothers, sisters, servants, and maids of Christ, and the social ethics resulting from this blessed tie, are neither products of wishful thinking nor ultimately a utopia. They have an ontological basis in God and the Lord.

Upon this ground Paul will make his appeal to Philemon. When God made it possible and real that the servant Jesus was made the Lord who will be universally recognized as such — who then is the slave owner at Colossae, and what chance has he to maintain an unbrotherly relationship to his slave?

Grace is the gift of God that Paul first mentions. The Greek word *charis* alludes to *Chairein* ("rejoice!"), the conventional good wish found near the beginning of letters, and in the NT in Acts 15:23; 23:26; and James 1:1 (cf. 2 John 10-11). Yet the "grace" *of God* (in the LXX *charis* is almost always the translation of Hebrew *ḥen*) is of another order and quality: (1) Grace is the nature and character of God himself. (2) It is his free gift, unfolded in manifold and surprising gifts *(charismata)* that are showered on elected persons. (3) It calls into being life, courage, and joy, by creating a community and generating gratitude. (4) Unworthiness is no obstacle to it and sin is overcome by it.

Often in the NT (so, e.g., in Rom 6:15) grace is the opposite of legitimate condemnation by God: a synonym of mercy. For instance, in James 2:13 and Luke 18:13 *eleos* (mercy) and the verb *hilaskomai* (to be gracious) take the place of words derived from the same stem as *charis*. Especially in Galatians, Romans, Philippians, and Ephesians, Paul fights the fiction that human beings can be right before God's eyes out of their own resources. Neither Jews nor Gentiles can be justified or can justify themselves — least of all by a meticulous fulfillment of "works of Law," that is, of selected commandments such as circumcision, Sabbath keeping, and dietary prescriptions (Gal 2:16; Rom 3:28; Eph 2:8-9). The will and promise of God that the Law be fulfilled in its totality is, according to Paul, fulfilled only through the coming of Christ and the outpouring of the Holy Spirit (Gal 4:4-6; Rom 8:3-4; 10:4; etc.).

Still, neither in the OT nor in the NT is grace dependent on human failure, rebellion, or idolatry. For it does not solely overwhelm, but it also precedes, sin. Therefore God is called gracious because he forgives sins, but sin does not increase grace (Rom 6:1-2, 15). Finally grace, the unshakeable goodwill, faithfulness, and mercy of God are not restricted to Israel who first experienced

God's grace. Grace is also overflowing to the Gentiles, as Paul the apostle of the nations untiringly proclaims, especially in Ephesians.

Peace is the other gift of God's blessing. This term, *eirēnē,* alludes in the benediction formula to the Semitic greeting *shalom (salem, salam).* Again the daily use of the wish for peace is overarched and lifted to a higher level by the mention of Jesus Christ. A central message of the NT is that through him "peace on earth" is now brought and proclaimed to God's people and to all the nations (Luke 2:14). According to Isa 9:5-6 (cf. Zech 9:9-10), the Messiah was to be the "Prince of Peace" whose Kingship was to have no limit in space and time. According to John 14:27, Jesus himself called the peace given by him "my peace," that is, the messianic peace (cf. Mic 5:4; Eph 2:14).

This peace gives rest to troubled and worried individuals. Haggai 2:9 (cf. Lam 3:17) speaks of "peace of the soul," and in Philem 7 and 20 Paul mentions the rest given to the hearts of the saints and to his own heart. However, there is more than only a psychic effect. In the Bible *shalom (eirēnē)* almost always means wholeness that embraces soul and body, individuals and society, Israel and the nations.

Therefore the mention of peace in the initial blessing of PHM anticipates the new relation between Philemon and his slave Onesimus. Though Paul does all in his power to intervene on the fugitive slave's behalf, the formula of blessing reveals his awareness that God alone is the source of the peace that is to be enjoyed in Philemon's household. The Pax Romana tolerated slavery in a slightly humanized form (see "Social Background," sec. III.B, pp. 18-23). The community established and united by God the Father, the messianic peace, and the family and household of God stands on more firm a foundation than an ideology or utopia would provide.

II. A CHRISTIAN — A GIFT OF GOD (VV. 4-7)

VERSE 4

I give thanks to my God always when in my prayers I ask him to remember thee.

Several features of this verse look surprising:
A. Paul speaks of *my* God rather than repeating the formula "God our Father" he had used in verse 3. His diction follows "Old Testament Psalm style" (E. Lohmeyer); when psalmists address God directly, they often say "my God" (Pss 3:7; 5:2; 7:1, 3; 59:1; 145:1; etc.). According to Matt 27:46 par., Jesus quoted on the cross from Ps 22:1: "My God, my God, why . . . ?" Paul also uses the same

form elsewhere (in 1 Cor 1:4; Rom 1:8; Phil 1:3; 1 Cor 14:18, variant reading), exclusively after writing "I give thanks." Obviously the apostle permits his readers to listen in to his personal conversation with God.

B. The plurality of senders ("Paul . . . and Timothy") notwithstanding, Paul writes the main part of his epistle in his own name, using the first-person singular of verbs "I . . ." and the singular of personal and possessive pronouns ("me," "my") rather than the plurals "we" and "our" (Phil 1:3; etc.). On the other hand, in Eph 1:16 his single authorship does not deter him from using the plural form of a verb. More frequently, however, the logical order is observed: first several senders, then plural forms of verbs and pronouns (1 Thess 1:2; 2:13; 3:9-10; 2 Thess 1:3; 1 Cor 1:4; Col 1:3; etc.).

C. Paul asks God to "remember *thee*," that is, to remember Philemon only. Are then the other persons named and addressed in Philem 1-2 simply bypassed and forgotten? Parallels to the replacement of an expected *plural* "you," "your" by "thou," "thee," and "thy" do not exist in the undisputed Pauline letters. Although in PHM (in the address, in a variant reading of v. 6, and in vv. 22 and 24) the group of recipients is remembered, the body of Paul's letter concerns one single person. In other letters that under Paul's name are directed to an individual, even to Timothy and Titus, reverse changes from the singular to the plural are never made. Still it is remarkable that in, e.g., Titus 2:1-9 the author almost dictates what has to be said to elders, young persons, and slaves.

Each of the particular features of the thanksgiving in PHM, if taken by itself, seems to be irrelevant. But combined they set a tone and create an atmosphere that are not only personal but also intimate. They reveal a specifically warm relation between Paul and God, between the apostle and Philemon, and between the slave owner and the congregation. Philippians and Second Corinthians witness to an analogous intimacy between Christ, Paul, and the whole congregation. The signal given in Philem 4 will be confirmed by almost every line of the following verses. When Onesimus reenters Philemon's house, he shall enjoy the same warmth that so far he has found only at Paul's side.

I give thanks to my God. Between the address and the body of most uncontested Pauline letters, a paragraph is found containing thanksgiving and intercession (P. Schubert, *Form and Function*, is indispensable for the study of all these passages). T. Y. Mullins, "The Thanksgiving," pp. 288-293, discusses the keywords used and concludes that Colossians is as authentically Pauline as PHM. Second Corinthians together with First Peter are exceptional: there a great benediction substitutes for a reference to personal thanksgiving. In Ephesians both are combined: the benediction is followed by thanksgiving and intercession. It is possible to consider all these passages demonstrations of the power of positive thinking. Alternatives would consist of the presentation of the results of a social and/or religious analysis, or of bitter complaint about the deplorable state of the church and the world. Among Paul's letters, only Gal 1:6-9, with its denouncement of the Galatians' fickleness and the threat of a curse, forms a conspicuous exception. Within the Pastoral Epistles, despite their urgent calls for prayer, only 2 Tim 1:13 resumes Paul's own thanksgiving and intercession. Whenever Paul expresses his thanks to God, he intercedes for a congregation. Then he considers and treats the community now addressed as a creature and gift of God, not as a result of his own or any other person's human labor. So also in Philem 4-7, Philemon is gratefully recognized as a gift of God.

The Greek word *eucharisteō* (to thank, to render thanks) is formed out of the same stem as *charis* (grace). It was pointed out in a note on verse 3 that "grace" includes, among several meanings, "gratitude." Indeed, according to, e.g., 1 Cor 1:4, the reason for thanksgiving is the grace given. In 1 Tim 1:12; 2 Tim 1:3; Heb 12:28, the phrase *charin echō* (lit. "I have grace") substitutes for the verb *eucharisteō*.

For Paul, gratitude is the basis and source not only of a person's relation to God but also of interhuman relations. No witness to the gospel, no mutual encouragement, no social ethics except on this foundation and out of this source! (See foremost Col 1:3, 12; 3:16-17; 4:2; cf. Eph 5:4; Phil 4:6.) Under the title "Thankfulness," the ethical part III of the Heidelberg Catechism of 1563 corresponds to this essential element of Paul's theology.

While in modern languages "gratitude" and synonyms often signify no more than a warm feeling or a mood hidden deep in the heart, *toda* in the Psalms (see C. Westermann, *Praise of God,* for texts such as Pss 22:22-31; 26:12) and *eucharistia* (thanksgiving) in the NT are public acts taking place in the midst of the congregation and calling everybody to join in. The version "I give thanks" is therefore better than "I thank" or "I am thankful." Paul offers an invitation in Philem 4 and its parallels to a life that reveals indebtedness to "the mercies of God" (Rom 12:1-2). His intention is certainly not a display of his personal piety. The prayer of thanksgiving and the conduct fitting such devotion come out of joy, and they are performed joyfully (Phil 1:3-4; Philem 7; etc.).

Always when in my prayers I ask him to remember thee. In following the precedent set by Paul himself (in, e.g., Rom 1:10; Col 1:9; cf. Phil 1:4; 4:6; 2 Tim 1:3), the words "I ask him" have been added to the original text. The apostle is not ashamed of depicting himself as a beggar before God. In 2 Cor 5:20 he speaks of himself as a man who in the name of the God stands begging before the congregation, and according to Rev 3:20, Jesus Christ himself is humbly knocking at the door and asking for admission.

Always. Interpreters are divided into three groups regarding the connection of this word with the foregoing and following words. Is Paul continuously

269

giving thanks (as he does according to, e.g., 1 Thess 2:13)? Among modern expositors, A. Suhl, E. Lohse, and J. Gnilka take this view. Or is he (as, e.g., Luther and Calvin assume, supported by Rom 1:9-10; 2 Tim 1:3) without cessation, by day and by night, reminiscing on those to whom he now writes? Or is this alternative misleading because thanksgiving and intercessory prayer are inseparable, complement one another, and are made simultaneously? Because the position of Greek *pantote* (always) is pendent in the midst of its environment, the last-mentioned option deserves preference. Then it must be concluded: when Paul prays he thanks; and when he makes a petition, it is out of gratitude (cf. Calvin and W. Estius; E. Lohmeyer states, "Ultimately there is no other form of prayer than thanksgiving").

To remember thee. The Greek original has the rather ponderous periphrastic form *mneian sou poioumenos* (making remembrance of thee). Also elsewhere (in 1 Thess 1:2; Rom 1:9; Eph 1:16; 2 Tim 1:3) this form substitutes for the simple verb "remember." In 1 Thess 1:2-3 both expressions are used in succession: the first is related to the persons of the Thessalonians, the second to their clearly demonstrated faith, love, and hope.

It is hardly fortuitous and meaningless that Paul likes to use the heavy formulation "making remembrance." In the Bible remembering and remembrance are in most cases more than just an intellectual process in which something of the past is retained and revived for the present and future time. (Pertinent secondary literature has been listed in AB 34, p. 147 n. 15.) Remembering also goes beyond the mere naming of a person or group in prayer. It can mean repentance, assistance to the poor and needy, celebration of communal thanksgiving, a life in faith, obedience, and hope (cf. Eph 2:11; Gal 2:10; Luke 22:19; 2 Tim 2:8). Several times in OT prayers, God himself is asked to "remember me" — or to remember his people, his word, his covenant, the land, the sacrifices offered, or the like (Judg 16:28; Jer 15:15; Jon 1:6; Pss 8:5; 25:7; 106:4). If he would remember sins, the petitioner(s) would be lost. The name Zechariah ("Yahweh remember!") expresses the confidence that from God much more than only recollection can be expected. When the prayer is heard, and when out of his grace God remembers the supplicant and his need or request, the effect does not remain buried in God's mind and head but is revealed in actions taken. This corresponds to an earlier observation: human gratitude cannot remain hidden in the psyche but breaks out in words and deeds. God who "remembers" intervenes in human affairs, he rushes to visit, to help, and to save those crying out of their misery. Also he defeats internal and external enemies by punishing sin and by repelling hostile armies.

To be included in Paul's prayer not only means for Philemon to be recommended to God's special protection and care. It also implies that the slave owner's reflections and decisions, his actions and omissions are watched by

God, who is protector, enabler, and judge at the same time. For better or worse, Philemon is in God's hands. Not only Paul's and other Christians' eyes are watching him.

Intercession is the strongest nonviolent means to encourage and to warn persons in possession of power. As all Christians are obliged to pray and intercede for the political powers that be (1 Tim 2:1-4), so Paul intervenes before God on behalf of Philemon, letting the man know of the substance of this prayer.

VERSE 5

For I am hearing of your love and faithfulness which you have toward the Lord Jesus and to all the saints.

I am hearing. The source of the oral information received by Paul on Philemon cannot be safely established. It is unlikely that Onesimus told the apostle of the many good things enumerated in Philem 5-7. The most likely reporter was Epaphras, who "revealed to us the spiritual love" of the Colossians whom Paul never had seen face-to-face (Col 1:8; 2:1). In question are also other church members who of their own will or forced by persecution moved from one city to another. Perhaps the names of some of them are contained in the greeting lists at the end of Colossians and PHM.

Only in the thanksgiving of PHM, although also in 1 Cor 11:18; 2 Thess 3:11, does the present participle "hearing" occur — in our translation "I am hearing." In Eph 1:15; Col 1:4; cf. 1:9, the aorist "having heard" is used. This may indicate that Paul repeatedly had received news about Philemon (H. Binder), perhaps through several persons. But unlike the faith of the Christians that according to the hyperbolic verse Rom 1:8 is proclaimed "in all the world," Philemon's faith and love are hardly discussed worldwide. All the more is Paul glad to hear again and again good things said about the owner of the slave Onesimus. First, it was Paul himself who persuaded Philemon to become a Christian (Philem 19). Then at one or another occasion or place, this convert had proved to be a personal friend and fellow worker (v. 1). And now the apostle has reliable information that Philemon can be trusted to obey voluntarily and abundantly Paul's request (vv. 14 and 21) and to welcome his visit (v. 22; cf. Phil 1:27). When in other letters the apostle speaks of hearing about persons he had previously met, the news received was not always good, as 2 Thess 3:11 and 1 Cor 11:18 show.

Your love and faithfulness which you have. The ugly duplication "you . . . which you have" and the somewhat surprising use of "having" are so conspicu-

271

ous in the Greek text that they had to be reproduced in the translation or else a particular accent set by Paul would be overlooked. Why a rather ungraceful style was chosen will be discussed after another unique feature of Paul's formulations has been observed.

The sequence of first *agapē* (love) and then *pistis* (faith, faithfulness, pledge) has no precedent in other Pauline letters. There faith is posited before love (Eph 1:15; Col 1:4, 8: cf. the relation between Rom 1–8 and Rom 12–15 and the triad faith-hope-love in 1 Cor 13:13; Heb 10:23-24, or faith-love-hope in 1 Thess 1:3; in 1 Tim 1:14; 6:11, faith is mentioned ahead of love, but in 4:12 love precedes faith). According to Gal 5:6, faith is distinctly the gift, the power, and the source manifested in love: "faith working through love." As observed in "Literary, Biographical, and Contextual Issues," section II, p. 106, spurious variant readings of Philem 5 restore the normal sequence.

In writing PHM, Paul had two reasons to deviate from his own usual pattern. As shown by P. Schubert in his book *Form and Function,* the thanksgiving parts of the Pauline letters announce and anticipate the substance of the later parts and main topics. Indeed, the purpose of PHM is to praise and to evoke love rather than to discuss faith and to protect it against its detractors and falsifiers. Certainly in verses 6-7 Paul will first speak of Philemon's *pistis*, then only of his *agapē*, but the noun "faith" never again occurs in the later verses.

Two other peculiarities in the Greek wording of Philem 5 are as perplexing and as easily overlooked as the mention of faith *after* love: unlike our translation, the possessive pronoun "your" (lit. "thy," i.e., Philemon's) is more immediately connected with faith than with love; and the relative pronoun "which" is in the singular *(hēn)* — as if it did not refer to the two preceding nouns love *and* faith, and therefore ought to be the plural *has*. Certainly among others, E. Lohmeyer and P. Stuhlmacher have good reasons to remark that both love and faithfulness are in mind. Indeed, the Greek diction makes evident that at this place love and faith are treated almost as one single thing, one single way, attitude, and act, perhaps as a hendiadys or as complementary and mutually interpretive synonyms (cf. C. Spicq, *Agape*, 2.302-306). Faith is then not related to love as theory is to practice, or dogmatics is to ethics; and the two ought not be carefully set apart. While Paul in Philem 5 poses love before faith, in 1 Cor 13:13 he affirms that love is even greater than faith. He elevates neither rock-hard confidence (as in Abraham's case, Rom 4:3-5, 18-22) nor an impeccable orthodox faith to the status of preconditions of salvation. When he wants to praise a Christian such as Philemon, he mentions his love *and* his faith.

Excursus: Love, Faith, and Faithfulness

In the closest parallel to Philem 5, Col 1:4, the Colossians' "faith in the Messiah Jesus" is mentioned at the side of, although immediately connected with, "the love which you have for all the saints." In 1 Thess 1:3 the "work of faith" is first remembered by Paul, the "labor of love" only later. Philemon 6-7 contain separate praises of Philemon's faith and love — in this order. Finally, together with most diverse interpreters of PHM, such as Calvin, W. Estius, E. Lohmeyer, E. Lohse, R. Bultmann (hesitantly in *TWB*, 6.212), and BDR, 477, the structure of Philem 5 may be considered a chiasm with the scheme a/b–b/ a. In this case the translation of this verse ought to read, "the love for all the saints and the faith you have in the Lord Jesus." Love and faith would point in different directions, and would be orientated toward different persons — one to the neighbors, the other to Christ.

Yet close study of the meaning and function of *pistis* in Paul's letters opens another possibility to describe the interrelation of faith and love. In many passages *pistis* should be translated "faithfulness," "loyalty," "fidelity," or "reliability." Small is the number of expositors of Philem 5 who propose this version. E. Lohse and H. Binder, together with nineteenth-century scholars such as H. A. W. Myer, G. Wohlenberg, and P. le Seur, decide against faithfulness. J. B. Lightfoot, however, is followed by C. F. D. Moule: both leave the issue open whether "faith" or "faithfulness" is the proper version. Moule concludes his discussion of the option "faithfulness, reliability" with great care: "It is possible, though not inevitable, to take *pistis* in the characteristically Pauline sense of 'trust' in the Lord Jesus." At any rate, even if for Philem 5 faithfulness deserves prior consideration, essential features of "faith" and its most frequent understanding need not be completely excluded. *Pistis* has indeed an epistemological and hermeneutical sense when it means the method of a perception opposed to sight, worldly knowledge, and wisdom (as in 2 Cor 5:7; Heb 11:1; 1 Pet 1:8; 1 Cor 1–2), and whenever it has the psychological meaning "confidence, assurance, trust, hopeful anticipation" (as in the description of Abraham's and the OT witnesses of faith in Rom 4 and Heb 11). Yet the ethical and practical quality of "faith" is extensively confirmed not only in several parts of the OT and NT, but also specifically by the apostle Paul.

In the OT, grace, truth, faithfulness, love and fear, righteousness, spontaneous goodness (*hesed*, going beyond explicit stipulations and obligations) are used with preference for denoting the proper attitude of keeping a covenant. Only God's *hen* (grace) and *hesed* toward the elect people on one side and the fear of God on the other are unilateral. The other terms describe reciprocal attitudes. In Paul's writings, the word "covenant" appears rarely — in PHM never. But what the apostle writes in Philem 6 about *koinōnia* (communication, community, sharing) and in verse 17 about being "partners" alludes to a covenant relationship.

By a covenant are held together God and his chosen people, the king of Israel with God and with his people, and all the members of Israel among one another. The covenant between husband and wife is at the same time illustration and application of all that is meant by "faithfulness," "love," "righteousness," and other terms. (See Hos 1–3, esp. 2:19-20; Jeremiah and Ezekiel, passim; Mal 2:14-16.) Connected with covenant promises given by God is the announcement of a Davidic Messiah (in, e.g., 2 Sam 7; Ps 89; Isa 11; 55:3-4). Paul alludes to pledges and hopes related to God's covenant and the Messiah to come when (in Gal 3:10-18; 2 Cor 1:20; 3:7-18; and elsewhere) he claims that Jesus Christ is the very incorporation of both God's promise and the human response.

In Rom 3:3 *pistis* cannot be translated "faith" but signifies God's "faithfulness": his loyalty is not abrogated by Israel's *apistia* (perfidy, unfaithfulness, disloyalty). In the same chapter (vv. 5 and 7), God's righteousness *(dikaiosynē)* and truth *(alētheia)* are synonyms of his *pistis*. Similarly, the old English word "troth" combines all these terms and their meanings in one single word. In other Pauline texts (1 Thess 5:24; 1 Cor 1:9, 13; etc.) God is frequently called "faithful" *(pistos)*. He keeps his promises according to the old and now renewed covenant (2 Cor 3). Current English versions and translations in other languages are wont to translate passages speaking of the Lord's *pistis* with the words "faith *in* Christ Jesus" (so in Gal 2:16, 20; 3:22, 26; Rom 3:22, 26; Phil 3:9; Eph 3:12). However, the version "faith *of* the Messiah" is not only as literal as the widespread translation "faith in Christ," but also fits better the gospel of justification by grace, not by works. The apostle does not make a given amount or quality of correct insight the basis or means of salvation; neither does the gospel attribute such a function to a wild psychic and emotional status. (Literature and arguments in favor of the version "faith [or faithfulness] *of* the Messiah" are mentioned in AB 34, pp. 224-225.) Hebrews and the book of Revelation name Jesus Christ "the faithful Son," "Highpriest," or "Witness," just as the OT distinguishes between faithful priests, kings, and witnesses, and those who misuse their office.

According to Gal 2:20, Jesus Christ's *pistis* is the love with which "he has loved me." This way Christ has fulfilled the whole law and all commandments (Rom 3:31; 8:3-4; 13:8-10; etc.). His obedience (Rom 5:19; 2:8) cannot be separated or clearly distinguished from his *pistis*. Therefore his faith is his faithfulness.

Paul fully reveals his ethical and practical understanding of the *pistis* of all Christians when in Rom 1:5; 15:26 he speaks of "obedience of faith" and in 1 Thess 1:3 of the "work of faith." As earlier quoted, according to Gal 5:6, faith works through love.

Just as faithfulness and obedience can describe all that God's covenant with his people requires, so can love. In, e.g., Deut 6:5; Rom 5:5; 8:28, love of God; in Lev 19:18; Gal 5:13-14; 1 Cor 13; Col 3:14; James 2:8; etc., love of the neighbor; and in Matt 22:34-40 love of God and of the neighbor is the sum of all commandments.

Because the foundation, source, and criteria of covenant-like conduct are found only in God himself and in his Anointed One, the members of God's people have faith and love (Philem 5; 1 Cor 13:1-3; Col 1:4; Ephesians; etc.) only when they are given to them: from God, through the Messiah, by the Spirit. Then the "Law of God is written on their hearts." What in Jer 31:31-34 is promised to Israel, is in Rom 2:14-15 (according to Augustine's interpretation of this text; cf. Rom 2:26-29; 5:5; Gal 5:22-23) applied also to the Christians of

Gentile origin. "In Christ" they are now "a new creation" (Gal 6:15; 2 Cor 5:17), true to their creation "in the image after the likeness of God" (Gen 1:26-27; Col 3:10; cf. James 3:9). The essence and prototype of the image of God is Christ himself (Col 1:15), and the Christians are boldly challenged to be "imitators of God" (Eph 5:1). Philemon, who by birth was a Gentile (as Philem 19 and the absence of OT references from PHM show), was such an imitator, according to verse 4.

Since "love" and "faithfulness" are ethical terms, Paul occasionally speaks of the "work" and the "labor" of *pistis* and *agapē* (1 Thess 1:3; 2 Thess 1:11). How much love has to endure and suffer is hymnically described in 1 Cor 13:4-7. In James 2:14-19, Paul is not caricatured or contradicted when the alternative between "having faith" and "having works" (of mercy) is ridiculed: "Faith by itself, if it has no works, is dead." In his foreword to Romans (1522 and 1546; WA *Deutsche Bibel,* 7.10-11), Luther observed that "to separate work from faith" is "as impossible as to separate burning and shining from a fire."

Hermann Binder (in his commentary on PHM, just as in his *Der Glaube bei Paulus,* passim, esp. pp. 83-108) disputes R. Bultmann's view that faith is a human answer to God's gift. With the purpose to uphold the Reformation teaching on salvation by grace alone, Binder defines love and faith as "divine actions . . . a sphere of salvation, . . . entities of salvation history . . . divine energies." He defines "salvation itself as objective reality" in which the individual is included. Love and faith cannot and must not be understood as pious works, contributed by chosen persons to their salvation. The man Philemon, so Binder argues, "stands in" the divine armor of faith and love; it is their givenness that "influences conduct," for "the power of God . . . founds the congregation." Similarly E. Lohmeyer comments on Philem 6: "Here faith does not mean the fullness of the human giving of oneself but the divine gift and power."

Indeed, some Pauline texts (such as 1 Thess 5:8; 1 Cor 16:13-14; 2 Cor 1:24; Rom 11:20) support this radical interpretation. In the final blessing of Ephesians (6:23), "peace . . . and love with faith" are distinctly gifts and powers of "God the Father and the Lord Jesus Christ" (cf. Philem 3). According to Gal 3:23, 25, *pistis* "has been coming" the same way as Christ, the offspring of the faithful Abraham, and at the fullness of time has been sent into the world (Gal 3:6, 16, 19; 4:4). The verse Gal 5:22 states explicitly that, among other things, love and faith are fruit of the Spirit. So they are not innate human capabilities and definitely not works of Law of which a Jew or Gentile might boast. "What have you that you did not receive? If then you received it — why do you boast as if it were not a gift?" (1 Cor 4:7; cf. 10:12; Rev 3:11). These words apply to Philemon as much as to the Corinthians. They have no other gifts than those granted out of God's sheer grace. In his thanksgiving to God, Paul speaks of this "having," just as in his *prayer* for the Colossians (1:4) he mentions that they

275

"have love." Paul's talk of love and faith is true to the nature of love and faith. It is realistic because it is rooted in thanksgiving and intercession rather than being a fruit of psychological or sociological analysis.

While Binder insists on the absence of any meritorious value of a person's love and faith, Lohmeyer observes that in PHM, unlike other letters, "not one word is said about the riches of love and the strength of faith." He concludes that the "carefully set down wholly general words" ("love" and "faith") reveal that "Paul knows but little of Philemon. . . . Despite all intended proximity, there remains a distance between the author and the reader." J. Ernst considers the mention of love and faith "an expression of edifying pietism." J. Gnilka suggests that a confessional formula was used for describing Philemon's status as a Christian.

Interpretations of this kind have a common trend. They assume that, for better or worse, in order to set Philemon into a favorable light, Paul puts some sort of hood over his head — a splendid cover that might as well adorn any other church member. But does the apostle really make disappear the individual face, the personal character, and the distinctive gait of the man Philemon? Should it be true that divine gifts, devotional diction, and liturgical formulae are in effect depersonalizing? If this were true of Paul's theology and pastoral work, then the apostle might be accused of caring very little for Philemon himself. His thanksgiving and intercession would then but incidentally pertain to the personality of the house owner and slave owner he addresses. The apostle would thank God solely for the hood imposed on Philemon, not for the man himself. Be it admitted: the military, managerial, institutional, including monastic and communist, treatment of human beings is known for placing a system of values and ideals, complete subordination to them and of efficiency in achieving them, high above the exigencies of personal life, experience, and performance. But mutual consolation and counseling, even care of souls among Christians, would be heinous if their aim and essence consisted in the production of a total soldier, a party member, a man in the gray flannel suit, a monk or a nun who has lost the personal identity in order to become a cogwheel in the machine of a totalitarian system. Religious adumbration of total functionality, adorned by a vocabulary that includes terms such as "God," "prayer," "love," and "faith," would certainly be the worst form of manipulating humanity. For the following reasons, Paul should not be accused of treating and praising Philemon this way.

When the apostle tells the man in Colossae how and why he renders thanks to God, he says first, in verse 4, that he asks God "to remember *thee*," and then only does he mention the love and faithfulness in which Philemon shares and from which others benefit. After the more detailed description of the effect of the slave owner's faithfulness and love in verses 6-7, Paul again speaks of what is effected "through *you*." Obviously thanks is given for a very specific person's (lit. "thy," in our translation "your") very particular love and faithfulness ("which you have"), not for an idea or abstraction of them in which Philemon is masked and strutting around. The apostle distinctly cares for the Colossian himself, just as in verse 1 he shows that he loves the man himself and also his function as a fellow worker.

Again, Philem 16 is anticipated. There Paul will ask Philemon to receive the slave as a dear brother (lit.) "in the flesh and in the Lord." In verses 4-7 the apostle does himself what he later asks Philemon to do: not to neglect very personal traits even when the function in the Lord's service is highly appreciated. Paul writes of himself, "The life I now live in the flesh I live by faith" (Gal 2:20), and he trusts that "the life of Jesus will be manifested in our mortal flesh" (2 Cor 4:11). Neither Paul's, nor Philemon's, nor Onesimus's, nor any Christian's unique earthly personality vanishes behind a screen of holy smoke. Just persons such as they are, are seized and used by God; for their total human existence prayers are raised to God. Their love and faithfulness establish them as distinct and irreplaceable personalities rather than hide them under uniforms and monastic or clerical garb.

If now the love and faithfulness of Philemon are strictly personal, bearing the marks of a human being's individuality and flesh, then they are neither unchippable granite blocks, nor perfect jewels, nor timeless ideas or virtues. Presupposed that Paul or another fellow Christian would ask Philemon about the quality and stability of his faith, he might well hear the answer, "I believe, help my unbelief" (Mark 9:24). Jesus Christ himself might have challenged him thrice with "Do you love me?" (John 21:15-17). Paul himself appeals to a congregation for whose existence he has thanked God: "Be watchful, stand firm in your faith, let all that you do be done in love" (1 Cor 16:13). To the Philippians, whom he loves more intimately than other congregations, the apostle writes, "For this I ask that your love shall overflow more and more in recognition and total perception." The apostle trusts that he can continue his ministry "for their progress and enjoyment of faith" (Phil 1:9, 25). Whoever loves and believes is not yet perfect. *Agapē* and *pistis* are in need of nourishment and growth; they have to be deepened and expanded; they undergo tests and accept suffering. According to the Gospels, Jesus said once to a person, "Great is your faith," and he spoke of that rare supreme love that lays down the life of the self for friends (Matt 15:28; John 15:13). When the confession made to Jesus with the words, "You are the Messiah, the Son of the living God," is declared a gift of God and fundamental of the church, the same man Peter who made the confession is soon enough addressed "Satan" (Matt 16:15-25). Of all people it is the believer and confessor who is exposed to loose faith in view of wind and waves; even Peter is saved by ever renewed grace alone (Matt 14:22-33; cf. Mark 10:38-40).

Paul's thanksgiving and intercession for Philemon is a *prayer* for the unfolding and ever new demonstration of love and faith, just as Luke 22:32 reports that Jesus *prayed* for the stability of Peter's faith and for his future conversion. It would have been superfluous for Paul to continue writing after verses 4-7 if Philemon's love and faithfulness had already been perfect in every dimension. The whole of PHM, including the visit of Paul in Philemon's house, most likely has the purpose "to supply what is lacking in your faith" and to "convey some spiritual gift to strengthen you, that . . . we may be comforted together through our mutual faithfulness, yours and mine" (1 Thess 3:10; Rom 1:9-12).

Toward the Lord Jesus and to all the saints. In the Greek text, two different (although practically synonymous) prepositions are used to show to which persons love and faithfulness are directed. Who is the object and substance of *agapē* and of *pistis?* As equivalent of *eis, epi, en* ("toward," "upon," "in," which serve the same function in parallel texts), in Philem 5 *pros* precedes "the Lord Jesus" and *eis* (lit. "into") substitutes before "all saints" for the genitive, which elsewhere is often used by Paul to denote the loved persons. (*Agapē eis* . . . also occurs in 1 Thess 3:12; 2 Thess 1:3; 2 Cor 2:8; Rom 5:8; Col 1:15; Eph 1:15.) The formula, faith *pros* the Lord Jesus, is never again found in Paul's epistles; faith *pros* God in 1 Thess 1:8 is the nearest parallel. The unusual employment of *pros* makes it improbable that in Philem 6 Paul literally, not to say thoughtlessly, cites a fixed formula and that, following a chiastic pattern, faith is related only to the Lord Jesus and love solely to all the saints.

As shown by the double commandment of love, the covenant made by God is kept only when the human covenant partner is included in the affection due to God. Election, forgiveness, reconciliation would be misunderstood and actually denied if they were considered a privilege granted for the benefit of individuals only — as if they did not by nature work out in an attitude of mercy, justice, and support of the neighbor. What the Gospel of Matthew (5:23-24, 43-48; 6:12, 14-15; 18:23-35; 22:34-38) and 1 John 3:13-18; 4:7-12 explicitly affirm, is also the aim of Paul's ethics. In faithful love for one another, Christians can and will bear with slander, persecution, and sufferings befalling them from outside. Faith working out in mutual love distinguishes their love of God and their faith in God from being sheer hypocrisy and pretension. The fact that the Messiah "has loved us . . . the church" (Eph 5:2, 25) is, according to Eph 2:14-18, demonstrated by the peace that has terminated all forms of enmity between humankind and God, and between the persons of Jewish and Gentile origin.

The formula "the Lord Jesus" is part of a traditional blessing and/or confession. In Philem 5 the formula reminds the slave owner that he has joined the community of those who proclaim by word and deed that "Jesus is Lord!" This confession anticipates what the chorus of all creatures in heaven and on and under the earth will take up and make their own (1 Cor 12:3; Phil 2:10-11; etc.).

To confess the Lordship of Jesus means to bow to the conviction that he who is in eternity and time God's Son and Image was sent out by God the Father, humbled himself to become a man and to obey as a servant, was ignored and despised, was ill-treated and crucified by the religious, political, and economical powers that be — that this Jesus was raised from the dead and enthroned on high in order to return in glory (Phil 2:6-11; 1 Cor 1:18; 2:8; 15:23-28). In verses 8-21 of PHM the slave owner Philemon will be urged to live up to his confession. By mentioning the substance of Philemon's faith, Paul reminds the earthly lord over one or several slaves of the high Lord Protector who is in charge: not only the apostle will plead for Onesimus; rather the Lord of all lords (cf. Rev 19:16) protects Onesimus and makes him worthy of a good reception.

The words "and all the saints" sound in Philem 5, as much as in Col 1:4 (cf. Eph 1:15; 6:18; etc.), like an Oriental exaggeration. How can one single church member, in as tiny a town as Colossae and in control of just one house, embrace by love "all" Christians? Two extreme attempts to answer this question call for a replacement by a third alternative.

1. P. Asting (*Die Heiligkeit im Urchristentum* [Göttingen: Vandenhoeck, 1930]) suggests that by "saints" (unless this term denotes angels) not all church members are meant but the church office bearers only. This interpretation favors clericalism and hierarchic tendencies. It forgets what in First Peter and in Reformation theology (and in a strong trend of modern Roman Catholicism) is said about the general priesthood of all believers.

2. John Calvin, true to his understanding of the commandment "love thy neighbor," puts emphasis on the word "all" in Philem 5 and explains that love is not so restricted to the saints that for others it could be nonexistent. He believes that it must embrace the whole human race. This exposition, however, throws the net too far out. Just as in the OT the resident foreigner is included (Lev 19:18, 34), so in Paul's ethical instructions love is always directed to a known person: to the neighbor, the brother, the sister, the members of the congregation, and the whole church. In agreement with Matt 5:43-48, according to Rom 12:17–13:10, love also includes the persecuting enemy and, in its own way, the officials of the Roman state. The entire human race is never mentioned as the persons or groups to be loved. Love always concerns people known through personal encounter and contact. (See in AB 30 and 30A the last Notes of Eph 1:15 and 4:2, and esp. AB 30A, pp. 459-462.) Brotherly love according to Paul is the attitude, the act, and sometimes the disappointing and painful experience that occur when the brother or sister in faith is accepted just as he or she is, when his or her faults or sins are not accounted for but forgiven (cf. 1 Cor 13:4-7). Love is ever new and always very special.

It is as singular and mysterious as each of the persons who are linked together by love, be it in one-sided or mutual affection. "Doing good to all persons when opportunity arises" is by no means excluded, but "those who are of the household of faith" have preference, as Paul affirms in Gal 6:10. The apostle does not describe love as a virtue of the soul that can be discriminately applied here or there. It cannot be splashed around, as it were, out of the full tank of a kind heart.

3. Most likely the formula "to all the saints" refers not only to all the local church members who assembled in Philemon's house. It reaches far beyond Colossae: visiting Christians are included, even migrating missionaries, prophets, delegates of the apostle to a near or far congregation. Some visitors may have come out of need in order to beg or ask a favor. For others an empty stomach, together with worn-out sandals and clothes, might have been a sanctimonious disguise used in order to exploit Philemon's hospitality. *Didache* 11 gives a vivid picture and warning of such visitors.

In addition, the term "all the saints" may be used to prepare the way and the reception not only of Paul, if the Lord wills that he comes around (v. 22), but even more of an earlier arrival: Paul's alter ego, Onesimus (v. 12, variant reading; 16-17). Certainly the fugitive slave is an ugly bird when he attempts to find a nest in Philemon's house and to be included in his love. As much as the apostle is deserving of the honor, Onesimus may look unworthy of it. But "love for all the saints" embraces high- and low-standing Christians equally. All of them Paul calls "saints."

VERSE 6

I ask that your faith communion be a source of energy to recognize all the good that is found in your congregation, in expectation of Christ.

The Greek text of this verse is fraught with heavy theological vocabulary, and is therefore extremely dense and complex. Since it defies a literal translation, it calls for paraphrasing additions if ever at least a part of its substance is to become intelligible. Inside the Pauline corpus, perhaps only Eph 4:16 contains as many puzzling problems of interpretation.

In his article "knowing, knowledge etc" in *TWB*, 1.689-719, Rudolf Bultmann (on p. 708) offers the following exposition: "The faith which Philem. shares is to be effectual in his recognition of all that is given to the believers and of what must foster union with Christ when it is expressed." NEB, JB, NJB, and other modern versions differ significantly from this paraphrase and from one another. As the number and weight of variant Greek readings show, already old church copyists had serious troubles with offering a comprehensible text. Among highly respected modern exegetes, C. F. D. Moule observes that Philem

6 is notoriously the most obscure verse in this letter, and that answers to the several questions posed by expositors "must remain obscure." H. Riesenfeld begins his contribution to the C. K. Barrett FS ("Faith and Love Promoting Hope: An Interpretation of Philemon 6") with the sigh: "Few passages in the New Testament have been interpreted and translated in so many different ways."

Should this invite despair, or should it be argued that Philem 6 is part of a prayer and that by nature the mystical mood and emotional atmosphere presupposed and promoted by adoration is opposed to grammatical, rational, logical, historical, etc., analysis? Or is it enough when only God understands Paul's words, and when readers of PHM gain a faint notion of how warmly Paul loves and recommends Philemon? The best way to face serious difficulties is hardly constituted by denying or avoiding them.

After due attention is given to the many various readings, at least three tasks emerge and have to be solved simultaneously: (1) Out of the cornucopia of multiple senses and possible shades of meanings inherent in the employed key words, that particular or compound significance has to be selected which is best recommended by the whole sentence and its context. (2) The most probable grammatical and syntactical connection between individual words and between the several parts of the whole verse requires elucidation. (3) As a result and summary of the preceding philological work, a translation has to be formulated that throws as much light as possible into the opaque jungle.

I ask that. The addition of "I ask" (in other versions, "my prayer is") follows the complementation made sometimes (in 2 Cor 1:11; Rom 1:8-10; Phil 1:4; 4:6; 2 Tim 1:3; cf. 1 Tim 2:1) by Paul himself; also it corresponds to the description of prayer in Eph 6:18. Not only a pious wish, to be introduced by "may," as, e.g., P. Stuhlmacher suggests, but the distinct aim and purpose of Paul's prayer are mentioned in the following (J. B. Lightfoot). Thomas Aquinas concurs in essence though not in method when he translates the Greek *hina* (that) as a consecutive conjunction, pointing out the hoped-for result in Paul's intercession.

Your faith communion. The Greek original is as strange and ambiguous as the English version here proposed. Other options are, e.g., "the sharing of your faith," "your sharing of faith," "your fellowship in our common faith." After love was mentioned before faith *(pistis)* in verse 5, now the essence of Philemon's *pistis* is unfolded before, beginning with verse 7, love *(agapē)* becomes the main theme. In verse 6 the nouns *koinōnia* (communion, communication, community, fellowship) and *pistis* (faith) are as closely joined and tied together as the Greek language permits: *koinōnia tēs pisteōs.* Obviously Paul intends to emphasize the communal character of Philemon's faith and to distinguish it from a privately invented, fabricated, or possessed virtue. For Paul faith is, specifically when he speaks of Abraham's and Christ's faith, never a matter related to and dependent on this or that individual only. Faith implies and expresses solidarity, just as does love.

What is actually meant by *koinōnia* and the cognate verbs, nouns, and adjectives *(koinoō, koinōneō, koinōnos, sygkoinōnos, koinos)?* Among the literature mentioned in BAG, *TWB,* and other theological wordbooks, H. Seesemann, *Der Begriff [Koinōnia] im Neuen Testament,* is still a classic. Calvin has asserted as clearly as Thomas Aquinas before him, that the noun means participation. It denotes primarily a dynamic interrelation created by sharing. However, just like English "communion" (or building), it can also signify the result of receiving and giving (namely, of the activity of constructing). In that case, a community or society is meant that has been established by participation — be it one-sided or reciprocal.

The communication and community signified by *koinōnia* binds and holds *persons* together. The Greek word does not denote the unilateral or mutual coherence of ideas or the combination or interaction of material things. (See the references given s.v. in LSLex; in the Pauline epistles, 1 Cor 10:16-18, 20 are outstanding examples; in the Johannine literature: 1 John 1:3-4). The bond joining together living persons may be material or spiritual. When it is spiritual, it yet finds physical expression. Friendship, education, worship, sexual intercourse, common suffering and joy, comradeship in war, games played together, bread shared or a sacrificial meal, a handshake can constitute and publicly manifest the partnership called *koinōnia.* Because sharing is essential, "participation" or an equivalent would be as viable a translation of the Greek term as "communication."

In Philem 6, *koinōnia* can be understood primarily in the passive sense. If so, then Paul emphasizes that what other Christians and all congregations had possessed first, was also received and shared by Philemon. Chrysostom refers to Titus 1:3, where the "common faith" *(koinē pistis)* is mentioned. On the other hand, Paul may intend to speak of the faith and the fruit of faithfulness, which radiate from Philemon so forcefully that they inspire and enrich others. Both interpretations are philologically justified and correspond to the context. For clarity's sake, many interpreters decide in favor of either the first or the second; but H. Riesenfeld (in the Barrett FS, p. 254) observes with good reason that "both alternatives make sense, and good sense." Therefore the translation of *koinōnia* must show that Philemon in both capacities, as a receiver and as a giver, is member of the community of "all the saints."

Still, among others J. B. Lightfoot, E. Lohmeyer, and C. F. D. Moule increase substantially the number of interpretive options. Not only the act, but the result of sharing, even the fellowship of other Christians created by faith, might be meant. Or the very specific faith communication between two persons only — Paul and Philemon — might be in mind, as signaled by the juxtaposition of "you" and "me" (in vv. 11 and 16) and other signs of personal cordial friendship. Further, some Pauline passages (1 Cor 1:9; 10:16; 2 Cor 13:13; Phil 2:1; etc.; cf. 1 John 1:3, 6, 7) that distinctly speak of the faith communion created and held together by God, Jesus Christ, and the Holy Spirit may be considered decisive. Finally, *koinōnia* is not limited to denoting a spiritual union. Physical actions and gifts, the provision of food and a place to meet and/or to sleep, not to speak of contributions made in cash, are sometimes meant by this noun. The cognate Greek words can point in the same direction. Practiced charity, even liberal giving as the essence of doing good, are mentioned several times (2 Cor 8:4; 9:13; Rom 15:26; cf. Gal 6:6, 10; 1 Tim 6:18; Heb 13:16). They are issues and demonstrations of faith. The hospitality offered in Philemon's house, the proven and expected goodness of the man and the reference to financial affairs in Philem 2, 14, 18-19, 22, support the last-mentioned interpretation of *koinōnia pisteōs*.

The manifold meanings should not be treated as mutually exclusive. And yet, a modern language version as comprehensive and multicolored as the Greek text of Philem 6 has yet to be found. The translation "faith communion" fails to reproduce the full sparkle and all the riches of the Greek, but it seeks at least to hint at the greatest possible number of fitting interpretations.

Be a source of energy. Thirty times in the Pauline letters do words formed out of the stem *energ* occur. They signify not only what the etymology (in-working) indicates. They certainly do not denote something that might remain completely hidden because it is solely internal and invisible. Rather these words denote the working out, the causation and the display of very specific events. According to Paul, God, God's word, God's power, love, and life, following James 5:16 also the prayer of the righteous, are sources of the energy that works in the Christians (Eph 1:11; 3:20; 1 Thess 2:13; Heb 4:12; etc.). Energy flows out of power *(dynamis)* and is sometimes mentioned in the same breath. The supreme demonstration of God's unique power is the raising of Jesus Christ (Eph 1:19-20; Col 2:12). When God "works in" human persons, he uses his dominion over all things to make their "lowly body conform to his [Christ's] glorious body" (Phil 3:21) and already now to raise Gentiles and Jews from spiritual death together with Christ (Eph 2:1-6; Col 2:12-13). He also effects in them the "willing and performing" so that they can work according to their salvation (Phil 2:12-13). By the same Spirit through which Christ was raised, the fruit of the Spirit is distributed and the love of God is poured out (Rom 5:5; 8:11; Gal 5:22-23). Now the Christians are enabled to experience and/or to do deeds of power (Gal 3:5). The apostle Peter as well as Paul himself are paradigms of this efficiency of God's power and grace (Gal 2:8; Col 1:29; Eph 3:7; cf. 1 Cor 15:9-10). On the other hand, Paul also speaks of evil forces at work over and in humankind. He mentions the energy "of the mystery of iniquity . . . of Satan . . . of sinful passions . . . of death" (in 2 Thess 2:7, 9; Rom 7:5; 2 Cor 4:12). Therefore his own and every Christian's life mean continuous labor, struggle, and warfare (Col 1:29–2:1; cf. Rom 7:14-25).

When in Philem 6 Paul asks God to inspire and manifest Philemon's faith communion, he hardly intends to insinuate an earlier lack of the slave owner's efficiency. Rather, out of gratitude for what the apostle has already heard, he prays to God that Philemon's faith be sustained and increased by ever new acts of communication and manifestation. According to Gal 5:6, it is love through which faith works out; according to W. Estius, it is works by which faith reveals its energy. Indeed, variant readings of Philem 6 refer to "every good work," while Philem 7 corresponds to Gal 5:6 and elaborates on love.

According to the Latin version of Philem 6, also following, e.g., BAG (s.v. *energēs*), J. B. Lightfoot, and E. Lohmeyer, the words *energēs genētai* (lit. "become effective") have the very specific sense of "becoming clear, evident, visible, manifest." Because the Greek text continues with a reference to knowledge (*epignōsis*), it might be argued that the effect of Philemon's faith influenced solely the perception, cognition, or understanding of the persons in the slave owner's environment. Perhaps the Latins had in their hands a Greek text that had *enargēs* (clear, evident, visible, manifest) instead of *energēs* (effective). Indeed, this reading would say little or nothing about a causation of changes in the total life and palpable experience of other persons. Still, a Greek MS reading *enargēs* has as yet not been discovered.

Actually, the effects denoted by *energēs* are motoric or causative as well as revelatory or cognitive. Both effects are co-inherent. Certainly Paul attributes immense relevance to "revelation" — not only to past but also to present and future revelation. The life of Jesus shall be "revealed" in the mortal body of the Christians (2 Cor 4:11), and the noble zeal of the Corinthians shown in Paul's favor, "shall be revealed" before God (2 Cor 7:12). But, as in the whole Bible so also Paul's writings, revelation is much more than a special way of information leading to intellectual knowledge and psychic stability. It is at the same time enlightenment of those ignorant *and* transformation of sinners. The effect of Philemon's faithfulness is therefore not limited to a show or announcement, but includes changes effective in the whole life of others.

To recognize (lit. "in knowledge"). In classical Greek the noun *epignōsis*, used here, and the corresponding *epiginōskō* can signify the acquisition or possession of full and perfect knowledge as distinct from a partial or superficial knowing (*gnōsis, ginōskō*). Indeed, according to 1 Cor 13:12 and Eph 4:13, complete knowledge comes no earlier than at the end, when Christ returns. But elsewhere the complex and the simplex nouns and the corresponding verbs are used as synonyms. According to, e.g., Col 1:4, 9-10, the Colossians of whose faith and love Paul has heard (and among whom Philemon is living), are still in need to be "filled" with *epignōsis* and to "grow" in it. J. B. Lightfoot believes that in Philem 6 *epignōsis* means "the complete appropriation of all truth and unrestricted identification with God's will." But Paul does not explicitly hint at a theological or philosophical, analytical or synthetical, pure or practical knowledge. Not even in the Pastoral Epistles, where the formula "knowledge of truth" *(epignōsis alētheias)* is repeatedly used, is a flawless perfection in mind.

When Paul speaks of knowledge and knowing, in most cases he reproduces the OT and later Jewish meaning of these words rather than their significance in Greek philosophical thought or in Gnostic literature (see AB 34, pp. 12-18, for a discussion of some problems posed by a Gnostic interpretation of Paul). In the Bible knowledge means acknowledgment, recognition, joyful awareness, acceptance, and respect of the otherness and nearness of a person or an object. The opposite of knowledge is infinitely worse than lack of intellectual perception, memory, and actual awareness. Not to know God is the conscious or unconscious act of blatantly *ignoring* the manifestation and will, the right and the might, the goodness and the mercy of God together with his gifts (see, e.g., Isa 1:3, and the promise that one day Israel will know God in Jer 31:33 and in Ezekiel passim). Knowledge does not only lead to an appropriate response to the person or thing known — it already *is* the right response. Being "an inward appropriation or experience . . . Christian knowledge carries in it a corresponding manner of life" (R. Bultmann, *TWB*, 1.706-707). According to H. Binder, the "recognition" to which Philemon is called means that he shall "realize the reality of salvation." On the other hand, knowledge of good and evil as promised by the serpent in Gen 3:5, is a gift only God gives — through the Law, as the rabbis are emphasizing. Always in the Bible, knowledge is a matter of life and death and affects a person's total life. It is never an act or a possession of the brain only.

This is manifest foremost in the use of the verb "knowing" for signifying sexual intercourse (Gen 4:1; 19:5; etc.) and for a summary description of the covenant relationship between God and his people (in Hosea, Jeremiah, and Ezekiel, in the NT in Gal 4:9; 1 Cor 8:2-3; 13:12; cf. Matt 11:27; John 10:14-15). Knowledge can therefore be identified with love and faithfulness. J. B. Lightfoot says in his comments on Philem 6, "To know is both to possess and to perform. . . . *epignōsis* is the result and the reward of faith manifesting itself in deeds of love." E. Lohmeyer, however, adds a mysterious dimension to the function of knowledge: "The way out of the transcendental realm of faith to the this-worldly realm of life and action is called knowledge of all the good."

In Philem 6 Paul does not say *who* is to recognize the energy and effect of Philemon's faith. (1) Philemon himself has been proposed: through doing good, even in his works, he might find a confirmation of his election by God's grace, and of his faith. (2) Or it could be Paul who hopes for an increase in his own knowledge through a response of God to his prayer that would validate his trust in Philemon. (3) Or the local congregation is expected to esteem Philemon even more highly than at present. It is to honor and to love him as a model Christian who demonstrates that and how faith works out in deeds of love. (4) Finally, Philemon's practiced faith may fulfill a missionary function: it can so deeply impress persons outside the congregation that "seeing your good works . . . they give glory to your Father in heaven" (cf. Matt 5:16; Phil 2:15; Eph 2:7; 3:10; 5:8-9; 1 Pet 2:12).

The wording of Philem 6 neither permits the exclusion of any of these interpretations nor prescribes the selection of just one of them. Calvin's exposition touches on every essential point: Faith "does not remain hidden otiose but through true effects reveals itself to humankind. Although it has its hidden seat in the heart, it communicates itself . . . through good works. . . . Knowledge of all the good is understood as experience. Paul prays that out of its effect faith be verified as being effective. . . . Whatever good is found in us, reveals our faith." On this basis, later Reformed divines developed the doctrine of the so-called *syllogismus practicus:* a believer's life, work, and success can confirm his or her eternal election by God.

All the good. A few ancient MSS and the Clementine edition of Vg. add after "good" the noun "work." In "Literary, Biographical, and Contextual Issues," section II (pp. 106-108), it was mentioned that this addition does not contradict Paul's teaching on justification by faith alone rather than by works of law. The reading "good work" looks good enough because of its concern for Philemon's and the congregation's ethics. Yet it hides or suppresses a strictly theological sense: the "good" may be not only a sum of God's commandments, but even more all the good done and given by God himself, through Christ and the Spirit.

The scholarly interpretations vary wildly and often contradict one another. JB translates "all the good we can do"; NEB has "all the blessing" (followed by "that our union with Christ brings us"). H. Binder refers to Phil 1:6 and speaks of "the good, that is, God's work"; he calls it "the entrusted good," "the power of God which founds, holds together and motivates the congregation." The same author repudiates the idea that "the good as such be meant in Philem 6." This is the opposite of E. Lohmeyer's opinion that this verse contains traces of pagan "philosophical ethics" and of "a breath of urban education." Philippians 4:8 ("whatever is true, honourable, . . . just, . . . pure, . . . lovely, . . . gracious, if there is any excellence . . . worthy of praise, think of those things") has often been quoted in support of the last-mentioned exposition.

H. Riesenfeld (in the Barrett FS, pp. 255-256) has made another original contribution. He argues that the frequent triad faith, love, and hope in Pauline writings (as in 1 Thess 1:3; 1 Cor 13:13; Col 1:4-5; cf. Heb 10:22-24) is the key to Philem 5-7: after love and faith have been mentioned in these three verses, hope seems still to be missing; but what is called "all the good" in verse 6 actually means hope; therefore once again hope completes the triad. Indeed, "the good things to come" are mentioned in Heb 9:11 and 10:1, and the words (lit.) "toward Christ" at the end of Philem 6 add an eschatological note to the whole of Philem 6, as if to confirm Riesenfeld's thesis.

However, theocentric and eschatological interpretations cannot simply eliminate the ethical sense of "all the good" in its present context. C. F. D. Moule observes that the "good" is usually mentioned by Paul "as something which is done or performed . . . rather than as a possession or the object of knowledge." The fact that "there is none that does good, no, not one" is lamented by a psalmist as well as by Paul (Ps 53:1, 3; Rom 3:10), and the urgent advice "depart from evil and do good" is one of the summaries of Wisdom ethics (e.g., Pss 34:14; 37:27). According to Heb 13:21 (NJB), it is God who prepares "you to do his will in every kind of good action"; and Eph 2:10 states, "In the Messiah Jesus we are created for those good works which God has provided as our way of life."

Regarding Philem 6, E. Lohmeyer observes that for both the Pharisees and Paul "knowledge" is the gift to do good and the task to perform it; but while for the Jewish teachers the Law is the object and principle of all endeavors, in the apostle's teaching ethics is so directly oriented to Christ that in effect Christ takes the place of the Law; Christ is the essence of all glory, rather than Israel's future glorious perfection.

Because antilegalistic and anti-Judaistic polemics are far from the purpose of PHM, other exposition may stand closer to the text of this verse. P. Stuhlmacher prefers the variant reading *en hymin* (in you) in Philem 6 and assumes that Paul speaks of the new heart given by God, that is, of the inscription of God's Law upon the heart of his people (cf. Jer 31:31-34). Indeed, in Rom 2:14-16 Paul speaks of that heart and that inscription which, when God holds judgment through the Messiah Jesus, will prove to have enabled even Gentiles "to do what the Law requires." Philemon was not a Jew by birth, but in Philem 6 Paul describes him de facto as a man with a new heart, who does what is good according to God's will.

The formula "all the good" can include a reference to everyday matters, even to the use of material things. This is plain in Gal 6:6: the apostle has material support in mind when he writes, "Anyone who is taught the word shall give a share of all good things to the one who teaches." Palpable actions and gifts are meant when Timothy is told to command "those rich in the present world . . . to do good, be rich in good works, to be liberal and generous," as a solid investment for gaining eternal life in the future (1 Tim 6:17-19). James 2:16 goes into details by mentioning "warming . . . nourishing . . . giving the things needed for the body." Indeed, the generalizing moral understanding of "(doing) all the good" would be vague if it did not include some hints at liberal gifts made for the benefit of needy persons. The texts just cited support H. Binder's exposition of "all the good" in Philem 6: "For the poor church members Philemon had an open hand."

Several expositors assume that Paul thinks of himself as the main recipient or co-beneficiary of the material support provided by Philemon. Among them, Sara Winter has produced an adventurous theory. In "Paul's Letter to Philemon," pp. 3-4, she suggests that "all the good" was done by the whole congregation of Colossae rather than by Philemon alone; this good was performed for the benefit of the imprisoned apostle; as the church's delegate, Onesimus had transported the gifts to their destination. Indeed, according to Phil 2:25 (cf. 4:15), another man, Epaphroditus, had been sent to the captive Paul as carrier of goods collected by the Philippians. Ms. Winter understands the words *en hēmin* (lit: "in us") in Philem 6 to mean "on our behalf, in our case, for us." However, because Onesimus was not baptized and was considered "useless" before he met with Paul (v. 11), such a man would hardly have been trusted enough to become a church envoy.

The remaining four words of Philem 6, (lit.) "in you" and "toward Christ," are in telegraph style. In consequence, they are prone to endure several different interpretations. Both formulae need be translated with paraphrasing additions if one clear sense rather than a fog of possible meanings shall emerge.

Which is found in your congregation (lit. either "in us" or "in you"; variant readings of the Greek text have either *en hēmin* or *en hymin*). When a Pauline letter was dictated or read aloud to a congregation or a copyist, there was little or no difference between the pronunciation of *hēmin* and *hymin:* the vowels *eta* and *upsilon* sounded like English "ee" (as in "see"). The reading "in us" has support in the possessive pronoun "our" in Philem 1-3. The competing "in you" is recommended by three occurrences of the plural "your" in verses 22 and 25. The quality and weight of Greek MSS having the one or the other reading are in balance; the numerical majority favors "in us" and is given preference by the Nestle-Aland and Greek New Testament editions. J. B. Lightfoot believes that "*hymin* has somewhat better support," but he decides in favor of *hēmin* as "being more expressive." Other Pauline letters frequently present the same textual problem. The difficulty of solving it from case to case is increased by Paul's inclination to mean himself when he writes "we" or "our." But not always are these plurals majestic. In, e.g., 2 Cor 4:12; 13:9, the apostle distinguishes sharply between "us" and "you," the death and weakness on Paul's side and the life and strength on the congregation's. Elsewhere, e.g., 2 Cor 1:3-7, he insists on the close connection between himself and the Christians he addresses. Is it then impossible or superfluous to ask for a decision whether in Philem 6 "in us" or "in you" ought to be preferred as the better reading?

E. Lohmeyer refers to the context and its parallels: elsewhere in his thanksgiving prayers Paul "does not lump himself into a unity with the congregation." To this observation may be added another. Presupposed that in Philem 6 spiritual rather than material goods are meant, the words "in us" might well imply that Paul thanks God not only for Philemon's but also for his own endowment with divine gifts, and consequently also for his own piety. Still, unlike the Pharisee in the temple whose boasting of doing good is portrayed in Luke 18:9-14, Paul never thanks God for granting him outstanding love and faithfulness. Whenever he expresses his very personal gratitude, then he refers to his transformation from a former persecutor of the church to a servant of Jesus Christ who is sent out to the nations. According to 1 Tim 1:12-16, he thanked God for making him the prototype of a sinner, an example of the gracious salvation of many others. The reading "in you" is therefore more probably authentic than the variant "in us."

However, the literal translation "in you" might easily obscure the proper sense of *en hymin*. For unlike in Greek, in English "in you" can be misunderstood to point to Philemon only, as indeed do the singular pronouns translated by "thee, thy" in our version of verses 2 and 4 and by "you, your" in verses 5-21. In Philem 6, "in you" *(en hymin)* denotes a local presence in a community of persons, even among the individuals and the assembly mentioned in the address in Philem 1-3. The next paraphrastic interpolation into the Greek texts consists of the words "which is found." This addition leaves it open whether the presence and unfolding power of the good divine gifts is meant or the performance of good deeds by Philemon.

Paul emphasizes that spiritual and/or material goods are to be perceived and enjoyed by a society on earth, even in the congregation at Colossae and in Philemon's house. Or else the goods might be sought or located in a cloud-cuckoo-land or in an invisible and merely ideal church. Certainly the new heart and the inscription of God's Law are a gift and a deed of God that pertain immediately to individual persons. Each one of them shall "through the Spirit be fortified with power (to grow) toward the inner man"; that is, "through faith the Messiah may dwell in your hearts" (Eph 3:16-17). In Philem 6, no less than in every chapter of Ephesians, Paul asserts that the congregation is the place in whose frame and to whose benefit God's effective power is felt at work — although it also works outside its limits.

On the basis of grammar and syntax, it is impossible to decide which precedent word or part of verse 6 is meant when Paul speaks of the power demonstration "in your congregation." Communion, faith, internal and external experiences, the mental recognition of all the good received from God and done by Philemon — each or all of these events may be in mind. Certainly Paul does not choose and combine so many heavyweight theological terms in order to speak of a pie in the sky. His concern is the social relations on earth for which Philemon bears a share of responsibility.

In expectation of Christ (lit. "toward Christ"). Tacked on to the already overloaded sentence, this phrase, too, permits and invites several expositions. In, e.g., Rom 16:5; 2 Cor 1:21; 11:3, the same formula *(eis Christon)* recurs at the end of an affirmation. Rather than containing an incidental afterthought or being a superfluous fill-in, its position at the end of Philem 6 and at the conclusion of the thanksgiving-and-intercession prayer of Paul reveals that the apostle wanted to have it read with emphasis.

The easiest way to explain the formula was chosen at the time of the church fathers by Vg., and more recently by F. F. Bruce. They consider the words *eis Christon* (toward Christ) a synonym of *en Christō* (in Christ). Most commentaries on Pauline epistles and on the Gospel of John, also the monographs on the theology of the NT, on Paul, and in specific on the phrase "in Christ," contain discussions of the riches accumulated in this expression. (See, e.g., AB 34, pp. 69-71, and the pertinent bibliography, on pp. 409-10.) The formula "in Christ" qualifies statements about God's eternal election, about the fulfillment of God's will on the cross and in the resurrection of Christ, and about the ethical freedom and responsibility of the Christians.

However, when the difference between the literal meanings of *en Christō* and *eis Christon* is taken seriously, Philem 6 takes on a unique character and glamor. Rather than a place that might be misunderstood as static ("in Christ"), a direction and forward movement of all the divine and/or human good is indicated by the word (lit.) "toward Christ." Among the alternatives for explaining the specific content and intention of Philem 6 are the following:

1. Communion *(koinōnia)* is defined as being "communion *with Christ*" (so, e.g., Calvin, R. Bultmann, C. H. Dodd as quoted by C. F. D. Moule, NEB, and others). Indeed, occasionally (as in 2 Cor 6:14; 9:13; Phil 1:5; cf. Rom 15:26; Phil 4:15) Paul speaks of communion (lit.) "toward" *(eis)* instead of using genitive forms of the partners in question. Only in 1 John 1:3, 6, 7 is *koinōnia* followed by the preposition *meta* (with).

2. *Pistis* (faith, faithfulness) is distinguished from subordination and attachment to other persons: it is "faith *in Christ*."

3. The direction of the energy working in Philemon and in the community is made clear: God's power, as it is manifested in Philemon's faith, urges and inspires giving witness "*to Christ*." To him alone, not to any other person; to his coming and deeds, to his death and resurrection, not to events that are caused and shaped by human activity. According to W. Estius, the good done by Jesus Christ is the cause of the good works performed by Christians, in his honor.

4. Estius adds another interpretation that dates back to Oecumenius and Theophylact and is later taken up with slight variations by, e.g., JB and NJB: "All

the good" done to a little brother of Christ is actually done *"to Christ"* or *"for Christ"* himself. The parable of the Son of man's surprising judgment over the sheep and the goats (Matt 25:31-46) speaks in favor of this exposition. "In the service, in view, in honor of Christ," or "as to Christ" (the Lord, and not to men; cf. Col 3:23; Eph 6:7), are in this case proper translations of *eis Christon.*

5. J. B. Lightfoot is rather vague when he paraphrases the formula with the words "leading to Christ as the good." E. Lohmeyer proposes a strictly eschatological interpretation, and later commentaries (with the exception of, e.g., J. Ernst and H. Binder) join him: as a part of Pauline thanksgivings, references to Christ's second coming *(parousia)* are made in 1 Cor 1:7; Phil 1:6. If the Lord's return for judgment is in mind, then the crisp words *"toward Christ"* mean in Philem 6 that Christ's future advent looms high and mighty above all the good that was done by Philemon among and for the Colossians, and also above the announced visit of Paul in Philemon's house (v. 22). Then the end of Philem 6 emphasizes that neither Philemon himself, nor Paul, nor a vote taken among the saints in Colossae will on the Lord's Day judge and reward the faith that was confessed and the good that was done. Jesus Christ alone will do this (cf. 2 Cor 5:10; 1 Cor 3:3-5; Rom 2:5-11, 16; Gal 2:2; Phil 2:16).

None among these five interpretations can be declared impossible. The paraphrase "in expectation of Christ" was chosen for our translation because it is, as the last exposition above listed, strictly eschatological. Philemon 6 illustrates and confirms that eschatology and ethics are inseparable and interdependent. (On American soil, esp. A. Wilder, *Eschatology and Ethics* and "Kerygma, Eschatology, and Ethics," has emphasized this connection.)

Hardly convincing are two other proposals: As already mentioned, E. Lohmeyer suggests that Paul intends to exalt deeds done for a higher goal, even for Christ's glory — deeds that excel above "works" performed for the glorious perfection of Israel. And A. Suhl believes that the reference to Christ in Philem 6 is "a cunning stylistic instrument of pressure" on Philemon. Still, although Paul can on occasion utter the threat to come with a stick (1 Cor 4:21), he does not transform Christ into a sledgehammer.

VERSE 7

Through your love, brother, I have received much joy and comfort, for through you the hearts of the saints are given rest.

To proceed from Philem 6 to Philem 7 is like leaving a somber medieval cathedral with its symbols of sincere devotion and its art treasures and stepping into broad daylight. Here is the first glimpse provided by PHM of the deep and warm feelings of the man Paul. Albrecht Dürer painted him as a grim fighter who, armed with a sword, thinks deeper and looks farther than others. For orthodox Protestant theologians, the apostle was the correct teacher of the doctrine of justification. The appreciation of several passages written by Paul has created such great difficulties to numerous Bible readers that some of them are inclined to confess, "I hate that man." Still, if nothing else, at least the form and substance of Philem 7 tell another story and require a different response.

With J. B. Lightfoot, this verse can be considered an integral part of the almost liturgical "thanksgiving" in Philem 4-7. Or, with E. Lohmeyer, it adds a personal corollary to supplement the prayer that ends with verse 6. This rather trivial issue cannot be dissolved by an either-or. It is, however, obvious that when Paul tells of his prayer, he lays his soul bare and lets Philemon and the co-addressees of PHM look into it. Equally in other letters, when the apostle talks and writes with the full authority entrusted to him, he does not hide that he is a human being, full of feelings. So Philem 7 permits readers even at the present time to meet the letter's author personally, not just the office bearer. Here Paul confesses how deeply he is moved and how pleased he is with the effect of Philemon's love. And yet, this summary exposition does not give us the right to gloss over other riches hidden in this verse — and some minor or major problems connected with them.

Through your love I have received much joy. The great majority of the minuscule (small letter) MSS (the numbers 33 and 1937 are among the exceptions) have "much grace" *(charin pollēn)* instead of "much joy" *(charan pollēn).* In the most important majuscule (capital letter) codices one reads, and the Latin and the Syriac versions presuppose, *charan* (joy). Variant readings waver between "grace" and "joy" also in 2 Cor 1:15 and 8:2. The different words that in Greek signify "grace," "thanks(giving)," and "joy" all stem from *char,* and have therefore cognate meanings. The person who dictated, the secretary who wrote a script, or both could easily mistake "grace" for "joy" or vice versa. In Philem 7, the MSS evidence speaks distinctly in favor of "joy," but there is no reason to forget that joy is a divine gift — not only according to Beethoven's Ninth Symphony. In, e.g., Luke 1:28; Acts 11.23 grace and rejoicing are woven together; in 1 Thess 3:9; Col 1:11-12 it is joy and thanksgiving; and in Phil 1:3-4 thanksgiving, intercession, and joy. The noun *charis* itself, which most frequently means "grace" in the NT, occasionally signifies "thanks" — so in the formula "thanks to God" (six times in the letters to the Romans and Corinthians), or in the phrase (lit.) "I have thanks" to God or to Christ (1 Tim 1:12; 2 Tim 1:3).

Excursus: The Joy of an Apostle

Joy and rejoicing play an important role in several Pauline letters. (For a survey of pertinent passages, see H. Conzelmann, *TWB*, 11.369.) The noun and the verb always have a good and positive character — except when the apostle speaks of the (malicious) joy that is based on injustice and grief suffered by a neighbor (1 Cor 13:6; 2 Cor 7:9), or when he urges those rejoicing in the goods of the present short time to live as though they were not rejoicing (1 Cor 7:30). Especially 2 Cor 1–2 and 7, and each chapter of Philippians, unfold the great function of joy in the life of every Christian.

The opposite of joy is tribulation, grief, suffering, and the temptation provoked by them. The joy given by God confronts all saints and protects them from despair. Although the God-given joy does not ignore or simply wipe out the reality of the opposites, it makes bearable what looks too heavy and cumbersome. The imprisoned Paul, not a man moving around freely, speaks in Philem 7 of his joy in Philemon's love. In 2 Cor 7:9-10; 13:9; Col 1:24, Paul mentions a grief that leads to repentance and to joy in one's own weakness and in sufferings endured (cf. 1 Pet 1:6, 8; 4:13; James 1:2).

How and on what grounds can such seemingly paradoxical statements ever be made? Explicitly in Phil 3:1; 4:4, 10 and implicitly in other letters, Paul speaks of joy "in the Lord." The substance of this joy is constituted by the person, the way, and the work of Jesus Christ. It comes from a personal source outside one's dear or deep self, not from a blocked wellspring of the human soul. "Rejoicing in the Lord" means, in view of the temporal succession of Christ's suffering, death, resurrection, and parousia, to accept and to go the way through much pain to radiant glory (cf. Luke 24:26; 1 Pet 4:13-14; etc.). According to John's Gospel (15:11; 17:13; cf. Heb 11:15; 12:2), this connection between suffering and glory is the reason for Jesus Christ's own joy. From it sprouts the "fulfilled" joy of the disciples.

When joy is founded in Christology, then it also has eschatological character. As in every one of Israel's festivals, so in the NT joy looks beyond the "remembered" past and the often dismal present. It is an anticipation of the future, even of the full revelation of God's glory. Paul looks forward to Christ's parousia with full confidence and therefore with joy. In, e.g., 1 Thess 2:19 "hope" and "joy" and a "crown of boasting" form a triad that cannot be split up.

Still the orientation to the future by no means prevents joy to accept and to celebrate present events and experiences. Repeatedly (in 1 Cor 16:17; 2 Cor 2:3; 7:6-7; Phil 2:28-29; 2 Tim 1:3-4) joy is evoked by the recent or instantly expected arrival of a gospel messenger or a church delegate — be it Paul, Titus, or Epaphroditus. If only the good news of Christ is preached, Paul "rejoices and will rejoice" (Phil 1:18). So also by his amply demonstrated love, Philemon is a cause of the apostle's joy. Indeed, for being filled with joy, Paul depends on fellow workers and on cooperative congregations. Without them no joy in the Lord! "You are my joy and my crown," "You are our glory and joy." Paul cannot thank God enough for the joy created in him by fellow Christians. He calls himself and his aides "fellow workers of your joy" (Phil 4:1; 1 Thess 2:19-20; 3:9; 2 Cor 1:24).

By writing "I have received much joy," Paul reveals that he does not consider his joy a natural or skillfully acquired psychic disposition, or a self-fabricated power of positive thinking, not to speak of a fluctuating and transitory sentiment. Joy is a gift of God, even of the Spirit (1 Thess 1:6; Gal 5:22; Rom 14:17). Just as in the case of love and faithfulness (Philem 5), it can be "had" solely when it is given. In Philem 7 Paul uses the aorist of "having" *(eschon)*, as if to refer to a specific, perhaps even a surprising event. Some important Greek MSS replace (lit.) "I had" by the majestic plural "we shall have" *(hexomen)* or by the subjunctive "let's have" *(echōmen)*. They underline that Paul's joy is not a deep-frozen state of mind or emotional disposition, beyond the danger of disturbances or loss. For the apostle, there is no doubt that a person must be continuously "filled with joy" by God or by fellow Christians (Rom 15:13; Phil 2:2; 2 Tim 1:4; compare the Fourth Gospel passim). Once, in Phil 1:25, the apostle talks of "progress and joy in faith" in the same breath. Obviously he knows that joy needs replenishment and increase. It can be augmented to such a level that not only Paul but also a whole congregation is "overflowing" with it (2 Cor 7:4; 8:2).

In that case, joy is what Luke calls "great joy" (Luke 2:10; 24:52; Acts 15:3; cf. 8:8; etc.). In Philem 7 Paul talks of "much joy," elsewhere (in 1 Thess 3:9; Rom 15:13; Phil 2:29) of "all joy." This formula might as well be translated "only joy, sheer joy" or "every kind of joy."

While in 1 Thess 3:9 the apostle, just as John the Baptist according to John 3:29, uses the phrase "rejoicing with joy," and while he occasionally employs *euphrainomai* (to be gladdened, to be cheered up), he does not have in his written vocabulary the words *agalliasis* and *agalliaomai*. This noun and this verb occur in the Psalms of the LXX and denote exuberant rejoicing, a climax of expressed joy, not only by the mien but also by sounds and body movements. The Gospels of Matthew, Luke, and John, also Acts, First Peter, and Revelation, mention this manifestation of joy without attempts at spiritualization. Still it is difficult to imagine Paul dancing, jumping high, and perhaps playing a cymbal as King David did when he brought the ark of the covenant to Jerusalem. Neither can he be easily fancied in more moderate movements as happily performed by rabbis with the Thora scrolls in their arms, at the day of *Simha Thora* (Joy of the Law). The apostle never encourages others to make a show of their enthusiasm. The sobriety and temperance recommended in the Pastoral Epistles when they use the words *nēphalios* and *nēphō* correspond to Paul's own lifestyle.

The moderation *(symmetria)* promoted by Greek philosophers and educators may have contributed to the Pauline reticence. Plato had written a special tract *(Philebus)* against those for whom joy depended on the consumption of food or drink or on activities devoted to Aphrodite. This kind of joy he called *hēdonē* and *terpsis* (bodily pleasure, base delight), and he emphasized that it is shared by animals who satisfy their lusts *(Phlb.* 11A; 67B). Still, Plato acknowledges that there are some pleasures to enjoy that "appertain specifically to the soul" and are "painless . . . pure pleasures of the soul herself," produced by some of the "sciences and arts and true opinions" (66C). According to this philosopher, reason and wisdom are instruments to perceive and judge what is good.

Aristotle *(NE* 2.5.1105B) counted joy, together with appetite, anger, fear, hate, pity, and other feelings that are accompanied by pleasure and pain, among the passions that are strictly opposite to the virtues. Some Stoics admitted that joy might be a "noble passion" *(eupatheia),* but only the wise could afford this feeling. When W. Estius emphasized that in Philem 7 Paul speaks of "grace not of pleasure" (of *gratia* rather than *gaudium*), he not only deviated from the Vg., which had *gaudium* as the translation of *chara,* but also endorsed the repudiation of the slightest trace of Epicurean hedonism that is characteristic of philosophical and theological moralists.

A social dimension is inseparable from the christological and eschatological, sober and personal traits that are essential of Paul's utterances on joy. In the teaching of Greek ethicists, the decision whether joy and pleasure of one or another kind ought to be sought was the individual's responsibility and privilege. At best, other reasonable and wise persons were accepted as teachers and/or companions of the right choice. However, at the basis and essence of Paul's display of joy lies not only the mutual sharing of joy created by the same cause, but also the joy different Christians find and have in one another. Paul, his coworkers, and all members of the congregation rejoice together, as members of one body. They participate in the tears, and so also in the joy, of each Christian (2 Cor 1:24; 1 Cor 12:26; Rom 12:15; Phil 2:17-18). Unless the congregation heeds Paul's call to "rejoice always" (Phil 4:4), the apostle himself cannot find or have joy. Yet not even the joy of others and in others created by the gospel and the Spirit prevents Paul from describing his joy in a way that reveals how much he gains by it for himself.

And comfort (kai paraklēsin). In verses 8-22 Paul will approach Philemon with exhortations and requests introduced by the verb *parakalō* (I exhort, entreat, or comfort, vv. 9-10). But first, in verse 7, Paul mentions "comfort" as a companion or as the primary explication of joy. Before he gives *paraklēsis* to another person, he describes himself as a recipient of it. In 2 Cor 7:4-9, 13-16, regarding Titus's activity and success, reception and passing on of *paraklēsis* are closely connected. In 2 Cor 7, joy, comfort, boldness, boasting, encouragement are mentioned side by side and interpret one another. So also in Philem 7 the joy received edifies and strengthens the apostle, to his own advantage. Later, in verse 20, he makes bold to express his confidence that from Philemon he will receive further personal profit, gaining rest for his own heart. Paul is not ashamed of mentioning his personal interest.

But in the second half of Philem 7, the apostle will prove to be altruistic. There he will affirm that solely the rest given to the heart of the Colossians is the cause of his joy and comfort. Still, the minute trace of personal pleasure, enjoyment, and gain that can be found in verse 7a and might malevolently be called self-centered or egotistic, reveals that even in his overwhelming altruism the apostle is a human being, not an angel. Yet Paul should not be suspected of hunting primarily for the peace of his own soul. When in, e.g., Gal 5:22 and Rom 15:13 joy is closely connected with peace, peace is, just as in the initial benediction (Philem 3, etc.), the dominion and victory of social wholeness, health, and well-being. This peace does not exclude but by far exceeds the personal feelings.

Three conclusions can be drawn. (1) The apostle is one of the fortunate persons for whom professional work and personal pleasure fully coincide. His occupation is his hobby and vice versa. (2) Paul wants urgently to effect a social change: the relationship between master Philemon and slave Onesimus shall never again be as it was before their separation. The request for a new common life is not founded on a just and bitter complaint about existing injustice, on a skillful investigation of the total social and economic situation, or on a programmatic sketch of a perfect, new world order. Rather Paul builds the petitions formulated in verses 8-22 on gifts of God that have been proven so strong and real that through Philemon both the apostle and the church have received much joy, comfort — and rest. The effect and evidence of God's blessing in history upon really existing persons make Paul uniquely confident and bold. On them he builds his case, rather than on the heat of burning personal compassion or furious anger, on a penetrating analysis of prevailing unjust conditions, on a well-made synthesis of its results, or on a new social theory. (3) The combined references to joy, comfort, and rest appeal to experiences of people assembled for a festival. In verse 7 Paul evokes the atmosphere of celebration. This way he sets the tone for speaking of the changes that will affect the whole life of a slave, an apostle, a community, and that might become a beacon in the prevailing darkness of the environment (cf. Phil 2:15; Matt 5:14-16).

For through you the hearts of the saints are given rest. While Paul's joy and comfort are personal, they are grounded in the well-being of other persons: through Philemon rest is given to the saints. In verse 20 the apostle will remind Philemon in imperative form of the slave owner's indebtedness: he owes rest to Paul's own heart, too. Even there the apostle may well think primarily of rest to be given to Onesimus: in verse 12 he declares that his own heart is Onesimus, and in verses 16, 17, and 22 he makes unmistakably clear that he expects a reception of the returning slave by "brother" Philemon that is as cordial and joyful as the welcome due or offered to Paul would and will be. A causal connection between rest given and joy erupting is repeatedly established in and outside of the Bible (see, e.g., Deut 12:9-12; Sir 6:28; *Barn.* 10.11). In 1 Cor 16:17 Paul speaks of his joy at the arrival of three Corinthian delegates who procured rest "to my spirit and to yours." Following 2 Cor 7:13, the apostle rejoices in the joy of Titus because his spirit is "given rest" by all Corinthians.

Paul employs the key word and treats the theme "rest" solely in the Corinthian letters and in PHM. In other parts of the NT, just as in the OT and in apocryphal books (in 1 Macc 9:57, etc.), "peace" often serves as a synonym and is unfolded in many dimensions. In the short benediction, peace forms a couple with grace. Elsewhere Paul uses a large number of additional nouns to describe the effect of Christ's work and of the proclamation of the gospel. Barnabas (10.11) maintains that God is the source of joy and rest. However, in the same passage Barnabas moves in the direction of individualization and internalization. In a daring interpretation of an OT dietary law, he affirms that to know the one who feeds you means to rest in him and to rejoice, and that to obey God's commandment is to find the pleasure of rest. A horrifying description of the opposite to finding peace and rest is offered in, e.g., Deut 28:65-68: a trembling heart, failing eyes, a languishing soul, fear for one's survival by day and by night, return to Egypt, and the frustrated attempt to sell oneself into slavery. Lamentations 5:5-18 mentions a yoke on one's neck, being hard-driven and weary, bearing the sins of the fathers, being forced into the role of slaves without delivery in sight, etc. It is noteworthy that in such utterances enslavement ranks high among the consequences of rest withheld and missing.

The question must be asked why only in PHM Paul speaks (twice — in vv. 7 and 20) of "giving rest to the heart(s)." Is he really thinking of no more than a refreshment of the Colossians' and his own innermost feelings (so, e.g., E. Lohse)? A look at the wider biblical context may reveal that the theme "rest" and the main topic of PHM — the brotherly reception and treatment of a slave — are in substance co-inherent.

Excursus: Rest

The OT and later Jewish background of Paul's use of the verb "giving rest" *(anapauō)* is discussed in the pertinent articles of biblical wordbooks and the literature there mentioned. Most important is O. Hofius, *Katapausis,* pp. 22-58. In the Hebrew Bible the nouns *enuḥa, manoah, sabbat,* in the LXX *anapausis* or *katapausis,* are used with preference for denoting "rest." Paul uses exclusively the word *anapauō,* which in the LXX renders the Hebrew *nuaḥ* and signifies "to cause to settle down, to give rest, to satisfy." Elsewhere in early Christian literature the Hebrew background is reflected in the composite verb *epanapauomai* ("to take, to find rest"; so in, e.g., Num 11:25-26; Luke 10:6; *Barn.* 4.13).

According to the OT, God's own rest on the day of creation (Gen 2:2) is the ground of all commandments, promises, and (provisionary) attainments of rest. God, whose throne is in heaven, will also dwell on earth: Canaan, Zion, the temple are the resting places he has chosen for himself (Deut 12:9, 11; Pss 11:4; 95:11; 132:7-8, 14; 1 Kings 8:16, 29-30; 1 Chron 22:18; etc.). However, in Isa 66:1 the confidence is being shaken that after the exile the rebuilding of Jerusalem's sanctuary by human hands will secure God's presence and rest at the temple site.

Deuteronomy and Chronicles emphasize specifically God's gracious will to let Israel participate in his own rest, that is, to find rest in his resting place. To dwell in God's house means to feel at home and to sing God's praise just as the swallow does (Ps 84:3-4). Indispensable helpers to finding rest in the Promised Land, on the chosen mountain, and/or in the central sanctuary are the elected servants of God, among them Moses, Joshua, David, Solomon (1 Chron 22:9 mentions Solomon only in contrast to the warrior David), and those called "wise." Many Prophets and especially the book of Deuteronomy insist that without obedience to God's covenant and commandments, there is no rest for Israel. Instead, there will be misery within the land and/or expulsion from it. According to Wisdom Literature, especially Jesus Sirach (6:28 and context), solely Wisdom brings rest and joy. The wisdom from the mouth of the Most High has searched for a resting place all over heaven, the abyss, the sea, and the whole earth; and to this wisdom finally Israel, the tabernacle, Zion, and the beloved city (Jerusalem) have been assigned as a dwelling place (Sir 24:3-12). E.g., Deut 4:6 and Sir 24:23 affirm that the Wisdom is the Law given through Moses. The rest given to those faithful in Israel presupposes that the call of Wisdom is heard and the Law obeyed. The rest affects and secures the place where one lives, the material things necessary for life, the relation to the neighbors, the health of the body, and the emotions of the soul. Just as peace, it embraces and aims at the wholeness of human existence, that is, dwelling in the land, enjoying its fruit, peaceful relations to neighbors and nations, and also a tranquil state of mind and soul. For a poor girl and widow such as the Moabite Ruth, it means to have the protection of a home and a husband (Ruth 3:1); for Israel, it is the result of the Good Shepherd's perfect care (Ps 23:2-3). Rest is the security, pleasure, and joy given by God to those chosen by him even while they live on earth. Once in the Dead Sea Scrolls (1QpHab 11.6-8), the Day of Atonement is called the day of rest: physical fasting is linked to spiritual renewal. In turn, phenomena of the lack of psychic rest are described in 1QH 7.29-31 and 9.4-6.

OT historiography, prophecy, and prayers reveal that rest and peace were but seldom enjoyed in Israel (see, e.g., Josh 11:19; 2 Sam 7:1; 1 Kings 8:56; Ps 55:9). As-yet-undefeated external enemies and neglect and/or oppression of justice and righteousness by kings and other ruling powers in the land stand in the way. But prophetic voices announce rest, and pious people hope for it — repeatedly in connection with the expectation of the promised messianic king. Always, except in late books, rest and peace are predicted and promised for the temporal historic future rather than for a coming eternal aeon. To repeat: they concern the whole life of the community rather than the psychic refreshment and good feelings of some individuals only (see, e.g., Isa 14:3; 32:18). However, in Job 3:13 and Sir 30:17, hardly also in Dan 12:13, the tomb is denoted as a place of rest, and no earlier than in some books of intertestamental and later Jewish literature does the soul find rest after death only. Some rabbis taught in their exposition of Ps 95:11 that the rest as yet withheld from God's people because of their rebellion, will be the privilege of those found worthy to have a share in the coming aeon, even in the new creation of heaven and earth and in the new Jerusalem. (For references see Hofius, *Katapausis,* pp. 44-47.) The pseudepigraphon *Joseph and Asenath* (7:9; 15:7; 22:13) speaks of God's own place of rest in the beyond, to which the elect will be admitted after death in order to receive eternal life. Other apocrypha, also Ps.-Philo (*Lib. ant. Bibl.* 28.6-10; 23.4), mention either an eternal abode prepared for those blessed, or a place for their souls only, or a temporary waiting room or treasury for the souls of those expecting to be rejoined by their bodies on the day of resurrection. (For a collection and discussion of pertinent other texts, see again Hofius, pp. 59-74.) While OT passages such as Isa 26:19; Job 19:25-27; Dan 12:2 affirm a bodily resurrection, they do not use "rest" for describing eternal life.

What does the NT contribute? At one single place, in Matt 11:28-29, the giving and finding of rest is by Jesus himself described in terms resembling statements made about Wisdom in Sir 24:19; cf. 6:28; 51:23-24: "rest" is the purpose and effect of his whole ministry. This rest is neither only local and material, nor solely psychic and spiritual, nor exclusively futurist and eschatological. The miracle stories, the proclamation of forgiveness, and the words about the coming kingdom and eternal life show this clearly. Though Paul calls Jesus Christ the Wisdom of God in 1 Cor 1:29, 30; cf. Col 2:3, he may not have known the exact wording of Matt 11:28-29. Still, when he expects that by Philemon his "heart [will] be given rest *in Christ*" (Philem 20), he reveals that for him, too, no one else than Christ is the herald and the place, the guarantor and giver, of rest.

"Rest" is most extensively discussed in Heb 3:7–4:11, in a midrash on the OT promise, the factual forfeiture, and the renewed promise of rest for God's people. In elaborating mainly on Ps 95:9-11, the author of Hebrews argues that because of Israel's hardness of heart, disobedience, unbelief, and sin, neither during the wilderness period nor under Joshua, nor ever since, could Israel find the rest that was kept by God himself and was foreseen for the people. Rather "today," only after and by the coming of Jesus, that Word of God is proclaimed, which calls for faith and affirms that "there still remains a sabbath rest for the people of God." Those admitted to it "enter God's rest and rest from their labors as God did from his" (Heb 4:9-10). In Hebrews the eschatological and temporal senses of rest are merged into one: the congregation lives now "in the last days" (Heb 1:2). This does not contradict the Christians' moving forward like pilgrims. They are waiting for the day when after "yet a little while" the redeemer will come and let them join the heavenly festival assembly of the angels (cf. Heb 10:37; chap. 11, passim; 12:22-23).

Post–OT Jewish traditions are taken up in the book of Revelation. In Rev 6:9-11 the souls of the martyrs are told to rest under God's altar "still for a short time" clothed in a white garment, before "after three and a half days" the martyrs are bodily raised and ascend into heaven. This will occur to the consternation of the enemies, as 11:11-13 emphasizes. According to 14:13; cf. 7:17; 21:4, rest begins after death only: "Blessed are the dead who die in the Lord henceforth. . . . they will rest from their labor." To the strictly futuristic eschatological hope for rest correspond the tradition of inscribing on tombstones "RIP" (*requiescat in pace*: rest in peace) and the concluding petition made in the *Requiem*: that God "grant eternal peace."

Among the apostolic fathers, Ignatius has written more than others about rest. According to Ignatius, rest is given by delegates and by whole congregations when they provide temporal relief to himself or to other communities. In his letters (*Eph.* 2.1; *Trall.* 12.2; *Smyrn.* 9.2; 10.1; 12.1), *anapsychō* ("to refresh," lit: "to revive the soul") is sometimes used as a synonym of *anapauō* ("to give rest"; cf. 2 Tim 1:16). Once in the NT, in Acts 3:20, the formula "the times of refreshment" *(kairoi anapsyxeōs)* has distinctly eschatological significance. But when the Antiochian bishop speaks of rest, he does not think of rest in the tomb or of eternal rest. Even when (in *Eph.* 2.1; *Smyrn.* 9.2; and *Trall.* 10.2) he mentions that to himself and others rest is given in every way *(kata panta)*, and when in *Trall.* 12.1 he replaces this formula by "in the flesh and in the spirit," his notion of rest is this-worldly.

Absent is an eschatological dimension also in the references to "rest" and "giving rest" of the Shepherd of Hermas (*Sim.* 6.2.7; 9.1.9; 5.4, 12). But what is lacking in Ignatius's letters and Hermas's books is fully present in *Barn.* 5.7; *2 Clem.* 5.5; 6.7; *Mart. Pol.* 1.1. Just as in Heb 4:4-10, so also in *1 Clem.* 59.3 and *Barn.* 15.2, 5, 7, God's own rest and resting place provide certainty to the promise of rest that is given to God's people.

An alternative to explaining NT and early postapostolic references to rest has been proposed ever since the history-of-religion school began to flourish. Instead of OT and later Jewish traditions, Gnosticism, especially Gnostic ideas of rest, supposedly mediated through Hellenistic Judaism in the form of Wisdom speculation, was now used as key to explaining several difficult NT texts. Among the pioneers of this experiment are E. Norden, *Agnostos Theos* (Stuttgart: Teubner, 1913, 1956), pp. 277-308, and T. Arvedson, *Das Mysterium Christi* (Uppsala and Leipzig: Wretmann, 1937), in their interpretations of Matt 11:25-29, and E. Käsemann in his commentary on Hebrews (*Das wandernde Gottesvolk,* esp. on pp. 40-45, where "The Gnostic Katapausis-Speculation" is discussed). Much more detailed than the books just mentioned is the survey on the manifold roles of rest in Gnostic writings that is offered in Hofius's *Katapausis,* pp. 75-90.

Main elements, although not common denominators, can be discerned. In Gnosticism "rest" is ultimately an attribute of the All-Father deity and is the essence of the primordial world of Light and Silence. Out of this world have flown the souls of persons now held captive and restive in the created universe and in their physical bodies. Through a Light-Messenger — in Christian Gnosticism: through Christ — the imprisoned souls are given knowledge of their divine nature and are led to the restoration of their true self by reunion with their origin. Already while living on earth, the Gnostic is in possession of the saving knowledge, anticipates freedom from the fetters of matter and death, and demonstrates his superiority above all worldly affairs. In summary, Gnostic teachings on rest amount to individual salvation of the soul through escape from the world.

Over the past decades, the gnosticizing interpretation of the Jesus-Logia found in Matt 11:25-29 has been seriously questioned and corrected. Finally Hofius (pp. 91-101) has collected convincing arguments to refute the notion that in Heb 3–4 Gnostic conceptions of rest are fundamental. Obviously, a reference to Gnosticism could also adumbrate rather than illuminate the meaning of "rest" in Philem 7 and 20. This letter's main concern is with the present world and the social relations, opportunities, and responsibilities from which a Christian cannot escape. On the other hand, the question remains on the table whether Paul does not internalize or psychologize or spiritualize the nature and effect of rest, perhaps with some support from biblical precedents. For instance, Ps 116:7; Jer 6:16; Matt 11:29 explicitly speak of rest for "the soul." In Philem 7 and 20 the heart that is put to rest is mentioned, and PHM ends with a prayer that the grace of Christ abide with "the spirit" of those assembled in the house of Philemon.

The hearts. (For the following see esp. the articles *raḥamim* and *splagchna* by H. J. Stoebe and by H. Koester in *THAT,* 2.762-768, and *TWB,* 6.549-559.) E. Lohmeyer suggests that the three references to the heart(s) in Philem 7, 12, and 20 mark the end of a stanza of four verses, with two lines per verse (vv. 4-8, 9-12, and 17-20). Against the reconstruction of such a poetic scheme speaks the absence of "the heart" from the end of the supposed third stanza, verses 13-16.

Just as much as Hebrew *raḥamim,* so also Greek *splagchna* originally has a physiological sense. These words denote the soft parts of the body, e.g., the heart, lungs, kidneys, liver, bowels of the sacrificial animals and/or of persons, also a mother's womb. In Acts 1:18 *splagchna* signifies distinctly human bowels. Most likely due to the physiological effect of a strong psychic emotion are the metaphorical meaning of this noun and the formulation of corresponding verbs. Frequently they denote the activation of human feelings and affections in general, or more specifically the origin and outbreak of strong emotions such as anxiety, anger, and wrath on one side, and of passionate love, pity, and mercy on the other. While the mercilessness of human enemies is often deplored, God's compassion and steadfast love are frequently invoked and praised in OT prayers (compare, e.g., Isa 47:6 with Isa 63:7, 15).

Although the Vg. version of Philem 7, 12, 20 translates *splagchna* "*viscera,*" in today's Western languages "bowels" would be absurd. Solely the adjective "visceral" still signifies a deeply affected emotional state. As Martin Luther states in his 1527 lecture on PHM, and as countless other Bible versions show, "heart" expresses what is meant by Paul.

In Hebrew and other Semitic languages, "heart" *(leb)* is as well the power source of physical life as the organ of human knowledge and intelligence, will and planning. It is also the seat of the feelings of pain, fear, despair, joy, courage, and sexual desire. The body, the soul, and the spirit of every human being depend on it (cf. F. Stolz in *THAT,* 1.862). In 2 Cor 6:11-12 Paul uses *splagchna* and *kardia* (heart) as synonyms; in 2 Cor 2:13 he speaks of relief for his spirit; and in 2 Cor 7:13, 15 *splagchna* and *pneuma* (spirit) are used as mutually exchangeable terms. Elsewhere Paul employs *nous* (mind) or *psychē* (soul) in the same sense. Sometimes in contrast to Greek anthropology, but in harmony with OT Hebrew and LXX (also with later Jewish usage inasmuch as it has withstood dualistic influences), each of these words signifies more than just a part of a person. They denote "the whole" of a person "in respect of the depth and form of feelings . . . the total personality at the deepest level" (H. Koester, *TWB,* 7.549, 555).

In Ps 16:9 and 1 Thess 5:23, the heart, soul, and body, or the spirit, soul, and body, are mentioned separately, without implying that three separable parts constitute the whole person. Each of these anthropological terms describes the whole of a man, a woman, or a child, although they refer to various vital aspects, forces, and functions of the human being. Jesus' logion about the relation between the eye, the hand, and the whole body expresses this drastically: if but one member is crooked, all members are affected (Matt 5:29-30; 6:22-23). In 1 Cor 12:14-21 and 29 and Rom 12:5, Paul writes of the analogous interdependence of the church members among one another. In consequence, when the apostle sends his own heart — the slave Onesimus — to Philemon (Philem 12), he transfers neither "a part" of himself (as NEB translates) nor his better ego (his soul in distinction from his body), but his total self. "Welcome him as (you will or would welcome) me" (Philem 17, 20, 22). In analogy, the *splagchna* of the Messiah Jesus that are the ground of Paul's yearning for the Philippians (Phil 1:8), are not just a part of the Lord, but his whole person with special emphasis on his affection, compassion, and love (cf. Gal 2:20; 2 Cor 5:14; Eph 5:2, 25).

The "rest given to the heart(s)" of which Paul writes in Philem 7 and 20 has to be distinguished from many sorts of rest mentioned in and outside of the Bible. It does not include the final termination of all labor, suffering, mourning, aching, not to speak of the abolishment of death, that is promised in, e.g., Rev. 14:13 and 21:4. Neither does it mean the finding of an intermediate resting place for the souls of those who are waiting for reunion with their not-yet-resurrected bodies. Not even victorious and/or righteous human kings such as David and Solomon, neither (after the coming of the Messiah Jesus) another praiseworthy "fellow worker of God" (cf. 1 Cor 3:9), can mediate according to Paul that kind of rest that God alone can and will give. The "rest" mentioned in Philem 7 and 20 is temporal; it is palpable when created by material gifts and yet also spiritual and soul warming because no person lives by bread alone. On the gift and experience of such rest, every strong and every weak, each hard-working and each much-suffering, human being depends for surviving on earth.

Through you. The rest given by Philemon is the fruit of love, faithfulness, goodness, and liberal sharing of earthly goods. What this host and benefactor contributes to the church has three special traits that do not exclude certain limitations. The rest bears the marks of the donor's character and capability, it is limited by space and time, and it is extended to only a restricted number of persons. The last-mentioned limitation has not yet been discussed:

The saints. Cf. verse 5: "all the saints." While Christians are taught in Gal 6:9-10 to "do good to all persons" as opportunity arises, the "members of the household of faith" have the first claim and give the first occasion to experience the fruit of untiring well-doing. When Onesimus reenters the house of his earthly master, Philemon's love of "*all* the saints" will be subjected to a test: the slave is now one of them.

While E. Lohmeyer denies that "specific acts of charity" from Philemon's side are meant, F. F. Bruce (p. 210) proposes that a special reason for the praise of Philemon is verse 7b: this well-to-do man had a way of doing good and sharing that did not embarrass the feelings of the recipients. At any rate, as soon as the OT Sabbath commandment and the importance of its observation in Jewish homes are remembered, it becomes obvious that Philemon had fulfilled, and is expected to continue fulfilling, the responsibilities of the *paterfamilias.* In the Deuteronomic version of the Sabbath commandment (Deut 6:12-15), the head of the household is obliged not only to keep rest for himself, but to give freedom from any work also to his children, his male and female slaves, his cattle and the sojourners. Unlike Exod 20:11, where the reason given is God's own rest after the completion of creation, in Deut 5:15 "remembering" (that is, celebrating; see the Note on v. 4, p. 270) the slavery endured by Israel in Egypt and the people's glorious liberation from it is the ground of the Sabbath rest. The preamble to the Ten Commandments, by which God declares himself the liberator of Israel (Exod 20:2; Deut 5:6), is in Deut 5:14-15 shown to be relevant also for all (Hebrew and foreign) slaves of both sexes. They are to be given on each Sabbath day a spiritual and physical share in Israel's redemption. Most likely because of the Sabbath commandment Paul combined in PHM the mention of the "rest" given or to be given with the request for special reception and treatment of a slave.

In Annotation 14 to the "Social Background," p. 100, a keen interpretation of the Sabbath law was cited. Philo of Alexandria (*Spec. leg.* 2.66-69) taught that the temporal rest that was to be granted to slaves on the Sabbath gave the slaves an occasion to entertain "still higher hopes," "to enjoy an ember or spark of freedom," and "to look forward to their complete liberation." Paul does not explicitly mention either the rest from slave work or the eventual manumission of Onesimus. Yet he formulates his praise of Philemon in a way running parallel to Philo's understanding of the Sabbath. The earlier-mentioned liturgical, joyous, and festival tone of the blessing in Philem 3 and the thanksgiving in verses 4-6 is continued *fortissimo* in 7 and the rest of the epistle, especially in 20. Specifically the slave Onesimus is to be granted joyful rest. The above-mentioned theological wordbooks confirm *unisono* the mutual affinity of joy, rest, peace, and freedom.

Brother. In the Greek original, unlike our version of the whole sentence, the warm personal address "brother" stands at the end of verse 7. In substance it corresponds to the adjective "dear" in verse 1 and reveals once again the intimate personal bond that unites Paul and Philemon and has also been expressed by the title "fellow worker." "Brother" and "sister" have an established place in letter openings. The plural "brothers" was a proper way of addressing a solemn Jewish or Christian assembly (Acts 13:15, 26; 15:7, 13; etc.). More than forty times in his letters Paul inserts the vocative "brothers" into the beginning of a sentence in order to give special emphasis to an appeal. Always he reminds of a knowledge possessed or refreshes the memory of those addressed, and/or calls for ethical conduct (1 Thess 2:1, 9; Rom 1:13; 12:1; etc.). While in Galatians, in proportion to the total vocabulary of the epistle, this appeal is made much more frequently than in other epistles, its absence from Colossians, Ephesians, and the Pastoral Epistles has been considered evidence of the spuriousness of these letters. (E. Schweizer, *Neotestamentica*, p. 429, uses this argument, unaware of the fact that it would call into doubt also the authenticity of 2 Cor 2–7 and Rom 2–6. In these chapters, the allocution "brothers" never occurs.)

The placement of the moving appeal "brother" at the conclusion of verse 7 deviates from normal Greek syntax (BDF, 474, 6; cf. 146-147). In verse 20 Paul will return to the usual order, which also is followed by writers and orators of his environment. The "emphatic opposition" (J. B. Lightfoot) of the vocative in verse 7 has but one analogy in Paul's letters: in Phil 4:1 "loved ones" *(agapētoi)* concludes a sentence.

When Philem 7 is read aloud, the tone of either an exclamation mark or a question mark after "brother" can be proper to Paul's intention — without detracting from the special closeness and warmth between the apostle and Philemon. "Brother!" — indeed, by God's and Christ's grace you have proven to be a good church member and personal cooperator. "Brother?" — please be consistent and live up to your gifts, your capability, and your good name when they are to stand the test of Onesimus's return. If nothing had been given to Philemon, or if nothing had ever been given away by him, nothing might be expected of him. H. Binder comments that the example given by Philemon is binding first of all for Philemon himself. In other words: noblesse oblige.

Paul's rhetorical and logical procedure in PHM becomes clear when the letters of Pliny the Younger are used for comparison; they, too, express concern for the return and reception of a runaway. The foundation laid by Paul in verses 4-7 for his request is unlike the arguments Pliny uses in his letters to Sabinianus (21 and 24; see Annotation 4 to "Social Background," p. 86). Pliny appeals to the patron's previous love and urges him to find his way back to that love: "You love the man and I hope you will love him again. . . . once he was dear to you." The writer admits that Sabinianus had been given just cause for anger, and that the servant eventually may give occasion for well-deserved new anger. But for the time being, the servant returning with intercessory letter 21 in hand should, in view of his sincere penitence and of his youth, be granted mercy and forgiveness. This all the more because the patron would torment his own gentle self by refusing to give pardon. By this mode of arguing Pliny gives to psychic potential and drama the same basic place and function that in PHM are attributed to the equipment of Philemon by God to follow a distinct way of life and conduct.

With some summary remarks the commentary of verses 4-7 can now be concluded.

For the apostle Paul, grace, prayer, love, faithfulness, and the attitude, performance, and effect of Christians such as Philemon are just as real and as much physically and spiritually experienced as are other realities that can be perceived and are accepted as unquestionable in the present world. Indisputable earthly phenomena are, for instance, Paul's imprisonment in Rome, Philemon's hospitable house in a small town of Asia Minor, the flight of a slave and his meeting with Paul, and the fact that the apostle now writes a letter of intercession. Paul is far from dreaming up a heavenly reality that might negate or exclude earthly conditions and events. Rather he reminds the readers of PHM that God has made himself felt here and now, and that there are good reasons to accept gratefully the consequences of the divine interference. As earlier stated, Paul proves to be a sober realist rather than a daydreaming utopist or a symbolist rich in fanciful imaginations. He presupposes that ever since the message of Christ has been preached and received in faith, there exists on earth a new society — however small or weak it be: Christians do form a structured community whose members are brothers and sisters because God is their Father. They are all fellow servants because Jesus Christ is their Lord.

This society is present and alive in the midst of the old aeon and its seemingly unshakeable and unchangeable structures. There are conflicts within the old order: Onesimus has run away from his master and might have to bear painful consequences. There are also attacks made by some Diaspora Jews and by Roman state officers on Christian missionaries and groups. Because Jesus Christ himself was executed by the Romans, in several parts of the NT Christians are encouraged not to take conflicts and persecutions for Christ's sake too badly, as if they were strange occurrences. Paul bears his imprisonment boldly. The worst dangers on the church's pilgrimage are the deviations from Christ's way. They are found inside the congregations and within each Christian. In Colossians and Ephesians every church member is admonished to resist and abandon the attitudes of "the old man" and to don "the new man" as he is created by God through Christ (Col 3:5-11; Eph 4:22-24). In analogy, in Philem 8-14 Philemon will be encouraged to live up to the mutual love of brothers and sisters of Christ. The slave owner is a captive of both God's and his own goodness, not a helpless agent of the contemporary slave system. For this reason (as of yore Theodore of Mopsuestia [2.275] and in more recent literature especially P. Schubert, *Form and Function*, p. 77, etc., have emphasized), key concepts appearing in Philem 4-7 such as prayer, love, community, brother, goodness, the heart, and rest return in verses 8-22.

Behind, under, and above all statements made in verses 4-7 about past experiences and works of Christians stands a great confidence: God and Christ themselves will continue and crown the work commenced in the congregation (cf. Phil 1:6). By his thanksgiving, Paul not only engages but almost obliges the Lord to carry out his work. In the case of Philemon and Onesimus: to care and to look for the fulfillment of Paul's urgent suggestions. Gratitude and trust are the basis of Paul's ethics and of his ethical counseling.

III. INTERVENTION FOR A SLAVE (VV. 8-14)

In the Greek text, Philem 8-14 constitutes one long sentence. Just as other extremely long literary structures, this sentence requires dissolution into several clauses if ever an English version shall be comprehensible. As a ring composition, the introduction (vv. 8-9) corresponds in substance to the conclusion (v. 14): the *character* of the plea made for Onesimus is described. The substance of the request is contained in the central verses 10-13. In turn, these four verses prepare the way for a more distinct expression of Paul's hope in verses 16-17.

Neither in verses 9-14 nor in the next subdivision of PHM, 15-20, does the apostle plead, as it were, from a safe distance. He does not pretend to be in the position of an objective judge over Philemon and Onesimus. In every verse (except 15 and perhaps 20) he speaks pointedly of himself, out of a total involvement with the person and the history of the master and the slave; both are his close friends. According to verses 4-7, the existence of the community of all the saints, together with the demonstrated vital function of Philemon in the congregation, is the presupposition of the removal of tension between these friends of the apostle. The bond of brotherhood and love can and will unite them. In verses 8-20 Paul insists that the way toward a brotherly relation between Philemon and Onesimus is not merely a bilateral matter. Paul, as advocate of both the master and the slave, belongs in the bond of love that shall unite them. A triangular rather than only a bilateral personal community is at stake. According to verse 17, Paul, Philemon, and Onesimus form a trio of inseparable partners. Such partners have equal duties and rights, share failures and successes, and are united in tears and in laughter.

VERSES 8-9

Therefore, although in Christ's service I feel completely free to command how you have to behave properly, for love's sake I rather make an appeal, just as the man who I am: Paul, ambassador of the Messiah Jesus and yet his prisoner.

Instead of jumping *in medias res* and clearly formulating what he wants Philemon to do with the returning slave Onesimus, Paul chooses a detour. Because the slave owner has proved to be a good Christian and because of the joy with which he has filled Paul, "therefore" the apostle rejects the possibility of a blunt order. Instead, he approaches the man with soft tones and as if on cat's paws. Before dictating or writing PHM, Paul had apparently pondered which way might be best. He confesses to have been tempted by the thought that the duties of a good man need be hammered and spelled out unequivocally, but he refused to decide for this procedure. He knows that the response to *what* a person says is often dependent on *how* the message is conveyed. In addressing Philemon, the apostle lives up to the advice and command given in Eph 4:15: to "speak the truth in love."

When Israel was groaning under the yoke of Pharaoh Ramses II, Moses, as an elect member of God's people, had to convey to the pagan ruler the divine command: "Let my people go!" (Exod 4:23; etc.). Indeed, in 2 Cor 3 Paul compares his ministry with that of Moses, and what the apostle has to say to Jews and Gentiles often resembles the uncompromising style and substance of the pronouncements of OT prophets. Radical reformers, among them Zwingli, Calvin, John Knox of Scotland, and Oliver Cromwell, spoke in a prophetic manner about and to oppressive civil governments, rather than in the way Paul chose in dealing with Philemon. Is, then, in writing PHM without prescribing the immediate manumission of Onesimus, Paul no longer the "Apostle of Liberty" (as R. N. Longenecker called him in his book *Paul, Apostle of Liberty*)? The warm, personal, and open-ended atmosphere of pastoral counseling that dominates PHM is certainly different from a rock-hard insistence on the principle of emancipation. Especially in Galatians (3:28; 4:21-31; 5:1, 13; etc.) Paul had proclaimed in unambiguous terms that in Christ not only Jews and Gentiles, male and female persons, but also masters and slaves are united, equal and free. The suspicion that Paul's teachings in matters of slavery are self-contradictory was already discussed in "Literary, Biographical, and Contextual Issues," section VII.B-C, pp. 170-200. Whether Paul's decision against a hard command, as it is made in Philem 8-9, contradicts the best of Paul's message and work has to be answered by a detailed study of these verses.

In Christ's service I feel completely free (lit. "in Christ I have much freedom"). The freedom *(parrhēsia)* of which Paul speaks at this place is the capability to speak up freely in the presence of a ruler or before a court. A slave, "having no voice" (see "Social Background," sec. III.B, p. 18, did not have this right. (For a comprehensive discussion of *parrhēsia*, see S. B. Marrow, *"Parrhēsia,"* pp. 431-446; cf. the exposition of Eph 3:12 in AB 34, pp. 347-348.) Paul calls himself in, e.g., Rom 1:1 a "servant" (or "slave") of the Messiah Jesus — of a Lord who does not muzzle his subjects but entitles and commands, encourages and enables them to open their mouths freely and courageously. According to a logion of Jesus, to the Acts of the Apostles, and to Paul's understanding of the apostolic ministry, it is the Spirit of God that provides the wisdom and the bravery for this free speech, be it before Jewish and Gentile courts, or within and to the congregations (see, e.g., Matt 10:18-20; Acts 4:8, 31; 1 Cor 2:13; 7:40; Eph 3:5, 7). Because it reveals confidence and is a pleasure to speak this way, in Philem 8 *parrhēsia* has often (e.g., in Vg.) been rendered by "confidence," and sometimes by "joyfulness." NEB paraphrases: ". . . I might make bold," and NJB: ". . . I have no hesitation." The paraphrase chosen in our translation stresses the dialectic between the authorization by Christ and Paul's self-consciousness.

In the Greek text, the adjective "much" before *parrhēsia* reminds one of the "much" before "joy" in verse 7. In both cases more than a relatively large quantity is meant: completeness and perfection beyond any restrictions are in mind.

Indeed, Paul's freedom is created and sustained by Christ himself and by no means stems from arrogance and presumption. But why does the apostle not simply remind Philemon of his authority *(exousia),* as several expositors suggest? According to, e.g., H. Schlier (*TDNT,* 5.883, 885), in Philem 8 *parrhēsia* is used "in much the same sense as *exousia,* because there exists a close connection" between both. E. Lohse translates *parrhēsia* "authority." Equally N. R. Petersen (*Rediscovering Paul,* pp. 179-180 n. 52; 190 n. 128) is convinced that at this place Paul "lends" the word *parrhēsia* "the connotation of authority," with the result that there is "little if any semantic difference between Paul's terminology, for either his appealing or his commanding." A sketch of some of the essential elements of authority in the NT can contribute to another exposition of Philem 8-9.

Excursus: Use and Misuse of Full Power

The noun *exousia* is derived from the verb *exesti* (it is allowed, it is possible). It occurs in the NT over one hundred times, e.g., five times in Romans and ten times in First Corinthians, for denoting, inter alia, the freedom or capability to choose and to act, and the full power, authority, and right to occupy a ruling position. In, e.g., 2 Cor 10:8-10; cf. 13:10, Paul affirms that it is not a sign of excessive boasting of his authority when he "frightens" those he addresses or when he "puts fear" into them. Indeed, he does not approach the fickle Galatians and the opponents in other congregations with a soft touch.

Still, in 2 Cor 10:8 and 13:10 the apostle qualifies the authority entrusted to him by the Lord: it is full power to build up, not to tear down. Paul can threaten to come to Corinth with stick in hand rather than "with love in the spirit of meekness" (1 Cor 4:21); yet instead of intending to "lord it over the faith" of the saints, he hopes to be "a fellow worker of your joy" (2 Cor 1:24).

Now, whoever makes use of the power and right of a gospel servant might misuse and abuse them also (*katachraomai;* 1 Cor 9:12, 18). The interpretation and the misapplication of the slogan *panta moi exesti* (all is permitted to me) by the supposedly Spirit-drenched Corinthians is corrected by Paul in 1 Cor 6:12 and 10:23. Obviously they turned what John 1:12 calls the "*exousia* to become children of God" into a moral free pass under the heading "Everything Goes." According to Matthew's and Luke's accounts of Jesus' temptations, not even God's Son was spared the idea to become omnipotent on earth by wanton use of the power conveyed by God. The disciples were given full power to preach, to forgive, to heal the sick, and to expel demons. But a hierarchical misuse was prohibited to them: they were instructed not to follow the example of the lords over the nations who ruled their subjects by brute power (Matt 10:25-28). Solely Jesus Christ is given by God unlimited authority (Matt 7:29; 11:27; 28:18; etc.). In various ways, not only the disciples and apostles but also Roman state officials are authorized by God to perform specific services (Matt 10:1; John 19:11; Rom 13:1-7).

Among the common features of the authority granted by God to his elect servants are the following: They are appointed to contribute to the redemption and liberation of persons suffering under heavy yokes; they endure hard temptations; they are, by some members of God's people and of the nations, met with suspicion and hostility. Finally, only by the same equipment as they are given to fulfill their task — by the Holy Spirit — is their authorization recognized and their ministry accepted (1 Cor 2:9-16; Matt 16:17; John 14:17; etc.). The whole of PHM, and verses 8-9 in particular, can be considered a discussion of the proper and improper use and recognition of authority.

The Reformers Luther and Calvin have elaborated on a special ethical message of PHM. In his foreword to this epistle, Luther (WA *Deutsche Bibel,* 7.292-293) states that here Paul "renounces his right," just as Christ, according to Phil 2:6-8, has given up his divine prerogative and as Philemon is to dispense with his legal claim on Onesimus. Calvin uses the same expression *(iure suo cedit),* yet without mentioning the christological foundation and making it a general principle of ethics. A great number of fighters for social justice proclaim that unjust social relations and conditions can be corrected only when the high and mighty are forced to renounce their power and their rights.

Still, it must be asked whether Paul, by preferring an appeal to a command, really intends at least at this occasion not only to forgo his authority, but also to encourage others to follow his example. If so, he would have proposed an ethic that in principle rejects legal power and right — in order to replace law and order by the impulses of love and voluntary decision. According to Acts 16:21, 37, 38; 23:27, the apostle did not renounce the privilege of Roman citizenship. What he writes in Rom 13:1-7 (unlike 1 Cor 6:1-8) does not support the notion that, because of the frequent misuse of legal powers and rights, Paul favored total renunciation of all legal claims and institutions.

In Philem 8 Paul renounces a specific use of freedom of speech *(parrhēsia),* not his authority *(exousia).* Both terms can denote apostolic privileges. The apostles' unique full power is never shared on an equal basis by other members of the early church. In several passages (1 Thess 2:2; 2 Cor 3:12; 7:4; Eph 3:12; 6:20; twelve times in Acts; cf. E. Lohmeyer, p. 184), *parrhēsia* is a special freedom granted to apostles only. Yet, according to 1 Tim 3:12, all ministers of Christ — following Hebrews and First John, all the faithful — participate in *parrhēsia*. There is a difference between full authority and confident speech: the first is a quasi-objective authorization by the Lord, the second is one among several subjective manifestations of the divine gift and task.

To ignore or reject the power and the right given by Christ would amount to rebellion. In 1 Cor 9:16-17 Paul himself confesses what in Acts 9:4, variant reading; 26:14 is said about the "hard" consequences of "kicking against the goad": he is under compulsion *(anagkē)* to preach the gospel, and he acknowledges that it is better to fulfill the entrusted ministry out of his free will. In 1 Cor 9:4-18 the apostle affirms that one of his voluntary and subjective responses to his divine appointment has been to renounce solely some ways to exploit it. Unlike "the other apostles and brothers of the Lord and Cephas" who on their journeys are accompanied by their wives, Paul travels alone. Like every respectable rabbi, but unlike other early Christian teachers, he works with his hands for his upkeep and does not claim physical support. He refuses to accept material means from the Corinthians, although he gladly accepts them from the Philippians (Phil 4:14-19; 2 Cor 9:1-5; cf. 11:7-11). This man would consider it a misuse of his authority if he claimed the right of a salary or reward.

In Philem 8-9 Paul actually renounces neither his right nor his authority. Rather he exercises his apostolic prerogatives in a very specific way, keeping intact his authorization to proclaim the liberty and equality of all true children of Abraham (cf. Gal 3–5). A literal translation of Philem 8 must therefore show that the apostle "has" the full power and freedom to give an order to Philemon (so, e.g., E. Lohmeyer, C. F. D. Moule, E. Lohse). For instance, J. B. Lightfoot, NEB, and P. Stuhlmacher give the text a wrong slant when they translate "having *(echōn)*" by the conjunctive "might have, would have," or the like. Paul's abstention from dictating to the slave owner a single course of action is the result of a personal decision and is made for a special occasion. Our translation, "I feel completely free," seeks to express the subjective element (and the risk!) in the method chosen by Paul. The apostle is aware that even in the possession of legitimate authority, in having a right and while being in the right, he is not automatically right in all cases, nor does he always do the right thing. He has to choose one of several ways, and he intends to decide for the best — in this case for rejecting what seems to be the easiest and most effective method.

To command. In other epistles of Paul, a command *(epitagē)* and the giving of an order *(epitassō* or *paraggellō;* a third synonym, *keleuō,* is a favorite of Matthew and the Acts of the Apostles but is never used by Paul) have by no means a connotation that is morally inferior to other modes of oral or written communication. The LXX uses the noun and the verb for denoting God's, a king's, or a general's method of making his intention known and having it fulfilled, and the apostle had no reason to consider commanding as bad in itself. Mark and Luke speak of the commands by which Jesus reveals his dominion over unclean spirits (Mark 1:27; 6:39; 9:25; Luke 4:36; 8:31) and forces elect persons to become his followers (Matt 4:18-27; etc.). All synoptic Gospels abound with examples showing the saving role of the Lord's blunt orders. In analogy, Paul speaks of the forceful subjugation *(hypotagē, hypotassō)* of principalities and powers to Christ's feet (1 Cor 15:25-27; Eph 1:19-21; etc.; cf. Phil 2:10-11). According to Paul's Capital Letters, the direct command of the Lord and/or God is to be heeded under all circumstances, while the apostle's counsels represent no more than his own opinions *(syggnomē* and *gnomē)* or a stimulus to evoke zeal and genuine love among the saints (1 Cor 7:6, 25; 2 Cor 8:8). In the liturgical conclusion of Romans, the "command of the eternal God" is the ground for the worldwide proclamation of the saving gospel. This command requires "obedience of faith" (Rom 16:26; cf. 1:5). According to 1 Tim 1:1 and Titus 1:3, the command stems from God or the Messiah, who is "our savior." It does not originate from a lawgiver who establishes his authority as an end in itself. To proclaim the will and command of God — be it in the form of an indicative, a participle, or an imperative — is therefore a way of gospel proclamation rather than an attempt to subjugate those listening to a dictate or a military order.

If Paul had intended to impress Philemon with the citation of a divine command, he might have quoted Lev 25:25-29, 39-46; Exod 21:2; Deut 15:12, that is, the Torah texts that prohibit harsh treatment of Hebrew slaves and prescribe their release after the sixth year of service. Also he might have alluded to Sir 33:13, "If you have a servant, treat him as a brother," or Sir 7:21, "Let your soul love an intelligent servant, do not withhold from him his liberty." Or he might have cited, as indeed he does in 1 Cor 7:10; 9:14; cf. 11:23; 14:37; Acts 20:35, a pronouncement made by Jesus or a commandment given by the Lord.

Why, then, does Paul refrain from conveying or giving an order to Philemon? Since it is most unlikely that Philemon or Onesimus or both were born Jews, or that the slave owner had been a proselyte, the quotation of a specific Hebrew law or wise counsel might have been bewildering but hardly convincing. Even if the apostle should have known anything of the description of Jesus' mission: "anointed to proclaim liberty to the captives, . . . the Jubilee Year" (Isa 61:1-2 is quoted in Luke 4:18-19), he still did not transform the promise into a command that any Christian could and should fulfill as well. To repeat: in no way does Paul seek to imitate Moses' stance before Pharaoh Ramses II.

Paul was not always as reticent and humble as he presents himself in

Philem 8-9. For in his earliest two letters — if both epistles to the Thessalonians are accepted as genuine — and in the latest letters circulated under his name, the Pastoral Epistles (except Second Timothy), the apostle repeatedly refers to commands given by him. They prescribe working with one's own hands (1 Thess 4:11; 2 Thess 3:10, 17) or other things; the explicit commands are given to the saints in the name of the Lord Jesus: Paul is confident that the members of the congregation "know" each one of them (1 Thess 4:2; 2 Thess 3:4). The need to repeat a prescription (e.g., regarding a married woman's apparel in public worship) is "not to the praise" of those addressed, according to 1 Cor 11:17. Titus is encouraged to pronounce the gospel, to admonish, to reprove (lit.) "with all command" (Titus 2:15; RSV, NEB, and NJB translate here *pasē epitagē,* "with all authority"). Unlike Philem 8-9, in 2 Thess 3:14 and Titus 2:15 commanding and exhorting are not opposites but belong together as mutual interpretations. A striking example of this coherence is found in Eph 5:33: "One by one, each one of you [husbands] must love his wife as himself, and the wife — *may* she fear her husband."

A development can be observed in Paul's attitude and diction. Early in his missionary activity ethical instruction by commandments was not strange to him. Then, as shown especially by Galatians and Second Corinthians among the Capital Epistles, Paul combined a rigorous display of his authority with the tone of humble pleading and begging. Paul appears to have been "learning by doing." In PHM he goes one step further, for here he plainly rejects commanding in favor of pleading. Directive counseling yields here to an appeal for voluntary individual ethical decision. As an experienced and wise counselor, Paul refuses to order around a "brother" and a "sister" (Philem 1-2, 7, 16, 20); they are not soldiers in basic training or marionettes. Rather, if they need advice and are treated as mature adults, pleading and entreating will be more effective than a display of naked authority. Together with the church fathers, Calvin emphasized this in his exposition of PHM. Finally, First Timothy and Titus show that soon enough — if not by Paul himself then yet in the early church by pseudonymous writers — the need was felt to return to the method of the early Paul.

Ignatius of Antioch (*Rom.* 4.3 and *Eph.* 3.1-2) reflects the picture of Paul presented in the Thessalonian correspondence and the Pastoral Letters. Apostles such as Peter and Paul "are someone great"; they "give commands" and "order you." Yet for his own person and position, Ignatius imitates Philem 8-9: "I do not give you commands *(ou diatassomai hymin)* . . . for though I am a prisoner for the Name, I am not yet perfect in Jesus Christ; for now I do but begin to be a disciple, and I speak to you as my fellow-learners. . . . But since love does not suffer me to be silent concerning you, for this reason I have taken upon me to exhort *(parakaleō)* you that you live in harmony with the will of God." "Peter and Paul . . . were Apostles, I am a convict; they were free, I am even until now a slave." J. Knox (*Philemon,* pp. 86-87) treats Ignatius, *Eph.* 3.1-2, as evidence of the bishop's literary dependence on PHM. But this presupposes that Philem 8-9 was misunderstood or ignored: Ignatius ascribes to Paul that right of command which Paul does not wish to display in PHM.

What Paul does not wish to dictate to Philemon, and what he yet expects the slave owner to do, is described by a very crisp and yet somewhat vague phrase:

How you have to behave properly (*soi to anēkon,* lit. "you do the proper thing"). These words signify all that is fitting, decent, suitable for Philemon's reflections and decisions, as well as for his attitude and his actions. The Vg. version, "what pertains to the matters at hand," reflects the etymological sense of *anēkon* but ignores the wider moral meaning of this word, and of its equivalents *kathēkon, prosēkon, prepon,* and *dikaion.* (See esp. M. Pohlenz, "To Prepon," pp. 53-92; cf. E. Lohmeyer's comments on Col 3:18 and Phil 4:8 in MeyerK IX, 8th ed. [1930], pp. 173-176, 156). These terms occur in Greek moral-philosophical literature; in, e.g., Cicero's discourses and in Horace's poetry; *decet, aptum est, decorum est* are the corresponding Latin terms. Originally aesthetic beauty, then a person's conduct appropriate to high or low status, was described by them; pleasure and joy are evoked by beauty and beautiful conduct. "Proper" was, for instance, an artist's recitation that displayed his gifts, corresponded to the subject matter, and pleased the audience. Or satisfactory performance of an official could be so labeled. Whatever proved to be wise in respect to prevailing conditions and by following reason and nature fulfilled the norms of decency. Just as a "gentleman" or a "lady," so also a person behaving properly in the ancient world was entitled to considerable leeway and freedom in deciding, from one opportunity to another, for a specific deportment. Epictetus (*Diss.* 3.7, 25; 4.10, 12) distinguished between different dimensions and applications of "the proper." In no case is casuistic legislation or shrill commands considered the means by which a conduct can be engendered that is dependent on voluntary harmony with unwritten standards.

But J. B. Lightfoot sees in *anēkon* "the ultimate meaning of moral obligation." The NEB and NJB versions translate "duty," and P. Stuhlmacher is not alone in elaborating on the concept *Pflicht,* a favorite in Kantian and later nineteenth-century German moral philosophy. In *TDNT,* 1.360, H. Schlier defines *anēkon* "Not merely what is fitting but that which is almost legally obligatory, although in a private matter." Elsewhere (in *TDNT,* 3.439) Schlier explains the synonymous *kathēkon* as a "general moral conviction rather than a specific command or order."

Such expositions cannot convince. For "duty" is, as the word says, something that is owed and therefore "due." An "obligation" arises solely when there is a debt or a code. Paul, however, speaks no earlier than in Philem 19 of a possible personal debt of Philemon. He never reminds him of a fixed oral or written code comparable to the Sectarian Rule of Qumran (1QS). Not even the *Haustafel* of Col 3:18–4:1, which might have been read aloud in the presence of Philemon, contains direct prescriptions about the treatment of a fugitive and later returning slave.

Actually, the phrase "commanding the proper thing" is a contradiction in terms and speaks of something that is absurd in itself. The Greeks called such a paradox an *oxymōron*. Paul, in turn, has confidence in Philemon's *voluntary* decision to take the right course (cf. Philem 14 and 21). The freedom granted by God to his children, the power of love inspired by the Spirit, and the voice of what in other letters is called the conscience *(syneidēsis)* are trusted to make Philemon do what is right and meet.

In his commentary on Phil 4:8, E. Lohmeyer explains the words "Finally, brethren, whatever is true ... honorable ... just ... lovely ... gracious, if there is any excellence, if there is anything worthy of praise, think about those things" by stating that "a natural morality" is *not* meant by Paul. Rather, just as in Jewish tradition, "these norms are plainly and simply given," and "the modality of their givenness is the religious experience (of God)." The same is true of Paul's reference to the *anēkon* in Philem 8. The will of God, the Lord, or Jesus Christ, or the custom of the saints, is in other texts sometimes explicitly mentioned by Paul when he discusses the right thing to do. (See 2 Thess 1:6; Eph 5:3, and in the *Haustafeln:* Col 3:18; 4:1; Eph 6:1-3; cf. *1 Clem.* 3.4 and 41.3-4). Certainly the apostle does not shy away from speaking in 1 Cor 11–14 and Rom 1:26 of things taught by nature or contrary to nature. Also he quotes (in, e.g., 1 Cor 9:7, 12; Eph 5:28-29; not to mention Titus 1:12) proverbs or commonsense sayings in favor of his ethical admonitions, sometimes side by side with Scripture texts. But solely by a *tour de force* can Paul be transferred into a promoter of natural revelation, of a law of nature, or of a pagan consensus on an ethics based on reason alone.

Several ethical Pauline texts mention a standard of the Christians' conduct: they have to find out and do the will of God and what is pleasing to him and to Christ, not to conform to the present world (Rom 12:2; 2 Cor 5:9; Col 3:20; Eph 5:10; cf. Heb 11:5-6; 13:21). God's and Christ's judgment (Rom 2:5-11; 14:10; 1 Cor 3:13-15; 2 Cor 5:10), rather than the opinion of moral philosophers, will decide the worth of human performance. Yet even before God's ultimate verdict is declared, humankind may be pleased by the conduct of Christians. As the earliest Jerusalem congregation enjoyed "favor among all the people" (Acts 2:47), so Paul exhorts the saints in 1 Thess 4:12 to "behave decently" (RSV, NEB, and NJB: to "earn respect"), and in Col 4:5 to act wisely among "those outside." The Christians shall "give no offense to Jews, Greeks and the congregation of God" (1 Cor 10:32). In Titus 2:9 slaves are admonished to "behave pleasantly *(euarestous einai)*" toward their masters, and according to Rom 14:18 a servant of God is both "well-pleasing to God and approved by humanity." It is to be concluded that the "proper" conduct expected of Philemon includes a missionary function; it does not only affect the slave owner's good name in the congregation and his future new personal relationship to Onesimus.

9. *For love's sake.* These words might serve as a title of the whole of PHM. A consensus on the exact meaning of this formula is not yet within sight. Paul may have thought of (a) God's or Christ's love; (b) the love for God or Christ; (c) the love demonstrated by either Paul, Philemon, or Onesimus; (d) the love of all the saints for one specific Christian or for the community of the saints. Also a combination of divine and human love would make good sense. Neither divine nor human love, neither the love of individuals nor its function for the building and growth of the community (see, e.g., Col 3:14 and Eph 4:15-16) can be separated or singled out from the rich meanings of this one word. Certainly the beginning of Philem 9: "for love's sake," refers back to the thanksgivings of verses 4-7 and reminds of their core. J. B. Lightfoot speaks of "the principle" and "of respect for the claims of love," but H. Binder warns of considering love "an abstract norm" because neither Paul nor Philemon can produce and achieve this "power . . . which in Christ streams upon the human beings."

At least three dimensions of Paul's appeal to love in Philem 9 can be distinguished.

1. The apostle expects that the same power that has distinguished Philemon in the past and up to the present will prove irresistible and motivate him in the future. Paul does more than only argue in a cogent way. He touches on the very nature of love. An affection and attitude that could be superseded or terminated would never be true love. The apostle hopes that just as faith and joy can increase, so also love will grow and flourish (cf. Phil 1:9). Since Philemon has demonstrated that he lives by love, he had better not do without it in his relation to Onesimus.

2. In the NT, love is repeatedly called the sum and fulfillment of all commandments and the whole Law of God. If Paul had passed on to Philemon just one or several individual commandments, the slave owner might have assumed that partial compliance with God's will could substitute for total loyal obedience. Those opponents of Paul who trusted in justification by selected "works of law" and "statutes" had succumbed to that error. (See esp. Gal 2:16; 3:2, 5, 10; 5:3, 14; 6:2, 13; Rom 1:5; 2:25; 3:28; 9:30-31; 13:8-10; Phil 3:9; Col 2:8; 3:14; cf. James 2:10.)

3. Love is often considered something soft and sentimental — as if it were bare of any direct influence on and power over the hard issues of social, economi-

cal, and political daily life. Paul, however, trusts that love will create a new relationship between the master Philemon and the slave Onesimus, the existing laws and customs of the slavery institution notwithstanding. When the runaway is received and treated as a "loved brother," a new structure of common life will emerge. If love is the basis of an "antistructure," as N. R. Petersen has emphatically stated, then it shapes a distinct society, built on a specific kind of law, order, and customs. According to Deuteronomy, the love of God is prominent among the ways in which God and his people keep the covenant. (Cf. W. L. Moran, "Ancient Near Eastern Background," pp. 77-87, and the passages listed in AB 34A, p. 665 n. 228.) Covenant is much more than a religious idea in the Bible: it is the foundation of a community and it shapes Israel's social, economical, and political life. The divine King is a "lover of justice," and the earthly king is praised when he acts as such a man (Pss 99:4; 45:6-7; 72:2, 7, 12-14; 82:1-3).

So also for Paul, Philemon's love without social conduct determined by love vis-à-vis Onesimus would be chimeric; if law and order in Philemon's house were not dominated by love, that house would betray love. It would remain subjugated to the passing-away system of the present world. Among recent scholars, a philosopher of law, Erik Wolf (in Wolf, *Rechtsgedanke und biblische Weisung,* pp. 65ff.) has spoken of "Confessing Church Law," and K. Barth (*Church Dogmatics* IV, pp. 676-826) has extensively discussed the order and the right *(Kirchenrecht)* that distinguish the congregations from other communities. The function given to love in Philem 9 warns of a Scylla and a Charybdis: Paul speaks neither of a church ruled by a lawbook such as the *Codex Juris Canonici,* nor does he promote a formless and spiritualizing concept of an enthusiastic brotherhood, as proposed by, e.g., Rudolf Sohm *(Kirchenrecht. Die geschichtlichen Grundlagen)* and Emil Brunner *(Misunderstanding of the Church).*

I rather make an appeal. As Philemon is not forced by a command to take a specific action, so Paul reveals that it is his own personal and subjective decision "rather" to choose a soft approach. In the service of Christ, the free man Paul asks for a free person's response.

The meanings of *parakalō,* which in our version of Philem 9 and 10 is translated "appealing," cover a wide field: "calling for help, inviting, summoning, entreating, pleading, urging, exhorting, charging, encouraging or warning, comforting, consoling and cheering up." A choice has to be made by interpreters, depending on the sentence and wider context in which the verb is being used. (See BAG; and G. Staehlin, O. Schmitz, and J. Behm in *TDNT,* 5.773-814.) Theological dimensions of the term are discussed in depth by, e.g., H. Schlier, "Vom Wesen der apostolischen Ermahnung," pp. 74-89, and by C. J. Bjerkelund, *Parakalō.* In the notes of Philem 7 it was shown that the cognate *paraklēsis* can sparkle with as many nuances. Sometimes they overlap. The frequent occurrence of these words in the Pauline letters (the verb fifty-four times, the noun twenty times) shows that they constitute a basic element in Paul's ethical teaching.

Excursus: Ethics Based on the Gospel

In Greek literature, the philosophers' and poets' "art of consoling" those in grief is much more broadly enfolded than other dimensions of *parakalō*. But in the NT the various groups of meanings of this term appear side by side and are sometimes merged. In the synoptic Gospels and Acts the approach of supplicants to men possessing power is often described by this word. In the Johannine writings the verb is missing, but the noun *paraklētos*, in the sense of "advocate" before God and humankind rather than of "comforter," is used as a title of the Holy Spirit and of Jesus (John 14:16, 26; 15:26; 16:7; 1 John 2:1). In the Pauline writings, other verbs are by a simple "and" combined with *parakalō*, either in order to specify and emphasize the significance of this verb or to add a complementary thought. In, e.g., 2 Thess 3:12 "commanding" *(paraggellō)* and in Titus 2:15 the words "by strict order" *(meta pasēs epitagēs)* provide an authentic interpretation of the intended meaning of *parakalō;* in 1 Thess 2:12 and 1 Cor 14:3, "encouraging, cheering up" *(paramytheomai, paramythia);* elsewhere (in Acts 20:21; 1 Thess 5:12, 14; 2 Thess 3:15; 1 Cor 4:16; Rom 15:4-5) the same is true of "admonishing, exhorting." Again, at other places verbs such as "asking, strengthening, building up, proclaiming, adjuring, reproving, rebuking" have the same function. (See *TDNT*, 5.796, for references.) Paul uses *parakalō* in at least four different senses:

(a) "Asking" or "entreating" is the proper meaning in 2 Cor 12:8 and 5:20, that is, standing as a beggar before God and humankind. (b) Almost thirty times in Second Corinthians, *parakalō* and *paraklēsis* signify the act and the gift of consolation. God is both the source of consolation in the present troubled time and the guarantor of eschatological and eternal comfort. Temporal consolation is effected by the words, the arrival, and the deeds of the apostle and other persons, as the above-mentioned Pauline passages show. (c) In, e.g., 1 Thess 2:3 (cf. Acts 13:15, 32; Heb 13:22; 1 Pet 5:12; Jude 3) the proclamation of the gospel is meant. There statements are made in indicative form about the fulfillment of Israel's hope through God; about the coming, death, and resurrection of Christ; and about the work and effect of the Spirit. (d) Finally, recognizable by imperatives or equivalent participles and infinitives in the context, *parakalō* signifies "exhorting, admonishing, urgent counseling." Repeatedly (in 1 Thess 4:1; Rom 12:1; Phil 4:2; cf. 1 Pet 2:11; yet in Gal 5 another purpose prevails) the verb marks the transition from the kerygmatic (proclamatory, creedal, dogmatic) first part of a Pauline letter to the ethical (parenetic, moral, didactic) section.

The common basis of Paul's prayer, proclamation, consolation, and exhortation is the justification and salvation given gratis by God, through Christ and the Spirit, to Jews, Gentiles, and Christians. Even when with the key word *parakalō* and by the use of imperatives Paul calls for a distinctive human conduct, namely, for good works, he never assumes that works can make righteous and serve as merits before God. Neither the Law itself nor the earlier-mentioned selective or a radicalized fulfillment of the Law

317

secures the attainment of salvation (Gal 2:16, 21; etc.). Still, Paul's insistence on Christ's grace and faith alone does not prevent him from speaking of the "Law written in the hearts . . . the law of faith . . . the Law of God according to the inmost self . . . the Law of the Spirit of life in Christ . . . the Law of Christ," or of "living under Christ's law" (Rom 2:14-15; 3:27; 7:22; 8:2; Gal 6:2; 1 Cor 9:21). For Israel, God's *Torah* was and is not a narrow prison exacting by force a legalistic performance. Rather it is a demonstration of God's election and love, and a benefit for the liberated people. For Jews, each *mitzvah* is an opportunity to do God's will today (cf. Deut 4:5-8; 33:3-4; etc.; cf. Rom 3:31; 7:12, 14; 10:4; 13:8-10). So also the Pauline admonitions stand on the basis of salvation through grace. God's free grace calls for the spontaneous service of those justified by Christ's faithfulness.

Greek moral philosophers referred to Socrates as a paragon of perfect virtue — but they did not know of specific saving events such as Israel's election and Christ's work that would authorize them to replace a moralist's "you must" by a magnanimous and loving "thou mayest." Especially R. Bultmann (*Theology of the New Testament,* 1.332-333, 2.79-82) and H. Schlier, in his essay on *Ermahnung* (cf. O. Merk, *Handeln aus Glauben*), have carefully elaborated on the irreversible sequence of God's gracious deed and the human response, of proclamatory indicatives and words of ethical imperatives. Yet, as among Greeks consolation can have the form of imperatives such as "cheer up, stop crying," so the NT contains extended texts — among them the Sermon on the Mount and the Epistle of James — in which imperatives are a way of proclaiming the gospel (cf. *TDNT,* 5.796-797, 799). Even urgent admonitions can communicate the message that God loves, trusts, and equips his elect people so much that he expects total gratitude, joy, and cooperation. Not in vain can a beggar's humble request and an authorized messenger's proclamation and exhortation be meant by the one single Greek term *parakalō*. A Christian such as Philemon is invited to respect evangelical ethics in which exhortation and consolation are hard or impossible to distinguish. A legalistic ethics would contradict a main element of NT preaching and teaching. In a note on verse 4, it was shown that gratitude is the motive of a Christian's personal and social conduct.

In his *Ep.* 95.65, Seneca carefully distinguishes *praeceptio, suasio, exhortatio,* and *consolatio* (prescription, persuasion, admonition, consolation) from one another. But in many other writings he combines and mixes all these modes of speech — no less than does the NT, although for different reasons.

In his monograph on *parakalō* (p. 188; cf. 120ff.), C. J. Bjerkelund declares Philem 8-10 to be the key to Paul's use of this word. He flatly rejects for verses 9-10 not only the versions "command" and "implore" but also an exposition that thrives on the logical deduction of an imperative from a preceding indicative. Instead, he proposes that here Paul expresses simply his confidence in the actuality of the brotherhood that constitutes the church. Indeed, verse 8 excludes the possibility that *parakalō* in verse 9 contains a hidden command, and beseeching or entreating would then be a fitting translation of *parakalō* (as suggested by, e.g., Vg., RSV, J. B. Lightfoot, E. Lohmeyer, H. Binder, P. Stuhlmacher) only if Paul, by calling himself a *presbytēs* and a prisoner at the end of verse 9, really intended to make Philemon weep with pity.

The translation of *parakalō* by "I (make an) appeal" follows NEB and NJB. It shows that the apostle intends to take Philemon by his honor (as it was described in vv. 4-7) and to tell him, in terms simultaneously complimentary, friendly, and urgent, in which direction to move. Also it cannot be excluded that Paul fostered a specific hope: that by Onesimus's return as a dear "brother," Philemon would be as much "comforted" as Paul was, according to verse 7, by the slave owner's good function in the congregation.

Examples taken from the history of interpretation reveal how Paul's kind way of approaching Philemon has been appreciated and applied to solving diverse acute problems. Ignatius, as cited above, imitates by his own attitude the humble stance fitting a servant and a prisoner: he can do no more than "exhort." In the foreword to his PHM commentary, Theodore of Mopsuestia (in the H. B. Swete edition, II [1882], pp. 261-262) discusses the general "usefulness" of this letter. First of all, this epistle teaches those "holding an ecclesiastic function, most of all those who appear to preside over the congregation," how to conduct themselves in their relation to those "joined to us by faith." Church leaders are to instruct the laity "with *modestia* (moderation, meekness), not on the basis of authority" — just as Paul in 2 Cor 1:24 rejected being a lord over the Corinthians' faith in order to be a cooperator of their joy. Similarly, Calvin affirms that the apostle's procedure is a model for church office bearers — but he advises those softly guided by the officials to remember that they actually owe to do more than is asked of them. According to Luther's PHM lecture of 1527, Paul confirms that it is easier to attract a person in a friendly way than to use force, for application of force has an embittering effect. W. M. L. de Wette simply speaks of "the amiable, genial *(gemuetliche)* personality of the apostle." In a cooler vein, A. Suhl speaks of Paul's "dialectic and play-off of authority and renounced authority." In turn, again and again N. R. Petersen *(Rediscovering Paul,* pp. 127, 131-133, 151-152, 161, 177, 188 n. 13) mentions a "mask" that Paul puts on now and puts off again later. The last-mentioned interpretation may be slightly supported by Gal 4:20, where Paul "would wish to change his voice." But it becomes questionable when it suggests that in conversing among themselves Christians should continuously assume diverse roles — as play actors do.

As the man who I am: Paul (lit. "being such a person as Paul"). Vg. has, without support in any as yet known Greek MS, *cum sis talis ut Paulus* ("because you [Philemon] are the same kind of person as I, Paul," or ". . . of the same quality . . ." — namely, an "old man"). Erasmus observes that the Vg. version is supported by Ambrose, namely, Ambrosiaster, but presupposes a crude solecism that "is never found among the Greeks." Indeed, if at all a Greek text ever intended to speak of Philemon's and Paul's equal quality, then it would have the wording *toioutō onti,* as fits the dative *soi* in verse 8. But all available Greek texts have the nominative *toioutos ōn* and thereby show that solely Paul is meant. While Erasmus as well as after him W. Estius accept the Vg. version as authoritative, both follow in their expositions the transmitted Greek reading — just as earlier Chrysostom and Theophylact had done — Jerome and Vg. notwith-standing! Estius noted that according to the Syriac version, an exact Latin translation would have been *cum sim talis* ("since I [Paul] am such a person").

Frequently in other letters, when the apostle discusses major questions of faith and life, he finds a reason and a way to speak of himself. So also in Philem 9 he interrupts the flow of thought and makes a short excursus concerning his own person. Only in the next verse does he begin to spell out for whom, for what cause, and with which expectation he makes his appeal.

The phrase "as the man who I am: Paul" is "unlike St. Paul's usual mode of speech" (J. B. Lightfoot). The Greek might as well be translated "just as I am . . ." or be paraphrased "qualified by my capability as. . . ." Elsewhere (in Gal 5:2; 2 Cor 10:1; Col 1:23; Eph 3:1) Paul also refers to himself. Then he formulates, *egō Paulos.* "His whole authority as an apostle" (H. D. Betz, *Galatians,* p. 258 n. 48) is mobilized by the introduction of Paul's name into the body of his epistles, just as by the title(s) with which the apostle introduces himself at the letter openings. Philemon 9 confirms an observation made earlier: in verse 8 the renunciation of giving a command does not mean a suspension of the apostolic authority.

Paul anticipates a question that might be posed no earlier than when the following verses are read. What right has the author of this letter to interfere in matters pertaining to a slave owner's private property, to peace and order in his house, and to his good standing among the townspeople? Is he making politics from the pulpit in order to effect social change? Or is he, in contradiction to his abstinence from commanding, yet treating Philemon as if he were a freshly recruited soldier or even a schoolboy? Paul answers by referring to his authorization from on high. According to his teaching, no one can nominate and make himself fit for the ministry of a wise counselor and comforter, and nobody is free to choose the appropriate methods at random. Finding and using the proper way of addressing other persons is a *charisma* (a gift of grace), according to Rom 12:8. When all church members are charged to counsel and comfort one another mutually (1 Thess 4:18; 5:11; 2 Cor 13:11), they are all treated as charismatics. Just as Paul needed to be comforted by God himself before and while he offered consolation to the saints (2 Cor 1:4; 7:6, 7, 13; Rom 1:12; etc.), so the church members receive and experience God's nearness and help before, and in order that, they become witnesses of it to their brothers and sisters. The source of all counsel and comfort is also its standard: it is "the Lord Jesus Christ and the love of the Spirit," "the meekness and gentleness of the Messiah" (Rom 15:30; 2 Cor 10:1). Unlike, e.g., 1 Cor 2:4, 12-13; 7:40, Paul does not claim in Philem 9 divine inspiration for the counsel to be given. Neither does he refer either to timeless general principles such as righteousness, equality, and freedom or to contemporary social, legal, or spiritual developments. Philemon's and other readers' potential questions are answered by the mention of love at the beginning of verse 9, and later in the same verse by the reference to the ministerial appointment through Jesus Christ and to the price paid for this ministry: captivity.

The Messiah Jesus' ambassador and yet also his prisoner. In crisp terms, whose arrangement in our translation resembles the contents and order of a Japanese visiting card, the apostle introduces himself — this time more extensively than in verse 1. After giving his name, he mentions his employer, describes his function as employee, and points out the circumstances under which he lives at present. Two main problems of interpretation have to be mentioned first:

1. Since the days of the church fathers and until the early seventeenth century, the Greek noun *presbytēs,* in our version "ambassador," was usually interpreted "old man." In consequence, the genitive "of the Messiah Jesus," which in the Greek text is posited after "prisoner" but may well qualify both *presbytēs* and *desmios,* was understood to pertain to Paul's captivity only. Already Theophylact suggested translating *presbytēs* "delegate," and Calvin, while retaining the version *senex* (old man), remarked that at this place *presbytēs* means "not the age but the office" of the apostle.

2. Regarding the substance and intention of these words of Paul, three alternative interpretations compete: (a) Paul offers two reasons to restore a part of that authority he seemed to have renounced previously. (b) By mentioning his age-conditioned weakness and humility, together with his actual suffering as a prisoner, he asks for pity rather than for obedience. (c) He combines a moderate authoritarian posture with a highly emotional plea for compassion.

In "Literary, Biographical, and Contextual Issues," p. 107, it was briefly mentioned that in some newer versions and commentaries "ambassador" or a synonymous term is preferred to "old man" for the interpretation of *presbytēs.* What is the philological basis of either translation, and which consequences of the version "old man" are hardly avoidable?

Lexicographical evidence at first sight favors a reference of Paul's advanced age. It seems to justify the Vg. version *senex* (old man). But the apostle's contemporary Philo of Alexandria (*Op. mund.* 105-106) distinguishes between an older (or elderly) man and an old man. In order to glorify "the wonderful plan in nature" occupied by the number 7, he refers to Hippocrates, who discussed 7 seasons of a man's life: a little boy until age 7, a boy till 14, a lad till 21, a young man till 28, a man till 48, an elderly man (*presbytēs*) till 58, and an old man (*gerōn;* Lat. *senex*) after that. According to this division of life in seven "*hebdomades*" of (with a few exceptions) equal length, Paul may have been between 49 and 56 years old when he wrote PHM. Then he was *not* yet a physically or spiritually weak person who depended on compassion and on moral and physical support by relatives and friends. When in Luke 1:18 Zechariah and in *Mart. Pol.* 7.2 Polycarp are called *presbytēs*, feebleness may indeed be in mind (cf. Hermas, *Man.* 8.10). But what in Titus 2:2-3 is said of "elderly men" and "women" contains no hints at bodily or mental frailty.

The longer form *presbyteros* (lit. "older") is usually chosen when the contrast to young people is in mind (see Acts 2:17; 1 Tim 5:1-2; 1 Pet 5:5). *Presbyteros* is also the technical term for the bearer of the office which to this day is called the ministry of an "elder," i.e., a "presbyter," be it in a Jewish congregation or council, or in a church. In the book of Revelation, "elders" is the title of the members of God's council, and outside the Bible, of civic and religious office bearers.

Because of the difference between *presbytēs* and *presbyteros*, Philem 9 supposedly alludes to Paul's advanced age. W. Estius assumes that Paul was actually younger than Philemon but had aged prematurely in consequence of the suffering inflicted upon him at the time of Nero.

Yet the same author declares that not even by emphasizing his age would the apostle have gained the right to give an order to an older man; therefore Paul had to add a reference to his captivity in order to increase the weight of the age argument. Among modern interpreters, H. v. Soden, M. Dibelius, H. Greeven, E. Lohse, and P. Stuhlmacher insist on translating "old" or "elderly man." G. Bornkamm (*TDNT*, 6.683) remarks that Paul "almost certainly means 'old man' here rather then 'ambassador.'" According to Thomas Aquinas, the apostle loves Onesimus, whom he has begotten when he was an old man, as much as the old Jacob loved Joseph. Among the implications of the version "old man" are the following: Concerning the place of origin and the date of PHM, Caesarea and especially Rome are supported and the Ephesus theory is weakened. Regarding the logic of the letter, and the picture emerging of Paul, first the apostle flatters Philemon (vv. 4-7), then he intimidates him with the menace of a command (v. 8), then he applies an emotional thumbscrew: in verses 9-10 he boasts that even in his advanced age and as a prisoner he has produced a child! All of this and more is then supposed to make Paul the author of the "beautiful" and "charming" letter to Philemon! Still, other Pauline epistles do not contribute to a picture of Paul that ultimately displays a lachrymose self-pity of the apostle.

As mentioned in "Literary Issues," p. 107, section II, more than 250 years ago Richard Bentley opened the door to an alternative exposition. By a bold conjecture, he replaced *presbytēs* with *presbeutēs* (envoy, ambassador, staff officer). Bentley's suggestion has no support in any ancient Greek MS or version, but in substance it reproduces Paul's self-understanding. In 2 Cor 5:2 and Eph 6:20 the apostle describes his ministry by the verb *presbeuō* ("serving as ambassador"; cf. Ignatius, *Philad.* 10.1). Moreover, independent of Bentley, it was pointed out by J. B. Lightfoot (and after him by, e.g., E. Haupt; E. J. Goodspeed; E. Lohmeyer; C. F. D. Moule; A. Suhl; C. J. Bjerkelund, *Parakalō*, pp. 119-120) that before and after Paul's time the original difference between *presbytēs* and *presbeutēs* had begun to vanish or became neglected. In, e.g., some LXX MSS (of 2 Chron 32:31; 1 Macc 13:21; 14:21-22; 15:17; 2 Macc 11:34; cf. Eusebius on Isa 18:2; Ignatius, *Smyrn.* 11.2) the two nouns are treated as interchangeable, i.e., they are used as synonyms. The translation of *presbytēs* by "ambassador" can therefore claim to be as literal as the time-honored "old man." If Paul wanted to refer to his office, not to his age, then a sentimental way of exhortation is out of the question, and together with it, also a renunciation of his rightful authority. Rather, in this case the apostle makes very specific use of his authority by showing that his full power has ample room for decency and kindness. In spite of the contrary assertion made by, e.g., O. Schmitz (in *TDNT*, 5.795), Paul does not have "almighty powers" and does not make felt "the weight of supreme authority." Rather, as, e.g., Lightfoot and Moule maintain, the reference to Jesus Christ (namely, to the "Messiah Jesus") pertains to both Paul's ministry as ambassador and his imprisonment, not only to the latter. Romans 15:30 and 2 Cor 10:1 have been cited before: Paul makes his appeal "by our Lord Jesus Christ and by the love of the Spirit," and "by the meekness and gentleness of the Messiah."

And yet also his prisoner. Ancient and modern versions of Philem 9 translate *nyni*, just as elsewhere the synonymous *nyn*, by "now." This translation is indisputable whenever (as, e.g., in the next verse) something "past" is opposed to the present. But it is unlikely that when Paul wrote PHM captivity was a new experience, in contrast to a former permanently enjoyed freedom. Whether this letter stemmed from Ephesus, Caesarea, or Rome — in each case Paul had previously seen prison walls from the inside. For instance, the brief imprisonment of Paul and Silas in Philippi, which in legendary form is described in Acts 16:23-34, was certainly but one among many even more painful incarcerations of the apostle (cf. 2 Cor 11:23). In Philem 9 *nyni* may well have another sense than the temporal.

According to LSLex (s.vv. *nyn* and *nyny*), the adverb "is sometimes opposed to what might have been under other circumstances." Then its sense is "as it is, as the case stands, or as a matter of fact." G. Staehlin (*TDNT*, 4.1106-1123, esp. 1108-1110) speaks of a "non-temporal *nyn*" that introduces a "logical antithesis," that is, intends with "very heavy stress . . . to oppose something factually valid to a hypothetical but erroneous assumption or an incorrect idea," and that reveals "a shift of meaning from 'in the present' to 'in actuality.'" With this significance, *nyn* and *nyni* frequently occur in classical and Hellenistic Greek, also in the LXX and the NT. (See 1 Cor 5:11; 12:18, 20; 13:13; 14:6; 15:20; Rom 7:17; Heb 9:26; Luke 11:39; Acts 20:22, 25.) In the Lukan, Johannine, and Pauline writings, the force of this word is often augmented by the addition of the conjunction *de* (but) or *kai* (and, also, especially). So in, e.g., John 11:22, the formula *kai nyn oida* is to be translated "nevertheless (or: even so) I know" and has nothing to do with an insight gained no earlier than at the present moment.

In the Greek text of Philem 9 both conjunctions, *de* and *kai*, follow on the antithetical "now." They sharpen the contrast between the previously mentioned ambassadorship and the imprisonment that looks so unfitting for a high official delegate. A seemingly absurd paradox is pointed out: An ambassador who cannot move around freely — how can he fulfill his ministry? And a captive who yet in his chains claims to represent that Lord before whom all knees will bow — why should he not make a ridiculous figure? How strong is the position of an ambassador normally, how weak that of a prisoner! In Eph 6:20, most likely with good humor, Paul explicitly calls himself an "ambassador in chains." More than elsewhere, in 2 Cor 11–13 he explains why the coincidence of the opposites, strength and weakness, is not absurd, but essential to his mission. Among the Corinthians, Jesus Christ is "not weak . . . but powerful" because "he was crucified in weakness, but lives by the power of God" (13:3-4). This Lord's grace is sufficient for the apostle because his "power is made perfect in weakness. I will all the more boast of my weaknesses, that the power of Christ may rest upon me. Therefore I am content with weaknesses, insults, hardships, and calamities; for when I am weak, then I am strong" (12:9-10). In other words, solely because, in Paul's assignment and in his person and life, strength and weakness are equally essential and factually inseparable, he is the crucified and risen Messiah Jesus' ambassador — not any other potentate's employee. The apostle's suffering as a prisoner demonstrates and validates his very special ministry and authority.

When, however, in Philem 9 *presbytēs* is translated "old man," and when Paul's imprisonment is considered a surprising recent event, then a permanent trait of his apostolate is ignored and replaced by a sentimental element. Then Paul applies emotional extortion in order to make Philemon comply with his plea.

VERSE 10

I appeal to you on behalf of my own child — him whom I have born in my chains [to be true to his name]: Onesimus [the Profitable].

Now, finally, Paul says explicitly why he writes to Philemon. He intends to intervene and plead in favor of the slave who bears a most meaningful name. In a modern legal or business letter, near the left top, the words "*re*, concerning, or in matters of . . ." would at once indicate the subject of the following script. Indeed, with his intervention Paul will do what is perfectly legitimate; he will not omit business aspects of the matter at hand. Still, Onesimus is not a thing or a piece of property but a person and a very close friend of Paul. Unlike Galatians, where Paul vehemently argues *against* "some" (anonymous) persons who by their teaching and example diverted the congregations from the gospel preached by Paul, in PHM the apostle acts as an advocate *(paraklētos) in favor* of one single man.

In making his plea, he follows the development of a friendly Oriental conversation and waits a long time before coming to the point. But when the name Onesimus finally turns up, he proceeds "with a miraculous affect of charity" (W. Estius). Usually the slave is depicted as a rascal in the commentaries. Presupposed that this image be true, Paul humiliates himself utterly: it is a slave, a fugitive, a thief whom the apostle calls his own son (Calvin).

Despite the clarity and emotional force of verse 10, several obscure or controversial elements require special attention.

I appeal to you on behalf of. Paul repeats the verb *parakalō* that he used in verse 9. Thus he gives it specific emphasis. By mentioning solely the origin and name of his protégé, but by not yet revealing his wish concerning the slave's future, Paul evokes the reader's curiosity. Still, J. Knox (*Philemon,* pp. 20-21) and, in his footsteps, S. Winter ("Paul's Letter to Philemon," p. 6) refuse to translate *parakalō peri* "I appeal in favor." They plead for the version "I ask for . . . Onesimus." As earlier mentioned, in 2 Cor 5:20 and 12:8, as well as frequently outside the Pauline letters, *parakalō* can mean "I ask, I beseech, I entreat." But only a few papyri (among them P. Oxyrrh. 1070) and, e.g., Appian (*Bell. Pun.* 136) have *parakalō peri* in the sense suggested by Knox and Winter, and solely a variant reading of 1 Thess 3:2 and the substance of Philem 13 can be quoted in support of this rather rare signification.

When Paul in his prayers asks God for something specific, and when in his admonitions he expects the saints to do or to give something, then the preposition *hyper* (not: *peri*), a final clause, an indicative, an infinitive, and/or an imperative follow *parakalō.* (See, e.g., 2 Cor 5:2; 12:8; 1 Cor 1:10; Rom 12:1.) In addition, if in Philem 10 the apostle had formulated, "I ask *hyper* (for) my child," he might have been understood to mean to write in the name of Onesimus, upon the slave's request, in place of the slave. B. M. Metzger (*The New Testament,* p. 234) suggests even this: After many misdeeds, Onesimus "was converted and wished to make restitution for the wrong he had done to his master. . . . He besought Paul to write to Philemon a reconciliatory letter on his behalf. Paul acceded to his request." However, since Paul chose to write *peri,* there is no evidence that Onesimus took the initiative for returning to his master. Paul's words "I send him back" (v. 12) may well tell a different story.

It has to be concluded that most likely in verse 10 Paul did not (yet) pronounce his ultimate intention, that is, to have Onesimus transferred to him, whether on the basis of a lend-and-lease arrangement with Philemon or of the slave's instantaneous manumission by his earthly master. Or else Paul's procedure would lose its sensitive and careful character.

The majority of interpreters (e.g., E. Lohmeyer; P. Stuhlmacher; H. Binder; U. Wickert, "Der Philemonbrief," pp. 230-238; N. R. Petersen, *Rediscovering Paul*, pp. 106, 179 n. 50) favor a translation of *peri* in the sense of "with reference to" or "in favor of." Our version, "on behalf of," seeks to combine both a sober business style and a warm plea.

My child. The use of the term "child" for the slave Onesimus reminds one of God's own words, spoken through Moses to the ruler of Egypt: "Let my son go that he serve me" (Exod 4:23). However, as stated in Philem 8, Paul does not wish to confront Philemon with a command, and he certainly does not seek to play God. Why then does he call Onesimus his "child" and, by the addition "my own" *(tou emou)*, lay "vivid emphasis upon his property-right" (H. v. Soden)? Two answers compete with one another in modern commentaries, or are considered reconcilable:

1. In the language of mystery religions and Gnosticism, the mystagogue, i.e., the priest initiating properly prepared and tested applicants into divine mysteries, is sometimes called the "father" of those saved by the grant of saving knowledge. Very little is exactly known of the elaborate rituals of regeneration. Sculptures, paintings, and magic papyri, esp. *Corpus Hermeticum* XIII, are used as sources for sometimes daring reconstructions and interpretations. Paul's metaphorical talk of himself as "father" and of the Christians converted by him as "children" (1 Thess 2:11; 1 Cor 4:14-17; Philem 10; cf. 1 Tim 1:2; Titus 1:4) can indicate his acquaintance with these religions and cults. Commentaries stemming from the history-of-religions school (e.g., H. Lietzmann's) rely on Paul's dependence on contemporary pagan religious ideas and practices, including the functions ascribed to one or several divine messengers and to the enactment of mythical stories and mystical experiences in mysterious sacramental actions. Indeed, in 1 Cor 4:1 the apostle calls himself a "steward of the mysteries of God," and, if M. Dibelius's interpretation of Col 2:18 (in his essay "Die Isisweihe bei Apuleius," pp. 30-79, esp. 55-65) is endorsed, then the Colossians (among them: Philemon) knew of initiation rituals.

However, in opposition to such pagan practices, Philo of Alexandria knows of but one mystery that counts: Israel's exodus from Egypt, the symbol of the soul's liberation from carnal bondage. Paul stands in the same front when he describes (esp. in the letters to the Corinthians, Colossians, and Ephesians; cf. 1 Tim 3:16) Jesus Christ, his death, his grace that overflows to the nations, as the one "great mystery." Still, neither the Jewish philosopher nor the

Apostle to the Gentiles refused to occasionally make use of a terminology current in mystery religions or in nascent Gnosticism.

Whenever the spiritual father-son relationship between Paul and Onesimus is explained on this background, grave consequences pertaining to the apostle's theology, especially his concept of salvation, can hardly be avoided. If in Philem 10 the apostle implicitly calls himself a mystagogue, then he elevates himself to the level of a mediator of salvation. In that case he makes daily hardships bearable and even human misdeeds invalid by effecting rebirth and guaranteeing immortality. Delphi priests could do no more for a runaway slave than serve as bankers for the regulation of the financial and legal dimensions of the case at hand. But Paul would then boast of effecting much more — although not at the exclusion of a financial settlement (Philem 18-19) — even of having made a new man of Onesimus. According to Acts 8:10, Simon Magus was such a miracle worker: he was considered an incorporation of the "Great Power," and many a "Divine Man" was esteemed equally high. But does Paul fit that company? Without any reference to mystery religions, e.g., W. Estius affirms that in Philem 10 Paul wanted to say, "I made him a Christian" *(Christianum feci)*. Yet the same expositor adds cautiously: Onesimus was begotten not for Paul, but for Jesus Christ; not by the apostle's but by Christ's power.

2. An alternative to the creative and sacramental function ascribed to Paul is offered by interpreters who rely more on Jewish than on pagan influence upon Paul. (Among them: E. Lohmeyer; F. Buechsel and K. H. Rengstorf, articles *gennaō*, etc; *paliggenesia, TDNT*, 1.665-675, 686-689.) In 2 Kings 2:12; 6:21; and 13:14, a prophet is addressed as father; in Judg 17:10 a priest is called father, and in 1 Sam 24:11; 26:17 the king is called "my father," his subject "my son." A teacher of wisdom gives instruction to his "son" (Prov 4:20; 19:27; etc.); the Qumran Teacher of Righteousness praises God for being installed as "father to the sons of grace," a "nurse of the sons of the sign" so that they "open their mouth like a suckling and rejoice in the nurses' bosom" (1QH 8.20-23). Matthew 23:8-10 shows that "rabbi," "father," and "teacher" were almost synonyms for properly addressing a person possessing spiritual authority. In rabbinical literature, those persons are compared to progenitors or are to be honored as fathers who (1) raise an orphan, (2) convert a Gentile by making him a proselyte, and (3) instruct younger Jews as teachers of the *Thora* (bSanh 19b; 99b; GenR 84 [53 b]. See StB III on 1 Cor 4:15).

There are also parallels in secular literature: in the realm of politics, a metaphorical parent/child relationship is attested by, e.g., Philo (*Leg. ad Gaium* 58): Macro, a general and high official under the Roman emperor Gaius, is accused of having boasted (according to the LCL translation) that "It is I, Macro, who made Gaius *(emon ergon Gaium)*, I am his begetter *(gegennēka)*, more or not less than his parents *(goneis)*. Not once only but thrice." Epictetus *(Diss.* 3.22.31), in turn, designates an educator as a spiritual father.

A comparison of these two derivations and explanations of the metaphorical meanings of the terms "father" and "child" leads to the following conclusion: If the OT and Jewish tradition is decisive, Paul ranks considerably lower than a mystagogue who in a mysterious way mediates new and eternal life. Then his contribution to Onesimus's present existence consists solely of the testimony he has given to God the Creator of all things and to Christ the sole mediator of salvation. Under the impulse of the Spirit, his prophetic and apostolic voice together with the wisdom of a good teacher has then contributed to making Onesimus a new man.

It is probable that Paul wrote about his spiritual fatherhood and the slave's spiritual childhood with Jewish precedents in mind. But it cannot be excluded that Gentile-born readers of his letters understood his words as an allusion to concepts used in pagan Hellenistic religion. The apostle appears to have been aware that calling Onesimus his "child" was not enough; for in the same verse he unfolds this term more broadly.

Him whom I have born in my chains [to be true to his name]: Onesimus [the Profitable] (lit. "whom I have begotten [or, born] in the chains: Onesimus"). A bushel of problems is contained in these words: the syntax of the Greek is so irregular that it defies exact reproduction in English, without paraphrastic additions.

(a) The decisive verb *gennaō* can signify "begetting" or "giving birth" or both. (b) Unless the Greek article before "chains" is ignored, it calls for a translation such as "these" or "my" chains. (c) The wordplay with the name Onesimus, which is certainly made in the next verse, probably begins already at the end of verse 10. (d) The central problem consists of whether Paul speaks here, as indeed other NT texts do, of rebirth, regeneration, and/or new creation.

Whom I have born. Because the preceding Greek noun "child" *(teknon)* has the neuter gender, punctilious Greek grammar requires the neuter relative pronoun. The replacement of "which" by the masculine "whom" will be discussed, together with other grammatical irregularities, below, at the beginning of the Note on "Onesimus," p. 337.

Regarding *egennēsa* (in our translation, "I have born"), only one thing is certain: just as the noun "child," so also this verb is here used in the metaphorical sense that is spread also among other Greek writers. Translators and expositors of PHM, ranging from the Old Syriac versions to N. R. Petersen's monograph *(Rediscovering Paul,* p. 128), almost universally agree that Paul thinks of himself as a father and that therefore the translation has to be "I have begotten," or "I fathered," or even — as an early Cotton Patch edition of Ephesians and Philemon has it — "I sired while in jail." J. B. Phillips gives Philem 10a the sound of a proud oral announcement of a baby's birth: "Yes, I have become a father though I have been under lock and key."

Still, with the words used in Philem 10b, not only a father but also a mother can notify friends of the birth of a healthy baby. In Gal 4:19-20 Paul describes himself as a mother who is "in travail" with the Galatians. A study of Paul's specific function in relation to Christians of his time can also prove relevant for the contribution made by leading later church members to the life and growth of the church.

Excursus: Inclusive Language of Procreation

In old and in modern Greek, in secular and in religious literature (including the LXX and the NT), *gennaō* signifies not only the brief moment in which a male person makes his contribution to creating a child. The verb also denotes the extended pain and labor endured by a woman when she gives birth. And sometimes, whether in the literal-physical or the metaphorical-spiritual sense, the combined creative energy of father and mother is meant.

1. *Paul the father.* In Eph 3:14-15 Paul affirms that he bows his knees "before the Father from whom each family in heaven and on earth receives its name." He recognizes the uniqueness of the heavenly Father in, e.g., the initial blessings of his letters (Philem 3; etc.) and when he emphasizes that God is addressed "Abba" (Gal 4:6; Rom 8:15). To this Father corresponds the temporal and eternal privilege of God's children. Paul's self-designation as father and of the believers whom he addresses as his children depends on his awareness of God's fatherhood and does not compete with it. Neither does it contradict or minimize the function of "Abraham our father," whose children walk in the footsteps of the patriarch's faith (Gal 3:7, 29; Rom 4:1, 12). Those among Abraham's true offspring who were born as Jews are and remain the patriarch's physical and spiritual children; those of Gentile origin enjoy full equality as adopted spiritual children.

In Matt 1:2-16a and Acts 7:8, *gennaō* signifies the physical act of begetting. The same verb denotes God's spiritual fatherhood whenever Ps 2:7 is quoted in the NT for describing Jesus Christ's unique origin and dignity. (See Acts 13:33; Heb 1:5; 5:5; and the "Western" readings of Luke 3:22.) In 1 John 5:1, *gennaō* occurs three times: God is the Father of those "believing that Jesus is the Messiah"; when they love this Father, they love his only begotten Son.

Another genealogy opposed to the line from God through Abraham and the Messiah to Paul and the Christians is offered in other passages (John 1:13; 3:6; 8:38-47; Eph 2:2; James 1:15). There the will of the flesh and of males, or the devil, the ruler of the atmosphere, or even desire and sin are described as the ancestors of all rebellious and death-bound persons.

In 1 Cor 4:14-15 Paul calls himself "father" in contrast to the influence of other religious leaders. Already in the Royal Psalm 2 (v. 7), where the emphatic Hebrew *'ani* . . . and the LXX's *egō* . . . call for a translation such as "It is I who have begotten thee," the competition of kingmakers other than Israel's God is faced. A variant reading of Philem 10 has the same emphatic *egō* and may as well be borrowed from Ps 2:7 as be dependent on the formula *ego hymas egennēsa* ("it is I who have begotten you"), which is found in 1 Cor 4:15. It cannot be demonstrated but is possible that in Philem 10 this variant contrasts Paul's spiritual fatherhood to another man's physical procreatorship. Philemon and a slave girl or woman might have been the biological parents of Onesimus (cf. "Literary, Biographical, and Contextual Issues," p. 138). If *presbytēs* in verse 9 is translated — all opposing arguments notwithstanding — "old man," then Paul in verse 10 went to the limit of boasting: not only did he defy and spite prison regulations, but by begetting a child very late in his life he also had overcome impotence. What Rom 4:19-20 and Heb 11:11-12 say about the effect of faith in the biological realm, this then Paul would use as a metaphor of his spiritual achievement. Still, in 1 Thess 2:11 Paul compares himself to a father and the Thessalonians to children — without any trace of antithetical or biological mental associations.

It is not known whether a sudden conversion took place when Onesimus visited Paul in prison or was his fellow prisoner. Probably Paul listened to the slave and spoke to him, consoled, informed, and instructed him over a period of time. The words "in the Messiah Jesus it is I who have begotten you through the gospel" (1 Cor 4:15) show about whom Paul was speaking and with whose blessing the apostle conversed with the runaway. In medieval paintings and sculptures, Jesus was conceived in the womb of Mary by the transfer of Word and Spirit from the angel into the virgin's ear. For Onesimus, baptism in the name of Christ may have been the sign confirming that the slave joined the community of other believers whom Paul also considered his children. But since in 1 Cor 1:17 the apostle asserts, "Christ did not send me to baptize but to preach the gospel," it is uncertain whether mainly or solely by his baptism Onesimus became Paul's child. If the decisive moment in Paul's and the slave's life should have been the instant when the slave began to speak in tongues, this manifestation of the Spirit might have preceded the baptism with water, or followed upon it (cf. Acts 8:12-17; 10:44-48; Gal 3:1-5). An exact method and date of Onesimus's conversion cannot be established by any interpretation of the term *gennaō*. But the creative role of the Word and the Spirit should not be disputed.

When a physical or spiritual father declares that somebody is his child, he performs an act that has great legal and moral consequences. According to the Codex Hammurabi (170-171) and the attached Sumerian Family Code, the bastard offspring of a slave owner, by being called by the master "my child(ren)," receive(s) the right and claim of inheritance. When in Ps 2:7 God pronounces publicly to Israel's king, "Today [I declare] I have begotten Thee," and when at Jesus' baptism and transfiguration such a declaration is renewed (Matt 3:7 par.; 17:5 par.), the heavenly Father declares his love and assumes full responsibility for the person addressed. Inalienable rights are bestowed on the "child" or "son." On an earthly, interhuman level, Paul does the same in favor of Onesimus. The slave receives a new legal status. Several dimensions of this status can be distinguished.

a. *The name*. The runaway slave has now a full name that includes a patronym. He can introduce himself as, and can be called by others, "Onesimus, son of Paul." So he is no longer a more or less anonymous "boy" but has his own dignity. Far from being any longer of unknown, dubious, or bad stock, he has a respectable father.

b. *The voice.* A child not yet of age was in Latin called *infans* (infant, mute, stammering, silly). For the duration of his slave status, a slave, too, had no voice but needed representation in public and before a court by a free protector if ever a grievance or a claim was to be given a hearing. In writing PHM, Paul fulfills the function of a spokesman and advocate for Onesimus, who is simultaneously his child and Philemon's slave. As soon as the slave's owner fully accepts the child status of Onesimus, the latter will be much "more than a slave" (Philem 16). As a recognized son of a free man who is also a Roman citizen, he will be entitled to lift up his voice and speak for himself.

c. *Payments.* A father is liable for damage caused by his children, a slave owner for losses inflicted on third persons through the misconduct or negligence of his slaves. Therefore, if Onesimus should be guilty of offenses, Paul offers to pay for him (vv. 18-19). On the other hand, Jewish law (Lev 25:25-28, as interpreted in rabbinic tradition; see "Social Background," sec. VIII.D, p. 50) contained a special provision: when a Hebrew had been captured by a foreigner or for other reasons had been enslaved abroad, the nearest relation was obliged to redeem the member of his family and people. God sets the precedent for true fatherhood by forcing Pharaoh to "let my son go" (Exod 4:23). In turn, as the promise of the land to Israel shows, the liberated person, be it a slave or a child, was entitled to share in the heirdom of the father and redeemer.

d. *Love.* A father bears great responsibility not only for the physical sustenance, but also for the climate in which a child grows up. Whether he loves his son or daughter is tested and revealed when he fulfills these obligations voluntarily, wisely, and gladly. Unlike Oriental, Greek, and Roman stories and laws that exemplify a father's right in extreme cases to hate or destroy his own children, the Bible proclaims God's indestructible fatherly love. This love is extended not only to Israel's king and to other individual servants of God, but also to his whole people and every member of it. God the Father in heaven shows what it means to help and be near a beloved son, whether the child be captive, in the wilderness, or in exile. Even the child's unbelief and rebellion are met with patience and pity. This father makes provisions, gives directives, soothes with consolations; he chastises with moderation because his steadfast love is never extinct. God's example is binding for earthly fathers, according to the Bible.

e. *Instruction and education.* In Israel, God's eternal and forever renewed covenant with his child Israel includes instruction given to fathers on earth: they have to tell and remind their children of the mighty deeds and gifts of God in the past, and of the directive *(Thora)* that remains valid in the present and the future. In dealing with his spiritual children, Paul acted "like a father with his children, exhorting, encouraging, and charging" the Thessalonians and "admonishing . . . his dear children" in Corinth. The apostle leaves it to his children to decide whether he shall come to them "with a rod, or with love in the spirit of gentleness" (1 Thess 2:11-12; 1 Cor 4:14-15, 21). This kind of "discipline and instruction" by parents is recommended in the *Haustafeln* (Eph 6:4; Col 3:20) as the opposite to provoking and discouraging the children.

f. *Belonging.* Whether Onesimus was originally a foundling, a bastard, a prisoner of war, or a debtor sold into slavery, as a child who owes his life to Paul he is also a child of God and of Abraham, the member of a family. Among the nations, earthly fathers can expose or forsake their children, and according to the Bible, even earthly brothers can lift their hands against their next of kin. But because Paul is the spiritual father of Onesimus, this child belongs now in a firm circle of brothers and sisters who are joined by love. Not only established church ministers such as Timothy and Titus have Paul for a father (1 Cor 4:17; cf. 1 Tim 1:2; 2 Tim 1:2; Titus 1:4). Every member in the household of God has the rank of a child of Paul, and even of a "brother" or "sister" of the apostle. They are "partners" enjoying equal rights. Philemon and the congregation assembled in his house are urged to act correspondingly (Philem 16-17).

g. *Gratitude.* Among Greeks and Romans it was considered the moral duty of a manumitted slave to support his redeemer if the latter became poor and despondent because of disease, old age, or financial loss. "Honoring father and mother," as the fifth of the Ten Commandments prescribes it, means above all caring for old parents. To those demonstrating such gratitude God will give long life. On the obligations of slaves redeemed by a relative from a foreign master, David Daube has elaborated (in his essay "Redemption," pp. 268-284, esp. 272-275): those "recovered" from slavery were bound for the rest of their lives to serve their redeemer. The ruler of Egypt was told to let God's son go "that he serve me" (Exod 4:23; etc.). While Paul abstains from giving a command to Philemon, yet in Philem 13 he intimates that he would wish Onesimus in the future to serve him in the gospel work.

So much for interpreting *gennaō* in the sense of "begetting." This time-honored understanding would be gloriously justified if only in Philem 10 Paul had followed the precedent of 1 Cor 4:15 and explicitly used the term "father." However, *gennaō* can as well denote what solely a woman can do in "giving birth."

Therefore it cannot be excluded that in Philem 10 the apostle intended to describe his *motherly* relation to the child Onesimus. While in many respects this would not make a serious difference, there are yet some distinctive implications of spiritual motherhood.

2. *Paul the mother.* "As one whom his mother comforts, so I will comfort you." These words describe in Isa 66:13 how God cares for Israel, and other OT passages confirm God's motherly nature, even his love and the many ways of his continuous help. J. Knox (*Philemon*, p. 21) translates *egennēsa* in Philem 10, "I have given birth." Above, reference was made to Gal 4:19, where Paul tells his "little children" that he is again "in travail with" them. In the NEB version of 1 Thess 2:7-8, Paul reminds the Thessalonians that "we were as gentle with you as a nurse caring fondly for her children. With such yearning love we chose to impart to you not only the gospel of God but our very selves, so dear had you become to us." Equally literal is the NJB translation, ". . . like a mother feeding . . . to share with you . . . also our own lives." According to 1 Thess 2:9, such "labor and toil, . . . working night and day" are the way a nurse or mother keeps her children free from want and trouble. No earlier than *after* these Pauline self-descriptions follow the already quoted verses 1 Thess 2:11-12, in which Paul compares himself to a father.

In the NT, the word *gennaō* denotes the mother's act of giving birth much more frequently than a man's contribution to procreation. Passive forms of this verb are frequently used in the sense of "born from a woman" (Rom 9:11; Gal 4:23, 29; Heb 11:23; Matt 1:16b; 2:1, 4; Luke 1:35; Acts 2:8; 7:20, 29; 22:3, 28; Job 3:3; 9:2, 32; 16:21), but only once (in Heb 11:12) with the meaning "begotten." Active forms seem to be preferred for the masculine act, but surprisingly often (in Gal 4:24; Luke 1:13, 57; 23:29; Acts 13:33; John 16:21) also serve to describe birth given by a mother.

Theodore Beza (*Annotationes*, p. 481) emphasizes that when Onesimus in verse 12 is called Paul's *splagchna* (lit. inter alia: "womb"; in our translation, "heart"), then a part of a mother's body provides the metaphor. As earlier mentioned, W. Estius compared Onesimus's relation to Paul with the embryo Jesus' place in the virgin Mary. Long before J. Knox, at least these two interpreters appear to have considered Paul the spiritual mother of the runaway slave. Because before, during, and after giving birth a mother provides and suffers and often rejoices more than the father, Paul's intimate relationship to Onesimus may be better expressed when *egennēsa* points out his motherly function. Revelation 12 speaks of Israel the mother who gives birth and protection to her child. In at least one regard, according to the Bible, both parents are equally responsible and efficient: they give instruction in the ways of the Lord (Prov 1:8; 6:20; etc.). In exceptional cases the mother (alone or supported by a grandmother; see Prov 31:1; 2 Tim 1:5; 3:15) can do the teaching. In the course of the church's history, e.g., the mothers of Augustine and John Wesley are shining examples. One of the reasons why the words "Outside the church — no salvation" almost attained the rank of a dogma was the conviction that whoever wants to have God as Father must have the church as mother (cf. Augustine, *Sermo* 57.2). Within the Roman Catholic Church, several types of Mariology have been developed to express and buttress the creative and saving function of the motherly church.

Paul's love and care for Onesimus loses nothing but is extolled maximally when in Philem 10 the words "child" and *gennaō* express a mother's extended physical and spiritual care, her patience, her gentleness, her suffering, and her self-giving. Then the earlier-discussed derivations of Paul's use of these terms either from mystery religions or from OT and later Jewish traditions become misleading alternatives.

And yet, if at the expense of a wise and legally relevant fatherly authority, solely a mother's endurance and emotion, sensibility and spontaneity, intuition and wisdom would be magnified, new problems can emerge. Two forms of churches have been developed over the centuries — and often they have clashed.

(a) There is an institutional type in which — by their jurisdiction, their orthodox doctrine, and their sacramental ministry — male priests determine all that is necessary for the birth and growth, the salvation and unity of church members. As a disciplined organization and founded upon Peter the Rock, the church is equated with the body of Christ and called "the pillar and bulwark of truth," as indeed is suggested by Matt 16:18-19; 1 Cor 12; Eph 1:23; 4:4, 15-16; 1 Tim 3:15; etc. (b) Opposed is another conception, in which the church and its members are understood and treated as the people of God, held together by love, compassion, and voluntary mutual subordination. Especially the Gospel and the epistles of John, but also many Pauline texts, foremost the description of the church as Christ's bride (in, e.g., 2 Cor 11:2; Eph 5:25-32), support this type. It contradicts all variations of male-dominated "church*man*ship."

Neither lexicographical evidence, nor the context, nor parallels to Philem 10 permit a one-sided decision between the first and the second interpretation and application. A combination of both seems to recommend itself as the way out of the dilemma.

3. *Father and mother. Gennaō* has a third significance: outside and inside the NT the verb can denote the combined reproductive activity of the two parents. The joined procreatorship can in fact also be described by the verbs *tiktō* and *apokyeō* (see Mark 14:21; John 3:6a; 1 Pet 2:2; 2 Pet 2:12; James 1:15, 18; also Matt 1:20?). In 2 Cor 12:14 Paul compares his rights and duties to those of "parents" *(goneis)*. Ancient literature contains examples of the same inclusiveness: In 1QH 7.20-22 the relation of a spiritual leader to his community is described by a combination of father imagery and mother imagery. According to 1QH 9.35-36, God himself "is a father for all sons of his truth" and "like a mother rejoices[?] over her baby." The earlier-mentioned boasting of General Macro, as recorded by Philo (*Leg. ad Gaium* 58), comes again to mind. In the Bible, the commandment to honor father and mother, in order to enjoy long life, gives the parents equal rights (Exod 20:12; etc.; Prov 10:1; 15:20; 17:25; Eph 6:1-3; Col 3:20).

Therefore, only an inclusive translation of Philem 10, e.g., "whom I have brought forth" or ". . . produced," might be really adequate.

For our commentary, the version "whom I have born" was given preference in order to draw attention to the ministry of a spiritual mother. This way at least a counterpoise is established against the self-overestimation of the men who have so far constituted the huge majority of church leaders and Bible interpreters.

Again, *gennaō* may yet include an entirely different sense. According to some commentaries on PHM, Paul is no less than the instrument of Onesimus's *regeneration,* namely, of his rebirth. In this case it would be irrelevant whether the apostle made his contribution in a fatherly or motherly spiritual capability. Ultimately what counts is then the result only: in Paul's presence and through his cooperation the slave became a "new creation," a "new man" (cf. Gal 6:15; 2 Cor 5:17; 1 Sam 10:6; Col 3:9-10; etc.).

4. *Rebirth?* In the NT, as in different ways in many religions and cultures, the seemingly most carnal, even the sexual sphere and its physiological manifestations, sometimes provide the imagery for describing events that can only be caused and shaped by a power far superior to an earthly male's and female's biological and spiritual capabilities. According to the Lukan and Matthean accounts of Jesus' nativity, that is, of the miracle of Christmas, the divine and the human realms more than only touch upon one another. Elsewhere, too, verbs and nouns signifying generation and birth are used to describe the miraculous events through which Jews and Gentiles received "the right *(exousia)* to become children of God." Many passages speak of "regeneration" and "rebirth" (John 1:12-13; 3:3, 5-8; 1 John 2:29; 3:19; 4:7; 5:1, 4, 18; 1 Pet 1:3, 23-25; James 1:18; Titus 3:5; cf. Matt 19:28. In *TDNT,* 1.666-675, K. H. Rengstorf and F. Buechsel discuss the pertinent texts).

According to the NT witnesses, the resurrection of Christ, the gift and work of the Spirit, and/or the preached word of God are the means by which the new life is given. In 1 Cor 4:15 Paul states that his own spiritual fatherhood is due to Jesus Christ and the gospel. In Rom 1:16 he calls the good news proclaimed by him, "the power of God for salvation to every one who has faith, to the Jew first and also to the Greek." As mentioned above, the apostle thanks God in 1 Thess 2:13 for the fact that the Thessalonians have received his sermon "not as the word of men but as what it really is, the word of God, which is at work in you believers." Paul's proclamation is verified and becomes effective by the Spirit and the power of God (Gal 3:3-5; 1 Cor 2:4-5, 13; etc.).

Foremost the words "born of water and the Spirit" (John 3:5) and the mention of "the water of rebirth and the renewing power of the Holy Spirit" (Titus 3:5 NEB) have been quoted, since the days of the church fathers to the present, to consider baptism the means and the moment of regeneration. Widely diverging exegetes of PHM, among them John Calvin and W. Estius, J. Knox (*Philemon*, p. 21) and P. Stuhlmacher, have therefore assumed that Paul became Onesimus's spiritual father and that Onesimus was regenerated and reborn because and when the apostle *baptized* the slave. But Paul's categorical denial of having been sent to baptize, together with the absence of a mention of baptism when he calls the Corinthians his children (1 Cor 1:17; 4:14-15), contradicts this assumption. Even if Paul himself had baptized Onesimus — as indeed in Corinth he had baptized "the house of Stephanas" (1 Cor 1:16) — it is most unlikely that by saying "I have born Onesimus" he presumed to have taken the place of God. For God alone could say to Israel's king, "Today, it is I who have begotten thee," or could make of Saul "a new man" (Ps 2:7; 1 Sam 10:6). Actually the apostle esteems himself and others no higher than as handymen and cooperators of God. He is but an agent of the creative Word of God, and of the power of the Holy Spirit. Therefore he claims as little as any other of Christ's first witnesses to fulfill the function that the Holy Spirit has in the nativity of Jesus, and that the "imperishable . . . seed" of the "Word of the living God" has in the regeneration of Jews and Gentiles (cf. Matt 1; Luke 1; Acts 1:3, 23; James 1:18; 1 Pet 1:23). When Paul speaks of the creation of the "new man" out of the "old," he never attributes to himself the power, skill, and effect of this transformation (cf. 1 Cor 15:22, 45-49; Eph 4:22-24; Col 3:9-11).

Instead of baptism, not only evangelical and pietistic interpreters (as mentioned in, e.g., "Literary, Biographical, and Contextual Issues," sec. VIII) place conversion, i.e., personal acceptance of Christ as Lord and Savior, in the foreground. The words "my child whom I have born" express then the miracle of personal conversion. This opinion can affect the interpretation of the whole of PHM. For it entails that neither a high-church emphasis on sacraments nor a social gospel or liberation theology can really be the source and standard of such a social change as God has in mind regarding the relationship between Philemon and Onesimus. Only rebirth by personal conversion counts in this case: Paul — a reborn Christian for many years; Onesimus — recently born anew; Philemon — expected to live up to his rebirth! Thus personal regeneration is declared the means and the presupposition of the brotherhood that in the house of the slave owner shall replace the crooked institution of slavery. However, it has been shown above (foremost in the "Literary Issues," sec. VI.C, pp. 141-150) that the text of PHM offers little or no evidence of Onesimus's sin, confession of guilt, later virtue, and other elements of personal conversion. The terms "rebirth" and "regeneration," in the sense they have in traditional church parlance, are therefore unfitting to describe Paul's relation to Onesimus.

From the text of PHM and the gist of the excursus on the language of procreation, only one thing can be safely concluded: Onesimus has become a disciple and very close friend of Paul. The apostle has given the slave a name and a voice; as only a father can do, he secures for Onesimus legal standing in society. And just as a mother does, so Paul shows his love by continuous care for the spiritual and physical well-being of the slave.

In my chains. Beginning with Vg. and resumed recently by, e.g., E. Lohse and P. Stuhlmacher, the Greek words *en tois desmois* seem to be adequately enough translated "in fetters" or "in prison." Not only the letter written to Philemon but also the "child" who is now sent back to the owner stems from a man who is held captive by the Romans. Paul's missionary and pastoral activity is not frustrated by physical impediments. On the contrary, the imprisonment has proven counterproductive. The evil endured by the apostle has really served to advance the gospel (Phil 1:12-14). As earlier stated, this is evidence for "strength in weakness" (2 Cor 12:9-10). The affirmation that, of all places, Paul has become father and mother in a prison may evoke admiration for the apostle, and perhaps even a smile on the face of every reader of PHM. In turn, a special light falls also upon Onesimus: because he was, as it were, hatched in prison, he may well be considered a jailbird for the length of his life. Exactly such a relation to chains is what Paul has in mind for Onesimus's future: may he help Paul spread the good news "in the chains of the gospel" (v. 13)!

However, the chains or prison of which Paul writes in Philem 10 consists not only of the irons, the wooden block, the stony walls fabricated by the Romans, and not only of the physical restrictions and sufferings inflicted on the body and mind of the captive. The Greek formulation contains the definite article and need therefore be literally translated, "in these chains" or "in my chains." NEB has "in this prison"; NJB, "while wearing these chains." Other passages (Phil 1:7, 13-14, 17; Col 4:18; cf. variants of Philem 10 and of Heb 10:34) speak explicitly of "my chains." Therefore the translation "my chains" deserves preference.

What RSV renders "my imprisonment" denotes indeed a distinctive kind of captivity that is not shared by all and sundry of the inmates of Paul's Roman prison. Already in Philem 1 and 9 Paul has declared himself a "prisoner of the Messiah Jesus." Above, in the exposition of these words, it was shown that Paul considered it a joy and honor to suffer physical imprisonment for the sake of Christ and the gospel. Regarding Onesimus, in the depths of his heart, the apostle hopes for a similar future.

[To be true to his name]: Onesimus [The Profitable]. The paraphrastic additions to the Greek text are necessary because of the peculiar grammar and syntax of the original text. In at least three ways Paul appears to deviate from normal Greek diction — probably in order to squeeze a maximum of meaning into a minimal number of words.

1. No problem would exist for a simple word-by-word translation if only the name "Onesimus" were placed immediately behind the term "child." Indeed, several modern versions choose an easy way out of the existing problem: they correct the seeming misplacement of the proper name by translating "of my child Onesimus whom. . . ." While this interpretation is smooth and makes good sense, it yet obliterates two facts: (a) In the Greek text the accusative case of the name *(Onēsimon)* does not fit the genitive case of "my own child" *(tou emou teknou)*. (b) The position of the name at the end of the whole verse gives it exceptional, not only incidental, weight.

2. To repeat an observation made earlier: punctilious grammar and syntax would require the relative pronoun at the beginning of verse 10b to have the neuter gender of the preceding Greek noun "child" *(teknon)*. But instead of *ho*, Paul has chosen the masculine "whom" *(hon)*, which fits the accusative of the male name, *Onēsimon*.

3. The verb *gennaō* (to beget, to bear) has two objects: "him whom" *(hon)* the apostle has procreated, and the name Onesimus. The second object is an attribute to the first: it reveals the identity and quality of the person of "whom" Paul will speak in the following. Linguistic parallels to such double accusative objects are found in, e.g., Gen 1:27: "God created them male and female," and in Mark 6:16: "whom I have beheaded: [him,] John." Analogous double objects are found in the Greek text of Philem 12, 15-16, and 17: (lit.) "whom I have sent back to you, him that is my own womb . . . that you have him back forever, no longer as a slave but much better than a slave: as a dear brother. . . . Receive him as me." The doubled accusatives (first to denote the proper object, then its attribute) correspond to good grammar and syntax, but are to be distinguished from the more widespread "attraction of the relative pronoun" (as found in, e.g., 2 Cor 1:4, 6; Eph 1:6; 4:1; cf. Luke 1:20; BDF, 294). If in Philem 10b that attraction were made, the pronoun would have the genitive form *hou* ("of whom," dependent on the genitive "of my child" in v. 10a).

In a singular way, J. Knox (*Philemon,* p. 21) has not only drawn attention to these puzzling elements but has also proposed an interpretation that does justice to the complex sentence structure. As shown by, e.g., Suetonius (*Galba* 13) and a Jewish tomb inscription (*CIJ* 761, mentioned by F. F. Bruce, p. 201), the adjective *onēsimos* was not only used for a slave but had eventually become the proper name also of free male and female persons. In Philem 10, i.e., even before the explicit mention of the contrast useless/useful in verse 11, Paul engages in a wordplay on this name. As if to say, *nomen est omen* (the name is a presage of the character), already in verse 10 the apostle indicates what kind of person he calls his child and sends back to Philemon. Knox explains the puzzling pronoun *auton* (him) in verse 12 by speaking of a "new Onesimus — Onesimus really himself." For before and during his flight this man was a living contradiction to the name that most likely he had been given by his master. Now Paul declares the slave a new person. Not to perceive this sense of Philem 10 means, according to Knox, "to miss the whole point."

Already Erasmus had drawn attention to the play on words. His observation that *onēsimos* is a synonym of *euchrēstos* (useful) in verse 11 was later almost generally endorsed. But W. Estius refused to believe that *euchrēstos* alluded to *onēsimos;* he pointed out that the idea of "profiting" emerges no earlier than in verse 20 and that no church fathers had spoken of a play on words. Still, it is probable that solely J. Knox's interpretation takes full account of the literary idiosyncrasies of the Greek text. Lest readers not acquainted with Greek miss what Knox calls a "pun" on the slave's name, in our translation the words "to be true to his name" and "The Profitable" have been added.

Who was this Onesimus? The few things known from the contents of PHM and from Col 4:9, and some of the many things unknown of this man, have been listed above (in "Literary Issues," sec. VI.C, pp. 141-150). A summary suffices at this place: He was a slave of Philemon, but it remains hidden whether he had been a war captive, bought, or house-born, and whether he was his master's only slave. He had been considered useless to and by his owner — a fact that does not demonstrate that, corresponding to the contemporary image of a Phrygian slave, he had a wicked character, was and had been lazy, impertinent, and rebellious. He may have been able to listen and to speak carefully, probably also to read and write. Therefore he may have possessed secretarial skills that, after being ignored by his earthly master, yet recommended him among other things to Paul as a possible future assistant. He had run away from Philemon, but it is unknown whether he really stole cash or valuables, for instance, in order to finance his flight. He found his way to the imprisoned Paul, but what he endured during his flight, whether he regretted his escape and hoped that Paul would intercede for him, is unknown. By the apostle he was sent back to his master, in the company of the free man Tychicus and with a warm letter of recommendation. Still, what became of him (a free man? a cooperator of Paul? bishop of Ephesus? collector and editor of Paul's letters?) cannot be safely established.

VERSE 11

In the past, he has been useless to you, but now he is useful to you and especially to me.

Taking his cue from the etymological sense "Onesimus," Paul admits that his protégé's name had been a misnomer because only now had it become a fitting designation. In the Greek original, verse 11 is no more than an appendix to verse 10 (lit. ". . . Onesimus, the former useless . . . but now . . . useful"). The independent clause chosen for our translation and the addition of the verbs "has been" and "is" underline an easily overlooked fact: only in verse 11 is the slave treated as a person in his own right, forming the subject of a sentence. In the subsequent verses he is an object. More explicitly he is the grammatical subject in Col 4:9. There this "faithful and dear brother" is charged and enabled, together with Tychicus, to carry a letter to Colossae and to give information of Paul's present condition. However, also in PHM, as a child of Paul, he has the right and dignity to be received as a "brother" and "partner" (vv. 16-17).

Useless . . . useful (achrēstos . . . euchrēstos). In classical Greek philosophy, potentiality precedes actuality. Verbal adjectives, as they are used in Philem 11, express basically a possibility or necessity rather than an accomplished fact. E.g., *agapētos, eklektos, didaktos, gnōstos, eulogētos* signify "lovable," "eligible," "teachable," "knowable," "praiseworthy." Still, already in classical times, and then increasingly in Hellenistic Greek, such verbal adjectives are used as replacements of aorist or perfect passive participles. Then they mean "beloved," "chosen," "taught," "known," "blessed." Some of them hide or lose completely the dynamic power of the underlying verb and become in fact adjectives, e.g., "dear," "elect," and "known." When this is the case, the addition of qualifying prefixes such as *a, dys,* or *en* (BDF, 65.3; 112; 117.1) is possible or necessary. The *agnōstos theos* of Acts 17:23 is the unknown or the ignored God — obviously not the God who *cannot* be known. Literally, *achrēstos* might mean that Onesimus "has not been used." But Paul means to say that he once had been "use*less*" and/or was despised and treated as such. So also in Philem 11, *euchrēstos* denotes the slave's present "useful" function rather than *chrēstos,* which might be understood to mean "used."

To be *achrēstos* is in Greek literature equivalent to being "bad," "wicked," "shameful," "painful" *(kakos, ponēros, aischros, lypros).* Just as *anonētos* (from the stem *onaimi,* cf. Philem 20) and the older form *achreios* (derived from *chraomai,* "to use"), this adjective denotes something or someone as worthless. Implied is the notion of "superfluous" *(perisson),* and sometimes the intention of blunt moral condemnation (see, e.g., Demosthenes, *Or. Phil.* 3.40; Ps.-Phocylides 37 [34]; Diognetus 4.2). In a parable Jesus describes the fate of such a "useless" servant: he is thrown into outer darkness. According to Luke 17:10, even those Christians who have done what they owed their master are to call themselves "useless." Epictetus (*Diss.* 1.19.19, 22) tells of a slave whose history in some regard resembles Onesimus's: he was employed for making shoes, was considered worthless for that task, and was therefore sold; then he became shoemaker at the emperor's court and was paid respect even by his former owner. What G. F. Moore (*Judaism,* 2.138) writes of hired servants may apply to the treatment of slaves too: "Men could not be set at women's work, nor women at men's, and when any special skill was required, the servant did that one thing and did not expect to be generally useful."

The opposite of "useless" is, in older and younger Greek literature, inter alia *chrēstos, euchrēstos, chrēsimos* ("useful," "good for use," "serviceable"; see, e.g., Plato, *Plt.* 3.411a; Josephus, *Ant.* 22.61; Hermas, *Vis.* 3.6.1, 5-7; *Man.* 5.1.6; *Sim.* 9.24.4). In 2 Tim 4:11 Mark is called "useful for service" at the apostle's side, and in the same letter (2:20-21) each church member is admonished to cleanse himself or herself from the soiling influence of heresy and heretics: in God's "great house" a Christian shall be a "vessel . . . for noble use *(skeuos eis timēn)*, sanctified and useful for the master, prepared for each good work." Still, there is also a warmer terminology: highest praise is expressed by the address, "You good and faithful servant" (Matt 25:21, 23). In his discussion of a slave's loyalty ("Sklaventreue"; see n. 31 to "Social Background," pp. 13-14), J. Vogt mentions tombstones erected by masters in honor of faithful slaves. In Col 4:9 Paul describes the slave Onesimus as "faithful and dear brother," rather than using the term "useful."

Ever since church fathers began to write scholarly interpretations of PHM, and still at the present time, the contrast made by Paul between Onesimus's former uselessness and his later usefulness has given occasion for vilifying and besmirching the slave's former character and conduct. The conviction is widespread that after continuously proving inept and careless, lazy and unprofitable in his daily work, this bad man had plotted his escape, had made provisions for it by theft, and had finally succeeded in running away. Together with verse 11, verses 15-17, 18-19 were exploited for material suitable to the fabrication of this image. In addition, Onesimus's former moral depravity was given a theological crown: it was called "sin." In turn, it has been held that this sin was no earlier overcome than after the slave's contact with a holy man, his repentance, his oral confession, the proclamation of forgiveness, possible works of satisfaction, and finally through reconciliation with the offended party.

Indeed, Pliny the Younger's letters to Sabinianus (see "Social Background," Annotation 4, pp. 86-87) speak extensively of the repentance and tears of a runaway man and contain many other heartwarming elements. Whether known or not to expositors of PHM, the substance of these letters seemed to supplement what in PHM is covered with the mantle of silence. Especially Luther (in his PHM commentary of 1527), Calvin (esp. on v. 16), J. B. Lightfoot, and pietistic interpreters of PHM have lustily elaborated on Onesimus's sin, wickedness, and obstinacy. Luther offers the boldest exposition: when Paul confesses Onesimus's sin, he boasts of the fact that out of one single evil a double good, and out of one single injustice a double justice, have been produced, in relation to both God and Paul. In analogy to Augustine's idea of a *felix culpa* (a guilt paving the way to salvation), Luther speaks of the *felix fuga* (the salutary flight) of Onesimus and alludes to the central theme of Paul (in Rom 1:18–5:21; Gal 2:15–3:29; Phil 3:6-16): the justification of the sinner by God's sheer grace. Thus Luther discovered in PHM the core of Paul's and the Reformers' message.

It is still possible that by contrasting Onesimus's present usefulness with his past uselessness Paul had something else in mind than the moral distinction between good and bad, or the theological difference between justification and condemnation by God. Philemon 11 might have a more subtle meaning than "This bad man Onesimus has now become a good boy," and a more specific sense than "Just as every Christian, so Onesimus has been saved by grace and faith alone." Thomas Aquinas does not refrain from speaking of the slave's "sin," but he observes that by choosing the term "useless" the apostle "speaks lightly of the guilt" incurred by Onesimus. G. Theissen (*Studien zur Soziologie des Urchristentums* [1979], p. 15) has the "impression that Philemon was not all too much damaged by the runaway slave." The liberation theologian J. Comblin (on p. 89 of his commentary on Colossians and Philemon, as described in "Literary Issues," sec. VIII.B.2, pp. 221-222) goes even further. He observes that the usefulness of a slave can never be "true utility." He implies that freedom is the presupposition of true usefulness and that Onesimus's former uselessness and his final escape do not make him ultimately sinful and guilty. In consequence, repentance and forgiveness would not be the prime requirement of an economically and socially exploited person who takes action aiming at liberation.

Common to the last-mentioned interpretations is the intention to reduce the general validity and applicability of the criterion "either useless — or useful." Such expositions, if they be true to the text of PHM at all, liberate Paul from suspicions or accusations such as the following: (a) In verse 11 the apostle pretends to utter God's ultimate judgment on the slave; and by sending him back (v. 12) he executes, at least on a temporary level, even that judgment. (b) Paul imposes on Onesimus's life history a black-and-white scheme. In, e.g., Paul's, Augustine's, Luther's, John Wesley's, and John Mott's *auto*biographical utterances, the use of crying contrast-colors for the description of the difference between the wicked past and the present blessed state is essential, deeply moving, and may even be convincing. But in Philem 11 Paul offers such a binary description not of himself but of a human companion who had been nothing but a poor slave. (c) Notwithstanding his parental concern and cordial intercession for Onesimus, Paul passes a general judgment on the slave without ever mentioning any early personal, specific, and subjective conditions and developments of the formerly useless man. (d) The apostle adopts the criteria of a classical slave owner for whom the servant is equivalent to an animated instrument or stands near a head of cattle that by its usefulness has at least to repay the investment made in its acquisition and maintenance. Naked utilitarianism appears to dominate Paul's own thought, and to be recommended to Philemon.

The earlier-mentioned works of F. Overbeck, A. B. Cleage, G. Kehnscherper, S. Schulz and the polemics directed against the supposedly archconservative and patriarchal apostle by some representatives of the women's liberation movement give expression to such complaints and condemnations. And yet, as soon as the contrast between useless and useful is subjected to closer examination, Philem 11 can also be read and understood in a less malevolent way:

Just as other Christians, Onesimus is called (in Philem 10) Paul's child. When the slave fled from his master, when he met Paul, and when he was sent back to his master, he was probably a young man, about twenty years old. According to psychological and pedagogical terminology (see, e.g., E. H. Erikson, *Childhood and Society* [1956], chap. III 7 [German trans., 1957, pp. 228-487]), he was a young adult, having outgrown the period of adolescence, but had not yet attained the creativity of a so-called mature man. Perhaps as a child Onesimus may have been expected and compelled, or may have attempted of his own will, to be of some use to others, and thereby to live up to his name. But eventually he proved to be, or at least was called, a useless person, a hopeless scoundrel, or a good-for-nothing. His self-awareness and self-esteem, the conscious formation of his identity, will have developed correspondingly. It is not known whether his flight was provoked by ever-growing inferiority complexes or in a moment of simple despair; it may have been a desperate attempt to save his self-respect and to find a useful place in contemporary society.

By describing the history and character of the slave as the way from uselessness to usefulness, Paul hardly intended to apply to and impose on the slave an inhuman and utterly unkind value system. Rather, in Philem 11 Paul did more than express the place and function of Onesimus in his environment and in the value judgment of a slave owner. He summed up crisply what the slave may have gladly heard said, by a person he respected. Verse 11 of the letter Onesimus was to hand to his master could reflect and confirm the slave's newly enhanced self-esteem.

The talk of "useless" and "useful" is then far from revealing a lack of love or complete personal acceptance. When a child, beginning with kindergarten, is incessantly urged and pressed to fit into the existing society, to perform and to produce what is expected of him or her, to be profit bearing and to serve as a cogwheel in a machine, then the child's potential or actual usefulness is distorted and misused. Paul, however, speaks out of his obvious love for his child. There is a usefulness that makes a person want to be accepted, to have a home and to be at home, and even to have a place in the world at large. Unemployed or unwillingly retired persons suffer from being or feeling useless. By being called useful, the person of Onesimus is neither wronged nor disrespected but highly rewarded and honored. Paul himself does not reveal any details of Onesimus's inner life. But in the following, he hints at the range of both Onesimus's inutility and profitability.

To you . . . to you and especially to me. Regarding lacking profitability, Philemon is solely noted as the party suffering damage. Verse 11 does not entitle the reader of PHM to declare the slave a bad man and sinner in every regard. The confession made to his father by the prodigal son, "I have sinned against heaven and before thee" (Luke 15:18, 21), has no equivalent in Paul's plea for Onesimus. As a slave, before his flight, Onesimus may have been a "useful" friend to fellow slaves and other persons in need — as was indeed the unjust steward to other dependent persons in Jesus' parable (Luke 16:1-9). During his flight, if he temporarily joined a robber gang, Onesimus may have been useful in contributing to the group's survival. Probably he also was never useless to Paul.

According to S. Winter's theory, Onesimus was sent out to Paul with gifts of the Colossian congregation. According to F. F. Bruce, he overstayed a legitimate leave of absence (see "Literary Issues," Annotation 3, pp. 227-228). These guesses would then only be well founded if Onesimus had been considered useful at least by the congregation in Colossae long before he met Paul. Then not even the possible damage suffered by the slave's owner could be serious: Philemon would not have been frustrated by the slave's consistently poor work before his flight, but solely by the loss of Onesimus's working power during his absence from Colossae and his stay with Paul. But Philem 10 shows clearly that Onesimus did not become a Christian before leaving Philemon's home, and the slave proved to be a "faithful and dear brother" no earlier than in Paul's company (Col 4:9). Therefore these theories are not convincing.

Onesimus's recently demonstrated use*fulness* pertains, according to Philem 11, to both Philemon and Paul. It also could be recognized by the first readers of Colossians. The slave was entrusted, together with Tychicus, with the assignment to bring the letter to the Colossians to the proper address and to inform of Paul's situation (Col 4:9). Obviously the already experienced utility of the man is expected to be extended into the future.

The ancient MSS of PHM describe Paul's and Philemon's share in the benefit from Onesimus's present and future service in slightly different ways. Crucial is the sense and the use of the little word *kai*. It can have the sense of "and" (when repeated: "both . . . and") or can mean "even, also, just." Some MSS of Philem 11 have *kai* twice, before and after *soi* (to you); they must be translated ". . . now useful both to you and to me." The returning slave is then declared equally useful to his earthly master as to his spiritual father. Still, a no less important and reliable other group of MSS omits the first *kai* and thus makes Paul the main beneficiary of Onesimus's usefulness. Recent interpreters of PHM such as J. Gnilka and H. Binder contradict one another in their preference for either one of the variants. The Nestle-Aland and Greek New Testament editions attribute to the first *kai* in Philem 11 "dubious textual validity."

Three arguments favor the variant that omits the first *kai*.

1. All Greek texts posit "to you" before "to me." This "exceptional order" contradicts "common Greek usage [where] the first person would naturally precede the second," according to J. B. Lightfoot. Indeed, the sequence *ti emoi kai soi* (in John 2:4 RSV translated, "What have you to do with me?" while in Greek the personal pronouns follow one another in the reverse order) would look more normal, and the Vg. version of Philem 11, *mihi et tibi* (to me and to you), restitutes the usual arrangement. Lightfoot concludes from Paul's extraordinary diction that the words *kai emoi* (and to me) express "an afterthought" (comparable to Phil 2:27, "God had mercy on him, and not only on him but on me also"). However, because in Greek sentences the most emphatical element is often posed at the end, Paul's explicit concern with his own benefit sounds like more than an irrelevant corollary.

2. In Philem 16 Paul tells Philemon to accept the slave as a brother, (lit.) "dear . . . most of all to me and how much more to you." It is hard to imagine how there can be "much more" than "most of all," but is it obvious that with his love for Onesimus Paul goes ahead of the love expected from Philemon? Relevant is also another parallel: as just cited, in Phil 2:27 the apostle writes, "God had mercy upon him [Epaphroditus, who had fallen ill and was near death], and not only on him but on me also, lest I should have sorrow upon sorrow." Certainly the danger in which Paul's helper was and the salvation of the patient through God's compassion were not belittled. But in the end, Paul's own gain by the healing of his friend is clearly emphasized.

3. Decisive is Philem 13. There Paul distinctly expresses his conviction and hope that "by serving me in the chains of the gospel" Onesimus would be better employed than if Philemon retained him for domestic work in the Colossian house.

Our translation, "useful to you and especially to me," does not hide Paul's self-interest behind a facade of altruism. In verse 17 Paul speaks of a partnership between himself and Philemon that seems to exclude superior interests of one of the associates. But in verse 20 Paul admits bluntly that he expects to "take advantage" of the slave's legal owner. Certainly the apostle does not intend to leave Philemon empty-handed or damaged in his interests. Rather Paul is convinced that by letting Onesimus work full-time in the service of the gospel, the slave's master will benefit too. For this master owes himself (supposedly for the length of his life) to Paul (v. 19), and the apostle is magnanimous enough to accept the useful Onesimus as a substitute for the service owed by Philemon (v. 13)! The transfer of the slave to Paul would mean more than only a moratorium for the repayment of Philemon's debt.

H. Binder deems it impossible that Onesimus could ever be useful at the same time to two persons living as far apart as the apostle and the slave's owner. He proposes to interpret the words "useful to you and to me" by speaking of utility demonstrated by "serving the church." This interpretation obfuscates the strictly personal triangular relationship between the captive apostle, the rights and duties of the slave owner, and the runaway and now returning slave.

In the past . . . but now. While in verse 9b *nyni* means "yet," in verse 11 the same word has the strictly temporal significance "now." This is always the case when, as in Philem 11, the enclitic *pote* (once upon a time) or the more precise *tote* (then, at that past or future time) is used as contrast. "Then" and "now" can be as radically mutually exclusive as either and or, black and white, evil and good, perishing and everlasting.

In Philem 11, the division line between the two is not explicitly mentioned. But what is not recorded by Paul, and is lacking in the text, has been substituted by some interpreters. If Paul had anything specific in mind, it certainly would have been a specific event rather than something abstract that would hover above or beyond specific historical occurrences and experiences.

One daring exegesis seeks to remain as close to the wording of the text as possible: reference is made to a matter of pronunciation. To Greeks and Romans of Paul's time, the word spelled *christos* (anointed) sounded the same as *chrēstos* (useful, serviceable, worthy, good, benign). For in oral communication, the Greek letters *iota* and *eta* ("i" and "ē") were hardly or not at all distinguishable. In consequence, in the first half of the second century, the Roman historiographer Suetonius (*Claudius* 25) writes that, instigated by a certain *Chrestus,* Jews continuously caused riots and were for this reason expelled from the city of Rome. Later in the same century, two Christian apologists (Theophilus of Antioch, *Ad Autolycum* 1.12, and Justin Martyr, *Apol.* 1.4.1, 4-5) stated that "the Christian *(to christon)* is sweet and useful and not to be ridiculed," and "the name of which we are accused" is "in reality the kindest *(chrēstotaton)*." For this reason, since F. C. Baur (*Paulus,* 1st ed. [1845], p. 478) to the present (e.g., S. Winter, "Paul's Letter to Philemon," pp. 4-5), some expositors have guessed that a second play of words is made in Philem 11: as in the past Onesimus was *achristos* (i.e., not yet a Christian), he was "useless"; now that he has become a Christian, he is "useful."

These authors have yet to produce evidence that *achristos* was ever used to denote a non-Christian, and that the word *euchristos* ever described a disciple of Christ, not to mention "a good Christian" or "very much of a Christian." As early as the third and fourth centuries, Tertullian (*Apol.* 3.5) and Lactantius (*Div. inst.* 4.7) denounced the replacement of *christos* by *chrēstos* as a plain error. Equally radical is J. B. Lightfoot's rejection of the alleged second play on words in Philem 11.

Together with a considerable number of other expositors, P. Stuhlmacher affirms that the slave's past and present are "separated by the event of conversion." Emphatic descriptions of the need, the character, and the effects of personal conversion are indeed widespread in Christian literature and appear in PHM commentaries as soon as an author engages in heartwarming embellishments. As earlier observed, the stories of the prodigal son and the accounts of Paul's conversion (Luke 15:11-32; Gal 1:13-16; 1 Cor 15:9-11; Phil 3:4-14; Eph 3:8; Acts 9; 22; 26) offer rich details and biblical precedents of the nature and consequence of this great event. But since neither repentance nor confession, neither forgiveness nor reconciliation or other elements vital for conversion are ever mentioned in PHM, it is doubtful whether the gap left open in this letter must be filled by the talk of personal conversion. In other parts of the NT, other moments and means of change from an evil past to a good present stand in the foreground. What happened and what was experienced in perhaps one hour, one day, or in a more extended span of time in an individual's life, may well be insufficient to cause the dramatic transition from the past to the present of which Paul speaks in Philem 11. Can the wider context throw light on a puzzle contained in this verse?

Excursus: The End of the Past and the Beginning of the Present, as Door to the Future

In Plato's books, events that have occurred at a specific time, except the death of Socrates and the experiences of the philosopher in Syracuse, do not play a major role. Aristotle discusses in his *Physics* (4.11.220a–6.6.237b) the interdependence of time, spatial motion, change, and measuring by numbers. Solely the eternal is not subject to changes conditioned by time. By the "now," time is both continued and divided. "Now" is a mathematical point that marks an end and a beginning, but is a fleeting and escaping moment, unable ever to be an absolute first (237b). Whatever is being changed now, was of necessity also subjected to change earlier (237a). A pessimistic vein comes to the surface when Aristotle quotes proverbs such as "time wastes things away" and "all things grow old through time." He concludes that "time is by its nature the cause . . . of decay . . . the condition of destruction rather than of coming into being" (221a; 222b). In analogy, Greek tragedies convey the message that a prediction or a curse can provoke a black fate and loom over the present, leaving no room for a better future. And when anywhere a golden age is mentioned as the background of later history, it is depicted as irretrievably past. Opposed to such views are those Stoics (G. Staehlin, article *nyn* in *TDNT*, 4.1106-1123, refers to H. von Armin, *Stoicorum Veterum Fragmenta* [Leipzig: Teubner, vol. 1, 1903, ##509; vol. 2, 190ff.) who assert that only the present has true being while the past exists no longer, and the future is not yet.

In the whole Bible, with the exception of part of the Wisdom Literature, time and history in general, and specific events in particular, are of singular importance. God's own nature and name are revealed by the events he creates. Whenever God reveals himself (e.g., to the patriarchs, to Moses, on Sinai, in the Holy Land, and in the exile), he announces and initiates extended time periods. They are embedded in the midst of the history of the nations, and they establish the identity of Israel together with the way and the mission of this people. Narration and announcement of events, rather than speculation, deduction, induction, and definitions, are the biblical way of speaking of God and his relation to Israel and the nations, to individuals and all creatures. Occasionally, in the OT as much as in nonbiblical literature, the evil present is nostalgically compared with the good old days, or the hope is expressed that the last things will be like the first.

"In the NT, however, the *nyn* [now] shines out with radiant splendor as compared with the *tote* [in the past]," as G. Staehlin observes (*TDNT,* 4.1116). The "now" not only opens the door to a future that is better than the miseries endured in the past. It also surpasses the blessings granted to earlier generations. What is given "now" anticipates eternal salvation and life (Rom 5:9-11; 2 Cor 6:2; Luke 4:19, 21; 1 Tim 3:2; 4:8; John 12:10-11; 16:5; 17:5, 13; etc.). It is exceptional for Paul to say "as always, so now" (Phil 1:20), and solely in typological OT interpretations (as in Gal 4:29; Heb 12:26; 1 Pet 3:21) does the present correspond to the past.

The now, even the new time that terminates the misery of the past and introduces future blessings, has an extended duration. As especially Oscar Cullmann has emphasized in almost all of his books, there exists a tension between "already" and "not yet" fulfilled eschatology. According to Paul Minear ("Time of Hope," pp. 337-361), the old and the new aeons are overlapping. The old is so weakened and defeated that — despite its surviving manifestations — it can only recede and vanish more and more in the past, while the new proves its victory by being consistently coming.

In several letters Paul unfolds distinctly by which events the past time is brought to an end and the new aeon is created. He speaks in three ways of the means by which the transition and change from old to new have been and are being effected:

1. A unique act of God, even the sending and coming of Jesus Christ and the Spirit, begins the new time at which all times, all promises, and all hopes are fulfilled (Gal 4:4-6; Eph 1:10, 13-14). The coming, the death, and the resurrection of Christ constitute the turning point from the past to the "now." Now sinners are once for good and all justified and sanctified, redeemed and reconciled by grace alone, even in "Christ" (1 Cor 1:30; etc.). According to, e.g., A. Nygren's *Commentary on Romans,* the central theological message of that epistle consists in the distinction between the old and the new aeons. Sin, the Law, and death have ruled the first, "but now" (Rom 3:21; etc.) God's saving righteousness has been revealed. Indeed, according to Paul, the temporal difference is but a signal of a glorious qualitative superiority of the "new covenant" (cf. 2 Cor 3:7-11). Now Jews and Gentiles who, each in their own ways, had been dead in trespasses and sins are redeemed, raised, and united to be free children of God (Gal 3–4; Rom 3:21–5:21; 11:30-31; Eph 2:1-7, 11-22; etc.). According to Paul, what has happened now does not reveal a change in God; for in all eternity it has been God's will, "in Christ," to love Gentiles as much as the Jews. But only now this secret *(mystērion)* has been revealed through the Spirit (Eph 1:4-14; 3:5-6; Col 1:26-27; cf. Rom 16:26).

Not only human beings are affected and changed by the grace and power manifested now. In and by and for Christ, also principalities and powers (i.e., invisible structures and institutions of creaturely existence) and *all things* that resist, prevent, or deny salvation have been and will be subjugated to the crucified and risen Christ's feet (Rom 8:31-39; 1 Cor 15:23-28; Eph 1:10, 19-23; 4:8-10; Col 1:15-20).

The dividing line or turning point between the old and bad past and the blessings of the good present is therefore a cosmic event and has quasi-objective character. It evokes a human response but is not fabricated by human potential or personal experience. Rather, while humanity was still sinful and inimical toward God and scandalously divided in hostile groups, Christ has died and has been raised for the sinners (Rom 5:6-10; 2 Cor 5:14-15; Eph 2:11-19). And while invisible and intangible powers were engaged in rebellion and in unjust and pernicious deeds, God has already enthroned his Son high above them (Phil 2:10-11; Eph 1:19-22; cf. Heb 2:5-9).

In Philem 11, no explicit reference is made to God's cosmic work of salvation, even to the redemption from the dominion of sin and death and other oppressive powers. But Paul can presuppose that, as a member of the Colossian congregation, Philemon has heard and is aware of the christological and soteriological substance of Col 1–3. Eight times the name of Christ occurs in PHM, and each mention can remind the slave owner of him who holds the whole world in his hands and has interfered in history in order to let the past be past and create a good new time, even the "now."

2. Paul also has another, a subjective and anthropological, way to speak of an event that terminates the past and initiates a present that has a future. G. Staehlin (in *TDNT,* 4.1113) speaks of a "cosmic turn which later takes place in the individual." The apostle Paul is an outstanding example of such a turn. Before this paragon and promoter of zealous "Judaism" was stopped and grasped by Christ, he persecuted Christians. But "now," in the light of what has happened to him and through him, he calls his former merits a "loss" and "excrements" (Gal 1:13-16, 23; Phil 3:5-14; cf. Rom 6:21). No longer does he know any person or even Christ "in a fleshly way" (2 Cor 5:16). By the grace of God and in the service of Christ, this man who had been useless to Christ and wrought havoc on Christ's people, and who even later declared himself "the least of the apostles," worked harder for the Lord than any other apostle (1 Cor 15:9-10). His own salvation through sheer mercy made him, according to Phil 3:17; cf. 1 Tim 1:15-16, a prototype of all to be saved. As slaves of sin, they, too, had gained nothing by their works — except shame. But "now," since they are freed from sin and placed into God's service, they harvest "sanctification and eternal life" (Rom 6:20-21). In 2 Cor 5:17; cf. Gal 6:16, those united with and in Christ are called "a new creation," for "the old things have passed away and new things have come into being." Similarly crisp is the formulation of Eph 5:8: "In the past you were darkness, but now in Christ you are light." More elaborate is the description of the Gentiles' past in Eph 2:11-12 and 4:17-19. The past time is overruled by the fact that "but now" they are included in the Messiah's realm, made honored members of God's household and equipped to conduct themselves worthily, wisely, and thankfully (Eph 2:13, 19; 4:1-3; 5:15-20).

Thus the unique and glorious intervention of God in human and cosmic affairs has radical consequences for the life of individuals and groups. What happened once for good and all on Calvary, at Easter and at Pentecost, is now, at God's own time, efficiently applied to human beings. Again and again, decisive events take place that completely change their life and their evaluation of their former life. They are equipped for a new life. In modern terminology, the turning point from the past to the present, from old to new, from hopelessness to confident trust, is ascribed to an encounter with God or with Jesus, and is called a religious experience or "personal conversion."

In order to effect this change on the subjective level, God always uses, especially according to Paul and the book of Acts, the same two instruments: the proclamation of the Word and the dispensation of the Spirit (Gal 3:1-5; Rom 1:16-17; 8:1-17, 26-27; 10:14-17; 12:6-8; 1 Cor 1:18–2:16; 12–14; 2 Cor 3; Eph 1:12-13; 3:5-7; 4:7-11; cf. Acts 2; 8:14-17; 10:44; 11:14-15; etc.; cf. Luke 3:22; 4:18-19). God appoints human agents to fulfill a service when a new person is to be created out of an old one. Samuel contributes to transforming the young farmer Saul into a "new man" (1 Sam 10:6) and in making out of the shepherd boy David the king after God's heart. Ananias's and Barnabas's assistance and friendship are as vital for the future apostle Paul as is the labor carried out and endured by Paul himself in the conversion and guidance of, e.g., the Corinthians. Such cooperators of God (1 Cor 3:9) would never say of themselves, "I made other persons new and useful" or "I have changed them." They just had to do their work — whether voluntarily or not (1 Cor 9:16-17). Whenever in the Bible the turning of an old into a new person is called regeneration or rebirth (e.g., in Ps 51; Ezek 36; John 3; First John; Titus 3:5), the context shows that the Messiah or the Holy Spirit performs the miracle. Not even inspiration can enable a human being to determine the moment and manipulate the conversion of another person. In the interpretation of Philem 10, it was shown that the fatherhood and motherhood of Paul that made Onesimus the apostle's child did not include the claim that the apostle achieved what only God can do.

3. When the word "now" is combined with an imperative, rather than used in contrast to "then" or "in the past," this adverb emphasizes that an act of obedience has to be performed forthwith and henceforth, at any place, day by day. In rare cases, *nyn* effects no more than a sharpening of the imperative: *age nyn* means "up now, come on now" (in James 4:13; 5:1; cf. Matt 3:15). More frequently a specific conduct is declared to be the consequence of the great ("cosmic") intervention of God and/or of the new creation of a person as described above under numbers 1 and 2. "After God has overlooked the times of ignorance, in the now time he commands all persons everywhere to repent" (Acts 17:30).

"Neither do I condemn you; go, and from now on do not sin anymore"; "But now . . . put off the old man with all his works and put on the new man" (John 8:11; Col 3:8-10; Eph 4:22-24; cf. Rom 6:19; 7:6; etc.). Day by day, human reflection, decision, and action can and shall answer and mirror God's almighty deeds in favor of the whole world and shall correspond to all that Jews and Gentiles have experienced when they heard the gospel and believed in the good news. They are expected and encouraged to be what they are by God's grace. The ethical "now" lasts from the first coming of Christ to his parousia, and it calls for an existential demonstration and confirmation, even by daily conduct — be it under benign or adverse circumstances. "We have this treasure in earthly vessels . . . even if our external person perishes yet our internal is being renewed day by day" (2 Cor 4:7-16).

By such obedience and courage the cosmic separation of the past from the present and the worldwide and personal change effected by God are fully recognized. This way the specific personal conversion is proven real and evident: it means a daily new beginning. At the same time, the dependence of all NT ethics on the above-mentioned future and eschatological change and transformation confirms an earlier-mentioned fact: the moment and means of change, the events, which constitute the door between the past and the present, are to be found not only in the past but are extended into the present and the future.

All biblical texts concerning the difference and regarding the transition from the past to the present are decisive for the interpretation of PHM and for the application of this letter's contents for future periods. An often unfriendly dispute between friends and foes, e.g., of the Social Gospel movement, the liberation theology, and the Anti-Racism Program of the World Council of Churches thrives on an alternative setting of priorities: Either it is stipulated that first the social and economical structures of this world have to be changed; then only conversion, faith, and love have a chance to follow. Or it is proclaimed that personal conversion and attainment to the status of a reborn Christian are the root of social change and will change the world. But Philem 11 does not encourage such use or misuse of Paul's letter. For the apostle, the simple fact is decisive and sufficient: Onesimus was useless and is now useful.

The experience of Onesimus is embedded in the cosmic change already effected by God, in the resulting personal changes in the life of sinners, and in the imperatives addressed to Christians. This sequence of events makes Paul describe Onesimus in the manner of Philem 11. Whatever may be thought and said of the runaway, the past has left the slave behind; it has no right and claim upon him, and does not entitle anyone to condemn and reject him. In analogy, in Gal 2:6 Paul parenthetically observes regarding those who have now an honorable position in the Jerusalem church, "What they were in the past, makes no difference for me." The past, to use a Pauline expression, is now "swallowed up" (cf. 1 Cor 15:54). Paul bluntly says of himself, "I am forgetting what lies behind and strain forward to what lies ahead." But does not the apostle urge the Gentiles to "remember" what they once have been in Eph 2:11-12 (cf. 4:17-19)? There his intention is certainly not to make the Gentiles wallow or welter in their past status. Rather he praises and wants them to praise their salvation by grace and by Christ alone. They are now saved from death in sin (Eph 2:1-9). "Now" they are accepted as members with full rights in the house of God (Eph 2:19-22). Equally Paul is so convinced of Onesimus's move from his past to the present, that he reckons firmly with the good reception of the slave in Philemon's house (Philem 16-17).

Certainly Onesimus's usefulness in that house will to a large extent depend on his good will, his skills, and his industry. But it will also be determined by the master: Will he or will he not recognize the slave's usefulness? Still, in verse 13 Paul more than only timidly suggests that Onesimus would be most useful if he were returned to Paul and assisted him in preaching the gospel.

VERSE 12

I send him back to you — him, that is my own heart.

Lit. "whom I have sent back. . . ." The textual transmission of this verse bristles with so many important variants that it cannot be established definitely which wording was Paul's own or corresponds best to his intention. Each of the variant readings gives expression to an understanding that prevailed at the time of the copyists of PHM or anticipated later interpretations. Our translation is based on the evidence of a small number of MSS (the first script of the fourth-century Codex Sinaiticus, the fifth-century Codex Alexandrinus, the ninth-century minuscule 33). Origen is the only source to confirm that already before the fourth century this reading was accepted. The Nestle-Aland and Greek New Testament editions decide in favor of this relatively short reading. These two recent editions of the Greek text arrange the textual material in their critical apparatus in diverging ways, but both draw attention to relevant alternatives.

The huge majority of Greek MSS, the early versions, and earlier and later commentaries before the rise of modern text criticism offer the variant that was discussed in "Literary, Biographical, and Contextual Issues," section II, pp.107-108: they add the words "but thou, receive him." A warm and friendly reception is in mind. Indeed, all MSS of a later verse, i.e., Philem 17, contain these words; there they must be considered authentically Pauline. But when they are used as early as in verse 12, then Paul gives the impression of fostering the hope that Onesimus ought to remain "forever" (v. 15) in his master's house — as a slave even while treated as "more than a slave: a loved brother" and "a partner" (vv. 16-17). Still, it is unlikely that Paul wanted to be understood this way: the clear structure and logic of PHM are muddled when the expected reaction of Philemon to the slave's return is anticipated in that part of the epistle that in actuality serves to describe solely Paul's intentions and feelings concerning Onesimus. No earlier than in the next part (vv. 15-21) does Philemon's hoped-for response become the main theme.

Other variants are supported by sometimes rather weak attestations:

1. The indirect object "to you" *(soi)* is either missing or replaced by "in your direction" *(pros se)*.

a. In some MSS it is omitted together with all the following words of verse 12. Then exclusively the statement "I send him back" is left standing. In this case Paul cares little for the person *to whom* the slave is returned — if only the slave is returned to his place! Then the apostle's personal relationship to Onesimus as revealed in the intimate parental vocabulary of verses 9-10 is not crowned by the equation, "this man is my heart." Despite his kind intervention for Onesimus, Paul then looks like a typical representative of law and order. His contribution to the problem of slavery would then consist mainly in the paradigm given by returning a fugitive slave to his legitimate master.

b. The opposite is suggested by those Greek texts and the versions that say the slave was sent *pros se*, that is, as an apostolic delegate to Philemon. A letter, a parcel, or a prisoner sent to someone would be a mere object. But envoys sent by Paul to diverse congregations are entrusted with honorable assignments and are therefore worthy of a decent and respectful personal reception. According to the reading *pros se*, Philem 12 does not reveal Paul's general attitude to slave flight, neither ought it be considered a timeless paradigm of how a law-abiding Christian has to treat any and every economical or political refugee, escaped prisoner, or striking laborer. The variant underlines what the context reveals at any rate: a very specific slave (vv. 9-11) is sent back to a very specific master (vv. 4-7), to be received in a very specific way (vv. 13ff.).

2. A great number of other divergent readings might well be of minor importance, yet they reveal or instigate sensitivity for hidden problems.

a. Several MSS omit the words "but thou," yet anticipate verse 17 by inserting the command "receive him."

b. Others fail to have in the center of verse 12 the emphatic "him" *(auton)* — perhaps for one of the following reasons: The copyist(s) considered the combination of the relative pronoun with the personal pronoun *(hon . . . auton)* a Hebraism (*'asher*, complemented by the personal affix at the end of the verb) that needed not be reproduced in Greek. Or, because the accusative "him" had a necessary place in the imperative sentence "but thou, receive him," the pronoun "him" was considered superfluous in the first half of the verse.

c. Again, in another group of MSS one reads ". . . I have sent *(epempsa)*" instead of "I have sent back *(anepempsa)*." Together with the above-mentioned variant *pros se*, this reading can indicate that Onesimus is an authorized messenger of Paul (cf. Th. Preiss, *Life in Christ*, pp. 32-42). In this case, Onesimus returns as Paul's apostle, rather than as the property and tool of Philemon, which he had been before his flight.

d. Finally, the explication "that is my own heart" does not have the same location and function in all MSS. When, as in the text used for our translation, these words follow "I have sent him back," they express according to some expositors primarily Paul's hurt and grief as caused by his losing the slave's company. But when they are (as in Vg.) included in the variant "but thou receive him," they underline the preciousness of the gift now placed in Philemon's hands and care. Despite obvious shades of difference, these two implications are not mutually exclusive.

3. The original script of PHM, which is not preserved, and the oldest Greek MSS did not interrupt the flow of a sentence with commas, colons, dashes, etc., and mark its end with periods or other signs. But in modern translations a comma here and a colon or dash there, and finally a period, question mark, or exclamation mark, facilitate the understanding of the original text. What in the latest Greek minuscule MSS and in modern versions is expressed by punctuation, corresponds to tendencies represented already in variant Greek readings.

Together with many Bible versions and PHM commentaries, the aorist *epempsa* (lit. "I did send" or "I have sent") is to be translated in the present tense: "I send back." For frequently in Greek letters, "the writer transposes himself into the time at which the recipient reads the script" (BDF, 334). Then the aorist tense of "sending," "writing," or other verbs is used at places where in other languages the present tense occurs. (Examples of this so-called "epistolary aorist" are found in Philem 12, 19; 2 Cor 8:18; Col 4:8; Eph 6:22; Phil 1:25, 28; Heb 13:22; Acts 23:3; Polycarp, *Phil.* 13.2.) In 1 Cor 14:37 Paul might have chosen this kind of aorist — but he uses the present tense *graphō* (I write). Exact literal translations (in the past tense) are necessary only when (as in Rom 15:15; 1 Pet 5:12; perhaps also in Philem 21) the Greek aorist *egrapsa* refers to the almost completed letter, to a distinct part of the present letter (as in Gal 6:11; 1 Cor 9:15), or to a previously dispatched script (as in 1 Cor 5:9; 2 Cor 2:3-4; 7:12; 3 John 9).

The substance of Philem 12 poses problems even graver than the many forms of the text transmission. The vulnerability of the apostle is laid bare, and not all of his interpreters are pleased with what they see. When Paul sends away his heart, he has to tear it out of his breast and thus injure himself fatally. And when expositors seek to heal the gaping wound, they proceed on different routes and end up with diverse results.

At first sight, Paul appears flatly to contradict himself: first he avers that he sends the slave back and then calls Onesimus his heart. The moving rhetoric of the apostle seems to signal a spiritual suicide. If not before, then certainly after the separation from his dear child, Paul must look like a heartless fellow. For Onesimus, after being so warmly introduced in verses 10-11, Paul's action might resemble a betrayal by a kiss. "Sending back" — this is what a supporter and promoter of the social-economical status quo would do with a runaway slave. "My heart" — this is a language fitting the whisper of lovers. Each of these two key words has provoked and needs intensive scrutiny.

"I send him back." In his PHM commentary of 1527, Martin Luther writes, "Whom I sent back — this is the epistle." Onesimus is restored to his master not in order to be manumitted but "to return into his pristine servitude, so that he serve two times better than before. You see, servanthood is not abrogated." Still, because Luther knows only the reading of Philem 12 that includes the words "but thou, receive him," the Reformer expects that the slave owner will heed Paul's intercession and that there will be "reconciliation" between the master and the slave. Analogous is Luther's interpretation of Gal 5:1 (1531/ 1535; WA 40 II, 3): "Christ has liberated us, not from any human servitude, or from the power of tyrants, but from God's eternal wrath. Where? In the conscience . . . not politically, not fleshly, but theologically and spiritually." In substance, John Chrysostom and Theodore of Mopsuestia, Thomas Aquinas and John Calvin, finally a host of more recent expositors argue similarly. H. Diem expresses his conviction that during the Peasants' War of 1525, Luther took the same stance as Paul in PHM: Christian freedom is not a program of social emancipation.

However, such interpretations presuppose a sharp contrast between Philem 12a on one side, and the biblical accounts of liberation by God, an explicit commandment of God, the mission and work of Jesus Christ, and some highlights of Paul's proclamation on the other side:

a. In sending the slave back, the apostle does not appear to be an "imitator" (cf. Eph 5:1) of that God who has redeemed Israel from the servitude endured in Egypt and from the Babylonian captivity, and who has pulled out and/ or will save (according to the Lamentation Psalms and Thanksgiving Psalms) the poor and needy who cry to him from the depth. Certainly in Hos 8:11; 9:3, and variant readings of 11:5, the threat is pronounced that because of its rampant sin the whole of Israel shall return to Egypt. Should then Paul presume that in his capacity as apostle he has to execute that menace and make Onesimus its prime victim?

b. In Isa 16:3-5 Israel is urged, and in Deut 23:15-16 the command is given, not to betray and extradite fugitives. Rather, escaped foreigners and slaves are to be given shelter and safe asylum: they shall enjoy the privileges granted to God's elect people. Again, as, e.g., 1 Sam 25:10-11 and 30:11 show, this humane commandment was not always (and perhaps never) obeyed. But even if this be true, it would hardly entitle Paul to join the company of its trespassers.

c. Paul's treatment of Onesimus also contradicts the social order established by the Essenes: they did not tolerate slavery in their midst. Honorable positions held by slaves in mystery communities and in funeral societies and other societies *(collegia)* could reduce the willingness of their lords to humiliate them continuously and might have increased a slave's self-esteem. All the more does it look amazing that Paul sent the slave back to his master.

d. Paul likes to call himself an apostle or a servant of the Messiah Jesus. Yet does he truly represent the master who, according to Luke 4:18-19, declared it his mission to announce liberty to the captives and to usher in the promised Jubilee Year? Jesus did heal the sick and expel demons, and did not send them back to their helpless doctors or commit them to an institution. In the service of that King, according to the Gospels and Acts, the disciples were given similar full power. Has Paul forgotten whose messenger he is?

e. The way Paul treats Onesimus appears to run opposite the apostle's own glorious pronouncements of the unity and equality of all who are in Christ (esp. Gal 3:28; 1 Cor 12:13; Col 3:11). Has he then forgotten what he said about "our freedom which we have in the Messiah Jesus," as children of the free Sarah and not of the slave girl Hagar, as citizens of the heavenly Jerusalem, as those who are "freed for freedom" rather than for "returning under the yoke of slavery" (Gal 2:4; 4:22-31; 5:1, 13; cf. Rom 6:18, 20, 22; 7:3; 8:2, 21; Eph 3:12, variant reading)? No trace appears to be left of Paul's counsel given to the slaves in 1 Cor 7:21: "If you can gain your freedom, avail yourself of the opportunity." Obviously, in all the texts just mentioned, freedom is also, but never exclusively, a spiritual matter.

Arguments and passages of this kind have been marshaled against Paul and have called forth more than only academic questions. The apostle's decision to send Onesimus back to his master has exposed Paul's moral conduct and example to criticism, if not to outright condemnation. F. Overbeck, G. Kehnscherper, black theologians, and others have not withheld their disgust of Paul's attitude toward slaves in general, and toward Onesimus in particular. If they are right, then this apostle is co-responsible for much of the injustice and suffering inflicted on uncounted oppressed and exploited people not only in the church, but also in families and states that are strongly influenced by Christian traditions. Notwithstanding the many charming elements of PHM, this letter is then a document that in substance antagonizes freedom fighters of all kinds.

Yet there are also entirely different interpretations of the words "I send him back." In one or another way they all amount to apologetics. In "Literary, Biographical, and Contextual Issues," section VIII.C.1-2, pp. 222-225, general indictments and defenses regarding PHM were enumerated. Now the possible basis of an acquittal on the grounds of Philem 12 is to be examined. Precisely this verse may leave several ways open for declaring Paul a wise and loving, compassionate and humane man who in his thought as well as action regarding Onesimus never really forgot or denied what he had written about the freedom, unity, and equality created by Christ.

1. The case of Philemon and Onesimus may be considered so totally unique that PHM can and must not be considered a precedent, but excep-

tional — so extraordinary and peripheral that a part of the early church did not treat this letter as a canonical book (see "Literary Issues," sec. I, pp. 104-106. Indeed, other Pauline epistles contain exhortations that run parallel to the "sending back" in Philem 12. Christians are told to subordinate themselves to the Roman state officials in Rom 13:1-7; 1 Tim 2:1-3; Titus 3:1, just as wives to their husbands, children to their parents, slaves to their masters, according to the *Haustafeln* (Col 3:18–4:1; Eph 5:21–6:9; 1 Tim 2:11-12; etc.). The force of the collateral witness of these "parallels" can be weakened when, e.g., Rom 13:1-7 is considered an (unconscious?) relapse of Paul into the pharisaical attitude of his past, or a non-Pauline interpolation into Romans. Also the testimony contained in Colossians, Ephesians, and the Pastoral Epistles (as of 1 Pet 2:13-17; 3:1-6) is often treated as voices of a Pauline school, rather than of Paul himself. In consequence, the "sending back" of Onesimus can be explained as an inconsistency of the apostle with his own proper preaching and teaching. The easiest explanation refers to the special task of Paul to proclaim *the Word* and to build the church, or it calls to mind the special conditions of the period in which he lived; the church was a tiny minority. P. Eicher (in *Auf der Seite der Unterdrückten*, p. 52 n. 82; cf. nn. 219 and 225 of "Literary Issues," pp. 215, 220) voices the attitude of Latin American theologians of liberation when he uses this argument and rejects attempts to draw "historizing conclusions of analogy" from Paul's situation to our present twentieth-century setting. No doubt the words "I sent him back" cannot be converted into a timeless Pauline, ecclesiastical, or general law, saying: Escaped slaves must be returned to their owners.

2. The sting is taken out of Paul's action when with J. Knox (*Philemon*, p. 21; cf. H. Schmauch and others) it is argued that the verb *anapempō* "in the New Testament period . . . was commonly employed to indicate the reference of a case to a higher court." Lexicographical evidence (from papyri, supported in the NT by Luke 23:7, 11, 15 and Acts 15:21; cf. Annotation 3 to "Literary Issues," pp. 227-228) can be quoted in support of the translation, "I refer him to you." Just as Jesus and Paul are deemed possibly innocent by lower judges and handed over to higher courts, so Onesimus is then sent back to his owner because Paul expects from Philemon a fair trial and treatment, based on the apostle's warm recommendation rather than exposing the runaway to uncontrolled outbursts of wrath and arbitrariness. This interpretation washes Paul's hands superficially only, and it suffers from a lack of plausibility. A prisoner was handed over to a higher court in shackles — but there is no indication that on his journey to Colossae Onesimus was fettered to Tychicus (cf. Col 4:7-9). In addition, Philemon's position was as little equivalent to the full power of a higher court as Paul's plea for Onesimus was comparable to the findings of a lower court. The final judgment to which the apostle would gladly submit him-

self, Onesimus, and Philemon is to be pronounced by God or Christ, not by any man (cf. Eph 6:8-9; Col 3:25–4:1; etc.).

3. Paul is thoroughly whitewashed if another exposition of "sending back" is accepted. Before John Knox turned a new leaf in the exposition of PHM, it was commonly assumed that Onesimus had run away from his master and was a fugitive when he came to Paul. Foremost the slave's "separation" from Philemon, as mentioned in Philem 15, his former uselessness (v. 11), and the damage caused by his thievery or other misdeeds (v. 18) appeared to be sufficient proof of Onesimus's vile character and flight. But already Knox himself expressed (on pp. 15-16) some doubts whether the slave had really run away. He called the escape story "a tentative theory . . . constructed on the meagre facts we have." Where Knox stopped short, P. Lampe ("Keine 'Sklavenflucht' des Onesimus," pp. 135-137) and B. M. Rapske ("The Prisoner Paul," pp. 187-203) took off to a keen flight. Both argued that Onesimus had made a perfectly legitimate journey with the intention to meet a high-standing friend of his master, even the apostle Paul, and to ask him for intervention. Indeed, some commentators on Greek and Roman law permitted slaves who felt ill-treated to take such a step. Vivianus, Paulus, and Ulpianus, juridical scholars living more than 120 years after Paul's time, can be quoted for this humane interpretation of contemporary laws (see *Digesta* 21.1.17.3 and 5; 21.1.43.1). Paul was then far from acting despicably when he sent Onesimus back. He merely fulfilled the slave's wish and hope by writing PHM and letting the slave bring this script to his master Philemon. If only some late and humane expositions of current law would guarantee that slave owners, police stations, slave catchers, and courts always actually followed the learned commentators! Then Paul would be not only thoroughly innocent but would prove to be a truly loving helper when he sent the slave back.

4. Again another interpretation is proposed by Sara C. Winter ("Paul's Letter to Philemon," pp. 2-10): According to Phil 2:25-30, a certain Epaphroditus had been sent out to Paul by the Philippians, carrying gifts of the Macedonian congregation to the apostle. The man was then "sent back" in order to be at home "received in the Lord," with joy and honor. So also, according to Winter, it is probable that Onesimus was carrying gifts from the Colossian congregation to Paul, and that now, as Philem 12 affirms, he is finally "sent back" to his hometown. Even this theory is not foolproof. As observed earlier, a slave who had not (yet) become a Christian and was considered "useless" (Philem 11) would hardly have been entrusted with money and other gifts collected by a congregation.

5. Other expositors assume that Paul's face can be saved when the questions are raised: What alternatives existed to sending the slave back? and, which consequences would have arisen if Onesimus had stayed with Paul? H. Koester

(*Einführung in das Neue Testament*, p. 509) is convinced that "Paul could not keep him [Onesimus] — for juridical and practical reasons." J. M. G. Barclay ("Dilemma of Christian Slave-Ownership," esp. pp. 176-179, 183) has elaborated on this: Onesimus would have felt rewarded for his flight; other slaves would have felt encouraged to run away and expect Paul's protection; they might have become Christians for other than spiritual reasons; Philemon would have suffered a financial loss because Onesimus could not and a Christian congregation (unlike Jewish relatives and/or communities; see Lev 25:47-49) would not pay for the slave's manumission; without the domestic help provided by at least one slave, a house church could hardly be hosted; among Paul's good reasons not to ask directly for emancipation were the remaining economical and moral obligations of a freedman to his master and the fact that solely communities "far removed from ordinary life," such as the Therapeutae and Essenes, attempted to fight slavery in principle.

Other reasons have been or might be added: Paul felt responsible for the future physical and moral welfare of Onesimus — if the slave had stayed with the apostle, the police or private slave-hunters might have apprehended him at any moment; the sociopolitical harmlessness and civic respectability of the Christian movement would have been jeopardized; an emancipated Onesimus would have been exposed to possible hunger, cold, and diseases, to the temptation to join a robber gang or to become a slave of his lusts.

Whatever grains of truth may lie in one or another of these speculations, they do not suffice to eliminate a possible tension and contradiction. On one side stands the fact that Onesimus was sent back without the direct request that his master manumit him; on the other, the Pauline statements (in, e.g., Gal 2:4; 4:22-31; 5:1, 13; Rom 6:18-22; 7:3; 8:2, 21) on the freedom and equality of all Christians. Is then Paul guilty of doing himself what he prohibited others to do when he warned them not to buckle under "the weak and poor elements of the world" and not to be "held captive under the yoke of slavery," i.e., to man-made human traditions and thus to sin and death (Gal 4:8-10; Rom 8:2; Col 2:6-23)? But another possibility also exists: the drama evolving between Paul, Onesimus, and Philemon may well be a test case. Later, in the interpretation of Philem 13, 14, 16, and 21, it will be shown that Paul has in mind a very specific kind of freedom that does not exclude service joyfully rendered. At this place, it may suffice to show that even in sending Onesimus back, Paul serves the cause of freedom.

1. *The freedom of the apostle.* According to PHM, it was Paul's free, personal, unique decision to send Onesimus back. No evidence exists to demonstrate that he was compelled by a law or by brute force to do so — or that he intended to pass a law for his time or for the future. Although Timothy, as coauthor of PHM, and the other cooperators who send greetings (vv. 1, 23-24)

will have concurred with the return of Onesimus to Philemon, Paul was taking and bearing a grave risk. How many things can happen on the slave's journey to Colossae, and how many at and after his arrival in Philemon's home! Paul had ventured far out when, according to verses 8-9, he abstained from giving a blunt order and restrained himself to uttering a plea. Obviously he used for himself the privilege to make his own decision before he granted it to Philemon. This liberty costs him dearly: it means separation from his dear child, his own heart (vv. 10 and 12b). But the price he pays for his decision and the vocabulary he uses for describing his relationship to Onesimus reveal that he acts out of spontaneous and responsible love, rather than in order to impose on the slave an unbearable yoke.

2. *The freedom of Onesimus.* In being sent back and while returning to Colossae, Onesimus is in the company of Tychicus (Col 4:7-9) — but not as a prisoner of war is escorted by an armed soldier, or a criminal by a policeman. Even if the slave was not the first to suggest that he return home, his journey would have been impossible without his free will and consent. Paul has "sent" several cooperators as delegates of himself from one place to another, and it cannot be demonstrated that any one of them went against his own will. In Philem 17 Onesimus is described as such a companion and representative of the apostle. It cannot be ascertained whether and how much the slave was fully convinced of the effectivity of Paul's letter to Philemon. Perhaps Onesimus reckoned that good service rendered to his master would pave the way either to returning to Paul definitely (cf. Philem 13) or to manumission, or to both. Certainly for Paul himself, the freedom of the children of God and of Abraham that he proclaimed was not only freedom from but also freedom for. After his encounter with Christ near Damascus, Paul was free not only *from* the Jerusalem authorities but also for them; e.g., he followed a special revelation that sent him to the city to report on his activities (Gal 1:15–2:10). So also Onesimus had reasons enough not to resent but to gladly accept his mission to Colossae, not on the basis of an enthusiastic impulse but after due consideration of other options. Then Paul would negate his own proclamation only if he robbed the slave of that freedom of decision that he uses for himself and grants to the slave's legal owner, according to verse 14.

3. *The freedom of Philemon.* Onesimus is sent back to a trustworthy friend of Paul, to a pillar of the community in which he lives. Philemon is neither rich enough to maintain several slaves, nor a tyrant who at random creates and uses laws to increase his own power and profit. Rather, according to Philem 1, 4-7, 9, ample evidence exists of *this* slave owner's love and faithfulness. He is used to serve "all the good" from which the members of the local church and "all the saints" benefit. In verse 21 Paul expresses his confidence in an "obedience" that goes beyond fulfilling the carefully phrased suggestions contained in PHM.

"Obedience of faith" (cf. Rom 1:5; 16:26) is a matter of ever new spontaneity. It holds the members of the church together by the bond of love that Paul calls "perfect" in Col 3:14. Where there is no love, there is no freedom, and vice versa. Freedom is the product, shape, and criterion of love, and love means freedom.

In verse 16 Paul will elaborate on the freedom in mutual responsibility and love, which is granted by God's grace and pertains to the physical as well as the spiritual dimensions of human life. A "two-realms doctrine," as fostered by Luther's exposition of PHM in 1527, in his commentary on Galatians, and by later Lutherans, contradicts Paul's teaching. According to Philem 14 and 16, the voluntary love with which Philemon is to receive the returning slave will embrace the slave (lit.) "in the flesh and in the Lord."

The second half of Philem 12 confirms that love is the sole motivation of Paul's intervention on behalf of Onesimus, and of the slave's return to his master.

Him, that is, my own heart. The choice of the translation "heart" for the Greek word *splagchna* (lit. "bowels") has been explained above in a Note on verse 7 (pp. 301-302). Among the expressions of his intimate and warm relationship to the escaped slave, the equation, Onesimus is my heart, is the most cordial. Paul might have written that the man is a part (so, e.g., G. Friedrich and NEB) or the better half of himself or of his heart; or that he loves him with his whole heart or with all his love; or that his soul loves him (Song of Sol 3:1-4); or that he loves him as himself or as his own soul (Lev 19:18, 34; Matt 19:19 par.; Rom 13:9; Eph 5:28; etc.; *Testament of Simeon* 4:6). In modern diction this would mean that he declares Onesimus to be his true love, even his sweetheart; that he now tears all his love out of his heart; that therefore he will henceforth feel empty of all vitality and joy. Actually, Paul says still more. Not only is he Onesimus's loving father, mother, and subtly pleading advocate, but he plainly *identifies* himself with the slave and the slave with himself. Onesimus "is made one with me so that henceforth also to you [Philemon] he is quasi the *alter ego*" (W. Estius). According to E. Lohmeyer, in Philem 12 "I and thou [Paul and Onesimus] have been made one person"; the formula used by Paul is "completely unique"; "the I of Paul is the thou of the slave" — so totally the apostle "empties himself." Lohmeyer may well exaggerate when he claims that this identification is a unique Pauline feature. E.g., during the Gulf War of 1991, an Iraqi woman told a reporter at a marketplace, "We love our Leader [Saddam Hussein], he is our heart" (quoted from the *Basler Zeitung* of February 12, 1991). It is to be admitted, however, that Paul's total self-identification with the slave goes far beyond the Stoics' and other humanitarians' sympathy with slaves. While the Stoics recognized that slaves, too, *have* a soul, Paul in fact confesses that Onesimus *is* his soul.

In other epistles the apostle transcends ordinary diction in similar fashion — yet exclusively in statements describing his relation to Christ. "I live, no longer I but Christ lives in me" (Gal 2:20); "for me, to live is Christ" (Phil 1:21); "the Messiah will be revealed, your life" (Col 3:4); "when Christ is in you . . . the Spirit is life through righteousness" (Rom 8:10). The OT contains analogies: e.g., when "God [is] our righteousness" has become the name of a king on whom the prophet's hopes are set (Jer 23:6), or when the Lord's Anointed is called "the breath of our nostrils" (Lam 4:20). Sirach 33:30-31 advises a slave owner, "If you have a servant, let him be as yourself . . . for as your own soul you will need him."

Because *splagchna* originally can mean a mother's womb and the embryo, Theodore Beza states (in his *Annotationes*, p. 481), "Paul transfers upon himself what properly fits a mother" when again he denotes Onesimus as his child. It was earlier mentioned that W. Estius made a comparison with Mary's relationship to her as-yet-unborn child. Indeed, according to Philo (*Jos.* 25), Jacob wailed the presumed death of his son Joseph, calling him "my *splagchna*" (in the LCL version: "my own flesh and blood"). At the time of Emperor Hadrian, Artemidorus of Ephesus (*Onirocriticus* 1.44) observed that "the children are called *splagchna*." The Peshitta version (fifth century) translates *ta ema splagchna* in Philem 12, "like a son of mine." However, Philo (*Leg. ad Gaium* 368) shows that other, less specific meanings had not been obliterated, and, e.g., J. B. Lightfoot, E. Lohmeyer, and H. Koester (*TDNT*, 7.558) have for Philem 12 the version "child." Still, calling Onesimus his child would but repeat the essence of verse 10. Actually the apostle's unique and special love for Onesimus even goes beyond his cordial care for other Christians whom he calls his "dear children" (cf. 1 Cor 4:14-15; 1 Thess 2:11).

Calvin speaks of the "miraculous goodness of Paul, considering that Onesimus had a rotten character and was a thief and vagabond"; this Reformer is sure that there was no way to fight Philemon's wrath more effectively than Paul's courage to direct the slave owner's anger at the apostle himself. Chrysostom asks rhetorically, "Which stone would those words not bend, not soften?" Luther (1527) observed, "How can he talk, this man!" and declared it impossible for Philemon not to return Onesimus to the apostle who so totally renounced his right. According to H. Koester (*TDNT*, 8.555), "it is as if Paul in the runaway slave came to Philemon in person with his claim to experience love." To repeat an earlier observation: when Paul sends his heart and as much as transfers himself to Philemon, he is much more than only the slave's advocate. The apostle himself is received when Onesimus is welcomed: "Welcome him as you would receive me" (v. 17). When Matt 25:31-46 is remembered, then the slave is at the same time representing Jesus Christ.

One part, however, of J. B. Lightfoot's interpretation has no support in PHM or other NT texts. He writes, "The great capacity for good which appears in the typical slave of Greek and Roman fiction, notwithstanding all the fraud and profligacy overlying it, was evoked and developed here by the inspiration of a new faith and the incentive of a new love. The genial, affectionate, winning disposition, purified and elevated by higher knowledge, had found its proper scope. Altogether this new friendship [with Onesimus] was a solace and a strength to the Apostle in his weary captivity which he could ill afford to forgo" (p. 379). This exposition goes far beyond the wording of the text. Certainly the possibility exists that Paul regretted the loss of the "solace and strength" received from a morally rearmed Onesimus. However, in verse 7 he explicitly speaks solely of the great joy and comfort that has already been evoked by the good contribution of Philemon to the life of the whole congregation. In Col 4:9 the escaped and now returning slave is indeed called Paul's "faithful and dear brother." But the title "my own heart" goes beyond such praise. Unlimited love for Onesimus and total dependence on him, full trust in him and extreme pain suffered by the separation from him — rather than hidden psychic treasures and accumulated credits — are essential of the deeply moving identification of Paul with the slave.

Now, when Paul sends away his true love, are they then never to meet again?

VERSE 13

I, for one, should have liked to keep him with me so that in the chains of the gospel he could serve me, substituting for you.

This verse bristles with surprising and puzzling statements, and divergent solutions of the puzzles have been proposed. Paul's wish is formulated equivocally. The notion that Paul may aim at a future complete independence and liberty of Onesimus from any human obligation is contradicted by the apostle's hope that henceforth the former fugitive will "serve me in chains." Personal service to the apostle is as much as equated with service to the gospel. The substance of Philem 19b is anticipated: properly the slave owner, not the slave, would owe full-time service to Paul. Each one of these embarrassing elements of verse 13 requires intensive discussion.

I, for one, should have liked (*ego eboulomēn*, lit. "it is me, who was willing"). The tone in which verse 13 begins is distinctly personal. It reminds one of the opening of verses 8-9. There Paul had mentioned — and rejected! — the temptation to misuse his authority by giving an order to Philemon. Now he admits that he had or has a personal wish, perhaps even a secret plan.

He alone ("I, for one") would have preferred something of which apparently other persons did not think, or had failed to suggest. Perhaps Onesimus expected to be sent back for good, in order to enjoy a better relationship with his Colossian employer. Perhaps Paul's cooperators and fellow prisoners deemed it undesirable or impossible that Onesimus stay longer in the apostle's and their company. The congregation living in the city of Paul's captivity may have exerted some pressure on Paul, advising that he separate himself from the fugitive, who had been harbored long enough. Agents of Roman law and order or privately employed slave catchers might have been about to discover who and what Onesimus was, and to transport him home in chains. In verse 15 the apostle intimates that perhaps God's own providence runs contrary to the wish uttered in verse 13. At any rate, Paul opens his heart and lets his own personal wish be known.

Is he, then, his warm love and concern for Onesimus notwithstanding, in the manner of a patriarch, desiring to dispose of the slave's future? A study of the form in which he expresses his wish can reveal how strong and how realistic are Paul's ultimate intention and hope.

Excursus: Different Kinds of Wishes

In the course of its use from Homer's time to Hellenistic times, the verb *boulomai* (to be willing, to wish, to desire) is sometimes a synonym of *thelō* or its equivalent *ethelō* (to be willing, to give consent, to decide, to decree). Still, it can also be slightly or sharply distinguished from the latter. In Philem 13-14 Paul uses both verbs, changing over from one to the other: "I should have liked to keep him" is obviously not the same as "I have decided to do nothing without your consent." As in earlier Greek, so also in Philo's writings, a difference between the two verbs can be observed. *Boulomai* can denote the free choice and preference of the gods (or of God): they are not subject to earthly limitations — their wish is their will. In turn, *(e)thelō* can signify consent as it is found among human beings. Or, *boulomai* and the noun *boulē* express a deliberate, rational, conscious decision. In, e.g., 2 Cor 1:16-17 *boulomai* does not mean an arbitrary resolve but is used as a parallel to *bouleuomai* (to determine, to resolve after deliberation). On the other hand, *(e)thelō*, just as the cognate noun *thelēma*, can signify an impulsive, unconscious, or natural inclination. But in early and late Greek literature, occasionally the reverse differentiations are also made. The NT distinctly prefers *(e)thelō* to *boulomai*: the ratio of the use of the two verbs is over 200 to 37. (For references, see the pertinent article in LSLex; G. Schrenk in *TDNT*, 1.629-633; 3.45-62; BDF, 359.2.)

For translating Philem 13-14, Vg. has in both verses the same verb, *volo* (to will, to desire), and thereby obfuscates a distinction between *boulomai* and *ethelō* that Paul obviously intended to make. Which difference? Because the apostle is the subject of both verbs, the contrast between God's free will and providence — to which indeed verse 15 will refer — and Paul's emotional and/or rational desire is not in question. Neither is there an indication that the apostle first speaks as a willful daydreamer, then on the basis of a realistic calculation. Rather the progress from the imperfect *eboulomēn* in verse 13 to the aorist *ēthelēsa* in 14 may signal the transition from a timid and a seemingly unfulfillable wish to a definitely made decision. Greek imperfect verbal forms suggest or permit at least three interpretations that need not be mutually exclusive.

1. The imperfect can replace the pluperfect, that is, it can describe an action or a state of being that is no longer real and decisive. In classical and later Greek, plusperfects occur "much more rarely than in Latin or German" (BDF, 347) — or in English. Still, the beginning of Philem 13 may be paraphrased, "Once upon a time, I alone had a wish which at present I foster no longer: to keep Onesimus with me." The Vg.'s version of *eboulomēn* has the pluperfect *volueram* ("I had been willing"), and among modern expositors E. Lohse believes that Paul's earlier wish had become known to others, before PHM was written. The apostle's great love for the slave (vv. 10 and 12b), supported by Onesimus's demonstrated usefulness to Paul (v. 11), would provide ample reasons for Paul's former but now discontinued wishful thinking. In this case, only later, for reasons not mentioned in PHM, would the apostle have decided to send the slave back to his master and to permit Philemon freely to decide over the slave's future (vv. 12a and 14). Such a change of Paul's mind would have analogies in the apostle's attitude toward frustrated travel plans. According to 1 Thess 2:17-18, it was Satan who prevented a first and a second decision of Paul. Twice he had planned to visit the Thessalonians after he had been (lit.) "made an orphan" by the temporary separation from them. What a daring reversal of roles: the spiritual father is "orphaned" for the duration of the separation, rather than his spiritual children! Instead of Satan, in 2 Cor 1:15-17 and Rom 1:10, 13, it is "the will of God" that forces the cancellation of Paul's earlier plans, hopes, or promises. While Paul obviously concedes that he has repeatedly changed his mind when he was forced to do it, he affirms in 2 Cor 1:18-20 that God never retracts a given word. In consequence, if and whenever in Philem 13 *eboulomēn* is understood in the sense of a pluperfect, the apostle has renounced carrying out a firm former wish.

2. The Greek imperfect tense can, however, reveal that Paul's earlier wish was no more than "conative": a tentative desire and expectation. In this case the beginning of Philem 13 ought to be paraphrased, if at some length, e.g., this way: "Although I knew that I would break existing laws, hurt Philemon's property rights, and/or risk any moment the intervention of official and private slave hunters, yet for a long time I have fostered the idea, and even now I am

trying and hoping, to retain Onesimus at my side." Among others, J. B. Lightfoot and C. F. D. Moule suggest this kind of exposition, and BDF, 359.2, mainly by reference to Epictetus's writings, proposes, "Properly I would, but I do or did not wish [to retain Onesimus]." If this be the proper sense, then Paul was aware that his secret wish was illusionary and chimeric, doomed to shatter under the impact of overwhelming facts of life.

3. The imperfect form *eboulomēn* can express the continuity of an urgent wish. According to J. Knox and S. Winter, Paul wrote PHM because he seriously and unceasingly hoped that the slave's owner would set Onesimus free and let him become an assistant to apostolic work. As previously mentioned, these two and other authors consider Archippus the owner of the slave and assume that Col 4:17 reveals the slackness of this master to implement Paul's sincere and permanent wish. The form *eboulomēn* need not necessarily mean that the uttered wish is admittedly unrealistic and has now been given up. According to Acts 25:22, King Agrippa once said to the procurator Festus, "I should like *(eboulomēn)* to hear the man [Paul] himself," and (although J. B. Lightfoot declares this wish unrealistic) Festus promises its prompt fulfillment. Most diverse expositions of Philem 13 support a translation that expresses the unbroken validity of Paul's wish. (Among them: Calvin; W. Ollrog, *Paulus and seine Mitarbeiter,* p. 106; U. Wilckens, *Das Neue Testament* [1970], p. 772; H. Binder; W. Schenk, "Der Brief des Paulus an Philemon in der neueren Forschung (1945-87)," pp. 1368-1369.) In effect, the apostle would in this case seriously "ask for" the release of Onesimus (as Knox had suggested), and not only, as he has done in verse 10, without becoming specific, "plead in favor" of the slave.

Still, even when Paul's wish is firm and constant, it is being phrased in a reticent, shy, and humble way. In the context the apostle acknowledges that three limits impede his desire: Verse 12: by sending back the slave to his master, Paul creates a fact that at least temporarily interrupts the useful assistance Onesimus has already begun to provide. Verse 14: the fulfillment of Paul's wish is made dependent on Philemon's own free decision. Verse 15: whatever Paul may intend and the slave's legal owner may decide, the outcome is determined by God's providence and guidance.

Each one of the sketched expositions of the imperfect tense "I should have liked" has its own advantages and yet poses problems. The first looks convincing because it makes the discussion of the second and third superfluous. But it suggests that, after dispatching the escaped slave back to his master and, according to Philem 12, commending a loving reception, Paul left Onesimus's future entirely in the hands of Philemon. The second recommends itself because it leaves to Paul the honor of being a pragmatic realist. But it does not answer the question why Paul should waste a whole verse on an idea that cannot be realized. The third is harmonious with the expression of love, concern, and care found elsewhere in PHM. However, if Paul had really intended to make an unchangeable and unmistakable wish known, a conjunction such as "but," "nevertheless," "however," or "yet" (*alla, de, plēn,* etc.) would have sufficed as a signal at the beginning of verse 13. The "sending back" of Onesimus would then have been devalued as a preliminary act.

Actually, neither grammar nor syntax, neither the context nor parallels can prove that any one of the three options mentioned, or any two in combination, are foolproof. It is therefore best to assume that with full intention Paul described his wishing or willing in an ambiguous way. He wanted to leave it to Philemon (and to the congregation in his house) to ponder and discuss the urgency and practicability of the expressed wish, and to find and enact a proper response. To repeat J. M. G. Barclay's ("Dilemma of Christian Slave-Ownership," p. 175) observation: PHM is "deliberately open-ended." While the apostle hopes that his plea and wish will be heeded, yet especially in verse 13 his counseling is distinctly nondirective. Philemon's right to self-determination is acknowledged and supported, as is, even more, God's overarching will and plan (vv. 14-15). By formulating "I, for one, should have liked . . . ," Paul almost hides and certainly only hints at his own opinion and hope. But precisely this way he reveals his concern, his responsibility, and his love — for both the master and the slave.

To keep him with me. While writing these words, Paul actually does not "keep" Onesimus (be it in Rome, Caesarea, or Ephesus), but he makes or permits the slave to return to Colossae, into the house and under the hand of Philemon. Paul's wish to retain the slave can be fulfilled by Philemon earlier or later. Either the owner makes the slave return to the apostle or, at the occasion of Paul's forthcoming visit in his home (v. 22), he permits or commands the slave to become Paul's permanent travel companion and coworker. E.g., Luther, K. Staab, A. Suhl, W. Bieder, H. Binder reject the first possibility. The absence of any reference to a back-and-forth journey of the slave favors the second.

How can Philemon let go of the slave, instead of either punishing him and keeping him forever for the fulfillment of slave duties or even retaining and treating him in Colossae as a dear brother? The apostle's wish as such is neither illegal nor illusionary. Contemporary law and custom contained several options for a slave's correct and socially accepted transfer from one person to another. So Philemon had not only to decide whether or not to release Onesimus into the care of Paul, but also which modality should be chosen for the eventual change of masters.

Excursus: Legal Options for Onesimus's Future

1. Philemon might sell the slave to Paul or — in view of the apostle's lack of sufficient funds — transmit Onesimus to him as a present.

2. He can hire out the man to the apostle, either in expectation of remuneration for the work done or free of charge, as was sometimes done among friends. Still, a "cessation of the Christian slave for a limited period of time is in legal respect by far not a manumission" (S. Schulz, *Gott ist kein Sklavenhalter*, p. 182).

3. The slave's owner may understand Paul's wish, however feebly it is expressed, as equivalent to a military conscription. Not only free citizens but also slaves were drafted into the army and navy in some emergency situations. Occasionally, especially when Paul calls some of his cooperators "fellow soldiers," the apostle does not shy away from military imagery.

4. Philemon may understand the wish of Paul as equal to a summons to the Roman emperor's court. Such a call could contain the prospect that the slave in question might ascend to the high civic status of an "emperor's freedman." The gospel preached by Paul was far from apolitical. It proclaimed an empire of a very specific kind, even the kingdom of Christ and of God (Col 1:13; 4:11; cf. 1 Cor 15:24; Gal 5:21; Eph 5:5; etc.).

5. In Philemon's eyes, the asylum temporarily given by Paul to Onesimus may have resembled the protection given by the Apollo temple at Delphi and by other officially acknowledged refuges for escaped slaves. The return of Onesimus to his owner would then be an interlude stipulated during the negotiations, between priests and owner.

6. If Philemon was acquainted with OT and intertestamental Jewish history, legislation, and practice at all, he might have "lent" his slave "to the Lord," just as did Hannah when she brought her child Samuel to the priest Eli (1 Sam 1:26-28). Or Philemon might have thought of the Netinim, i.e., of those sometimes foreign-born persons who were "given by the Lord" or "given to the Lord" for doing lower temple services (Yebamoth VIII 3,76b; Kidd J 4, 342; cf. *TWAT*, vol. 5 [1986], pp. 709-712, and above, Annotation 9, pp. 94-96, to "Social Background").

7. If the slave owner in Colossae had known of a rabbi-pupil relationship as cordial as that between Gamaliel II and his scholarly slave Tabi, he might have found pleasure in sponsoring Paul and Onesimus's cooperation for the churches' benefit. If ever Paul would have considered legally to adopt the slave, Philemon might have added his blessings.

8. Finally, Philemon might have become so overwhelmed by Paul's warm intervention, or so disgusted with Onesimus's former conduct and uselessness, that he was willing to swallow the material loss and manumit the slave on the spot. Eventually homelessness, hunger, cold, diseases, and other miseries had to be faced by the freed or expelled man, as described in moving terms in, e.g., Gen 16 and 21 (concerning Hagar and Ishmael) and by Epictetus (*Diss.* 4.1, 37). At the time of Emperor Augustus, public order and safety was so seriously threatened by the exploding number of manumitted slaves that laws were passed that limited the number of possible releases. (See above,

"Social Background," sec. III.B, pp. 18-23; and sec. VII, pp. 41-53.) The repentant runaway in whose favor the noble Pliny the Younger intervened (in *Ep.* 9.21 and 24; cf. "Social Background," Annotation 4, p. 86) was an escaped *freed*man, no longer a slave — and yet he appears to have had reasons to take to his heels. Unlike the biblical prescription saying that a slave had the right to refuse his manumission (Exod 21:5-6; Deut 15:16-18), Greek, Roman, and Asia Minor laws did not secure a slave's right to remain in the master's home. Still, under given conditions a slave might prefer enduring known evils to an unknown future after manumission.

In Philem 13 Paul asks neither explicitly nor implicitly for Onesimus's manumission by Philemon. But verses 14-17 and 21 appear to reveal that Paul aims at nothing less than the slave's full legal emancipation: Philemon is given the freedom to decide — and manumission of the returning slave is among the possibilities. God may have separated the slave from the master in order to reunite them as (free!) brothers: Onesimus is called (lit.) "no longer a slave but more than a slave"; Paul, Philemon, and Onesimus are to be (equal?) partners; and the abounding obedience of Philemon to the contents of Paul's epistle may well consist in the permission granted to the slave to go out free.

The question whether or not the whole of PHM has been or has to be understood as a plea for manumission will be discussed below, in an excursus on the words (lit.) "no longer as a slave" that stand at the head of verse 16 (pp. 412-416).

The list of eight viable legal and biblical options has no claim on completeness, but the omission of formal legal manumission is conspicuous and requires an explanation.

Excursus: Why No Plea for Manumission?

Many expositors of PHM (some names were enumerated in n. 112 to "Social Background," pp. 41-42, and in the "Literary, Biographical, and Contextual Issues," sec. VIII.A, pp. 200-214. have assumed that Paul wrote PHM in order to move the slave owner not only to receive the returning servant kindly but also to manumit him. If this could be proven, Paul would indeed be an early member and protagonist of abolitionism, the Social Gospel movement, and liberation theology. Then it might be claimed that he fought slavery in principle and that any other interpretation reveals the expositor's bourgeois, if not capitalistic, mentality and contributes to future oppression and exploitation. Whether it pleases or displeases, it has to be accepted as a fact that in PHM there is "not one single word" expressing the wish or command that Onesimus be legally emancipated (E. Lohse, p. 206; cf. P. Stuhlmacher, pp. 40-41).

By not taking, in the middle of the first century C.E., an explicit abolitionist stance, Paul actually proved to be a wise man who sought the best for Onesimus's future. The confidence Paul expressed in this spiritual son in verses 10-12 does not permit him to be placed among those Stoic teachers who praised the inner freedom of the slaves but warned of their seduction by carnal lusts after manumission. (See "Social Background," sec. VI, pp. 33-41) There were also church fathers (among them Ignatius, *Polyc.* 4.3, and Tertullian, *De cor. mil.* 14) who warned of the immoral conduct of liberated slaves.

Rather Paul was probably fully aware that in exceptional cases only the life of a freed man was better than the conditions and daily experiences in the house and under the power of a reasonable master (see above, "Social Background," sec. VII.D, pp. 49-53). There were slaves who were manumitted in order to save their owners the expense of their maintenance in economically difficult periods. Others were freed because of their old age, sickness, laziness, carelessness, impertinence, or lack of loyalty. Such persons often faced unemployment, hunger, and homelessness. Even when a slave had been a useful, good, and faithful servant, he remained, by contracts called *paramonē* or *pactum,* for three or more years economically and morally in obligation to the patron. For the duration of his life, a redeemed Jewish slave was indebted to render service to his redeemer — just as Israel was liberated from Egypt in order to serve God (Exod 4:23; etc.). On the plane of interhuman relations, biblical law (Exod 21:5-6; Deut 15:16-18) gave a slave who had been permitted, enabled, or condemned to "go out" the right to remain enslaved to his master. Enduring the evils known could be preferred to unknown future evils. (Cf. Annotation 16 to "Social Background," pp. 101-102.) So also PHM does not support an ideology of freedom at any price. And never in other letters does the apostle presume that everything will be all right if only and as soon as a person gains economical, political, and social freedom.

What, then, has Paul in mind for Onesimus, if manumission is not his target?

That in . . . chains . . . he could serve. The selection of these few words from the second half of Philem 13 seems to be arbitrary. In addition, their composition into a crisp statement of intention appears to make Paul look like a grim and brutal supporter of slaveholders, oppressors, and exploiters, wherever they be found. Indeed, the words omitted at present will be given due attention soon enough. They may mitigate the shock caused by Paul's suggestion that Onesimus's future shall be a life of service rendered in chains. Still, all and everybody's human feelings smart when Paul reveals that the alternative to returning home and remaining Philemon's slave is definitely not freedom from servanthood but further service.

The distinctly biblical connection between freedom and service provides the background of Paul's talk of the slave's future service in bonds.

Excursus: Freedom in Order to Serve

A digest of classical Greek philosophical and political thought, and of its reflection in Hellenistic literature, is offered in the *TDNT* articles on service and on freedom (H. W. Beyer, *diakoneō,* etc., in 2.81-83; K. H. Rengstorf, *doulos,* etc., in 2.261-269; H. Schlier, *eleutheros,* etc., 2.487-496, offer excerpts from the writers of dramas, from Plato and Aristotle, and from the Stoics and Epicureans). Freedom means self-determination (*autokrateia),* as opposed to the bondage of slaves and their shameful and unhappy position in society. In the ethical and political systems discussed by those philosophers, democracy is sometimes considered the best form of a state because it permits full citizens — not everybody! — the enjoyment of equal rights *(isotēs, isonomia, parrhēsia)*. Early within the development of careful reflection is the observation and request that these citizens obey and serve the law of the community *(nomos)* and God. E.g., Plato *(Ep.* 8.354e) demonstrates that to serve no one and to behave absolutely *(pantē pantos)* free leads to tyrannies. "Overshooting servitude and freedom are thoroughly evil, while in due measure they are entirely good." In the middle lies the "service to God" because "the law is God for reasonable persons, [as is] pleasure for the fools."

Later the concept of freedom sometimes develops in other directions: then it can signify the right of the free and wise citizen to live and behave as he pleases, or to resist the decisions arising out of passions, or to withdraw from all obligations to the community. A wise person can demonstrate royal dignity by retiring into the spheres of his inner life. Then he can find "rest of the soul." E.g., H. Greeven *(Das Hauptproblem der Sozialethik in der neueren Stoa und im Urchristentum)* has elaborated, just as also more briefly H. Schlier *(TDNT,* 2.496-502, and other authors in monographs), on the differences between Stoic thinking and NT ethics of freedom.

In the Orient, slavish religious and political devotion is not treated as a shame; rather it is an honor to stand in the service of a high-ranking person. Because of its election by God and its redemption from the Egyptians and later from the Babylonian bondage, Israel is instructed that serving God and the neighbor in mutual love is the essence and guarantee of life, and that there is no freedom from foreign oppressors and unrighteous and merciless neighbors except by faithful service. Both the king and the people owe such service to God and to one another, and they obey God's commandments to their own good. A few OT and NT key texts suffice to exemplify that freedom and service are inseparable.

Israel is led out of Egypt because it is God's servant and in order to serve the Lord (Lev 25:42, 55; Exod 4:23; etc.). As shown above ("Social Background," sec. VIII.C.2-3, pp. 67-70), to be redeemed means to leave the bondage to a bad master and enter the good Lord's service, in order to be safe under his protection. According to talmudic exegesis, God himself renders the lowest services to Israel in order to set his people free and secure its freedom. Edited under the impact of the Deuteronomic reform, the accounts of Israel's kings state emphatically that rulers of the Northern and Southern Kingdoms who disobey God's commandments are misusing their full power and lead the people into sin and perdition. For priests and Levites there were codes of conduct that were binding for them only. Jesus Christ, while sharing in God's own majesty, "emptied himself, taking the form of a servant" (Phil 2:7). Several stories of the Gospels record that he was sent and chose to live as a servant and to fulfill such duties that even his disciples considered despicable (Matt 20:24-28; Luke 22:24-27). According to John 13:4-17, he washed his disciples' feet and declared this utter self-humiliation an "example" given to his followers. Paul follows this paradigm: he calls himself a "slave of the Messiah Jesus" (Gal 1:10; Rom 1:1) as well as "a man free from all men" (1 Cor 9:19-23), and he teaches the Corinthians that they are at the same time Christ's freedmen and his slaves (1 Cor 7:22). In Rom 6:12-23 the apostle sharply distinguishes between a bad and a good freedom, and also between a pernicious and a fruitful servant. In the past the Romans had been "free from the control of righteousness" (NEB, v. 20), serving their desires as obedient slaves of sin, producing works of which they are ashamed, and finally inheriting death, the wages of sin (vv. 21 and 23). But now they "have been freed from sin, made slaves of righteousness," even "of God" (vv. 18 and 22). Now grace, no more sin, is king over them, so that they can live as "slaves to obedience" (v. 16) and give their body and their members "to serve righteousness for sanctification" (v. 19). Thus they will harvest "eternal life" (v. 22). When in Gal 5:1 and 13 Paul passionately reminds the Galatians that they are liberated "for freedom," he makes clear that liberation *from* a misunderstood law, from sin, from death and other powers of oppression does not exhaust his message. In the OT as well as in Paul's letters, the criterion and apex of liberty is the freedom *for* which God's people is elected, redeemed, and called. As, e.g., H. Schlier (*TDNT*, 2.499) has shown, the Holy Spirit is the life-giving power that convinces the Christians and enables them to live up to the freedom granted (see esp. Rom 8:2, 4, 9). To sum up: true freedom is demonstrated solely in and by the service rendered to the good Lord, and through works of love performed for neighbors. Briefer is a Latin dictum: *Deo servire summa libertas* (to serve God is supreme freedom).

Not a law, not even an amnesty, but exclusively the freedom, which was proclaimed by Jesus Christ, was made public worldwide through the gospel and was confirmed by the gift and work of the Spirit, which he sends out to lead Christians into humble and obedient service. Philemon is in verse 14 declared free to make his own decision. Not despite but because of this assurance, he is in verse 21 expected to act in "obedience." Similarly, Onesimus is a free man because he is the spiritual child of the free Paul (according to Gal 3–4, also of God and of the free Abraham and Sarah). All the more is Paul confident that he is and will be a useful servant (Philem 10, 11, 13). Greek and Roman philosophers, poets, and ethicists who were unaware of God's history with Israel and its culmination in the work of Jesus Christ and the Spirit had no reason to concatenate freedom and service in the way of the Bible. When Paul in Philem 13 envisages for Onesimus a future life in servanthood, he applies to him the same life order as was and is valid for Israel, for Christ, and for all Christians.

In the chains of the gospel he could serve me. In verse 11 Paul wrote that Onesimus had become "useful to you [Philemon] and especially to me." Thus a certain limitation of his profitability was indicated. According to verse 12, Paul's spiritual child was sent back to Philemon only. So also, according to verse 13, the slave's expected future service is to be rendered to a specific person: to "me" (the apostle), and for a unique cause: "the gospel." By the gospel its servant is fettered in a seemingly horrible way: "in chains."

At first sight the apostle's wish to retain Onesimus at his side and employ him as his personal servant looks egotistic. A certain amount of selfish interest can even then be discerned, when with E. Lohmeyer it is assumed that Paul appeals to the "right" possessed by the apostles "to have a personal servant near them" (cf. Acts 13:5; Phil 2:30). Certainly Paul hopes to benefit from the work done by a servant. But even this hope seems to assign to Onesimus a place and function in society that makes him subordinate to the will, wishes, and whims of a master. Still, these impressions may well be deceptive.

By the manner in which Paul has described his captivity in verses 1 and 9 and spoken of his joy and consolation in verse 7, he has revealed that he completely identifies himself with the mission he has to accomplish. "What has happened to me has really served the advance of the gospel" (Phil 1:12). Critical readers of Paul might be inclined to speak about an overinflated self-consciousness, but (as esp. J. Munck, *Paul;* cf. K. Stendahl, *Paul,* have shown) the relation between the person of Paul and his ministry approximates identification. Paul's personal involvement in the incorporation of the Gentiles into God's people is at least as close and unbreakable as that between Moses and the gift of the Law to Israel. Both persons fulfill an indispensable function in the so-called history of salvation *(Heilsgeschichte).* Paul himself describes in 2 Cor 3:7-18 parallels and differences between the glorious ministry *(diakonia)* of each one of them. In each case the person of the chosen servant of God represents the cause for which he stands. So also personal servants of Paul, as are, e.g., enumerated in Acts 13:5; 19:22, always assist him in his mission work. Philemon 13 distinctly confirms that service to the gospel is service to Paul, and vice versa. But what exactly does this apostle understand by "serving" and "service"?

Excursus: Service according to Paul

The verb "serving" *(diakoneō),* which Paul uses for describing Onesimus's future position and function, and the cognate nouns "servant" and "service" *(diakonos* and *diakonia)* are among several verbs and nouns signifying the place of and the work done by persons subordinate to others, be it by choice or under the influence of historical events. *Douleuō* can mean "being a slave or a hired employee"; *hypēreteō:* "offering assistance to a master, or to another kind of superior"; *leitourgeō (= ta laita ergeō):* "fulfilling a ministry to the public." The term chosen by Paul in Philem 13 *(diakoneō)* signifies originally "serving at the table" (so, e.g., in Matt 4:11 par.; 8:15 par.; Luke 22:26-27; John 2:5, 9; Acts 6:2, cf. 4). Table ministry included many different duties: providing food and beverage, inviting guests, laying the table, cooking the meal, serving it to those present, cleaning the table and the dishes, and sometimes accompanying the guests home in the light of a torch. A Hebrew slave could, however, not be expected to wash the feet of the arriving visitors. Most of the work done by a *diakonos* was manual and esteemed low: as menial. Plato *(Grg.* 517-518) calls the constructive political work done by Athens's former statesman in favor of the citizen "servile and menial and illiterate (lit. unfree) *(douloprepēs, diakonikos, aneleutheros),*" because it pertained to the body only and "left no room for justice and temperance," as they are necessary for the soul. As the NT example of Martha shows, chares (or chores) were often left to women (cf. Mark 1:31 par.). The service load *(pollē diakonia)* caused by the presence of numerous guests could turn out to be a sorrow-filled caring, even an overload that prevented listening to ongoing table talk (Luke 10:38-42). On the other hand, in Jerusalem, as Acts 6:1-6 shows, the apostles' time and energy were so absorbed by preaching the word of God that widows in need were neglected during the daily distribution of food. Therefore special deacons *(diakonoi)* were appointed and ordained to do the administration and manual work without which extended works of love cannot be performed. Philippians 1:1 and 1 Tim 3:8, 12 show that the ministry of deacons (probably also of deaconesses, 1 Tim 3:11) became institutionalized also outside Jerusalem. This service presupposed a special gift of the Holy Spirit. It was charismatic according to Rom 12:8, and it left the spiritual leadership of the congregation (by diverse ministries of the Word) in the hands of other charismatics, even of the apostles, prophets, teachers, and bishops. In Acts 20:17, 28 the titles of bishops and presbyters occur as synonymous, but the Pastoral Epistles and Ignatius bear testimony to later developments. A monarchic function was attributed to the bishop. Finally the ordained and consecrated clergy was sharply distinguished from the so-called laity.

The occurrence and function of the words formed from the root *diakon* in the undisputed Pauline letters do not encourage an ecclesiology built on a hierarchical system. Unlike, e.g., in *1 Clement,* servants of God who served one another or the whole congregation were not yet compared to military officers or other occupants of an office; they were not separated from the folks by a monopoly of rights and duties. E.g., the Colossians had to urge Archippus to fulfill a "service" that he had neglected to carry out (Col 4:17). Certainly this *diakonia* was hardly technically limited to a deacon's obligations. For the words derived from the root *diakon* have in Paul's diction a much wider sense:

Christ is called a "servant of those circumcised," but he is not a "servant of sin" (Rom 15:8; Gal 2:17). The mission and work of the apostle Paul reveal that he himself is a "servant" and fulfills a "service." He serves God, Christ, the gospel, righteousness, and this "in Christ" and/or by the power of the Spirit. He does it never to his own benefit but out of love for the congregations (2 Cor 3:3-9; 4:1, 8-9; 11:6, 15, 23; Rom 11:13; 15:25; Eph 3:7; Col 1:23, 25). Facing the manifold physical and spiritual needs, men and women assist him as colleagues rather than as underlings. Together with Paul they are "fellow workers of God" and will be rewarded by God himself (1 Cor 3:5-15).

This does not exclude a division of labor. The Holy Spirit provides the workers with manifold "gifts" to perform their service to the life and unity of the "body of Christ," even the church (1 Cor 12:5; Rom 12:7). In the lists enumerating the several manners of serving, the ministries fulfilled by preaching, teaching, and counseling have priority (1 Cor 12:4-11; Eph 4:11-12; cf. Rom 12:3-8; Pastoral Epistles, passim), and the very specific contributions made by individuals are fully recognized. E.g., the distinct service work of Timothy is cited in 1 Thess 3:2; 1 Tim 4:6; 2 Tim 4:5; of Apollos in 1 Cor 3:5; of Phoebe in Rom 16:1-2; of Stephanas in 1 Cor 16:15; of Epaphras in Col 4:12; and

of Mark in 2 Tim 4:11. But a hierarchical system, corresponding to a military, govern-
mental, or business pecking order, is not established by the differentiation. No servant
except Jesus Christ is in any sense superior to others. Rather Paul considers and treats
each Christian and every congregation as drafted into service and equipped for the ministry. According to Eph 4:12 (cf. Heb 6:10), all of them are in the "service" of God and
one another. In Phil 2:30 Paul goes so far as to assert that the saints owe him personal
service to benefit his apostolic ministry. (In this verse *leitourgia* is used instead of
diakonia.) At any rate, "serving" is both the privilege and the obligation of *all* the saints,
without any distinction of higher from lower service ranks. All of them have to live up
to their salvation with fear and trembling (cf. Phil 2:12).

The collection Paul organizes in the mainly Gentile Christian congregations for
the benefit of the Jerusalem church is called *diakonia* in 2 Cor 8–9 and Rom 15:31. This
denotation reveals that the original sense of this word ("waiting at the table") was never
completely obliterated. It reminds one of the fact that in the early church all the diverse
ministries that met the needs of the congregation had their roots, their center, and their
criterion in the celebration of the Lord's Supper. In Gal 2:11-14 and 1 Cor 10–11, Paul
insists on the eucharistic communion of Jews and Gentiles, rich and poor, high and low,
and thereby shows that all Christians alike are guests and servants at the Lord's Table.

Onesimus's service, as envisaged by Paul for the slave's future, can certainly include work done with the hands, but needs by no means be restricted to manual
labor. The apostle uses a formula that denotes the width and the narrowness of
the expected service — as well as the cost of faithful discipleship:

In the chains of the gospel. In the Greek texts, the noun "chains" *(desmoi)*
distinctly alludes to the Pauline self-description as "prisoner" *(desmios)* in
verses 1 and 9. Paul had more than solely his physical and legal captivity in Roman hands in mind there — also the spiritual bondage by and to "the Messiah
Jesus." Now, in verse 13, Paul speaks of "chains of the gospel," probably in a similar sense. Three interpretations can be distinguished, without excluding one
another.

1. E.g., the NEB and NJB versions suggest that Onesimus's expected service was restricted to work to be done during the present imprisonment of the
apostle by the Romans. Indeed, in verse 10 Paul calls his physical and spiritual
captivity "my chains," just as also Ignatius (*Trall.* 12.2) writes of "my chains."
P. Stuhlmacher suggests that Onesimus's service would consist of daily valet
work, and of maintaining contact with the outside world. Still, the apostle need
not have thought of solely housekeeping and secretarial duties that would enable him to do his own church building and mission work. He may have found
Onesimus "useful" also for fulfilling independent tasks, as a colleague rather
than an amanuensis. In that case, the slave was not just to continue under the
new employer the more or less domestic work done once at the orders of

Philemon. Neither would he be condemned, together with some probably all-too-loquacious women, to "keep silent in the congregation" and to abstain from "teaching and wielding any authority" (cf. 1 Cor 14:34; 1 Tim 2:12). Rather he would then assist and support Paul by being also, of his own right, a preacher and teacher of the gospel. The "chains of the gospel" do certainly not exclude the combination of manual services with verbal proclamation and counseling. Earlier the possibility had been mentioned repeatedly that the slave Onesimus became finally bishop of Ephesus.

2. The "chains of the gospel" may hint at future suffering. Almost all parts of the NT show that heralds of the gospel and less conspicuous believers were slandered, reviled, persecuted, and laid in chains. Staying with Paul and serving him involve for Onesimus the serious consequences of becoming an inmate of a state prison. He even may have to work under the conditions usual for a chain gang. There is no reason to assume that Paul's "child" shied away from such a future. In turn, the apostle makes Philemon realize that by letting Onesimus serve Paul, he would not dismiss the slave into an easy and comfortable life. Neither Paul, nor Onesimus, nor Philemon is spared the cost of discipleship. Calvin insists in his exposition of Philem 13 that those working for the testimony of the gospel will be "martyrs of Christ," and he enumerates "exilations, prisons, calumniations, deprivations of property" among the modalities of persecution. He concludes, "whoever refuses to participate in them, separates himself from Christ himself." Less harsh but substantially similar is E. Lohmeyer's interpretation: the dignity of the service to the gospel is augmented when the service is performed "in the chains of the gospel. Paul ties him [Onesimus] together with the cause of the gospel and the grace of martyrdom."

3. Also possible is a brighter understanding of "the chains of the gospel." According to Matt 5:11-12, Jesus had pronounced God's blessing over those reviled, persecuted, and slandered, and had invited them to rejoice and be jubilant in view of the great reward awaiting them. In, e.g., Col 1:24 Paul bluntly affirms, "I rejoice in suffering"; in Eph 3:13 he declares that his tribulations are the "glory" of the congregation; and in Eph 6:20 he jokingly equates his (iron) fetters with an ambassador's (golden) chains. Ignatius considers it a glory and an honor to be imprisoned for Christ's sake. He calls the chains binding him "spiritual pearls." To be exposed to death means: "Near the sword is near to God; with the wild beasts is with God." Also he warns of being haughty toward slaves, but advises, let them "endure to the glory of God" (*Eph.* 11.2; *Smyrn.* 4.2; *Polyc.* 4.3; additional utterances in praise of captivity are collected by, e.g., J. B. Lightfoot). In his exposition of PHM (1527), Luther declares, "Those chains are precious in the eyes of the Lord." Applied to Onesimus's eventual future service to Paul, this would mean that, even when suffering cannot be avoided, the slave will occupy a place of honor and will be richly rewarded by God himself. How

can Philemon ever begrudge his slave such a privilege? To summarize: the mention of the gospel chains increases the pressure on the slave owner to fulfill the wish that Paul utters so cautiously.

Substituting for you. There is more than only one viable translation of the words *hyper sou* that in the Greek text stand in the center of Philem 13.

NEB gives a version that corresponds to a frequently held opinion: "as you would wish." Indeed, in the majority of cases when *hyper* occurs in the NT, especially also in the Pauline letters, this preposition has lost its original local sense ("over" or "beyond") and signifies "in the name of, in favor of, with reference to, or, on account of." (See H. Riesenfeld, *TDNT*, 8.705-715.) Therefore, philological reasons permit the assumption that Onesimus's hoped-for service to Paul and the gospel would be both permitted and authorized by Philemon. It would then fulfill a wish not only of Paul but also of the slave's owner. The overfulfillment of Paul's hopes and desires, as mentioned in verse 21, would possibly consist of material and moral support given to the servant who would be working for Paul. In verse 20 the apostle actually admits that — perhaps in this way — he would "take advantage" of his friend Philemon.

Another interpretation, however, has still heavier implications: e.g., NJB translates, "he could have been a substitute for you." If this version be correct, Paul appears willing to accept Onesimus's service as replacement of the labor that ought to be carried out by the slave's legal owner himself. Would such a hint be friendly or vituperative? J. B. Lightfoot writes, "With delicate tact the Apostle assumes that Philemon would have wished to perform these friendly offices in person, if it had been possible" (cf. E. Haupt and E. Lohse). But H. Binder does not intend "to cover up what properly no listener to Paul should miss hearing: at bottom, Paul approaches Philemon with a quasi reproach. Onesimus would have to do . . . in your stead, what essentially would be your own duty." (Cf. A. Schweitzer, *Die Mystik des Apostels Paulus* [1930], p. 321.)

As a matter of fact, in the Hellenistic age *hyper* invades the spheres of *anti* ("instead of"; H. Riesenfeld, *TDNT*, 8.507, 512-513). Contemporary law permitted under certain circumstances a freeborn man who had been drafted for public work or military service to delegate an able-bodied slave as replacement. When at the dictation of a sender a scribe writes a letter, he sometimes remarks at the end that the document was written "for" *(hyper)* the employer by ———. In analogy, a postscript to Paul's letter to the Romans bears the remark, "written through *(dia)* Tertius." In 2 Cor 5:20 Paul calls himself an ambassador who represents Christ or substitutes for him *(hyper Christou)*. The apostle receives the gifts brought to him by Epaphroditus, Stephanas, Fortunatus, and Achaicus as full payment of the Philippians' and Corinthians' open debt *(hysterēma)*. (In Phil 2:30 and 1 Cor 16:17 the preposition *hyper* is not used, but the representative function of the delegates is obvious.) According to Philem 20, finally, Philemon owes nothing less than himself to Paul — which means that he is indebted to deliver much more than what he might amortize by cash payments and/or temporary services.

Because verse 20 follows soon after verse 13, the second of the above-mentioned interpretations deserves preference. Paul considers Philemon a man who for the length of his life is obliged with soul and body to do full-time service, in the chains of the gospel at the apostle's side. And now, in verse 13, he is graciously permitted to let Onesimus take his place. There is a way in Greek to denote replacement or substitution unequivocally. If Paul had chosen to write *anti sou* instead of *hyper sou,* all ambiguity would have been avoided. For the less frequent preposition *anti* means distinctly "in place of, in exchange for, or in return for" (as, e.g., in 1 Thess 5:15; 1 Cor 11:15; Rom 12:17; Matt 20:28; Luke 11:11). Onesimus would then have served vicariously in Philemon's stead, and the slave owner would have been as much as honorably dismissed from service and would henceforth "owe" the apostle nothing. The goal and result of slave insurrections before Paul's time, also of later social and political revolutions, was frequently a reversal of the tables. The high and mighty were forced to do menial work, and formerly oppressed people were placed in the positions of power. In Philem 13, however, Paul suggests something else than such a simple change of roles. He prefers writing *hyper sou* instead of *anti sou* because Philemon shall not fancy himself to be released from duty by letting Onesimus enter Paul's service.

What Paul probably had in mind is a special kind of representation. When he sends the slave as his delegate and representative to Philemon and expects an adequate reception and treatment of him (vv. 16-17), he reveals that he himself will be present and welcomed when Onesimus has returned to his master. So also Jesus Christ is in person fully present when his messengers and the little brothers are either repudiated or charitably received. They do not replace an absent person but re-present him who has sent them. In analogy, when Onesimus substitutes as servant of Paul and the gospel, then Philemon remains conscripted for service and fulfills his interminable duty. The slave owner is not permitted to enjoy happy riddance of his debt, but will have continuously to demonstrate his "obedience," e.g., by honoring Onesimus as brother and by doing the domestic work necessary to host Paul (vv. 16, 20-22).

VERSE 14

But I have decided to do nothing without your consent so that the good you do not be as if by coercion, but voluntary.

The section Philem 8-14 is a ring composition: at the end, the substance of the beginning is resumed. In verses 8-9 and 14, alternatives are mentioned that seemed open to Paul and that he yet rejected in favor of a strictly personal decision. The whole passage also has a climactic character. After the reticent and soft start that culminated in humble "pleading," Paul has clearly formulated what he "should have liked." Now he announces a final decision: Philemon is given the freedom to decide for himself. Is, then, the apostle kinder and more magnanimous toward the master, who is a freeman, than to the slave who is being sent back?

I have decided. As earlier observed, the aorist *ēthelēsa* (I have decided) stands in contrast to the imperfect *eboulomēn* (I should have liked) in the preceding verse. The tense now chosen by Paul is hardly to be explained as "literary aorist," although indeed (in vv. 13, 19, 21) such aorists are used. They call for the translation, "I send back, I write, I am writing." But in verse 14 Paul expresses a decision made once and definitely, even before he started to write PHM.

The resolve to let Philemon make up his own mind does not preclude the apostle from speaking in the imperative: "Receive him . . . charge it to my account . . . give my heart rest . . . get a guest room ready" (v. 17; cf. vv. 12 [variant reading], 18, 20, 22). Paul appears to contradict himself paradoxically when with equal emphasis and conviction in verse 14 he affirms, if not the slave owner's autonomy, then at least his freedom of decision, and later in verse 21, the confidence in the same man's "obedience." Is the affirmation of free will hypocritical, or is it illusionary wishful thinking when a slave owner is trusted to heed the hints given in PHM in Onesimus's favor? A choice between these alternatives is certainly only superfluous when Paul aims at *voluntary* obedience. Below, in the Notes on verse 21, this particular kind of obedience will be discussed. Verse 14 opens vistas but does not yet close the issue.

In this verse Paul explains why he sends back Onesimus and thereby, at least temporarily, renounces fulfilling his wish to retain him at his side: he would have deprived the slave's owner of the opportunity to make a decision of his own.

Nothing without your consent. The personal decision that Paul by no means wants to limit or obstruct is at this place called *gnōmē.* This Greek noun is formed out of the same stem as *ginōskō* and *gnōsis* (to know, knowledge): it signifies the root and the mode, the means and the result of rational perception and intelligent thought. Whenever in secular and religious literature this noun occurs, different contexts determine which of the possible translations or paraphrases is appropriate (see LSLex and BAG, s.v; R. Bultmann, *TDNT,* 1.691 nn. 7 and 9, and pp. 717-718): (a) intelligence or its use in careful rational pondering and deliberating; (b) a disposition or inclination of a person's mind and character; (c) an opinion, judgment, decision, proposal, or counsel based on reason, or, more seldom, on emotion; (d) consent with the opinion, will, or at-

titude of other persons, with the stipulation of a contract, or under the requirements of law and custom. The rational essence of *gnōmē* is pointed out by, e.g.,
the fifth century B.C.E. orator Antiphon (*Or.* 5.92): "An unwillingly committed
lapse *(hamartēma)* is due to coincidence *(tychē)*, a willing lapse to *gnōmē.*"

Aristotle (*NE* 3.2.1111b) admits the existence of different opinions in regard to heavenly and earthly matters, and regarding things possible and impossible. He emphasizes that human freedom of choice pertains solely to *the means*
to achieve a given end. Examples of the significance "personal opinion" or
"counsel" (as opposed to "command") are found in 1 Cor 7:6, 25-26, 40; 2 Cor
8:10. When Paul warns of divisions emerging within a congregation, *gnōmē* signifies the conviction and intention shared with other church members (1 Cor
1:10). In Acts 4:32 full harmony is described when it is stated, "they were one
heart and one soul." "Consent" was chosen for our translation because Paul appeals to something better than a freewheeling opinion that would be bare of respect for another person's innermost thoughts and hopes. Paul has good reasons not to appeal explicitly to emotions and feelings such as pity, compassion,
or other precursors and followers of forgiveness. Philemon's knowledge, insight, and intellect shall have their say and their way. In the exposition of the
words "recognition of all the good" in verse 6, it was shown that "knowledge,"
according to Paul and most parts of the Bible, means the awareness and the wisdom to relate to persons and things and to behave adequately. Almost always,
knowing and knowledge signify more than only a mental act or an intellectual
conviction. (Cf. the interpretation of Col 1:9-10 in AB 34B.)

When in Philem 14 Paul's friend is given the freedom to form his own
gnōmē and to act according to his finding, he is declared responsible and capable. He is free to ponder motivations and implications, to weigh various means
to achieve his goal, to make a wise selection, and to follow the way he deems
best for himself, for Paul, and for Onesimus. Main options open to the slave
owner have been listed in the second excursus under verse 13 above (pp. 367-
369). What Paul expects of Philemon is, to borrow a phrase from Immanuel
Kant, that he "have the courage to make use of [his] own intellect."

There is a close relationship between *gnōmē*, as used in Philem 14, and the
"conscience" *(syneidēsis)* mentioned by Paul in other texts. Both are a gift of
God and are presupposed in Christians. (According to Augustine, Paul refers in
Rom 2:14-15 to the Gentile Christians *rather* than the pagan Gentiles' conscience, as the allusion to Jer 31:33, i.e., to God's eschatological people, shows.)
A common stem links the words *gnōmē* and *syneidēsis* together: both indicate
the presence and the effect of a given knowledge. Also the Latin *conscientia* and
its equals in Western languages express an awareness that is shaped by what a
person knows. How is it known? Micah 6:8 (cf. Deut 10:12-13; etc.) affirms
clearly: by the revelation of God only. "He has showed you, O Man, what is

good. . . ." The NT affirms that the same revelation is summed up by Jesus Christ and implanted into human hearts by the Holy Spirit.

Instead of speaking of Philemon's *gnōmē,* Paul might as well have mentioned his conscience. He has full confidence that the slave owner will let his conscience speak and will obey its voice, rather than a passing mood or whim. The free will and conscience proclaimed is, as the words "so that the good you do" reveal, orientated exclusively to the good. The conjunction *hina* (so that) is used in both its final and its consecutive senses. A freedom from God, without God, or against God would never have been designated by the term *gnōmē.*

In analogy, Epictetus has been admired and imitated by many teachers of ethics when he asserted that human will and decision are free only when a higher wisdom and will prevails over individual preference. "All will be free according to the will *(gnōmē)* which is at the same time yours and God's." (Quotations from Epictetus's *Dissertations* and *Enchiridion,* which culminate in this sentence, are easily accessible in H. Schlier's article on freedom, in *TDNT,* 2.494.)

But following J. Knox's above-mentioned understanding of "sending back," *gnōmē* would in Philem 14 mean the judgment to be passed by Philemon in his capacity of ultimate judge over Onesimus's future. Paul's wish to retain the slave would then be equal to a lower court, an overrulable verdict. Philemon would not only be a party to but also the judge in questions of his private possessions. Since he certainly shall not judge in the manner of an autocrat and tyrant, he would be bound by a law; God, the supreme judge, would be left out of the picture. Actually, the text of Philem 14 asserts solely the freedom of Philemon to decide according to his conscience.

The good you do. The Greek formula *to agathon sou* (lit. "your good") is unique in the NT: a *hapax legomenon.* As the article before the "good" shows, the adjective is transformed into a substantive, as is often done in Greek literature (and in the NT in Gal 6:11; Rom 3:8; 8:3; 13:8; Luke 6:45; Matt 5:37; etc.; cf. BDR, 263). The possessive pronoun "your" which in the Greek text follows upon the adjective turned into a noun, reminds one of the phrases "your love and faithfulness which you have" in verse 5 and "your faith communion" in verse 6. In the last-mentioned verse, too, the possessive "your" was immediately linked up with "the good." Paul had expressed his thanks to God for Philemon's very personal and specific participation in those spiritual gifts that were also given by God to the congregation. Now, in verse 14, the apostle expresses his hope that after receiving PHM, the slave's owner will continue deciding and acting in the service of the good.

RSV, NEB, and NJB follow and anticipate those interpretations that render *to agathon sou* by "your goodness," "your kindness," or equivalent nouns (in German: *deine Güte* or *deine Gütigkeit*). In Hebrew, *ḥesed* is the cordial and outgoing, spontaneous and compassionate, liberal and overwhelming character disposition and social attitude that goes beyond the mere fulfillment of a contract's or family bond's requirement. This significance need not be totally excluded from Paul's mind. Yet the reference to coercion and voluntariness in the context discourages the version just quoted: a quality of character can neither be imposed by force nor be the result of a single voluntary decision.

Most likely Paul intended to speak of one of three things, which all have to do more with doing the good than with being good or having a firm character. *To agathon sou* may mean:

1. One specific deed, one among other "good works." In Eph 2:10, in the Pastoral Epistles, and in, e.g., Matt 5:16, such works are mentioned. Paul distinguishes them from "works of law," which cannot justify either Jews or Gentiles (Rom 3:28; Gal 2:16; etc.; cf. AB 34, pp. 244-251). From Philemon Paul would then expect one specific good work (a particular *Guttat*, according to BDR, ZB, H. Lohse, and others): the sending back of Onesimus to Paul. H. A. W. Meyer and M. Dibelius/H. Greeven are convinced that Paul's mention of a good work actually includes and expresses a petition for Onesimus's return to the apostle. W. Bieder argues that sending back the slave would be the "better" choice for Philemon to make, for "ever again in its relation to the better it is decided what is good." Earlier it was observed that other interpreters considered manumission that "good" which the slave's owner had to do upon receiving PHM.

2. An unspecified, lifelong devotion to do good work. Sometimes (in 2 Thess 2:17; Rom 2:7; 13:3; cf. Phil 1:6) Paul speaks of "good work" in the singular and means distinctly more than one single action. In 2 Cor 9:8 and Col 1:10 he urges the saints to be "overflowing and fruitbearing in every good work," and in 1 Thess 1:3 and 2 Thess 1:11 the term "the work of faith" reveals that in Paul's understanding faithfulness is an activity, far removed from a quietistic or merely passive attitude toward the Lord Jesus and all the saints (cf. Phil 1:5-7). Faith is the one and only attitude that counts for both the present life and eternity. Similarly, John 6:27-29 elaborates on the distinction between the singular and the plural of *ergon* (work) by stating, "Do not labor for the food which perishes, but for the food which endures to eternal life which the Son of man will give you. . . . What must we do, to be doing the *works of God?* . . . This is the *work* of God, that you believe. . . ."

3. Finally, Philem 14 may have to be slightly paraphrased by a brief addition: "the good you do." In this case, the actual performance of the good, not just the intention, the voluntariness, and the decision to live out of faith and according to it, decides over the quality of Onesimus's character as well as of his work. In the NT, diverse Greek words are used for emphasizing that the good has to be "done." In Mark 3:4 *agathon poieō;* in Acts 14:17 *agathoergeō;* in 1 Pet 2:14-15, 20; 3:6, 17 *agathopoieō;* in 1 Pet 4:19 *agathopoiia* denote the mental and

physical activity that not only aims at the good but also achieves it. If Paul means this by (lit.) "your good," then he does more than only appeal to a certain choice to be made, and an action to be taken after Onesimus's arrival. In this case he is asking for an ever new pondering, searching, weighing, finding out, deciding, and performing. Not at the first try may a patent solution offer itself and be readily grasped. Unforeseen problems can arise and take turns with unexpected opportunities. A decision made now with a good conscience may later have to be revised partially or totally. Philemon alone, a member of the congregation of the assembled community of Christians, may propose the best way to choose.

The last interpretation has the widest range. It includes the tenable results of the alternatives, and it corresponds best to the context. It suggests a type of pastoral counseling that is at the same time realistic-pragmatic and liberating. Does it also include egotistic elements that allude to either Paul's or Philemon's self-interest and profit? J. B. Lightfoot has suggested that by "your good" is meant "the benefit arising from thee [Philemon], i.e. the good which I [Paul] should get from the continuous presence of Onesimus [with me], and which would be owing to thee." Also, it might be argued that in some cases slave owners welcomed an opportunity to get rid of a troublesome slave, that Paul hoped for an improvement of Philemon's domestic peace by his separation from the slave, or that he wanted to make the slave owner think of a rich heavenly reward. Indeed, there are biblical passages revealing that what is good in God's eyes is ultimately good also for God's children. Still, the conclusion cannot be drawn that "good" is solely what serves self-interests.

Paul has a special term for describing how the good to be done becomes known. In 1 Thess 5:21; Gal 6:4; Rom 12:2; Phil 1:10, he denotes by the verb *dokimazō* the process of searching, probing, testing, deciding, and enacting by which is discovered the will of God for the present time, and what pleases him in eternity. (In AB 34A, pp. 568-569 and 603-606, reasons are mentioned why in the just-mentioned passages this verb has to be translated "finding out by experience.") In Philem 14 Paul permits and encourages his friend in Colossae to search for the good and to stick his neck out boldly in taking action fitting to his finding.

The next verse will reveal that Paul does not pretend for sure to know God's will for himself, Onesimus, and Philemon. He cannot quote a divine command, and he will not give an order for describing which way Philemon has to decide and to go. But since according to Phil 1:6 Paul is "convinced that he who began his good work in you will bring it to completion," and because Philemon has already served the best interests of the congregation (Philem 6), the apostle has no doubt that the slave owner will decide wisely and responsibly.

E. Lohmeyer, J. Ernst, J. Gnilka are among those interpreters who assume that "the good" to be done by Philemon agrees with the contemporary popular-philosophical conception of the good. But what H. Binder asserts may be true to a specific feature of most Pauline references to the good: it does not suffice just to speak of "human goodness, good work." For just as in verse 6, Paul actually speaks of "the good of God which gains power over a person and which then also may be called 'his' good. In question is here therefore the personal involvement of Philemon in the good will of God."

As especially Rom 7:14-23 shows, the apostle is fully aware of theological, biographical, and psychological problems in the decision-making process: "The Law is spiritual, but I, being a fleshly creature, am sold under sin. . . . What I don't will, this I do," etc. In Philem 14 the apostle gives yet another hint of the modality of that process:

Not as if by coercion . . . but voluntarily (me hōs kata anagkēn alla kata hekousion). Elsewhere, Paul does not frequently speak of the contrast between yielding to pressure on one side and freewill decisions and actions on the other. More unique to and central to this message and his ethics are other alternatives: flesh or Spirit, sin or grace, supposedly meritorious works or service to God out of gratitude, this world or the next, etc. Nonbiblical ethics has little use for such terminology. All the more, the rejection of force and pressure and the clear-cut decision in favor of spontaneity and voluntarism seem to link the apostle's preference to a tenet of idealistic philosophical ethics. Even when philosophers and moralists do not know or like Paul's Old Testament roots and the christological and soteriological ground of his ethics, they seem to uphold in essence the same distinction between coercion and voluntariness — the perennial issue of human freedom of will is at stake. English "voluntary" (cf. its German equivalent: *freiwillig*) is derived from Latin *volo* (to will) and denotes a freedom that is willing to defy all pressures.

Is it then necessary to assume that in Paul's opinion constraining coercion is always bad, while voluntary decision and action are always to the good? Or does yet a subtle form of determinism still have the last word? Is it, e.g., rather easy for Paul, the Roman citizen, to speak to the slave owner Philemon of freedom of will, because free decision is a privilege of the high and mighty, perhaps also of the bourgeois class, while it is a luxury the poor and needy are not given to enjoy? First an excursus on the role of coercion, then another on the essence of voluntariness are indispensable for the appreciation of the special message of Philem 14. (For the following see, in addition to philosophical and other dictionaries, especially the articles by W. Grundmann on *anagkē*, Fr. Hauck on *hekōn*, and H. Schlier on *eleutheros* in *TDNT*, 1.345-347; 2.469-470; 2.448-503. They provide access to the treatment of these topics in Greek literature.)

Excursus: Coercion in Greek Philosophy and in the Pauline Letters

In Plato's *Cratylus* (420de), Socrates offers an etymology of the Greek word *anagkē* (necessity). He derives it from *an' agkē iōn* (going through a ravine). More likely is, however, a non-Greek, perhaps Celtic origin of the word. Plato ascribes to sin (or, to error: *hamartia*) and to lacking knowledge *(amathia)* the pressure exerted by *anagkē* — which can also be called "brute force *(bia)."* Greek dictionaries show that at least four meanings of *anagkē* can be distinguished:

1. Synonyms of *anagkē* can be *moira* (lot) and, in later Greek, *heimarmenē* (destiny). These terms signify Fate, the supreme power enthroned high above all deities and requiring unconditional and unlimited respect. Fate is inevitable, invincible, and unchangeable, "a force which defies all knowledge . . . controls all things and . . . conditions reality" (W. Grundmann, *TDNT*, 1.345). Socrates (Plato, *Prt.* 345d) quotes a poet saying, "Not even the Gods battle against necessity *(anagkē)."* Sometimes the unknown and unavoidable is called "bitter *(pikra)."* Erinys, Klotho, Lachesis, and Atropos are the executioners in diverse ways, together with a host of Erinyes. There are no means to influence Fate — except when by magic means its resistance is tried. Still, death finally demonstrates its omnipotence. Only in rare cases may a friendly face of Fate penetrate the dark clouds. The goddess Tyche (Fortuna, good luck) is cultically worshiped, and attempts are made to influence her mood. Male and female children were named after her, but never after *anagkē*.

2. Any form of exerting *anagkē* can be called *anagkazō* or *biazō*. This is the way a tyrant and carnal need (such as erotic desire) make their powers felt. The wantonness and arbitrariness of heinous pressure of any kind call for resistance of freedom-loving and wise citizens. In Greek thought both are found: a monistic concept of an all-embracing cosmic principle of *anagkē* that makes rebellion hopeless, and a dualistic concept that ascribes to reason, the spirit, or the soul the capability and duty to engage in resistance. In his *Metaphysics* (5.5.1115ab), Aristotle offers a purely rational definition of "the necessary" and denies that anything compulsory is attached to eternal and unmovable things.

3. *Anagkē* may arise primarily from the needs and the weakness of the human body and from the miserable circumstances a person has to endure, before death brings final release. Greek ethicists are fully aware that the great majority of human beings, including heroes, wise scholars, and paragons of virtue, do not succeed in letting the immortal soul and its high aspirations be victorious over the requests and lusts of the body, and over the vicissitudes emanating from wicked persons and adverse conditions. Since the time of Plato, solely Diogenes and Socrates are described as shining examples of the soul's victory over the feeble body.

4. *Anagkē* is good and welcome when it issues from reason. Then it fights ignorance, error, foolishness, and unlogical thinking. In a friendly or a pointed dialogue, good sense and convincing arguments presented by wise persons "force" a less enlightened debater to yield to the "necessary" conclusion.

Turning to Paul, it cannot be expected that he ever means by *anagkē* blind Fate.

His faith in the one living God, the creator of heaven and earth, the savior and judge of Jews and Gentiles, leaves no room for either a dualistic or a monistic worldview. In Philem 15 he will distinctly allude to God's providence, not to fate. All the more, he uses the word *anagkē* and its cognates in several other senses.

In 1 Cor 9:16-17 the apostle speaks of a coercion exerted by God and/or Christ. Upon the former persecutor and devastator of Christ's flock (cf. Gal 1:23; 1 Cor 15:9; 1 Tim 1:16), the task is imposed to preach the gospel. (According to Acts 13:46, "it was necessary" *[anagkaion]* that the word of God be spoken "first to the Jews, then also to the Gentiles.") When Paul fulfills his assignment willingly (or: voluntarily, *hekōn*), he knows that he will be rewarded. But even when he is unwilling *(akōn)*, he yet has to carry out his mission. In Acts 26:14 and a variant reading of 9:6, Paul's conversion near Damascus is described in similar terms and Paul is forced into the service of Christ, for "it is hard for you, kicking against the goads" (NJB). *Anagkē* is in the hand of God also when the singular or the plural of this noun signifies present or future misery, distress, or calamity. The tribulations endured by the apostle and the congregations are far from being haphazard strokes of Fate. They are "messianic woes" (1 Thess 3:7; 5:3; 1 Cor 7:26; 2 Cor 6:4; 1:7; 12:10; Matt 24:8 par.; Luke 21:23; Acts 2:24; Rev 12:2). Not even the "necessity that scandals will come" (Matt 18:7) is ascribed to a power above God. In analogy, the synoptic Gospels contain many sayings of Jesus according to which "it is necessary" *(dei)* that suffering precede the glory to come. Paul mentions once also a necessity created by God in regard to the difference of the many members and the need of their cooperation. According to 1 Cor 12:22-24, by God's arrangement the parts of the human body as well as the members of the congregation are so composed and mutually interdependent that it is necessary that those seemingly weaker are worthy of the greatest honor.

A special problem is posed by Paul's reference to necessity *(anagkē)* in Rom 13:5. In this verse the apostle bids the Christians of Rome to subordinate themselves to the political authorities. As the middle form "subordinate yourselves" shows, Paul thinks of *voluntary* obedience, rather than of an enforced submission.

Elsewhere Paul speaks of a *perforce* subordination — yet without using the noun *anagkē* or the verb *anagkazō*. According to Rom 8:20-21, all creation has been subjugated to futility, without the concurrence of their free will or consent *(ouch hekousa,* variant reading, *thelousa)*. Yet this subjugation is not final: there will be a day when the creatures are "set free from bondage to decay and obtain the glorious liberty of the children of God." Other passages (1 Cor 15:25-27; Col 2:14-15; Phil 2:10-11; Eph 1:19-20; cf. 1 Pet 3:22; Heb 2:8; Matt 11:27 par.; 28:18 as also Rom 13:1-2) speak of the enforced subordination of the principalities and powers, i.e., of the invincible and yet manifest constituents and structures of creaturely life, including the state and death. The crucifixion, the resurrection, and the parousia of Christ are the means by which God bereaved them of this claim for omnipotence.

On the other hand, for human beings the death, the resurrection, and the second coming of Christ are, according to Paul, already at the present time the source of freedom, of appeals to freewill decisions and actions, and of the enablement to take up and to bear responsibility in diverse social settings. (The version of 1 Pet 2:18; 3:1 that has been chosen by, e.g., REV: ". . . be submissive . . . ," is misleading because it suggests re-nouncing the freedom for which Christians have been liberated, and withdrawal from active responsibility.)

In Rom 13:2, 3, and 5 Paul elaborates on the motivation for voluntary submission and cooperation: not only "fear" of the judgment and wrath (of God and/or of the state officials) shall motivate them, but "also . . . the conscience." As previously stated, that conscience *(syneidēsis)* is in Pauline writings that sharing of knowledge, that awareness of God's will and deeds that is given by the Spirit into new hearts (see, e.g., Rom 2:14-15; 1 Pet 2:19). Christians are privileged to know that God has exerted and is exerting power over political rulers. He uses them for a specific purpose: instead of displaying a wanton autonomy, they are to be "servants of God," by rewarding the good and punishing the evil (Rom 13:1-5; cf. 1 Pet 2:14). In his essay "Lob und Strafe durch die Obrigkeit. Hellenistisches zu Röm 13,3-4," W. C. van Unnik has shown that Paul was far from justi-fying or glorifying each and every form of civil government. The qualified rewarding and punishing is an element of enlightened contemporary Hellenistic philosophy of the state. Thus it is the essence of what today is called a constitutional and legal government, or in German: a *Rechtsstaat.*

In consequence, the *anagkē* mentioned in Rom 13:5 is a good force: it goes out from God, just as does the necessity laid upon Paul to preach the gospel. It is made per-suasive by Paul's logical argument. It calls not only for respect stemming out of fear, but for the response of the conscience. In summary, it aims at voluntary submission and ac-ceptance, rather than at grumbling connivance and doggish crawling. According to 2 Cor 5:14, the "love of Christ" is a similarly compelling force. It makes Paul draw logi-cal and ethical conclusions *(synechei hēmas, krinantes touto . . .).* In Heb 7:12, 27 *anagkē* is the force of a logical conclusion. How are Christians to react to it? The obedience that flows out of knowledge of the gospel and of free will is most eloquently described in Eph 6:5-8; cf. Col 3:22-24. Slaves shall, conscious of God's coming judgment, do their work "with fear and trembling, in singleness of heart . . . as servants of Christ, doing the will of God from the heart *(ek psychēs)* . . . with a good will *(eunoia)."*

References to the force applied to and by the human body have an entirely differ-ent meaning. In Gal 2:3, 14; 6:12 Paul rejects passionately the attempt to "force" Chris-tians to become circumcised. The apostle concedes in 1 Cor 7:37 that a biological drive *(anagkē)* can cause a man to insist on sexual intercourse with "his virgin," which also is permitted, mutual consent presupposed, to married couples (1 Cor 7:3-5).

In another group of statements Paul does what he "considers necessary" *(hēgoumai anagkaion)* in caring for the congregations founded by him. According to Phil 1:21-26; 2:5, he sends out cooperators to prepare his visit, and he holds out in his present captivity, because staying alive is "more necessary" for the Philippians than the fulfillment of his desire "to depart and be with Christ."

In view of the variety of meanings in which Paul speaks of a cogent necessity, the "coercion" rejected in Philem 14 might be understood in several different ways. Still, there is one pair of chapters that may serve as a fitting key to this central verse of PHM: perhaps each of the chapters 2 Cor 8–9 was originally a part of separate letters addressed to Corinth. Their combination in Second Corinthians increases the resemblance to

Philem 14. In 2 Cor 8–9 Paul asks, and he compiles a great number of reasons, for a liberal and well-planned collection for the saints in Jerusalem. In 2 Cor 8:1-5 he attributes it to the "grace of God" that the afflicted, utterly poor, and yet joyful Macedonian Christians have "overflowed in a wealth of liberality *(haplotēs)*" and contributed to the collection "beyond their means of their own free will *(authairetoi).*" In verses 7-9 he urges the Corinthians to live up to their already demonstrated "overflowing in faith, in speech, in knowledge, in eagerness and in your love for us" (cf. Philem 5-7!). In proof of this they are now, too, to overflow in the present act of grace. In 2 Cor 8:8 (as in Philem 8) Paul explicitly abstains from giving a command, in order in the next verse to argue that the Christians live from "the grace of our Lord Jesus Christ," who "though he was rich, yet for your sake became poor, so that by his poverty you might become rich." In the parallel passage 2 Cor 9:7, the apostle does not renounce giving a command but calls sadness and compulsion *(lypē* and *anagkē)* unfitting motivations of liberal giving. Each Corinthian shall contribute "according to the choice made by his own heart *(kathōs proērētai tē kardia)* . . . for God loves a cheerful giver." Just as in PHM, in these verses the voluntary decision and action are (1) closely related to God's and Christ's grace, (2) stimulated by a seemingly inexhaustible plentitude of supporting arguments, and (3) destined to work out for the best of the Christian community. Remotely parallel to such a quest for voluntariness is 1 Pet 5:2: the church elders are urged to tend "the flock of God not by constraint but willingly *(mē anagkastōs alla hekousiōs).*"

Nowhere does Paul teach or insinuate that human beings are sinning because they are under coercion to do so. Sin is a fact, but not a necessity. When the apostle confesses that — against his better knowledge and intention — he follows "the sin that dwells" in him, he obeys a will and a law that are strictly opposed to God's "spiritual law" (Rom 7:14-23; cf. 8:2).

In consideration of the various senses that *anagkē* and its derivatives had in contemporary secular Greek as well as in Paul's diction, it is hard to decide whether one single specific meaning prevails in Philem 14. A coercion emanating from God or from the logic of the context, from Roman legislation or from the apostle's special situation, from external or from internal forces may be in Paul's mind. In his 1527 lecture, Luther considered it sufficient to decry the compulsion exerted by the pope and the synagogue. The apostle himself appears to be aware of a inherent problem in the use of this term in the context of PHM:

Easily overlooked but potentially highly relevant is the word *hos* (in our translation: "as if") that is posed before "under coercion" but not repeated before "voluntary." Vg. renders it correctly by *velut* (as, just as, as if it were, seemingly), and J. B. Lightfoot elaborates on this qualification of *anagkē.* Paul "will not suppose that it [the good effected by Philemon] would really be constrained; but it must not even wear the *appearance (hōs)* of being so." In support of his interpretation, Lightfoot quotes Paul himself and Pliny the Younger: in

2 Cor 11:17 Paul admits that for a while "I speak not according to the Lord, but as if in foolishness *(ou kata kyrion, all' hōs en aphrosynē)*." The second-century Roman official writes in *Ep.* 9.21, "I am afraid that you will think that I am using pressure *(vereor ne videar non rogare sed cogere)*." According to LSLex, s.v. *hōs*, this word is used as an adverb, as a conjunction between two clauses, or as equivalent of a preposition, that is, it can introduce a comparison; prepare for the mention of "anything extraordinary"; serve as synonym of *hoti, hina, hopōs* (because, in order that, so that); designate "the reason or motive of the action"; or indicate that a round number follows. What Paul in Philem 14 actually wants to exclude is the assumption that brute force, the way it is usually understood, can ever be the cause, the motor, or the instrument of a good decision and action. In 2 Cor 11 the apostle had permitted himself, for a short time, to speak like a crazy fool. In Philem 14 he reveals by the little word *hōs* how sensitive he is to misunderstandings.

Still, the question can be posed whether the whole of PHM does not exert a very subtle form of coercion on the slave owner. As earlier quoted, A. Suhl explains Paul's procedure as a combination of candy-and-whip treatment, approaching extortion. N. R. Petersen (*Rediscovering Paul*, pp. 265 and 290) believes that there would have been "no need of such an array of manipulatory techniques — if Paul would have been as confident of Philemon's response as he claims" in verse 21. H. Binder, too, admits that Paul exerts "internal coërcion." At first reading, perhaps even Philemon might have understood the apostle this way. But there can be a gap between an author's intention and the reader's interpretation, and in case of conflict the author's purpose is more important. In verses 8-9 and 13-14 Paul makes unmistakably clear that he does not wish to impose, as if by coercion, his own will on Philemon. A study of *anagkē*'s opposite — "voluntary" — will provide more clarity.

Most amazing is a linguistic feature that makes the apostle's diction look less than beautiful. Paul changes over from the noun *anagkē* to the adjective *hekousios*. A pedantic literal translation of Philem 14 would read, ". . . not according to necessity (or: coercion, etc.) . . . but according to voluntary." Atticist Greek writers would have put it *kat' anagkēn* and *kath' hekousion* — as indeed also LXX Num 25:3 has the formula *kath' hekousion*. Good Greek style offered several possibilities to Paul for sticking to the rules. He might have formulated: (a) *kata to hekousion,* transforming the adjective into a noun, by the addition of the article (cf. *to agathon* in Philem 14); (b) *kath' hekousion tropon* or, . . . *gnōmēn,* i.e., one of the formulae used by, e.g., Sophocles, Thucydides, papyri, Philo; (c) *hekousiōs,* the adverb form that often (e.g., in 1 Pet 5:2) contrasts with *anagkōs.*

Paul's ugly deviation from normal Greek style might be explained as a feature of the Hellenistic rather than classical Greek in which he and other NT authors express themselves. The most striking example of a diction running wild is found in Rev 1:4: for denoting the divine origin of blessing, the author writes there, *apo ho ōn kai ho ēn kai ho erchomenos* (lit. "from the being one and the was and the coming one") — how barbaric a manipulation of Greek grammar and syntax! Incomplete, so-called *anacoluth* sentences occur often in Paul's letters (e.g., in Gal 2:4-5 and 2:6). Still, in each case good reasons had probably existed for choosing extraordinary language.

In the earlier-mentioned passage (*Cra.* 420de), Plato's Socrates adds to the etymology of *anagkē* a literalistic interpretation of the opposite "voluntary." *Hekousion* is traced back to the verb *eikō* and is explained as a motion corresponding ("yielding") to the human will *(boulēsis)*. What Paul understands by voluntariness in Philem 14 can be best explained when it is compared with the sense and function of *hekousios* in the Greek literature of his environment.

Excursus: Free Will in Philosophical Ethics and in the Greek Old Testament

According to Plato (*Prt.* 345de), "no wise man . . . will allow that any human being errs (or sins: *examartanō*) voluntarily or voluntarily performs shameful and evil works. But they know that all who do the shameful and evil things, do them against their will." Later in the same tract it is stated, "To prefer evil to good is not in the human nature." The dialogue in which Socrates utters these words ends with leaving it open whether or not knowledge and love of virtue are teachable. Socrates tends to teach that virtue, if only its essence be known, can be taught and will overcome the deceitful pleasures and effects of base desires and faulty arguments. In turn, in, e.g., *Leg.* 3.697, 701, and *Resp.* 8.562-563, Plato describes the degeneration and shameful transformation of freedom into licentiousness and anarchy.

Aristotle discusses (in his *NE* 3.1-5, 1109b-1115a) extensively the relation between external compulsion and voluntary choice. Unlike Plato, he makes a distinction between intentional and unintentional wrongdoing. Ignorance is at the root of unwillingly committed deeds only. (H. Schlier, in *TDNT*, 2.469, quotes also *Ethica Magna* 1.12.1118a for the difference between willingly committed and involuntary wicked acts.) In the case of lacking consciousness, the door is open to pity, repentance, and pardon. Voluntary is an act for which the moving principle lies in the agent. But what is done voluntarily can as well be vicious or virtuous, for human beings "make themselves responsible for being unjust." A person "can be unjust voluntarily. . . . vices of the soul and body are voluntary. . . . vices that are blamed must be in our own power." Thus in *NE* 1113b; 1114a, Aristotle corrects the "partly false and partly true . . . saying: No one is voluntarily wicked." A mature person is equal to neither a child nor an animal. Therefore neither a mere opinion or wish, nor anger nor appetites suffice to declare voluntarism always right. Freedom of will pertains solely to the making of a choice based on careful deliberation. Choice made on the ground of a rational principle decides on the proper means to achieve a good purpose. "Because a good man adopts the means voluntarily, virtue is voluntary, vice will also be none the less voluntary." In other words, not only the way to heaven, but also to hell, is paved with voluntary acts. According to Aristotle, it depends on ever new decisions and actions whether a person gradually becomes and finally is just or unjust. Voluntarism and free choice as such are not highest goods.

Socrates, Plato, and Aristotle teach that freedom can thrive only in the frame of a free *polis* (city, state). The state form in which freedom has its best chances is democracy (e.g., Plato, *Resp.* 8.362b; Aristotle, *Pol.* 4.4.1291b; *NE* 5.10.1134b). In such a state, freedom is based on law, and law on reason. Without respect *(aidōs)* for good law — no freedom! For freedom means both to rule and to be ruled (Plato, *Menex.* 86d; Aristotle, *Pol.* 6.1.1317b). We repeat: misuse of freedom is made and a degeneration takes place when freedom is equated with unbridled liberty in the pursuit of each individual's good pleasure.

Thus obedience to just laws is a demonstration of freedom, and freedom means to bear responsibility for the community. Following Ps.-Plato's *Definitions* (412d and 415a), freedom means "Mastership of one's own life, autocracy in every regard . . . liberty to use and to acquire (or, to possess) things." Neither Plato's nor Aristotle's teachings are recognizable in such definitions.

Contemporary and later Stoic philosophers are prolific in their discussions of true and false freedom. Freedom rightly used is a beautiful and glorious gift from which the individual and the state will benefit. Enslavement and other forms of coerced subjugation are the opposites. Epictetus's (ca. 50-130) teachings may serve as an example (as found in his *Dissertations* and *Enchiridion,* and excerpted conveniently by H. Schlier in *TDNT,* 2.493-496). Free in his decisions and actions is the wise man. He no longer follows, but despises, the urgings and passions arising out of desires, anxiety, anger, sympathy, astonishment, fear of death, and the like. He has a highly developed self-consciousness. He lives as he wills *(boulomai);* by his self-knowledge he determines himself; his soul is controlled by its own dogma rather than by imposed doctrines; his decision *(gnōmē)* is God's decision; freed by Zeus (or by Reason), he can show others that he is lord, is part of God, a son of God, and or even God himself. Because of the riches of his inner life, he is sovereign over the cosmos, his body, and the strokes of bad luck.

Some Stoic doctrines were prone to be misused in favor of unlimited individual liberty, of contempt for existing laws, and of total withdrawal from the obligations of the outside world. In addition, the rapidly developing natural sciences seemed to support a determinism that left little or no room for individual freedom and autonomy. Also, Epicureanism developed in a direction that contradicted the classical idealistic affirmation of the freedom of the soul and the will.

The ancient discussions were continued and enriched with new dimensions, especially by Augustine, the medieval discussions on voluntarism and merits, the controversy between Erasmus and Luther, the *Confessio Augustana* (XVIII), and many later elaborations on the *concursus* of divine providence and human free will. According to Immanuel Kant, freedom is the ground of the good, and God, freedom, and immortality are postulates of practical reason, i.e., of ethics. Modern psychological studies have influenced legal court practice: the knowledge (or awareness) of the difference between good and evil, the capability to decide in favor of the good, the energy to transform the decision into action, and reaching the intended goal are now distinguished. Sociological studies are limiting even more the space of free decisions and actions. Materialistic ethics can be so legalistic and deterministic that it leaves no room for idealism. Finally J.-P. Sartre's affirmation that human beings are *condemned* to be free seems to announce the doom of optimistic discussions of free will.

On the sketched line of developing Western philosophical ethics, Paul's appeal to Philemon's free decision has its place but is still not fully explicable. For there is still another context that may have influenced the apostle: the Jewish heritage with which he was acquainted thanks to his rabbinic studies and his participation in Israel's worship. Indeed, in the Greek Bible of his time, the LXX, *hekousios* (voluntary) and its cognates and synonyms occur occasionally with specific senses.

1. In most passages the adjective — with or without mentioning an offering explicitly — denotes a freewill sacrifice, as it was offered sometimes on the basis of a vow in addition to the bloody, cereal, or wine offerings prescribed for the festival days. The voluntariness of such gifts is in Num 15:3 described by the formula *kath' hekousion*, which very slightly changed is also used by Paul in Philem 14. Voluntary sacrifices were a stable and essential element of temple worship (as shown by Lev 7:16; 23:38; Num 29:39; Deut 12:6; Ps 53:8 = MT 54:8, RSV 54:6; Ezra 3:4-5; 7:16-17; 8:28). Forms of the Hebrew stem *nadab* stand behind the LXX *hekousios*. By daring linguistic procedures, the verb *hekousiazō* and the noun *hekousiasmos* were formed to signify the act and the result of a voluntary offering. Noncanonical writings of the intertestamental period (such as Jth 4:14 and 16:18; *Testament of Levi* 9:7) show that, before the destruction of the Jerusalem temple in 70 C.E., this kind of sacrifice was continued. Philemon may have been expected to let Onesimus work with Paul, as a kind of spiritual sacrifice.

2. In other LXX and later Jewish texts, the donation of silver, gold, building material, and labor for the construction of the tent of meeting, or of the temple in Jerusalem, was also "voluntary" (Exod 36:3; 1 Chron 29:6, 9; 2 Esdras = Ezra 2:68-69). By decree, according to 2 Esdras = Ezra 7:13-20, King Artaxerxes of Persia did more than permit the transfer of silver and gold, which the Jewish people and priests had collected for buying sacrificial animals to be slaughtered in the reerected temple. He and the Persian government even made their own contributions for the same purpose. Thus, Gentiles volunteered to support the worship offered at the Jerusalem temple! So also Philemon was not prevented from contributing a part of his possession to the building and maintenance of God's spiritual temple, the body of Christ, the church.

3. In the Septuagint, a series of diverse voluntary actions is mentioned. All of them are performed, as the freewill sacrifice and donations, in the service of God and/or for the benefit of the community. The brave and energetic Deborah is joined voluntarily by the princes and the people of most of the twelve tribes for the battle against the Canaanite king Jabin. Paul speaks (in Philem 2; etc.) of "fellow soldiers" who assist him in the (spiritual) combat in which he is engaged. Those 10 percent of the Jews who, after returning from the exile, decided to live in the still-destroyed city of Jerusalem are praised by the people because they do it voluntarily (*hekousiasmenoi*, 2 Esdras 21:21 = Neh 11:2). There is a group of militant Hasidim, i.e., of precursors of the later Pharisees

and Zealots, who together with other devoted persons "voluntarily stick to the Law" (*hekousiasmenoi tō nomō*, 1 Macc 2:4). Fourth Maccabees 5:23 speaks of those who "endure willingly all the affliction."

When voluntariness in one of these senses is mentioned, an expression of surprise, joy, and gratitude is sometimes found in the context. Free will is not considered a capability innate in every human being and ready to emerge from the natural resources of the psyche. Rather, whenever its origin is unfolded, it is described as a precious gift of God: the creation of a new heart and the inspiration with a new Spirit. In LXX Ps 50:12, 14 (= MT 51:12, 14; RSV 51:10, 12), "David" asks God, "Create in me a clean heart . . . and renew an upright spirit into my inwards. . . . hold me upright with a guiding spirit." LXX Jer 38:33-34 (cf. MT; RSV 31:33-34) contains the promise that God will put the Law into the thought *(dianoia)* of his people and "write it upon their hearts," so that no longer will they need to teach one another to "Know the Lord." Ezekiel 36:26 resumes this pledge: "A new heart I will give you, and a new spirit I will put within you, and I will take out of your flesh the heart of stone and give you a heart of flesh." The psalmic and prophetic texts do not use the word "voluntary," but they reveal clearly the origin of the free will with which God will inspire his servants.

4. Finally, the LXX knows also of a misuse of free will. An enemy covers you with "voluntary kisses" (Prov 27:6; cf. Matt 26:48-49 par.). Voluntary are the sins committed with "uplifted hands" (Num 15:30-31). According to Philo *(Deus immut.* 128), those who sin this way are condemned by their conscience and "incur woes forever beyond healing." In the Symmachus version of Job 31:33 (unlike MT and, e.g., RSV), Job expresses his conviction never to have committed such a sin. On the other hand, 2 Macc 14:3 reports that the former high priest Alcimus, a man of disreputable character, had voluntarily defiled himself. Thus the LXX concurs with Aristotle: sometimes a sinner, as if to manifest abounding wickedness, sins consciously and voluntarily.

Again, other sins are committed unwillingly *(akōn,* not *hekousiōs).* Lacking knowledge *(agnoia)* or error *(plēmmeleia,* lit. "making a false musical note") are repeatedly used as synonyms of unwillingness. (See Lev 4:2-3, 22, 27; 5:17-18; 22:14; Num 15:24-27; Ezek 14:39; only in LXX, not in MT, also Ezek 42:13; Eccles 5:6; cf. Philo, *Mos.* 1.273; *Deus immut.* 1288; Luke 23:34; Acts 23:5; etc.)

The LXX probably offers the key to understanding why in Philem 14 Paul chose the surprising formula *kata hekousion.* Voluntary sacrifices, freewill contributions to building and maintaining the temple, and other spontaneous acts in the service of God and the people were probably in his mind, and he expected from Philemon a corresponding decision and action. Elsewhere (e.g., in Rom 12:1; Eph 2:20-22; 4:16) Paul speaks indeed of spiritual sacrifices and of contributions to the building of the congregation.

However, the possible or probable intention of Paul need not automatically have met with Philemon's comprehension and appreciation. Unless the slave owner had been a proselyte for a long time before he became a Christian, he hardly could know enough of OT legislation and history to perceive the subtle hint given by the Pauline choice of words. Still, he understood Paul properly as soon as and if only he remembered that solely because of demonstrated bondage in love and faithfulness (Col 3:14; Philem 5-7, 9) he is addressed as a free man and entitled to make his own decision. The freedom of which Paul speaks is qualified by love and faith. It does not contain the permission to run wild and end up in libertinism and licentiousness, or in contempt and oppression of a brother such as Onesimus.

Has Paul then established, at least in the issue of a social change in Onesimus's future status, a principle of voluntarism? H. Binder explicitly denies the existence of such a principle, but H. Diem and especially J. Comblin (pp. 89-92, 102) come near to affirming it. They emphasize that the brotherhood of master and slave, as described in verse 16, can only be realized where and when human decisions are made voluntarily. Comblin draws a far-reaching conclusion: as not even Old Testament slave legislation, not to speak of the "deutero-Pauline" *Haustafeln,* could and did really change the lot of slaves, so no law introduced and carried out by a social revolution has ever effected enduring and beneficial change. Marxistic theory and practice presupposed that no rich and mighty man has ever renounced his power voluntarily. Social change was therefore considered impossible without the dictatorship of the proletariat and the use of violence. Comblin, who together with other liberation theologians is accused of Marxist tendencies, reveals his infinite distance from Marxistic doctrinairism: he rejects the use of all forms of violence for effecting political change. His interpretation of Philem 14 shows that the "coercion" rejected by Paul may well pertain not only to the motivation of Philemon's decision-making process, but also to the means of opening a new future to Onesimus. According to Paul, brute force can never be the path leading to brotherhood. The rejection of coercion and the freedom granted in Philem 14 imply that Philemon will abstain from coercing anyone who does not share in his opinion. He has no monopoly on free will.

By renouncing all ways of violence in PHM, Paul does not pretend to proclaim a general doctrine of nonviolence. The apostle offers neither a Christian doctrine on slavery or on its abolishment. He is not and he cannot play legislator to the church or the world. He does not proclaim moral principles, but when counseling a Christian, and in view of the communal life and order of the Christian congregation, he trusts the power of persuasion, the conscience and the Spirit. If Paul were a cleric and Philemon were a subordinate layman, a hierarchic decree or definition would release the slave holder from responsibility. Paul, however, writes as one brother does to another. The free choice left to Philemon is as well a sign of confidence as the entrustment with great responsibility.

The quasi-intramural character of Paul's appeal to voluntariness does not condemn the church to a ghetto existence. For through its brotherly life and order the church shall be a city on the mountain and a light to the world (Matt 5:14-16; Phil 2:15; Eph 5:8; etc.).

IV. THE COST OF BROTHERHOOD (VV. 15-20)

Finally, in verses 15-20 of his Epistle to Philemon, Paul formulates what he expects his Colossian friend to do. Philemon shall welcome the returning Onesimus as a brother and partner, and Paul will recompense the master for any damages suffered.

The friendly address (vv. 1-3) had been followed by praise of God, who had given Philemon as a precious donation to the local congregation and to the apostle (vv. 4-7). Next, the character of Paul's intercession for Onesimus was pointed out: a humble plea rather than a brusque command (vv. 8-9). Then only were the protégé and Paul's special relationship to him described (vv. 10-11), and Paul's painful separation from Onesimus was contrasted with the apostle's timid wish to keep the runaway at his side (vv. 12-13). Finally, the decision over the slave's future was entrusted to Philemon's conscience and decision (v. 14). And now, introduced by a heavy-weighing preamble regarding God's providence (v. 15) and concluding with a personal financial pledge and the expression of confident hope (vv. 18-20), in verses 15-17 Paul spells out, in the form of imperatives, his distinct counsel and request. He gives urgent advice, and he trusts that it will be implemented by Philemon directly after the slave enters Philemon's house.

In all subsections and verses of this part of PHM, Paul proves to be aware of the price to be paid for a complete change of the social relationship between a master and a slave — if ever dominion, oppression, and exploitation are to be replaced by brotherhood and partnership.

VERSE 15

Perhaps for this purpose he has been separated [from you] for an hour: that forever you hold him properly.

The exact meaning of the two verbs and the two time spans requires scrutiny before the function of verse 15 within the whole of PHM, and perhaps within Pauline ethics in general, can be elucidated.

Separated. Originally, and in the NT exclusively, the verb *chōrizō* has a local sense. Often (e.g., in Acts 1:4; 18:1; Rom 8:35, 39; 1 Cor 7:10-11; Matt 19:6 par.) it signifies departure from a city or termination of a firm relationship such as constituted by love and/or marriage. Outside the NT, the separation of the soul from the body in the hour of death can also be meant.

According to Calvin, Paul "wisely moderates everything by calling the flight [of Onesimus] a departure." Following a hint given by Chrysostom, W. Estius emphasizes that Paul plays down (in Latin: *extenuat*) the escape: it was not really a flight but a brief separation only. Luther (1527) draws the conclusion that in contrast to the devil, who magnifies even little sins, the Holy Spirit diminishes sin by "excuse and dilution *(excusatio* and *attenuatio) . . .* for this Spirit is *forgiveness* of sins and takes them totally away." This does *not,* however, according to Luther, imply "that Paul wants to liberate him [Onesimus) from servitude." While E. Lohmeyer agrees with the opinion that "the mildly forgiving expression [he was separated] removes from the past event all embarrassing elements *(alle Peinlichkeit)* and legal consequences," he yet is convinced that Paul intends to ask for the manumission of the runaway and now-converted slave.

S. Winter, P. Lampe, and B. M. Rapske (their essays were mentioned in "Literary, Biographical, and Contextual Issues," Annotation 3, pp. 227-228) disagree with such interpretations. Because the passive "he has been separated" does not contain a value judgment but solely a statement of fact, the theory was developed that Onesimus was never a fugitive, but brought gifts of the Colossian congregation to Paul or made a legitimate journey to Paul in order to ask for the apostle's intercession.

Still, with H. Binder it is to be considered much more likely that by using the passive form, Paul did not intend to "veil" what is declared by a majority to be the slave's "guilt" of escaping. Rather, by this passive form and by adding the purpose "that . . . you hold him," the apostle intended to speak of successive events arranged in God's providence. Reasons for this introduction of the term "providence" will be given below in a more extensive Note on "he has been separated."

Hold him properly. The Greek verb *apechō,* here translated "holding properly," reminds of the cognate *katechō* (to hold fast, hold back, hold down, detain, possess) in verse 13. It is possible that merely for stylistic reasons Paul changed over from the first to the second; in that case he had in mind the same kind of "keeping" or "holding." However, at the end of verse 15 *apechō* may mean a manner of possession that is distinct from the sense of *katechō* in verse 13. For (a) originally *apechō* denotes a spatial separation and signifies "keeping off, or away from" or "being distant"; (b) frequently this verb is used as a metaphor in the sense of "hindering," "desisting," or "abstaining"; (c) in commercial-legal documents, it signifies "receiving payment in full" or ". . . against a receipt." In the NT, each one of these senses occurs. Once, in Mark 14:41, the meaning is obscure.

In the first edition of his monograph on Philemon (1935), John Knox had referred to meanings *(a)* and *(b)* and concluded that Paul expected Philemon to turn the temporary separation into a definite and final separation from Onesimus. Similarly in the second edition (1959, p. 22), Knox still suggests that the full wording of Philemon 15b might or should have been "in order that you might freely relinquish your claim to him forever." This interpretation of verse 15b eliminates the slightest trace of a possible contradiction between this verse and verse 13, i.e., with the wish of Paul to retain Onesimus at his side for apostolic service. By implication Philemon is then told to manumit his slave. However, the assertions made by Paul in verses 8-9 and 14 regarding the freedom of decision granted to Philemon would then be turned by verse 15b into a hypocritical farce. The temporary interruption would be declared a prelude, if not also a justification, of the definite separation of master and slave. At best, the brotherhood and partnership described in verses 16-17 would have to find expression in a friendly farewell — not in a welcome party.

Not only outspoken critics of Knox's thesis (e.g., H. Greeven, "Prüfung der Thesen von J. Knox zum Philemonbrief," pp. 373-378) but also enthusiastic admirers (such as S. Winter) have therefore totally rejected this interpretation of *apechēs*. In the final edition of his monograph (1960, p. 23), Knox himself has withdrawn from his earlier position. Still, he suggests that the comma usually placed at the end of verse 15 must be omitted, so that the text of verses 15 and 16 forms one single sentence, saying "you may have him back no longer as a slave, but. . . ." E. Lohse, quoting from O. Merk *(Handeln aus Glauben)*, comes to a similar result: "Onesimus is no longer the property of his master which he was according to Roman law."

Indeed, if Paul's sole purpose in "sending him back" (v. 12) was the termination of his slave status, the sting is taken out of Onesimus's return to Philemon. The early church fathers', Luther's, Calvin's, and the later conservative scholars' exegesis and application are then proven wrong, and Paul can no longer be suspected or accused of conforming to contemporary law-and-order standards by dispatching Onesimus back to his master, so that forever his neck and back might be bent under the yoke of slavery.

Calvin added a special note by remarking that before Onesimus's flight, "Philemon did not really possess the slave *(non vere possidebat)*." The substance of this remark recurs in J. Comblin's commentary (1986) for another reason. The Reformer argues that before his escape Onesimus was a mean and perfidious fellow of whom his master "could not draw convenient profit *(non poterat ipso commode frui)*," and that now "the usefulness of the flight" has become manifest; the escape became for Onesimus the occasion to be "corrected," to become "a new man" and to return to his master as a brother. Different is the argument proffered in socio-critical terminology by the liberation theologian Comblin: in the past Philemon had never truly been Onesimus's owner; for no person can really be in possession of another person and treat him or her as though a piece of property. When Philemon now accepts Onesimus as brother, it is no longer with the claim that he is owner of this man.

Our paraphrasing translation of Greek *apechēs*, "hold him properly," relies on one of the assured lexicographical meanings of *apechō*, and it proposes a minor and a major alternative to interpretations so far offered. First, in contrast to Paul's original desire (and temptation?) to keep and hold Onesimus at his side (*katechō* in v. 13), Paul in this case intends to speak in verse 15 of Onesimus's staying in the house and service of Philemon on a new basis and under new conditions. When Onesimus is treated as a brother and partner in agreement with the substance of verses 16-17, his position will be unlike that of slaves in the huge majority of contemporary households or businesses. And yet there will be no open conflict with the existing legal, economical, and social aspects of the master/slave relationship. Second, by implication but sufficiently clearly, Paul makes Philemon realize that in the past, in his capacity as a slave owner, he has failed to treat Onesimus "properly," even as a brother and partner. If it be God's will that Philemon henceforth keeps and holds Onesimus at all, then the proper means to enjoy the company and the service of Onesimus is to honor and love, to protect and cherish him as a man of equal dignity and worth.

In "Literary, Biographical, and Contextual Issues," section VI.B and C (pp. 138-139, 143-144) the possibility was mentioned that the escaping slave had not been a thorough rascal, but that his master had not behaved "properly" to him. The *Haustafeln* as well as 1 Pet 2:18 presuppose that not all, if any, Christian slave owners behaved always as paragons of wisdom, virtue, and humanitarian standards.

For an hour . . . forever. The rhetorical device of contrasting pairs has been skillfully used in verses 8-9, 11, 14. It will be employed again in the following verses. In Philem 15 the formula *pros hōran* (for an hour) is used idiomatically, just as in John 5:35; 1 Thess 2:17; Gal 2:5; 2 Cor 7:8. In Mark 14:37 and Rev 17:12 the absolute accusative *mian hōran* (for one hour) only seemingly intends to denote the time span of sixty minutes; actually, either several hours or even the period of several years can be meant. (Cf. G. Delling, *TDNT*, 11.680-681; for the following see esp. H. Sasse, *TDNT*, 1.197-209.)

The adjective *aiōnios* ("everlasting, eternal"; in our translation: "forever") may have more than solely a temporal meaning, and has therefore been variously interpreted in commentaries on Philem 15. Already in verse 14 Paul has changed over from the formula (lit.) "according to necessity" to the opposite, (lit.) "according to voluntary." Equally in verse 15 he switches over from a noun to an adjective, with the effect of puzzling the reader. Possible expositions have to be discussed in some detail.

1. The accusative *aiōnion,* which in the Greek text immediately precedes the object *auton* ("him," i.e, Onesimus), may be understood as a masculine. Then it is a qualification of the returning slave. This man's future would then be described by a double sense of the same adjective, and it would be left to Philemon and later readers of PHM to decide whether Paul had in mind (a) the permanent (Calvin: *perpetuo*) slave status, or perhaps a similar servant position on Philemon's premises, or (b) the representation of something divine and eternal in the same house. In the second case, Onesimus would establish a presence of eternity in his master's home, which would be comparable, e.g., to the function of visiting angels (Gen 18; Heb 13:2) or — if pagan notions still survived in the family of Philemon — similar to the place occupied by an ancestor shrine, a Penate (house god), or a house altar. In the first case, Onesimus would be condemned by Paul, by God himself, or by both, to be a slave for life and become a permanent fixture in his earthly master's residence.

The context suggests and supports neither of these extreme interpretations of *aiōnios.*

Still, expositions exist that offer other reasons for and applications of the title "eternal" as it is here seemingly given to Onesimus. E.g., Calvin reminds of Onesimus's wicked past conduct; while living in a pious and holy house, the slave had boasted of misdeeds. Calvin assumes obviously that the slave had refused to be baptized when Philemon was baptized with his whole house: "he had intentionally withdrawn himself from God and eternal life." Now he returns to his master as a new man. J. B. Lightfoot, after having described Onesimus as a typically lazy, bigmouthed, unreliable, and generally bad Phrygian slave, asserts, "He departed a reprobate; he returns a saved man. . . . Since he left, Onesimus had obtained eternal life, and eternal life involves eternal interchange of friendship. His services to his old master were no longer barred by the gates of death." Even N. R. Petersen (*Rediscovering Paul,* pp. 73-74), his dominating sociological concern notwithstanding, comes near to using moralizing and pietistic language when he observes that "the runaway slave is returning as a new man . . . virtually clean as a result of his conversion." H. Binder follows A. Suhl by suggesting that by *aiōnios* Onesimus is described as a "man of new quality in a new dimension." Indeed, the man who has become Paul's "child" (vv. 10, 12) is by implication, according to Gal 3–4, also Abraham's and God's child. And the same person who formerly belied his name Onesimus (Profitable), returns now to his early master as a man worthy of his name.

Still, did Paul really want to say that the returning Onesimus would bring a whiff of eternity into Philemon's house? Actually, it is far from certain that in verse 15 *aiōnios* really is used as an adjective adorning Onesimus with "eternal" quality. In the LXX, the NT, and the apostolic fathers, "eternal" is an attribute of God and of God's riches and gifts; also it occurs where eschatological hopes are described. "Eternal" are the covenant made by God, the glory and the spirit of God, the salvation and redemption wrought by God, the kingdom established and ruled by God, the gospel and the consolation announced in it, especially the life and inheritance given by God. In addition, God's judgment, the human guilt, punishment, and perdition, also the fire of hell are called "eternal." The only *persons* described in the Bible by this adjective are God the Father, his Son — and the Holy Spirit. In this book, those Greek precedents are not followed that attribute eternity to the world, to the immortal soul, or to a defunct, or even living, Roman emperor. If Paul had called the returning slave "eternal," he would have used this term in a most extraordinary way. No wonder that another interpretation has been proposed:

2. Grammar and syntax permit an explanation of the form *aiōnion* not as the masculine accusative, but as a neuter that can be used as equivalent to the adverb (cf. BDF, 243). In Philem 14 the formula *kata hekousion* had indeed to be translated "voluntarily." In this case, instead of a quality of Onesimus, the modality of Philemon's action of receiving and holding the returning man is in the apostle's mind. E.g., W. M. L. de Wette and J. Knox understand *aiōnion* in the sense of an adverb. If this be correct, then primarily or solely the divine gifts of love and faith, together with the freewill decision made, in obedience to his conscience, by Philemon, are the presupposition and means for the proper reception of the returning fugitive. Both would be denoted: the unlimited duration and the religious basis and quality of the new social relation between master and slave, as they are created by God's gifts. By treating Onesimus in the manner described in some detail in verses 16-17, Philemon might then be said to participate in the (eternal) essence of God and Jesus Christ himself, and he might be called an imitator of the heavenly Father's and his Son's perfection. The earthly master rather than his slave would then secure the divine presence in Philemon's house. Philemon would be urged once again to reveal and confirm that he is a good Christian — inspired by the same "eternal spirit" that made, e.g., the Messiah offer himself as a blameless sacrifice to God (cf. 1 Pet 2:15, 21; 4:16; Heb 9:14; etc.).

The adverbial understanding of *aiōnion* need not totally exclude the interpretation that treated "eternal" as an attribute of Onesimus. Paul might wish to say that the arriving Onesimus *and* the receiving Philemon would meet and treat one another in a mode motivated by the eternal God and his eternal gifts.

On the other hand, general philological and specific contextual evidence for the adverbial employment of *aiōnion* hardly exists. Neither in secular nor in biblical diction are there precedents of, and parallels to, a human decision and action deserving to be called "eternal." Indeed, no law can forbid or prevent Paul from using the term in an extraordinary, perhaps unique way at this place. But as long as other alternatives exist, it is precarious to base an exposition on this possibility alone.

3. RSV and NJB translate *aiōnion* "for ever"; NEB: "for good." A great number of other versions use the same or an equivalent terminology. They reproduce the original, nonphilosophical, and nonreligious meaning of the adjective, that is: "perpetual, lifelong, enduring," whether a past, present, or future time span is in mind. The Greek adjective is derived from *aiōn* (period of existence, lifetime, age, generation). Since Heraclitus and Empedocles, this noun has played a role in philosophical discussions. In, e.g., Plato's *Timaeus, aiōn* is distinguished from *chronos* (time) because it means timeless, ideal eternity. A god *Aion* occurs in post-Christian Gnostic literature.

H. Sasse goes (in *TDNT,* 1.209) probably too far when he makes Philem 15 say Onesimus is to be a "slave for life." For Paul may well have realized as much as Jesus (according to John 8:35), that "the slave does not remain in the house forever"; only the son remains forever *(eis ton aiōna).* P. Stuhlmacher's comment on Philem 15 is somewhat reticent and yet clear in the rejection of the religious meaning of *aiōnios:* "There is no sufficient reason . . . [together with, e.g., E. Lohmeyer and E. Lohse] to relate the term solely to the new Christian relationship of the master to the slave"; for Paul speaks of "the piece of property" that belongs to Philemon and is returned to him "for time unlimited." J. Gnilka and J.-F. Collange come to a similar result: for a given time — which only God determines! — Onesimus is returned and to be held by Philemon. Most apodictic in his defense of the translation "for good" or "permanently" is C. F. D. Moule: "It must not be . . . assumed that *aiōnios* is here intended to carry a deeper meaning . . . of some condition transcending time. . . . The deeper relationship is described in the next verse."

In summary, the third variant of interpreting emphasizes exclusively the temporal extension, even the permanence, of Onesimus's future life in Philemon's company and house. The translation "forever" neither loads up nor replaces the unlimited period with a religious or moralistic halo above the head of Onesimus and or/Philemon. According to J. M. G. Barclay ("Dilemma of Christian Slave-Ownership," p. 172), the differences between scholarly interpretations culminate at exactly this point.

Among the reasons favoring the version "forever" are the following:

a. Legal and commercial contracts state either the limitation to a given time span or the unlimited duration of the agreement. E.g., God's covenant with all his creatures, with Israel, and with David is called "eternal" (in Gen 9:16; 17:7; Exod 31:16; Lev 24:8; 2 Sam 23:5). According to Philem 15, temporal ("for an hour") was the legal and personal bond holding Onesimus and Philemon together in the past. Irrevocable "forever" are the brotherly reception, place, and treatment of the returning man. Because the qualitative difference of Onesimus's future status is in verse 15 sufficiently described by the words "holding properly," and in verses 16-17 by the mention of love, brotherhood, and partnership, the rather laborious and onerous digressions made by several expositors regarding the moral development and progress of the runaway man and his and/or his master's Christlike future conduct miss the point Paul wanted to make when he used the term *aiōnios*.

b. According to OT legislation and its talmudic interpretation, debt servitude ended for Jewish slaves after maximally six years, or it was terminated at the dawn of the Jubilee Year. But a Hebrew slave entitled to manumission had the right as a lifelong servant to remain in his master's home. By the ceremony of ear piercing he became a slave "forever." Foreign ("Canaanite") slaves, however, could be bequeathed by the owner and inherited by the heirs "forever" (MT: *le'ōlām, 'ōlām*; LXX always: *eis ton aiōna*, Exod 21:5; Deut 15:17; Lev 25:46). From his rabbinical training Paul certainly knew that a Jewish slave who loved his master and the master's family was entitled to choose staying in his master's home "for life." By renouncing manumission, he could avoid a possibly uncertain, drab, dark, and miserable future. After becoming apostle of the Messiah Jesus, Paul could no longer reserve a privileged treatment for Jewish slaves only. Rather he proclaimed that by Jesus Christ Jews and Gentiles were made family members in the household of God, and fellow citizens of God's first-chosen people (Gal 3:28; Eph 2:13-19; etc.). When the apostle succeeds in persuading Onesimus voluntarily to return to his master (v. 12), and when he expects that in the future this master and this slave will never again be separated, he reveals the conviction that — consciously or unconsciously — a humane element of Israel's slave legislation will be implemented by Philemon — although without a bloody ritual such as ear piercing and circumcision.

c. As earlier mentioned, the expectation that Onesimus will stay in Philemon's house "forever" appears to contradict Paul's wish to keep his "child" and "heart" near him (vv. 10-13). Easy ways out of the impasse, or a detour around it, have been proposed by several expositors: Paul's personal wish was so tenuous that the apostle finally abandoned it. Or: *aiōnion* has no more than a spiritual and religious sense and means "eternally" rather than "forever." Or: the temporal and the spiritual senses of the adverbial *aiōnion* are combined and reconciled. According to, e.g., W. Estius, each form of servitude ends with the present life, but Christian brotherhood remains in eternity. According to J. B. Lightfoot, Onesimus was to stay with Philemon "for all time and for eternity," bound to him by the "eternal exchange of friendship." Also it might be argued that Paul's utterances on his imprisonment (in vv. 1, 9, 13) combine both a temporal or this-worldly and a spiritual, otherworldly sense. Chrysostom crisply comments on verse 16 by stating that Philemon had gained Onesimus as a brother "as well in time . . . as in quality."

Yet the observation of a detail in verse 15 reveals that for reasons of his own Paul acknowledges a tension between the substance of verses 13 and 15: he contradicts neither himself nor pure logic. For he dares facing a contradiction of God's own will to an apostolic wish:

He has been separated. The aorist passive form of the verb *chōrizō* (to separate) contains the key to solving the seeming irreconcilability of verse 15 with verse 13. Just as Chrysostom, also Thomas Aquinas, Luther, Calvin, W. Estius, and the majority of modern interpreters see in verse 15 a reference to God's *providence.* When the Greek passive *echōristhē* is assumed to substitute for the middle *echōrisato* ("he separated himself" or "he separated in his own interest"), then Onesimus is made the logical subject of verse 15a and God is left out of the picture. Indeed, the Vg. version is *discessit* (he departed, he removed himself). Rather surprising interpretations are offered by NEB: "you lost him," and NJB: "you have been deprived of him." Vg. suggests the mischievousness of Onesimus's departure: the stroke of bad luck suffered by Philemon. It is not certain, however, whether at this place Paul really intended to ascribe the separation to a decision made by the slave alone, or to an accident having occurred in Onesimus's or in Philemon's life. Although in Hellenistic Greek passives can replace middles and vice versa, the biblical usage of the passive, without an added reference to the agent, suggests that Paul wanted to say as much as "God has separated him from you, in order that you. . . ." In fact, in verses 3-4 Paul had explicitly mentioned God and Christ as the source of grace and peace, and he had thanked God for making Philemon a good Christian. Why does he not do the same in verse 15?

The reason for substituting a passive verbal form for the mention of God is explained by, e.g., G. Dalman (*Die Worte Jesu,* p. 184) as "shyness to mention God's name." The passive often circumscribes God's name in the LXX, the NT, and talmudic literature. By some scholars it has been called *passivum divinum.* It is used in order to prevent magical and other misuse of the Name, as it is prohibited by the third of the Ten Commandments. To mention a few examples: Matt 5:4, 7, 9: "they will be comforted . . . obtain mercy . . . be called sons of God . . ."; 7:1-2: "you will be judged . . . measured"; 7:7-8; 12:31-32: "it will be given . . . opened . . . forgiven"; 1 Cor 6:11: "you are sanctified . . . justified"; 15:42-43: "it is sown . . . it is raised"; 1 Tim 3:16: "He was revealed in the flesh, was justified in the Spirit."

Applied to the exposition of Philem 15, this means: Paul affirms that the relationship between master Philemon and slave Onesimus is constituted by far more than the reciprocal conduct of these individuals. It is distinct from the perennial problems inherent in the institution of slavery, wherever and in whatever form they are manifested. There is a third party that decides over the course of the evolving drama. God himself reigns over and directs all things and events, whether they be good or bad, painful or pleasant, ephemeral or long lasting, issuing from wisdom or foolishness. Unlike numerous other verses in PHM, in verse 15 Paul omits mentioning also a fourth party: himself. His own contribution to the events is evident: after meeting Onesimus with conspicuous results, he sends the man back to his master with a warm intercessory letter, and it is he who draws attention to the overarching providence of God. Not only past events are subject to this providence, but also the wish of the apostle to retain Onesimus, the decision to send him back, and the freewill reaction of Philemon to seeing Onesimus at his doorstep and to reading PHM.

Narrative, prophetic, hymnic OT and NT passages often assert that God reveals his omniscience and omnipotence by turning even evil things that had been plotted, performed, and suffered by human beings to a good end. In their commentaries on PHM, e.g., Chrysostom, Thomas Aquinas, and Estius consider the patriarch Joseph's words as a precedent to Philem 15: "It was not you who sent me here, but God . . ."; "You meant evil against me, but God meant it for the good" (Gen 45:5-9; 50:20). God himself "kills and brings to life" (1 Sam 2:6), and in his name Jeremiah has to "pluck up and break down, to destroy and to overthrow, to build and to heal" (Jer 1:10). "Who has commanded and it came to pass, unless the Lord has ordained it? Is it not from the mouth of the Most High that good and evil come?" (Lam 3:37-38). "I am the Lord, and there is no other. I form the light and create the darkness, I make weal and woe. I am the Lord, who does all these things" (Isa 45:6-7).

This Lord even assumes personal responsibility for the scandalous deafness, blindness, and hardened heart of the people he will finally save (Isa 6:9-10; 12:1-5). God's thoughts and ways are so much higher than human designs and so different from human performance, that even those sent into exile because of their defection from God will go out from their captivity with jubilation and all creation will break out into applause (Isa 55:8-13). Convinced of being in the care of God the Shepherd, a member of God's people confesses, "Even though I walk through the valley of the shadow of death, I fear no evil; for thou art with me. . . . I shall dwell in the house of the Lord forever" (Ps 23:4-6).

According to the NT, even the heinous extradition and execution of Jesus Christ have been willed by God and used for the salvation of Israel and the world (Mark 8:31 par.; Acts 2:22-24; 3:13-26; 5:30-32; etc.). When the question is asked whether a man is born blind because of his own or his parents' sin, Jesus rejects the alternatives and gives a reason to be verified in the immediate future: "The works of God shall be manifested in him." Indeed, the man is healed by Jesus and becomes a bold witness to his Savior, according to John 9. Paul, too, testifies to the marvelous rule of providence. His captivity in Roman hands "has really served the advance of the gospel" (Phil 1:12).

Such events and pronouncements show that the providence of God is not exhausted by permitting or causing evil things to happen. Rather, the providence that gives leeway to human wrongdoing and suffering aims at a surprising final intervention and manifestation of God. Only from the purpose and the end of the way on which God leads his people can and do individuals draw the conclusion that the events preceding that end have been willed and directed by God himself. In the Bible, both the history of Israel and the nations, and the life of individual persons, are explained in the light of not only their origin but also their purpose and end. To the etiological (or protological), a teleological understanding is added. So also in Philem 15 God's providence is, under the proviso of that later-to-be-discussed "perhaps," made responsible for the separation in order to point out that from the beginning God had reunion in mind. The separation took place "for this purpose . . . that you hold him properly." Because the end will reveal and justify the means chosen by God, Onesimus's painful past dramatic separation from Philemon is but a prelude to the future warm reception and treatment of the same man.

J. Knox (*Philemon*, 2nd ed., p. 22) has radically rejected this interpretation. He considers it impossible that in the same letter Paul should ask for the release of Onesimus and his transfer into gospel service, and ascribe to God's providence the future permanent life and service under this earthly master's supervision and hand. Knox argues that in the majority of the Pauline letters containing the phrase *dia touto* (in our translation: "for this purpose"), these two words point backward rather than forward: "*eis touto* [not *dia touto*] was Paul's way of connection with a final clause." Therefore, according to Knox, the free decision of Philemon mentioned in verse 14 was firmly expected to correspond to the apostle's wish as formulated in verse 13 — rather than to entail the future permanent slave-status of Onesimus.

This reasoning is not convincing. Several times in Paul's letters (in Rom 4:16; 13:10; Eph 5:17; cf. 1 Tim 1:16; 2 Tim 2:10), *dia touto* points forward, or (as in 1 Thess 3:5; 2 Thess 2:11; 1 Cor 4:17; 11:30; Rom 13:6) it is impossible to distinguish a retrospective from a prospective sense. In consequence, however hard it may be to swallow for an expositor of PHM, a possible tension and contradiction between verses 13 and 15b cannot be ruled out.

Still, at least one feature distinguishes the substance of verse 15 from that of the just-quoted biblical passages that speak more or less explicitly of God's providence. In those texts *human* misdeeds and/or misery were shown to be overruled by God's mercy. In Philem 15, however, the brief and grievous separation caused by God has to yield to the long-lasting and friendly reunion and common life of two human persons. There and here, God's providence is operative in historical events and becomes manifested in them. But in Philem 15, more than elsewhere, the responsible, active share of God's human partners is emphasized. Under the roof of God's providence, Onesimus has disrupted his relationship to Philemon, and in verse 15b Philemon is the grammatical subject. It is he who gives shape and expression to a restored, reformed, and even totally changed common life with his servant. So Paul indicates that providence calls forth responsible human action and conduct: "You [Philemon] [shall and will] hold him [Onesimus] properly."

Therefore the reference to God's omnipotence and omniscience does not promote a fatalistic determinism that would deny human failure and guilt or responsible human choice and action. Neither does Paul plant or support a cheap optimism that might rely on a glorious happy end, disregarding omissions made and deeds committed by those living under the sun that God makes rise over the evil and the good.

Excursus: Providence, Free Will, and Human Responsibility

Scholastic and later Orthodox theologians have used the term *concursus* to denote the interrelation and actual cooperation of God's absolute rule and the contingent human behavior. They were not the first, neither the only ones, to seek a reconciliation between divine omnipotent providence and the weakness and problematic of all human responses.

The Tannaite rabbi Aqiba (d. 135 c.e.) is quoted in the Mishnah tractate Aboth (V 19; in H. Danby's edition, V 16) as saying, "All is foreseen, and free will is given, and the world is judged by goodness, and all is according to the amount of work." (Hardly reliable variant readings of this text either insert "not" before "according to . . ." or omit "amount of.") Among others, Maimonides (h. Teshuba III 1 and V) has discussed what appears to be a contradiction between the two assertions, and the attempt to reconcile them. Jewish writers in Paul's historical environment defy commonsense arguments and philosophical objections. They are convinced that predetermination by God and full human responsibility belong together. God has created the necessity that one of the Two Ways be followed: either the Good or the Bad Impulse, either the Spirit of Darkness or the Spirit of Truth (see, e.g., Sir 15:11-20; Midr. Bereshit XXVII 4, on Gen 6:6; b. Kidd 30b; 1QH 12.15.12-20; 1QS 3.13–4.26; CD 2.2-13). In different ways, other texts (such as Sir 16:15-30; 23:20-21; 33:10-17; 39:17-21; *Psalms of Solomon* 5:1-18 [15]; 9:1-10 [5]; *1 Enoch* 41:8; 98:4; *Assumption of Moses* 12:4-13; *2 Baruch* 15:5-8; 19:1-4; Josephus, *BJ* 2.162-163, concerning the Pharisees' teaching) combine God's omnipotent providence with the freedom of choice given to humankind. Because of (rather than in spite of) the coherence of God's eternal will with the ever new decisions to be made by his children, God's judgment is righteous.

So also the third petition of the Lord's Prayer, "Thy will be done on earth as it is in heaven," means both the fulfillment of God's intention and foresight by God himself and the doing of God's will by humanity, including the acceptance of suffering. The election of God's people by sheer grace equips the liberated persons to serve God. Even when they disobey and are punished, they will yet be a light to the nations. Instead of quenching freedom by giving direction through the gift of his Law and by his irresistible way of shaping history, God in his freedom frees his people to make free decisions and to take bold actions.

Not even the freedom-loving ancient Greeks, who stood up for the autonomy of individuals and political communities, refused to tie freedom to the rule of reason and to the respect for the laws of the *polis* (city, state). Modern theologians reject any claim upon total human autonomy and yet affirm freedom, as two citations show. Karl Barth writes (in his *Church Dogmatics* I/2, p. 313), "Faith . . . does not mean merely the superseding but the abolishing of man's self-determination. It means that man's self-determination is co-ordinated into the order of the divine predetermination. In faith, it loses its autonomy outside this predetermination. . . . The . . . ultimate and really serious determination for the believer is that which proceeds from Jesus Christ." In a discussion, Paul Tillich stated crisply: "Freedom is only where there is destiny, destiny only where there is freedom."

Philemon 15 and the context of this verse show that observations of this kind, their dogmatical or philosophical ring notwithstanding, correspond to Paul's theology and anthropology.

Referring to God's will, as is done in Philem 15, is not always a holy or necessary enterprise. Dictators and demagogues often raise the claim in their speeches that they are exactly informed of the divine providence and have therefore the full power to tell the people what they must expect and do. There are biblical prophets who, it is said, have "stood in the counsel of the Lord" (Jer 23:18, 22). But there exist also prophets and clerics who are not qualified to pass on secret information and to give direction to people sitting at their feet. It is not impossible that in Philem 15 Paul attempts to exert some pressure on Philemon in order to induce him to treat in a friendly way the man who in verses 11-12 was introduced as the apostle's child and heart. Still, Paul neither takes the stance of a demagogue nor dons the garb of a cleric for putting the fear of God into Philemon and making him obey.

In addition, it is one thing to subordinate oneself completely to being "set apart" before one's birth for a later gracious and dramatic "call" into the service of the gospel (Gal 1:15-16), and another to subordinate another person to what, for reasons good or bad, is considered God's providential guidance.

After his dramatic encounter with the risen Lord near Damascus, the former persecutor of Christ and devastator of Christian congregations could not help speaking of the "necessity" laid on him (1 Cor 9:17; cf. 15:8-10; 1 Tim 1:15-16). From then on he knew that it was God's "will that all persons be saved," whether they be Jews or Gentiles, high- or low-standing (1 Tim 2:4, 6, etc.). To God's will, rather than to his own or other persons' will and decision, Paul ascribes his life as an apostle and in the service of Christ (Gal 1:1; Eph 1:1; etc.). Also, when he comes to speak of frustrated travel plans and promises (as in 1 Thess 2:17-18; 3:10; 2 Cor 1:15-17; Rom 1:9-13; 15:22, 32; Phil 1:8; 2:24; cf. Acts 16:6), he recognizes God's hand in the delays or cancellations, rather than calling the obstacles met "one of those things" that are due to a hostile fate or human failure.

In ethical contexts Paul affirms that the eternal will of God embraces equally all members of the congregation. "This is the will of God: your sanctification" (1 Thess 4:3), and sanctification depends on justification (1 Cor 1:30; 6–11; Rom 5–6; etc.). God wills "that all men be saved and come to the knowledge of truth" (1 Tim 2:4). Should then in Philem 15 Paul really intend to subordinate Philemon to a divine providence whose direction was and is first revealed and known to the apostle only?

Perhaps for this purpose . . . that . . . (tacha gar dia touto . . . hina . . .). Far from pretending that he has looked over God's shoulders and into his cards, and far from claiming an authorization to ordering Philemon around, Paul drastically reduces the weight of his reference to providence.

The word *tacha* (perhaps) introduces the reference to God's will. Verse 15 begins with the expression of tentativeness, openness for alternatives, and tolerance for other opinions. Paul abstains from directive counseling because he deems it possible that, by briefly separating Onesimus from Philemon, God had provided for something other than fulfillment of the apostle's wish as it was uttered in verse 13.

Originally, since Homeric times, *tacha* has the adverbial meaning "presently, forthwith." But especially when there is an optative, with or without the modal particle *an* and/or the adverb *isōs* following it, an action is introduced whose implementation is contingent, that is, dependent on conditions that have not yet been met. In the temporal sense, *tacha* occurs neither in the LXX nor on papyri. *Tacheōs* (at once, fast), the adverbial derivate from *tachys*, replaces *tacha* in the NT as well as in other literature. On the other hand, *tacha* can have a nontemporal significance and mean "perhaps," pointing out "any contingency from probability to a bare possibility" (LSLex, s.v.), in contrast to that which is certain *(asphalēs)*. In this sense *tacha* is used in Wis 13:6; 14:19; Rom 5:7; Philem 15. In Luke 20:13 *isōs* has the same function and meaning.

If in Philem 15 Paul had added the particle *an* and/or substituted *isōs* for *tacha,* not only the lack of certainty but outspoken irony might be expressed. Then the translation would have to be "Should perhaps . . . ?" and this question would have been an ironical parenthesis to be answered by a definite no! The same negative reaction of the readers might also be evoked if (as in Rom 5:7, variant reading) *tacha* were replaced by *molis,* variant reading *mogis* (hardly). In this case Paul himself would utter in Philem 15 his opinion that God did *not* provide Onesimus's final and definite return to Philemon. NJB, however, translates *tacha* "I suppose" and thus lets the apostle express the opposite tentative thought. The voiding of the Greek text suggests neither affirmation nor negation of the purpose of God's providence. Paul expresses by *tacha* exclusively his ignorance and uncertainty, and no twinkle of the eye reveals his personal stance.

How, then, can this apostle be so timid and humble? Elsewhere he claims that "Christ is speaking in me" (2 Cor 13:3) and is not ashamed of acting and writing with authority in all matters concerning faith and life. A key to explaining the surprising "perhaps" is offered by OT texts.

In substance, Hebrew *'ulay* stands behind Paul's "perhaps." In sentences speaking of God's will and future acts, *'ulay* is an indication of unpredictability and lack of certain knowledge (Num 23:3, 27; Josh 14:12; 1 Sam 6:5; 14:6; 2 Sam 16:12; 2 Kings 19:4 = Isa 37:4; Amos 5:15; Jer 21:2; Jon 3:9; Zeph 2:3). Sometimes (in 2 Sam 12:22; Joel 2:14; Jon 3:9; Esther 4:14) *mi yōdēaʿ* ("who knows?") reveals the same absence of a well-founded conviction; it can be combined with *'ulay.* Ernst Jenni (in Jenni-Westermann, *THAT,* pp. 79-82) emphasizes that "the consciously humble attitude of a person reckoning with the sovereign freedom of God" is expressed as "a more or less hesitant or confident hope," "while yet being distinct from the uncertainty of human beings in face of a capricious despot" or "an irrational stroke of fate." According to Esther 4:14, Mordecai has let Esther know that relief and deliverance may certainly "rise for the Jews from another quarter," but "who knows" whether *she* has not come to royal dignity at a time like this, just because *she* has to contribute to the salvation of the Jews? Only in rare cases (as in Hos 8:7; Jer 51:8; Isa 47:12; 1 Kings 18:17) does *'ulay* have an ironical undertone.

In his exposition of Philem 15, Jerome states that God's judgments are hidden and that therefore it is audacious to make fail-safe pronouncements about them. Indeed, in this verse Paul does more than abstain from pretending to possess omniscience. He subordinates both his own wish to retain Onesimus for gospel service (v. 13) and the result of Philemon's free decision (v. 14) to the wisdom and goodness of God's providence. Thus he does not appeal to providence in order to support a personal desire. Neither does he wish to exert pressure on Philemon to decide in favor of the apostle's personal hope. Paul bears the risk and is willing to pay the cost (vv. 18-19) for seeing his noblest intention being overruled by God himself. He deems it possible that God's providence runs contrary to the best human wishes and hopes — although they sound so excellent and reasonable. The apostle is ready and willing to be refuted and put to shame by God's decision and plan. Without swallowing all too hard, he is prepared to let Onesimus forever stay with his earthly master — even if this means that in this single case the slave owner's natural inclination to repossess his property should be in harmony with God's providence.

How and when will Paul ever know what God's will is? As much as every Christian, he has to "find out by experience what is pleasing to the Lord . . . what is the will of God, what is good and acceptable and perfect" (*dokimazō* . . . ; Eph 5:10; Rom 12:2; etc.). When in the triangular interrelation between Paul, Philemon, and Onesimus the runaway slave's future is at stake, Paul is willing to accept Philemon's reaction to the letter addressed to him as test, proof, experience, and sign that reveal what God himself wills and plans. So it was neither hypocrisy nor fakery when in verse 14 the apostle permitted and encouraged Philemon to decide freely. It is not enough to yield to a suggestion or to punctually carry out a commandment — not even when it stems from an apostle. Philemon, too, has to "obey God rather than men" (cf. Acts 5:29). As the interpretation of verse 14 has shown, Paul is confident that the consciousness ("of God!"; 1 Pet 2:19) will direct Philemon to decide wisely.

Certainly, to the options open to Philemon described above (see the Excursus "Legal Options for Onesimus's Future," pp. 365-366), one more has to be added in light of verse 15: the owner of Onesimus may have to follow God's will by disregarding the wishful thinking of Paul described in verse 13 and retain the slave in his house. Not even in that case does Paul pity himself for the disappointment and the personal loss suffered. He does not grate his teeth and succumb gruntingly. Neither does he deliver or condemn Onesimus to the fate of remaining a slave for life. Rather, he cares all the more for his protégé. As if he had never thought of anything other than Onesimus's permanent future at Philemon's side, he describes in verses 16-17 the termination of the former master/slave relationship by the bond of brotherhood, love, and partnership. At the latest when Paul comes to be a guest in Philemon's house (v. 22), he will see with his own eyes how well the return of Onesimus has worked out to the best of all parties concerned. However Philemon will decide, the returning Onesimus is a "gift of God" (H. Binder), not a present made by the apostle. In Philem 4-7 Philemon himself was described as such a gift, made by God to both the church and the apostle.

At this place, finally, the question can be answered whether or not in verses 13 and 15 Paul flatly contradicts himself. Undeniable is a certain logical tension. But Paul's logic is far from opaque or brittle. For he is, just because he is an apostle, willing to accept God's contradiction against his best-meant personal wishes and hopes. He is prepared to be reproved as a fool and to be confounded by God, and he expects that even this way Onesimus's future will be bright and good.

Therefore, in PHM Paul neither suggests nor decrees that Onesimus be

Philemon's slave for life. The apostle's personal wish and hope is another way of employment, another sort of service to be fulfilled by his "child" (v. 13). Paul's advice to all slaves among the church members was to grasp any chance to become manumitted (1 Cor 7:21). And yet the apostle Paul is ready to yield to God's providence — even when and if it runs contrary to human wishes and advice.

VERSE 16

No longer as [if he were just] a slave, but [because he is] more than a slave: a brother who is loved most of all by me, yet how much more [to be loved] by you, both as the person he is and because of the Lord.

This verse is the core and highlight of PHM. Here, finally, Paul clearly formulates what he expects his friend Philemon to do. This verse and the next offer a vision on the social change Paul has in mind — but a political or economical program of action is beyond his horizon. "Loving," "brotherhood," and "partnership" are key terms in the following. An extensive and intensive exegesis will have to show what relevance these three forms of communion have for the interrelation between Philemon and Onesimus, and what impact eventually they may have for easing or solving social tensions between weak and strong, poor and rich, powerful and powerless, seemingly independent and utterly dependent persons and groups in later periods. Certainly verses 16-17 are an appeal to all Christians to accept and to follow another life-order than was previously valid in their environment. In fact, here Paul challenges and encourages all church members so to shape their community that it becomes a lighthouse in a dark world (cf. Matt 5:14-16; Eph 5:8; Phil 2:15; 1 Pet 2:9, 12).

The apostle's call for brotherhood comes from the heart and is deeply moving. It may well signal a step forward in the history of sound interhuman relations — away from unrighteousness, oppression, exploitation, and conflict and toward the stilling of physical and spiritual hunger, an attempt to establish peace on earth.

Yet at least one question must be asked and requires an answer: Is not Paul perhaps a daydreaming victim of illusion, far removed from all that can be realized in common daily life? In other words: Is not the substance of Philem 16 a utopia? Also it may be asked whether an employer such as Philemon is really so free to decide as Philem 14 presupposes, and whether Onesimus is in so totally dependent a position as to be at best the beneficiary of some goodies granted to him, but by no means to be an agent claiming and protecting his own human rights.

First, some preliminary observations regarding the literary form of verse 16. This verse is formulated in quasi-telegram style; it is replete with rhetorical contrast-pairs; it appeals to emotion in a way that could soften a stone. By these means it conveys the message that love can and will completely change the social, political, and economical interaction between persons separated by seemingly insurmountable walls. According to Paul, love is far removed from being a sugarcoating spread over social institutions that will not have their foundations shaken, and that resist changing the supposedly indisputable property rights and power positions of the high and mighty.

On the other hand, the clarity and incisiveness, together with the warmth and beauty, of the substance of Philem 16 do not preclude the presence of ambiguous formulations and of obscure corners in the Greek text. To avoid misunderstandings in an appropriate English version, it is necessary, at the beginning of the verse, to make paraphrastic additions; at its center, to insert an extensive word history of the term "brother"; and at its end, to choose a very free translation. In his essay "Paul, Philemon and the Dilemma of Christian Slave-Ownership," pp. 173-174, J. M. G. Barclay has succinctly listed varieties of possible interpretations. The exposition of Philem 16 has to be much more intensive and extensive than the exegesis of other verses.

Verse 16a

No longer as [if he were just] a slave, but [because he is] more than a slave.

Ever since commentaries on PHM have been written, and so also in this exposition, Onesimus has been designated as a "slave" and Philemon as his "master." But unlike the address "you slaves . . . you masters" *(hoi douloi . . . hoi kyrioi)* found in the *Haustafeln*, those titles are missing in PHM — probably for some good reason (cf. Petersen, *Rediscovering Paul,* pp. 93-97): Paul did not intend to confirm his two friends in their present social status and appellation; he did not wish to nail them down to it. Onesimus — a slave? "No longer!" The depreciative treatment held fitting for such a person and state is utterly unsuitable, if according to God's providence Onesimus has to stay forever with Philemon. The latter — a master with unlimited rights over his servant? — is impossible, for Onesimus is "more" than the slave he once had been.

Does, then, Paul aim at the immediate manumission of Onesimus and press Philemon to decide forthwith to release the returning man into social and economical independence and freedom? If so, the author of PHM would have an honorable place among ancient and latter-day abolitionists and might well be suspected by many of being a political leftist. If not, he might look like an advocate of the social-political status quo and of its oppressive institutions and exploitative structures. Faced by these alternatives, the expositors of PHM and Pauline ethics have come to divergent results. The issue is not just academic; it touches on the lives and hopes of the rich, the middle class, and their un-counted victims. The controversy is sometimes conducted so passionately that the mutual polemics tend to detract from the honor of the opponents — by putting them to shame, by indicting them of bad faith, and by considering their ethical teaching and stance immoral, if not pernicious.

On what evidence are these mutually exclusive opinions based?

Excursus: Does Paul Ask for Manumission?

Above (see "Social Background," n. 112, pp. 41-42, and "Literary, Biographical, and Contextual Issues," sec. VIII.A, pp. 200-214; also occasionally elsewhere) the names of expositors have been mentioned who rejected the hypothesis that Paul wrote PHM in order to move Philemon to legally emancipate his runaway slave. E.g., M. Dibelius and H. Greeven (p. 107) declare, "The juridical aspect of the matter is not at all in view." But H. Koester (*Einführung in das Neue Testament*, p. 569) argues that while Onesimus might well be "a brother without being manumitted," the words at the end of Philem 16, (lit.) "both in the flesh and in the Lord," are hardly less than "a recommendation of manumission." The same opinion is expressed already by E. Lohmeyer; yet he adds, "The idea of brotherhood consecrates anew *(weiht neu)* the original relations between master and slave. . . . The idea of brotherliness has begun to lift up *(aufheben)* and to re-vive by faith a legal-social interrelationship." (Obviously the German verb *aufheben* is here used in the threefold sense it has in G. F. W. Hegel's philosophy: to elevate, to pre-serve, and to annul.)

Among the arguments in defense of either stance are the following:

1. *Pro Manumission*

a. If Paul really cares for his "child" and "heart" (vv. 10 and 12), and if he really considers Onesimus a "loved brother" of himself, the free Roman citizen, and of the free man Philemon, then anything less than full emancipation is unthinkable and would be morally intolerable. The young man can then no longer be treated as anyone's personal property, comparable to a tool or a head of cattle, and he can no longer be expected to suffer the fate and do the work of a mere slave. The Hebrew text of Sir 7:21 begins with the words, "Love an intelligent servant as yourself"; the LXX version of the same verse starts out by saying, "Let your soul love . . ."; and both texts draw the conclusion, "do not withhold from him his freedom." In consequence, if Philemon is as excellent a Christian as he is depicted in Philem 4-7, he must manumit the returned slave.

b. "The truth of the gospel" that is preached by Paul and perverted by the inter-vention of "false brothers" consists of the proclamation and actualization of the free-dom for which Jews and Gentiles have been redeemed by Jesus Christ, and it excludes further subjugations under the yoke of slavery (Gal 1:7-9; 2:4; 4:9; 5:1-13). "The Jerusalem above is free, and she is our mother" (Gal 4:26). This freedom message can and must not be spiritualized or evaporated into a sanctimonious mist. It means not only freedom from misunderstanding and misuse of God's Law, neither only eschatological freedom from sin and death, not to speak of the freedom of the soul and the inner life as proclaimed by Stoic teachers. Justification, liberation by Christ have in Paul's theology sociopolitical character. Those justified by grace do eat at the same table (Gal 2:11-21). "There is neither slave nor free . . . for you are all one in the Messiah" (Gal 3:28; 1 Cor 12:13; Col 3:11). In 1 Cor 7:21 Paul says to slaves: "If you can gain your [social!] freedom, avail yourself of the opportunity."

c. The *Haustafeln* appear to negate the request for the abolition of slavery: even when they are members of God's people, lords remain lords and slaves are exhorted to endure the present situation and to do their work faithfully and enthusiastically. But uncounted scholars of the nineteenth and twentieth centuries (among them, Petersen, *Rediscovering Paul,* pp. 97-98) dispute the Pauline authenticity of these household codices. Indeed, if Paul is not fettered to the ethics of the *Haustafeln,* then by sending Onesimus back (Philem 12) he must have something better in mind than a condemnation to slavehood "forever." To cite the apostle's own words, the man is to be "no longer . . . a slave" (Philem 16).

d. Paul may or may not have known the substance of the so-called Nazareth Sermon as it is recorded in Luke 4:16-21. In that synagogue address, Jesus had quoted Isa 61:1-2: "The Spirit of the Lord is upon me . . . to proclaim liberty to the captives." He had announced that now, with his coming, the Jubilee Year of the Lord (Lev 25) had begun. According to Matt 20:25-28 and parallels, Jesus had declared that every one of his disciples was to be a servant, rather than rule over fellow men by wielding power and displaying authority. Certainly known to the apostle was what early and late parts of the OT say about the exodus, and what in Lev 25 is prescribed and promised as a crown of the Sabbath Year: liberation and manumission. Paul, too, announces, "Behold, now is the day of salvation" (2 Cor 6:2). In conclusion, if ever Paul was a faithful servant and an apostle of the Messiah Jesus, he simply *had* to obey his Master's voice by asking for Onesimus's legal release.

e. When the apostle places faith, hope, and love as high as he does in 1 Cor 13; etc., he means more than psychic, mental, and emotional general attitudes. These gifts of the Spirit effect a change of life in its totality and immediately affect each person's function and place in society. A thief shall steal no more; a lazy person shall do manual work; a fornicator and an exploiter have no place in God's kingdom and shall be removed from the congregation; whoever loves litigation before a court shall prefer the mediation by wise fellow Christians; those who are used to participating in pagan temple festivals shall cease and desist from having a part in idol worship; a glutton and a drunkard shall change his habits (Eph 4:28; 5:5; 1 Thess 4:11; 1 Cor 5:11, 13; 6:1-2, 9-10; 10:19-22). If, then, Paul presses for so grave, vital, and total changes in the life and conduct of other Christians — how could he tolerate that Philemon remain owner of a "brother"?

f. Even if it be admitted (1) that the time was not yet ripe for an absolute command or request for manumission, or (2) that the expectation of the near parousia

413

made immediate social change irrelevant, or (3) that there existed some inclination toward accommodation to existing Jewish and non-Jewish concepts of law and order, together with the yearning for a peaceful and quiet life — even in those cases Paul can be understood as asking in PHM for Onesimus's manumission. J. A. Bengel and then again, e.g., J. B. Lightfoot (p. 177) and B. M. Metzger (*The New Testament*, pp. 23-24) declare that at least the great "principle" of universal equality and brotherhood was established in PHM, an ideal that ultimately had to lead to the termination of the inhuman slave system.

But however plausible such reasoning may sound — it has not been generally accepted.

2. *Contra Manumission*

a. Nowhere in PHM does Paul *explicitly* instruct or beg Philemon to grant liberty to Onesimus. Whether it pleases or displeases later readers of this letter, there were at least two strong reasons not to write "one single word" (cf. E. Lohse, p. 206; P. Stuhlmacher, pp. 40-41) in favor of immediate manumission, though neither Paul nor most expositors of PHM mention the arguments in so many words: (1) if after his legal emancipation, because of given circumstances, Onesimus could not return to Paul and become the apostle's cooperator, or (2) if he could not return to his original fatherland and family, then he might have been exposed to the miseries described by, e.g., Epictetus (*Diss.* 4.1.37).

b. The freedom Paul writes about in other letters is not a freedom at any price and for any arbitrarily chosen purpose. E.g., Seneca (*Ep.* 47), Ignatius (*Polyc.* 4.3), and Tertullian (*De cor. mil.* 13) warn of manumission because the freed person is prone to become a slave of carnal lust. Paul abstains from this argument. The slave quoted by Epictetus had at first been convinced that everything would be all right as soon as emancipation had been granted. Paul's conviction is not the same: free is he or she when he or she is called in the service of the good lord, and when he or she shoulders all the greater responsibilities. The apostle's and his fellow workers' life confirm what might be called "freedom by serving."

c. In Rom 13:1-7 Paul exhorts Christians voluntarily to subordinate themselves to the civic authorities. In 1 Cor 7 he confirms that even in their present civic status, women and slaves stand in Christ's service. The fact that Onesimus is being sent back to his master (Philem 12) is one of the reasons the assumption that the *Haustafeln* are spurious and/or contradict Paul's freedom message must be questioned.

d. The announcement of freedom and the redemption and reconciliation by Jesus Christ are, according to the Gospels, no obstacles to the declaration that, e.g., Caesar is to be given what is Caesar's (Matt 22:21). The parable of the unjust steward and his lord makes of a wise and even shrewd servant an example of how all disciples of Christ ought to behave in times of crisis (Luke 16:1-13). In John 19:10-11, Pilate's authority to act as judge is declared a gift of God. The slave legislation contained in the books of Exodus, Deuteronomy, and Lev 25 does not prohibit the members of God's people to own or be slaves. However, for the duration of bondage, the OT forbids treating slaves with "harshness" (Lev 25:43, 46, 53-55), the way, e.g., Sarah treated the slave girl Hagar (Gen 16:6). Sirach (7:20-21 and 33:30-31) advises a wise master to treat all slaves (not only fellow Jews) with fairness and to love them as "brothers." Job (31:13-15) asserts that he has not rejected the cause and the complaints of his male and female slaves; for God is not only their supreme judge but also the common Father of Job and his servants. Aristotle and the Stoics had argued in a similar way; a slave can be a friend.

e. A statement leading directly to the conclusion that Paul considered the institution of slavery as a sin cannot be found in the Pauline letters. The slave system is, to use Pauline terminology, one of the "principalities and powers" that have been corrupted by the sin committed by Jews and Gentiles and have become enemies of God and humankind. Being creatures of God, they are not sinful by nature. Because they have rebelled against God and are stronger than human individuals and groups, they can be subjugated and restored to order by no one other than God and Christ alone. According to Paul, they have been, they are, and they will be so defeated and so used that they cannot separate God's children from God's love (Gal 1:4; 1 Cor 15:24-27; Rom 8:38-39; Eph 1:19-23; 2:14; 3:10; 6:10-17; Col 1:15-20; 2:15; etc.; see AB 34, pp. 170-183). Therefore, the mere fact that a person owns property, and among his property one or several slaves, does not automatically make him or her a sinner. Neither is it sinful to have to live under the yoke of slavery. Or else the Bible would never call God "Lord," Jesus "Master," or describe the chosen people as God's and/or the Messiah's property and servants. With God's help sin can be recognized, confessed, and forgiven. Distorted and misused structures can*not* confess that they have sinned, and it is never said that they are or will be forgiven. Whether sexuality or marriage, parenthood or political authority, economical or social dependence, physical or psychical force is meant by the term "principalities and powers" — it is always persons who are forgiven, never institutions. So also PHM was written to make sure that Onesimus be received kindly and respectfully, and be treated as a brother. There are no indications that Paul wanted to condemn Philemon for the mere fact that he owned a slave, or to deprive him of supposed or factual civil rights, as they existed at his time. The question answered in this letter is: *how* to make use of such rights, rather than whether they have any validity in the life of a Christian and the congregations.

f. Even if Paul were whitewashed by the affirmation that at least "in principle" he promoted the abolition of slavery, it remains true that according to the apostle Jesus Christ died and rose for something better than the establishment of principles and lofty ideals. Even the way to hell can be paved with noble principles.

The reasonings just listed pro and contra Paul's intention to persuade Philemon to manumit Onesimus, and other arguments that have been or might be added, appear to have about equal weight — so much so that one might speak of a stalemate in the discussion. No wonder that humility, or despair, or both, not to mention lack of concern and care, have motivated some expositors to consider a choice for either side inadvisable or impossible. Why should not *docta ignorantia* (admitted lack of scholarly knowledge) be preferred to a seemingly sterile continuation of an ongoing debate that after all may well reveal negative and positive prejudices regarding the need, desirability, or possibility of radical social change?

If ever a way out of the impasse is to be found, then, it will probably come with the help of a close and minute scrutiny of style and structure of verse 16a. Strange and easily overlooked peculiarities remind one of similar features in verse 14b: (lit.) "not as if by necessity, but according to voluntary." (1) A negation precedes an affirmation and is opposed to it; (2) the negation is toned down by the addition of the multifaceted particle *hōs* (as if), which in the following affirmation is not repeated; (3) the affirmation is expressed in unusual form.

Wanton manhandling of good grammar and syntax is found in verse 16 that has no parallel in verse 14. Paul writes *ouketi hōs doulon* — but because verse 16a is syntactically dependent on the final clause beginning with *hina* and ending with the subjunctive *apechēs* (lit. "in order . . . that you hold him"), Paul ought to have phrased *mēketi hōs doulon*. Both formulations signify (lit.) "no longer as a slave." But in correct Greek, negations that contain *ou* or *ouk* (not), *ouk eti* (no more) or *oudeis* (nobody), are preceded and/or followed by the indicative mood of a verb, or by a noun or an adjective. Also, in questions to be answered affirmatively, *ou*, etc., is the proper way of excluding an alternative. On the other hand, the negatives *mē, mēketi, mēdeis* (not, no longer, no one) are found in combination with subjunctives, optatives, infinitives, imperatives, and frequently with participles. In addition, *mē*, etc., introduce questions to be answered with "no."

In Philem 16 Paul breaks these rules. J. B. Lightfoot has drawn attention to this irregularity. Elsewhere Paul shows that he masters the Greek language sufficiently to respect the rules and heed them. In Philem 14b the good done by Philemon shall not be a result of "coercion" *(hina mē . . . kata anagkēn . . . ē)*. In 2 Cor 5:15, in the final clause, "that those who live might live no longer for themselves *(hina . . . mēketi . . . zōsin . . .)*," he uses *mēketi*. The same is true of Eph 4:14: (lit.) "that we be no longer babes *(hina mēketi ōmen nēpioi)*." Certainly, Paul may be benevolently excused or mischievously accused of ignorance or sheer negligence of those rules that were scrupulously respected by Atticists — even those authors who attempted to dam the flood of Greek grammar irregularities spread worldwide in the Hellenistic age. Still, it is more probable that for a specific purpose the apostle at this place, as at others (see, e.g., Gal 2:4-6), exposed himself to the disapproval and scorn of pedantic grammarians.

Most likely the choice of the supposedly improper *ouketi* is a signal: Paul intended to speak of facts, not of a mere possibility, desirability, or faint expectation. What has actually happened to Onesimus, and what has become of him — this is the ground of the apostle's intervention and hope for the future status and treatment of Onesimus. In Paul's eyes and soon enough in Philemon's eyes too (if only they be opened!), Onesimus *is* (lit.) "no longer as a slave, but more than a slave: a brother who is loved." J. B. Lightfoot may provoke protest, but he is probably true to the text when he remarks: "The negative clause [at the beginning of v. 16] is . . . wholly independent [of the final clause in v. 15b]. . . . It describes not a possible view of Philemon, but the actual state of Onesimus. The 'no more as a slave' is an absolute fact, whether Philemon chooses to recognize it or not." What Lightfoot says of the termination of Onesimus's former status pertains equally to Paul's positive statements: now the returning Onesimus is "more than a slave: a brother. . . ." In verse 11, seemingly no more than his social place and function were sketched in very general terms: "in the past . . . useless . . . but now useful." In verse 16, his very being is described, which counts more than value judgments on the performance of a worker. So also in verses 10 and 12, it was stated as a fact that Onesimus has become and now is Paul's "child" and "heart."

J. B. Lightfoot has come to his daring interpretation by forming the theory that verse 16 is grammatically independent of verse 15. J. Knox, however, had achieved a similar result just by insisting on the intimate coherence of these two verses: "There is no need to be a comma" between the last word of verse 15 and the first of verse 16. The printed editions of, e.g., Vg., the Greek New Testament and Nestle-Aland, and versions such as RSV, NEB, NJB, ZB, Sec B have a comma or a colon or other punctuation at this place. Our translation follows NEB when it uses the parenthetical long dash (—) for marking both the relative independence of verse 16 from verse 15 *and* the coherence between these two verses. A total separation is excluded because no fewer than four accusative forms in verse 16 directly depend on the pronoun "him" *(auton)* in verse 15.

No longer as [if he were just] a slave. The bracketed words added to the Greek text in our translation suggest that in Philemon's house, in legal and economic regard, Onesimus may have remained in the position of a slave. For the following two reasons the paraphrastic version is necessary if ever a translation is to express unequivocally what Paul intended to say at this place.

The Greek does not contain a verb, either at the beginning of verse 16 nor in the subsequent phrase (lit.) "but more than a slave." Grammarians call this omission an ellipsis. Sometimes it included features of an "asyndeton" and/or a "parenthesis." Usually in an ellipsis one or another mood or tense of the verb *eimi* (to be) or *gignomai* (to become) — be it an infinitive or an imperative, an indicative or a participle, a subjunctive or an optative — would make the sentence complete (BDF, 127-128, 414). As earlier observed, the structure of verse 16a is analogous to that of 14b. There the negative and the affirmative predicate, (lit.) "not by necessity but according to voluntary," had been linked to the subject "the good you do" by the subjunctive *ē* (that be, that may be). When verse 16a is to be rendered in English, Greek syntax permits the interpolation of *different* moods of *eimi* (to be): of the optative *eiē* (might be), the subjunctive *ē* (be, may be) for the negative part, and the participle *ōn* (while, because, although being) for the affirmative part. If the nominative *doulos* (slave) were found in the Greek text instead of the accusative *doulon*, the imperative *estō* ("he shall be" or "he must be"), too, might complete the sentence. The context must determine the choice to be made by the translator. It was already shown that the grammatically dubious form *ouketi* (no longer) was a signal for the *facts* rather than mere possibilities described in verse 16a.

There exists still another element of the wording of this part of verse 16 that is surprising and has to be pointed out. For it requires the insertion of two paraphrases: "if he were just" and "because he is."

Hōs (as) is found, just as in verse 14, in the negating statement only, (lit.) "no longer as a slave"; it is not repeated in the immediately following assertion, (lit.) "but more than a slave." Indeed, if Paul had omitted this particle before speaking of a slave for the first time in PHM, he would have affirmed that Onesimus *is* already a free man or *is* at once to be freed from the yoke he has been bearing. Obviously, in the Greek and in the Western languages *hōs* (as, *als*, *comme*, etc.) has often little weight — except where it is used in the function of a conjunction or as introduction of a comparison. But in the Note on the phrase *hōs kata anagkēn* (lit. "as by coercion") in verse 14, it was shown that among its many meanings and functions, *hōs* can limit or diminish the noun, the adjective, the adverb, or the whole clause that follows it. Then the supposed adequacy and validity of an expression or statement is put into question.

In Philem 16a, this is probably the case, just as in Philem 14. Seen before Onesimus's meeting with Paul and his becoming a Christian (through the eyes of Philemon, of the church members meeting in the Colossian house, and of the Jewish and other non-Christian neighbors), that man had been and still was nothing but a slave — certainly not a brother of his master. As a slave, he was despised rather than loved. His self-esteem could not be different; not even by his escape could he avoid being eventually discovered and even caught as the missing "slave." For all who spoke about him and had to do with him, including fellow slaves, he was "just a slave" and nothing more. E.g., H. Grotius and J. F. L. Flach have suggested that the Greek words *hōs doulon* be complemented by *monon* (only), so that the translation should be "no longer only as a slave." In this case Onesimus, while nominally and legally remaining a slave, would yet in Paul's and hopefully in Philemon's judgment no longer be just a supposedly inferior member of the human society. This proposal has been rejected by, e.g., W. M. L. de Wette, H. A. W. Meyer, and more recently J. M. G. Barclay — that is, by those inclined to ignore a specific function of the particle *hōs*.

When E. Lohmeyer observes that the first words of verse 16 "avoid . . . the full force of the word 'slave,'" he sticks closer to the Greek text than N. R. Petersen (*Rediscovering Paul,* pp. 95-96), who assumes that "by implication" *hōs* also qualifies the noun "brother" and the following words. Petersen believes that all three titles, "slave" and "brother" and "partner," are "role-names." Yet Paul intends to describe what by the grace of God Onesimus now actually *is.* In the past his true identity was hidden. He could not be true to his own self as long as he was counted and treated "only" or "just" as a slave. Then he had played a role, and in that role he was "useless" (v. 11). An actor playing the role of Oedipus or Hamlet may be a complete failure on the stage — so much so that he is reproached, has to despise himself or quit the occupation to which he was never really called. No earlier than after the show is over may his very nature and identity, his true character and capabilities, become apparent.

So also Paul informs Philemon in verse 16 that the returning Onesimus has shed the disguising and disfiguring costume he was wearing "as a slave." The poor show he once made is finished and definitely over. Now the true identity is revealed. By placing *hōs* exclusively into the statement that negates the continued validity of the past, and not again before the words "brother" and "partner" in verses 16-17, Paul shows that in being a brother and a partner Onesimus is *not* play acting. Indeed, Petersen himself avers (on p. 188 n. 111) that in Paul's theology, "the reality of the world as seen from within the world is replaced by the reality seen from within the church. For Paul, there is only one reality."

In other Pauline writings, too, the same restrictive and relativizing function of *hōs* can be observed and is followed by an opposite that is not marked by the same particle. E.g., 2 Cor 6:8-10: "We are treated as *(hōs)* imposters, and yet are true; as *(hōs)* unknown, and yet well known . . ."; 1 Cor 7:29-31: "Let those who have wives live as though *(hōs)* they had none, and these who mourn as though *(hōs)* they were not mourning. . . ." However, in other passages *hōs* does not indicate a limited validity: 2 Thess 3:15: "Do not look at him as *(hōs)* an enemy, but warn him as *(hōs)* a brother"; 1 Cor 7:25: "as *(hōs)* one who by the Lord's mercy is trustworthy"; 2 Cor 6:4: ". . . as servants of God we commend ourselves in every way"; Eph 6:5-6: "Obey your earthly lords . . . as slaves of Christ"; 1 Pet 2:16: ". . . live as servants of God"; 4:10-11, 15-16: "as good stewards of God's grace . . . as speaking words of God . . . not as a murderer or thief . . . but as a Christian."

Our paraphrase of verse 16a, "no longer as [if he were just] a slave," follows the philological precedent set by 2 Cor 6:8-10 and 1 Cor 7:29-31. In consequence, in harmony with the substance of the lord/slave passages in the *Haustafeln,* in Philem 16 Paul does *not* ask for manumission, and yet has in

mind a most honorable position of the slave in his master's family and home —
a status that not only totally excludes a treatment deemed adequate for a head
of cattle or a tool, but can also motivate the servant to be a faithful and even enthusiastic cooperator. Before Paul spells out details at the center and end of
verse 16, he offers a very general description of Onesimus's newly achieved and
future esteem and function in society:

But [because he is] more than a slave. A similar statement is made much
later, in the spirit of the age of Enlightenment and Freemasonry, in a Mozart
opera: "Er ist ein Prinz — noch mehr: er ist ein Mensch" [he is a prince, but
even more: he is a man]. The Mozart text is grammatically and syntactically
complete: twice it contains the verb "is." Paul's formulation is elliptic, anacolu-
thic, and far from a model of linguistic clarity and beauty. As already mentioned, the multiple choices offered to interpreters of elliptic Greek texts make
it possible to complement the two parts of Philem 16a by different moods of
the verb "being." For the first half (lit. "no longer a slave") the tentative "if he
were" recommended itself; for the second half (lit. "more than a slave") the
causal "because he is" corresponds to the factual sense of *ouketi* ("no longer").
In a similar way, a new state is set in opposition to a former in Gal 4:7: "You are
no longer a slave but a son," and in Eph 2:13 and 19: "You who in the past stood
far off have been brought near. . . . you are no longer strangers and sojourners,
but you are fellow citizens with the saints and members of the household of
God." So also Onesimus *is* in Philemon's household worthy of a treatment appropriate to a child of Paul and a brother of Philemon.

What is the significance of the word "more," when the future status and
treatment of Onesimus are to exceed the supposedly normal place and role of a
slave? Originally Greek *hyper,* here translated "more than," is an adjective with
the local significance "over" or "above." Paul might have spelled *hyper doulon* as
one single word: *hyperdoulon.* Indeed, LSLex, s.v., refers to a contemporary of
the emperors Hadrian and Antoninus Pius: Apollonius Dyscolus, who (in *De
syntaxi* 330.13) uses the noun *hyperdoulos* (super-servant). In 2 Cor 11:5; 12:11
Paul utters his disgust of "super-apostles *(hyperlian apostoloi)*." LSLex proposes
for the translation of the ancient grammarian's text, "a slave and more." In the
1742 edition of his *Gnomon,* J. A. Bengel mentions the same second-century
passage; he confesses not to know the meaning of *hyperdoulon,* neither whether
it is relevant for the interpretation of Philem 16. It was earlier stated that in
later editions Bengel understood "more than a slave" to mean as much as
libertus (freedman).

LSLex, s.v., shows that the preposition *hyper* has issued in a rich delta of
nonlocal meanings. Whenever a genitive follows, it signifies, e.g., "on behalf, instead, because of, or, concerning." When *hyper* is combined with an accusative,
it means "beyond, exceeding": a captain is taller and stronger than *(hyper)* the

crew members on a ship (Plato, *Resp.* 6.488a); certain feats are possible, not beyond *(hyper)* human nature (Plato, *Leg.* 839d). For Philem 16, where *hyper* introduces the accusative *doulon*, BAG suggests the version "as something better than a slave." Thus this dictionary hints at a *qualitative* difference. The translations "more than, superior to, or, beyond . . ." are recommended by Matt 10:24 (a disciple is "not more than his teacher, neither a slave than his lord"); Acts 26:13 (lit. "more brilliance than the sun's"); and Gal 1:14 ("I advanced . . . beyond many of my own age"). Outside the NT almost never, but in 2 Cor 11:23 distinctly, *hyper* has the function of an adverb ("are they servants of Christ? . . . more am I!"). The same is the case in Matt 10:37: "Who loves father and mother . . . more than me, is not worthy of me." In Phil 3:4 the sentence structure resembles 2 Cor 11:23 closely, but instead of *hyper egō* Paul writes *egō mallon* — ("I in a higher degree" or "for a better reason") — as if to show that he can use *mallon* as a synonym of *hyper*.

In verse 16 Paul does not explicitly mention *why* a specific dignity distinguishes the returning Onesimus from the humiliating contempt in which he was held while he was treated "just as a slave," and from the punishment and wanton ill-treatment often imposed on a slave. In the preceding verse, however, a hint at God's providence is unmistakable, and in verses 10-11 Paul is far from ascribing to himself his spiritual parenthood and the replacement of Onesimus's lacking utility by the present usefulness. Paul does not speak of his own miraculous power that has proven effective. Neither does he expect Philemon to elevate Onesimus over the slave status. For even if Philemon should decide for manumission, the emancipated man would hardly in every aspect have been "no longer a slave, but more than a slave." A legally released slave was called *exeleutheros* or *apeleutheros* ("freedman"; cf. 1 Cor 7:22) — but he was occasionally still named his patron's *doulos* ("slave" or "servant"). By running away from his master, Onesimus may have hoped to leave the slave status behind, in order to become henceforth "more than a slave." Yet such an expectation could prove futile as soon as he was caught by omnipresent catchers, or if need compelled him to return voluntarily to his master. On his own, he could neither extricate himself from slavery nor rise high above it. Not even his so-called conversion was a creative effort and success of his own doing. Without God's grace and some assistance by Paul, he would have remained a slave: even a runaway slave.

As God himself, and he alone, is the redeemer of Israel from Egypt and the transformer of Saul into a "new man," so also God alone has made Onesimus to be "more than a slave." Especially in Rom 5:6-10, the apostle states emphatically that "while we were still weak . . . ungodly . . . sinners . . . enemies . . . Christ has died for us." Onesimus is, to quote 2 Cor 5:17 (cf. Gal 6:15), a "new creature" because by God's grace he is "in Christ," and not because it may someday please Philemon to receive the returning man as a brother. An even more extended paraphrase of Philem 16a would have the wording ". . . because by the grace of God, he is. . . ." In any case, every modern language version of this verse should show that it is a fact — not just a desirable possibility — that Onesimus is now "more than a slave." The fact of his new being and identity reveals that human guilt accumulated by Onesimus and/or Philemon before God's intervention has been overcome, and that the cry or whimper of Onesimus had been heard as much as the complaint of the enslaved people of Israel before its liberation.

The substance and the form of Philemon's and Onesimus's future life together is outlined in the continuation of Philem 16.

Verse 16b

A brother who is loved.

This translation of the Greek accusative *adelphon agapēton* is preferable to the flat version "dear brother" or the funeral-style "beloved brother." For whenever in the NT *agapētos* (beloved, dear) is placed after rather than before "brother," "son," or "child," the misunderstanding of a potentially merely formal expression of endearment is excluded. (Compare Matt 3:17 par.; 17:5; 2 Pet 1:17; Luke 20:13 par.; 1 Cor 4:14, 17; 15:58; Phil 2:12, variant reading; Eph 5:1; 6:21; James 1:16, 19; 2:5 with Eph 6:21; Col 4:7, 9; 2 Tim 1:2; 2 Pet 3:15.) In the accounts of Jesus' baptism and transfiguration, the article between "son" and the *agapētos* emphasizes the genuine great and total love of God the Father for his Son. In English, the version "who is loved" in Philem 16 is preferable to the use of an adjective or participle because it emphasizes the act of loving and prepares for the following description of the love shown for Onesimus.

Agapētos is the verbal adjective of *agapaō* (to love). This form means, if literally translated, "worthy of love, lovable," corresponding to the Latin gerund *amandus*. In Hellenistic Greek, the original and classical gerundial sense is frequently lost and the gerund is "fixed as an adjective" (BAG, s.v.) and has no longer the "living formative power" (BDF, 65.3) inherent in the verb from which the verbal adjective has been formed. So also English "dear," at best, from afar, reminds of the act of loving. On the other hand, in harmony with contemporary and later Greek writers, Paul can also use the verbal adjective as the equivalent of the perfect passive participle or vice versa. In 1 Thess 1:4 and 2 Thess 2:13, the Christians are called "brothers loved by God" and " . . . by the Lord" (*ēgapēmenoi hypo theou, . . . hypo kyriou*). Therefore, according to Philem 16, Onesimus is not only "dear to" Paul and Philemon, but is actually and in all the future loved and/or to be loved, in fulfillment of the commandment "love thy neighbor as yourself." Such love is the "bond of perfection" or "band of completeness" (cf. Col 3:14); its everlasting character is described in 1 Cor 13. Love is the first and the best gift of the Spirit according to Gal 5:22 (cf. 1 Cor 12:31; Rom 5:5). God himself (First John passim) and Christ's love for the church (Eph 5:2, 25; etc.) are origin, model, and criterion of this love.

When addressing or speaking of fellow Christians, Paul often calls them "brothers" without adding "who are loved," or "loved ones" without continuing with "brothers." Obviously each one of these words can be sufficient for expressing Paul's mind. Why does he in Philem 16b sew two seams when one is strong enough to hold the strain? A look at some of the riches and possible weaknesses of the noun "brother" can help to show that Paul has far from chosen a trite pleonasm.

Excursus: Dimensions and Limitations of the Term "Brother"

The following is a supplement to "Literary, Biographical, and Contextual Issues," section VIII, pp. 200-225. There the historic development of the exposition and application of the whole Letter to Philemon has been sketched. Now attention is to be focused on the one word "brother" only. Because this term has a central place and function in PHM, this letter is one of the documents that in the face of grave social tensions intends to pave a way to justice, reconciliation, and peace. Paul speaks of this way and of its goal without fearing to ask for a utopia.

Hebrew *'aḥ* (brother) is often used as a synonym of *rēa'* (neighbor). In other Semitic languages equivalent terms, in Greek foremost *adelphos,* frequently the plural *adelphoi,* mean brothers as well as sisters. Close relatives and friends, too, can be so denoted. Therefore the "brotherhood" now to be discussed includes the mutual interrelation of sisters, and the close communion between brothers and sisters, sisters and brothers.

A. Slaves Called Brothers outside the Epistle to Philemon

In a Note on Philem 1 (pp. 247-248), some indications were given of the use of the noun "brother" at Paul's time. See LSLex, s.v.; BAG, s.v.; H. v. Soden, *TDNT,* 1.144-146; A. v. Harnack, *Mission and Expansion,* 1.405-407; P. Minear, *Images of the Church,* pp. 165-172. R. Gayer (*Die Stellung der Sklaven in den Paulinischen Gemeinden und bei Paulus,* pp. 237-245) offers a convenient summary of the use of "brother" for a slave in ancient literature.

The noun "brother" signifies not only familial or tribal consanguinity, but is frequently also used as a metaphor, meaning spiritual congeniality and/or social equality of rank. In those communities and societies that were open to both masters and slaves, and that could be joined on a voluntary basis only, the members considered and treated one another as brothers. Evidence is scarce that the Essenes, the initiates in mystery cults, and the constituents of a collegium (a society formed for providing decent funerals, some education, sportive or cultural entertainment) orally addressed one another as brothers. Still, discriminating prejudices and practices were not tolerated in these groups: not only the free but also slaves could be elected as officials, and inscriptions reveal how high the mutual esteem of the members was.

When the book of Acts tells that the early apostles began speeches to the congregation or to the Sanhedrin with the address "brother," it does not attest to a universal use of this term. Rather the apostles took over an address expressing both respect and solidarity, which was current especially among contemporary Jews. Among the Gentiles, as has been described above ("Social Background," sec. VI, pp. 33-41, and Annotations 7-8, pp. 92-94), Sophists and Stoic philosophers had elaborated on ideas that were promoted also by tragedians and Aristotle. They argued that Zeus, the common father of all humankind, and Nature and/or a human mother's womb made all human beings brothers. The air that all of them needed for breathing; the soul, as distinct from the body; the capability for being virtuous; finally the death shared by all persons alike confirmed that ultimately free persons and slaves were all equals (see esp. Epictetus, *Diss.* 1.13.3-4; 3.24.16; 4.1). Slave legislation enacted under the Roman emperors attempted to protect slaves from the excesses of evil masters. Even some humane features are not absent from it (see "Social Background," sec. III.B, pp. 18-23). But the axe was not yet laid at the roots of the institution of slavery as such.

In the OT laws on slavery and in Mishnaic and talmudic tradition (see "Social Background," sec. VIII, pp. 53-83, and Annotations 2, 10-16, pp. 84-85, 96-102), some slaves were protected from "harsh treatment."

Solely a slave of Hebrew origin was equal in rank to "a hired servant and sojourner." He could not be kept forever by the Jewish owner and had the right to be redeemed by the next of kin, according to Lev 25:39-55. In these verses, the fellow Jew who has sold himself because of debts he could not pay is never called "slave," but always "brother." In Lev 19:18 and 34, the commandment "love the neighbor as yourself" includes the strangers who sojourn with the Jews in their land; it is mindful of the fact "that [the Jews] were strangers in the land of Egypt" and that the Lord is "[their] God." Without distinguishing between "Hebrew" and "foreign" ("Canaanite") slaves, the Hebrew text of Sir 7:20-21 and 33-31 advises not to abuse a faithful, devoted, and intelligent servant but to "love him as yourself," not to "withhold from him his freedom," and to "treat him as a brother." When Job (31:13-15) describes how he dealt with male and female slaves, he does not use the terms "brother" or "sister" but argues that God formed them in a mother's womb — God who is his and their judge. Therefore Job did not ignore the slave's cause or reject his or her complaints. God is the father and creator of all human beings, as is plainly asserted also in Mal 2:10 (cf. Deut 32:6). All the more is mutual faithlessness among God's elect creatures under judgment. Philo (*Quod omn. prob.* 79) reports that the Essenes "denounce the owner of slaves, not merely for their injustice in annulling the statute of Nature, who motherlike has born and reared all [human beings] alike, and created them genuine brothers, not in mere name, but in very reality, though this kinship has been put to confusion by the triumph of malignant covetousness which has wrought estrangement instead of affinity, and enmity instead of friendship." So clear-cut and consistent have the Essenes been, according to Philo, that "not a single slave is to be found among them, but all are free, exchanging services with each other." From the Midrashic tradition of later centuries, E. E. Urbach ("The Laws regarding Slavery," p. 26) quotes Sifra Betar 7: "You shall treat him [the Hebrew slave] with brotherly love." In the context, the command is explained by reference to the biblical words "If there be sold unto thee a brother" (Deut 15:12).

Now, Onesimus is a Gentile by birth but a brother in Christ. Just as for Jewish writers it was more important to show love for a brother than to exploit him as a slave, so according to Paul, Onesimus is "more than a slave: a brother who is loved."

I. Mendelsohn (*Slavery*, p. 123) considers the brotherly attitude shown by Job "the first condemnation of slavery as a cruel and inhumane institution" — a condemnation that was "based on the moral concept of the brotherhood of man." Mendelsohn declares that the rejection of slavery in principle occurred in Israel "for the first time in the ancient Near East" (pp. 177ff.). So also, as already mentioned, J. B. Lightfoot affirms that at least "in principle" PHM has prepared the way toward worldwide slave emancipation. However, among Jewish scholars, e.g., E. E. Urbach (pp. 4 and 93-94), and among Christian church historians, especially F. Overbeck ("Über das Verhältnis der alten Kirche zur Sklaverei im Römischen Reich," passim) have collected evidence sufficient to mute self-praise as it has arisen out of the synagogue and the church.

The conclusion is necessary that, by calling the slave Onesimus a brother, in the best case Paul has joined a humanitarian movement that existed and was developing well enough before and at his time. Having or not having religious foundations, this movement finally issued in the request and sometimes in the victory of widespread legal slave emancipation. "There was nothing especially revolutionary in the fact that Paul treated the slaves as human beings" (J. M. G. Barclay, "Dilemma of Christian Slave-Ownership," p. 184).

At Paul's time a house-born slave, whether begotten by his master or by another slave living in the same house, and whether or not the master was motivated by philosophical, economic, legal, or biblical stimuli, sometimes enjoyed the position, the privileges, and even the dignity of a brother. He might not be called "brother" by his lord, and he would certainly not address the boss as "brother." In fact, slave children nurtured, raised, and educated together with the patron's legitimate children could grow up as brothers of the legitimate offspring. In some cases they were installed by testament as coheirs and/or permitted to marry a free daughter or son of the house.

If Philemon had heeded the advice of wise and humane Gentiles and Jews, that is, if in his own and in his slave(s)' interest he had treated his servant(s) as brother(s), Onesimus might not have run away. In the sections on lord/slave relationships, the *Haustafeln* contain elements that have precedents or parallels in contemporary Jewish and/or Gentile ethical directives. Onesimus need hardly have fled if only his master had behaved toward him as a righteous, decent, and fair employer.

Still, Paul does not take up only contemporary Greco-Roman and Jewish thought and practice suggested to him, to all Christians, and so to Philemon, too.

B. Distinctive Features of Brotherhood

Philemon 16 is the only text in the NT in which a slave is explicitly called "brother," and solely in 1 Tim 6:2 is the relation between Christian masters and slaves summed up by the words "they are brothers." Neither in the unity formulae (Gal 3:28; 1 Cor 12:13; etc.) nor in the *Haustafeln* found in Col 3:18–4:1 and Eph 5:21–6:9 are the terms "brother" and "sister" even used. But in the context, this address or description does occur, and always the love of God and/or natural love is the tie that binds them together. *All* members of the congregation form "in Christ" one family, the house or household of God and of faith (cf. Gal 6:10; Eph 2:19-22): former Jews and Gentiles, whether male or female, unmarried or married, parents and children — and so also free masters and dependent slaves. They are brothers and sisters because all of them are children of God, children of Abraham, and wherever Paul has worked successfully, children of Paul. Sometimes they are also called "members" of the body of Christ, or parts of the building erected by and for God (e.g., stones) or "branches" of the tree planted by God (e.g., 1 Cor 3:5-10; 12:12-27; Rom 11:16-24; Eph 2:20-21; 4:11-16; 5:30; Col 1:6, 10; cf. 1 Pet 2:5; John 15:1-8). The latter terms seem to be less warm than "brother" and "sister." But always, as Paul shows especially in 1 Cor 3 and 12, their function in the service of the community is as essential and indispensable. No Christian is an island, but God's family has equals who are loved and to be loved.

When in the Gospels and Epistles of the NT the terms "brother" and "sister" serve as honorable description of a member of the church, at least eight constitutive elements can be distinguished. Each is relevant for understanding what Paul has in mind when in Philem 16 he calls Onesimus brother.

1. *The OT basis of family terminology.* The members of the people of Israel had unique reason to consider one another a brother and to heed the laws, the prophetic and other wise counsels prescribing brotherly conduct. Indeed, not only families, tribes, professional groups, nations, and religions have shown or at least required special solidarity. An actual or fictional common physical ancestor and mythical tales of descendance from one or two deities served to support claims of a special election, destination, and obligation. Idealistic, especially Stoic, thinkers of the Hellenistic times sought to pierce narrow limitations. They declared Zeus (or Reason) the father and Nature the mother of *all* humankind, slaves and masters included (see above, "Social Background," sec. VI, pp. 33-41). Thus they combined a naturalistic with a theological reason for all human beings' brotherhood, and they added an anthropological argument: each living person consists of soul and body. By striving for virtues and battling to overcome the body's carnal desires and passions, the soul could prove true to its divine origin.

The reasoning presented by OT writings is different. Why are, according to, e.g., Lev 25:35-55, the Hebrew slaves called brothers and to be treated without harshness, "not as slaves" but like temporarily employed servants? Because they are servants of that Lord God who has liberated the whole people of Israel from the yoke of Egypt (vv. 39, 42, 46, 55). In other passages (in 2 Sam 7:14 and parallels in First Chronicles; Ps 89:26; Isa 63:16; 64:8; Jer 3:4, 19; 31:9; Mal 1:6; 2:10), God is called "Father" or invoked as "Father," and (in Deut 1:31; 8:5; Ps 103:13; Prov 3:12) he is compared to a father. Instead of myths or a dualistic anthropology, events created and shaped by God encourage Israel to call God Father and treat one another as brothers. Constitutive for the existence and form of Israel are very specific events: the creation of heaven and earth by the same God; the election of the patriarchs and of people stemming from them; the exodus from Egypt, the Sinai legislation, the conquest of the land promised by God, and the appointment of judges and kings; the mercy and judgment shown to Jerusalem and the temple when disobedience and misdeeds prevented the establishment of justice and peace; the Babylonian captivity and the return from the exile; the ups and downs in the period of the Greek and Roman occupation of the land; the foundation of synagogues in the Diaspora and the rise and fall of manifold Jewish religious and political groups, including associations of friends called *ḥaburoth.*

Equally, the church owes its origin and specific order and mission to singular events: the fulfillment, crisis, and crown of Israel's history in the advent, ministry, death, and resurrection of the Messiah Jesus; the gift of the Spirit that inspires the proclamation of the gospel to Jews and Gentiles and holds the new Christian congregation together. Neither universal human needs and capabilities to meet them, nor an internal power for surviving as a closed tribal, national, cultural, and/or religious minority society, can explain or replace the particular foundation and structure of the church. Slander and persecution from outside make the church suffer. Errors seem to take it apart. But it has a mission that cannot be quenched. Tensions, errors, and crimes in its midst are chastised. Yet, while the congregations are historical societies and while their life on earth is exposed to uncounted criticisms and catastrophes, it is still the eschatological future that already now determines its very being, its ethics, and its order. The Christians' true life is high above them. They still have to "seek" it, for it is "hidden with the Messiah in God." They shall not fall victim to cynicism or despair: "When the Messiah, your life, is revealed, then you will also be revealed with him in glory" (Col 3:1-4; cf. 1 John 3:1-3). Present and future conformity with Christ crucified and risen (Rom 8:29; Phil 3:10, 20-21), even with the firstborn brother, means: "not to be conformed to the present world" (Rom 12:2).

To summarize: in both the OT and the NT, the fatherhood of God as demonstrated by powerful interventions in the course of history is the presupposition of a community of brothers. By God, out of sheer grace and through the election of specific persons, a brotherhood has been founded and sustained on earth. This foundation and this source transcend the barriers of biological consanguinity. They defy the alternative: either compulsive necessity or a series of accidents. Except perhaps in Acts 17:28, the alleged kinship between divinity and humanity is thereby contradicted.

As earlier mentioned, N. R. Petersen (*Rediscovering Paul,* pp. 151-163) called the NT church an "antistructure" opposed to the organized societies on earth. According to Matt 20:25-28, its main characteristic is the renouncement of rulership by power, in favor of mutual service. Other passages call love or faith or humility the mutual bond holding this particular society together.

2. *The trinitarian origin of the new covenant brotherhood.* In the NT, the brotherly community (*adelphotēs;* 1 Pet 2:17; 5:9) is most frequently called "church" or "congregation" (*ekklēsia*). It is composed of Jews *and Gentiles,* not of fleshly descendants of Abra-

ham only. It understands itself and its mission as a fulfillment rather than a displacement of the promises, commandments, and hopes given to Israel.

Jesus' parable of the wicked vinedressers (Matt 21:33-46, esp. vv. 41 par. and 43) and Paul's radical turn to Gentiles (Gal 2; Rom 1:5; 11:16; etc.; cf. Acts 13:46-47; 18:6; 28:28) have often been interpreted as an announcement of the total rejection of the rebellious first-chosen people of God and the substitution of a mainly Gentile Christian community. But the new covenant promised in, e.g., Jer 31:31-34 to Israel and mentioned at the institution of the Lord's Supper (Matt 26:28 par.), in 2 Cor 3:6, and repeatedly in Heb 8–9, does not mean that God abandons his bride and wife Israel in order to be free for another covenant partner. Rather God renews and fulfills the covenant promise given to Israel by expanding the reach of the covenant and including Gentiles into the full communion with his people. Now the church in which Jews and Gentiles are united is Christ's bride (Eph 5:25-27; cf. Rev 21:2, 9; 22:17). Especially in Rom 11:1 and 29 the idea is rejected that God might have rejected his people and revoked his call. According to Rom 11:16-17, the patriarchs and/or Israel are the holy root or the stem into which Gentiles have been grafted. Ephesians 2:16-22 and 3:6 assert that only in company with Israelites are Gentiles near God, citizens in God's realm, constituents of God's household, sharers in the heavenly heritage, members of the body of Christ. Correspondingly, in 1 Pet 2:9-10 and elsewhere the church is described by a series of terms that before Christ's coming had been reserved for Israel only.

Ancient priestly legislation had prescribed and rabbinical practice had respected that by circumcision even a pagan slave could become a member of Israel. In Eph 2:11-16 and Col 2:11 Paul declares that Christ's death on the cross was the bloody ritual by which Gentiles have joined the community of the elect people. Again: because they are children of God the Father and of Abraham, they are brothers of one another. If there were no theology (speech to and about God), there would be no sociology of brotherhood.

From the beginning the early church and its members addressed God as "Abba, Father" or as "Our Father in Heaven." In the chapter "Abba" in his book *The Prayers of Jesus* (pp. 11-66), Joachim Jeremias presents materials illustrating the origin and diverse forms of this title. He may overemphasize the difference between Jewish traditions and Jesus' own employment and interpretation of this address. Also, he did not intend to elaborate either on the trinitarian foundation of the invocation "Father" or on the existence and life of the brotherhood formed by God's children.

According to Gal 4:4-6 and Rom 8:15-17, the cry "Abba, Father" is raised to heaven after and because God has sent his Son and poured out his Spirit. Now former Jews and former Gentiles pray this way together; they are fellow heirs of Christ. Explicitly 1 Cor 12:4-7 mentions the Spirit, the Lord (Jesus Christ), and God (the Father) in succession. They equip the Christians with manifold gifts, hold them together, and make them cooperate as "members" of one body — as if to say: God's unity in diversity and diversity in unity enable the Christians to enjoy diverse gifts of God. The blessing pronounced over them in 2 Cor 13:14 anticipates, although in an unusual arrangement, later trinitarian creeds: "the grace of our Lord Jesus Christ and the love of God and the communion of the Holy Spirit be with you all."

Without God the eternal Father, without the coming of Jesus Christ at the time of fulfillment — of him who is the "Firstborn Brother" (Rom 8:29; Col 1:15, 18; Rev 1:5) — and without the ongoing dispensation and powerful work of the Spirit, the church would not be, or not destined and equipped to be, a community of brothers. But it is God who has created children not only of Jewish origin but also among the nations. It is Christ who was "not ashamed to call brothers" those assembled in the congregation (Heb 2:11-12; cf. Matt 25:40) and who has died even for the weakest among these brothers (1 Cor 8:11; Rom 14:15). No one is a Christian without hearing the gospel of this "Son of David" (cf. Rom 1:3) and without the presence and work of the Holy Spirit (e.g., Gal 3:2; 1 Cor 2:9-16; 12:1-31). The "full spiritual blessing" that makes Jews and Gentiles beloved children of God, fellow heirs of Christ, and members of one body is described by reference to God the Father, to Jesus Christ, and to the Spirit in Eph 1:3-14 (cf. 4:4-6). If the same Spirit by which Christ was raised from the dead was not working in them, they would be raised to new life neither already now nor on the last day (Rom 8:11; cf. Eph 2:4-6).

According to the four Gospels, Jesus spoke to God no fewer than 170 times in his prayers, and spoke about God to small and large audiences by calling him "Abba, Father" or "Our Father."

The same God who is his Father is also their Father. "I ascend to my Father and to your Father, and to my God and to your God" (John 20:17). The disciples shall not be called "rabbi . . . father . . . teacher," for they "are all brothers" (Matt 23:8-11). Once he himself is converted, Peter is charged to strengthen his brothers (Luke 22:32). Especially in the writings of Luke and in the Gospel of John, the same emphasis is laid on the presence and operation of God's Spirit as in Gal 4:4-6 and Rom 8:14-17. Jesus is born and is equipped to work and to suffer as the son and servant of God, because the Spirit has come upon Mary and him too (e.g., according to Luke 1:35; 3:22 par.; 4:18; Acts 10:38; John 1:32-34; 3:34). By the same Power those chosen by him will receive the promised Spirit and become children born from above and led into all truth (Luke 3:17 par.; 11:13; 24:49; Acts 1:8; John 1:12-13; 3:4-8; 7:38-39; 14–16; 20:22). Only in Matthew (28:19) does the risen Lord instruct his disciples to baptize new disciples from all nations "in the name of the Father and the Son and the Holy Spirit." All Gospels proclaim in their own way what also the Epistles assert: Christians form a special, even a brotherly community because God, the Lord of Israel and all the world, has revealed himself through his Son and his Spirit.

Because in the NT God's fatherhood, Christ's sonship, and the Holy Spirit are relatively often mentioned in the context of baptismal texts, it is not amazing that soon enough, in dogmatic thought and liturgical experience, baptism was declared the means of grace by which persons willing to join the church became God's children, Christ's brothers and mutual brothers, inspired, pacified, and united by the Spirit. Still, it is questionable whether the NT really considers baptism an effective symbol or sacrament. God's fatherhood is demonstrated by the incarnation of God's eternal Son who becomes the Firstborn among many brothers and does amazing works in the power of the Spirit. God and his Son pay for this revelation by suffering the rejection and crucifixion of Jesus. But God's Spirit is not defeated: Jesus Christ is raised from the dead and all over the world believers call "God our Father" and accept and treat one another as brothers.

In Philem 1, 2, 7, 16, and 20, Timothy, Philemon, and Onesimus are called brother, and Apphia sister. The ground of this kind and intimate appellation is mentioned in verse 3: it is the "grace and peace . . . from God our Father and the Lord Jesus Christ." The Holy Spirit is not explicitly mentioned in this formula. But love and faithfulness praised and expected, and the life history of all persons concerned give, according to this letter, ample evidence of the Spirit's operation (cf. Gal 3:2-5; 5:22-23; 1 Cor 2:14-16; etc.).

3. *True and false brothers.* Among the disciples of Jesus who belonged together as brothers was Judas Iscariot. Early in the OT the story of Cain's murder of his brother Abel is narrated. There are accounts of Esau's almost fratricidal relationship to Jacob and the resulting animosity between the peoples of Edom and of Judah (see esp. Obad 10-14). In two parables Jesus compares the attitudes of two unequal sons of the same father (Matt 21:28-31 and Luke 15:11-32). On the other hand, the brother-pairs Simon and Andrew, James and John were disciples of Jesus. James, the brother of the Lord, was honored as a pillar of the Jerusalem church (Gal 1:19; 2:9), and the author of the Epistle of Jude introduces himself as "brother of Jesus." Obviously, while physical kinship can result in the sharpening of contrasts and in enmity, it need not prevent spiritual harmony. Not all kindred is true kindred (Matt 12:48-50 par.; cf. 13:55-57 par.; Luke 11:27). What counts is the birth from above or rebirth (John 1:12-13; 3:3-8; cf. 1 Pet 1:3; Titus 3:5).

In Gal 2:4 and 2 Cor 11:26 Paul speaks of "false brothers" *(pseudadelphoi).* These men appeared to be "servants of Christ" pretending to be "apostles of Christ" and interpreters of the same gospel (2 Cor 11:13, 23; Gal 1:6-9). They insisted on the circumcision of Gentiles entering the community of Christians, and on other legal acts of obeisance to the Law. According to 2 Cor 11:22 (cf. Phil 3:5), they were "Hebrews." In Gal 2:4 Paul affirms that they entered the Christian congregation by the back door: they were "hustled in" and "had sneaked in" *(pareisaktous . . . pareisēlthon).* "Coming from James" (Gal 2:12), i.e., from Jerusalem, they most likely pretended to be delegated by James and authorized by the Jerusalem congregation. Acts 15:1 and 5 speak of an opposition to Paul arising from members of the mother church. But the claim to be authorized was explicitly disavowed by Peter and the so-called Apostolic Decree (Acts 15:10, 24). Paul, in turn, condemns the fake brothers and apostles *(pseudapostoloi)* and warns of them in the sharpest possible terms (see Gal 1:6-9; 2:4; 5:12, 15; 6:12; 2 Cor 2:3-5, 13-15; Phil 3:2).

The consequence, however, must not be drawn that the Jews worshiping in the temple and synagogues were defined as "false brothers." The book of Acts reports (in, e.g., 1:16; 2:29; 3:17; 6:3; 13:26, 38) that Peter and Paul used the formal address "brothers" or "men, [dear] brothers" *(andres adelphoi)* with equal respect and sincerity when speaking to assembled Jews and to meetings of Christians.

No more than a nominal brother *(adelphos onomazomenos)* is he who, while being a member of the congregation, "is immoral in sexual regard, immoral or greedy, or an idolater, reviler, drunkard or robber" (1 Cor 6:10; cf. Eph 5:5). Christians cannot avoid that, "outside" the congregation, in "this world" such a way of life is chosen; God will judge such persons. But because they "have no inheritance in the kingdom of God's

Messiah," they are to be "driven out . . . from among you." The Christians have to have no dealings with them, not even to eat together with them (Eph 5:5-7; 1 Cor 5:9-13). Paul himself states an example: although bodily absent, he has already passed judgment on a member of the church of Corinth who has done what not even Gentiles permit: having sexual relations with his father's wife. "In the name of the Lord Jesus, in the assembly of you [the saints in Corinth] with my spirit, with the power of our Lord Jesus, you are to deliver such a man to Satan for the destruction of the flesh, that his spirit may be saved in the day of the Lord Jesus" (1 Cor 5:1-5).

The mention of idolatry in the cited passages shows clearly that not all "false brothers" are of Jewish origin. A wholesale condemnation of Judaism and Judeo-Christianity as promoted by Marcionism and the Tübingen school of NT interpretation would discredit and contradict not only the words and deeds of the Jew Jesus (cf. Gal 4:4; Rom 1:3; 9:5; Matt 1–2; Luke 1–3; etc.) but also the origin and work of the twelve apostles and Paul himself.

Other NT passages concerning so-called "church discipline" and "excommunication" of scandalous and unrepenting church members have been discussed in AB 34A, pp. 592-598. In 2 Thess 3:14 the warning of immoral conduct, especially of the refusal to work for gaining one's living, is summed up by the words, "If anyone [of those addressed as brothers in the context] refuses to obey what we say in this letter, note that man, and have nothing to do with him."

It may be passages such as this that motivated Fr. J. Hinkelammert (*Ideological Weapons,* pp. 144-152) and N. R. Petersen (*Rediscovering Paul,* e.g., pp. 99, 222) to suggest that Philemon must be excommunicated from the congregation if he does not understand PHM as a request for Onesimus's manumission and fails to release the slave into freedom. As a member of the Colossian congregation, Onesimus himself would have to assist in the expulsion of Philemon! Still, 2 Thess 3:14-15 continues by saying that the brother refusing to obey Paul's letter is to be so treated "that he may be ashamed. Do not look upon him as an enemy, but warn him as a brother." These words recommend a procedure other than instant excommunication. When Paul uses the words "brother" and "loved" as exchangeable synonyms, or when he combines both terms as in Philem 16, then the idea of church discipline is certainly not on his mind.

Since "the specific relationship of brothers is that of love" (H. v. Soden, article *adelphos,* etc., *TDNT,* 1.145), the nature of this love is to be discussed next.

4. *In the NT, brother love signifies friendship.* A. Nygren, *Agape and Eros,* and others have sharply distinguished between unselfish, self-giving *agapē* (love that does not depend on the qualities of the chosen recipient), the reciprocal *philia* (friendship that unites persons of equal disposition and standing), and *erōs,* the desiring and consuming homosexual, heterosexual, or intellectual love (cf. AB 34B, pp. 715-720). Actually, in the NT neither the noun *erōs* nor the verb *eraō* ever occurs, but *agapaō* (to love) is repeatedly used in the sexual and in a much wider sense. Neither the OT nor the NT makes a clear-cut distinction between friendship and love, or between a friend and a brother. "Brother" is the most intimate way of describing or calling a dearly loved friend. And friends are mentioned together with brothers. Brothers and friends are the persons for whom one cares (2 Sam 1:26; Prov 17:17; Pss 35:14; 38:12 [RSV 11]; 122:8). In Exod

33:11 Moses is indirectly addressed as "God's friend," and James 2:23 refers to a text (hardly to Isa 41:8) in which Abraham was called "God's friend."

According to the canonical Gospels, Jesus never addressed his disciples with the words "my brothers." But according to the Fourth Gospel, Jesus repeatedly spoke of his friendship for them. He called them "friends" *(philoi)* and "no longer slaves" (John 15:14-15) — just as in Philem 16 the title and honor of a brother replaces the treatment "as a slave." Jesus demonstrates his supreme love for the friends by giving his life for them, by letting them know all that he has heard from the Father, and by interceding for them. In turn, they prove to be his friends by doing what he tells them, by bearing ever-lasting fruit, and by loving one another (John 15:13-17). John the Baptist is compared to a friend of the bridegroom (John 3:29), and Lazarus is called by Jesus "our friend" *(philos)*, while also Mary and "the Jews" observe that Jesus is loving and has been loving *(phileis, ephilei)* him (John 11:3, 11, 36). In John 21:15-17, finally, the verbs *phileō* and *agapaō* (both mean "to love") are used as synonyms.

There are examples in Greek and Roman history and literature showing that friendship was sometimes estimated more highly than brotherhood — perhaps because it was considered even better and stronger, more spontaneous and more inventive than the obligations established by birth and protected by moral expectations.

When Aristotle *(Pol.* 1.1255b and *NE* 8.11.1161b) and Seneca *(Ep.* 17 and 18; *Ben.* 3.18-20) declared it possible that a master becomes his slave's "friend" or has "a friendly feeling" *(adfectus amici)* toward him, they had hardly anything less in mind than those Hellenistic writers who promoted the idea that masters and slaves were, or at least could be, brothers. The Greek noun *philadelphia* (etymologically "love-brotherhood") contains in one word the love fostered among friends with the mutual love of physical and spiritual brothers. Eventually the description of ideal social conduct led to the formulation of not only an adjective and proper name *(philadelphos)* but a social structure. Cities received the name Philadelphia. In the NT, no reproach falls on the congregation assembling in the Asia Minor town of that name (Rev 1:11; 3:7-10). Christians are urged to practice *philadelphia* in their community (1 Thess 4:9; Rom 12:10; 1 Pet 1:22; cf. 3:8; 2 Pet 1:7; Heb 13:1). In essence *philia* can be a synonym of mutual *agapē*.

Applied to Philem 16, this means: If Philemon loved the returned slave for no other reason than that a brother in Christ has a moral claim on decent treatment, he would never fulfill the apostle's expectation. The last words of Philem 16, (lit.) "in the flesh and in the Lord," will confirm this interpretation: the returning escapee will then only be a "brother who is loved," when the master and the slave will be spontaneous, cordial, and faithful personal friends.

5. *Love by all means.* Brotherly love is far from restricted to the realms of emotion and intellect. W. L. Moran ("Ancient Near Eastern Background," pp. 77-87) has demonstrated that in ancient covenant agreements love is a basic element and motivation. Out of the love of God for Israel, this people is elected; led out of Egypt; given the command-ments, the Promised Land, and its king; protected from enemies; and blessed with rain and peace. So also Israel "shall love the Lord your God with all your heart, and with all your soul" not only, but also "with all your might" (Deut 6:5), that is, with all its earthy possessions and in every way conceivable. The love for the brother and neighbor shall be

no less total. Even the seemingly weakest covenant members — in Deuteronomy: the poor, the slaves, and in some aspects also the Levites — are protected by the commandment of love: unless justice, equity, a livelihood are secured for them, they are not treated as brothers. To love means to care for *all* needs of a covenant member, be they material, psychical, or spiritual.

So also Paul has received from many a "loved brother" and through their hands not only consolation for his soul, sympathy, and intercession. He has also accepted material gifts that helped take care of his daily needs. Using the material care of the Philippians (Macedonians) for himself as a shining example, he urges the Christians in Rome and Corinth with their collection of earthly goods to acknowledge the spiritual indebtedness to the "poor of saints" in Jerusalem (Phil 4:14-16; Rom 15:27; 2 Cor 8:1-4; 9:2; cf. Gal 2:10). Paul's own brotherly love for both Philemon and Onesimus is displayed in Philem 18-19: the apostle promises, if need be, to pay in cash for the damage caused earlier by Onesimus.

6. *Differences among brothers and their works.* There are languages that employ diverse nouns for denoting an older, a younger, and a twin brother. Even in the absence of a distinctive terminology and when brothers "live well and pleasantly in unity" (cf. Ps 133:1), the word "brother" signifies not only a certain physical, professional, or spiritual equality but often includes the recognition of small or great differences. Are some brothers actually or by pretense more equal than others? The privileged position of the firstborn is reflected in stories about the contest for inheritance of property and status. In the Bible, both Israel and God's Messiah are sometimes called God's "firstborn." The ill-treatment of Joseph by his brothers as well as the contempt in which "weak" brothers or members were held in the congregation (1 Cor 8; 11:22; 12:22-23; Rom 14–15) illustrate the treatment of those considered inferior. On the other hand, the loving, tolerant, and edifying way in which F. J. Dostoyevsky describes the Karamazov brothers shows how exciting and important the difference between brothers may be.

What counts are the place and function of a brother or sister in the body of a family or congregation and the work actually done by him or her. Paul, who in 2 Pet 3:15 is called "our brother who is loved," ascribes his work to the grace of God not working in vain in him, and he is convinced that he has worked harder than any other apostle (1 Cor 15:10). Because it pleased God to give each member of the human body and each member of the body of Christ its own place and function, its own indispensable gift and task, no church member is less worthy than others (1 Cor 12:4-11, 18-30). Those whom Paul calls brothers and sisters and recommends to the care of other Christians are all distinguished by specific services rendered, be they to Paul or to one or several congregations. While the spiritual gifts and the tasks given to them vary widely, and while their achievements are of many sorts, they are all coworkers of God and their works are subject to God's (or Christ's) ultimate judgment (1 Cor 3:5-15; 2 Cor 5:10).

In the eight chapters of the two letters to the Thessalonians, the term "brother" occurs proportionally more often than in other Pauline letters. Paul expects that all brothers do work (1 Thess 4:11; 2 Thess 3:6-13). He speaks of "the work of faith" and "the labor of love," and he describes himself as a prototype of proper conduct. In 1 Thess 5:12 (RSV) he distinctly beseeches the brothers to "respect those who labor among you and are over you . . . esteem them very highly in love because of their work." In 1 Cor 12:28-31 he mentions among those "installed by God and equipped with the gifts of the Spirit, first apostles, second prophets, third speakers," etc. (cf. Rom 12:6-8). N. R. Petersen (*Rediscovering Paul*, p. 174; cf. section "Some Sociological Implications of Paul's 'Work' Metaphors," pp. 109-124) refers to such texts in order to conclude that in the church, "within this social body, there is a hierarchy of positions." Indeed, different works are done, different services rendered. Yet this plain fact is hardly reason enough to speak of a "hierarchy" existing among brothers. Jesus had, according to Matt 20:25-27, admonished his disciples to serve one another and not to imitate earthly rulers. Paul calls himself "the least" and (lit.) "more least" among the apostles (*elachistos, elachistoteros;* 1 Cor 15:9; Eph 3:8). His fully developed apostolic self-consciousness notwithstanding, he follows his own advice: "In humility count others better than yourselves" (Phil 2:3; cf. Rom 12:10).

Therefore, even if Onesimus has to be Philemon's servant again and obey him as slaves in the *Haustafeln* are told to subordinate themselves to their masters, the returning fugitive loses nothing of his dignity and rank in the kingdom of God and in the church. In God's plantation, on his building ground, in his temple and household, one works as a planter while others have to water and to harvest. One may serve as an architect laying the foundation while others have to erect a house or a temple. Some are stewards, supervising fellow employees, and others fulfill a dependent function. In each case those called "brothers" or "loved," or both, are coworkers of God and are to respect and serve one another mutually (1 Cor 3:5-13). So also Onesimus is declared to be "useful" to both Philemon and Paul, without having to be ashamed of serving.

7. *The mutual responsibility of strong and weak brothers.* The qualifications "strong" and "weak" can have various significances. A conflict in every human being is described when the strong spirit is opposed to the weak flesh (Matt 26:41). Because of human failure to fulfill God's will, the law has proven impotent and become weak, while the Holy Spirit fulfills its requirement (Rom 8:3-4). In Rom 5:1-10 the terms "weak" and "godless" and "sinners" and "enemies" are used as synonyms, yet God's love is demonstrated as victorious by the death of Christ for even such persons. By becoming weak and poor, Christ himself has in the form of a servant revealed God's power, and from his crucifixion in weakness he was raised by the power of God in order that those "weak in him" shall "live with him by the power of God" (2 Cor 8:9; 13:3-4; cf. Phil 2:6-11; Heb 5:2; Matt 20:28; etc.). Paul is not ashamed of his weakness, but knows that God's "power is strong in those weak" (2 Cor 10:10; 11:29-30; 12:9-10; cf. Gal 4:13). Being "weak" can mean suffering a physical disease (Gal 4:13; Phil 2:26), being imprisoned by the Romans (Philem 1; etc.), making a poor show as a person and orator (2 Cor 10:10).

Not only the servant Messiah and the apostle Paul are "weak" as long as they are judged by human standards. Also the majority of the Corinthian congregation, and probably of other churches too, consists of people esteemed to be neither wise nor powerful nor of noble birth. Yet they are chosen and called by God in order to shame those wise and strong and to permit no boasting other than in and of the Lord (1 Cor 1:26-30). Jesus called the members of God's people "little ones"; and according to Matt 6:30 par.; 11:11; 14:31, he knew how defective their faith was. Even within the congregation, some are considered weak in faith, others strong in faith, again others have fallen sick (Rom 14–15; 1 Cor 8:7-13; 11:30). Also a brother can fail to carry out his task: according to First and Second Corinthians, Timothy had not succeeded in building up and steering the congregation in Corinth the way Paul hoped he would. Titus was sent later — and he, only, met with success. Yet Paul sent cordial "Pastoral Epistles" to both. Other cooperators are mentioned in the greeting lists attached to many letters. All fellow workers depend on spiritual gifts given by God (1 Cor 12:4-30; Rom 12:5-8). Paul acknowledges that the function of some is more hidden or despised than that of others, but he declares the most degraded members' function most vital and honorable (1 Cor 12:22-24). In 1 Cor 12:7 Paul avers that no one is a member of the church, a brother or a sister, without being given a gift and a task for the common good.

Therefore in, e.g., 1 Thess 4:18; 5:11, all of them are charged to comfort, encourage, warn *(parakaleō)*, and edify one another mutually. In the *Haustafeln* and in PHM, it is shown how a Christian in the (strong) social position of a slave owner has to conduct himself with a brother who works as a slave; and how the socially weaker is to serve the earthly master. Voluntary subordination of one to the other is in Eph 5:21 required before Paul goes into details.

In addressing the masters, Paul tells them to "give the slaves whatever is right and fair *(to dikaion kai tēn isotēta)*" and to "stop using threats" (Col 4:1; Eph 6:9).

In Philem 15-16, this attitude to the slave is indicated by the term "holding properly" *(apechō)* and by the reminder that Onesimus is "more than a slave: a brother." By no means are those Christians who own a house to "put to shame those having not" a house, a respected social position, or the freedom to meet on time for the celebration of the Lord's Supper (1 Cor 11:27). When Paul turns to the slaves, he appeals to them to do honest work from the depth of the heart (Col 3:22–4:1; Eph 6:5-7; 1 Pet 3:1-7). Married women are called the "weaker sex" (lit. "weaker vessel") and are instructed to subordinate themselves to their husbands, "just as Sarah obeyed Abraham," while husbands are to live "considerately" *(kata gnōsin)* with their wives and to "pay honor" to them.

This does not mean that the interrelation between the socially stronger and weaker members of the congregation is to be determined on the one side solely by the activity of the stronger, however just, humane, and kind it may be, and on the other by the submissive passivity of the weak partner. A social club may have active and passive members. But according to, e.g., 1 Cor 12; 2 Cor 5:5; Eph 1:13-14, 17; 4:7-12, in a congregation all members are charismatics, that is, persons inspired, equipped, and activated by a spiritual gift to participate in a life of mutual service.

The exchange of brotherly exhortation and consolation (later called *mutua consolatio fratrum*) mentioned in, e.g., 1 Thess 4:18; 5:11, is an essential part of that service. Since according to Philem 16 Onesimus is a brother of his master, he will have the right and duty not only to obediently do manual or secretarial work, but also to use his voice and, if need be, to speak up to his master. Because Onesimus "is sent" by Paul to Philemon, and because Philemon is bid to receive him as he would receive Paul himself (vv. 16b + 17b), this "brother" has a quasi-apostolic mission to fulfill in his master's home.

Rephrased in the spirit and language of liberation and Minjung theology, this means that not only slaves and the enormous number of other oppressed persons are in need of liberation through Christ and the gospel so that they have enough food to live and enough honor to do meaningful work with joy. Rather, those wielding economical and political power in society, too, wait for liberation from the yoke of their idols. How can they ever become free? It is God who can and will authorize and equip "the people," that is, "lowly and weak persons," to carry the good news for the high and mighty, whatever their position in the church and in the world. The socially and ecclesiastically well established Philemon may have to learn a few things from "brother" Onesimus and thereby begin to become a better man.

At any rate, brotherhood cannot be regulated by a set of conditions and rules. It must be perpetually learned and tested and improved. It is not a state or a status of being, but movement toward becoming and a search for perfection.

8. *An example for all the world.* The distinct society called the brotherhood of God's children is not an end in itself but is destined to fulfill a missionary function. Certainly they can also enjoy an intramural and personal advantage. Two persons or groups who "in Christ" are members of the congregation no longer are to impose upon one another or to suffer mutual segregation, discrimination, contempt, and enmity. According to the unity formulae (Gal 3:28; etc.) and the *Haustafeln,* Jews and Greeks, whether male or female, husbands and wives, parents and children, masters and slaves are the first to enjoy the fruit of conciliation and peace. But the mutual love and respect of Christians and the new life order given to the congregation, if ever they correspond to Christ's and the apostle's word, are as conspicuous to their environment as was, e.g., the exodus of Israel to Egypt and other nations. The lifestyle of people called Christians will speak at least as clearly, and probably even more convincingly, to non-Christians as words (cf., e.g., 1 Pet 3:1-4). Brotherhood and a conduct revealing *philadelphia* (brotherly love) are certainly never a possession or privilege of the church. What the Christians are by God's grace and what the intramural order of the church is, is destined to be radiant, and to serve for the benefit of all humanity and all the world. Those praying with Christ to "Our Father" and called Christ's and mutual "brothers" are instructed and equipped to be a light to the world and salt of the earth (Matt 5:14-16; cf. Isa 42:6; 49:6; Acts 26:18, 23; Phil 2:15; Eph 5:8-9; 1 Pet 2:9).

In 1 Tim 6:1 those church members "who are under the yoke of slavery" are specifically exhorted to "regard their masters as worthy of all honor, so that the name of God and the teaching [of the apostles] may not be defamed." As 1 Tim 6:2 shows, not only Christian slaves had "believing masters." Among both Christian *and* non-Christian lords *(despotai),* there were not only good and dependent but also crooked (or harsh, unjust, *skolioi*) masters, and to all of them slaves had to subordinate themselves by "doing good," as a testimony to Christ (who suffered without being guilty). In analogy, masters give a witness to their Christian and non-Christian slaves by showing through their treatment of the disputed persons that they know of the impartial judgment of God expected of both lords and servants (Col 3:24-25; Eph 6:8-9).

The same missionary responsibility is shared by husbands and wives. Because a married woman cannot "know" whether she will "save her husband" by moving him to become a Christian, and because the same is true of a husband having an unbelieving wife, they are not to break up their marriage but stay together; only when the pagan partner insists on divorce is consent to the separation to be given (1 Cor 7:12-16). According to 1 Pet 3:1-2, the Christian wives of husbands "disobedient to the word" may win them over by their conduct, without words. First Corinthians 7:14 speaks of the sanctification of children by a Christian father or mother — and in Mal 4:5-6 it is promised that the forerunner of the expected Lord, Elijah, "will turn the hearts of fathers to the children and the hearts of the children to the fathers."

In summary: the titles "brother" and "sister" include the engagement in missionary responsibility for the sake of persons outside the present household of God. As there may be some false brothers inside the community, so there may well be an enormous number of potential future brothers outside the walls of the church. An apocalyptic vision is applicable also to the nature and order of the biblical concept of brotherhood: the gates of the heavenly Jerusalem stand open by day and by night for admitting Gentiles (Rev 21:23-25).

When Onesimus left Philemon by stealth, he was not yet a member of the congregation meeting in the house of the model Christian Philemon. Most likely the slave had not been treated with brotherly love. Even when Philemon should be inclined to remember Onesimus's past, his not being a Christian, his uselessness, the possible damage caused by the man who ran away — the host of the Colossian house church has yet to welcome and treat the returning fugitive as a brother. Whether and how he complied with Paul's urgent intercession can only be guessed. But literary sources permit an outline of responses to the high calling for a fraternal life that has been given by the church in later times.

C. Ideals and Reality of Brotherhood in the Church's History

The history of the church is anything but a glorious demonstration of fraternal conduct motivated in and demonstrated by pure love. As in the NT epistles, including Rev 2–3 and in their own way each of the Gospels, from the beginning errors and quarrels, ambition and jealousy, suspicion and hypocrisy, separation and scandals plagued the church — no less than other groups and associations founded on well-meant principles. Had Jews and Gentiles really occasion to observe how different the life of Christians was because they loved one another exceedingly? In its description of the essence of the church, the third article of the Apostles' Creed calls the church *communio sanctorum* ("the communion of saints" or "participation in holy things") — but neither love nor brotherly solidarity is explicitly mentioned.

Still, the questions were raised and discussed: For what reason and by which means is someone a brother or a sister? Who is worthy of the honorable title? And, above all, how do people live together and what is the shape of a communal life even when brotherhood and sisterhood are taken seriously?

Not only in the early church but also later, the continuity and solidarity with Israel was much less emphasized than distinctive elements. God the Father, Jesus Christ the Firstborn Brother, the experience of the Holy Spirit who united Jews and Gentiles were declared the solid ground upon which the church stands and grows. Those joining the Lord's Prayer's "Our Father . . ." and being baptized in the name of the Father, the Son, and the Holy Spirit were considered brothers and were expected to be such. Personal and communal prayer connected with the baptism administered by the church was the means to become and the sign to recognize a brother.

Yet what about the great number of non-Christians in the church's environment and the less numerous and still dangerous groups of heretics? Most remarkable in the early church is the repeated citation of the LXX text of Isa 66:5: "Say to those who hate and detest you, 'You are our brothers *(adelphoi hēmōn)*,' in order that the name of the Lord be glorified and they be put to shame."

E.g., Justin Martyr (*Dial.* 96) proudly declared that even to all Jews and Gentiles who curse the Christians, "we [Christians] say: 'You are our brothers.'" In several sermons on the Lord's Prayer, Augustine (*Sermones* 56-59) pointed out that this prayer, especially the address "Our Father," is first of all a confession of faith *(symbolum)* and then also a prayer. Christians are brothers because the Son of God has made them participate in his sonship. They are brothers because they have the same Father and because Christ does not shy away from calling his servants "brothers." "Under that Father, the master and the slave . . . the Emperor and the soldier . . . the rich and the poor are brothers — not only of Christ but also of one another." The church father is aware that heresy and schisms seem to disrupt the family of those who believe in God, the common Father, who pray to him saying "Our Father," and who are baptized. In his *Enarratio in Psalmum* 32 (= Ps 33 in MT, RSV, etc.), Augustine calls "those far" not only "the pagans who do not yet believe in Christ," but also "those split off from us who confess the same Head and are yet separated from his body." How shall Christians behave in this relationship toward the latter? "Let us grieve for them *(doleamus)*, brothers, as for our brothers. Whether they are willing or unwilling, they are our brothers. Then only they would cease to be our brothers, if they ceased saying 'Our Father.'" Heretics and schismatics say to us, "you are not our brothers and call us pagans. They even want to rebaptize us, claiming that we don't have what they give. . . . By not recognizing our baptism, they deny that we are their brothers." Yet the prophet (cf. LXX Isa 66:5) said, "to those who say to you 'you are not our brothers,' say 'you are our brothers.'" Even those the apostle Paul had to reproach, he spoke of as brothers and addressed them as such (in 1 Cor 6:8; 7:15; Rom 16:10). By no means must they be rebaptized, for even the brother who was dead and lost has been found and lives again (Luke 15:32). In *Ep.* 2.87.5-6 Augustine declares that the whole Christian earth, except one's own self, would have to be condemned if heretics were not accepted as Christians, and in *Ep.* 2.23.2 anabaptism of a heretic is declared to be "a sin in every aspect" and "a most immense crime." Finally, in his Heptateuch interpretation, the church father states (*Ad Exod* 10:23), "it is noteworthy that also any man can be called man's brother" — yet without drawing the conclusion that every human being is to be loved as much as the fellow Christians.

In the time between Justin Martyr and Augustine, and afterward, there were groups inside the churches and at the margin of those eventually called orthodox that were composed of persons dissatisfied with the realization of community by and in the organized church. These groups resented the absence of measures to keep the congregation clean from the immoral conduct of clerics and laypersons, and from the defilement by heretics (see for the following, e.g., the articles on "brotherhood," "monasticism," the several monastic orders and other communities calling their members "brothers" in, e.g., *RGG*, 2nd ed., 1.1032-1036, 1425-1426; 4.1070-1081, etc.).

Already in ancient Israel, minority movements and groups had called for a restoration of brotherhood, and had attempted to implement it in their life. The Rechabites (see Jer 35, etc., and, e.g., *IDB*, 4.14-16; *ABD*, 5.632-633) wanted to uphold the ideals and customs of a nomadic community, in opposition to decadent city life, as it developed under Canaanite and other non-Israelite influence. Eventually a Rechabite group was formed among Levite singers; some of their members may have married into priestly families and participated in the sacerdotal temple service. Less ready for compromises was the covenant community of the Essenes in settlements founded "in the wilderness." Its members intended to be the remnant of God's people. Although married, they led an almost monastic, strongly disciplined life. Calling themselves "Sons of Zadok," they showed utter contempt and hatred for the "wicked priests" of the Jerusalem temple — although or because the latter claimed to stem from the same ancestor Zadok and were called "Sadducees." The feeling was probably mutual.

Similar protest movements originated and sometimes flourished among Christians. The monastic movement can be understood as a bold attempt to take seriously, to understand literally, and to organize practically what Philem 16 and other NT passages say about brotherhood. A lifestyle can reveal deeper appreciation and fuller obedience than learned commentaries and dogmatic formulations.

Beginning in Egypt and spreading over eastern and then also western regions, around inspired and inspiring leaders, communities were formed by formerly ascetic eremites and anchorites, preferably in remote places. *Fratres eremiti* (eremite brothers) founded monasteries in order to serve God totally and without concessions to worldly conduct, as a perfect brotherhood. Abbots, strict obedience, and rigorous discipline soon replaced the originally charismatic community life. An immediate dependence of the Christian monastery on, e.g., the Qumran settlement and its rule (1QS) cannot be demonstrated. But similarities to Vedic, Brahman, Buddhist, Hindu, and other Eastern religious experiments and experiences are obvious.

At a supposedly safe distance from temptations of the flesh, from the presence of members of other groups, from the burdens and allurements of possessing private property, and from the distraction and absorption by the care for daily needs, a chance was sought for prayer, meditation, and concentration on the "one thing needful" (cf. Luke 10:42).

In about 529, Benedict of Nursia founded the monastery on Monte Cassino. While learning from earlier monastic regulations, he refined them thoroughly. The so-called Benedictine Rule became basic for uncounted other monasteries and convents of the early and the classic Middle Ages. Discipline, meditation, withdrawal from the world were by Benedict combined with the requirement of handwork: *ora et labora* (pray and work); in this order liturgies, including sacred music, were developed. Care of souls and favor of all needing help, sometimes also missionary activity in faraway lands, were part of the brothers' and sisters' obligations. The fraternal life of the Benedictines and similar orders included cultivation of fields and forests, gardens, orchards and vineyards, and was a model for all those willing to learn. Thus a vital contribution was made to culture in the widest sense of the term. By the collection of manuscripts and scholarly study, by education offered in low and high schools, by the establishment of hospitals and the performance of other works of charity, the monasteries demonstrated that brotherhood not only meant common prayer and hard work, but also benefited those who did not take the vows of a monk. They gave living, existential, and historical evidence of the practicability and creativity of common brotherly life — as Paul had envisioned it in PHM for Philemon and Onesimus. Certainly the apostle did not foresee that Philemon's house would in the future be a monastery, but he expected it to be a light for the world, as indeed some later monasteries have been. In their own way, monasteries demonstrate that brotherhood is not only different from the so-called secular life and social order, but also contrasts with the structure and conduct of the great organized and established churches.

The great achievement of the monastic movement did not prevent the occurrence of internal corruption and decay on the one side and of criticism from lay groups and clerics on the other. Some monasteries became rich, tolerated luxury, owned slaves, and conducted their worldly affairs after feudal patterns. They oppressed and exploited dependent farmers and craftsmen and made them serfs. Beginning in the early ninth century, a monastic reform movement radiated from the Abbey of Cluny. New orders and monastic settlements were founded that made poverty a precondition of perfect obedience to Jesus' and the apostles' example and command. Francis of Assisi called not only human beings his brothers and sisters but also other creatures of God, e.g., the sun. Returning to ascetic discipline and fulfilling the task of public preaching were declared essential. Mendicant (beggar) orders were founded. Competition and strife arose among the exploding numbers of medieval brotherhoods. Because they set different priorities, the monastic movement split up — at least in the Western Church. In 1215 the Fourth Lateran Council forbade the establishment of new orders, and in 1274 the Second Council of Lyons made the validity of rules for monks and sisters dependent on papal approval. Still, the call for a reform not only of monasteries but of the whole church resounded loudly and clearly throughout the following centuries. Ever new brotherly communities were being formed in order to take up the challenge; they opened their doors also to laypersons.

In the thirteenth century, the lay movement called the Brothers and Sisters of the Free Spirit combined at least three concerns: quietistic mysticism, an anticlerical and antisacramental stance, and the pursuit of sociopolitical reforms. They were suspected of moral lasciviousness and suffered heavily from the measures taken by the Inquisition. In the middle of the fourteenth century, the Bohemian-Moravian unity of brothers took up the reform ideas of Jan Hus but intended, as "Brothers of the Law of Christ," to replace the violence of the militant Hussites by imitation of Christ's gentleness, poverty, patience, and love of enemies. Because the selected lay priests and bishops in congregational assemblies established a church order of their own, they were not officially recognized as an order and left the Roman Church. They had contact with the Reformers, but did not join a Reformation church. When their homeland, former Czechoslovakia, was re-Catholicized by the Hapsburg emperors of Vienna, they had to leave the country and survived in exile only. There, the great scholar, ecumenist, and pedagogue Johann Amos

Comenius became one of their bishops. The majority of today's Protestant churches in the Czech Republic and Slovakia insist that their provenance is from the Unity of Brothers.

Another group was formed under the name Brothers of Communal Life *(fratres communi vitae)*. Beginning about 1460, "Brother-houses" were built in Holland, on the Nether Rhine, and eventually all over Germany. These Brothers did not become monks, nor did they subordinate themselves to quasi-monastic rules, but simply lived and labored together, endeavoring to realize brotherhood.

The Reformers of the sixteenth century condemned monasticism summarily. Its emphasis on works and on perfections was decried as a denial of justification by grace and faith alone; its special ethics and forms of piety appeared to denigrate the worth of the laity's life; and it was easy to point out signs of moral decay, even among the beggar orders. In consequence, numerous monks left their monasteries and as many nuns their convents.

In addition, by decree of some civic authorities, a great number of friaries and nunneries were closed down. In 1532 Luther was asked by a brother of the Communal Life to give his opinion and judgment on the brothers' basic principles, so that they would no longer be condemned from pulpits, expelled from their houses, and forced to change their garb. Luther commended them warmly for leading an honorable life and having an honest and disciplined congregation. "Your way of life," he said, "as long as your teaching is poor and you live according to Christ's gospel, pleases me marvelous. If only the monasteries were of such kind, or at least, some of them today! I dare not wish many things, for if all were such, the church would be all too happy" (Luther, WA *Briefe*, VI, 1897, 1900, 1901, pp. 248-249, 254-257). The Reformation churches certainly did not follow this wish: they were organized in various ways, but never as a distinct brotherhood. Only on the so-called left wing of the Reformation was a brotherly manner of living, worshiping, and working together at a certain distance from established churches considered essential for a true and real Christian. E.g., Jacob Hutter (d. 1536) fled together with his Anabaptist friends from Tirolia to Moravia and joined there a likeminded group. The latter was much later labeled "communistic," but had intended no more than to live after the pattern of the earlier Christians. The great Protestant churches joined the Roman Catholics in tactics employed against such groups. Their members were tortured, drowned in water, or burned on the stake. And *Bruderhöfe* founded and maintained by the Hutterite Brothers survived — first in Russia and also in North and South America. To this day they demonstrate that devoted service to God, renouncement of private property, and hard communal labor can work.

The age of Counter-Reformation, of religious wars, and of the formation of Lutheran and Calvinistic orthodoxy contributed little to promote fraternity within diverse great churches. Once more, Paul's appeal to Christians that they live together as brothers (as it is made, inter alia, in Philem 16) was not heeded. The *Societas Jesu*, the Jesuit order founded stepwise in 1521/34/39/40, placed unlimited obedience to the pope, strict military discipline, influential activities (in honor of the virgin Mary) in education and at princely and royal court and on the mission field above the development of a warm fraternal life. Brothers and sisters of charity did less conspicuous work to benefit the sick and the poor.

In the Protestant churches the rise of pietism led to a rediscovery: brotherhood and sisterhood were essential and natural for all who by experience had met the crucified and resurrected Lord. "Societies" *(Sozietäten)* were founded in order to form within the frame of the great churches "little churches" *(ecclesiolae in ecclesia).* Count Nikolaus Ludwig von Zinzendorf took up traditions of exiled members of the Bohemian-Moravian unity of brothers. In *Herrenhut* (Saxonia) he established the *Brüdergemeine,* which soon enough developed and became a worldwide church, having its own clergy, constitution, and hymnal. Christocentric theology and worship, personal faith and piety, brotherly relation between all members, intensive diaconal and educational work at home, and mission in faraway countries are to this day among the distinctive marks of the "Moravian" *Gemeine.* In Germany, most of its members retain active and fruitful membership in one of the *Volkskirchen.* In Great Britain and America they have received recognition as a "free church." Among the names chosen by the hundreds of existing denominations, the self-designation *Brüdergemeine* is closest to the early Christian description of Christianity as a "brotherhood" (1 Pet 2:17; 5:9). At this place it suffices to mention that there are also numerous sectarian groups that timidly or daringly seek to restore this early Christian social bond.

When, beginning in 1933, all Protestant churches in Germany were exposed and in part yielded to the temptations and pressures of National Socialism, a group of pastors, laymen, and professors gathered at Barmen and pronounced a theological declaration that soon enough was called the Barmen Confession and became basic to the movement and eventual organization of the Confessing Church. In resisting the introduction of the *Führer prinzip* (leadership principle) of the totalitarian state in the churches', and the congregations', structure, articles I and II of that confession affirm that Jesus Christ lays claim on the Christian's total obedience. Article III declares, "the Christian Church is the *congregation of the brethren* [our emphasis] in which Jesus Christ acts presently as the Lord" and "has to testify . . . with its faith as with its obedience, with its message as with its order, this is solely his property. . . ." Article IV draws the conclusion that "the various offices in the Church do not establish a dominion of some over the others," and that the church cannot and is not "permitted to give to itself, or allow to be given to it, special leaders vested with ruling powers." (Quoted from the translation by A. C. Cochrane, *Reformed Confessions of the Sixteenth Century* [Philadelphia: Westminster, 1966], appendix, pp. 333-336.)

The movement and organization called Confessing Church suffered slander and political as well as theological condemnation from the established *Volkskirchen,* which succumbed to the Nazi pressures. Up to four hundred "confessing" ministers and laymen were imprisoned at times, and some of them died as martyrs.

As long as the struggle lasted, pastors in the Confessing Church called one another "Brother ———— ," and the leadership lay in the hands of *Bruderräte* (brother councils). After the defeat of Hitler's Germany and the end of the Third Reich, the appellation "Brother" degenerated to *Herr Bruder* (Mr. Brother). A restoration of earlier conceptions and forms of the church took place, so much so that once more the idea and realization of a brotherly church were quenched.

As already mentioned in the Note on Philem 9 (pp. 316-317), Emil Brunner (*Misunderstanding of the Church*, esp. pp. 10, 17, 84; German original 1951) had followed the tracks laid by law professor Rudolf Sohm when he argued passionately that the church is a spiritual community, "a pure fellowship of persons . . . of brothers held together solely by faith and love, not by institutional ties or laws." On the other hand, Karl Barth himself, the author of the text of the Barmen Confession, while maintaining that in essence the church is a brotherhood and should have an order expressing brotherhood, did not endorse the repudiation of all law and order in the church. In his extensive discussion of "church order" (in *Church Dogmatics* IV/2, pp. 676-726; German original 1955), he is willing to follow Erik Wolf in describing the church as a "brotherly Christocracy" and, with some hesitation, as a "Christocratic Brotherhood" (p. 680). This definition leaves room for spontaneity and free development while yet opposing disorder and chaos. The church as a whole and each local congregation stand under law that is unlike all other laws. But *Kirchenrecht* (church law) does not, as it were, automatically contradict the nature of the body of Christ and its high calling on earth. As long as church law and order are continuously corrected by the Word of God and the Spirit, the church "will show that its law is true law; a law which on the basis of the Gospel proclaims the Gospel" (p. 726; cf. 721). It may even be exemplary as "a pattern for the formation and administration of human law generally, and therefore of the law of other political, economic, cultural and other human societies" (p. 719).

Because of the influence on the great churches' tradition and attitude from conservative forces, voices such as E. Brunner and K. Barth are seldom heard and even more rarely heeded.

However, the church is not the only social community to attempt a fraternal society, or to obstruct and oppress advances toward its realization.

D. Fraternities outside and against the Church

Among the ideals and sociopolitical goals of the French Revolution (such as *union, concorde, fidelité, justice, liberté, loi, loyauté*), *fraternité* has a prominent place. In 1792 a Parisian delegate to the National Assembly proposed the formula *"union, fraternité, liberté, égalité"* and in 1793 he proclaimed, *"liberté, égalité, fraternity ou la mort!"* The famous triad — a tricolor form of the word — reappears in the constitutional document of the *Deuxième République.*

The theoretical foundation of the revolution had been laid by the Encyclopedists and other outstanding representatives of the Age of Enlightenment. The teachings and examples given by Catholicism and Protestantism for a brotherly social order were considered so insufficient or repulsive that it appeared necessary to tap other sources. The ancient Stoics, especially Cicero, had spoken of Zeus's or reason's universal fatherhood and the brotherhood and basic equality of all human beings. J.-J. Rousseau had done much to popularize the term *fraternité:* the humanity of humankind rested on the universality of pity and sympathy. Voltaire's arguments in favor of a better society were less warm and emotional. After having received his higher education at a Jesuit college, he argued as a true rationalist, with piercing analysis and biting irony, against Christendom and for a better society.

The French revolutionaries also had practical examples before their eyes. There were the medieval and still existing guilds, formed of urban craftsmen, tradesmen, or journeymen. Their members considered one another as brothers. Above all there were the Freemasons, who consciously harkened back to the masons who built and maintained the cathedrals. In 1717 they constituted the Great Lodge in London and began to admit for membership selected ("accepted") persons concerned with the building of a spiritual temple. The Freemasons organized themselves as an educated, tolerant, and humanitarian brotherhood. They developed a rich, symbol-laden ritual and used secret signs for recognizing one another. Soon they spread all over Europe and beyond the Atlantic. Royalty, great poets, and musicians were among their members, and their influence was at all times widespread. Forming character and personality and working for a justly organized society and international relations were among the purposes of the lodges.

Among the actual revolutionaries who in and after 1789 played a prominent role were the Jacobins — so-called because they met at first at the former Dominican friary bearing this name. According to Hannah Arendt (*Über die Revolution*, pp. 21 and 318; cf. also *Lexikon zur politischen Sprache in Deutschland*, pp. 252-281), "they carried the word brotherhood always in the mouth, while they founded terror regimes." Among them, Maximilien Robespierre is best known. A disciple of Rousseau in his criticism of the social-political status quo, he turned the revolutionary convictions into dogmas, and as head of the Welfare Committee and with the help of the Revolution Courts, shaped politics correspondingly. He did as rigorously as the Inquisitors had done with their dogmas. In 1793 Robespierre reformulated the human rights, but in 1794 he was executed, like so many children of the revolution, devoured by the forces he had cut loose.

His method to introduce fraternity corresponded to what was later called the "dictatorship of the proletariat."

The spiritual and practical protagonists of the French Revolution were not anti-religious in principle. Most of them were Deists rather than atheists or materialists. In 1783 and 1784 triumphant festivals were celebrated in honor of divine nature, reason, and the supreme being. But on the basis of the radical rejection of all that was represented by the hierarchy, the monasteries, and the laity of the Catholic Church, the slogan *écrasez l'infame* was coined, the religious orders were closed and prohibited by decree, and many monasteries were ransacked. The conviction was transformed into practice that charitable hospitals and educational works would be better carried out by civic organizations. The mutual address *citoyen* rather than *frère* was one of the many works of the triumph of political over familial and ecclesiastical concern. Laicization became a catchword of great attractiveness. The expropriation and secularization of church property was so profitable for the political power that, especially beginning in and since 1803, even nonrevolutionary European states followed the example given by France. Thus ended one great attempt at doing better in matters of brotherhood than the official church, the monasteries, the free churches, and the sectarian groups.

In the American Constitution, Bill of Rights, and Federalist Papers, "brotherhood" or an equivalent warm term does not play a conspicuous role. Was brotherhood considered too familial, homey, and intimate a concept to be realized in the political, social, and economic documents? One may observe the same omission and ask the same question in view of other democratic constitutions.

In the October 1917 revolution in Russia and in states that were subsequently built on the Marxist ideology, the appellation "comrade" rather than "brother" was intended to express the freedom, justice, and equalities for which socialists were hoping and fighting. Already in the ancient slave uprisings and wars, as above described in "Social Background," section V, pp. 31-33, and Annotation 6, pp. 88-91 the terminology of brotherhood is hardly prominent. Did it sound too bourgeois to suit the taste of militants? Here and there streams of blood were the price of revolutionary attempts at forming a new society.

In his early writings Karl Marx had not envisaged that this method was to be chosen. At least he wanted to be a humanist and to work for the humanization of nature, insofar as nature seemed to permit that man be a wolf to his fellowman. So also "the real Socialist [today] could elicit . . . from the doctrines of the Marxist classics the faith in justice and brotherliness . . . a faith which had been buried underground long ago by government practices of Socialism as it existed in reality" (our translation of an essay of Inge Markovitz, Faculty of Law, University of Texas, Austin, in *Die Zeit* [Hamburg], January 17, 1992). Until expelled by their party, the communists Roger Garaudy in France, Milan Mahoveč in Czechoslovakia, and other convinced socialists had endeavored in vain to restore a human faith to socialism. They could not prevent that continuous violations of human rights and economical mismanagement contributed more to the collapse of that form of brotherhood and the majority of those states that called themselves socialist.

What fraternities and sororities contribute to American campus life need as little be discussed at this place as the wine produced by a California firm under the name Christian Brothers. This appellation takes a holy name in vain as much as, e.g., one Italian financial institute called Banca de Spiritu Sancto.

E. Conclusion

The examples collected in the foregoing extensive excursus reveal that Paul was not a daydreaming illusionist when he appealed to Philemon to treat the returning slave Onesimus as a brother. Before the apostles' time others had spoken of a brotherly and friendly relationship between master and slave. The Christian congregations hoped to realize brotherhood between all the members, though deep crisis shook the communities. After the death of Paul monks and nuns, lay groups, free churches, and sects founded houses and institutions that required or permitted a brotherly common life. In addition, around cathedrals and near other ecclesiastical edifices secular brotherly associations began to flourish. The French and the socialist revolutionaries intended to pay more than only lip service to the ideal of a society of free and equal brothers, citizens, and/or comrades. But the bloody methods employed for implementation seem to discredit even the best purposes.

It is easy, and most likely foolish, to sneer at the shortcomings and failures of most, if not all, attempts hitherto made to realize brotherhood in social and political, economical and cultural relations. And it would be incorrect to consider Paul's plea for "brother" Onesimus one more example of a mission that failed. When the Bible speaks of the frustrated building of the Tower of Babel, it does not scoff. And when Jesus looked at the really existing Jerusalem, he wept. The words of Jesus "you are all brothers," and the proclamation of Paul that Onesimus is "more than a slave: a brother," will still be heard as valid challenge as long as the Gospels and the Epistles are essential parts of the churches' Holy Scriptures. As will be shown later, in the interpretation of Philem 16c, Paul was fully aware of the weakness of the human nature and all human enterprises. But he did not deem it utopia to serve and to imitate Jesus Christ, the firstborn brother of all humankind.

Only in Philem 16 does Paul call a slave explicitly "brother." Since elsewhere co-operators of Paul who perform a specific service are preferably named "brother," the question cannot be avoided: Which specific contribution can and will the returning Onesimus make to the life of Philemon — if ever he is to be "useful" (v. 11) and "loved" (v. 16)? Certainly brotherhood cannot remain unilateral! Onesimus can bring honor to his name "Profitable" by much more than resuming the work he had done before his flight. And Philemon can desire advantage from the slave's presence, which would exceed the profit drawn from any other skillful, industrious, and faithful servant.

In the spirit and language of Latin American liberation and Korean Minjung theology, a grave conclusion is necessary: slaves and other oppressed, exploited, and poor persons are by far not the only ones to need liberation through Christ, the gospel, and a radical change of the social order. But also all those possessing riches and wielding power. While a clergy — siding with the ruling forces — fails to make a deep impression on, e.g., generals, the political victims, "the people," are equipped and charged to carry the gospel to those high and mighty and to liberate them from their presumption and malice.

According to Paul's best-known letters, every person, whether Jew or Gentile, needs forgiveness of sins, salvation by Christ's blood rather than self-salvation by the misunderstood and misused law of God, and redemption from eternal death. For everyone the spiritual freedom has immediate consequences in the social setting of his or her own life. But Philem 16 makes it explicit that salvation and redemption, freedom and equality are divine gifts far too precious to be left to the handling of even so good a Christian and so legal a slave owner as Philemon. When this man receives and treats Onesimus as a brother, he receives, according to verse 17, a person "sent back" (v. 12) by Paul who is to be received the same way the apostle hopes to be received. Not only brother Paul but also brother Onesimus will have to show and tell brother Philemon a few things relevant to faith and life, and the latter will have to listen to and follow good advice and proposals. If this be applied to twentieth-century conditions, it means that professional philosophers and social scientists, pastors and theology professors, politicians and industrial managers, trade unionists and revolutionaries have no monopoly on representing and proclaiming a social order that would deserve to be called free and just and peaceful.

The words following the term "brother" in Philem 16 reveal why and how Paul expects Philemon to live up to the common life of brothers.

Loved most of all by me, yet how much more by you. In harmony with the information given by specialists in Greek grammar and syntax, the datives *emoi* and *soi* are usually considered and translated as datives "of interest" or "of relation," or "of community." There are also — as books and classical and later Greek show; e.g., A. Kaegi, *Kurzgefaßte griechische Schulgrammatik,* pp. 113-116, and BDR, 192-197 — "ethical," "instrumental," "modal," and "causal" datives: versions of verse 16 such as "but a dear [or loved or beloved] brother *to* me and . . . *to* you" can claim to be literal. Indeed, for verse 11 the proper version is "useless to you . . . useful to me and . . . to you." But at this place the version "dear" converts the love shown into a quality and attribute of Onesimus and thereby obfuscates and hides what actually is a miracle for the loved person and needs to be renewed day by day. Grammatical and syntactical reasons exist for concluding that Paul wants to say more than only that Onesimus generally is considered a dear fellow, and therefore also incidentally or providentially, he is dear to me and to you. The unusual free version, "who is loved by me and you," was chosen to bring out the joy of being motivated and driven to love another person, the joy of experiencing the act and attitude of loving, the formative and creative power of love on the formerly unloved but now cherished neighbor, and perhaps also the pain, the risks, and the costs of loving. Decisive for translating the datives in Philem 16 "*by* me" and "*by* you" are philological observations.

The words following in the Greek text after *agapētos adelphos* are either a comment on both the verbal adjective *agapētos* (lit. "loved") and the noun *adelphos* (brother), or they are meant to explain primarily one of the two. If the complete title were in mind, or solely the noun "brother," the genitives "of me" and "of you" *(emou* and *sou)* would have been appropriate. But seldom is the person called a "brother to . . ." when the term "brother of . . ." will do. It is more likely that Paul intended to specify primarily the verbal adjective, and to place emphasis on those who actually were "loving" Onesimus. He might have used the genitive forms for speaking of himself and Philemon. After the verbal adjective *eklektos,* Paul has in Rom 8:33 the genitive *theou* (those elected of God or by God); in 1 Cor 2:13 *en didaktois . . . anthrōpinēs sophias logois* (in the words taught of or by human wisdom) is opposed to *en didaktois pneumatos* (in the things taught of, or by, the Spirit). Genitives are often also attached to adjectives (see BDR, 183, 194 n. 5; cf. 117.2). In Philem 17, however, Paul did prefer datives.

After verbal adjectives where the longer form having . . . *teos* rather than the short and much preferred . . . *tos* is affixed to the verbal stem, in classical and later Greek the so-called dative with the passive can be used instead of *hypo* (by) with the genitive. It denotes the agent who performs what the verbal stem says (BDR, 64 n. 5). E.g., in Plato, *Resp.* 2.358a, *agapēteon tō mellonti makariō esesthai* signifies "what is loved (or desired) by him who would be happy." Within the NT, only in Luke 5:38 and Mark 2:22, variant reading, is the longer form retained: *blēteon* means "must be thrown." For expressing the same gerundive sense, the shorter form can also be used, as in Acts 26:23 *pathētos* signifies "capable of suffering," and in 2 Pet 2:14 *akatapaustos,* "unable to find rest." *Agapētos . . . emoi kai soi* may presuppose solely the passive sense "loved," or the plain significance "dear" of the verbal adjective *agapētos.* Yet it also may retain or revise the original gerund sense "(worthy) to be loved." Philemon 16 contains two features that not only aggravate the existing problem but also may contribute to its solution:

1. Verses 10-13 unquestionably say that Paul is convinced of loving Onesimus more than does anybody else: the now returning slave is "loved most of all *(malista)* by me." How, then, can the apostle continue, "how much more *(posō mallon)* by you"?

After all, neither an adverb nor an adjective can be passed by a higher degree or intensity once its superlative has been used. Indeed, wild flowers of rhetoric are displayed when in Eph 3:8 Paul combines the superlative and the comparative degrees in order to call himself *elachistoteros* (lit. "more least"; in the AB 34 version: "less than least") of the apostles and prophets, and when around the turn from the second to the third century Sextus Empiricus (*Math.* 3.54; 11.406) coins the super-superlative *elachistotatos* (lit. "the leastest"). Third John 4 surprises the readers with the doubled comparative of *megas* (great): *meizoteros* (lit. "greaterer"), as does Paul (in 2 Cor 7:13) by the formula *perissoterōs mallon* (lit. "more overflowing more").

Does, then, Paul in Philem 16 attempt to puzzle Philemon or to humor him, and so coax him elegantly into love for Onesimus, unaware that oxymoronic and paradoxical statements do *not* automatically produce the desired effect?

2. How can Paul state that Onesimus *is* already "loved" by Philemon, even before the runaway has reentered his master's home, and before Philemon has read and taken to heart the apostle's epistle? If *agapētos* has the passive sense of "loved" and would be equivalent to the perfect passive participle *ēgapēmenos* (cf. 1 Thess 1:4; 2 Thess 2:13), it might correspond to the Hebrew "prophetic

perfect," i.e., to a narration using verbal perfect forms for describing what will occur in the future only. But it is doubtful whether Philemon's knowledge of prophetic speech was sufficiently developed to understand a Hebraism included in Paul's diction.

A patent solution of the first puzzle has repeatedly been proposed: the term "most of all" *(malista)* is not to be understood in the "superlative," but in the "elative," sense. (See, e.g., E. Lohmeyer, E. Lohse, H. Binder; cf. BDR, 60. J. Knox, *Philemon,* p. 24, remarks that the superlative "may represent simply a courteous exaggeration," while Moule quotes Lightfoot for speaking of "an enthusiastic illogicality" and decides in favor of an elative version such as "exceedingly, immensely." NEB translates *malista* "very dear"; NJB "especially dear.") Paul then says as much as, "I love Onesimus extremely"; or, "he is my best friend, and you, Philemon, are free and welcome to do even better." While this exposition corresponds to the apostle's intention, it takes some of the bite out of the formulation he has chosen. It is possible to retain the affirmation of Paul's maximal and Philemon's still greater love with the combined answer to both problems: when Paul wrote Philem 16, as much as elsewhere when he speaks of loved (or dear) brothers, he had not completely forgotten the original gerund sense of the verbal adjective *agapētos.* The same incomparable and supreme love that the apostle already has fostered in the past and still has and reveals in the present is also a possibility and necessity to be acknowledged and realized in the future even better by Philemon. To use Latin terms: Onesimus is already superlatively *amatus* ("loved"; Vg.: *carissimus . . . maxime*) by Paul, but Philemon will find out that this is not enough: even more *amandus* (to be loved) is the returning slave by his master. Paul has so much confidence in Philemon (v. 21) that he almost treats the anticipated love-relationship between this patron and this servant as an established fact. The apostle's heart cries out loud enough in favor of Onesimus — how then could Philemon not let his own heart speak even more clearly, when "perhaps" by God's providence he receives him, to "hold him forever" (v. 15)?

Just as Paul in verse 11 had indicated *to* whom Onesimus was first useless and later useful — to Philemon and to the apostle — so now Paul and the recipient of PHM are mentioned as the persons by whom the returning escapee is loved. According to Paul, love is always personal, specific, concrete, and unique, since not everybody loves the same person. There has to be someone who confesses to be a lover and behaves as such. True love has a history; it has high and low points; it is not always romantic but bears risks and is exposed to temptation and threats; it means involvement and engagement in the whole being and life of the beloved, even when his or her character and conduct are less than perfect, seem to entitle one to grievances (cf. 1 Cor 13:4-7), and are a burden requiring great patience and humility on the side of the lover (cf. Gal 6:2; Eph

4:3). Love makes no conditions and gives no prescriptions or orders; it seeks permanency and needs daily renewal. It is costly and never cheap (in AB 34A, pp. 459-462, and in the Notes and Comments on Eph 5:21-33 in the same volume, these and other elements of Paul's concept of *agapē* [love] are more extensively described). No one can love everybody, neither can anyone be loved by everybody. But love is so revealing and so creative that the conclusion can be drawn: tell me whom and how you love, and continue by telling by whom you are loved — and I will tell you who you are. The bond of brotherly love joins not only Paul, Philemon, and Onesimus together; it also discloses who and what each one truly is. Paul's love for Onesimus has had its history, just as Philemon's love for the same will still develop through highs and lows. The apostle is not so self-conscious and vain as to depict himself as a perfect and ideal lover who flawlessly imitates God's and Christ's love (as described in, e.g., Rom 5:5; 8:31-35; and Eph 5:25-27). He expects that Philemon will love Onesimus even more and better.

According to Paul, the messenger of grace and faith, of freedom and justice, of equality and unity in Christ, there can be no lasting change in social relations unless there be love abounding, and there can be no love at a cheaper price than full personal involvement in the history, the strengths, and the weaknesses of the stronger and weaker partners of human society.

By courageously living out the unfolding — however stepwise and incompletely — not only of the love of God and Christ, but also of their mutual brotherly love, Paul and Philemon and Onesimus and other members of the congregation give a proof to the whole world that not even cruel power structures and institutions such as slavery can prevent radical change of interpersonal relation. Paul does not presume that *he* will make the world a better place to live in. But he describes the community of believers as a body that is called to testify publicly to the power of love in all dimensions of personal and social life. As if — for his own reasons and in his own terminology — he wanted to affirm: love makes the world go round!

Verse 16c

Loved . . . both as the person he is and because of the Lord.

A literal translation of the Greek words *en sarki* and *en kyriō* would be "in the flesh" and "in the Lord," but in order to avoid obscurity, ambiguity, and possible misunderstandings, a free version is here proposed. Only at this place within the Pauline writings are these two formulae combined into a two-edged double formula. Both of its members seem to stand here on an equal level and to occupy equal rank, as the conjunction *kai . . . kai* (both . . . and) shows. Elsewhere "flesh" and "the Lord" or equivalent terms often appear as opposites (see pp. 459-460). No less than the whole intention and understanding of PHM, perhaps also of the whole message of Paul, may well depend on a philological and theological explication of this double formula. Not in vain does N. R. Petersen (in his book *Rediscovering Paul*) quote these words untiringly. H. Diem (in the FS for Theodor Dipper) has made them the title of his essay on Philemon: "Onesimus — Bruder nach dem Fleisch und in dem Herrn." Above all, the character and essence of the love of which Paul speaks not only in PHM but in all his letters, is in Philem 16 elucidated in a unique way.

In syntactical regard the double formula "in the flesh and in the Lord" depends on the preceding words of verse 16 that declare that Onesimus is a brother, loved and to be loved by Paul and Philemon. Still, not only the returning slave is qualified by these words. Also the two persons here mentioned who love Onesimus and who certainly have no monopoly on loving this man are existing "both in the flesh and in the Lord." Finally, the very love itself, which binds the three together, is shown to be shaped and conditioned by the flesh as well as by the Lord. Another analysis of the syntactic place and function would attach the double formula to a verb: either to the subjunctive "hold him properly" *(apechēs),* which in verse 15 denotes God's own eventual purpose, or to the imperative "receive him" in verse 17 (cf. v. 12, variant reading). Most likely Paul is concerned not solely or primarily with Onesimus "in the flesh as well as in the Lord"; the influence of the flesh and the Lord on Paul and Onesimus deserves equal attention.

Because of the Lord. The second half of the double formula contains hardly any problems that were not also posed by the words "in the Lord," "in Christ," "in Jesus," and "in the Messiah Jesus" in other Pauline letters. Just as elsewhere, so also in Philem 20a and b, the formula "in the Lord" has probably the same meaning as "in Christ" *(en Christō).* The reference made by Paul in Philem 16 to Christ needs at this place a brief discussion only. Variants will be discussed first, and very briefly only. Meanings and accentuations were collected in the Comment on Eph 1:1 in AB 34, pp. 69-71, and a selection from the immense pertinent literature is offered on pp. 409-410.

The Greek preposition *en,* which originally had a local sense, is not only by Paul often used in this same wide sense as is characteristic of Hebrew *bᵉ.* In view of the contexts in which the formula "in Christ," etc., occurs, it is possible to distinguish between mythical and mystical, historical and eschatological, proclamatory and hortative, ethical and existential, sacramental and ecclesiastical meanings, and a purely instrumental sense can never be excluded. For Philem 16 a paraphrase such as "because of the Lord," "for the Lord's sake," "in obedience to the Lord" is to be preferred to, e.g., "as a Christian," "in the framework of the congregation," in "Christian love." For the person of Jesus Christ and the decisive function of his personal work and will ought not vanish amid a general attitude of Onesimus or of love, and must not be simply identified with the church or an ethical principle. Jesus Christ the Lord is the church's one foundation and its only redeemer and head, but he does not dissolve himself into the church.

To be more specific, and by using parallels for paraphrasing the last few words of Philem 16, Paul's intention may be summed up in the following way: (a) In Christ, brother Onesimus is eternally elected by God to be holy and blameless (cf. Eph 1:6-7). (b) Christ has died for this brother too (cf. 1 Cor 8:11; Rom 14:15), so that he is now dead to sin but alive to God in the Messiah Jesus (cf. Rom 6:11). More elaborate and hymnic would be the interpretation: "God, who is rich in mercy — for he loves us — with all his love — just because Onesimus was dead in his lapses, God has made him alive together with the Messiah: by grace he is saved as much as we all are; for God has in the Messiah Jesus raised and enthroned him in the heaven" (cf. Eph 2:4-6). Although it was earlier shown that in PHM Paul, unlike Pliny the Younger, does not above all plead in favor of the runaway for pardon, yet an application of a prose passage is not inappropriate: "It is fitting for you, Philemon, to bear Onesimus and to forgive him if you have a complaint against him. As the Lord has forgiven you, so also you forgive him. . . . Put on love. . . . Let the peace of the Messiah rule in your hearts, for which you were also called in one body" (cf. Col 3:13-15). As it need not worry Onesimus, it also need not bother Philemon, that he who was called to faith was and even now still is a slave. For whoever is called (in, by, and for the Lord) is a freedman of the Lord, just as a person called while being free is yet a slave of Christ (cf. 1 Cor 7:21-22). Master and slave are destined to live a life worthy to the Lord, pleasing in all things (cf. Col 1:10). Just as all Christians, they are brothers who, united by their baptism with the Spirit and having confessed their union by the baptism with water, have put on Christ, are willing to put him on day by day, and are expecting to be clothed over with the new man definitely in the resurrection (cf. Gal 3:27-28; 1 Cor 12:13; Rom 6:4; see AB 34A, pp. 536-545). Already now they are wearing Christ's colors and are engaged in the same internal and external struggles (cf. Rom 13:14; Eph 6:10-17; etc.). They have a share in the sufferings of Christ (cf. Col 1:24; 2 Cor 4:10-13), but are confident also to share in his glory (cf. 1 Thess 4:16; 1 Cor 15; 2 Cor 5:1-10; etc.). To use terminology found in the synoptic Gospels: what is done to the little brother Onesimus, even if it were no more than offering him a cup of water, is done to Jesus Christ (cf. Matt 25:31-46; 10:42; Mark 9:41).

Whenever Jesus Christ or the Lord is explicitly mentioned in PHM (that is, in vv. 1, 3, 5, 6, 8, 9, 16, 20, 23, 25), such explanations and applications are implicit. Therefore in verse 16 the formula (lit.) "in Christ" is so rich and comprehensive that it forms the nucleus and summary of all that Paul has to say as a herald, a teacher, and a counselor. In the work the apostle does among Jews and Gentiles, and in the sufferings he endures for his Lord's and the gospel's sake, he wants to praise Jesus Christ alone.

All the more amazing is it that in Philem 16 "the flesh" is mentioned before, and in conjunction with, "the Lord." By these two unequal partners the reception of Onesimus in Philemon's house and the love for the returned slave have to be motivated and shaped. It would seem that "the Lord" includes and provides so inexhaustible a richness of meanings and benefits, of motivation and orientation, that the weak, fallible, deficient, corrupted, and death-bound "flesh" cannot or must never be mentioned in the same breath and for the same purpose.

As the person he is and . . . (lit. "both in the flesh and," or, "in the flesh as well as . . ."). For the following, an unusual exegetical procedure was chosen. In order to arouse sensibility for possible misuses and misunderstandings of love, the story of a personal encounter and experience will be told first. An excursus comparing voices from the history of interpretation will be the next step, which in turn will be followed by another excursus devoted especially to one among Paul's manifold references to "flesh." Finally, practical consequences will be drawn for the everyday relation between Philemon and Onesimus — applications that may not have lost their actuality even after social conditions and institutions have changed.

At an interfaith conference, in the course of a friendly private chat between official lectures and seminars, a Jewish scholar asked me a question that has stuck in my memory as follows: "How come you study our history-literature, traditions, achievements, and difficulties with so great a concern and so much sympathy, even with love and understanding, while you belong in your own tradition and community and share in convictions and customs other than ours?" My response went something like this: "I love you because you are under the special protection of Jesus Christ. Whatever you believe and say, however your worship and your daily life is shaped, and especially the persecutions you suffer and which have culminated in Auschwitz, all of this and more makes you transparent for our Lord, who was and is a Jew. In this light and because of him, I would and I do love you under all circumstances."

My partner's reply was a shocking surprise for me: "Thank you for *that* kind of love! Obviously you don't really care *for me,* my ups and my downs, my personal history and feelings yesterday, today, and tomorrow. You ignore or bypass the problems I have with myself and my environment, my sorrows or pains, what makes me sad and what may make me glad. Your concern is for an image you have made of me for your own use. Of real interest for you is solely something above, behind, and beyond my own self. Any member of my people might just as well as I fit into your vision and find your loving sympathy. I don't call this attitude 'love' and can do without it."

The story has no conclusion, least of all a happy ending. Obviously my reply was understood as equivalent to, e.g., a romantic lover's confirmation to the sweetheart: "I love you only because you are a member of a noble or rich family from which one day I can inherit wealth; in the meantime, I am not so poor a match after all!" Because I caused the Jewish partner to feel that I loved him solely "because of the Lord" or "in the Lord," I was to a great extent guilty of evoking the gross misunderstanding. A brother and a neighbor has the right to be loved in his own right, as a specific and unique person.

When in Philem 16 Paul speaks of a love that is not only founded and exemplified by Jesus Christ but is also true to the flesh of the lover and loved one, he reveals his subtle sensibility for Onesimus's reaction to the love demonstrated by the apostle himself and by Philemon. Whether for good or poor reasons, the feelings of the returning slave and brother might be deeply hurt. He might imagine that he is loved only out of a sense of duty, exclusively in conformity with the congregation's expectation, or solely as an occasion to give or increase heavenly reward. As an individual person, he might feel left standing in the cold rain, uncertain whether he could say to Philemon "Just as I am, I come to thee," and could receive a welcoming bear hug.

The concatenation of the references to Onesimus's person and to the Lord, by which Paul elaborates on the love "owed according to God's commandments" (cf. Rom 13:8-10) to brother Onesimus, by no means belittles love for Christ's sake. But it reveals the apostle's sensitivity for the feelings of Onesimus, and prevents misunderstandings that can emerge when charity seems to be abounding. Even love richly spent in the name of Christ can be humiliating and dehumanizing. When it ignores and does not care for the idiosyncrasies of those loved, be it their history, their problems, their temptations, their weaknesses, their failures, their sadnesses — or their capabilities, virtuous achievements, and joys — then it uses the neighbor as means to achieve a higher end. But just because of Christ, Onesimus is not a fata morgana toward which to move with open arms. Neither is a halo painted around his faith nor a hood or garment used for hiding his identity "in the flesh." Instead of being calculatingly chimeric, ideologic, or superhuman, the love Paul has in mind is realistic, pragmatic, and therefore true to both Jesus Christ and humankind.

Especially by mentioning the flesh in Philem 16, Paul shows that love *(agapē)* is so great, so deep, so total as to include, embrace, and sanctify *erōs* (passionate love, desire) and *philia* (friendship). In his book *Eros and Agape*, A. Nygren promoted the widespread thesis that the differences between these terms, e.g., between unselfish love and natural desire or sympathy, are much greater than the eventual common or reconcilable elements (see AB 34A, pp.

715-720, for arguments and literature pro and contra this assumption). But when Paul describes Onesimus as a man "loved . . . in the flesh," he speaks of an intimate and warm person-to-person relationship. For married people this includes psychic harmony and sexual intercourse (Eph 5:21-33; cf. 1 Cor 7:1-5). But because in, e.g., Rom 1:18, 26-28, together with the Jewish tradition and unlike Plato, he declares the homosexuality, especially the pederasty, spread among Gentiles an element and consequence of human ungodliness and unrighteousness, the mention of love "in the flesh" cannot possibly mean homosexual intimacy.

At any rate, with his total person Philemon can and shall let Onesimus feel that as and in and with his total being he is accepted. This way Paul himself loves his spiritual child "most of all." In 1 Cor 13:4-7 the apostle lists, in the context of the highest and most beautiful praise of love, a great number of things and events that love has to bear patiently and with undying hope. In Eph 4:2 the church members are described as a potential burden that has to be "born patiently in love," and in Gal 6:2 he mentions the loads that have to be taken from the shoulders of fellow Christians. Paul knows that it is not always easy to love a brother and neighbor. But whether the mode of the love and the loved is sour or sweet, under all external and internal circumstances Onesimus is to be loved not only for Christ's but also for his own sake, free of any sort of compulsion. As Paul has wisely stated in Philem 8-9 and 14, such love cannot be prescribed or commanded or made dependent on certain conditions. It is always spontaneous, voluntary, and in need of renewal. Or else, even if allegedly demonstrated in the name of the Lord, such love is neither genuine nor complete nor a pleasure for either partner.

This proposal for an interpretation of Philem 16 does not exclude the need to compare it with alternatives.

Excursus: Other Interpretations

Aristotle (*NE* 8.11.1161a-b) is convinced that a slave can be his master's friend and that such a friendship will prevent injustice as it prevails in tyranny. However, the philosopher adds, this friendship will not be extended to "the slave qua slave" — as such he is "a living tool, and the tool is lifeless" — but "qua man," i.e., "in so far as he is a human being." Seneca (*Ep.* 47, esp. 1, 16 and 18-19) wants to show how a sensible and well-educated master need hunt for friends among free persons only, but can find them at home and can live on friendly terms (*familiarites*) even with his slaves. When he does this, he will be respected and loved by his servants, rather than feared (*colere, amare, amor* are opposed to *timere* and *timor*). To be ignored are people who say, "they are slaves." For in fact they are "human beings . . . comrades . . . unpretentious friends . . . our fellow-slaves, if one reflects, that Fortune has equal rights over slaves and freemen alike." According to both Aristotle and Seneca, the humanity of the slave makes friend-ship and love possible, if not also necessary. Because he is human, his slave status does not really matter. The distinction and combination that Paul makes between love for Onesimus "in the flesh and in the Lord" is of another order. He adds to the anthropo-logical and psychological arguments of the philosophers the reference to Jesus Christ's rulership. Ignatius of Antioch (*Trall.* 12.1) speaks gratefully of congregations whose del-egates have "give(n) him rest in the flesh and in the spirit." If he had written " . . . in the flesh and the (Holy) Spirit," his formula would be a remote parallel to Philem 16c. But Ignatius uses the terms in their anthropological sense. By spirit he means the human spirit of which also Paul speaks in, e.g., 1 Thess 5:23; 2 Cor 7:1; Gal 6:18; Philem 25. Paul mentions sometimes even the human person in its totality and under every aspect (cf. Ps 16:9: "My heart . . . my soul . . . my body"). In Philem 16, "flesh" covers all physical, psychic, historical, and social factors constituting a personality. But unlike the Ignatius text, an explicit reference to the Lord is added.

Ever since Jerome and the Greek Fathers, and continued even in the Middle Ages, in the Reformation period, and down to the present day, a cosmological or sociological combined with moralistic interpretation of the term "flesh" has been prevailing. E.g., Theodore of Mopsuestia interprets "flesh" as "that temporary status which in the pres-ent life is occupied," and in which in consequence of his conversion, and change of mor-als *(dia ten tou tropou metabolēn, mores suas denudans),* Onesimus would serve his mas-ter faithfully.

Regarding the sociological character and consequences of this exposition, it cor-responds to an earlier-cited interpretation of 1 Cor 7:21: "Even if you have a chance to gain your freedom, you should prefer to make full use of your condition as slave" (JB; similar translations and some of their promoters were mentioned in "Literary, Bio-graphical, and Contextual Issues," sec. VII.C, pp. 191-200). Just by remaining a slave, Onesimus is then "useful" (cf. Philem 11). As in the context of 1 Cor 7:21 God's call and the liberation through Christ are the presuppositions of obedient slave service, so in Philem 16 the words "and in the Lord" (in our version "because of the Lord") are then explained as the ground of the affirmation, the continuation, even the sanctification of the slave status. A personal and moral dimension of the terms "in the flesh" and "in the Lord" is by no means obliterated. Since in biblical diction "flesh" often means the weak, corrupt, or sinful state of the nature of humankind and is therefore opposed to the Spirit or the Lord, the fleshly Onesimus who is loved for Christ's sake is then the sinner who is saved, the bad man turned into a good man. Ultimately, the message of Philem 16 is then this: let your old Adam be changed into the new man, and love the justified sinner; then the social problems will solve themselves without prescription or laws.

A few examples can reveal different accentuations made with this combination of sociological, moral, and theological expositions.

Luther (in his PHM commentary of 1527) understood "flesh" as a description of Onesimus's identity under civil law *(iure gentium):* he is a slave. But solely because of Christ, who dwells in the slave, he is a praiseworthy Christian person, even a brother, and he serves Philemon as a brother.

Calvin uses Philem 16 not only for elaborating in strong terms on Onesimus's former wickedness, but also on God's mysterious ways and powers to make another man of the worthless slave. In Calvin's eyes Onesimus is "a marvelous specimen of repentance."

W. Estius reports that several expositors understand the formula "in the flesh" to refer to the common Gentile origin of Onesimus and Philemon; if Onesimus had been born a Jew, he would have to be called Paul's rather than Philemon's fleshly brother. Estius also mentions others who interpret "in the flesh" as that brotherhood that would in the flesh signify membership in the same household, but he prefers the exposition of the church fathers: "healed from his former wickedness *(a priori nequitia correctus),* [Onesimus] is or can be held worthy to be entrusted with worldly affairs and services." To Paul, he is most dear as a spiritual brother only (fit for spiritual service; cf. Philem 13); by Philemon Onesimus can be loved "even more" because he fulfills a double service: in the flesh he performs "businesses" of the present world, and in the Lord he acts "in spiritual matters." Estius succinctly sums up the earlier and later understanding of PHM when he writes, "this passage [v. 16] does not mean that by the law of the Christian religion the slave status is abolished — as was much later arranged by Christian princes, in honor of the holy religion." But in agreement with Gal 3:28 ("In him there is neither slave nor free"), Christian slaves were by Christian masters to "be received and embraced with brotherly affection, that is, as brothers in the Lord. 'You are all brothers' said the Lord himself, Matt 23[:8]. That this brotherhood does not abolish slavery, the same apostle [as wrote Gal 3:28] teaches in 1 Tim 6[:1-2]: 'Those [slaves] who have believing masters, shall not despise them because they are brothers, but shall serve them all the more, because they are believers and beloved.'"

J. A. Bengel (in the eighth edition of his *Gnomon Novi Testmenti* [1887], as quoted by P. Stuhlmacher, p. 62) follows the tradition that understands "in the flesh" as meaning "as a slave," but because at the beginning of Philem 16 it has been stated that Onesimus is "more than a slave," this formula now means "he is freedman in the Lord: a brother." Already in the first edition (1742), Bengel had declared that the love is extended to the brother and friend, not to the slave. According to Bengel, "in the flesh" means then: by legal manumission of him who still seems to be a slave.

H. Koester (*Einführung in das Neue Testament* [1980], p. 569), too, solves the puzzle by speaking of manumission: when Onesimus is not manumitted, he is a brother in flesh; he is only a brother in Christ when he is emancipated. In even more radical form, the same opinion is expressed by the liberation theologian J. Comblin: according to his Portuguese PHM commentary (esp. pp. 40 and 99), the gospel is distinct from an abstract discourse or idea, for the term "in the flesh" reveals that it pertains directly to human life, feeling, aspiration, and social relations and structures of the world. These words show that "slavery will be destroyed in its concrete and material reality."

The huge majority of commentaries and monographs do not go so far. Common to them is either talk of the two spheres in which a Christian lives, or the splitting up of a Christian's personality into two identities, corresponding to the two dominating realms. The local sense of the preposition *en* (in) has led to the separation of a "sphere of flesh" from a "sphere of the Lord"; and as persons living "in" both realms, Christians were depicted as having a double existence. Both interpretations are combined. If so, the result is that for an individual's complex personality, the given or freely chosen influences of the environment are decisive and responsible.

For instance, together with H. A. W. Meyer (1859), J. B. Lightfoot distinguishes between "two spheres alike . . . the affairs of this world and . . . the affairs of the higher life. In the former . . . Philemon had the brother for a slave; in the latter he had the slave for a brother." (C. F. D. Moule speaks of "an ordinary human" and the contrasting "specifically Christian level." NJB calls the first "the natural plane"; H. Binder: "natural existence" and "everyday life," as distinct from the "Christ-sphere.") N. R. Petersen (*Rediscovering Paul*, pp. 96-98, 174, 289ff.) speaks of "two domains" or "spaces" and distinguishes between the worldly order of the master-slave relationship and the order prevailing in the church. The words "in the flesh" then connote "the social as well as the moral 'space.'"

Petersen refers to Conzelmann (*An Outline*, pp. 208-212) in order to demonstrate that in Philem 16 and other contexts the words "in Christ, the Lord" mean "in the church." Each of the "two domains" has its own social relations and structure. Paul announces in Philem 16, unlike the message of 1 Cor 7:21-24 and the supposedly non-Pauline *Haustafeln*, that in the church "the structural ground of the [worldly] master-slave-relationship is 'undercut,'" with the effect that Philemon has to take action: presumably by legally freeing Onesimus. The term "in the flesh" then connotes "the social as well as the moral space, of the world." According to E. Lohse, "the earthly relationship" in which Onesimus in the flesh is a slave, the property of his master, is now surpassed by the union "in the Lord." The slave who returns home is now a brother.

When R. Bultmann (in *Theology of the New Testament*, 1.190-269) describes humanity "prior to the revelation of faith," he repeatedly calls "flesh" "the sphere" (on pp. 234-237; cf. 154, 151). In this sphere human beings move; it marks out the horizon or the possibilities of human action and experience. As Gal 2:20; Phil 1:22; and 2 Cor 3:10 show, to live "or 'to walk in the flesh' means nothing else than simply 'to lead one's life as a man,' an idea which in itself does not involve any ethical or theological judgement but simply takes note of fact, not a norm but a field or a sphere," even "the sphere of the humanity natural and transitory." E. Lohmeyer translates, in his version of Philem 16, *en sarki* (in the flesh) simply by "in life" *(im Leben),* but according to Bultmann, not only "facts" present within natural life and verifiable by everyone, but also another possible point of view hovers behind the formulae "according to" or "in the flesh" in other passages: "the sphere of the flesh can also be regarded as the sphere of sinning. So regarded . . . it is not merely the earthly transitory contrast to the transcendental-clerical God, but opposes God as his enemy." Then "life 'in the flesh' is a spurious life." Whenever explicitly or implicitly life in the spirit, in Christ, or in faith is the antithesis to life in the flesh (as in, e.g., Gal 2:20; Rom 7:5; 8:4-9; Gal 5:16-25), flesh is "regarded as a sphere of sinning. . . . It stamps an existence or attitude not as natural-human, but as sinful." In Bultmann's wake, E. Schweizer (article *sarx*, etc., in *TDNT*, 7.28-105, 119-138) speaks of the "circle of purely human relation . . . the whole of human existence, both its bodily and its intellectual functions." With this he contrasts the "sphere of God" that "invades" or "from without breaks into" the sphere of man. He observes that indeed only in Philem 16 are these two spheres linked by the conjunction *kai* ("as well as" or "and"). Already E. Lohmeyer had pointed out how unique this linkage of "flesh" and "Lord" is in Paul's letters. As little as Bultmann, Lohmeyer had spoken of *two* "spheres." In *TDNT,* 7.123-124 and 138, Schweizer observes concerning the sphere of the flesh that "in Hellenism . . . OT-Oriental [cosmic] dualism . . . combines with that of Greek naturalism," and that references to Christ's saving appearance "in the flesh . . . , i.e. in the earthly sphere" presuppose "the Hellenistic idea of the two spheres." Indeed, no doctrine of two spheres can pretend to reproduce a message that is combined solely or uniquely in the New Testament. For the translation and exposition of Philem 16, Bultmann (in his *Theology of the New Testament,* 1.236) proposes a revision that elucidates the personal rather than a spherical intention of Paul's utterance on love "in the flesh and in the Lord." Probably in order to exclude the misconception of "flesh" as a "mythological . . . demonic being" or in the physiological sense of "sensuality" (p. 238), he translates "both as a person and as a Christian." In the same vein, NEB renders *en sarki kai en kyriō,* "as man and as Christian," while NJB combines spheric with a personalistic interpretation by writing, "on the natural plane and in the Lord."

Four critical remarks can be made to such interpretation of the flesh and the Lord in this verse. (a) Whenever "spheres" are considered essential, allusion appears to be made to a possible war and reconciliation as if between atmosphere and stratosphere. But within Christ now his kingship forms a sphere, and a quasi-cosmic star war and star peace is certainly not in Paul's mind at this place. (b) When the higher, even the Lord's, sphere is explained to be formed by or to be coextensive with the church or with church membership, then the church is overestimated: it is no longer the people, the body or bride of Christ, but is identified with the Lord himself. (c) The term "[a] Christian" transforms into the attribute of a human being, what by the formula "in the Lord" is proclaimed as the redemption and rule, the gift given and the order established by one person alone: the Lord. (d) The insertion and occurrence of the particle "as" in recent Western versions (not in the Vg.!) supports the notion that, just as an actor who changes masks and costumes, so also Onesimus (and those loving him: Paul and Philemon too) plays not only a double role but actually consists of two persons at the same time, each having his own identity. Indeed, especially in Rom 5–8 Paul teaches that a Christian's present life is constituted by two rules and two laws that are in conflict and turn the individual into a battlefield. The old Adam is distinguished from the new (also in 1 Cor 15, Eph 4, and Col 3). Never are the two rulers, laws, natures, and destinies depicted as a harmonious pair; according to Paul, it is impossible playfully or in an earnest manner to change from one to the other and back again. The victory gained by Jesus Christ on the cross and in the resurrection does not permit the wavering of the believers; rather they have to decide and to battle and to overcome every day anew. All the more again, the question is burning: How can the apostle in Philem 16 place the words (lit.) "in the flesh" and "in the Lord" harmoniously side by side? Certainly he knows and teaches that when a decision between Christ and Belial is necessary (see 2 Cor 6:14–7:1), no Christian can serve two masters at the same time, and that the payment of taxes to Caesar is subordinate to the obedience to God (cf. Matt 6:24; 22:15-22 par.; Rom 13:1-7; Acts 5:29; 1 Pet 2:17; John 19:10-11). Among Protestant exegetes, one possible way of combining a dualistic distinction of two domains (which resemble the rabbinic differentiation between two aeons) with a Janus-faced anthropology has gained widespread influence: the Lutheran *Zwei-Reiche-Lehre* (doctrine of two realms). Rather than better or more elaboration on this doctrine by post-Reformation Lutherans, Martin Luther's "Weekday Sermons on Matt 5–7" are a good illustration (in the following, the references are to the edition in the WA, vol. 32, 1906, 299-544. For an English version, see *Luther's Works,* American ed., ed. J. Pelikan [vols. 1-30] and H. T. Lehmann [vols. 31-55] [St.Louis: Concordia; Philadelphia: Fortress, 1955ff.], 21.3-294). These sermons are a wonderful and indispensable tool for understanding the Sermon on the Mount, but they also contain passages that, if applied to the interpretation of Philem 16, lead to strange conclusions.

In two manners Luther affirms that in a Christian "two different persons become equal in one" (p. 316), and that we must "learn carefully to make a distinction between the two persons which a Christian must bear on earth" (p. 391; cf. pp. 393, 439-440, 530).

1. All human beings *(Menschen)* are created and born equal, be they men or women, young or old. God "clothes and adorns" these creatures by making them "another person . . . a divine person having a divine *Amt.*" (By *Amt* Luther understands an established position in society with emphasis more often on authority possessed and wielded than on a service or ministry fulfilled.) On, e.g., page 316 he speaks of the *Amt* of a child, father, master, prince, servant, or citizen. It is Luther's conviction that the Sermon on the Mount is not addressed to persons in an *Amt,* but exclusively to "the individual, natural person [revealing] what everybody shall do for himself . . . in relation to the other," in order to keep a "pure heart" (pp. 309-310, 316, 324, 374-375, 387-389, 392-393).

2. Luther further distinguishes between the "relation" in which the Christian stands to the emperor's rule and to Christ. He cannot avoid being a "world-person" with "his body and his property," and as such he is not "called a Christian but a father, master, prince etc." But for his own person, according to the Christian's life, he is only and exclusively *(gar allein)* "under Christ" — while "in relation to his servant he is another person." Thus a "Christ-person" or Christian is distinguished from a "world-person," while yet both are created in every single Christian (pp. 390-391). "Neither man nor woman, young or old, master, servant, prince, farmer, citizen . . . is called 'a Christian.' A prince may well be a Christian, but he need not rule as a Christian, and as a ruling person he is not called a Christian, but a prince. The person may well be a Christian, but his being a Christian does not pertain to his *Amt* or principality. . . . Therefore each human being on earth has two persons, one for him [or her] -self, bound to no-one but God himself. Then a worldly person, by which he is bound to other people." The "Sermon on the Mount" and all other sermons of Christians say nothing about the manner in which "a worldly person is to act and live" but speak about how as a Christian you should live correctly in relation to God (pp. 439-441).

According to both two-in-one-person doctrines, the Beatitudes, antitheses, and later passages of the Sermon on the Mount are directed not to listeners having an *Amt.* Yet only in the first is natural humanity considered the addressee, while solely in the second addressees are consoled, instructed, admonished, and encouraged by Jesus Christ.

Both exclusions of those occupying a worldly *Amt* are held together by Luther's doctrine of the two realms, which, unlike the different persons, are never two-in-one but always and everywhere must be radically distinguished and separated. Christ has "nothing to do with the fools or those who . . . do not discern Christ's from the world's rule and doctrine" (p. 375) "but brew and mix them together as the Pope has done with his doctrine and rule" (p. 391). They "did not really know that the two pieces, the worldly and the spiritual state or the realm of Christ and of the world . . . ought be separated" (p. 387; cf. pp. 473-474). "We have been placed into another higher essence *(Wesen)* which is a divine, eternal realm in which we have no need of the things belonging to the world, but in which everybody for himself is in Christ a Lord over both the devil and the world" (p. 389).

When Luther interpreted the Sermon on the Mount in these terms, he certainly did not think and speak of that obedience to the love commandment that Paul had in mind when he asked Philemon to follow and surpass the apostle's love for Onesimus (lit.) "in the flesh and in the Lord." The two persons and two realms that the Reformer had distinguished are joined by a "both . . . and," and neither Paul with his apostolic *Amt* nor Philemon with his earthly *Amt* as a master, nor Onesimus in his status of being "more than a slave: a brother," is exempt from the perfect bond of love.

On the other hand, those later expositors who saw the words "in the flesh" as a reference to the slave status of Onesimus or to his wickedness before his conversion, appear to have split up the need of and the questions about a good social order into a dualistic, be it cosmological, soteriological, or psychological, scheme.

Excursus: Paul Honors the Weak Flesh

For the following, see especially BAG, s.v. *sarx;* R. Bultmann, *Theology of the New Testament,* 1.232-246; E. Schweizer, *TDNT,* 8.98-105, 109-110, 119-138; R. Jewett, *Paul's Anthropological Terms,* pp. 455-456; W. Schmithals, *Die theologische Anthropologie des Paulus;* H. G. Kuhn, "New Light on Temptation," pp. 94-113; A. Richardson, *Theological Wordbook,* pp. 83-84. For the OT and later Jewish usage, see especially F. Baumgärtel, R. Meyer, *TDNT,* 7.10, 105-108, 110-114; N. P. Bratsiotis, article *basar,* in *TWAT,* 1.850-867. In all Pauline letters the noun *sarx* (flesh) occurs ninety-one times, and two adjectives signifying "fleshly" *(sarkikos* is sometimes, esp. in variant readings, used as equivalent to *sarkinos)* occur nine times (according to R. Morgenthaler's *Statistik,* p. 58). In variant readings of, e.g., 2 Cor 1:12; cf. Heb 7:16; Rom 7:14; and 1 Cor 3:1, 3-4, the two adjectives are exchanged, perhaps because they were considered synonyms. In the undisputed writings under Paul's name, the noun is used seventy-two times, and only in them are the adjectives found.

In, e.g., 1 Cor 6:18-20; 15:35-40; 2 Cor 4:10-11; Phil 1:20-21, 24; Eph 2:11-16; 5:28-32 (cf. Gal 4:13-14; 2 Cor 12:7 where "flesh" obviously means "body"), the nouns "flesh" and "body" interpret one another mutually.

A. Dependence on the Old Testament

Especially in Rom 6–7 the term "members" and "flesh" occur and "flesh" substitutes for body. Without awareness of Paul's rootage in OT traditions, Paul's manifold and specific utterances on the "flesh" cannot be understood. Already the LXX frequently translates the Hebrew *basar* either "flesh" or "body."

A clear-cut chronological development of the meaning of *basar* cannot be discerned in the history of Israel and its literature. Therefore in the following, references to earlier and later passages are mixed. Excluded will be the passages describing which "flesh" (or "meat") is suitable for sacrifices and profane use, as will the later Aramaic noun *guf.* The term *basar* denotes — except when also animals and other living beings are included — the whole of human existence inasmuch as it is corporal and visible. When in later Hebrew humankind is called "flesh and blood," when in Job 10:11 skin, flesh, bones, sinews are distinguished (cf. Ezek 37:6), or when at early or late times cultic rituals such as circumcision are discussed (e.g., in Gen 17), *basar* describes a part of the body. In and by the flesh human procreation takes place; flesh can signify biological and ethnic origin and relationship. The invisible things constituting a person, e.g., the human spirit, soul, and heart, describe the totality of human existence as much as the tangible flesh and body. Also animals count among "all flesh." While there are not only references to God's Spirit but also to the soul and heart that seem to be anthropomorphical, and while God's eyes and ears and bowels are repeatedly mentioned, there is no indication that God has or is flesh. God's eyes are not of flesh; his way of seeing is unlike a man's (Job 10:4). "Flesh" denotes the difference of humankind from God (Isa 31:3; Jer 17:5; Job 10:4; 2 Chron 32:8; Ps 56:4; Eccles 12:7), its total dependence on him, and its limitation. Without continuous inspiration by God's Spirit, there is no creaturely life, be it for humans, animals, or plants (Job 12:10; 34:14-15; cf. Gen 2:7; 6:3, 17; Ps 104:30). Yet even in its dependence, flesh was created by God (Isa 45:11-12; 64:8; Pss 119:73; 138:8; Job 10:8-13) and is, just as all his works, "very good" (cf. Gen 1:31). The human creatures are dependent on him alone. They are made from dust and will return to it; they pass like a wind or breath and do not come again; they perish, dissolve, and vanish like grass (Gen 3:19; Lam 3:4; Isa 40:6-7; Ps 78:39; Job 33:21; Prov 5:11; Zech 14:12).

Especially when human creatures are meant by the term "flesh," rather than also animals and plants, as in most cases where "all flesh" is mentioned, then often both Israel and the nations are in mind, and this in their weakness, lack of sufficiency and autarky, finitude and mortality. Both those who claim to know Israel's Lord and those who have not seen him are also inclined to serve the creatures instead of the creator, idols instead of God; to hate, oppress, and kill their neighbors and to yield to carnal temptations. According to the OT, but unlike, e.g., R. Bultmann's and E. Schweizer's description of "the sphere of flesh," there is no reason to speak of "the possibility" of human sin against God and humankind. Even if the flesh is fallible, the recourse to the "fallibility of that which God has created" is never taken in the OT, nor does it serve as an excuse and plea for mitigating circumstances. Rather, solely the crude and catastrophic fact is stated that "all flesh" has actually corrupted its way upon the earth and "has filled the earth with violence" (Gen 6:12-13; cf. Gen 3–4), and prophets denounce the crisis effected not only by the nations, but also by Judah and Israel. It is not the result of self-analysis of the creatures when their subjection to sin is proclaimed, but God's judgment on humankind and all creation is proclaimed. Neither by creation nor by nature but by the continuously "evil inclination of the thoughts of the human heart" (cf. Gen 6:5;

8:21) has flesh become so corrupt that it falls under God's condemnation. But the failure to fulfill its purposes has caused God to hold bloody judgment over all flesh and take the peace from humankind (Jer 12:12; 25:31; 45:5; Isa 66:24; cf. Gen 6:13, 17; 7:21). The vocabulary of the Dead Sea Scrolls includes (e.g., the fragment 1QH 13.13, 18, 19; 17.25; 1QM 12; 1QS 11.9) terms such as "spirit of the flesh," "guilt of the flesh," "iniquity of the flesh," in opposition to the Spirit given by God.

There are persons who accept sickness, exile, devastation, and other miseries as an act of God and respond to it by crying to God out of the depth (see, e.g., Ps 22; 109:22-26). They confess their weakness, sin, and defection from God. Psalm 38:3, 7: "There is no soundness in my flesh . . . no health in my bones, because of my sin." Psalm 143:2: "No flesh is righteous before thee" — this is the confession of a man who calls himself God's "servant." In many psalms, and especially in the book of Lamentations, at Yom Kippur and on other days of repentance, not only do individuals confess their weakness and failure but the people join in confession, lamentation, and prayer for help, and in thanksgiving. Even Job, who declares himself innocent of the crimes while his friends suggest he is the cause of his misery, accepts God's judgment. Still, neither condemnation nor confession and lamentation exhaust the richness of the OT utterances on the "flesh."

God is and remains "the Lord, the God of all flesh" (Jer 32:27). God's people have rebelled against God despite his marvelous deeds and humble punishment; but "he being compassionate, forgives their iniquity. . . . he remembered that they were but flesh" (Ps 78:38-39 in its context; yet not only Israel is protected by God: "To thee shall all flesh come" [Ps 65:2]). "He gives food to all flesh" (Ps 136:25). "Let all flesh bless his holy name for ever and ever" (Ps 145:7). The psychosomatic unity of humankind becomes apparent in several statements: "My soul thirsts for thee; my flesh faints for thee" (Ps 63:1). "My heart and flesh sing for joy to the living God" (Ps 84:2). When God's wind, the Spirit, blows upon dry bones, they are clothed with sinews, flesh, skin, and they will breathe and live (Ezek 37:6: the bodily resurrection seen in the vision signifies the restoration of Israel). "All the Glory of the Lord will be revealed and all flesh shall see it together. . . . Then all the flesh shall know that I am the Lord, your savior and your redeemer" (Isa 40:5; 49:26). While in, e.g., Isa 31:3 flesh and the Spirit constitute the strongest possible contrast, Joel 3:1-2 (cf. 2:28) contains God's eschatological promise, "I will pour out my Spirit on all flesh, your sons and your daughters . . . even upon the men-servants and maidservants."

Thus even much more is announced than what God promised by the covenant made after the flood with "the earth" and "every living creature of all flesh" (Gen 9:8-17). Then God had sworn never again to destroy all flesh as he had done by the flood. Through Isaiah, Deutero-Isaiah and, e.g., Joel, the same Lord gives to Israelites and to Gentiles the promise that God's Spirit will be upon them. And many psalms express the conviction that the nations, too, will know God and participate in his worship. In 1QS 11.12-13 the confession is made, "Behold if I should totter, God's mercy will be my salvation. If I stumble in the iniquity of the flesh, I shall be set aright through God's righteousness ever enduring." The history that the OT tells of the relationship between the Lord and the flesh culminates in the promise of God's mercy, grace, and gracious gifts from which all creatures shall benefit and which will make them jump with joy.

E. Schweizer has (in *TDNT*, 7.97-105) clearly shown that in ancient Greek literature the quality of being flesh can mark the difference between human beings and the
gods, but that "flesh" is basically *anthropologically* corrupt, describing that part of humankind that is inferior to the human soul, spirit, and reason. In the OT, however, the
relation to God, the Creator and Redeemer, is essential. The same triumph of grace over
all flesh that the OT ends with, is in Paul's theology the basis and starting point for
speaking of both the flesh and the Lord in as positive a combination as he does in
Philem 16.

B. Relying on Christ Incarnate, Crucified, and Risen

Among the occurrences of the noun *sarx* (flesh) and the adjective "fleshly" *(sarkinos* or
sarkikos) in Pauline letters (eighty-one times in those generally accepted as authentic),
the best known are those with a devaluing tone and context. For this reason the apostle
has been frequently understood and sometimes highly esteemed as a promoter of a
dualistic, be it Platonic, Stoic, Gnostic, Manichean, or a later idealistic and/or ascetic,
ethics that left little or no room for a high estimation of the human body. Such interpreters took the joy out of the temporal, fallible, and corrupted conditions under which
all human beings live their lives. What Philem 16 says about living and/or loving "in the
flesh *and* in the Lord" shows that here Paul does not consider flesh the cause and seat of
misery and mortality of creatureliness, neither (as Luther sometimes did) as an "old bag
of maggots" *(alter Madensack)* (cf. Rom 7:23). Also the Lord is not described as ruler
over a faraway realm that must absolutely be distinguished from the present world. On
what, then, is the apostle's double formula based?

1. The Christological Basis

Fundamental is the great event of the Messiah Jesus — who, "being equal to God . . .
emptied himself, taking the form of a servant . . . having been born like other persons . . .
found in a human form . . . became obedient to death even death on the cross" and was
therefore highly exalted by God himself — that is hymnically praised in Phil 2:6-11.
This hymn may be quoted from a church tradition, or it may have been composed by
the apostle himself. At any rate, in prose style the same confession of Christ's humiliation, this time by inclusion of the word "flesh," is also made in Rom 8:3 in the RSV:
"God has done what the law, weakened by the flesh, could not do: sending his own Son
in the likeness of sinful flesh and for sin, he condemned sin in the flesh." The same emphasis is laid on the incarnation and death of the Son of God in Col 1:22: "[Christ] has
now reconciled you in the flesh through his death"; in Eph 2:14, 16: "in his flesh [he has
wiped out all] enmity . . . through the cross in one single body. In his own person . . .";
and in 1 Tim 3:16: "He was manifested in the flesh, vindicated in the Spirit."

Other NT passages, not published under Paul's name, concur: 1 Pet 3:18, cf. 4:1:
"The Messiah suffered once for all . . . put to death in the flesh but made alive by the
Spirit"; Heb 2:14-16 RSV: "Since . . . children [of God] share in flesh and blood, he him-
self likewise partook of the same nature, that through death he might destroy him who

has the power of death. . . . surely it is not with angels that he is concerned"; Heb 5:7: "In the days of his flesh, he offered up prayers and supplications" (cf. Heb 10:15-26). According to Acts 2:26-27, 31, David's confidence that his "flesh will dwell in hope" (cf. Ps 16:9) is fulfilled in Christ's resurrection: "He was not abandoned to Hades, nor did his flesh see corruption." Outstanding among all statements that connect Jesus Christ immediately with flesh is John 1:14: "The Word became flesh and dwelt among us, full of grace and truth; and we have beheld his glory." The references to Jesus Christ's "flesh and blood" in John 6:51-58 are not only to his incarnation, but especially to his death, by which death-bound sinners receive eternal life. Therefore it is probable that in John 1:14a the term "flesh" includes also the sacrificial death of the Son of God. The following words about living in a tent and seeing the glory and the fullness of grace and truth refer to events taking place in Israel's origin (see esp. Exod 33:7-23; 34:6-8) and in the context of cultus. John the Baptist is quoted for hailing Jesus as "the lamb of God who takes away the sin of the world" (cf. John 1:29, 36). To him who is incarnate and will be crucified, the Father has given "full power over all flesh" (John 17:2). The salvation proclaimed in the NT depends on the coming, praying, working, suffering, and dying of God's Son "in the flesh." For Paul and Matthew, Luke, the authors of Hebrews (7:14) and Revelation (5:5), it was most important that the Son of God was born on earth and according to the flesh, not from any human but from a Jewish woman. In most cases when Paul uses the formula "according to the flesh" *(kata sarka),* this term depreciates the value of all and every flesh, or of actions and conduct dictated by flesh. So also the Fourth Gospel emphasizes that no child of God is born "of blood nor of the will of the flesh nor of the will of man"; that all which is "born of the flesh is flesh, and that [exclusively] which is born of the Spirit is spirit"; in short: that "the flesh is of no avail" (John 1:13; 3:6; 6:63 RSV; cf. Rom 9:8). But for Paul and others it is also essential to narrate and to proclaim that "according to the flesh," the Messiah Jesus stemmed "from the seed of David," more specifically, from the tribe of Judah, and so from the people of Israel (Rom 1:3; 9:5; Luke 1–3; Matt 1–2; Heb 7:14; Rev 5:5). For he was "king of the Jews" — this even Pilate might have known when he fixed the inscription on Jesus' cross — not even a pretender could be of pagan origin. By letting his Son be fully and truly human in the form and tradition of Jewish generation, according to Paul, God in person had shown himself faithful to his one people he had chosen for becoming the light of the nations and chastised. Even after Christ was crucified and the gospel was rejected by many Jews, "Israel according to the flesh" (1 Cor 10:18) and its Bible show the church the way to serve God and that, even when Christ's incarnation led to his crucifixion "in weakness" (2 Cor 13:4), there was reason enough to honor a man "born of a woman" (Gal 4:4) — without succumbing to the temptation "to boast of the flesh" (cf. 2 Cor 11:18). But all those willing to boast shall boast of the incarnate and crucified Lord, not of themselves, rather than put their confidence on immediate descendance from Abraham and/or the permanence of prescribed rituals (such as circumcision and dietary laws) that affect the body (1 Cor 1:29).

Without the resurrection of Christ, neither Paul nor early Christianity would have known that any one person living, and that events taking place "in the flesh" or "according to the flesh," could constitute the foundation and beginning, the mediation and instrument of the salvation of "all flesh," be it Jewish or Gentile. In turn, the authors of NT writings were convinced that Christ was resurrected bodily and physically, as truly in history as he was born and crucified and buried in history. His resurrection was resurrection of the flesh. Of the (empty!) tomb speak not only the Gospels (cf. Acts 2:29-33). The risen Christ is, according to Luke 24:38, not a spirit, e.g., of the spiritual power mentioned in Eph 6:12. For a "spirit has no flesh and bones as you see me having." Paul, too, knows he was buried and no earlier than after three days raised and seen again (1 Cor 15:5; cf. Rom 6:4; Col 2:12). The resurrected was seen, heard, and touched by hands, and ate meals with his eyewitnesses, according to the last chapter of the Gospels (cf. Acts, e.g., 1 John 1:1-3). Ignatius emphasizes in *Smyrn.* 3.1-2 that he was in the flesh even after the resurrection and that his disciples, by touching and believing him, were "mingled both with his flesh and his spirit." According to Ignatius, *Eph.* 3.2, he is "one physician, who is both, flesh and spirit in God, in man, true life, in death. . . ." In 2 Cor 5:16 Paul seems to affirm the opposite: (lit.) "From now on we don't know anyone according to the flesh; even if we have known Christ according to the flesh, yet no longer we know [him this way]." By these words the apostle does not mean that the so-called historical Jesus, or Jesus the Jew, or Jesus as he was treated by the Jews, is irrelevant for faith and proclamation. Solely a nonspiritual way of knowing him (cf. John) is sharply rejected, so the exposition of, e.g., Calvin (in his commentary on Second Corinthians); J. A. Bengel (in *Gnomon*); A. C. Headlam (*St. Paul and Christianity*, pp. 51f.); C. A. A. Scott (*Living Issues in the NT*, pp. 3-4); P. Schubert (*NT Study and Theology*, pp. 565-566); C. F. D. Moule (in *Jesus and Man's Hope*, ed. D. Y. Hadidian et al., p. 30; cf. P. Minear, in Hadidian, p. 26); R. Bultmann (*TDNT*, 1.237-238); E. Schweizer (*TDNT*, 7.131). According to Gal 4:9; 1 Cor 8:2-3; 3:12; cf. John 10:14, a true and relevant knowledge of God and Christ presupposes that those who know are aware of being first known by God in Christ.

In summary, what the Hebrew Bible said of the fundamental and overarching Lord, the grace and mercy of God, is, according to Paul, manifested in the person of the Lord Jesus Christ. The apostle, and with him the other above-mentioned NT authors, gives testimony to what is called the "philanthropy of the savior God" (Titus 3:4) and more recently (by, e.g., K. Barth), "the humanity of God" (cf. book of same title; Richmond: John Knox, 1960).

2. Experience in One's Own Life

The christological care communicated in many utterances on flesh permits and encourages Paul to appreciate very highly his own life and activity "in the flesh." Autobiographical statements reveal this: Gal 2:20: (lit.) "What I live now in the flesh I live in the faith of the Son of God who has loved me and given himself for me"; Phil 1:20-24 RSV: "I shall not be at all ashamed, but . . . with full courage now as always Christ will be honored in my body. . . . For to me to live is Christ, and to die is gain. If it is to be life in the flesh, that means fruitful labor for me. . . . My desire is to depart and be with Christ. . . . But to remain in the flesh is more necessary on your account"; 2 Cor 4:10-11: "[We are] always carrying in the body the death of Jesus, so that the life of Jesus may also be manifested in our bodies . . . in our mortal flesh"; 2 Cor 12–13: because Christ "was crucified in weakness, but lives by the power of God" (13:4), Paul bears with "the thorn given in my [his] flesh, a messenger of Satan, to harass me, to keep me from being too elated"; he accepts God's decision that "my grace is sufficient for you, for my power is made perfect in weakness," and he will "all the more gladly boast" of his "weakness" that the power of Christ may rest upon him. "For the sake of Christ, then, I am content with weaknesses, insults, hardships, persecutions and calamities; for when I am weak, then I am strong" (12:7-10). The apostle expects "that no one may think more of me than he sees in me and hears from me," and in order to make himself corporally seen he plans and announces visits again and again (e.g., Phil 1:26). He reminds the Galatians of the reception they gave him once when he was in bad shape. "It was an illness that first gave me the opportunity to preach the gospel to you, but though my illness was a trial to you, you did not show any distaste or revulsion — instead, you welcomed me as a messenger of God, as if I was Christ Jesus himself" (Gal 4:13-14 NJB). Paul endures his sufferings as a minister of the gospel for the sake of such Christians who have never seen him: "in my flesh I complete what is lacking in Christ's afflictions" (Col 1:24; 2:1).

To the positive and even joyful way Paul accepts his present bodily existence belongs the solidarity with relatives, even with "Israel according to the flesh" (1 Cor 10:18). Notwithstanding the catastrophic rejection of Christ and the gospel by the Jews, of which Paul writes in 1 Thess 2:14-16, he affirms in Rom 9:3 (NJB): "I could pray that I myself might be accursed and cut off from Christ, if this could benefit the brothers who are my own flesh and blood" (lit. ". . . my consanguineous according to the flesh"). Jesus Christ's own unshakeable faithfulness to God's first elected people is mirrored in the destination of the gospel, first to the Jews and also to the Gentiles. Certainly of the gospel, which announces that the Jew Jesus is the savior of the world, Paul is "not ashamed" (Rom 1:16-17). This does not mean that the apostle could not boast of his own Jewishness: he claims to have reason for confidence in the flesh, and even more so than others, for he was "circumcised on the eighth day, of the people of Israel, of the tribe of Benjamin, a Hebrew born of Hebrews, as to the law a Pharisee, as to zeal a persecutor of the church, as to righteousness under the law blameless." But he wisely abstains from it: "We worship by the Spirit of God and make Christ Jesus our only boast, not relying on the flesh *(en sarki)*" (Phil 3:3-5). What Paul says about his own life, work, weakness, and suffering "in the flesh" or "in the body" pertains also to all members of the church.

3. Applied to All Christians

A few passages suffice to show that, except for the unique and prototypical function of the apostolic ministry, all Christians share in the same relation to Christ and to their own flesh and body as does Paul. Often when Paul says "we," the congregation is included. Before their resurrection, their house (namely, body and/or congregation) is a tent in which they groan, yearning for a habitat coming from heaven. While "at home in the body, they are exiled from the Lord." Paul knows and proclaims that "flesh and blood cannot inherit the kingdom of God" (1 Cor 15:50). Neither can it raise from the dead Jesus Christ for itself. But this statement is made immediately after, in 1 Cor 15:35-

49, the apostle has extensively and with the help of daring comparison argued that the resurrection is bodily, even the resurrection of flesh. The future body will be different from the present life in the flesh: it will be "imperishable . . . in glory . . . in power . . . spiritual." It will not destroy and annihilate the present fleshly body but will "clothe over" (2 Cor 5:2-4a; 1 Cor 15:53-55) what is material and weak and has proven inept and impotent to fulfill God's law (Rom 8:3). What is mortal will die because of sin (cf. Rom 6:23), and even death itself will be "swallowed up by life" (2 Cor 5:4; 1 Cor 15:54-56). When the new body is called "spiritual," this does not signify that it consists of a new matter. Rather, spirituality means here total sustenance, direction, control, and glorification by the Spirit of God and Christ so that weakness, rebellion, illness, distortion, and rejection of God's will are left behind.

The pouring out of God's Spirit over all flesh (Joel 3:1; etc.) determines not only the essence of eternal life. Already now the saints are no longer "in the flesh but in the Spirit" (Rom 8:9; cf. 7:5), for they are "sealed" by this Spirit (2 Cor 1:22; 5:5; Rom 8:23; Eph 1:13-14; 4:30; cf. Gal 3:2; 4:6; etc.). Though their bodies be "dead through sin," there is yet this Spirit at work in them to give to their bodies "life through righteousness" (Rom 8:10-11). While Christians still walk "in the flesh," they are yet free to walk not "according to the flesh" (2 Cor 10:2-3). "Through the body of Christ . . . who was raised from the dead," and having confessed in baptism that through Christ's death they are dead to sin in order to "live for God and the Messiah Jesus," they are freed and equipped already now with conduct to live a new life (Rom 6:1–7:7). It is, as is stressed in 1 Pet 3:21, not by the baptism with water that "the dirt of the flesh" was removed from the people elected by God. Also they were not cleaned by a handmade circumcision, but all wickedness of "the human body was cast off in the circumcision of the Messiah" (Col 2:11) — even that circumcision of Jews and Gentiles performed on the cross of Jesus (see AB 34B, on Col 2:11). Then and there they have died to sin, with and in Christ in order to be raised with him (cf. Rom 6:5-11). Therefore what they have done in the body, even in their present life, whether it be "good or evil," will count before "the judgment seat of Christ" (2 Cor 5:10). While they "have time," they are called upon to "do good to all, especially to those who are of the household of God" (Gal 6:10). Just when they have to endure suffering in their body, they know that it is "Christ's sufferings to which they are made to 'conform' in order also to be conformed to the body of his glory" (Phil 3:16, 21; Rom 8:29; cf. 2 Cor 4:10-11; Rom 8:17-18; etc.). First Peter 4:1-2 (RSV) combines Christ's suffering directly with the sufferings of all Christians by using in close succession three times the formula "in the flesh": "Since therefore Christ suffered in the flesh . . . whoever has suffered in the flesh has ceased from sin, so as to live for the rest of the time in the flesh no longer by human passions but by the will of God." More honor and good can hardly be shown to the flesh, although 1 Pet 1:24 boldly quotes the Second Isaiah, "all flesh is like grass."

According to Paul, even material possessions such as money or food are owed by Gentile Christians to saints in Jerusalem to serve them with the gift of "fleshly things" for the "spiritual" goods received from them (Rom 15:27; cf. 2 Cor 8:9). The apostle feels entitled to reap material (fleshly) benefits in exchange for the spiritual things he has sown (1 Cor 9:11).

Corresponding to these appreciations of the flesh on a much longer, even universal, scale are the statements made in Rom 8:19-22 and Col 1:15-20 about the liberation and reconciliation of all creatures of God. Just as Christians are "groaning" while they still live in their earthly tent far from God, so also all creation "groans" under the consequences of sin (2 Cor 5:2; Rom 8:22-23). Flesh is not explicitly mentioned in these passages, but it is distinctly proclaimed that not only human beings but also what the OT calls "all flesh" will be finally redeemed. In the OT story of the flood, which presupposed the human guilt in the corruption of all flesh, salvation of the universe was anticipated. The OT and NT promise and expectation of a "new heaven and a new earth" (Isa 65:17; 66:22; Rev 21:1; 2 Pet 3:13) reveal that there is hope for the flesh, its deficiency and defection, weakness and fall notwithstanding. The very existence and composition of a local church such as the Corinthians demonstrate that God "has elected . . . what is weak in the world."

How can Paul's positive statement on the flesh and the human body, especially his hope that God "keeps the spirit and soul and body [of the saints] sound and blameless" (1 Thess 5:23), be reconciled with his bitter complaint of his own present existence in the "body of death" (Rom 7:24), and his crushing condemnation of the works and the value of all flesh (e.g., Rom 3:9-20)?

4. Mercy Triumphs over Judgment

Paul's condemnation of flesh is most outspoken when he, following, e.g., Gen 6:3; Isa 31:3; Ezek 3; etc., compares the flesh and its effect to the Spirit and its fruit (Gal 3:3; 5:16-25; 6:8; 1 Cor 2:4–3:3; Rom 7:5-6; 8:1, variant reading; 8:4-6, 9-14). Some Greek writers spoke of the contrast between the human flesh and soul or spirit. If in this interpretation (cf. Matt 26:41 par.) the Holy Spirit is left out of consideration, the desperate sigh, "the Spirit is willing but the flesh is weak," has a proverbial and generally accepted sense. Epicurus believed in the possibility of their cooperation in harmony, but he was readily, without sufficient reason, much maligned by, e.g., Plutarch, Epictetus, and not only Stoic but also Jewish and Christian writers. For a fairer interpretation of genuine Epicurism, see N. W. DeWitt, *Epicurus and His Philosophy;* cf. E. Schweizer, *TDNT,* 7.102-104.

According to Paul, neither the human soul nor the individual or communal human spirit constitutes the ultimate contrast to flesh and fleshly things and actions. Just as in the OT, "each soul" *(pasa psychē)* can be used almost as equivalent of "all flesh." In 1 Cor 2:14 the "psychic" *(psychikos)* man is as inept as the fleshly and foolish persons mentioned in 1 Cor 3:1. As long as they are not "spiritual," i.e., taught by God's spirit, they cannot grasp "spiritual" things, even the mystery and wisdom of God: Christ crucified (1 Cor 1:18–2:16). First Peter 1:22 makes an analogous application: even the souls of the Christians are in need of purification by "obedience to the truth for a sincere love."

The same is true of the human spirit. Only once (in 1 Cor 5:5) does Paul express the hope that it may be saved on the Lord's day, even after the flesh of the same person has been delivered to destruction. In the context he maintains that he can be present in the spirit, even during his bodily absence (1 Cor 5:3-4; cf. Col 2:5). He knows that his own and the saints' spirit can be given rest by outside events (1 Cor 16:18) — obviously not out of internal resources. He appeals to the communal spirit of meekness and unity in which all are to share (Gal 6:1; 1 Cor 4:2; 14:32; 2 Cor 12:18; Phil 1:27; cf. 1 Pet 3:4). But neither the individual nor the communal spirit is identified with the Holy Spirit. The spirit of the Christians (mentioned in 1 Thess 5:23; Gal 6:18; Philem 25) needs cleansing from defilement as much as their flesh (2 Cor 7:1).

For Paul, the Holy Spirit is not the only powerful opponent of the flesh and fleshly things and actions. Mentioned are also: the Lord (2 Cor 11:17-18), the grace of God (2 Cor 1:12), God's wisdom (1 Cor 1:24-26), his power (2 Cor 10:4), his promise (Gal 4:23-29; Rom 9:8; cf. his word, Isa 40:6, quoted in 1 Pet 1:24-25), the faithfulness and obedience of Christ (Gal 2:20; Rom 8:3), etc. The opposition and mutual warfare are so radical that it hardly makes sense to speak of an occasional or basically "neutral" sense of the term "flesh." Rather, just as, e.g., Leviticus and Ezekiel show, there is no neutral ground between pure and unpure, holy and profane. In the face of God, who condemns all flesh because of its corruption, nothing seems to be left but the bitter complaints and lamentations of many psalmists, and of Job, which Paul gathered up by crying: "Wretched man, who I am! Who will deliver me from the body of death?" (Rom 7:24), that have encouraged many an existentialist of, e.g., the twentieth century to glorify self-pity, anxiety, meaningless, and despair.

Indeed, the depreciative and condemnatory statement made by Paul about the flesh covers many fields, of which some examples can suffice at this place. Before the Son of God is sent out, the flesh is so weakened by sin that it cannot fulfill what the Law requires (Rom 8:3-4). Only a fool can build his confidence on his birth and descendance from a certain people, or can boast of special moral or religious achievements and distinctions resulting from his natural ancestry (2 Cor 11:1-18; Phil 3:3-8; cf. Gal 1:13-15). In vain he relies on worldly and fleshly knowledge and wisdom (1 Cor 1:18; 3:3; 2 Cor 1:12; 5:16). "Works of the flesh" are the results of evil desire and carnal lust that exclude their performance from inheriting the kingdom of God (Gal 5:19-21; etc.). Most Gentiles and all Jews agreed in condemning them. But also the observance of a mere selection from the divine commandments that particularly pertain to the body (e.g., circumcision and dietary prescriptions) called "works of law" is denounced by Paul as an inept means for becoming justified (Rom 3:28; Gal 2:16; Eph 2:11; etc.; cf. Heb 9:13, 16; 8:13). To sow in the flesh means to reap corruption from the flesh (Gal 6:8; cf. Rom 6:23). While the formula "in the flesh" need not always have a pejorative sense (see, e.g., R. Bultmann, *TDNT*, 1.135-138), the term "according to the flesh" — except when it refers to Christ's birth — has a condemnatory undertone. And yet, Paul's theology and anthropology are by far not sufficiently exhausted by quoting such texts. For he speaks of a Lord and a Spirit of a distinct kind: the Lord who is and remains creator and redeemer of all flesh and the Spirit that is to be poured on all flesh and will raise it from death, however tempted, failing, sinful, and subject to death it may be. According to Heb 5:7, "in the days of his flesh Jesus offered up prayers and supplications, with loud cries and tears, to him who was able to save him from death." The Lord's Prayer presupposes that the Father in heaven can and will even on earth be revealed as the gracious God who sanctifies his name, establishes his kingship, carries out his will not only in heaven but also on earth, and who therefore provides the daily bread, grants the forgiveness, shows a way out of temptation and delivers from evil all those who will shamefully forever perish without God's continuous and final intervention in behalf of the weak flesh.

Paul's seemingly pessimistic anthropology stands on a very specific basis and is protected by a particular roof. The ground and the shelter are constituted by the grace of God, which is revealed in Christ and by the Spirit. Whatever Paul calls flesh and whatever he has to say about the depravity of flesh is said within the proclamation of grace. Because the flesh was created by God, it remains under God's protection. God alone knows how to handle what is weak and fallible and what has fallen into corruption. When he acts on it out of his anger, his mercy yet is so great that no one is entitled to despise or condemn the life "in the flesh" and "in the body." Rather, all flesh has reason to rejoice and give thanks. In Rom 7:24-25 (NEB) Paul speaks not only of himself when he cries out of the depth of misery, "Miserable creature that I am, who is there to rescue me out of this body doomed to death?" Just as in many OT psalms of lamentation, despair has not the last word: he answers his question immediately: "God alone, through Jesus Christ our Lord! Thanks be to God!" (cf., e.g., Ps 22:1-21, 22-31). It may be concluded that, according to Paul, not only a sham "wisdom manifested by willing piety and humility and severe [ascetic] treatment of the body leads [only] to gratification of the flesh" (Col 2:23) and is devious because Christ has reconciled former sinners "in the flesh of his body" (Col 1:22), but that also self-satisfaction by verbal and doctrinal denouncements of the flesh can contradict the essence of the apostle's message; this does not prevent Paul from exerting rigorous self-discipline (1 Cor 9:24-27 RSV, *hypopiazō mou to sōma kai doulagōgō,* "I pommel my body and subdue it, lest after preaching to others I myself should be disqualified"). At a peak of his rhetoric, Tertullian *(De resurrectione carni* 9, our translation) called the flesh "Christ's sister": "Far be it that God forsake the work of his hands [the flesh], the protégé of his genius, the receptacle of his inspiration, the crown of creativity, the heir of his liberality, the priest of his worship, the soldier of his testimony, the sister of his anointed: we have known that God is good, but that he is best we have in addition learned from Christ. . . . He loves the flesh which is nearest to him in so many ways, although it is weak . . . imbecile . . . dishonorable . . . corrupt . . . condemned. . . . Why do you accuse the flesh of those things which expect [salvation from] God, hope in God, are honored by him, which he supports and helps? I would dare say unless these things had happened to the flesh, the goodness, grace, mercy and all-beneficent power of God would have been void."

Tertullian adduces most diverse parts of the Bible for his panegyric on the flesh: the double commandment of love; the perfection of God's strength in weakness; the sick, not the healthy, who need a doctor; the most honorable treatment of the supposedly dishonorable members of the body; Christ's mission to seek and save that which is lost; God's pleasure in the repentance and life rather than in the death of the sinner; and God's power to wound and to heal (Matt 22:37-40; 2 Cor 12:9; Luke 5:31; 19:10; 1 Cor 12:23; Ezek 18:23; Deut 32:39).

A summary of the preceding excursus can be decisive for the interpretation of the last words of Philem 16. We have asked the question, How can the same Paul who so often devalues the flesh and all things fleshly combine the terms (lit.) "in the flesh" and "in the Lord" by "both . . . and" and put both, as it were, on an equal level, the standard of love shown and to show to Onesimus? An answer can now be given, consisting of four points.

1. After God, Christ, and the Spirit have given the flesh great honor, as OT and NT texts reveal, Paul cannot afford solely to depreciate and condemn all that is flesh and occurs in the flesh. Rather — though for a reason and in a form different from those of, e.g., artists, sportsmen and sportswomen, beauty queens, and hedonists — the apostle, too, honors the flesh. When he addresses himself to Jews and Gentiles, he is not ashamed to give testimony to the Lord who had become incarnate, had suffered in his body and died on the cross, who was corporally raised as the firstborn among many brethren (cf. Rom 1:16; Matt 10:33). God's and Christ's mercy has been manifested to benefit all flesh. In Col 1:15-20 the apostle reminds the Colossians that it was God's will to create and reconcile all things in heaven and earth in Christ, through Christ, and for Christ. Among the created and reconciled things and persons are Paul, Philemon, and Onesimus — even what they are, do, and endure "in the flesh" as unique historical individuals. The love that holds and will hold them together rests upon the love by which these fleshly creatures are loved by God (cf. 1 John 4:7-13, 19-21).

2. The love for Onesimus of which Paul speaks embraces the total person of the formerly useless and now returning slave. "Flesh," as much as "soul," "spirit," "mind," or "heart," denotes the whole person (including the past, present, and future behavior, the evident weaknesses, failures, and disappointments enumerated in, e.g., 1 Cor 13:4-7), and not only a part of it. Certainly the so-called "conversion" of Onesimus; his place in the church as a "Christian," or "brother"; and his present and future usefulness (v. 11) will have provided the occasion for loving him. Still, he is not to be loved for those reasons only — as if love might be reduced or withdrawn whenever Onesimus does not live up to expectations. True love is not a conditional gift and bond, but accepts the neighbor, brother, and sister just as they are.

3. Above it was shown that in Philem 16c the mention of *sarx* (lit. "flesh") sometimes has been considered a reference to the slave status of Onesimus in distinction from his membership in the congregation. But Paul did not write "love . . . as a slave and as a Christian." In this verse the apostle distinguishes neither, on a worldwide scale, the realm of worldly institutions from the realm of Spirit or of the church, nor in individual believers an allegiance that is based on love for a servant from love for a fellow Christian. Such a division would permit the limitation or even suspension of one of the two loves in favor of the

other. However, not only, e.g., the Gospels speak of the one shepherd who is to be obeyed and followed (John 10:1-16) and the impossibility of serving two masters at the same time (Matt 4:8 par.; 6:24 par.), but Paul, too, excludes dancing at two weddings or serving two Gods in, e.g., 1 Cor 8:4-6; 10:19-22; 2 Cor 6:15.

4. Not even respect for and subordination to state officials, of which Rom 13:1-7; Matt 22:21 par.; 1 Tim 2:2-4; 1 Pet 2:13-17 speak, permit us by analogy to see in Philem 16c a tacit endorsement or sanctification of the contemporary institution of slavery; for the commandment and admonition to pay taxes and honor state officials is always grounded in the institution of the state by God. To formulate it with John 19:11: "You would have no power over me, unless it had been given to you from above." So also in Philem 16c the mention of love (lit.) "in the Lord" reveals why even (lit.) "in the flesh" Onesimus is "no longer [just] a slave" (v. 16a). As Philem 13 shows, at the bottom of his heart Paul hopes that Philemon will eventually permit Onesimus to leave his present master, not for a wanton freedom, but in order to serve Paul in the gospel work.

VERSE 17

Therefore, since you have me as partner, welcome him as you would receive me.

In verses 8 and 9 Paul had announced that he was not "commanding," but only requesting. Up until verse 17, he has used no imperative. Then in verses 18, 20, and 22, he seems to choose a language that he has just sought to avoid. The apostle expects *obedience* from Philemon, as verse 21 shows. How obedience and autonomy, requesting and "commanding," are related will be further discussed in the excursus "Freedom and Obedience," pp. 487-490.

Verse 17, like verse 18, is introduced by the Greek conjunction *ei*. The meaning of the word is different, however, in the two respective instances. While in verse 18 *ei* introduces a conditional clause, in verse 17 it gives the grounds for the following argumentation, and is to be translated "since" (for this usage see BDR, 372.1, and LSLex, p. 481).

The particle *oun* is a transitional one, indicating hereafter certain intervening observations — that the author is returning to the main theme, the slave Onesimus's journey back to his master Philemon.

Verses 17-19 contain a multiplicity of juridical and financial technical terms from ancient commercial language. Some of these are *adikein* (to "wrong" someone), *opheilein* (to "owe" someone something), *ellogein* (to charge to someone's account), and the entire verse 19. The noun *koinōnos* (partner) is also being used with a special meaning.

S. Winter ("Paul's Letter to Philemon," pp. 11-12) understands *koinōnos* as a juridical *terminus technicus.* She interprets verse 17 as "an explicit appeal to a form of partnership contract under Roman law, named *societas (koinōnia),* entered into for the purpose of pursuing a specific goal." Winter appeals in her explanation to J. P. Sampley (*Pauline Partnership in Christ,* esp. pp. 11-20, 79-81). For such a *societas:*

> Consent of the parties was binding; no witness or notification of authority were required. The contract was, however, legally binding and fully subject to court process. The partners were bound by the contract simply to exert themselves on behalf of the agreed-upon goal of the partnership. There were no specific rules governing behavior of the partners, with the exception that it was required that all profits and losses be shared by all partners. There were no restrictions on who could enter into consensual *societas,* and even slaves could become full partners with any person and thus acquire rights of court process with respect to the partnership. (Winter, p. 11)

As an example of such a partnership, Sampley cites the agreement between Paul and the community in Philippi.

If Winter is correct, the concept *koinōnos* would bring the equality of rights between slave Onesimus and his master to striking expression. However, such a juridically defined contract between Paul and Philemon, in which Onesimus is to become a partner, remains hypothetical. The letter does not make any other allusion to this. Sampley rightly remarks: "The letter is so brief and the evidence is so limited that we cannot with any degree of certainty conclude whether Paul actually had a formal *societas* with Philemon" (p. 79).

Koinōnos (partner) does not have in Greek only the special sense that Winter adduces. It can also mean, more generally, "business partner" or "coworker," and does not necessarily imply the equal standing of the partners (cf. Luke 5:10).

In the Septuagint, the word describes someone who shares something with someone else (cf. Prov 28:24; Isa 1:23; cf. in the NT, Matt 23:30), or else a person with whom an alliance is formed (Mal 2:14). In Sir 6:10, the *koinōnos* as a simple "table companion" is distinguished from *philos* (friend) in that the former does not "stick by you" in time of need.

In the Pauline writings, the word occurs five times. In 1 Cor 10:18, 20 it is used in a context of worship. It describes, besides, someone who suffers the same fate as another (2 Cor 1:7; Heb 10:33). In 2 Pet 1:4 *koinōnos* denotes someone to whom a share in something falls. Thus, the meaning of this concept can be very specific as well as very general.

With its juridical, commercial concepts, it is true, the context of Philem

17 suggests an understanding of *koinōnos* in a "commercial" sense. But since no compelling linguistic grounds are at hand for Winter's interpretation, I prefer the translation "business partner" in the wider sense.

The manner of the "business relationship" is now described more closely. The content of the clause introduced by the conjunction *ei*, to be interpreted causally ("since"), reflects on verse 19b, where we have "Not to mention your own *debt* to me, your total self."

Welcome him (lit. "receive him"). The interrelationship between the words *proslambanein* (receive) and *koinōnos* occurs only here, it is true, in the New Testament. But it is not unusual in the Greek language. As an expression of commercial speech, it can mean "accept someone as partner" or "take someone as one's partner" (see LSLex, s.v.; Lohmeyer, p. 189 nn. 5, 6). However, *proslambanein* does not require this juridical sense. The verb can simply mean "receive someone as a guest" (see Acts 18:26). In this denotation, the verb leads smoothly into the following context. Finally, Paul sends the (runaway) slave Onesimus back, and furthermore announces his visit to Philemon in the near future.

As you would receive me (lit. "as me"). Does Paul mean, as you would receive me as a *Roman citizen;* or as an *emissary of Christ;* or as a *guest,* with all the rights and comforts of a guest; or as a *member of the house church* that meets in Philemon's home?

All of this fits Paul's attitudes. None of these possibilities is readily to be excluded.

According to Winter's presentation, to be sure, where *koinōnos* designates an equal partner in a *societas,* the meaning of the second part of Philem 17 is unambiguous. It contains the demand that Philemon receive Onesimus into this *societas* as an equal partner, *just as* Paul is an equal partner. According to Winter, this shows "the extent of the shift that Paul is requesting in the latter's relationship with Onesimus — from an owner-slave relationship to one of equal partnership, to an equal sharing in the profit and loss of the endeavour" (p. 12).

A more general interpretation is possible, however, and even more likely (see above, on Winter's thesis). Paul expressly demands, at the end of the letter, "Get a guest room ready for me." Philemon will understand this request in connection with the one in verse 17b. Still, the "as me" is not to be understood without reference to the noun, *koinōnos,* which gives the whole verse a special coloring in the context of the abundant series of juristic and commercial concepts. If *koinōnos* refers to Philemon's debt to Paul as it is indicated in verse 1b, then what is said here is, Receive him as a creditor receives his debtor to whom he forgives an entire debt.

But what does this mean concretely? Once more, nothing is said of manumission. Nor does the particle *hōs* (as) permit an unambiguous decision in this respect: *hōs* (as) can mean "as if," so that it is not unconditionally presupposed that Philemon is to receive Onesimus as a "free man" because Paul is not a slave. If anything, the Greek *hōs*, in this verse, is to be interpreted against the background of its use in verse 16 (". . . no longer *as* a slave"). See also *in loco*, pp. 419-420.

Although it is not expressly demanded that Onesimus's status as slave be abolished, it is certainly the case that Paul will have had changes in mind in the dealings between lord and slave. The question is surely: How does Paul think a Christian would treat his slave? But the question is not explicitly answered in the Letter to Philemon.

Excursus: To Be a Sibling *and* a Slave or Master

Our investigations (see esp. the excursuses "Why No Plea for Manumission?" and "Does Paul Ask for Manumission?" pp. 369-370, 413-416) have repeatedly supported the hypothesis that Paul has not offered a brief for the abolition of the institution of slavery. But what did it mean, in the mind of the apostle, for the mutual dealings of master and slave if they are both Christians, and thereby siblings?

One is struck by the fact that, in the surely authentic Pauline letters, there are no explicit observations on how Christians are to deal with their slaves who are also Christians, or how slaves who have become believers are to relate to their owners who are now their siblings. Paul's silence is surprising on this point, since it is not readily imaginable that there were no difficulties in the mutual relations of these groups of persons.

Only a few texts may permit cautious conclusions that could provide a little progress in the solution of this problem.

As we have shown, Philem 17, in which Paul demands that Philemon receive his runaway slave "as me," is not very helpful. Nothing can be concluded from verse 17 other than the demand that the slave not be punished, but be received in a friendly fashion. A fugitive slave could expect severe punishments from his owner. "Flogging and branding were common, and there was in practice no limit to the punishments an angry master might impose" (J. M. G. Barclay, "Dilemma of Christian Slave-Ownership," p. 170). The time following the reception of the slave is in no way dealt with in this statement.

Statements in First Corinthians, on the other hand, are more meaningful for the series of questions under discussion. If slaves became Christians in Christian households, they then belonged to one and the same house community with their owners, and crucial changes were made in the slave-lord relationship. In 1 Cor 12, Paul compares the Christian community with a body. In verse 13 he expressly emphasizes that the *one* Spirit is equally at work in each member, regardless of whether that member is a Jew, a Greek, a *slave*, or a free person. And so Paul obviously is taking into consideration that in the community a slave, on grounds of his or her qualification or calling by the

Spirit, becomes an apostle, a prophet, a teacher, or a wonder-worker (v. 29). At the least, in the gathering of the community the case is conceivable that a slave might admonish, instruct, correct, or console a master.

Of course, an equality of lords and slaves in the community gathering could be called into question from the assertions in 1 Cor 11. Paul rebukes the community in Corinth because, in the gathering for the Lord's meal, some carry their "own meal" along, so that "one is hungry, the other is drunk." Paul would solve this deplorable state of affairs in his instruction "to eat and to drink at home," and then to gather for the Lord's meal.

It is strange that Paul does not call for equal portions at the meal, in order to further the table community of the different social groups. This could cast doubt on the supposition that, at least in the gathering of the community, Paul must surely have insisted on the equality of lords and slaves through the practice of a community table. This sort of meal community was everywhere frowned upon in the world around (Seneca, *Ep.* 47.2-8). At very least, we would be well advised to be cautious about hasty conclusions from assertions like 1 Cor 12:13 (cf. Gal 3:28) regarding the dealings between lords and slaves in everyday life.

In 1 Cor 12, however, Paul is attacking Hellenistic forms of the worship meal, in which it was customary to bring along one's various dishes. The diners did not begin their meals together. The Lord's meal, by contrast, was rooted in the Jewish meal usage, whose special earmark was the common inception, consisting in the breaking of the bread. Paul has obviously regarded this custom of the *common* beginning as unnegotiable, in order to maintain at least the *Lord's meal* as a *common* meal. At the same time, the usage of the breaking of the bread distinguishes the Lord's meal from other, pagan (worship) meals. (See K. Berger, *Manna, Mehl und Sauerteig*, pp. 106ff.; cf. also G. Theissen, "Soziale Integration und sakramentales Handeln," pp. 290-317.)

The special character of the Lord's meal, which was rooted in Jewish tradition, was for Paul obviously incomparably more serious than the question of the table community of the everyday, ordinary meal. But is this any indication that, for Paul, the question of the concrete relationship between slaves and owners as siblings in everyday dealings, apart from the community gathering, had no essential importance?

The Letter to the Colossians might offer further answers here. But one must keep in mind that the authorship of Colossians is disputed. In Colossians, we find, in the "house catalogue," express instructions to slaves, as well as to slave owners, who are Christians. The terse instruction to the "lords" leaves the question open whether the author is thinking of slaves who are Christians, or of pagan slaves. However, the admonitions to the slaves suggest that they are being given advice in their behavior toward unbelieving "lords." Thus, in Colossians as well, we may expect only a very terse answer to the question of how far, and how, a sibling bond through the faith between slaves and lords ought to influence the dealings of these persons with each other.

But at all events there *are* statements in Colossians that give instructions to believing lords and believing slaves that relate to behavior *outside* the community gathering.

If Colossians is an authentic Pauline letter, then its statements acquire special meaning in a framework of the presentation of the Letter to Philemon, since Philemon and Colossians were both addressed to Christians of the same place and are very nearly contemporary. If Colossians is a pseudo-Pauline letter, in any case it has been composed almost at the same time, and probably is very nearly Pauline in content. It reveals, then, an early step in the further development of Pauline thought by the young church.

In Col 3:22–4:1, both slaves and "lords," who believe in Christ, are admonished. These admonitions stand in the context of a "house catalogue" of instructions. The special form of the admonitions must be closely observed if we are adequately to assess their content.

In the first edition of his commentary on Colossians, M. Dibelius proposed the thesis that early believers — compelled to concentrate on everyday life by the delay of the parousia — went back to the old house catalogues for the sake of their parenetic content, especially of Jewish propaganda, and only superficially Christianized the same.

K. Weidinger, a pupil of Dibelius, then developed this thesis further. He adduced proofs that in Judaism as well, although only in the Diaspora, there were "duty catalogues" whose content was the relationships between spouses, parents and children, friends and relatives, slaves and slave owners (Weidinger, *Die Haustafeln*, pp. 23-27). His investigation of the schema of the house catalogue in the philosophy of Hellenism (pp. 27-50) led him to the conclusion that, with the house catalogue, a piece of Greek popular ethics was at hand that, by way of Stoic propaganda, was continuously urged, and thus survived.

This thesis has found wide recognition, and has been expressly discussed. (For the history of the investigation, see AB 34B, "Excursus: *Haustefeln*," pp. 462-475.) D. Lührmann ("Wo man nicht mehr Sklave oder Freier ist," pp. 53-83; see also Lührmann, "Neutestamentliche Haustafeln und antike Ökonomie," pp. 83-97) has indicated a major flaw, consisting in the fact that the Dibelius-Weidinger hypothesis is unable to explain the triple group women-children-slaves, and the reciprocity of the admonitions, from a unitary tradition, any more than this is possible on the basis of the Hellenistic catalogues of duties.

As J. E. Crouch *(Colossian Haustafel)* has acknowledged but a single piece of evidence from the source material brought forward by Weidinger (Seneca, *Ep.* 94), so for Lührmann precisely this evidence plays a salient role. This is not isolated testimony, holds Lührmann; rather it belongs to the entirely different tradition of the writings "on the economy." These writings deal with the art of household administration. "On the economy" indeed refers, as in Seneca, *Ep.* 94.1, to that part of philosophy "that gives special prescriptions for each life role: . . . it communicates to the husband how he is to behave vis-à-vis his wife, to the father, how he should rear his children, to the lord how he should rule his slaves" (Lührman, "Neutestamentliche Haustafeln und antike Ökonomie," p. 85; as other important texts, this author cites Aristotle, *Pol.* 1; Ps.-Aristotle, *Oec.* 1; Philodemus of Gadara [ed. Jensen, 1906]; Hierokles, *Kleine Schriften* [Hildesheim: H. Dorrie, 1973], pp. 311-467). In terms of social history, the "writings on economy" lead, Lührmann holds, to "house" as a social and economic concept — in Greek *oikos/oikia*, Latin *familia*, Hebrew *beth*. Indeed, holds Crouch, "house," or "household," in this sense, is not just one more socioeconomic concept among many, but is "the elementary and economic form *simpliciter*, not only of antiquity, nor indeed of the New Testament, but presumably of all pre-industrial sedentary cultures" (Lührmann, "Neutestamentliche Haustafeln und antike Ökonomie," p. 87). Were we to set the house catalogues of Colossians and Ephesians in connection with these traditions, we should have the advantage of being able to explain both the triple schema (women/children/slaves) and the reciprocity of admonitions, on the basis of a unitary tradition. This arrangement, says Lührmann, leads to a new assessment of the New Testament house catalogues. *Pace* Dibelius and Weidinger, we should not have to assume a "bourgeoisization" of primitive Christianity. Rather, Lührmann goes on, they contain, since economy was a part of politics, a latent political reference (Lührmann, "Wo man nicht mehr Sklave oder Freier ist," pp. 79-80; K. Thraede, "Zum historischen Hintergrund der 'Hausafeln' des NT," pp. 359-368, has developed this approach; see also AB 34B, pp. 462ff.).

The key thought of the *Haustafel* in Colossians is doing *everything* in Jesus' name (Col 3:17). Colossians 3:16 indicates ethical behavior within the community, and this range is broadly extended in 3:17ff. — a consequence of Colossians's dominating conception of the already present cosmic lordship of the Messiah (cf. Col 1:12ff.). That, to this end, besides behavior in the community (Col 3:16), with "everyday" living included, the form of a catalogue of ethical admonishments is selected addressing constitutive groupings for a *household*, is suggested by the meaning of "household" as the elementary and social form of economy. The "household" was *the* everyday living space of the members of the Christian community. The schema of the writings "on the economy" that designates the reciprocity of admonitions as one of its characteristics was akin to the postulates of the ethics developed in Colossians, which likewise stresses the "social" element (see Col 3:11). The context of the house tables in Colossians describes an ethics altogether orientated to the Messiah, and brings this to expression through the picture of the putting on of the "new person," by which the Messiah may actually be meant. Under the characteristics of this "new person" are, e.g., love, humility, and meekness (Col 3:12), which, it strikes one, are qualities of God or the Messiah. The demand is for manners of behavior that stand in relation to the characteristics of the "new person" (and thereby of the Messiah) that were presented previously. From the "revealed mystery" (Col 1:26), it is specified how Christians' "new" conduct ought to look. This occurs inasmuch as altogether well known concepts like "obey," "be subordinate," and "to love" are fulfilled in their content by the Messiah and his actions.

As the house tables are addressed to members of the ancient household, here slaves are addressed, but not slaves on the plantations, in the work in the mountains, or in the mines. The mere fact of the presence of these admonitions shows that the author does not mean to attack the institution of slavery. For the author of Colossians, the institution of slavery was no very great problem. It goes without saying, then, that what it means to have put on the "new person" (cf. esp. 3:11) can become evident in the relation of slave to lord or lord to slave. That where this new person is put on there is neither slave nor free, then, does not mean for the author of Colossians the abolition of slavery, but is for him the demand so to shape dealings with each other that it becomes clear that the Messiah takes slaves as well as lords into his service, in order to proclaim that he, the Messiah, is *the Lord* over all things. (Cf. also 1 Cor 7:22: "For the slave who has been called is a freed person in the Lord, just as the free one who is called is a slave in Christ.")

The striking fact that women are admonished with regard to their husbands, children with regard to their parents, and slaves with regard to their lords, with a disequilibrium of detail in the admonition to slaves, becomes more understandable if we keep in mind the situation of slaves who had left the religion of their lords and become Christians. Thus the Christian community is exonerated of the reproach of inciting disobedience, and disturbing the order of the households in question. D. L. Balch, in his *Let Wives Be Submissive,* has shown that there were stereotyped Roman reproaches against foreign worship to the effect that they destroyed the order ("harmony") of the "households," which in turn were regarded as a prerequisite for a civic order. In the face of such a wholesale imputation, the Christian community was obviously keen to emphasize that it had no desire to set slaves against their lords (or incite wives against their husbands and [adult] children against their parents).

The house table required of slaves not to refuse obedience to the Messiah, and to be ready even to suffer injustice. Conversely, lords are admonished, "Give [your] slaves what is right and fair. After all, you know that you, too, have a Lord, in heaven." E. Lohse (p. 231) indicates that this was a constant thought in popular philosophical instruction, and that therefore everyone knew what was to be understood under these concepts as a norm of moral conduct. To be sure, the indication that the *lords,* too, have a Lord in heaven is scarcely a mere reminder that they must one day give an account of their behavior to their heavenly Lord. The admonitions to slaves containing the statement to the lords that they too have a Lord, are probably underscoring that the lords, too, are "slaves." Paul expressly writes in 1 Cor 7:22: "Whoever is called as a free person is a slave of Christ." But then account will have to be taken of the fact that here the behavior of the *Lord* Christ with his slaves ought to be taken as a model for the behavior of earthly lords with their slaves (cf. Matt 18:21-35). However, clear statements formulating this thought in the behavioral instructions to the "lords" are lacking. The admonition to slaveholders remains extremely terse. Consequences to be drawn from the details of the house tables are left to them, as Paul, too, leaves it to Philemon to translate his "general" admonishments into concrete conduct where Onesimus is concerned.

VERSE 18

If he has wronged you in any way or owes you anything, charge this to my account.

The conditional sentence beginning here may be hypothetical. The conjunction *ei* (if) does not necessarily introduce an established fact, but can altogether readily describe a simple possibility that is not fixed as a reality. (For this use of *ei,* cf. Gal 1:6ff.; 2:18, 21.)

Paul does not further explain what he is referring to. (1) Has Onesimus stolen from his master, and fled with gold coins and/or jewelry? (Cf. LCL, *Select Papyri,* vol. 2, no. 234, pp. 137-138, cited in "Social Background," Annotation 5, p. 87.) (2) Or is Paul referring to the damages that Philemon has suffered through the loss of the work of this former slave? (3) Or does Paul possibly mean a debt that Onesimus had once brought into debtors' servitude and was to "work off"?

For possibility 1 there is no further evidence in the letter. This possibility remains hypothetical, and supposes Onesimus to be a thief. *Adikeō* (to "wrong" someone) and *opheileō* (to "owe" someone something) are not euphemisms for to "steal" (cf. H. A. W. Meyer, p. 340). Nor does the fact that we have a double usage here, "wrong . . . owe," likely justify P. Stuhlmacher's assumption (p. 49) that Onesimus has damaged his master in his escape not only by depriving him of himself, but by stealing money (?). The redoubling can just as well emphasize that Paul means this assertion with complete earnestness.

Solution 2 would be ruled out only if, with Winter, we deny Onesimus to be a fugitive slave — scarcely a likely solution. Winter indicates: "Although this letter consists of a mere twenty-five verses, it exhibits the form of a Pauline epistle precisely." To be sure, despite their function of thanksgiving, verses 4-7 present no indication to support the "runaway slave hypothesis" ("Paul's Letter to Philemon," p. 3). Even prescinding from the fact that the entire expression of gratitude can be interpreted as a description of Paul's expectation that Philemon will receive the fugitive slave in friendly fashion (and even send him back to Paul), Winter's presentation of Philem 11 is scarcely convincing. She interprets verse 11 ("He has been useless to you, but now he is useful to you and especially to me") as a simple play on words, and it "need not function literally outside the word play" (p. 4). Of course, that Onesimus was sent to an imprisoned Paul, with gifts from the community of Colossae, as Winter thinks, is improbable on the basis of the clear assertions in verses 9-10, according to which Onesimus only through Paul became a Christian and therefore is designated by him as "useful" (see further, the presentation on vv. 10-11).

The most far-reaching consequences for the interpretation of Philemon are of course contained in solution 3 above. If Paul is referring to "damages" incurred by Philemon that Onesimus had brought into (debtors') slavery, then what we have could be an indirect introduction to Paul's ransom of the slave and demand for his manumission.

With such indirect demand, it would have to be assumed that it was compelling. Otherwise, further grounds would have been necessary. Then, of course, it would have to be supposed that Philemon was a Jew. Only a Jewish slaveholder was compelled, by the law of God, to free a debt slave "as soon as the slave's relatives or the slave in person paid for his or her value or covered the not yet amortized debt." A non-Jewish slaveholder, by contrast, could not be compelled to accept such payment and to free the slave in question (see "Social Background," sec. VIII.D, pp. 72-78).

Thus, this solution presumes two hypothetical assumptions, and would have required that Paul expressly demanded Onesimus's manumission some-where in the letter, which is not the case. This solution is not likely to be the correct one. Also, it would have been expected that Paul had specified not only the amount of the debt but also the amount of the selling price of the slave.

Charge this to my account. The usual form of the Greek verb applied here is *ellogei,* from *ellogeō.* Paul applies the less current form *elloga,* from *ellogaō.* Some textual critics have exchanged this form for the more common one.

The verb is a *terminus technicus,* with the denotation, "to take into ac-count." (See proofs in E. Lohse, p. 284 n. 2.) See further the presentation of the following verse.

VERSE 19

With my own hand I, Paul, write this. I myself shall pay up — not to mention your own debt to me: your total self.

With my own hand I, Paul, write this (lit. "I wrote . . ."). The aorist used here, *egrapsa* (I wrote), is the "epistolary" aorist. The writer mentally shifts to the sit-uation of the addressee and thinks of the writing being done as already com-plete and now sent and received.

As we have no original manuscript of the New Testament letters, it is dif-ficult, if not impossible, to decide whether Paul has written with his own hand only verse 19a, or verses 19-25, or indeed the entire letter. O. Roller (*Das Formular der paulinischen Briefe,* p. 592) represents the last opinion, and P. Stuhlmacher (p. 50) has embraced it as well. Roller and Stuhlmacher point to the wording of verse 19, which contains more than what we usually have with Paul, who ordinarily only signs off with a greeting in his own hand appended to the dictation, and therefore regard it as likely that Paul has written the whole letter in his own hand. Granted, we find this autograph closing greeting in the surely authentic Pauline letters only in First Corinthians (16:21). In the letters whose Pauline authenticity is contested, it occurs in Col 4:18 and 2 Thess 3:17. We must also notice that the occasion of the mention of the autograph hand-writing is the special juridical form of the declaration in verse 19.

The answer to this problem will remain hypothetical, and will contribute little to a better understanding of the letter. What is decisive is that Paul in any case has written verse 19a with his own hand and expressly emphasizes this. Thereby the statement in verse 18 ("Charge this to me") becomes legally bind-ing.

The "receipt" issued by Paul in this place in the letter to Philemon, and provided with his signature, is called in Greek a *cheirographon. Cheirographa* were issued by debtors themselves, on their own initiative, without the collaboration of a notary, and personally signed. Should the debtor be unable to write, and a representative undertook the signature, this was expressly noted. (See A. Deissmann, *Licht vom Osten*, p. 281, and AB 34B, "Excursus: The 'Bill of Indictment' against Us," pp. 369-372.) In Col 2:14 as well, the concept *cheirographon* occurs, although not in this specific juridical meaning.

With this "receipt," Philemon could have required damages of Paul in the courts (cf. P. Lampe, "Keine 'Sklavenflucht' des Onesimus," pp. 136-137). The fact that Paul does not hold a simple promise before the house community as adequate, but chooses a legally binding form, may be an indirect but clear indication of the consequences for Paul in case Philemon fails to grant the apostle's "request" to receive Onesimus as a beloved brother. In the Pauline communities, the principle obtains not to bring conflicts "among siblings" before secular courts (1 Cor 6:1ff.). So, does Paul wish to indicate here that he will treat Philemon as an unbeliever, in case the latter fails to receive his onetime slave as a sibling?

I myself shall pay up. The Greek verb *apotinō* occurs in the New Testament only in this locus. It has the meanings "to pay," "to pay in full," and "to pay a penalty," as well as "to reconcile" and "to revenge." The word is a juristic *terminus technicus* for the payment of monetary penalties or damages. Lohse (p. 283 n. 4) adduces, as an example of this usage, a contract for an apprenticeship (P. Oxyrh. 2, 24-28) in which it is established that the father of the apprentice is liable for one silver drachma in damages *(apotinō)* for each day that the latter is absent from work.

Not to mention your own debt to me: your total self (lit. "not to tell you that also you owe me yourself"). Were verse 19b immediately attached to verse 18, the translation would be indicated, "Credit this to me, (19) not to tell you that you owe. . . ." Analogously, the expression "not to mention" *(hina mē legō)* in 2 Cor 9:4 translates, "lest we — not to mention you [pl.] — be shamed." Paul would then have sought to make it clear that the obligation of his debt, and his intervention on behalf of Onesimus, have been meant, as far as financial terms are concerned, purely rhetorically (cf. BDR, 495.3 n. 4).

The insertion, verse 19a, "I, Paul, write this," contradicts, it is true, this interpretation. It would be superfluous in this case. And too, the "separation" of the expression "not to mention" from verse 18 as occasioned by this insertion renders the interpretation above rather improbable.

The style-form introduced by the words *hina mē legō* (". . . not to mention . . .") is called *paralepsis*, "preterition." "The speaker asserts that he or she is passing over something that is actually mentioned" (BDR, 495.3). Thereby the apparently incidental element is specially emphasized.

Once more Paul uses a verb, *prosopheilō*, that has a technical fiscal, juridical meaning. It not only designates personal obligation, but is a technical term for a reciprocal, legal, financial obligation (see the evidence from the papyri in Lohse, p. 284 n. 8). While the root *opheilō* is used thirty-eight times in the New Testament (see AB 34A, pp. 631-632), the composite, *pros-opheilō*, occurs only here.

Paul is obviously unwilling to abandon the plane of legal obligation, although the statement that now follows is scarcely any basis for suit in a secular court. In this fashion Paul lends emphasis to these assertions. Elsewhere as well, Paul uses altogether juridical concepts in ecclesial space, borrowed from the area of "private property" (cf. esp. Rom 1:14; 15:26ff.).

But what does he mean here? He gives no explicit indication how Philemon has been bound by debt vis-à-vis himself.

Whether Paul has saved Philemon's life or his honor; whether he has hidden him from pursuers; whether he has helped him in some extreme need, perhaps by standing his bail bond; or whether Paul has proclaimed the gospel to him so that he came to faith in Christ — all these open questions can have only speculative answers. Since Paul can presume that Onesimus knows what he, the apostle, is referring to, no conclusions can be deduced from the general character of the statement.

But at all events, this reference seems to indicate that Paul and Philemon have met personally. In that case, it can at least be maintained with some degree of probability that Paul has brought Philemon to a personal appreciation of the gospel. Of course, Paul refers to a special circumstance. The preaching of the gospel alone can scarcely be meant, since then the plurality of the members of the communities founded by Paul would be in the same obligation to Paul as Philemon. Presumably, therefore, Paul is reminding Philemon of some special effort in his behalf, perhaps indeed that he has baptized him, which would have been unusual (cf. 1 Cor 1:16-17). As we have already said, however, a sure answer to the question is not possible.

The words "You owe me yourself" could be bringing to expression that Paul regards Philemon as his debt slave. Against this background, then, his "request" would be interpreted: Philemon should send Onesimus back to Paul in order that he, instead of his master, should serve Paul (v. 13). In Asia Minor, at the time of Paul, it was possible for a slave to substitute for someone else, so that the latter would go free.

Onesimus, however, is now identified by Paul expressly not as his slave, but as his child. Indeed, nowhere does Paul call any one of his coworkers *doulos mou* ("my slave"). But he does speak of those who accompany him as "serving" him (see, e.g., Phil 2:30). In this connection it is to be observed that, for Paul, to "serve him" and to "serve the gospel" have the same denotation (see above, pp. 372-373, and esp. the excursus "Service according to Paul," pp. 373-374).

Provided that Paul is alluding to Philemon's having become acquainted with the gospel through Paul, and having been baptized by the apostle, Paul is not using, with the words "You owe me yourself," the slave-master metaphor but is referring to the relationship of child and father. Not only does Plato (*Laws* 717b) stand for the principle that all persons are *owed* to their procreator, but in the New Testament as well, the conceptualization is represented as "going without saying that a son serves a father" (see esp. Luke 15:11ff.). Paul calls the Christians in the communities founded by him "his children" (cf. 1 Cor 4:14; Gal 4:19). Likewise he calls close collaborators son or child (1 Cor 4:17; cf. 1 Tim 1:2, 18; 2 Tim 1:2; 2:1; Titus 1:4).

Thereby, *for one thing*, the apostle's special status among his collaborators is brought to expression. Paul *sends* his coworkers to execute tasks in communities that he is not in a position to fulfill at the time, or to keep up contact during times of imprisonment (e.g., 1 Cor 4:17; Phil 2:19). Paul determines whether a collaborator is deserving or not to accompany him on a journey (Acts 15:37ff.). He announces his arrival, and warns that he will brook no arrogance (1 Cor 4:18). He demands imitation of *himself* (1 Cor 4:16). Granted, he expressly distinguishes his words from commands of the Lord — but then, at once, he indicates his own words as given by the Spirit, and equates them, for all practical purposes, with Jesus' commandments (1 Cor 7:40).

For another thing, it is made clear, with the father-child image, that the obedience demanded by Paul (in his special function among his coworkers) is fundamentally to be distinguished from that of a slave. "His children" obey of their own free will, for the sake of the gospel, so that in this respect "father" and "child" stand on the same level: both *serve* the gospel, and thereby the one Lord. The declaration in Phil 2:22 illustrates this by way of an example: "For as a child with his father, *he serves* the gospel *with me*." Paul has applied the crisp distinction implied here between slave and child in another connection in Gal 4:1-7. The same distinction is likewise clear in the parable, already mentioned, of the "prodigal son." In Luke 15:29 the elder son reproaches the father with having dealt with him as a "slave": "Behold, so many years I serve (*douleuō*) you" — and the father responds, "All that is mine is yours as well," thereby eviscerating the reproach, inasmuch as his reply distinguishes the service of a slave from the "service" of a son.

VERSE 20

Yes, brother, I myself like to profit from you in the Lord. Give my heart rest in Christ.

The Greek interjection *nai* (yes) has a strong reinforcing function. This is how it is used in oaths, as well. As in Matt 10:9; Luke 11:51; Phil 4:3; and Rev 14:13, the particle in our present verse introduces a clause that brings to a head what has previously been said (cf. also H. A. W. Meyer, p. 342). Both of Paul's requests, to keep Onesimus (v. 13) and/or to see him accepted by Philemon as a "beloved brother," receive emphasis. The demand here expressed would be fulfilled only with Onesimus's reception by Philemon as Paul wishes. Thus, Philemon's margin for maneuver, as expressed in verses 14-15, remains intact.

But here as well, Paul indicates his wish to see *both* requests fulfilled. *Onaimēn* (I like to profit) is a form of the verb *oninēmi,* which has the same root as the name Onesimus. The verb occurs only here in the New Testament. Paul would have had other words at his disposal in order to express the same content: thus it is probable that *oninēmi* has been consciously selected in order to refer to the name Onesimus, as well as to the wordplay in verse 11. Paul would "like" to profit by Philemon, as Philemon profits from Onesimus, the now "profitable" one.

The verb *oninēmi* not only denotes "to have profit," but also a consequence arising from this, namely, "to be glad" (see the evidence in LSLex). The formula shaped by this word, "I should like to be glad of you," is current outside the New Testament (see Stuhlmacher, p. 51). But as Paul has filed the concrete request with Philemon that he send Onesimus back to him, to Paul, and as this request, here once more, is taken for granted as accepted, the more concrete denotation, "to profit," has been selected in the translation. J. B. Lightfoot (p. 410) adduces a series of examples in which the verb is used for "filial offices." This denotation would have fit my recommendation for an interpretation of verse 19b, according to which a comparison of "owner/slave" is less likely: rather "parent/child" is the thought. To be sure, this meaning of *oninēmi* is dependent on the context. The verb is not an express *terminus technicus* for "filial offices."

Paul's striking "selfishness," expressed in this verse, is connected with his notion of the identity of his person with service to the gospel (see pp. 372-373). It was probably to forestall misunderstandings that he appends "in the Lord," which is translated in this connection as "in the Lord's service" (cf. v. 13).

Give my heart rest in Christ. In verse 12 Paul had called Onesimus not only his child, but also his "heart" *(ta ema splagchna).* Accordingly, *splagchna* could be understood as a synonym for Onesimus. Against the background of Old Testament expressions, according to which *anapauō* describes the Sabbath rest (see the excursus "Rest," pp. 297-301; cf. LXX Lev 25:2; Deut 5:14), this expression would then suggest the interpretation that a demand is placed on Philemon that he set Onesimus free. The basis for such an interpretation, of course, is too scant. For one thing, nowhere in the letter does Paul explicitly demand that Onesimus go free. For another, the expression at hand is too "formulaic" for such a specific and far-reaching interpretation to have to be stipulated. It is also questionable whether Gentile Christian Philemon would have understood such an explicit reference to an Old Testament theme. It is therefore to be assumed that Paul ranges himself in the series of the holy persons named in verse 7 who were edified by Philemon. Such refreshing edification is also awaited by Paul. See further our explanation of verse 7.

V. CONCLUSION (VV. 21-25)

1. Willing Obedience (v. 21)

VERSE 21

I am writing this to you out of full confidence in your obedience, knowing that you will do even more than I ask for.

The key word, "obedience," seems to indicate that Paul has now definitively abandoned the plane of "request" and returned to that of "command." P. Stuhlmacher, it is true, holds such a conclusion as inadmissible, since Paul argues from the commandment of love, and consequently, it is here *besought* that Philemon should see fit to comply with the will of God as rendered explicit in Christ (p. 52). Lohse (pp. 286-287) is of the same opinion — that the words of the apostle bind the addressee of the letter by the commandment of love. P. Ewald's translation (p. 282) is altogether different: "In confidence that you have an open ear." In this fashion, holds Ewald, the problem of a possible contradiction between verse 9 ("Although . . . I am . . . free to command, . . . for love's sake I rather make an appeal") and verse 21 is solved.

The translation proposed by Ewald is philologically justified (see below).

The noun *hypakoē* is very rare apart from biblical Greek, and occurs primarily in late sources (cf. MMLex, 650). Paul uses it eleven times; in the New Testament as a whole it occurs fifteen times. It can denote the obedience of a slave to an owner (Rom 6:16), or can even describe the entire work of Christ (Rom 5:19). As a description of the Christian's existence, *hypakoē* is equated in Rom 1:5; 16:26 with "faith." The genitive in the expression "obedience of faith" here is the so-called *genitivus epexegeticus*.

In the Septuagint, the substantive occurs only in 2 Sam 22:36, where God is the subject of the *hypakoē*.

An explanation of the range of meaning of this word will be further helped by an investigation of the verb *hypakouein*. This verb denotes the meanings "to give ear," "to hearken," "to give answer" when questioned, or indeed "to answer one's expectations." In a special sense, it can denote "to obey" on the part of dependents (examples in LSLex). Both the general and the special meaning are found in the Septuagint. Frequently the Hebrew verb *shm'* is translated by *hypakouō*. The word can mean "hear and obey," in which case a relationship of superordination and subordination is presupposed (e.g., Gen 41:40; 1 Macc 12:43; 2 Macc 7:30). But it also means simply "listen to," without the "listener's" being in a subordinate position (e.g., Gen 16:2; Prov 17:4; 29:12). In the book of Job, the verb preponderantly has the meaning of "to answer" (Job 5:1; 9:3; 14:15; etc.). Thus, *hypakouein* also means to "hear prayers" (Prov 15:29; 2 Macc 1:5). Further, the verb describes a person's correct attitude toward wisdom (e.g., Prov 1:24; 2:2). In the papyri, we likewise have examples of the special meaning "submit," "obey," as well as the general "to listen," "to give answer," "to answer" (see MMLex, 650).

Paul uses *hypakouō* not only in a more comprehensive meaning, in which it denotes the Christian's existence (Rom 6:16, 17; 10:16; Phil 2:12; cf. 2 Thess 1:8), but also the meaning "obediently follow" (Rom 6:12; cf. 2 Thess 3:14), or indeed "obey" (spoken of a slave: Rom 6:16). Granted, the verb is applied relatively seldom in the uncontested Pauline letters (four times in Romans, once in Philippians).

Now, what meaning is before us here?

Excursus: Freedom and Obedience

Neither the view that Paul is falling back into an imperative speech nor the choice of a general translation ("to have an open ear"), in order to solve a contradiction between verses 8-9 and 21, does justice to Paul's intent.

The following detailed considerations are intended to show that the frequently observed tension between verses 8 and 21 is far less serious than appears at first sight. The danger is great of an interpretation in terms of anthropological and theological presuppositions that are not those of Paul. (Cf. for the following, K. Berger, *Historische Psychologie des Neuen Testaments,* esp. pp. 83-105.)

The Old Testament knows no special concept for "freedom," "liberty." This does not mean, however, that Paul must necessarily have drawn his conceptualizations of "freedom" from other traditions. The thematics of freedom are handled extensively in the Old Testament. In the prologue to the Decalogue, the code "to lead out of the house of slavery" is applied. The freedom described can be characterized as follows. (Cf. esp. F. Crüsemann, *Bewahrung der Freiheit.*)

1. The giver of this freedom is Yahweh. Thus, the bond between Yahweh and the people is constitutive of the freedom described.
2. The freedom described has a real material and social foundation. It presupposes liberation from forced labor, and at the same time possession of one's own land, which provides security for one's existence.

3. The freedom code is applied as an introduction to a series of commandments. The thought is therefore presupposed that "freedom" obliges obedience to the one bestowing this freedom.

The description of the concept of freedom with the reference to the "leading out of Egypt" undergoes a new interpretation in later texts, ascribed to the "priestly" writings (cf. esp. F. Crüsemann, *Die Tora*). With these texts, one must begin with the fact that they did not arise before the time of the exile. The exile is presupposed in them. After the loss of the land, the goal of leading the people out of Egypt is the binding of this people to God. Separation from the land recedes into the background. This is made clear by declarations like, "I am YHWH, and I lead you out of the forced labor of Egypt, and redeem you from slavery, and lead you with outstretched arm and with great judgments. And I take you to me as a people, and I shall be to you a God, and you shall know that I am Yahweh, your God, who leads you out of the forced labor of Egypt" (Exod 6:6-7; cf. 29:45). In the priestly theology, the exodus is interpreted differently than in the preexilic literature. "Not the existence of free and incontestably possessed areas, nor the political liberty of the people is indicated with the Exodus, but separation from other peoples and from their mores, and thereby an ordering to God, nearness to God. This nearness is the *Gestalt* of the liberty for which the concept 'Exodus' stands" (Crüsemann, p. 253). Freedom is inconceivable otherwise than in its intimate connection to commandments through whose observance the close bond between YHWH and the people is preserved.

But this new interpretation of the exodus means no interiorization of freedom that no longer has any interest in political and social reality. Since YHWH is the giver of the land and has remained its proprietor, this land cannot be expropriated by others forever. But as possessor of the land, God can have sold it for a time (Lev 25:23). Thus the obligation arises to take steps for the return from the exile, including the creation of laws that take account of God's proximity and the status of the people. One is struck by the juridical considerations formulated in this connection, the legal rules regarding slavery. Not only the land but also the liberated people are God's possession. Through the leading out from Egypt, they have become "God's slaves." This juridical relationship serves to ground the prohibition of holding a fellow Israelite in lifelong slavery. The "enslavement" to YHWH, then, means not the transfer of certain relationships of lordship to the picture of God and the relationship with God, but a summons to an alteration in these relations of lordship. This is a "first, significant step toward the abolition of slavery altogether, and its transformation into wage-earning labor" (Crüsemann, p. 353).

Alongside the Old Testament tradition, which was doubtless known to Paul, the thematics of freedom were also extensively handled in other traditions of the Greek-speaking Diaspora of the time of Paul. Here the Stoa and Cynicism must be especially mentioned. S. Vollenweider observes: "With *eleutheria* [freedom, liberty], we have a concept before us that precisely in the first and second centuries A.D., as a watchword for political ideas or as a spiritual and religious salvation word, combines a multiplicity of elementary human hopes and ideas" (*Freiheit als neue Schöpfung*, p. 15). Epictetus defines freedom as follows (*Diss.* 4.1.1): "That one is free who lives as he will, who is not constrained or restrained, nor can be overcome — whose striving is unhindered, whose willing and unwilling ever reach their goal." Such freedom is possible, according to Epictetus, only when one's own will is in conformity with God's. And this in turn is possible only in the knowledge and acceptance of God's commands. Freedom can materialize only where the individual willingly attaches to the divine will. Even a slave can share in this liberty.

In the Stoa, as in the Old Testament traditional material, there is a close connection between freedom and the observance of a law.

Of course, law is not to be regarded as a homogeneous quantity. Especially with thinkers influenced by Cynic thought, a differentiation occurs in the concept of law. Thus, a Dio Chrysostom, for example (from Prusa in Bithynia, ca. 40-120 C.E.), distinguishes a written law that aims at the creation of fear from the true law of Zeus, inscribed in the soul. Freedom is then defined as freedom from the written, tyrannical law, and as willing concord with the law inscribed in the soul (*Or.* 76.3).

One of the great Jewish authors of Paul's time is Josephus. For him, the old Jewish insurrectionist against the Roman hegemony, reflecting the history of his people, "*Israel's freedom*" is "precisely a leading motif of his historical work" (Vollenweider, *Freiheit als neue Schöpfung,* p. 133). In the second book of the *Jewish War* (pp. 345ff.), Josephus records an address of Agrippa that reveals the elements of Josephus's conceptualization of freedom. In this address Agrippa urgently warns against starting any war in order to wrest liberation from the Roman hegemony by force. The strength and extent of the Roman territories are described. As there is no ally in view for a war of liberation, the only thing left is to rely on God's support (p. 390). But since in a war against the Romans, as experience shows, the commandments of God — namely, the Sabbath commandment — must be violated, one cannot count on divine assistance (p. 394). Thus, the conclusion is supported that the Roman lordship has only become possible through God's will. In this situation, revolution has nothing to do with love of freedom. "But who has once been defeated, and then becomes disloyal, is an arrogant slave, not a lover of liberty *(phileutheros)*" (p. 356).

The concept of freedom represented here (from which Josephus does not diverge) shows, first, that freedom is conceptualized against the background of foreign hegemony: freedom is freedom from the tyranny of the Romans. As has already been observed in the comparison of the Decalogue with the priestly (exilic) interpretation of the code for freedom, here too the weight of foreign lordship returns, and in the foreground we have the close connection between liberty and God's will as well as commandments. Josephus is clear (*Ant.* 4, pp. 177-193): he has Moses, in a farewell speech shortly before his death, admonish the people to observe the commandments that God has given through him. As until now God has procured through Moses that his people were able to do his will, so in the future it will be possible through the high priests, and leaders of the people, and those at the head of the tribes. In this connection we read: "Be sure, as well, that obedience is the best liberty."

For Josephus, no contradiction obtains between freedom and obedience to God's commands. Obedience also includes obedience to those who bear the responsibility for the observance of the divine law.

Now, what is the aspect of Paul's concepts on freedom with respect to these traditions? The apostle has developed no completely new concept of freedom. His concepts are inserted — where the relationship of freedom, obedience, and the will of God is concerned — into the framework of the available understanding of freedom.

For Paul, persons do not belong to themselves. They are *always* in a relationship of possession and rule. The Christians in Rome, formerly subjected to the power of death and sin (Rom 6:6ff.), become in their baptism *slaves* of God (Rom 6:22). In this connection freedom means being free *from* the power of sin, in order to be free *for* a service under the lordship of God. The experience of being enslaved to sin does not arouse in Paul a desire for liberty in the sense of absolute autonomy. He suffers from knowing the law (of God), wishing to do it, and yet not doing it. From this Paul draws the conclusion that he stands under a relationship of lordship that determines his activity without his being able to do anything against it (Rom 6:14-20). In the Letter to the Romans, Paul uses the image of a house in this connection ("the sin that *dwells* in me" [Rom 7:20]). In the background is the concept that the occupant of a house determines what happens there (cf. for this image, 1 Cor 3:16; 6:19; 2 Cor 6:16). Paul sees a solution for this dilemma only in an alteration of the relationship of lordship and possession. If the Holy Spirit, or else Christ, "dwells" in him, the discrepancy between willing and knowing the law and activity contrary to the law can be abolished. This abolition means, for Paul, freedom. So it is entirely possible for Paul to compare his liberation from the slavery of sin with the image of the purchase of a slave (by a good master from an evil one) (1 Cor 6:20).

The apostle's actual problem with slavery, then, lies in the question of who the lord of a slave is. When God is the "master," freedom, on the one hand, and lordship and obedience, on the other, are not basically exclusive alternatives. Against this background, we begin to understand that, for the apostle, the concepts of freedom and obedience were not mutually exclusive contradictions, even when Paul does not use the concepts of "liberty" and "obedience" in the same context. When it is a question of doing the *will of God,* and thereby God's command, the alleged tension between verses 8-9 and 21 is far less dramatic and meaningful than is sometimes assumed. When it comes to obedience to the will of God, there is no contradiction, in the apostle's understanding, if "liberated" persons command and obey one another.

Knowing that you will do even more than I ask for. This phrase has raised the question of whether Paul is enjoining Philemon, as the sibling of a returning slave, to set the latter free. J. B. Lightfoot observes that "slavery is never directly attacked as such" in Philemon, but that "principles are inculcated which must prove fatal to it" (p. 411). E. Lohmeyer explains that what the "more" is, is left to Philemon, but that this freedom is given a clear direction by what has already been said (pp. 191-192). According to Lohmeyer, Paul supports the concept that, since Onesimus is returning as a sibling, Philemon ought to follow out "the implications 'in life,' that is, to set him free" (p. 189). N. R. Petersen argues in the same way. His extensive sociological and exegetical investigations lead him to the conclusion that Paul is not attacking "the institution of slavery, nor even the participation of a believer in it. Rather he attacks only the participation in it of a believing master and his believing slave" (*Rediscovering Paul*, p. 289). For Petersen, it follows that Onesimus's "*being* a brother to Philemon means that he cannot also *be* a slave to Philemon in any domain" (p. 289), even outside the church.

For Dibelius and Greeven (p. 107), on the other hand, the juridical side is simply not under consideration, and thus there is no allusion to the slave's manumission (cf. Lohse, p. 287).

A decision among these opinions is difficult. Paul is nowhere explicit as to what *he* means by "doing more." At least three possibilities must be named in terms of a manumission, and they are very different. (See "Social Background," sec. VII, pp. 41-53.) (1) Philemon is to set Onesimus free for service to the gospel with Paul. (2) Philemon is not only to receive Onesimus in friendly fashion in his house and house community, but also to assign him an office in the community. (3) Paul wishes Philemon not only to send his slave back to him, Paul, but also to provide him with clothing, food, and money, in order to care for Onesimus in such a way as, e.g., the community in Philippi does for Paul.

The list could certainly be extended. As to the question of manumission, the present passage offers no further explanation. There is no further information given beyond the discussion of this problem in verses 12, 13, and 16. (See esp. the excursuses "Why No Plea for Manumission?" and "Does Paul Ask for Manumission?" pp. 369-370, 413-416.)

The most obvious thing seems to be to see verse 21b in connection with the request in verse 13. With gentle emphasis, the apostle once more recalls how very much he wishes that Onesimus *not only* be received by Philemon as a brother, but also be sent back to him, Paul.

P. Stuhlmacher seeks to learn — if Paul's opinion cannot be surely determined — how Philemon reacted to Paul's request, and thereby can have understood Paul. He adduces Col 4:7-9: "Tychicus will tell you all the news about me; he is a beloved brother, a faithful minister, and a fellow servant in the Lord. I have sent him to you for this very purpose, so that you may know how we are and that he may encourage your hearts; he is coming with Onesimus, the faithful and beloved brother, who is one of you. They will tell you about everything here."

Stuhlmacher proceeds on the supposition that, with these statements in Colossians, it is a matter of a personal tradition worked out by the author of the letter — that these verses cannot be a deutero-Pauline construct, and that they must have been composed *after* the Letter to Philemon. He concludes that Onesimus, in the time since the composition of the Letter to Philemon, must have been in Paul's service. "Philemon has therefore indeed done more than was immediately enjoined upon him. He has decided to set Onesimus free to serve Paul and the mission" (p. 54).

But if we assume that Colossians is an authentic Pauline letter, or if we embrace the view of E. Schweizer that Philemon is a composition of Timothy on Paul's commission, then the chronological position of Colossians after Philemon is not as certain as P. Stuhlmacher holds (p. 53 n. 137). The detailed list of greetings in Colossians, which *sets forth* the individual collaborators, then, indicates that Colossians was delivered to its addressees together with the Letter to Philemon, so that a detailed presentation of the greeters in Philemon would have been superfluous.

For the differences between the two lists of greetings in Colossians and Philemon, see below.

2. Paul's Visits and Personal Travel Plans

VERSE 22

One more thing: Get for me a guest room ready. Because all in your community pray for me, I hope that God will grant me to you as a present.

The expression "One more thing" is a rendering of the Greek adverb *hama*. It describes the simultaneity of various actions (e.g., Acts 27:40), indicates a secondary intent (Acts 24:26), or concretizes an antecedent statement (Col 4:3). In 1 Tim 5:13, in the framework of an enumeration, the adverb has the meaning of "besides."

An understanding of the meaning of *hama* in this passage as indicative of the (near) simultaneity of Onesimus's reception and the requested readying of the guest room is without foundation. Thus, neither is the conclusion imperative that Paul has been taken into custody in the vicinity of Colossae, and was therefore certainly not in Rome (cf., e.g., H. A. W. Meyer, p. 243).

The expression *hetoimaze xēnian* occurs outside the New Testament as well (Ps.-Clement, *Hom.* 12.2, cited by Stuhlmacher, p. 54). *Xēnian* means "shelter," "guest room," or in the abstract, "hospitable reception." It remains open whether Philemon is to prepare a guest room in his house or provide for Paul's maintenance with a fellow member of the house community.

The very fact that the matter of Philemon's fugitive slave Onesimus is dealt with not in a private letter to Philemon, but in an open letter to the community in Colossae, must have exerted a certain pressure on Philemon. Paul had made this matter a matter of the church, so that Philemon must respond for his good or bad behavior before the community. To boot, Paul now announces his visit. This is at least "gentle compulsion," as Lightfoot remarks (p. 411). According to Petersen, Paul's Letter to Philemon "makes authority an issue because it puts the congregation in the position of having to become conscious of the gap between local and translocal authority, if not ultimately to decide for one authority rather than the other." Through the announcement of his visit, "the issue of authority becomes immediately concrete for the congregation, . . . for his arrival will be the occasion for a showdown on the question of whose authority ultimately governs the social life of this church" (*Rediscovering Paul,* p. 300). The chopped, short imperative, "Get for me a guest room ready," underscores this connotation. But it is also to be observed that Paul stresses not his mistrust but his trust in Philemon, and is sure of the prayers of the community for his release. If Colossians is an authentic Pauline letter, then Paul's visit is not only to be seen against the background of Paul's return of the slave Onesimus, but his visit emphasizes his statements concerning the close connection he assumes between himself and the little community in Colossae (see esp. AB 34B, notes to 1:24ff.). What is only assumed in Colossians, is to be verified by a visit.

Because all in your community pray for me, I hope that God will grant me to you as a present. Paul counts on his release on grounds of the prayers of the community in Philemon's house. The conclusion from this statement that Paul's imprisonment is a loose one, or Rome is the place of his imprisonment (cf. Acts 28:17ff.), is not sufficiently well grounded. In the Letter to the Philippians, Paul realistically considers the possibility of a mortal outcome of his imprisonment, but at the same time relies on being released because of his necessary service among the Philippians (Phil 1:18-26).

The travel plans here laid out are difficult to reconcile with the information we have from the authentic Pauline letters and Acts. From Acts — prescinding from Paul's brief arrest in Philippi — only two imprisonments of the apostle are known, in Caesarea and in Rome. These occur after the composition of the Letter to the Romans, in which Paul announces that he is to come to Rome, thereupon to travel *westward,* to Spain (Rom 15:23-24: "But now, with no further place for me in these regions, I desire, as I have for many years, to come to you when I go to Spain"). If Philemon was written in Caesarea or Rome, then Paul has changed the plans he transmitted to the Romans, and has gone once more from Rome *eastward.* To whatever extent authentic information on Paul's activity is worked out in the Pastoral Letters, the probability of the correctness of such an assumption rises. In First Timothy and Titus, Paul's activity in Ephesus, in Macedonia, and on Crete is presupposed. The data in the Pastoral Letters thereby presuppose a situation to be dated at the earliest after the Roman imprisonment reported in Acts 28. These descriptions cannot be reconciled with the data from Acts and from the authentic Pauline letters (cf. W. G. Kümmel, *Einleitung in das Neue Testament* [Heidelberg: Quelle & Meyer, 1964], pp. 330ff.). However, the reliability of the data in the Pastoral Letters is uncertain and disputed.

At the same time, the possibility must be considered that Paul was arrested before his imprisonments in Caesarea and Rome, without concrete reports thereof existing and surviving (cf. 2 Cor 11:21ff.). Whether in 1 Cor 15:32 (". . . had I only with a view to this life *fought with wild animals at Ephesus*") Paul is making a direct reference to an arrest in Ephesus is uncertain. Probably this expression is a graphic expression for serious confrontations that brought the apostle into life-threatening circumstances. An arrest in this connection is conceivable. If Philemon was actually composed at Ephesus, there is no longer any necessity for postulating a change in the travel plans announced in the Letter to the Romans. To be sure, the Pauline letters contain no unambiguous indication of any rather long imprisonment at Ephesus, nor does Acts know of any such occurrence (see also "Literary, Biographical, and Contextual Issues," sec. V, pp. 121-128).

3. Greetings (vv. 23-24)

VERSES 23-24

Epaphras, my fellow prisoner in the Messiah Jesus [in Jesus' service], sends greetings to you, [as do] my fellow workers Mark, Aristarchus, Demas, and Luke.

All names in the list of greetings in the Letter to the Colossians (4:10ff.) occur as well in the list of greetings in Philemon. However, the name "Jesus the Just" is omitted in Philemon.
Lohse accepts a suggestion by E. Amling ("Eine Konjektur im Philemonbrief," pp. 261-262) to which he ascribes high probability: in the Greek, instead of reading the dative *Iēsou*, the nominative *Iēsous* is to be read, so that the following translation would be correct instead: "Greetings from Aristarchus, my fellow prisoner in the Messiah, Jesus, Mark. . . ." In this case the greeting list of Paul's collaborators would be fully identical in Colossians and Philemon. Granted, the "conjecture" in question is attested in no extant textual variant.

The order of the greeters is different in Colossians and Philemon. While in Colossians Aristarchus stands in first place, in Philemon Epaphras is named first. The grounds for this are to be sought in the fact that, in Philemon, Epaphras is Paul's "fellow prisoner," while in Colossians Aristarchus has this place. In both lists of greeters, Mark is named in the second place. In the last two places, in Philemon, Demas and Luke are listed, in Colossians Luke and Demas.

Compared with the greeting list of Colossians, that of Philemon is shorter. In Colossians more individual collaborators of Paul are presented. Only under the supposition that Colossians is a pseudo-Pauline letter is Lohse's position enlightening, that the short list in Philemon was later reworked by the author of Colossians and presented in the resulting form in order to "gain credit for his writing as a composition of the Apostle's" (p. 248). However, if we suppose that Colossians is an authentic Pauline letter, or at least was composed by a collaborator of the apostle in his commission as a companion of Paul (thus Schweizer, *Der Brief an die Kolosser,* pp. 20-28), then Philemon presupposes Colossians, and a more explicit presentation of persons named would have been superfluous, as it would already have been made in Colossians.

Epaphras is called a "fellow prisoner" *(syn-aichmalōtos). Aichmalōtos* originally meant "prisoner of war." It is not unusual for Paul to borrow concepts from the military area (cf., e.g., Philem 2; Phil 2:25).

The following interpretations are possible. (1) Epaphras was arrested like Paul and taken into custody. (2) Epaphras volunteered to share Paul's imprisonment. This would indicate fairly slack conditions of imprisonment, allowing collaborators of the apostle to take turns sharing his imprisonment with him. (3) As in Rom 16:7 the concept *synaichmalōtos* is used in a transferred sense; its meaning in Philemon, too, could be "prisoner in obedience to the Messiah Jesus." Of course, it is to be observed that the Romans passage may originally have belonged to another letter, which may very well have been composed during an imprisonment.

Since in Philem 1 *and* 23 Paul refers to his own imprisonment, interpretation 3 is rather improbable. If Colossians is an authentic letter of Paul, then at best interpretation 2 would be in order. In that case, Paul finds himself in fairly slack conditions of an investigative detention, as we have in Acts 28.

Epaphras is named elsewhere in the New Testament, in Col 1:7 and 4:12. The name is probably a shortened form of Epaphroditus. However, there is no very suggestive evidence for identifying Epaphras with that Epaphroditus from Philippi who is mentioned in Phil 2:25; 4:18. Information about Epaphras is spare. According to Col 4:11, he was of non-Jewish extraction. He belonged to the community at Colossae (Col 4:12), and brought to Paul the heartening reports of the Colossian Christians. He has not only proclaimed the gospel in his home city, but has also taken on responsibility for the communities in the cities of Laodicea and Hierapolis, Colossae's neighboring cities (Col 1:7; 4:13). He can be viewed as the missionary of Lykostales, in which these three cities lay.

According to Col 4:10, Mark was a cousin of Barnabas, and of Jewish origin (cf. Col 4:11). If this interpretation is correct, then he is fairly surely identical with the John Mark named in Acts 12:12, 25; 15:37, 39. According to the report in Acts, the Christians gathered in his mother's house, in Jerusalem. He himself was taken along by Paul and Barnabas from Jerusalem to Antioch and from there on Paul's "first missionary journey." But Mark left them in Pamphylia. For this reason Paul hesitated to take him once more as his companion on the "second missionary journey." This caused strife between Paul and Barnabas, which led to a separation of their ways. Mark and Barnabas sailed for Cyprus, and Paul selected Silas as his new companion. The discord between Paul and Mark seems to have been smoothed over by the time of the composition of Philemon.

Aristarchus is named only here and in Col 4:10 in the Pauline corpus. According to the latter passage, he was of Jewish extraction. Acts has him coming from Thessalonica, and accompanying Paul at the end of the "third missionary journey." Aristarchus was the companion of Paul at Ephesus, and was seized by the people incited by goldsmith Demetrius and dragged to the theater (Acts 19:29). In Acts 27:2 he was taken by the imprisoned Paul on his voyage to Rome.

Nor is a great deal known of Demas. His name occurs in Col 4:14 and 2 Tim 4:10 as well, therefore where Luke, too, is named. Second Timothy has it that Demas left Paul and "grew fond of the world."

In Col 4:14 Luke is presented as the "beloved physician." His name is used otherwise only in 2 Tim 4:11. If ecclesiastical tradition since the end of the second century is to be credited, Luke the physician, a companion of Paul, composed the Gospel of Luke and the Acts of the Apostles.

Paul calls the persons named his "collaborators," his "fellow workers" *(synergoi)*. For this concept see the notes to verse 1, pp. 251-253.

4. Benediction (v. 25)

VERSE 25

The grace of the Lord Jesus Christ be with the spirit of you all.

As also in his other letters — Romans is the only exception — Paul closes his writing with the wish for grace for his addressees. For the content see our presentation of verse 3.

The wording corresponds to Phil 4:23. In the other letters this wish for grace is formulated both more briefly and more at length. Some manuscripts read, "The grace of *our* Lord Jesus Christ." The possessive pronoun is also applied in 1 Thess 5:28. A subsequent interpolation of the pronoun in Philemon is more likely than its deletion.

Here, as also in Gal 6:18 and Phil 4:23, instead of the simple "with you," Paul writes "with your spirit." "Thereby he follows Jewish anthropology: when the latter speaks of the *pneuma* [spirit], it means the human being with will, capacity for sensitivity, and vital force, a being standing before God" (Stuhlmacher, p. 56).

The plural of the possessive pronoun makes clear once more that Paul has understood his letter not as a private one, but as one to the *community* in Colossae.

Bibliography

I. ANCIENT SOURCES

Aeschines (ca. 397-322 B.C.E.): *Oratio in Timarchum*

Antiphon (2nd half 5th cent. B.C.E.): *Orationes*

Apollodorus Comicus (4th/3rd cent. B.C.E.): *Fragmenta*

Appian (2nd cent. C.E.): *Romanes historiae*

Aristophanes (ca. 446-385 B.C.E.): *Ecclesiazusae*

Aristotle (384-322 B.C.E.): *Nicomachean Ethics; Politica; Rhetorica*

Ps.-Aristotle (2nd half 4th cent. B.C.E.): *Oeconomica*

Athenaeus (end 2nd cent. C.E.): *Deipnosophistae*

Bion (2nd cent. B.C.E.): *Fragmenta*

Chrysippus Stoicus (281-208 B.C.E.): *De concordia*

Chrysostom, John (354-407): *De statuis*

Cicero (106-43 B.C.E.): *De officiis; De provinciis consularibus; Paradoxa Stoicorum; Pro Rabirio; Perduellionis reo; Pro Valerio Flacco*

Clement of Alexandria (died before 215 C.E.): *Stromata*

Clement of Rome (ca. 96 C.E.): *1 Clement; To the Corinthians*

Columella (2nd half 1st cent. C.E.): *De re rustica*

Corpus iuris civilis (Codex Justinianus)

Dead Sea Scrolls: Covenant of Damascus

Delphi Inscriptiones (ca. 3rd cent. B.C.E.–3rd cent. C.E.), in Corpus "Inscriptiones Graecae," vol. 8 (Berlin: W. de Gruyter), and in Ecole française d'Athènes, Fouilles de Delphes III (Paris: Boccard, 1909ff.)

Ps.-Demosthenes (4th cent. B.C.E.): *Ad Neaeram*

Digesta Justiniani (Codex Justinianus), ed. P. Bonfante, C. Fedda, et al. (Milan: Formis Soc. Editr. Libreriae, 1908)

Dio Cassius (2nd-3rd cent. C.E.): *Historia Romana,* I-IV, ed. T. Mommsen and A. Watson (Philadelphia: University of Pennsylvania Press, 1985)

Dio Chrysostom (1st cent. C.E.): *Orationes*

Diodorus of Athens (4th cent. B.C.E.): *Periegeta*

Diodorus Siculus (1st cent. B.C.E.): *Bibliotheca historica*

Diogenes Laertius (3rd cent. C.E.): *De clarorum philosophorum vitis*

Dionysius of Halicarnassus (1st cent. B.C.E.): *Antiquitates Romanae*

Epictetus (ca. 50-130): *Dissertationes*

Epiorates (4th cent. B.C.E.)

Euripides (480-406 B.C.E.): *Helena, Hecuba, fragmenta, Supplices, fragmentum Alexandros*

Festus Grammaticus (2nd cent. C.E.): *Grammatica*

Gortyna, Law Code (between 550 and 400 B.C.E.); ed. A. C. Merriam in the *American Journal of Archaeology* 1 (1885): 324-350, and 2 (1886): 24-45

Gregory of Nazianzus (ca. 329-390): *Orationes*

Hecaton (Panaetius Rhodius): *De officiis*

Heraclitus Ponticus (4th cent. B.C.E.): *Athenaia*

Hermes, Shepherd of (1st half 2nd cent. C.E.): *Similitudes; Mandates*

Horace (65-8 B.C.E.): *Satires*

Ignatius (1st to early 2nd cent. C.E.): *Epistulae*

Isaeus (1st half 4th cent. B.C.E.): *Orationes*

Isocrates (436-338 B.C.E.): *Panegyricus; Epistulae; Areopagitica*

Josephus (ca. 37-97): *Antiquitates; Bellum Judaicum; Contra Apionem*

Julius Caesar (100-44 B.C.E.): *Bellum Civile*

Juvenal (ca. 58-138): *Satires*

Lactantius (3rd-4th cent. C.E.): *Divinae institutiones*

Livy (59 B.C.E.–17 C.E.): *Historia*

Macrobius (ca. 400 C.E.): *Saturnalia*

Menander (343-290 B.C.E.): *Fragmenta*

Musonius (1st cent. C.E.): *Epistulae,* in Stobaeus (5th cent. C.E.), *Eclogae*

Ovid (ca. 43 B.C.E.–17 C.E.): *Amores; Ars amandi*

Paris Papyri, in Notices et Extraits XVIII 2, ed. Brunet de Presle (Paris, 1865)

Pausanias (2nd half 2nd cent. C.E.): *Periegesis*

Philemon Comicus (ca. 4th-3rd cent. B.C.E.): *Athenaia, fragmenta*

Philo Judaeus (ca. 20 B.C.E.–50 C.E.): *Quod omnis probus liber sit; De decalogo; De specialibus legibus; De virtutibus; De vita contemplativa; Hypothetica*

Plato (ca. 428-348 B.C.E.): *Gorgias; Leges; Phaedo; Phaedros; Politeia (= Respublica); Politicus; Protagoras*

Plautus (ca. 251-184 B.C.E.): *Bacchides; Miles gloriosus*

Pliny the Younger (ca. 61-113): *Epistulae*

Plutarch (50-120): *Vitae: Coriolanus, Cato, Crassus*

Polybius (ca. 210-120 B.C.E.): *Historiae*

Poseidonius of Apamea (ca. 135-51 B.C.E.): *Historia*

Select Papyri, Loeb Classical Library (1956)

Seneca (ca. 4 B.C.E.–65 C.E.): *Epistulae morales; De ira; De clementia; De beneficiis; De constantia sapientis*

Sextus Empiricus (2nd cent. C.E.): *Adversus Grammaticos; Adversus Mathematicos; Parrhoneae hypotyposes*

Solon (ca. 640-560 B.C.E.): *Elegiae*

Sophocles (496-406 B.C.E.): *Hecuba, fragmenta*

Stobaeus (5th cent. C.E.): *Eclogae*

Strabo (63 B.C.E.–19 C.E.): *Geographia*

Suetonius (75-150): *De grammaticis et rhetoribus*

Sumerian Laws

Tacitus (ca. 50-120): *Annales*

Terence (ca. 190-159 B.C.E.): *Comoediae sex*

Tertullian (ca. 170-222): *De corona militum*

Thucydides (460-396 B.C.E.): *History of the Peloponnesian War*

Varro (1st cent. B.C.E.): *De re rustica*

Vettius Valens (2nd cent. C.E.)

Xenophon (ca. 436-354 B.C.E.): *Memorabilia Socratis; Oeconomicus; Hellenica* (= *Historia Graeca*)

Ps.-Xenophon (4th cent. B.C.E.): *Athenaeus*

II. TEXTS

1. Biblical Texts

Biblia Hebraica Stuttgartensia. Edited by K. Elliger and W. Rudolph, cooperantibus H. P. Rüger and J. Ziegler. Stuttgart: Deutsche Bibelstiftung, 1967-77.

Novum Testamentum Graece. Edited by K. Aland, M. Black, C. M. Martini, B. M. Metzger, A. Wikgren. 26th ed. Stuttgart: Deutsche Bibelstiftung, 1979.

Septuaginta, id est Vetus Testamentum graece iuxta LXX interpres. Edited by A. Rahlfs. Stuttgart: Deutsche Bibelgesellschaft, 1935.

Synopsis quattuor Evangeliorum, Locis parallelis evangeliorum apocryphorum et patrum adhibitis. Edited by K. Aland. 9th ed. Stuttgart: Deutsche Bibelstiftung, 1976.

2. Apocryphal Texts

Apokryphen und Pseudepigraphen des Alten Testaments, Die. In Verbindung mit Fachgenossen hg von E. Kautzsch. Vols. 1-2. Darmstadt: Wiss. Buchgesellschaft, 1975.

Hennecke, E. *Neutestamentliche Apokryphen in deutscher Übersetzung.* Vols. 1-2. Edited by W. Schneemelcher. 3rd ed. Tübingen: Mohr, 1959, 1964.

Testamenta XII Patriarcharum. Edited by M. de Jonge. Leiden: Brill, 1954.

3. Other Literature

Corpus reformatorum. Brunswick: Schwetschke, 1895-. Reprint, New York and London: Johnson; Frankfurt: Minerva, 1964.

Corpus scriptorum ecclesiasticorum Latinorum. Brunswicke: Schwetschke, 1895. Reprint, New York and London: Johnson; Frankfurt: Minerva, 1964. Cited as CSEL.

Cramer, J. A., ed. *Catenae Graecorum Patrum in Novum Testamentum,* VII. Oxford: Typographia Academia, 1844.

Danby, H. *Mishna.* Oxford: University Press, 1933.

Gnosis, Die. Vol. 1, *Zeugnisse der Kirchenväter.* Edited by C. Andresen. Zürich and Stuttgart: Artemis, 1969.

Josephus, Flavius. *De bello Judaico* (Der Jüdische Krieg). Gr.-dt. Vols. 1-3. Edited by O. Michel and O. Bauernfeind. Munich: Kösel, 1959ff.

Loeb Classical Library. Edited by E. H. Warmington. London: Heinemann; Cambridge: Harvard University Press.

Luther, Martin. *Werke.* Kritische Gesamtausgabe. Weimar, 1883ff.

Mackail, J. W. *Select Epigrams from the Greek Anthology.* London, New York, and Bombay: Longmans, Green, and Co., 1906.

Orphicorum Fragmenta. Collegit O. Kern. Berlin: Weidmann, 1822.

Patrologia Graeca. Edited by J.-P. Migne. Paris: Migne. Cited as MPG.

Patrologia Latina. Edited by J.-P. Migne. Paris: Migne. Cited as MPL.

Philo von Alexandria. *Opera quae supersunt.* Edited by L. Cohn and P. Wendland. Vols. 1-7. Berlin: De Gruyter, 1896-1930.

————. *Die Werke in deutscher Übersetzung.* Edited by L. Cohn, I. Heinemann, M. Adler, and W. Theiler. Vols. 1-7. Berlin: De Gruyter, 1909-64.

Sylloge Inscriptorum Graecorum. 3rd ed. Leipzig, 1915-24.

Texte aus Qumran, Die. Hebr.-dt. Edited by E. Lohse. 3rd ed. Darmstadt: Wiss. Buchgesellschaft, 1981.

Theodore of Mopsuestia. *Commentaries on the Pauline Epistles.* Edited by H. B. Swete. Vol. 2. Cambridge: University Press, 1882.

III. GENERAL REFERENCES

Aland, K., and B. Aland. *Der Text des Neuen Testaments.* Stuttgart: Deutsche Bibelgesellschaft, 1982.

Bauer, W. *Griechisch-Deutsches Wörterbuch zu den Schriften des Neuen Testaments und der übrigen urchristlichen Literatur.* Nachdruck d. 5. Aufl. Berlin: De Gruyter, 1971. Cited as Bauer-Lex.

Beyer, K. *Semitische Syntax im Neuen Testament.* Vol. 1, *Satzlehre Teil 1.* StUNT 1. Göttingen: Vandenhoeck & Ruprecht, 1962.

Blass, F., and A. Debrunner. *A Greek Grammar of the New Testament and Other Early Christian Literature.* Translation and revision of 9th-10th German edition by R. W. Funk. Chicago: University of Chicago Press, 1961. Cited as BDF.

————. *Grammatik des neutestamentlichen Griechisch.* Revised by F. Rehkopf. 14th ed. Göttingen: Vandenhoeck & Ruprecht, 1976. Cited as BDR.

Encyclopedia of Religion and Ethics. Edited by J. Hastings. 13 vols. New York: Scribner's, 1908-27.

Encyclopedic Dictionary of Roman Law. Philadelphia: Philosophical Society, 1953.

Gesenius, W., E. Kautzsch, and G. Bergsträsser. *Hebräische Grammatik.* Reprint of the 28th ed. Leipzig, 1909; Hildesheim: Olms, 1962. Cited as GK.

Gregory, C. R. *Textkritik des Neuen Testaments.* Vols. 1-3. Leipzig, 1900-1903.

Hatch, E., and H. A. Redpath. *A Concordance to the Septuagint and the Other Greek Versions of the Old Testament.* Vols. 1-3. Reprint from the edition of 1897. Graz: Akademische Druck- und Verlagsanstalt, 1975.

International Encyclopedia of the Social Sciences. New York: Macmillan and Free Press, 1968.

Interpreter's Dictionary of the Bible, The. 4 vols. Nashville: Abingdon, 1962. Cited as *IDB.*

Jenni, E., and C. Westermann, eds. *Theologisches Handwörterbuch zum Alten Testament.* Vols. 1-2. 2nd ed. Munich: Kaiser; Zürich: Theologischer Verlag, 1975. Cited as *THAT.*

Kaegi, A. *Kurzgefaßte griechische Schulgrammatik.* Berlin: Weidemann, 1966.

Kuhn, K. G. *Konkordanz zu den Qumrantexten.* Göttingen: Vandenhoeck & Ruprecht, 1960.

Kühner, R. *Ausführliche Grammatik der griechischen Sprache.* Vols. I.1 (1890) and I.2 (1892) revised by F. Blaß. Vols. II.1 (1898) and II.2 (1904) revised by B. Gerth. Hannover (and Leipzig): Hahn.

Lexikon zur politischen Sprache in Deutschland (= Geschichtliche Grundbegriffe I). Edited by O. Brunner et al. Stuttgart: Klett, 1974.

Liddell, H. G., and R. Scott. *A Greek-English Lexicon.* Reprint of the 9th ed. of 1940. Oxford: Clarendon, 1977. Cited as LSLex.

Mayer, G. *Index Philoneus.* Berlin: De Gruyter, 1974.

Metzger, B. M. *Der Text des Neuen Testaments.* From the English translation of W. Lohse. Stuttgart: Kohlhammer, 1966.

———. *The Text of the New Testament: Its Transmission, Corruption, and Restoration.* 3rd enlarged edition. New York: Oxford University Press, 1992.

Morgenthaler, R. *Statistik des neutestamentlichen Wortschatzes.* Zürich and Frankfurt: Gotthelf Verlag, 1958.

Moulton, J. H. *A Grammar of New Testament Greek.* Vol. 3, *Syntax,* by N. Turner. Edinburgh: Clark, 1963.

Moulton, J. H., and G. Milligan. *The Vocabulary of the Greek Testament.* Reprint of the 1930 edition. Grand Rapids: Eerdmans, 1980. Cited as MMLex.

Pauly-Wissowa. *Real-Enzyklopädie der classischen Altertumswissenschaft.* Edited by A. Pauly (1839ff.). Revised by G. von Wissowa et al. (1894ff.). 1st ser., 24 vols. (1894-1963). 2nd ser., 9 vols. (1914-67). 12 suppl. vols. (1903-70).

Preisigke, F., and E. Kießling. *Wörterbuch der griechischen Papyrusurkunden mit Einschluß der griechischen Inschriften, Aufschriften, Ostraka, Mumienschilder usw. aus Ägypten.* Vols. 1-3. Berlin: Selbstverlag d. Erben, 1925. Cited as PreisigkeLex.

Richardson, A. *A Theological Wordbook of the Bible.* 5th reprint ed. London: SCM, 1956.

Schwyzer, E. *Griechische Grammatik. Auf der Grundlage von K. Brugmanns Griechischer Grammatik.* Vols. 1-3. Munich: Beck, 1934ff.

Theological Dictionary of the New Testament. Translated and edited by G. W. Bromiley. Grand Rapids: Eerdmans, 1964-76. Cited as *TDNT.*

Theologisches Wörterbuch zum Neuen Testament. Edited by G. Kittel and G. Friedrich. Vols. 1-10. Stuttgart: Kohlhammer, 1933-79. Cited as *ThWNT.*

Vollständige Konkordanz zum Griechischen Neuen Testament. Unter Zugrundelegung aller modernen kritischen Textausgaben und des Textus receptus. Neu zusammengestellt unter d. Leitung v. K. Aland in Verb. mit H. Riesenfeld, H. U. Rosenbaum, C. Hannick. Vols. 1-2. Berlin: De Gruyter, 1980.

Wigram, G. V. *The Englishman's Hebrew and Chaldee Concordance of the Old Testament.* 5th ed. Grand Rapids: Zondervan, 1970.

IV. COMMENTARIES TO PHILEMON

Bengel, J. A. *Gnomon Novi Testmenti.* Tübingen: Schramm, 1742.

Beza, Theodore. *Annotationes majores in Novum Domini Nostri Jesu Christi Testamentum.* 1594.

Bieder, W. *Der Philemonbrief.* In *Prophezei.* Zürich: Zwingli Verlag, 1944.

Binder, H. *Der Brief des Paulus an Philemon.* Theologischer Handkommentar zum Neuen Testament 11/2. Berlin: Ev. Verlagsanstalt, 1990.

Bleek, F. *Dr. Friedrich Bleek's Vorlesung über die Briefe an dei Kolosser, den Philemon und an die Ephesier.* Edited by F. Nitzsch. Berlin, 1865.

Bruce, F. F. *The Epistles to the Colossians, to Philemon, and to the Ephesians.* NIC. Grand Rapids: Eerdmans, 1984.

Caird, G. B. *Paul's Letters from Prison.* Oxford: University Press, 1976.

Calvin, John. *Commentarius in epistolam ad Philemonem* (1551). CR 80. *Calvini opera,* 52.441-450.

Carson, H. M. *The Epistles of Paul to the Colossians and Philemon: An Introduction and Commentary.* Tyndale New Testament Commentaries. London: Tyndale Press, 1960; 5th ed., 1970.

Chrysostom, John. *In epistolam Philemonem commentarius.* MPG 62.701-720.

Collange, J.-F. *L'épitre de Saint Paul à Philemon.* Geneva: Labor et Fide, 1987.

Comblin, J. *Epistola aos Colossenses è épistola a Filemon.* Petropolis, Brazil: Vozes/Imprensa metodista/Editora sinodal, 1986.

Dibelius, M., and H. Greeven. *An die Kolosser, Epheser, an Philemon.* 3rd ed. HNT 12. Tübingen: Mohr, 1953.

Eisentraut, E. *Des heiligen Apostels Paulus Brief an Philemon.* Würzburg, 1928.

Erasmus. *Opera omnia VI.* Leiden, 1705 (= Hildesheim, 1962). Cols. 977-980 (= Basel: Froben, 1535, 702-704).

Ernst, J. *Die Briefe an die Philipper, an Philemon, an die Kolosser, an die Epheser.* RNT. Regensburg: Pustet, 1974.

Estius, W. *In omnes Divi Pauli apostoli epistolas,* pp. 880-886. Paris: Quesnel, 1652.

Ewald, P. *Die Briefe des Paulus an die Epheser, Kolosser und Philemon.* KNT 10. Leipzig: Deichert, 1905.

Flatt, J. F. von. *Vorlesungen über die Briefe Pauli an die Philipper, Kolosser, Thessalonischer und an Philemon.* Edited by C. F. Kling. Tübingen, 1829.

Friedrich, G. "Der Brief an Philemon." In *Die kleineren Briefe des Apostels Paulus,* edited by H. W. Beyer, P. Althaus, H. Conzelmann, G. Friedrich, and A. Oepke, pp. 188-196. 10th ed. NTD 8. Göttingen: Vandenhoeck & Ruprecht, 1965.

Grotius, Hugo. In *Annotationes in Novum Testamentum* II, pp. 779-796. Paris, 1646. Reedited, Paris, 1759, pp. 831-837.

Haupt, E. *Die Gefangenschaftsbriefe.* KEK VIII and IX. Abt. 8 bzw. 7 Aufl. Göttingen: Vandenhoeck & Ruprecht, 1902.

Hofmann, J. Ch. K. von. *Die Briefe Pauli an die Kolosser und an Philemon.* In *Die heilige Schrift neuen Testaments zusammenhängend untersucht,* IV, 2. Nördlingen, 1870.

Holtzmann, H. J. "Der Brief an Philemon, kritisch untersucht." *ZWTh* 16 (1873): 428-441.

Jerome. *Commentariorum in Epistolam ad Philemonem Liber Unus.* In MPL, 26.635-656.

Knox, J. *Philemon among the Letters of Paul.* Rev. ed. New York: Abingdon, 1959; originally published, 1935.

Lapide, C. a. *Commentaria in omnes Divi Pauli epistolas, Ultima Editio aucta et recognita,* pp. 816-830. Antwerp, 1656.

Le Seur, W. *Der Brief an die Epheser, Kolosser und an Philemon übersetzt und ausgelegt.* Bibelhilfe für die Gemeinde NT 10. Leipzig, 1936.

Lightfoot, J. B. *Saint Paul's Epistles to the Colossians and to Philemon.* London: Macmillan, 1875.

Lohmeyer, E. *Die Briefe an die Philipper, an die Kolosser und an Philemon.* 13th ed. KEK 9/11. Göttingen: Vandenhoeck & Ruprecht, 1964. Ergänzungsheft von W. Schmauch.

Lohse, E. *Die Briefe an die Kolosser und an Philemon.* KEK 9/2. Göttingen: Vandenhoeck & Ruprecht, 1968; 2nd ed., 1977. ET, Philadelphia: Fortress, 1971.

Luther, M. *Annotationes Lutheri in epistolam Pauli ad Philemonem.* 16-18 December 1527. WA, 25.69-78.

Manen, W. C. van. "The Epistle to Philemon." In *Encyclopedia Biblica.* New York, 1902.

Meyer, H. A. W. *Kritisch Exegetisches Handbuch über die Briefe Pauli an die Philipper, Kolosser und an Philemon.* Göttingen: Vandenhoeck & Ruprecht, 3rd ed., 1859; 4th ed., 1874.

Moule, C. F. D. *The Epistles of Paul the Apostle to the Colossians and to Philemon.* CGTC. Cambridge: University Press, 1968. Reprint of the edition of 1957.

Schlatter, A. "Der Brief an Philemon." In *Erläuterungen zum Neuen Testament* II, pp. 861-866. Stuttgart: Calwer, 1909.

Soden, H. von. *Die Briefe an die Kolosser, Epheser, Philemon; die Pastoralbriefe.* HC 3,1. Freiburg: Mohr, 1891.

Staab, K. *Die Gefangenschaftsbriefe.* 3rd ed. RNT 7. Regensburg: Pustet, 1959.

Strack, H., and P. Billerbeck. *Kommentar zum Neuen Testament. Aus Talmud und Midrasch.* Vol. 3. 7 unv. Aufl., pp. 625-631. Munich: Beck, 1979.

Stuhlmacher, Peter. *Der Brief an Philemon.* EKK 18. Zürich and Brunswick: Benziger Verlag; Neukirchen-Vluyn: Neukirchener Verlag, 1975; 3rd ed., 1989.

Suhl, Alfred. *Der Brief an Philemon.* Zürich: TVZ, 1981.

Theodore of Mopsuestia. *In epistolam B. Pauli ad Philemonem.* In *Theodori episcopi Mopsuesteni in epistolas B. Pauli commentarii II,* edited by H. B. Swete, pp. 258-285. Cambridge: University Press, 1882.

Thomas von Aquin. *Super Epistolas S. Pauli Lectura.* 8th ed. Rome, 1953.

Vincent, M. R. *The Epistles to the Philippians and to Philemon.* ICC. Edinburgh: Clark, 1897; 5th ed., 1955.

Wette, W. M. L. de. *Kurze Erklärung der Briefe an die Colosser, an Philemon, an die Ephesier und Philipper.* KEH II/4. Leipzig: Weidmann, 1847.

V. LITERATURE ON THE EPISTLE TO PHILEMON

Amling, E. "Eine Konjektur im Philemonbrief." *ZNW* 10 (1909): 261-262.

Barclay, J. M. G. "Paul, Philemon and the Dilemma of Christian Slave-Ownership." *NTS* 37 (1991): 161-186.

Couchout, P. L. "Le style rhythmé dans l'épître de Saint Paul à Philémon." *RHR* 96 (1927): 129-146.

Diem, H. "Onesimus — Bruder nach dem Fleisch und in dem Herrn. Die Botschaft des Apostels Paulus an Philemon in ihrer dauernden Aktualität." In *Evangelische Freiheit und kirchliche Ordnung. Freundesgabe anläßlich des 65. Geburtstages von Theodor Dipper,* edited by Landesbruderrat der Evang. Bekenntnisgemeinschaft in Württemberg, pp. 139-150. Stuttgart: Steinkopf, 1968.

Dormeyer, D. "Flucht, Bekehrung und Rückkehr des Sklaven Onesimus. Interaktionale Auslegung des Philemonbriefes." *Der Evangelische Erzieher* 35 (1983): 214-229.

Goodenough, E. R. "Paul and Onesimus." *HTR* 22 (1929): 181-183.

Greeven, H. "Prüfung der Thesen von J. Knox zum Philemonbrief." *ThLZ* 79 (1954): 373-378.

Harrison, P. N. "Onesimus and Philemon." *AThR* 32 (1950): 268-294.

Holtzmann, H. J. "Der Brief an den Philemon, kritisch untersucht." *ZWTh* 16 (1873): 428-441.

Knox, J. "Philemon and the Authenticity of Colossians." *JR* 18 (1938): 144-160.

Lampe, P. "Keine 'Sklavenflucht' des Onesimus." *ZNW* 76 (1985): 135-137.

Müller-Bardoff, J. "Philemonbrief." In *RGG,* 3rd ed., 5.331-332.

Mullins, T. Y. "The Thanksgiving of Philemon and Colossians." *NTS* 30 (1984): 288-293.

Petersen, N. R. *Rediscovering Paul: Philemon and the Sociology of Paul's Narrative World.* Philadelphia: Fortress, 1985.

Rapske, B. M. "The Prisoner Paul in the Eyes of Onesimus." *NTS* 37 (1991): 187-203.

Reid, J. "The Message of the Epistles: Philemon." *ExpT* 45 (1933/34): 164-168.

Riesenfeld, H. "Faith and Love Promoting Hope: An Interpretation of Philemon 6." In *Paul and Paulinism, FS C. K. Barrett,* edited by M. D. Hooker and S. G. Wilson, pp. 251-257. London: SPCK, 1982.

Schenk, W. "Der Brief des Paulus an Philemon in der neueren Forschung (1945-87)." In *Aufstieg und Niedergang der römischen Welt* II, *Der Prinzipat,* XXV 4, edited by W. Haase and H. Temporini, pp. 1339-1395. Berlin and New York: De Gruyter, 1987.

Soesillo, D. "The Story Line in Translating Philemon." *BT* 34 (1983): 424-426.

Spiegel, J. F. *Ich will Freiheit. Der Weg des Sklaven Onesimos.* Wuppertal: Oncken, 1992.

Suhl, A. "Der Philemonbrief als Beispiel paulinischer Paränese." *Kairos,* n.s., 15 (1973): 267-279.

White, L. "The Structural Analysis of Philemon." *SBL Seminar Papers* (1971), I, pp. 1-47.

Wickert, U. "Der Philemonbrief — Privatbrief oder apostolisches Schreiben?" *ZNW* 52 (1961): 230-238.

Winter, S. "Paul's Letter to Philemon." *NTS* 33 (1987): 1-15.

VI. OTHER LITERATURE

Aland, K. *Neutestamentliche Entwürfe.* Munich: Chr. Kaiser, 1979.

Ateck, Nain Stifan. *Justice and Only Justice.* Rev. ed. Grand Rapids: Eerdmans, 1989.

Balch, D. L. *Let Wives Be Submissive: The Domestic Code in I Peter.* SBL Monograph Series 26. 1981.

Baron, S. *A Social and Religious History of the Jews.* 2nd ed. New York: Columbia University Press, 1952.

Barrett, C. K. *The New Testament Background: Selected Documents.* London: SPCK, 1956.

Barrow, R. H. *Slavery in the Roman Empire.* London: Methuen & Co., 1928. Reprint, New York, 1968.

Bartchy, S. S. μᾶλλον χρῆσαι: First-Century Slavery and the Interpretation of 1 Cor 7:21. SBL Press, Diss. Series 11. Missoula, Mont., 1973. Cited as *Mallon Chresai.*

Barth, K. *Der Römerbrief.* 1st ed., Bern: Bäschlin, 1919. 2nd rev. ed., Munich: Kaiser, 1921.

———. *Church Dogmatics.* Edited by G. W. Bromiley and T. F. Torrance. Authorized translation. Edinburgh: Clark, 1936-77.

Barth, M. *Ephesians: Introduction, Translation, and Commentary.* AB 34 and 34A. Garden City, N.Y.: Doubleday, 1974.

Barth, M., and H. Blanke. *Colossians: A New Translation with Introduction and Commentary.* Translated by A. Beck. AB 34B. New York: Doubleday, 1994.

Baur, F. C. *Paul the Apostle.* London, 1875. German original: *Paulus der Apostel Jesu Christi.* Edited by E. Zeller. 2nd ed. 1867.

Beker, E. J., and J. M. Hasselaar. *Wegen en Kruispunten in de Dogmatiek,* IV. Kampen: Kok, 1987.

Bellen, H. "μᾶλλον χρῆσαι (1 Cor 7,21) — Verzicht auf Freilassung als asketische Leistung?" *JAC* 6 (1963): 177-180.

———. *Studien zur Sklavenflucht im römischen Kaiserreich.* Wiesbaden: Steiner, 1971.

Ben-Chorin, Schalom. *Paulus. Der Völkerapostel in jüdischer Sicht.* Munich: dtv, 1970.

Berger, A. Article on diverse aspects of slavery. In *Encyclopedic Dictionary of Roman Law.* Philadelphia: Philosophical Society, 1953.

Berger, K. *Historische Psychologie des Neuen Testaments.* SBS 146/147. Stuttgart: Verlag Katholisches Bibelwerk GmbH, 1991.

———. *Manna, Mehl und Sauerteig. Korn und Brot im Alltag der frühen Christen.* Stuttgart: Quell Verlag, 1993.

Betz, H. D. *A Commentary on Paul's Letter to the Galatians.* Philadelphia: Fortress, 1979.

Binder, H. *Der Glaube bei Paulus.* Berlin: Evangelische Verlagsanstalt, 1968.

Bjerkelund, C. J. *Parakalō. Form, Funktion und Sinn der parakalō- Sätze in den paulinischen Briefen.* BTN 1. Oslo, Bergen, and Tromsö: Universitetsforlaget, 1967.

Bloch, I. *Die Prostitution I.* Berlin, 1912.

Boff, Leonardo. *Church, Charisma, and Power: Liberation Theology and the Institutional Church.* Translated by John W. Diercksmeier. New York: Crossroad, 1985. Portuguese original: Petropolis, Brazil, 1981.

Bömer, F. *Untersuchungen über die Religion der Sklaven in Griechenland und Rom.* Vols. 1-4. Mainz: Verlag der Akademie d. Wiss. u.d. Lit., 1958-63.

Bonhoeffer, A. *Epiktet und das Neue Testament.* Giessen: Töpelmann, 1911.

Bonhoeffer, D. *Sanctorum Communio.* Vol. 1. Munich: Kaiser, 1986.

Borg, M. J. "A Renaissance in Jesus Studies." *Theology Today* 45 (1988): 280-292.

Bornkamm, G. *Paulus.* Stuttgart, Berlin, Cologne, and Mainz: Kohlhammer, 1969.

Brockmeyer, N. Review of *Studien zur Sklavenflucht,* by H. Bellen. *Gnomon* 46 (1974): 182-187.

———. *Antike Sklaverei.* Erträge der Forschung 116. Darmstadt: WBG, 1979.

Brunner, E. *The Misunderstanding of the Church.* London: Lutterworth Press, 1954.

Brutchel, J. *Die Maria-Marta-Erzählung.* BBB 64. Bonn: Hanstein, 1986.

Buber, M. *Two Types of Faith.* Translated by P. Goldhawk. New York: Harper, 1961.

Buckland, W. W. *The Roman Law of Slavery.* New York: Cambridge University Press, 1908. Reprint, 1979.

Bultmann, R. *Theology of the New Testament.* New York: Scribners, vol. 1, 1951; vol. 2, 1955.

Calvin, John. *Institutio Christianae Religionis.* 1559.

Carrington, P. *The Primitive Christian Catechism.* Cambridge: University Press, 1940.

Cascopino, L. *Daily Life in Ancient Rome.* New York: Bantam Books, 1971.

Cerfaux, L. *La théologie de l'Église suivant Saint Paul.* Paris: Du Cerf, 1965.

Cleage, A. B. *The Black Messiah.* New York: Sheed & Ward, 1968.

Conzelmann, H. *Der erste Briefe des Paulus an die Korinther.* KEK 5. 1969.

————. *An Outline of the Theology of the NT.* London: SCM, 1969.

Conzelmann, H., and A. Lindemann. *Arbeitsbuch zum Neuen Testament.* Tübingen: Mohr, 1975; 5th ed., 1980.

Crook, J. *Law and Life of Rome.* Ithaca, N.Y.: Cornell University Press, 1967.

Crouch, J. E. *The Origin and Intention of the Colossian Haustafel.* FRLANT 109. Göttingen: Vandenhoeck & Ruprecht, 1972.

Crüsemann, F. *Bewahrung der Freiheit. Das Thema des Dekalogs in sozialgeschichtlicher Perspektive.* Munich: Kaiser, 1983.

————. *Die Tora. Theologie und Sozialgeschichte des alttestamentlichen Gesetzes.* Munich: Kaiser, 1992.

Csányi, D. A. *Optima Pars.* Studia Monastica 2 (1960), pp. 5-78.

Cullmann, O. *Einheit durch Vielfalt: Grundlegung und Beitrag zur Diskussion über die Möglichkeiten ihrer Verwirklichung.* Tübingen: Mohr, 1986.

Dalman, G. *Die Worte Jesu.* Leipzig: Hinrichs, 1930.

Daube, D. "Redemption." In Daube, *The New Testament and Rabbinic Judaism.* London: Athlone Press, 1956.

Deissmann, A. *Licht vom Osten.* 4th ed. Tübingen: Mohr, 1923.

————. *Light from the Ancient East.* New York, 1927. Reprint, Grand Rapids: Baker, 1965.

————. *Paul.* Torchbook 15. New York: Harper, 1957; German original 1912; 2nd ed., 1927.

DeWitt, N. W. *Epicurus and His Philosophy and St. Paul and Epicurus.* Minneapolis: University of Minnesota Press, 1954.

Dibelius, M. "Die Isisweihe bei Apuleius." In Dibelius, *Botschaft und Geschichte,* pp. 30-79. Tübingen: Mohr, 1956.

Duff, A. M. *Freedmen in the Early Roman Empire.* 2nd ed. Cambridge: Heffer, 1928; reprint, 1958.

Eicher, P., ed. *Neue Summe Theologie.* Freiburg: Herder, 1989.

Eicher, P., and N. Mette, eds. *Auf der Seite der Unterdrückten. Die Theologie der Befreiung im Kontext Europas.* Düsseldorf: Patmos, 1989.

Eichholz, G. *Die Theologie des Paulus im Umriss.* Neukirchen: Neukirchener Verlag, 1972.

Elert, W. "Redemptio ab hostibus." *ThLZ* 72 (1947): 265-270.

Ellis, E. E. "Paul and His Co-Workers." In Ellis, *Prophecy and Hermeneutics in Early Christianity: New Testament Essays,* pp. 3-22. WUNT 18. Tübingen: Mohr, 1978.

Ellis, M. H. *Towards a Jewish Theology of Liberation.* Grand Rapids: Eerdmans, 1989.

Erikson, E. H. *Childhood and Society.* 2nd ed. New York: Norton, 1964.

Filson, F. V. "The Significance of the Early House Churches." *JBL* 58 (1939): 105-112.

Finley, M. I. "Slavery." In *International Encyclopedia of the Social Sciences,* 14.307-313. New York: Macmillan and Free Press, 1968.

————. *Ancient Slavery and Modern Ideology.* London: Chatto & Windus, 1980; German trans., *Die Sklaverei in der Antike.* Munich: Beck, 1981.

Finley, M. I., ed. *Slavery in Classical Antiquity.* Cambridge: Heffer, 1960.

Galenus (ca. 130-200 c.e.). In *Medicorum Graecorum opera,* edited by C. G. Kuhn. Leipzig: Cnoblochius, 1821-33.

Gayer, R. *Die Stellung der Sklaven in den Paulinischen Gemeinden und bei Paulus.* Bern and Frankfurt: P. Lang, 1976.

Gielen, M. "Zur Interpretation der paulinischen Formel *Hē kat' oikon ekklēsia.*" *ZNW* 77 (1986): 109-125.

Gnilka, J. *Der Kolosserbrief.* Freiburg: Herder, 1980.

Goodspeed, E. J. *New Solutions of New Testament Problems.* Chicago: University Press, 1927.

————. *The Meaning of Ephesians.* Chicago: University Press, 1933.

————. *The Key to Ephesians.* Chicago: University Press, 1956.

————. *Introduction to the New Testament.* Chicago: University Press, 1957.

Grant, R. M. *A Historical Introduction to the New Testament.* London: Collins, 1963.

Greeven, H. *Das Hauptproblem der Sozialethik in der neueren Stoa und im Urchristentum.* Ntl. Forschung 3. Reihe, Heft 4. Gütersloh: Bertelsmann, 1935.

————. "Die Sklavenfrage." In Greeven, *Das Hauptproblem der Sozialethik,* pp. 28-61. Gütersloh: Bertelsmann, 1935.

Gülzow, H. *Christentum und Sklaverei in den ersten drei Jahrhunderten.* Bonn: Habelt, 1969.

Guthrie, D. *New Testament Introduction.* 3rd ed. Leicester: Inter-Varsity Press, 1970.

Gutiérrez, G. *A Theology of Liberation, History, Politics, and Salvation.* Translated and edited by Sr. C. Inda and J. Eagleson. Rev. ed. with a new introduction. Maryknoll, N.Y.: Orbis Books, 1988; originally published, 1973.

Hadidian, D. Y., et al., eds. *Jesus and Man's Hope.* Vol. 2. Pittsburgh: Pittsburgh Theological Seminary, 1971.

Harnack, A. von. *Mission and Expansion of Christianity.* Vol. 1. 2nd ed. London: Williams & Norgate, 1908.

Headlam, A. C. *St. Paul and Christianity.* London: Murray, 1913.

Heinrich, P. "Das Sklavenrecht in Israel und im alten Orient." *Catholica* 11 (1934): 201-218, 267-290.

Hinkelammert, Fr. J. *The Ideological Weapons of Death: A Theological Critique of Capitalism.* Translated by Philip Berryman. Maryknoll, N.Y.: Orbis, 1986.

Hofius, O. *Anapausis.* WUNT 11. Tübingen: Mohr, 1970.

———. *Katapausis. Die Vorstellung vom endzeitlichen Ruheort.* WUNT 11. Tübingen: Mohr, 1970.

Holl, K. "Die Geschichte des Wortes Beruf." In Holl, *Gesammelte Aufsätze zur Kirchengeschichte,* 3.189-219. Tübingen: Mohr, 1928.

Jeremias, J. *The Prayers of Jesus.* SBT, 2nd ser., vol. 6. Naperville, Ill. Allenson, 1967.

———. *Jerusalem in the Time of Jesus.* Philadelphia: SCM, 1969.

Jewitt, R. *Paul's Anthropological Terms.* Leiden: Brill, 1971.

Johnson, A. *The One and the Many in the Israelite Conception of God.* Cardiff: Wales University Press, 1961.

Jülicher, A. *Einleitung.* 3rd-4th ed. Tübingen and Leipzig: Mohr, 1901.

Kairos Document. Rev. ed. Grand Rapids: Scotavil Publishers and Eerdmans, 1986.

Käsemann, E. *Das wandernde Gottesvolk.* Göttingen: Vandenhoeck, 1937.

———. *Essays on New Testament Questions Today.* Philadelphia: Fortress, 1960.

———. *Exegetische Versuche und Besinnungen.* Vols. 1-2. 6th ed. Göttingen: Vandenhoeck & Ruprecht, 1970. Cited as *EVB.*

———. "Grundsätzliches zur Interpretation von Römer 13." In *EVB,* 2.204-222.

Kehnscherper, G. *Die Stellung der Bibel und der alten christlichen Kirche zur Sklaverei.* Halle, 1957.

Kippenberg, H. G. *Die Entstehung der antiken Klassengesellschaft.* Frankfurt: Suhrkamp TB, Wiss. 130, 1977.

Klauck, H. J. *Hausgemeinde und Hauskirche im frühen Christentum.* SBS 103. Stuttgart: Katholisches Bibelwerk, 1981.

Klees, H. *Herren und Sklaven.* Wiesbaden: Steiner, 1975.

Koester, H. *Einführung in das Neue Testament.* Berlin and New York: De Gruyter, 1980.

Krauss, S. *Talmudische Archäologie,* pp. 83-111, 491-503. Leipzig: Fock, 1911.

Kuhn, H. G. "New Light on Temptation, Sin and Flesh in the NT." In *The Scrolls and the NT,* edited by K. Stendahl, pp. 94-113. New York: Harper & Brothers, 1957.

Kümmel, W. G., P. Feine, and J. Behm. *Introduction to the New Testament,* vol. 14. Rev. ed. translated by A. J. Mattill, Jr. Nashville and New York: Abingdon, 1966.

Lambertz, M. *Die griechischen Sklavennamen.* Vienna: M. Lambertz, 1907.

Lampe, P. *Die stadtrömischen Christen in den ersten beiden Jahrhunderten.* WUNT II:18. Tübingen: Mohr, 1987.

Lauffer, S. *Die Bergwerkssklaven von Laureion.* Vols. 1-2. Mainz: Verlag der Akademie der Wissenschaften u. Lit., 1955, 1957.

―――. "Die Sklaverei in der griechisch-römischen Welt." *Gymnasium* 68 (1961): 370-395.

Lemche, N. P. "The Manumission of Slaves — the Fallow Year — the Sabbath Year — the Yobel Year." *VetT* 24 (1976): 38-59.

Lietzmann, H. *An die Korinther, I und II.* 3rd ed. HNT 9. Tübingen: Mohr, 1931.

Longenecker, R. N. *Paul, Apostle of Liberty.* New York, Evanston, and London: Harper & Row, 1964.

Lührmann, D. "Wo man nicht mehr Sklave oder Freier ist. Überlegungen zur Struktur frühchristlicher Gemeinden." *WuD.NF* 13 (1975): 53-83.

―――. "Neutestamentliche Haustafeln und antike Ökonomie." *NTS* 27 (1981): 83-97.

Luther, M. WA *Deutsche Bibel,* vol. 7 (= E. Th. Bachmann, ed., *Luther's Works,* vol. 25. Philadelphia: Fortress, 1960).

―――. *In epistolam S. Pauli ad Galatas commentarius.* WA, 40 I and II.

―――. *WA Briefe,* vol. 6.

―――. "Von der Freiheit eines Christenmenschen." *WA,* 7.20-38.

Lyall, F. "Roman Law in the Writings of Paul — the Slaves and the Freemen." *NTS* 17 (1970): 73-79.

Manson, T. W. *The Servant Messiah.* Cambridge: University Press, 1953.

Marrow, S. B. "*Parrhēsia* in the New Testament." *CBQ* 44 (1982): 431-446.

Marxsen, W. *Einleitung in das Neue Testament.* Gütersloh: Mohr, 1963; 2nd ed., 1964.

Massingberde-Ford, J. *Revelation.* AB 38. New York: Doubleday, 1975.

Meeks, W. A. *The First Urban Christians.* New Haven: Yale University Press, 1983.

Mendelsohn, I. *Slavery in the Ancient Near East.* New York: Oxford University Press, 1949.

―――. "Slavery in the OT." In *IDB,* vol. 4 (1962), pp. 383-391.

Merk, O. *Handeln aus Glauben. Die Motivierungen der paulinischen Ethik.* MthSt 5. Marburg: Elwert, 1968.

Metzger, B. M. *The New Testament: Its Background, Growth, and Content.* New York and Nashville: Abingdon, 1965.

Meyer, E. *Geschichte des Altertums.* Vols. 3-4. Berlin and Stuttgart: Cotta; Darmstadt: WBG.

Michaelis, W. *Einleitung in das Neue Testament.* Bern: BEG Verlag, 1966.

Milton, J. *Paradise Lost.* Edited by A. W. Verity. 3rd ed. Cambridge: University Press.

Minear, P. S. "The Time of Hope in the NT." *ScotJT* 6 (1953): 337-361.

———. *Images of the Church in the New Testament.* Philadelphia: Westminster, 1960.

Moore, G. F. *Judaism in the First Century of the Christian Era.* Vol. 2. Cambridge: Harvard University Press, 1901; 7th ed., 1954, pp. 18-19, 135-138.

Moran, W. L. "The Ancient Near Eastern Background of the Love of God in Deuteronomy." *CBQ* 25 (1963): 77-87.

Morrow, G. R. *Plato's Law on Slavery in Its Relation to Greek Laws.* Urbana, Ill.: University Press, 1939.

Munck, J. *Paul and the Salvation of Mankind.* Richmond: John Knox, 1959.

Nilsson, M. P. *Geschichte der griechischen Religion.* Vol. 2. 2nd ed. Munich: Beck, 1974.

Norden, E. *Agnostos Theos. Untersuchungen zur Formengeschichte religiöser Rede.* Stuttgart: Teubner, 1913.

Nygren, A. *Agape and Eros.* Vols. 1-2. Swedish original 1930/36. Abbreviated English translation, London: SPCK, 1932/38/39. Reprint, Philadelphia: Westminster, 1953.

———. *Commentary on Romans.* Translated by Carl C. Rasmussen. Philadelphia: Muhlenberg, 1949; Swedish original 1944.

Ollrog, W. H. *Paulus und seine Mitarbeiter. Untersuchungen zur Theorie und Praxis der paulinischen Mission.* WMANT 50. Neukirchen-Vluyn: Neukirchener Verlag, 1979.

Overbeck, F. "Über das Verhältnis der alten Kirche zur Sklaverei im Römischen Reich." In Overbeck, *Studien zur Geschichte der alten Kirche,* pp. 158-230. Chemnitz: Schmeitzner, 1899.

Pauly-Wissowa. *Real-Enzyklopädie der classischen Altertumswissenschaft.* Edited by A. Pauly (1839ff.). Revised by G. von Wissowa et al. (1894ff.). 1st ser., 24 vols., 1894-1963. 2nd ser., 9 vols., 1914-67; 12 suppl. vols., 1903-70; vol. 7, pp. 95ff.; vol. 13, pp. 136ff.; suppl. vol. 6, pp. 194-1068.

Pedersen, J. *Israel.* London and Oxford: Oxford University Press; Copenhagen: Povl Branner, vols. 1-2, 1926; vols. 3-4, 1940. Esp. 2.500-501, 579, 583-584.

Phillips, J. B. *Letters to Young Churches.* New York: Macmillan, 1960.

Pierce, C. A. *Conscience in the New Testament: A Study of Syneidesis in the New Testament: In the Light of Its Sources, and with Particular Reference to St. Paul, with Some Observations regarding Its Pastoral Relevance Today.* London: SCM, 1955.

Pohlenz, M. "To Prepon." Nachrichten von der Gesellschaft der Wissenschaften in Goettingen, Phil.-Hist. Klasse I. Berlin: Weidmann, 1933.

Preiss, Th. *Life in Christ.* SBT 13. London: SCM, 1954.

Rädle, H. "Untersuchungen zum griechischen Freilassungswesen." Diss., Munich, 1968.

Ragaz, L. *Die Bibel — eine Deutung.* Vol. 6, pp. 86-95, esp. 92-93. Zürich: Diana-Verlag, n.d. (written between 1941 and 1943). Reprint, Fribourg and Lucerne: Edition Exodus, vol. 4, 1990.

Reformed Confessions of the Sixteenth Century. Translated by A. C. Cochrane. Philadelphia: Westminster, 1966.

Rengstorf, K. H. *"Doulos."* In *TDNT,* 2.261-280.

Richter, W. "Seneca und die Sklaven." *Gymnasium* 65 (1958): 196-218.

Robert, A., and A. Feuillet. *Introduction à la Bible,* II, *Nouveau Testament.* Tournai: Desclée, 1959. ET, *Introduction to the New Testament.* New York: Desclée, 1965.

Robinson, J. A. T. *Redating the New Testament.* London: SCM, 1976.

Robinson, T. A. "Grayston and Herdan's 'C' Quantity Formula and the Authorship of the Pastoral Epistles." *NTS* 30 (1984): 282-289a.

Roller, O. *Das Formular der paulinischen Briefe.* BWANT, ser. 4, vol. 6. 1933.

Roon, A. van. *The Authenticity of Ephesians.* NovT Suppl. 34. 1974.

Rostovzeff, M. I. *Gesellschaft und Wirtschaft im römischen Kaiserreich.* Vols. 1-2. Leipzig: Quelle u. Meyer, 1929.

———. *Gesellschafts- und Wirtschaftsgeschichte der hellenistischen Welt.* Vols. 1-2. 1942. Reprint, vols. 1-3, Darmstadt: WBG, 1955-56.

Safrai, S. "The Jewish People in the First Century." In *Compendium Rerum Judicarum ad Novum Testamentum I 1-2,* edited by M. de Jonge, S. Safrai, et al., 1.509-513, 2.624-630. Assen: van Gorcum, 1974, 1976.

Sampley, J. P. *Pauline Partnership in Christ.* Philadelphia: Fortress, 1980.

Schlier, H. "Vom Wesen der apostolischen Ermahnung." In Schlier, *Die Zeit der Kirche. Exegetische Aufsätze und Vorträge,* pp. 74-89. Freiburg: Herder, 1956.

Schmithals, W. *Die theologische Anthropologie des Paulus.* Stuttgart: Kohlhammer, Taschenbuch 1021, 1980.

Schrage, W. *The Ethics of the New Testament.* Edinburgh: Clark, 1987; Philadelphia: Fortress, 1988.

Schubert, P. *Form and Function of the Pauline Thanksgivings.* BZNW 20. 1939.

————. *NT Study and Theology.* Religion in Life 14. 1944/45.

Schulz, S. *Gott ist kein Sklavenhalter, Die Geschichte einer verspäteten Revolution.* Zürich and Hamburg: Flambert/Furche, 1972.

Schweitzer, A. *The Mysticism of Paul the Apostle.* New York: Holt, 1931.

————. *Die Mystik des Apostels Paulus.* Tübingen: Mohr, 1981. Reprint of 1st ed. of 1930.

Schweizer, E. *Neotestamentica.* Zürich: Zwingli-Verlag, 1963.

————. *Der Brief an die Kolosser.* 2nd ed. EKK 11. Zürich, Einsiedeln, and Cologne: Benziger; Neukirchen-Vluyn: Neukirchener Verlag, 1980.

Scott, C. A. A. *Living Issues in the NT.* Cambridge: University Press, 1933.

Seesemann, H. *Der Begriff [Koinonia] im Neuen Testament.* Gießen: Töpelmann, 1933.

Selwyn, E. G. *The First Epistle of St. Peter.* London: Macmillan, 1946.

Sevenster, J. N. *Paul and Seneca.* Leiden: Brill, 1961.

Sherwin-White, A. N. *Roman Society and Roman Law in the New Testament,* pp. 78-98. 3rd ed. Oxford: Clarendon, 1969.

Sloan, R. B., Jr. *Favorable Year of the Lord: A Study of Jubilary Theology in the Gospel of Luke.* Austin, Tex.: Schola, 1977.

Sohm, Rudolf. *Kirchenrecht. Die geschichtlichen Grundlagen.* Leipzig, 1892.

Sokolowski, F. "Fees and Taxes in Greek Cults." *HTR* 47 (1954): 153-164.

————. "The Real Meaning of Sacral Manumission." *HTR* 47 (1954): 173-181.

Spicq, C. *Agapē in the New Testament.* Translated by Marie Aquinas McNamara and Mary Honoria Richter. Vols. 1-3. St. Louis: Herder, 1963-66.

Steinmann, A. "Zur Geschichte der Auslegung von I.Kor 7:21." *Theolog. Revue* 16 (1917): 340-348.

Stendahl, K. *The Bible and the Role of Women.* Philadelphia: Fortress, 1966.

————. *Paul among Jews and Gentiles.* Philadelphia: Fortress, 1976.

Strack, H. L., and P. Billerbeck. *Kommentar zum Neuen Testament aus Talmud und Midrasch.* 6 vols. Munich: Beck, 1922-61. Cited as StB.

Theissen, G. "Soziale Schlichtung in der korinthischen Gemeinde." *ZNW* 65 (1974): 232-272.

————. "Soziologie der Jesusbewegung." *ThExH,* n.s., 194 (1977).

————. *Studien zur Soziologie des Urchristentums.* Tübingen: Mohr, 1979. ET, Edinburgh: Clark, 1990.

————. "Soziale Integration und sakramentales Handeln." In Theissen, *Studien zur Soziologie des Urchristentums,* pp. 290-317. WUNT 19. Tübingen: Mohr, 1983.

Thielicke, H. *Theologische Ethik* II. Tübingen: Mohr, 1955.

Thiessen, H. C. *Introduction to the New Testament.* 3rd ed. Downers Grove, Ill.: InterVarsity, 1970.

Thomas Aquinas. *Opera Omnia,* XXI. Paris: Vivès, 1876.

———. *Summa Theologica*, I, II 2. Paris: Lethie/Leux, 1926.

Thraede, K. "Zum historischen Hintergrund der 'Haustafeln' des NT." In *FS für B. Kötting, Pietas*, edited by E. Dassmann and K. Suso Frank, pp. 359-368. *JAC*, suppl. vol. 8. Münster: Aschendorff, 1980.

Trocmé, A. *Jesus and the Nonviolent Revolution*. Translated by M. H. Shank and M. E. Miller. Scottdale, Pa.: Herald, 1973.

Trummer, P. "Die Chance der Freiheit. Zur Interpretation des μᾶλλον χρῆσαι in 1 Kor 7,21." *Biblia* 56 (1975): 344-368.

Unnik, W. C. van. "Lob und Strafe durch die Obrigkeit. Hellenistisches zu Röm 13,3-4." In *Jesus und Paulus*, FS W. G. Kümmel, edited by E. E. Ellis and E. Grässer, 2nd ed., pp. 334-343. Göttingen: Vandenhoeck & Ruprecht, 1978.

Urbach, E. E. "The Laws regarding Slavery, as a Source for Social History of the Period of the Second Temple, the Mishnah and Talmud." In *Papers of the Institute of Jewish Studies London*, edited by J. G. Weiss, 1.1-94. Jerusalem: Magnes Press, 1964.

Vaux, R. de. *Ancient Israel, Its Life and Institutions*. Vol. 1, pp. 80-96. 2nd ed. New York: McGraw-Hill, 1965. French original, 1.125-140.

Vogt, J. *Sklaverei und Humanität*. Wiesbaden: Steiner, 1965.

———. "Zur Struktur der antiken Sklavenkriege." In *Sklaverei und Humanität*, pp. 20-60. Wiesbaden: Steiner, 1965.

———. *Ancient Slavery and the Ideal of Man*. Oxford: Blackwell, 1974.

Vollenweider, S. *Freiheit als neue Schöpfung. Eine Untersuchung zur Eleutheria bei Paulus und in seiner Umwelt*. FRLANT 147. Göttingen: Vandenhoeck & Ruprecht, 1989.

Waldstein, W. *Operae Libertorum. Untersuchungen zur Dienstpflicht freigelassener Sklaven*. Stuttgart: Steiner, 1986.

Wallon, H. *Histoire de l'esclavage dans l'antiquité*. Paris: Hachette, 1847, 2nd ed., 1879.

Weber, M. *The Protestant Ethic and the Spirit of Capitalism*. London: Allen & Unwin, 1930.

Weidinger, K. *Die Haustafeln. Ein Stück urchristlicher Paränese*. UNT 14. Leipzig: Hinrichs, 1928.

Weizsäcker, C. *Das Apostolische Zeitalter der christlichen Kirche*. Freiburg, 1886; 3rd ed., 1902.

Wendland, H. D. *Ethik den Neuen Testaments*. 3rd ed. NTD, suppl. vol. 4. Göttingen: Vandenhoeck & Ruprecht, 1978.

Wengst, K. "Versöhnung und Befreiung." *EvTh* 36 (1976): 14-26.

Westermann, C. *The Praise of God in the Psalms*. Richmond: John Knox, 1965.

Westermann, W. L. "Sklaverei." In *Realenzyklopädie*, edited by Pauly-Wissowa, suppl. vol. 6, pp. 894-1068. 1935.

———. "The Freedmen and the Slaves of God." *Proceedings of the American Philosophical Society* 92 (1948): 55-64.

———. *The Slave System of Greek and Roman Antiquity.* 3rd ed. Philadelphia: American Philosophical Society, 1964.

———. "Masters and Slaves." *Interp.* 27 (1973): 259-272.

Weth, R. "Diakonie am Wendepunkt." *EvTh* 36 (1976): 263-279.

Wiedemann, T. *Greek and Roman Slavery.* London: Croom Helm, 1981.

Wilckens, U. *Das Neue Testament.* 2nd ed. Gütersloh: Mohr, 1976.

Wilder, A. *Eschatology and Ethics.* 2nd ed. New York: Harper, 1950.

———. "Kerygma, Eschatology and Social Ethics." In *The Background of the New Testament and Its Eschatology,* edited by W. D. Davies and D. Daube, FS C. H. Dodd, pp. 509-539. Cambridge: University Press, 1956.

Wolf, E. *Rechtsgedanke und biblische Weisung.* Tübingen: Mohr, 1947.

Wolff, H. W. *Anthropologie des Alten Testaments.* 3rd ed. Munich: Kaiser, 1976.

Woodhouse, W. J. "Slavery." In *ERE,* vol. 11 (1920), pp. 612-618.

Yavetz, Z. *Slaves and Slavery in Ancient Rome.* New Brunswick, N.J.: Transaction, 1988.

Zahn, Th. *Sklaverei und Christentum (in) der alten Welt,* pp. 116-159. Heidelberg: 1879.

Zeitlin, S. "Slavery during the Second Commonwealth and the Tannaitic Period." *JQR* 53 (1962/63): 185-218.

Index of Modern Authors

Index of Subjects

new creation, 186, 334, 348, 421, 469
new order of life, 144, 199, 347
new person, 186-88, 397, 421, 479
Nicholas of Cusa, 149
noblesse oblige, 304
nonviolence, 210, 393
now, 347-49, 350

obedience, 72, 136, 153-57, 180, 253, 274,
  349-50, 359-60, 371, 377, 473; of faith,
  311, 487; and freedom, 488-91; voluntary, 155, 191, 378, 385-86
obligation, 313, 484
occupation and status, 195
Oecumenius, 290
"old man," 107, 305, 321-24
oneness, 180-81, 186-87
Onesimus:; as apostolic delegate, 136,
  352; baptism, 330, 335; becoming
  bishop, 208, 226; character and conduct, 141-49; conversion, 330, 334-35,
  346, 472; discipleship, 336; eventual
  emancipation, 135; freedom, 359; as
  gift of God, 409; as guilty, 226-27;
  identity, 419-20, 459, 472; legal options, 367-68; loved by Philemon, 447-
  50; as more than a slave, 420-22, 425;
  name, 114, 119, 141, 328, 330, 336-38,
  398; as not a fugitive, 227-28, 357, 395;
  not manumitted, 417, 457; as Paul's
  child, 361; as property, 396-97; urged
  to renounce rights, 135; usefulness,
  223, 351, 371, 396, 434, 446, 472;
  wicked past, 340-41, 398, 480-81
orders, 155

pagan worship meals, 477
Panaetius, 92
paradoxes, 116
participation, 282
partnership, 410, 474-75
passivum divinum, 402
past, 345-50
patriarchalism, 254
Paul, 130-36; asking for manumission,
  412-16; as child of his time, 224; on
  coercion, 384-88; as conservative, 193-
  97, 201, 212, 219; ethics, 228-29, 383;

fatherhood, 111, 133, 161, 326, 329,
  335, 485; on the flesh, 466-67, 472; on
  freedom, 358-59; humility, 224, 243,
  408; identifies himself with Onesimus
  and Philemon, 166; imprisonment,
  132, 133-34, 243-45, 374, 494-95; as
  liberation theologian, 194-97; meetings
  with Onesimus, 146-47; as mother,
  329, 332-34; renounces apostolic authority, 113, 160-61, 167, 244, 309-10;
  sends Onesimus back, 351-58; on service, 372-74; weakness, 324, 434;
  wishes, 362-66, 408-9; on women, 254-
  56
peace, 174, 178, 184, 267, 436
Peasants' Revolt, 206, 354
Pelagius, 255
Pergamum, 89
persecution, 230
Philemon (book): date and place, 121-28;
  drama, 115, 128-30; Hebrew elements,
  117-18; in history of interpretation,
  200-214; humor, 118-19; as official
  church letter, 113-15; place in canon,
  202-3; as private letter, 112-13, 114-15;
  rhetorical devices, 115-19; structure
  and logic, 119-21; text, 104-5, 106-8;
  vocabulary, 108-9
Philemon (person), 137-41; freedom,
  359; obligation to Paul, 483-85; profitable to Paul, 486; proper response,
  200-201
philosophy, consolation of, 33-41
Phoebe, 255
pietism, 239, 442
pleading, 312
poor, 132
Poseidonius, 92
poverty, 216-17, 238-39
power, 283, 308-9
powers, 217, 415
prayer, 269-71, 278, 305
presbyter, 322
priesthood of believers, 279
Prisca, 255
prisoner, 243-45; of Jesus Christ, 245-47
private slavery. *See* house slavery
Promised Land, 67, 432

Index of Ancient Literature

Index of Ancient Literature

Odyssey		
17.322-323	10n.19	

Horace
Satires
2.7.83 — 38n.104

Isaeus
Orationes
8.41 — 13n.29

Isocrates
Panegyricus
123-124 — 44n.120

Josephus
Antquitates
1–4 — 57n.154
3.280-286 — 76n.216
3.281-282 — 71n.197
3.282 — 57n.154
3.282-285 — 74n.211
4 — 490
13.257-258 — 100
16.1-5 — 57n.152
16–17 — 58n.162
18.5-22 — 78-79n.219
18.21 — 79n.221
20.181 — 96
20.206 — 96
22.61 — 340
454–455 — 57n.154

Bellum Judaicum
2.119-161 — 79n.219
2.162-163 — 405
4.508 — 101

Julius Caesar

Bellum Civile
1.34 — 45n.123

Juvenal

Satires
6.219 — 17n.44
6.219-224 — 86

475ff — 17n.44

Livy
Historiae
8.28 — 7n.13
35.49.8 — 6n.9, 34n.95
36.17.5 — 6n.9
36.17.15 — 34n.95

Macrobius
Saturnalia
1.11.13 — 9n.18

Musonius
Epistulae
66.2 — 17n.45

Ovid
Amores
1.14.16ff — 17n.44

Ars amatoria
3.239ff — 17n.44

Philo
De decalogo
167 — 14n.31

De Josepho
25 — 361

De opificio mundi
105-106 — 321

De specialibus legibus
2.66-69 — 100, 303
2.67 — 14n.32
2.122 — 59n.165
2.122-123 — 59n.164, 75n.215
2.123 — 96
3.138 — 79n.221
3.141-143 — 16n.38
4.3 — 57n.154
4.4 — 72n.204

De virtutibus
123 — 14n.32

124 — 26n.72, 29n.78
125 — 29n.79, 61n.172

De vita contemplativa
70-72 — 78n.219

Embassy to Gaius
58 — 327, 334
368 — 361

Hypothetica
frag.11-18 — 78n.219

Moses
1.273 — 392

On the Unchangableness of God
128 — 392
1288 — 392

Quod omnis probus liber sit
41 — 23n.60
48 — 18n.47
48-57 — 79n.221
75-80 — 78n.219
79 — 79n.221, 424
156-157 — 50n.136

Plato
Epistulai
8.354e — 370

Cratylus
420de — 384, 389

Gorgias
491e — 23n.62
517-518 — 372

Leges
3.697 — 389
6.776-778 — 10n.19
6.776d — 13n.31
6.777bc — 88
6.777b-e — 15n.37
7.793c-794a — 15n.37